THE
STRUGGLE for PALESTINE

THE

STRUGGLE for

PALESTINE

By J. C. HUREWITZ

GREENWOOD PRESS, PUBLISHERS
NEW YORK   1968

TO
MIRIAM

Preface

THIS BOOK was first intended to be merely a study of the impact of World War II on Arab and Jewish politics in Palestine. But it soon became apparent that political developments in Palestine between 1939 and 1945 were understandable only in relation to the earlier history of the mandate, particularly to the period from 1936 on. Moreover, the political trends in the local Arab and Jewish communities had begun by that time to converge with world-wide currents. This book, then, turned out to be an analysis not only of Arab and Jewish politics in Palestine, but of political repercussions in the Arab and Jewish worlds, their growing involvement in Big-Power politics, and the consequent progressive breakdown of the Palestine Mandate. This is, therefore, a study of the Palestine problem since 1936 against the background of a world distracted by the ordeals of an approaching war, the war itself, and the fumbling for peace.

With the exception of the epilogue the text was substantially completed in July 1948. In the two years that I devoted to its preparation I was constantly reminded of the difficulty of obtaining a perspective which will stand the test of time when dealing with a problem so close at hand. Equally challenging has been the endeavor to avoid the pitfalls of partisanship. Emotions on the subject of Palestine have run high, so that only a very small percentage of the enormous literature dealing with the issue can be considered dispassionate. I have spared no efforts to present the conflicting viewpoints as fairly as possible, but I have also tried to relate these viewpoints to one another and to the larger factors involved.

During three years of research and residence in Palestine and the surrounding Arab lands between 1937 and 1940, I managed to acquire a firsthand knowledge of the local aspects of the problem. My experience was further enhanced by three years of wartime government service in Washington where I served as Palestine expert, first in the research and analysis branch of the Office of Strategic Services and later in the intelligence branch of the Department of State. Here I was provided with an exceptional opportunity to keep abreast of Palestine developments and to

7

become conversant with the Big-Power aspects of the problem. In the summer of 1949, moreover, I served as political affairs officer in the Department of Security Council Affairs at Lake Success and was thus enabled to examine at close quarters the handling of the Palestine problem by the United Nations.

To the Social Science Research Council, which provided a grant for the preparation of the greater part of this study, I am most grateful. I am especially indebted to E. A. Speiser for his original suggestion that I embark on this venture and for his subsequent encouragement, and to Salo W. Baron for his counsel throughout. I also wish to thank Mrs. Margaret Arakie, Henry Steele Commager, William Epstein, Harold W. Glidden, Abraham Halkin, Arthur Jeffery, Harold J. Jonas, Ismail Khalidi, and Arthur Lourie for constructive criticism on parts or all of the manuscript. Needless to add, I alone am responsible for the interpretation and conclusions. I wish to express my gratitude to the Agudas Israel World Organization, the American Jewish Committee, the British Information Services of New York, the Institute of Arab American Affairs, the Jewish Agency for Palestine, the New York Public Library, the New York State Library at Albany, and the Zionist Archives—all of which gave me ready access to the materials at their disposal. To David de Porte, who so skillfully executed the sketch maps, the Hagstrom Company, which so carefully followed my instructions in the preparation of the end-paper maps, and Miss Helen Fraser, who so patiently put together the Index, I must express my appreciation. I am especially grateful to the owners of Valatje Kill Farm, who provided ideal working arrangements. Finally, I am most deeply obligated to my wife, whose devotion above and beyond the call of matrimony made this book possible.

New York City
January 6, 1950

Table of Contents

List of Maps

PART ONE

THE SHAPE OF THE PALESTINE PROBLEM IN 1936

CHAPTER 1

The Origins of the Mandate
and Its Operation

THE ESTABLISHMENT OF THE MANDATE

PALESTINE, as a modern geographic and political unit, was the creation of
World War I and its peace settlement.[1] In the preceding four centuries
this territory formed part of the Asiatic provinces of the Turkish Empire.
Following the stabilization of the Turkish provincial boundaries in 1864,
the area later known as Palestine was divided between two separate provinces. Economic and political penetration by the major European powers
into the Asiatic portion of the Turkish Empire grew after the end of the
eighteenth century in direct proportion to the steady decline of the Sultan's authority. Between 1839 and 1916 Arabia was largely drawn into the
orbit of Great Britain. A partial ring had been formed around three sides of
the Peninsula by British acquisition of direct or indirect controls over
Egypt, the Sudan, Aden Settlement and its hinterland, and the several small
principalities along the southern and eastern coasts of the Arabian main-
land.

When the time arrived for the final dismemberment of the Turkish
Empire at the close of World War I, the area of European contention had
been reduced to the Fertile Crescent or the Asiatic provinces north of
Arabia, and the contenders to Great Britain and France. Although the two
Western allies eventually agreed on their respective zones of influence, the
traditional practice of direct annexation was now abandoned, owing to
United States insistence. Instead, the former Turkish provinces were con-
verted into mandates under the auspices and supervisory jurisdiction of the
League of Nations. On April 25, 1920, the Principal Allied Powers at the
San Remo Conference allotted the mandate for Syria and Lebanon (later

the Levant States) to the trust of France and the mandates for Mesopotamia (later Iraq) and Palestine to that of Great Britain. All three were created Class A mandates, which was intended to signify that their inhabitants were nearly ripe for self-rule and that their period of dependence would therefore be of comparatively short duration.

The mandates for the Levant States and Iraq recognized these countries as provisionally independent and enjoined the tutelary powers to facilitate the progressive development of full sovereignty. No such clauses were included in the mandate for Palestine because of British wartime commitments to the Zionists. Parleys had taken place in 1916–17 between the Zionist Organization and the British Government with the knowledge and consent of the United States. The British Cabinet finally approved for issuance on November 2, 1917, by Foreign Secretary Arthur J. Balfour a declaration of sympathy with Jewish Zionist aspirations, which was subsequently endorsed by the other Allied and Associated Powers. The preamble of the mandate for Palestine acknowledged "the historical connection of the Jewish people" with Palestine and "the grounds for reconstituting their national home in that country." Great Britain was made responsible by Article 2 of the mandate "for placing the country under such political, administrative and economic conditions as will secure the establishment of the Jewish national home . . . and the development of self-governing institutions." Article 4 provided for the recognition, as a public body, of a Jewish agency to cooperate with the Palestine Government "in such economic, social and other matters as may affect the establishment of the Jewish national home and the interests of the Jewish population in Palestine." Furthermore, the Palestine Government was bound by Article 6 to "facilitate Jewish immigration under suitable conditions" and to "encourage . . . close settlement by Jews on the land."

The mandate for Palestine was framed unmistakably in the Zionist interest. The preamble, it was true, repeated the stipulation of the Balfour Declaration that "nothing should be done which might prejudice the civil and religious rights of existing non-Jewish communities in Palestine." It was also stated in Article 2 that the mandatory was to be responsible "for safeguarding the civil and religious rights of all the inhabitants of Palestine, irrespective of race and religion"; and in Article 6 that the promotion of Jewish immigration and land settlement was not to prejudice "the rights and position of other sections of the population." However, these clauses merely qualified the mandate's primary purpose—the establishment of the Jewish National Home. This was borne out not only by Zionist contentions, Arab complaints, and the British Royal Commission's confirmation but by textual evidence in the mandate itself. Arabic was declared one of the three official languages of the country. But not once were the Arabs mentioned by name.

Still, the concept of a national home was unprecedented in international law, and the mandate failed to clarify its meaning. Nowhere was it laid down whether the national home would merely be the vehicle for the creation of a Jewish state; or whether it was to be an end in itself; or, if the latter, at what stage the national home might be regarded as established. The ultimate definition, it was obvious, would be determined primarily by the way in which the British used their wide authority, the extent to which the Zionists responded to their opportunities, and the degree to which the Arabs offered resistance.

The feeble attempts of 1918–19 to bring Arab and Zionist claims into alignment produced no lasting results. But the Arabs of Palestine were not at first organized for a political struggle. Indeed, the history of Palestine Arab resistance to the mandate was shaped by the rise of the local national movement, which grew steadily in strength and numbers after its birth at Haifa in December 1920. The Arabs formed an overwhelming majority of the population of Palestine. They had been in actual possession of its land for more than a millennium. Consequently, the nationalists resented the fact that the Palestine Mandate did not conform to the principle of self-determination. Nor was the resentment watered down by British and Zionist arguments that Palestine as a land containing shrines sacred to three world religions could not be considered purely Arab; that the Arabs had long since ceased to rule it; that in any case the Allied Powers were free to dispose of territory which they had liberated; and that the Jews' ancient title to the country was sealed as permanent by Biblical promise. To the Muslims Jerusalem was next in holiness only to Mecca and Medina, and Palestine was Islamic by divine right of occupation.

From the start the Palestine Arab nationalists contended that the mandate violated Article 22 of the Covenant of the League of Nations, which embraced Palestine in the mention of "certain communities belonging to the Turkish Empire [that] have reached a stage of development where their existence as independent nations can be provisionally recognized." This interpretation was not accepted by the British, who pointed out that the language of Article 22 was permissive, not obligatory. The Palestine Arab nationalists also charged that British wartime pledges to the Zionists were not binding because they were given subsequent to the assurances received in October 1915 by the Sharif of Mecca from Sir Henry McMahon, the British High Commissioner for Egypt. McMahon had written that his government would support Arab independence in the Asiatic provinces of the Turkish Sultan "within those frontiers wherein Great Britain is free to act without detriment to the interests of her ally, France." That this reservation concerned only Lebanon, the nationalists insisted, was further confirmed by the specific exemption in the McMahon letter of those "portions of Syria lying to the west of the districts of Damascus, Homs, Hama and Aleppo." With this contention, too, the British took issue. They maintained that Palestine lay outside the area slated for Arab independence, on the ground that in October 1915 France had claimed Palestine as well as Lebanon and Syria.

Similar ambiguities attached to the boundaries of Palestine. At the Paris Peace Conference the Zionist Organization requested that the lower reaches of the Litani River, the western slopes of Mount Hermon, and the lower Yarmuk Valley be included within the northern frontier. But owing to French obduracy, most of this zone was awarded to the Levant States. The Zionists also demanded that the eastern frontier of Palestine be determined by the Hijaz Railway, which ran from Dar'a through 'Amman to Ma'an. This would have provided a sizable stretch of fertile land on the eastern bank of the Jordan River. This territory, however, was already assigned to the provisional Arab government at Damascus, headed by Amir Faysal, the third son of the Sharif of Mecca. After the French forcibly terminated the Faysal Government in July 1920, the British annexed the southern region to Palestine, which now extended from the Mediterranean to Mesopotamia. Five months later the first draft of the Palestine Mandate was completed and was intended to apply to this entire region.

By August 1921 a new article was inserted into a revised draft of the mandate which empowered the mandatory "to postpone or withhold application" of the provisions regarding the Jewish National Home from the territory east of the Jordan.[2] In the interval between the two dates Amir 'Abdallah, Faysal's older brother, had been installed at 'Amman as temporary head of the new government of Transjordan. The Colonial Office explained in June 1922 that the decision to excise Transjordan—which was nevertheless to remain a part of the Palestine Mandate—from the field of the national home was made in accordance with the McMahon promise of 1915. The Zionists formally assented to this arrangement. Yet they regarded the separation of Transjordan as merely a temporary measure and repeatedly tried to reopen the question of Jewish settlement there.

THE MANDATE IN OPERATION

Despite the crystallization of Arab and Zionist grievances against the mandatory, the Palestine Mandate was ratified by the Council of the League of Nations on September 29, 1923. As a nonmember of the League, the United States formally approved the mandate in a special convention concluded in December 1924 with Great Britain. The attitude of the United States, however, was severely circumscribed by its isolationist foreign policy. The Department of State, admittedly, had secured assurances of equal treatment with League members for the economic interests of American nationals in the mandated territories. But when both houses of Congress had passed in 1922 a joint resolution favoring the establishment of the Jewish National Home in Palestine, the House Committee on Foreign Affairs made it clear that this resolution "expresses our moral interest. . . . [and] commits us to no foreign obligations or entanglements." [3]

The pressure of European rivalry, which might have become a fundamental obstacle to the peaceful operation of the Palestine Mandate, was now temporarily quiescent. France had obtained its sphere of influence in the Levant States and guarantees of a share of the oil production of the Mosul district in Iraq. Great Britain had completed its encirclement of the Arabian Peninsula and thereby became the predominant political force in the Near East. Until 1936 the British position of supremacy in the Near East was not challenged by any major European power. Under these circumstances London enjoyed relative freedom from outside interference in evolving its policy toward Palestine, subject only to review by the League of Nations. From the start Great Britain's primary interest in Palestine was strategic: to retain control over the territory as a buffer on the eastern flank of the Suez Canal and as an indispensable element of the imperial defense network in the Near East. The loose wording of the mandate provided the United Kingdom with an elastic instrument, but at the cost of growing strife between Arabs and Zionists and increasing hostility of both toward the United Kingdom.

Despite the failure to obtain explicit assurances for the evolution of an independent Jewish government over Palestine, the Zionist spokesmen nevertheless regarded this as the mandate's basic purpose. It was, therefore, of utmost importance in their eyes that the Jews should come to outnumber the rest of the population and to acquire ownership of most of the land. Only when these objectives were realized would the Zionists demand self-governing institutions for the country as a whole. But the Palestine Arab nationalists were determined above all to frustrate the creation of a Jewish state. They consequently urged the complete stoppage of Jewish immigration and, in the course of time, of Jewish land acquisition. They insisted that the Palestine Arabs were the only legal heirs of the Turkish Empire, that they were already mature for political freedom, and that the national home experiment should be abandoned. In these respects the political ideologies of the Arab nationalists and Zionists remained constant, though their political tactics were opportunistic. The British, in turn, within the flexible limits of the mandate, veered and tacked with the wind.

Great Britain began to pare down Zionist privileges as early as the first statement of mandatory policy on Palestine. This was issued over the signature of Colonial Secretary Winston Churchill on July 1, 1922, a few weeks before the approval by the Council of the League of Nations of the mandate's final draft. [4] The Churchill Memorandum, it was true, declared that the Jews were in Palestine "as of right and not on sufferance." Nor were the Zionists displeased with the official definition of the meaning of the Jewish National Home as "the further development of the existing [Palestine] Jewish community, with the assistance of Jews in other parts of the world, in order that it may become a centre in which the Jewish people as a whole may take, on grounds of religion and race, an interest and a pride." The instrument of policy then informed the Arabs that the mandatory never contemplated "the disappearance or the subordination of the Arabic population, language or culture in Palestine" or even "the imposition of a Jewish nationality upon the inhabitants of Palestine as a whole." Moreover, Jewish immigration would be limited by "whatever may be the economic capacity of the country at the time to absorb new arrivals," so that "the immigrants should not . . . deprive any section of the present population of their employment."

For the record, then, the Arabs obtained from the mandatory what they had not been given in the mandate: group recognition by name, the pledge of nondomination by the Jews, and regulated instead of unrestricted Jewish immigration. Off the record, the Zionists knew that there was "nothing" in the Churchill Memorandum "to prohibit the ultimate establishment of a Jewish State, and Mr. Churchill himself . . . told . . . [the Palestine Royal Commission of 1936–37] that no such prohibition was intended." [5] Thus the mandatory was endeavoring to win Arab confidence without dissipating Zionist good will. But the Arab nationalists refused to be mollified. In April 1920 and May 1921 the nationalists had expressed their enmity toward Zionism by sponsoring anti-Jewish riots. Then in August 1929 there occurred even more serious Arab assaults on Jewish areas of settlement.

Following an investigation of the disorders and a subsequent inquiry into the problems of immigration and land settlement, the mandatory issued in October 1930 a new basic policy statement, known as the Passfield White Paper. [6] British obligations to Jews and Arabs under the mandate—the establishment of a Jewish National Home and the protection of the rights of the non-Jewish community—were declared to be "of equal weight" but "in no sense irreconcilable." The White Paper went on to state that under existing conditions "there remains no margin of land available for agricultural settlement by new immigrants." Stricter land transfer and immigration controls were accordingly recommended. The organized Zionist reaction, the attacks in Parliament by the Conservative and Liberal parties, and pro-Zionist pressure from the British dominions, however, caused the Labor Government in February 1931 to explain away most of those features of the new policy objectionable to the Zionists. This took the form of an "authoritative" interpretation of the Passfield White Paper in a public letter from Prime Minister J. Ramsay MacDonald to Dr. Chaim Weizmann, the president of the Zionist Organization and the Jewish Agency for Palestine. [7] The Prime Minister

denied that the mandatory was considering any prohibition "of acquisition of additional land by Jews" or "of Jewish immigration in any of its
categories." Yet the theory of dual obligation was not repudiated. Nor
was the disputed instrument of policy replaced by another White Paper.

The mandatory never expressly revealed what ultimate constitutional
arrangement was visualized. Its efforts to institute self-government on
a countrywide basis, however, suggested that London had in mind the
gradual emergence of a unitary, Arab-Jewish state. As early as October
1920 the first High Commissioner, Sir Herbert Samuel, formed an Advisory Council, composed of ten British officials, four Muslim and three
Christian Arabs, and three Jews. The Advisory Council was an interim,
nominated body, enjoying only the right to discuss proposed legislation,
and was dissolved in February 1923. In the meantime, the mandatory had
published an order-in-council, which served as the constitution of the
Palestine Government. An elected Legislative Council, for which this
document provided, never came into existence, since the Arab nationalist leaders refused to participate. Nor was the High Commissioner able
to resuscitate the nominated Advisory Council, owing to the resignation under nationalist pressure of most of the Arab appointees. The question of creating a Legislative Council was reopened early in 1929, only
to be shelved after the disorders later in the year. The mandatory took
no further step to encourage self-rule for the country as a whole until
1935–36, when the proposal for a Legislative Council was put forward
for the final time.

The mandatory government in Palestine was, meanwhile, designed after
the model of the British Crown Colony. The military regime, which
had administered the country from the time of the British occupation in
the last year of the war, was replaced by a civil government under a
High Commissioner on July 1, 1920. Jurisdiction over this government
was transferred from the Foreign to the Colonial Office early in the
following year. The High Commissioner held the title of commander-
in-chief and was endowed with broad executive and legislative powers.
An Executive Council constituted his cabinet. A larger Advisory Council
was used primarily for formal endorsement of proposed enactments. For
administrative purposes the country was divided into districts, gradually
reduced in number from ten to three, each headed by a district commissioner.[8] The district commissioners and the members of the two
councils were British officials, as were the heads of the government departments. The mandatory introduced modern governmental machinery
where none existed before. It overhauled the legal system; set up departments of health, education, and agriculture; provided modern means of
communication and built new roads. But in the central government and
in the districts Arabs and Jews were entirely unrepresented on the au-

thoritative level. Hence, the administration was at its best benevolent and at its worst autocratic.

Still, Jews and Arabs were accorded a considerable measure of autonomy. The mandate (Articles 14–16) stated that the several religious communities were to enjoy religious and educational freedom. When these provisions were pooled with others relating to the establishment of a Jewish National Home, the Jews were also able to make out a good case for political autonomy. As a result the Jews assumed more and more quasi-governmental functions and, in the course of time, created an administrative apparatus in which the national and secular features took precedence over the religious. In an effort to obtain Arab cooperation and later in pursuance of the theory of dual obligation, the mandatory offered the Arabs similar privileges. While the Arabs did not organize themselves on a basis comparable to that of the Jews, the national movement came to exercise a powerful influence over the Arab Community. By 1936 Arabs and Jews in Palestine owed greater allegiance to their respective national leaders than to the Palestine Government. As their separate, competing, political institutions became more firmly anchored, the prospects of Arab-Jewish harmony grew dimmer. Besides, attempts by the mandatory to apply the principle of equal treatment merely intensified the separation and the rivalry, for after a while Jews as well as Arabs questioned British sincerity. Dual obligation also came to mean government by arithmetic. Government employment and subventions were determined not on merit or need, but on the relative numerical proportion of Arabs and Jews and the contributions of each to the public treasury. This hardly promoted good government. As the Palestine Administration became increasingly inefficient, it was less and less able to cope with the local political situation.

A more serious aspect of the Palestine problem derived from Britain's indecision. The Arab nationalists discovered that they were able to obtain concessions by refusing to cooperate in the implementation of the mandate and by resorting to political violence. The Zionists for their part found that by appealing to British public opinion and to Parliament they could induce policy decisions in the Zionist favor. There were also indications by 1936 that the two contestants were learning each other's tactics. The precedent of pressure and counterpressure, once established, was destined to complicate future efforts to settle the Palestine question on its intrinsic merits. Finally, the very existence of rival Arab and Zionist lobbies on the international scene was threatening to entangle the Palestine problem with larger world issues.

Meanwhile the basic aspects of the Palestine problem had changed by the mid-1930's. The question of whether or not a Jewish National Home should be established was no longer theoretical. The national home already existed. The issue now posed was whether or not it had been fully established, and for its further development the Zionists could muster powerful arguments. The alarming spread of anti-Jewish feeling in Europe after Hitler's rise to power in 1933 coupled with the stringent immigration laws in the Western Hemisphere and the British dominions increased the pressure for Jewish emigration to Palestine. Nearly 300,000 Jews had already settled there under the international guarantees of the mandatory regime. Most of them had left close relatives behind in Europe. The Palestine Jews had no faith in their personal safety or in the security of the national home under the rule of a hostile Arab majority. Besides, the economic fabric of the national home had been built upon international pledges that Jewish immigration would be facilitated. This structure might be seriously undermined, if no newcomers arrived.

The Palestine Arabs on their side viewed the benefits accruing to their countrymen from Zionist investments as unwelcome gifts from foreign intruders. Moreover, the nationalists pointed to the fact that predominant elements in the national home practiced economic exclusiveness; that the relative number of Arabs employed by Jews was steadily declining; and that no Arabs were allowed to work on nationally-owned Jewish land. By the mid-1930's an entire generation of Palestine Arabs whose political education was confined largely to learning about the alleged injustices of the mandate was coming of age. They constituted the rank and file of the national movement, which was more emphatically antagonistic to Zionism than ever before. The nationalists were persuaded that only the Zionists stood between the Palestine Arabs and self-rule. The progressive achievement of independence on the part of the Arabs in the near-by countries served to deepen this resentment.

As for the mandatory, its interests had grown apace. Construction was completed by 1933 of a modern harbor at Haifa. Two years later that city became the terminus of a pipe line for transporting crude oil from Iraq to the Mediterranean; this pipe line was owned by the Anglo-Iranian Oil Company, a majority of whose stock was controlled by the British Government, and the concessionaire obtained free rights of transit through Palestine. British capital had been invested in concessions for the generation of electricity and the extraction of chemicals from the Dead Sea. An airport had been built at Lydda and a seaplane base on the Sea of Galilee, furnishing links in the British air services to the Near East and beyond. Palestine also acquired by 1936 added significance in the over-all British defense system in the Near East. Following the grant of independence to Iraq in 1932 and to Egypt four years later, the United Kingdom's military, naval, and air bases in these countries were guaranteed by preferential treaties. However, the renewal of these privileges upon the lapse of the agreements was at best problematical. London was therefore forced to place greater reliance on preserving its military rights in Palestine. Palestine (and Transjordan) furnished centrally located bases, from which British forces could operate radially. Moreover, Haifa could supplement or, in case of need, replace Alexandria as a naval base in the southeastern Mediterranean, and the Negeb (southern Palestine) might be used as a substitute for the Canal Zone in the defense of Suez.

CHAPTER 2

Demographic, Economic, and Social Components

THE JEWISH population of Palestine grew steadily in the second half of the nineteenth century through the arrival of immigrants, drawn to the country for religious reasons. After 1882 the persecution of Jews in eastern Europe, principally Russia, and the beginnings of Zionism increased the rate of influx. The number of Jews had enlarged from about 12,000 in 1845, double that in 1882, and 47,000 in 1895 to nearly 85,000 in 1914. During World War I the Jewish population declined to an estimated 65,000 in 1919 or roughly 10 per cent of the total in the country. Between September 1920 and December 1936 some 280,000 Jews migrated to Palestine with mandatory authorization, bringing the number of Jews to 404,000 or close to 30 per cent of the over-all population. Jews from Poland headed the list of newcomers. The influx reached its peak after 1932, when the sharpening anti-Jewish feeling caused an abrupt rise in the immigration from central Europe. Between 1933 and 1936 the size of the Jewish Community, or *Yishuv* (settlement), as it had come to be known, expanded by 83 per cent as a result of the arrival of 166,000 settlers. Among the immigrants were also Jews from the near-by Arab and more remote Oriental countries, attracted to the national home because of the greater economic opportunities.

Although the government determined the immigration quotas, the Jewish Agency allocated the visas. For this purpose the Agency's immigration department maintained offices in the larger cities of Europe. High priorities were given to young Zionists, trained in agricultural and manual work and educated in the use of Hebrew at special camps operated by various branches of the Zionist Organization. Owing to the accent on youth, more than 85 per cent of the Palestine Jews were less than forty-five years old and the average age was less than twenty-seven in 1936.

At first, the immigrants had settled chiefly in the four "holy cities" of Jerusalem, Hebron, Safad, and Tiberias. But by 1914 the Jews had founded forty-four villages, whose 12,000 inhabitants, or 14 per cent of the Jewish total, continued unchanged throughout World War I. As a result of the centralized planning of the postwar years, the number of villages multiplied to 203 in 1936 and their population to 98,000, or 24 per cent of the total. Aside from Jerusalem and its immediate suburbs, the area of Jewish settlement was mainly confined to a small district southeast of Jaffa, the Coastal Plain from that city to Haifa, the Valley of Jezreel, and eastern Galilee. Two-thirds lived in Tel-Aviv, Jerusalem, and Haifa. Indeed, Tel-Aviv, which started out as a northern suburb of Jaffa in 1909, had become the largest city in the country by 1936, with an all-Jewish population of about 150,000. The Jewish population expanded by almost 400 per cent between 1914 and 1936; the area of Jewish-owned land enlarged by less than 200 per cent, from approximately 110,000 acres to 308,000. This represented about 4.6 per cent of the country's over-all land area.

The character of the Yishuv was determined largely by the Ashkenazim or Jews of north, central, and eastern European descent. They constituted more than three-fourths of the Jewish population. The Sefardim or Jews from Mediterranean countries formed somewhat less than one-tenth. Jews of Yemeni, Kurdish, Persian, Bukhari, and other Oriental extraction made up the rest. The diverse origins of the immigrants were reflected in the cultural disunity of the community. The Ashkenazim and the Sefardim had been bitter rivals ever since the late nineteenth century and still maintained separate religious institutions. The cultural and social discord between the eastern and central Europeans lost little of its shrillness in transit from the Continent. Finally, a Yemeni or Iraqi Jew had less in common culturally, economically, and socially with the Jew of German or Russian origin than with the Palestine Arab.

Turkish sources estimated the Palestine Arab population in 1914 at 600,000. By 1919 the number had dwindled to about 580,000; by the end of 1936 it had jumped to some 968,000, an expansion of nearly 67 per cent in less than two decades. The improvement in health conditions—the drainage of swamps and the introduction of modern methods of sanitation, water supply, and medicine—through Jewish and mandatory efforts reduced the rate of infant mortality and increased the longevity of the country's entire population. At the same time the high Muslim birth rate remained comparatively stable. Although the relative proportion of Arabs to the rest of the Palestine population shrank from about 90 to 70 per cent between 1919 and 1936, the Arab absolute growth exceeded the Jewish by nearly 50,000. Furthermore, the annual average of Arab natural increase rose steadily. In the five-year period between 1931 and 1935 it passed the 20,000 mark, as compared with the Jewish average of less than 5,000. Hence, unless Jewish immigration equaled at least 15,500 a year, the proportion of Arabs was likely to rise once more.

While the Palestine Arabs possessed a common cultural heritage, their community was divided along religious lines. The Muslims set the economic and social pace in the Arab Community even more than the Europeans in the Yishuv. For the most part the Palestine Muslims—almost 863,000 in December 1936—were adherents of Sunni or orthodox Islam, whose affairs were administered by a Supreme Muslim Council. Outside the Council's sway were some 4,000 Matawilah, a Shi'ite Muslim sect living in northern Galilee and retaining close relationships with their coreligionists in Lebanon. In the same region as the Matawilah lived some 10,000 Druzes, whose religion contained elements of both Shi'ite Islam and Christianity and who were recognized by the government as a separate community. The 95,000 or so Christian Arabs of Palestine were fragmented into numerous sects. About 47,000 belonged to the Greek Orthodox Church under the local jurisdiction of the Jerusalem Patriarchate. Of the approximately 41,000 Roman Catholics, slightly more than half adhered to the Latin Church with their own Patriarchate at Jerusalem. The rest belonged to various Eastern or Uniate churches. The two most important were the Greek Catholic or Melkite with a following of some 15,000 and the Maronite with roughly 3,700. The remaining Christian Arabs were attached either to the Syrian Orthodox (or Jacobite) Church or to the various Protestant churches founded by European and American missionaries.

The Arabs were concentrated in the hill districts of central and northern Palestine, although they retained a substantial hold on the Coastal Plain. In these regions were located most of the 850 Arab villages, where in 1936 some 670,000 *fallahin* or peasants lived. Moreover, there were about 67,000 seminomadic, Muslim Beduin, located mainly in the Negeb. The percentage of Muslims living in the towns rose from 23.5 in 1922 to 25.9 in 1936, about two-thirds living in Jaffa, Haifa, Gaza, Jerusalem, Hebron, and Nablus. As for the Christian Arabs, they tended increasingly to form the most urbanized section of the country's population. From 75.4 per cent in 1922 the proportion of urban Christians grew to 78 per cent in 1936, more than half residing in Jerusalem, Haifa, and Jaffa. However, the typical Arab town, it must be stressed, ranged in size from about 3,000 to 15,000 inhabitants. Thus, such Muslim towns as Ramlah and Lydda had populations of 10,000 to 15,000, while Janin, Beersheba, and Baysan had less than 5,000. Similarly, the population of the Christian towns of Nazareth and Bethlehem did not exceed 10,000, while that of Ramallah and Bayt Jala did not even reach 5,000.[1]

The driving force behind the Jewish economy was the effort to enlarge the absorptive capacity of the national home. To this end the Jews had invested over $400,000,000 in Palestine between 1919 and 1936. Of this sum about 10 per cent represented capital outlay for industry. In 1936 nearly nine-tenths of the 5,602 Jewish manufacturing establishments were still of the handicraft variety. These small firms, however, constituted only 7.4 per cent of the total capital investment. The arrival in the mid-1930's of many central Europeans, possessing managerial and technical knowledge and bringing with them machinery and capital goods, spurred the rate of industrial growth. The number of industrial employees, which had expanded from 4,750 in 1921–22 to 10,968 in 1929, reached 28,616 in 1936. The value of industrial output, which had been less than $12,000,000 in 1929, passed $42,000,000 by 1936. Jewish industry primarily produced consumer goods for the domestic market; specialized production for export, such as the extraction of Dead Sea chemicals, remained the exception.

In the early 1930's Palestine's largest item of export was citrus fruits. By 1936 private Jewish investment in citriculture amounted to at least $75,000,000, or nearly double that in industry, although the flow of capital into this type of agriculture fell off drastically after 1936. For the promotion of intensive, diversified farming the Jewish public bodies spent about $40,000,000 by the mid-1930's. Immigrants wishing to become farmers were encouraged to form collective or cooperative villages. There were eighty-two such villages in 1936, and their relative number was on the increase. These villagers were provided with land purchased by the Jewish National Fund, a subsidiary of the Zionist Organization; with long-term, low-interest loans for mechanized farm equipment and other initial capital outlay by the Palestine Foundation Fund, the fiscal arm of the Jewish Agency for Palestine; and with expert advice by the Agency's agricultural research station. As a result, the number of Jews gainfully employed in agriculture multiplied from 4,000 in 1922, to 12,300 in 1931, and 32,000 in 1936. Of the last some 12,000 were hired workers, mostly employed in citriculture.

The Anglo-Palestine Bank, which virtually served as the official bank of the Jewish National Home, was in 1936 second in size only to Barclay's Bank, the banker for the Palestine Government and the agent for the Palestine Currency Board. In that year there were as many persons engaged in commerce and transport as were employed in agriculture. The Palestine Electric Corporation, in which the Jewish Agency was one of the largest stockholders, began in 1926 to supply electric power to the entire country except the Jerusalem area. The Yishuv was by far the principal consumer, and an index of Jewish economic progress was the rise in the corporation's sale of electricity from 2,344,000 kw-hr in 1926 to 65,496,000 ten years later. Industry and irrigation each consumed roughly one-third of this supply.

The economic progress was characterized from the start by a strong labor movement. Its nucleus was a number of young eastern European socialists who had immigrated into Palestine in the decade before World War I. The two basic doctrines to which they dedicated themselves with a religious fervor were the "conquest of labor" and the "conquest of the land." By the first they meant their opposition to the "exploitation" of labor and their belief in "self-labor." The second involved the conviction that the Jewish masses should be "productivized" and the economy "normalized" by a deliberate directing of new immigrants to farming and manual labor, since in the two millennia of Jewish "exile" from Palestine, they argued, Jews had become estranged from the land and from manual employment. These labor zealots also insisted on the exclusive employment of Jews on land and in industry owned by Jews, to enable more Jewish workers to find their place in the national home. This was essential, they contended, because Jews could find few employment opportunities in the government and none from the Arabs, nor could they, owing to their higher standard of living, compete with Arab labor in an open market.

Some 4,400 workers, mostly farmers, who espoused these views founded at the end of 1920 the General Federation of Jewish Labor in Palestine, commonly known as the "Histadrut." Its membership, restricted to men and women over the age of eighteen "who live by their own labor without exploiting others," had grown in sixteen years to 87,000, or about three-fourths of the Jewish labor force. Another 15 per cent were enrolled in six smaller labor federations. The unorganized workers were mostly Sefardim and Orientals. The labor federations sponsored a wide variety of cooperatives, which by 1936 were some 770 in number. Most of the cooperatives were subsidiaries of the Histadrut, which, aside from the government, had become the country's largest single employer.

The economic developments in the Yishuv were bound to affect the Arab economy. The Jews may have spent as much as $75,000,000 on land alone. Although a considerable share, particularly in the earlier years, went to Lebanese and Syrian landowners, probably much more than half constituted a direct transfer of capital to the Palestine Arabs. In addition, the payments by Jews to Arabs for agricultural produce, building materials, wages, rents, and services expanded until they reached an estimated peak of $13,750,000 in 1935. Nor was the acquired capital siphoned off by the government, as had been the case in Turkish days, for the mandatory had both regularized taxation and lowered the rates. Finally, the application of government revenue to domestic services—extension of all-weather roads, harbor development, and improvement of communications—aided the Arab as well as the Jewish economy.

The most visible economic changes in the Arab Community occurred among the upper and middle classes. Investment in citriculture spiraled upward until the Arab-owned plantations covered 33,750 acres in 1936, as compared with a combined Arab-Jewish acreage of only 7,500 in 1918. Other newly acquired capital went into construction and the production of building materials to meet the demands of the enlarging population. By the mid-1930's Arab manufacturing had branched out from the traditional textile, soap, and olive-oil industries to a variety of consumer goods. The bulk remained handicraft shops, but the number of firms using power-driven machinery multiplied from seven in 1921 to 313 in 1935. Home industries, common fifteen years before, were on the wane. Forward strides in commerce and finance were suggested by the growing percentage of the Arab national income attributable to trade and transport and by the appearance of the community's first two banks, which served as bankers to the local Arab national movement. Finally, opportunities increased noticeably in the liberal professions—education, medicine, law, white-collar government employment, and journalism.

Yet the Muslim peasantry, in the last analysis, controlled by sheer weight of numbers the rate of Arab economic change. About 85 per cent of the fallahin were still illiterate in 1936 and slow in learning modern farming methods and the use of power-driven equipment. Moreover, a majority were in a state of unproductive indebtedness to moneylenders, to whom they paid interest at rates varying from 30 per cent a year to 50 per cent for three months. Perhaps as many as 40 per cent of the fallahin lived on *musha'a* land, or land owned collectively by all the families of a village and redistributed periodically in widely scattered fragments. This practice destroyed the incentive for soil improvement and precluded mechanization and irrigation. Probably another 25 per cent of the peasantry were tenant farmers, paying over a third of their income as rent to absentee landlords, to whom they generally stood in a semi-feudal relationship. The remaining fallahin possessed clear title to their land. But, for the most part, their holdings were permanently broken up into disconnected segments.

With a view to clarifying titles to all land, especially rural, the government began in 1928 to reform the method of land registry. That the fallahin might be relieved of throttling debts, the mandatory also enacted laws against usury, encouraged borrowing from government-approved banks, and reduced taxes on grain. By 1936 some seventy Arab cooperatives, mostly agricultural credit societies, had been formed under government auspices, and diversified farming was being promoted by the government department of agriculture. While these reforms were still rudimentary by 1936, the doubling of the country's population since the close of the war had added considerably to Arab farm income. As paved highways pushed their way through rural areas, the fallahin turned more and more to cultivation of crops for the expanding urban markets. Arab vegetable production alone had multiplied by some 400 per cent since 1921. Seasonal employment in the towns and work on the large citrus groves enabled many peasants to eke out their incomes. Although the Arab villages were able to support a population of 670,000 in 1936, as compared with 470,000 in 1922, the peasants were still living at a subsistence level.

Many fallahin, drawn by the multiplying economic opportunities, migrated to the towns. The Arab urban population accordingly grew from 194,000 in 1922 to 298,000 in 1936. The emergence of a substantial proletariat was accompanied by the beginnings of a labor movement. In the early 1920's the Histadrut sponsored joint Arab-Jewish unions among employees of the Palestine Government and of the mixed Arab-Jewish municipalities. At Haifa in 1927 the Histadrut established the Palestine Labor League, for the purpose of organizing Arab workers in private industry. But seven years elapsed before the Labor League opened its only branch, at Jaffa. Meanwhile, in 1925 Arab workers at Haifa had already founded their own Palestine Arab Workers Society, which in the early 1930's formed affiliates in Jaffa and Jerusalem. Some of its leaders, mostly Christians, were former members of the Arab-Jewish unions; others belonged to the middle class and were anxious to win the organized workers over to the national movement. By 1936 the total Arab enrollment both in mixed and purely Arab unions had not yet reached 5,000. Still the Palestine labor movement was relatively more advanced than in any of the near-by Arab countries except Lebanon.[2]

SOCIAL DEVELOPMENTS

The Palestine Jews demonstrated a determination to take care of their own social needs. The community had its own university at Jerusalem, a technical institute at Haifa, and a network of teachers' training, trade, agricultural, secondary, and elementary schools. The Jewish public school system was able by 1936 to provide elementary education for almost all the children in the community. The Jews had set up hospitals, clinics, and infant and child welfare stations; they maintained laboratories and promoted medical research; and they organized campaigns for combating tuberculosis, malaria, and trachoma. Subsidies from the Palestine Government were small in comparison to the scope of these projects. Most of the funds still came from supporters abroad, particularly American Jews, although the Yishuv itself progressively assumed greater responsibilities for the upkeep of the establishments.

Credit for these achievements was due in large measure to organized labor, which cared for many of its own needs. The Histadrut's medical insurance plan embraced more than one-third of the entire community, supported a chain of hospitals, dispensaries, and medical stations in all of the towns and most of the villages, and had a budget in 1936 even larger than that of the government health department. The Histadrut also maintained an unemployment fund and jointly with the Jewish Agency sponsored a semipublic works program to create jobs for the unemployed. Interest in the Histadrut's social doctrines was continually spread through publications and a system of schools conducted by its political factions. Its power was also enhanced by a large rural backing —approximately 85 per cent of all Jewish farmers eligible for membership. In fact, the socialist farmers of the cooperative and collective villages, though comprising only one-seventh of the Histadrut's total enrollment in 1936, exercised a disproportionate influence. These "pioneers," as they were called, had played a leading role in founding the Histadrut and had contributed more than their share of labor Zionist theoreticians. Their villages were linked together in federations within the Histadrut, so that the socialist farmers were able to present greater unity than the urban workers. Social progress in the cooperative and collective villages took the form of innovation. Farmers in both practiced the principle of self-labor. In the cooperatives the individual farmer lived in his own home and worked for his own profit. In the collectives, however, each member shared the village income according to his requirements and received no monetary payments. Decisions were made at regular meetings by a majority vote of all the members. Many new immigrants were attracted by the security and social equality which the collectives offered, so that their number was growing more rapidly than that of the cooperatives.

These social experiments did not tell the whole story. Thus the Oriental Jews remained crowded in urban slums. Here affiliation with labor unions was uncommon, and social, hygienic, and sanitary standards were low. Here also was to be found most of the illiteracy that existed in the Yishuv—13.9 per cent, according to the government census of 1931. The presence of the underprivileged Orientals tended to encourage class consciousness in an otherwise fluid society.

There were as yet no hard and fast social cleavages in the Yishuv, despite the economic stresses between organized labor and the advocates of free enterprise. The creation of a class of landed gentry seemed to have been obviated by the concentration of land ownership in a national institution. Nor were there any signs of an industrial or financial aristocracy. If a privileged group existed at all, it was the Histadrut, whose numerical and organizational superiority enabled its members to protect their vested interests and obtain special favors. Within the Histadrut, as in the community at large, the pioneers still enjoyed the greatest prestige. These former urban intellectuals constituted the hard core of the nascent Jewish peasantry and were accordingly regarded as the backbone of the emergent Jewish nation. Nevertheless a new social elite was already beginning to manifest itself by the mid-1930's, as the second and third generation of Palestine-born Jews reached maturity. On them, it was generally felt in the community, would depend the future of the national home.

The Arab Community for its part was characterized by a rigid, centuries-old class system. At the top of the social scale was a small circle of Muslim, landowning families. Next came the embryonic middle class, consisting of Christian Arabs and a growing number of Muslims primarily engaged in commerce, manufacturing, citriculture, and the professions. However, it was often impossible on purely economic grounds to distinguish the middle class from the landed aristocracy, many of whose members were employed by the mid-1930's in typical middle-class pursuits. By far the largest grouping comprised the fallahin and the urban workers. At the bottom were the Beduin, the second biggest class, who remained for all practical purposes outside the scope of community affairs.

The Muslim Community was atomized by clannish separatism. The basic social unit of all classes was the patriarchal, closely knit clan, each headed by its *shaykh* or chief. The clans formed ramified associations, usually pyramidal in construction. The shaykhs in the smallest villages attached their clans to more influential ones in the largest village of the district. These, in turn, were linked with powerful landowning families in the towns. In instances of debt or tenancy the clannish chiefs had little choice but to affiliate with their creditors or the owners of their land. Where the shaykhs were free to choose, they normally elected those associations which could render the greatest advantages—protection against blood feuds and Beduin raids and intercession with the government for the promotion of their interests.

The persistence of the clannish networks into the mandatory period enabled the Muslim oligarchy, even though surpassed in wealth by many middle-class families, to retain its position of social dominance. The middle-class families—a majority Christian—were not effectively organized to challenge this authority. Besides, the Christian Arabs could not hope to replace the Muslim landowners in social prestige in a predominantly Muslim society. Nevertheless, the traditional clannish structure was already being undermined, as the government provided the countryside with greater security than it had ever known and as the isolation of the villages was broken down by modern communications and increasing economic reliance on the towns. In the urban areas the process of dissolution was even more advanced, for there were concentrated the Westernizing influences—the factories, trade unions, schools, hospitals, and government departments. There the clannish bonds loosened most swiftly among the newly urbanized peasantry. They had broken away from their ancestral villages, without any preparation for the semi-Westernized conditions of their new environment. Many were now living in slum districts even worse than those inhabited by the Oriental Jews.

Meanwhile, Muslim clannishness combined with Christian sectarianism to retard the integration of the Arab Community and the development of a sense of community-wide social responsibility. This was reflected in dependence on non-Arab help for education and health. About three-quarters of the 54,000 Muslim children attending school in 1936 were enrolled in government institutions; substantially more than one-half of the 22,400 Christian children in establishments maintained by foreign missions. With this assistance almost all the Christian boys and girls of school age received some education, as compared with only 25 per cent of the eligible Muslim children; and of the latter nearly four-fifths were boys. Moreover, secondary schools were relatively few, and for university and professional education Palestine Arabs were forced to go to Lebanon and Egypt or to Europe and America. Similarly, the government and the foreign missions provided the hospitals and clinics, the maternity and infant welfare services.

Still, the Arab Community had made substantial progress, especially in the educational field. Arab children attending schools had grown from less than 15 per cent in 1920 to about 30 per cent in 1936. In the latter year nearly 12,000 Muslim girls, including about 1,500 in the villages, were receiving some schooling. The number of sectarian schools maintained by the Christian Arabs had risen from 58 in 1928 to 99 in 1936 and the pupils from 4,600 to 9,300. In the same period the number of schools operated by the Muslim Arabs had expanded from 75 to 175 and attendance from 4,700 to 14,600. Equally significant was the spread of Muslim interest in education. Of those who had applied in 1936 for admittance to government-operated town and village schools, 59 and 48 per cent, respectively, had to be turned down owing to inadequate facilities. The census of 1931 revealed that only 57.7 per cent of the Christian Arabs and 14.4 per cent of the Muslim Arabs could read and write. Though no later statistics were available, the subsequent extension of Arab education doubtless led to higher literacy rates among both sections of the Arab population.

The Arab and Jewish communities, it was clear, were moving forward at different rates and in different directions. From the human components to the economic and social forms, the dissimilarity of the two was almost complete. By 1936 the Yishuv consisted by and large of a population which was European in origin and thus derived much of its material and intellectual vitality from the West. The Arab Community, comprising almost entirely an indigenous population, was Oriental and possessed economic and cultural patterns in common with the Arabs of the near-by countries, or the Arab East (*al-Sharq al-'Arabi*), as their own writers have designated it. Though thrown together by circumstances, the communities were essentially ignorant of each other. Hence, the Hebrew newspapers were beyond the reach of nearly all Arabs, and the Arabic press could be read only by relatively few Jews. The Zionists invariably talked of the need for uninterrupted colonization. But in Arabic the word meaning "colonization" (*isti'mar*) also connoted "imperialism." Even if all other conditions were favorable, and they obviously were not, the language barrier itself discouraged social intercourse and intensified the introversion of the Arabs and the Jews. Consequently, neither branch of the Palestine population made its plans with reference to the other, except in a negative or incidental sense. At all events, the economic and social needs of both were far from identical. The Jews were confronted with the problem of maintaining their predominantly Western standard of living; the Arabs with the problem of raising the masses above the subsistence level. The Jews were faced with the problem of welding immigrants of widely scattered backgrounds into a social unity; the Arabs with the problem of preserving their traditional values while adjusting to Western forms. It was therefore only natural that two sets of political institutions should have come into being to serve the differing needs of the two communities.[3]

CHAPTER 3

The Political Structure
of the Yishuv

EVEN MORE important than the economic and social developments was the political aspect of establishing the Jewish National Home. Zionist theory taught that the difference between the Jews and other peoples lay in the fact that the former were everywhere a minority. This universal minority status, which the Zionists labeled "the Jewish problem," gave rise, in their view, to the political, economic, and social insecurity of the Jews—the spreading and threatening phenomenon called anti-Semitism. The primary function of the Palestine Mandate, insisted the Zionists, was to solve the Jewish problem by "reconstituting" the Jewish National Home in its "ancestral land." The national home, moreover, would be reconstituted only when the Jews had become a majority in Palestine and could determine the form of its government. Then in one country the Jews would be masters of their own affairs; and the Jewish state would become a center of Jewish life, culture, and influence throughout the world.

In the face of growing Arab opposition, the accredited Zionist leadership had agreed by 1931 to the principle of "complete parity." By this was meant a government in which Arabs and Jews would be represented equally "without regard for the numerical strength of either people." The Jews "did not wish to be dominated in Palestine," it was explained, "but neither did they desire to dominate." Also to allay Arab fears the spokesmen for the main body of Zionists no longer openly claimed a Jewish majority. Instead they shifted their emphasis to uninterrupted immigration. "Any demand for a limitation of the size and expansion

38

of the Jewish population in Palestine," it was stated, "was absolutely unacceptable." [1] Hence, so long as the Jews remained a minority in Palestine, the Zionist policy-making bodies seemed to regard as premature any overt discussion of either a Jewish majority or a Jewish state. Yet for most Zionists the principles of nondomination and complete parity still connoted in the mid-1930's the eventual establishment of a Jewish state, and, in their own words, the Jewish National Home was "a Jewish state on the way." [2]

In order to gain experience in statecraft the promoters of the national home insisted upon managing its affairs. For this purpose they created administrative machinery, which, since it was not sovereign, was only quasi-governmental. Furthermore, this governmental arrangement was intricate in the extreme, because it had to provide for the representation not only of the Jews in Palestine but of their supporters abroad, non-Zionist as well as Zionist. The two concepts—Palestine Jewish Community and Jewish National Home—were not identical. The community encompassed only those Jews permanently residing in Palestine. It had a constitutional life of its own embodied in the Jewish Community regulations of the Palestine Government and in the peculiar political practices which the Yishuv evolved. The national home, a broader formula, included the Yishuv but also established a special relationship between the Jews the world over and those of Palestine. This relationship was written into the Palestine Mandate. The Zionist Organization and the Jewish Agency for Palestine furnished the apparatus for world Jewish participation. Eventually a time might arrive when the Yishuv would become the national home, when the duplication or division of administration and policy-making would disappear. But that goal would not be attained until the national home reached its full growth and developed either into an independent state or into an autonomous part of an independent state. In the meantime, the community and the national home remained interdependent, corporate entities.

The community government came into being in 1920 when the first election was held. But its status was not formalized by law until the Palestine Government enacted the Jewish Community regulations in December 1927. The franchise was granted to all persons over twenty with at least three months' residence in the country. An Elected Assembly, chosen by secret ballot, was invested with the highest authority and was required to convene at least once a year. Between sessions its powers were delegated to a National Council, appointed by the Assembly from its own ranks. The Council, in turn, nominated from among its members an Executive, charged with the actual administration of the community. Membership in the community and assessment for its administrative upkeep were voluntary. In the regulations the government designated the Yishuv as a religious community. But in practice the Jewish Community administration was national and secular. In fact, a group of religious fundamentalists, who opposed the secular emphasis and the provision for female franchise, opted themselves out of the organized community from the beginning.[3]

In accordance with Article 4 of the mandate, the Zionist Organization was alone responsible for the administration of the national home until 1929 and, thereafter, in collaboration with the Jewish Agency. The Zionist Organization was an international body which was founded in Switzerland in 1897 and by 1935 had branches in nearly fifty countries. Membership was open to any Jew above the age of eighteen who endorsed the basic tenet of Zionism—"to create for the Jewish people a home in Palestine secured by public law"—and who paid the nominal yearly dues. These numbered 976,000 in 1935. The supreme Zionist organ was the biennial Congress, which made general policy decisions and elected the General Council, the Executive, the President, and the Zionist representatives to the Jewish Agency. The General Council (or Actions Committee), which met at least once every six months, was empowered to determine over-all policy within the wide latitude of Congressional decisions. The Executive was responsible for implementing resolutions passed by the Congress and the General Council. The Executive's seat was located in London from 1919 until 1935 and was then transferred to Jerusalem.[4]

The Zionist president automatically became the president of the Jewish Agency for Palestine, which was created in 1929 to enlist non-Zionist Jewish support for the national home. While the non-Zionists "were strongly opposed to anything which approached the idea of a National State," [5] they were nevertheless anxious to assist in the further growth of the national home as a Jewish cultural and religious center. For their part, many Zionist leaders were equally desirous of broadening the base of world Jewish backing of their cause. After five years of negotiations the enlarged Jewish Agency came into existence and took over from the Zionist Organization responsibility for directing the affairs of the national home.

Provision was then made for equal representation by non-Zionists and Zionists on the governing hierarchy of the Jewish Agency—a Council, an Administrative Committee, and an Executive—which paralleled that of the Zionist Organization. The Agency Council convened biennially at the close of the Zionist Congress, charted future policy, and appointed the Administrative Committee of forty members. This Committee met at the same time as the Zionist General Council in order to exercise supervisory authority over the Agency's activities. The implementation of policy, as determined by the Council and the Administrative Committee, was placed in the hands of the Executive with main offices at Jerusalem.[6] According to the usage of the Zionist Organization, its delegates on the Agency Executive were nominated from among the members of the corresponding Zionist organ. Indeed, non-Zionist representation and influence in the

Agency tended to diminish, and by 1935 there were twice as many Zionist as non-Zionist members on the Agency Executive.

Here, then, was the elaborate machinery of Jewish quasi-government in Palestine. The Executives of the Yishuv's National Council, the Zionist Organization, and the Jewish Agency, concerned as they were with the day-to-day business of administration, were the most important organs. The National Council's jurisdiction in the 1920's was confined to social and religious matters. In the early 1930's it was extended to those of education and health, which previously had been controlled and financed by the Zionist Organization and the Jewish Agency. For purposes of close liaison between the Yishuv and the Zionist Organization, the National Council was permitted after 1923 to appoint two representatives to the Zionist General Council.

The Zionist Executive, after 1929, concerned itself principally with directing the internal affairs of the Zionist movement and managing the Jewish National Fund—the Zionist land-purchasing instrument. The Jewish Agency, on the other hand, promoted, supervised, and financed the further development of the national home. Under this arrangement, it was clear, the Agency was the mainspring of Jewish quasi-government. Since the Zionists within the Agency were far more powerful than the non-Zionists, the members of the Zionist Executive, in their individual capacities as heads of various Agency departments, were able to execute the policy of the Zionist Organization.

Thus, the Zionists in 1936 directed the Agency's political department, which operated essentially as the foreign office of the quasi-government. The political department negotiated, respectively and in varying spheres, with the Palestine Government, with Great Britain through its London office, and with the League of Nations through its Geneva office on all matters affecting mandatory policy toward the national home. The political department's section on Arab and Oriental relations endeavored to establish contact with the neighboring governments. Indicative of the weight of this key department was the fact that the chairman of the Agency Executive headed it and that its London office was personally directed by the president of the Agency. Zionists also managed the financial, labor, trade and industry, and statistics departments. The only departments headed by non-Zionists in 1936 were those for agricultural settlement, organization, and the settlement of German Jews, while that for immigration was directed jointly by a Zionist and a non-Zionist.

The Palestine Jews, who by the mid-1930's administered their own community affairs and outnumbered all others on both the Zionist and Agency Executives, were thus receiving valuable experience in self-rule. The various departments of the quasi-government were staffed with residents of the Yishuv, so that a core of civil servants was also being trained.

Moreover, ever since the first Arab anti-Jewish outbreaks in 1920, the Palestine Jews had expanded their secret illegal militia, called *Haganah* (defense), for the purpose of defending exposed areas of Jewish settlement, where the Palestine Government's security measures had proved inadequate. Hence, the Jewish quasi-government even had a military arm which in 1936 consisted of an estimated 10,000 trained and armed members. The future support of the quasi-government was ensured by the schools, which constituted one of the most effective instruments of nationalism. "From this education 'melting-pot'," observed the Royal Commission of 1936–37, "emerges a national self-consciousness of unusual intensity." By and large Jewish teachers believed it was their mission [7]

> to foster a sense of devotion to the task of rebuilding a Jewish nation on its ancient homeland. . . . From the age of three or four years, when children enter the kindergarten . . . pride . . . in the National Home as an exclusively . . . Jewish achievement of the present is the dynamic centre-point of their whole intellectual development.

THE MULTIPLE-PARTY SYSTEM

An overwhelming majority of the Palestine Jews recognized the authority of the quasi-government. Competition for control of its administration was keen, for with it went the right to determine policy, to manage the large and growing national wealth, and to negotiate with the Palestine and British governments for changes in mandatory legislation. Opportunities for winning such control were given in the elections of the Zionist Organization, which were held biennially, and in those of the Yishuv, which were held irregularly. The electoral system, although one of proportional representation, bore little resemblance to that in Britain or the United States. It was based not on geographical districts but on the so-called party "lists" or tickets. The candidates on these tickets were usually chosen not by a party caucus but by the party machine. The voter cast his secret ballot not for a particular candidate but for a particular party.

In the case of community elections, an electoral unit was established, when all the returns had been tabulated, by dividing the total number of ballots by the number of seats in the Assembly. The electoral unit for Zionist elections was fixed by the Zionist General Council. But voters in the Yishuv enjoyed preferential rights, since their unit was only half the size of that prevailing elsewhere. Each party was allocated as many delegates, either to the Elected Assembly or the Zionist Congress, as it had received multiples of the electoral unit in votes cast. The individual party was then permitted to name its own delegates and to award its "surplus" votes to any other party of its own choice in order to fill the remaining vacant seats. Finally, since no provision existed for by-elections to the

Yishuv's Assembly, any vacancy was automatically filled by the party of the retiring delegate.[8]

Unlike the political parties in the United States, the essential feature of most of the Jewish political groups was their carefully formulated and rigidly upheld program. The key political plank of these platforms dealt with the eventual structure of the national home: whether it was to be theocratic, socialist, or capitalist, and whether it was to become an independent, unitary government or an autonomous province of a binational (joint Arab-Jewish) state. The adherent either endorsed the party program in its entirety as expressing the will of the majority or withdrew, usually banding together with like-minded dissidents to form a new party. The parties customarily sought to promote specific economic interests —the Histadrut and its manifold enterprises, private industry, trade, citriculture, or the like. Each party had one or more organs to give continuing expression to its views.

The most broadly representative body of each party was the annual (or biennial) conference (or convention), to which all fundamental policy questions were submitted for approval. Between sessions the highest organ was the more manageable council, which usually met quarterly to review party activities and problems. Policy making and routine administrative work were entrusted to a small, compact central (or executive) committee (sometimes called presidium), appointed by the council from among its own members. As a rule party caucuses insured a united stand by the party delegates on the organs of the quasi-government, although on issues which were not especially controversial provision was occasionally made for minority oppositions.

The Jewish multiple-party system in Palestine, similar to that of France in the late 1930's, was distinguished by a highly organized, vocal, and mutually hostile left and right, and a weak, disorganized center. The very heterogeneity of the Palestine Jews tended not only to preserve political diversity but also to foster it. The east Europeans drifted toward the leftist or rightist parties, while those from the German- and English-speaking countries inclined to provide the leadership and following of the less cohesive centrist groups. The Sefardim had established in the 1920's and early 1930's their own separate units within the European-controlled parties. Others were organized in their own semipolitical association, known as the National Representation of the Sefardic Jews in Palestine. The articulate Yemeni Jews joined either the labor parties or their own semipolitical societies. But most Yemenis and other Orientals were entirely nonpolitical and remained disorganized.

As is characteristic of the multiple-party system, no one group ever achieved an absolute majority of votes in the community elections; and in the Zionist balloting such a situation did not exist after 1929. Consequently, the executive organs, with one exception, had always been managed by loose coalitions. However, by 1936 the secular socialists, through their domination of the Histadrut, became the most powerful single party and were able to exercise the foremost influence on the formulation of national policy. Furthermore, there were two oppositions. The first comprised the parties which acknowledged the jurisdiction of the quasi-government but were set against those in power. The second consisted of the dissident political groups, which refused to have any dealings with the quasi-government and resisted both the coalition in power and the first opposition.

THE PARTIES

The number of Jewish political parties and factions in the Yishuv was in constant flux through fission and fusion. There were ten in 1936, each uniting two or more sub-groups. The parties fell into four classes—labor, centrist, clerical, and rightist. With the exception of the communist and the religious fundamentalist factions, they owed allegiance to the Zionist movement. With the further exception of a revolutionary socialist and a militant rightist group, they recognized the authority of the quasi-government.

The labor parties were identified with the Histadrut. There were labor factions outside its orbit. But these were intimately associated with other political groups which did not have an exclusively labor slant. The three main parties belonging to the Histadrut were socialist. They originated in Europe, ranged in emphasis from moderate to radical, and taken as a unit constituted the left.[9] By far the largest was the Palestine Labor Party or Mapai, as it had come to be known in the Yishuv.

Mapai's influence by 1936 was much greater than was suggested by its 12,000 enrolled members. In the latest election of the Histadrut in December 1932, Mapai obtained exclusive control over the Executive of the labor federation, which established policy, and over its secretariat, which administered the federation's multifarious activities. In the 1931 community balloting, Mapai returned 31 of the 71 delegates to the Elected Assembly and occupied two of the eight seats on the National Council Executive, including that of the chairman. Mapai and the world Zionist union with which it was allied, as the most powerful single group in the coalition Executives of the Zionist Organization and the Jewish Agency, also played a leading role in these bodies. David Ben Gurion (1886–   ), chairman of the Executive of the Jewish Agency, Moshe Shertok (1895–   ), co-director of its political department, and Eliezer Kaplan (1891–   ), its treasurer, were Mapai representatives.

The party, which was affiliated with the Second International, espoused socialist doctrines of a reformist or gradualist variety. Mapai champions saw no problem in encouraging the investment of private capital in the national home, provided the areas of Jewish settlement were thereby extended and employment for Jews created. As socialists they opposed investments "used for speculation, for raising land prices, and for the exploitation of cheap labor." [10] Their ultimate political objective was the organization of Palestine as an independent, socialist Jewish state. Within Mapai the strongest unit was the pro-British Faction C, whose leaders and members derived for the most part from the towns and were chiefly responsible for the close relations which had been established with the British Labor Party. The smaller, leftist Faction B, composed principally of members living in collective villages, constituted an internal opposition.

Allied with Mapai as a labor bloc in the Yishuv and the Zionist Organization were the Young Watchman (*ha-Shomer ha-Za'ir*) Party and the world Zionist union bearing the same name. Ha-Shomer ha-Za'ir was dedicated to revolutionary socialism; its platform interwove Marxism with Zionism. Its members considered themselves an integral part of the world proletariat striving to replace "the capitalist system with its private profit and the exploitation of the many for the good of the few" by a new economic and social order in which class distinctions would disappear.[11] The party program called for the conversion of Palestine into an independent, socialist, binationalist (Arab-Jewish) state, but otherwise endorsed the official Zionist principles of a Jewish majority and equal representation. The advocates of this position believed that the Jewish National Home, as a politically autonomous unit of a binationalist state, would be capable of supporting itself and of absorbing most of the Jews throughout the world.

The party's stronghold in the Yishuv was the National Collective, a federation of collective villages with a total membership of about 4,500. An urban branch, called the Socialist League, was formed in 1935. Ha-Shomer ha-Za'ir was affiliated until 1939 with the International Bureau for Revolutionary-Socialist Unity and maintained contact with the Independent Labor Party in Britain. Ha-Shomer ha-Za'ir's influence in the community at large was considerable, despite the fact that it was not represented on any of the executive organs of the quasi-government.

Somewhat smaller and much less influential was a second Marxist party, known as the Left Zionist Workers. The party was launched by a group which had seceded from the Zionist Organization in 1920 and sought *rapprochement* with Soviet Russia. Having been rebuffed by the Comintern between 1920 and 1928, it subsequently became anticommunist but retained a strong anti-British bias. It also remained outside the "bourgeois-dominated" Zionist Organization, because the party did not desire its program to be "diluted in the general stream of romantic ideologies." The Left Zionist Workers preferred their status as an independent proletarian movement "standing firmly on the ground of the class struggle [and] . . . working hand in glove with the international proletariat." Consequently, the party creed promoted the establishment of a Jewish proletariat throughout the world for whom it demanded full "national, political rights in all countries." The party's members were almost entirely concentrated in the towns and generally spoke Yiddish, not Hebrew. In fact, a small Hebrew-speaking faction withdrew from the party in 1936 and was absorbed by Mapai.[12]

On the extreme left were the communist splinter factions, outlawed by the Palestine Government and the Yishuv. While a few of the Jewish communists were followers of Trotsky, most of them belonged to the Stalinist Palestine Communist Party. Organized in the early 1920's chiefly by Jews of Russian origin who had broken away from the Left Zionist Workers, the Communist Party was the only one in the country with a mixed Arab-Jewish enrollment. From the start it featured a consistent anti-British and anti-Zionist line. Leveled against Britain were the charges that the mandatory, in complete disregard of its international obligations, was holding the local population in political and economic bondage, backing the reactionary elements in the two communities, and encouraging Arab-Jewish strife. Zionism was condemned as a tool of British imperialism, "a counter-revolutionary movement of the Jewish big bourgeoisie." In the Arab-Zionist controversy, the Jewish communists supported the Arab position. The Communist Party was therefore unable to entrench itself in the Yishuv and its membership in 1936 probably did not exceed 1,000.[13]

Less articulate than the left were the parties of the center. These so-called general parties resembled the American political parties in that they were not committed to an inflexible ideology. Any Zionist not already owing allegiance to a particular party automatically became a general Zionist. In the 1920's the general Zionists dominated the Zionist administration. Having been surpassed in strength by the labor bloc in 1931, they formed their own world Union of General Zionists. Its founding program stated that the union would be guided only by national, not sectional, group, or class interests. It pledged to support "the union and intensification of the creative forces of labour and capital in the service of the nation." Nevertheless, a world conference of the union in Poland in August 1934 adopted an anti-labor platform. This act split the organization into two separate bodies. The conservative wing retained the original name. The liberal wing, adhering to the original tenets, called itself the Confederation of General Zionists.[14]

In Palestine the Confederation was called the General Zionist A Party. It pursued an independent line in quasi-governmental politics, standing at times behind organized labor and at others behind private enterprise. The party founded its own labor faction, known at the time as the Zionist Youth, which was affiliated with the Histadrut. The total General Zionist A membership, including that of the labor subsidiary, probably did not exceed 5,000 in 1936. However, since most Anglo-American Zionists were nonpartisan and, therefore, commonly supported the progressive General Zionist A Party, it was strongly represented in the quasi-government. Three of its members sat on the Executives of the Zionist Organization and the Jewish Agency, including Dr. Chaim Weizmann (1874–   ), who was president of both bodies.

The conservative Union of General Zionists was known in the Yishuv after 1935 as the General Zionist B Party and became the champion of private enterprise. Associated with it were the Farmers Federation and the Palestine Manufacturers Association, representing respectively the private Jewish citrus and industrial interests. The party also had its own labor faction, called the Organization of the General Zionist Workers, which remained independent of the Histadrut. The active membership of the General Zionist B Party was somewhat smaller than that of the progressive group, and its single delegate on the Agency Executive characteristically directed the department of trade and industry.

The labor and general parties were either indifferent or hostile to religion. In an effort to counteract these secular tendencies there had emerged by 1936 two clerical parties, one Zionist and the other non-Zionist. The religious Zionist party, ha-Mizrahi, belonged to a world Zionist union of the same name which had been founded in 1902. The Zionist mission, Mizrahi champions believed, was to solve not only the problems of the Jewish people but also those of its religion. Judaism, they went on to declare, was a distinct system of life which inextricably blended nationalism and religion. Of the two elements religion was the more significant, for the Jewish faith constituted "Israel's unique contribution to modern civilization." The Mizrahi program accordingly proposed that "historic" Palestine be transformed into an independent Jewish state which would become the authority of Jewish religious law and in which the Jewish religious practices would be universally respected and observed. In the transitional period the Mizrahi Party considered itself the custodian of religion within the Zionist movement and attempted to make the traditional observance of the sabbath, holidays, and dietary laws binding on all Palestine Jews. This was the price it exacted for agreeing to participate in the coalition Executives of the quasi-government. Opposed to the party's middle-class orientation was the Mizrahi Labor Federation, founded in Tel-Aviv in 1921 by a group of workers who rejected the secular Histadrut. The Mizrahi Labor Federation engaged on a much smaller scale in many of the same activities as the Histadrut. But it also functioned as a semi-independent political faction within the Mizrahi Party. Indeed, the labor faction with its 5,300 members in 1936 surpassed in numerical strength the middle-class section of the party, which probably had fewer than 4,000 members in Palestine at that time.[15]

More rigidly fundamentalist than the Mizrahi Party was the non-

Zionist Agudat Israel (Society of Israel) World Organization. The Agudists were convinced that Zionism, as a secular movement, basically challenged their own theocratic conception of Jewish life. Palestine had originally been granted to the Jews by the Lord, ran the Agudist thesis, in a "sworn eternal covenant," so that His chosen people could live there in accordance with the letter and spirit of the Mosaic Law. The Jews had been driven out of the country because of their sins. But God had pledged that Palestine would eventually be restored to the Jews by divine intervention through the promised Messiah. Only then could Palestine, comprising the territorial boundaries described in the Bible, become an enduring Jewish state. Agudist support in Palestine, weaker than that of the Mizrahi Party, came principally from the so-called "old Yishuv"—those Jews who had settled in the country for purely religious reasons before the Zionist rise to power. Consequently, the Agudists refused from the outset to recognize the authority of the quasi-government.

Under the impact of the Zionist industrialization there appeared among the Agudists for the first time laboring elements. Many of these workers were drifting into the Mizrahi Labor Federation and even into the secular Histadrut because of the greater economic security. To check this trend the Agudists formed their own Agudat Israel Labor Federation in 1933. The Agudist Federation followed closely the course, but had not yet reached in 1936 the stage of development, of its Mizrahi prototype. The Agudist labor organization also operated as a political group and was inclined to take a position much nearer to Zionism than that of its parent body. Nevertheless, it remained an opposition faction within Agudat Israel. The Labor Federation's membership in 1936 was probably less than 3,000.[16]

On the extreme right were the Revisionist Party and its outgrowth, the Jewish State Party. Both were as intransigent as the clerical groups, and both were dedicated to an aggressive, militant brand of Zionism. The world Union of Revisionist Zionists, with which the party in Palestine was affiliated, was formed in 1925 by Vladimir Jabotinsky (1880–1940), Russian-born journalist and Zionist leader. Jabotinsky had resigned from the Zionist Executive two years earlier. At that time he accused his former colleagues, especially Weizmann, of lacking political realism and of submitting without cause to the mandatory's efforts to curtail its pledges to the Jews. He gathered to his banner an increasing number of disaffected elements, who devoted themselves to the thorough revision of Zionist leadership, tactics, and program. Between 1925 and 1929 the Revisionists stubbornly opposed the admittance of non-Zionists to any share whatsoever in the administration of the projected Jewish Agency. Only a part of the Revisionists actually withdrew from the Zionist Organization in 1929. Those who remained, however, including Jabotinsky himself, refused to abide by the decisions of the Zionist Congress. Thus, at the 1931 Congress Jabotinsky introduced a resolution recommending that the Zionists openly demand a Jewish state on both sides of the Jordan. Although the resolution was defeated, the Revisionist Party thereafter adopted the proposal as one of its basic planks. In 1935 Jabotinsky formally resigned from the Zionist Organization and set up his own New Zionist Organization.

From then on the Revisionists were relentless in their criticism of the "old" Zionists and their "timid and shortsighted leaders," who, it was asserted, no longer spoke for "the whole or even the majority of Zionist Jewry." The Revisionists talked in extravagant terms about "liquidating the Diaspora" and about populating Palestine and Transjordan with eight to eighteen million people. They advocated that Jewish labor federations exclude non-Jewish workers from membership and be entirely divorced from politics. The Revisionists condemned the "class-war" or labor pioneers as detrimental to the national interest and proposed that a "national pioneering movement" be created. Under this scheme, at least half of the annual Jewish immigration into Palestine would comprise "national pioneers," young Jews between the ages of twenty-three and thirty-five, who would be required to devote a certain period to the national service. At its completion they would be provided by national funds with homes and with the means to set up their own independent livelihood.[17]

Nearly two-thirds of the Revisionists lived in Poland in the mid-1930's. The Palestine branch fluctuated in size, winning members from and losing them to such parties as the General Zionist B and the Mizrahi. The Revisionists founded their own National Labor Federation in 1933, as a means of dissuading their followers from joining the Histadrut. Still the party remained a small minority in the community and its enrollment probably did not reach 5,000 in 1936. It displayed little initiative after the British banishment of Jabotinsky from Palestine in 1929 and followed implicitly the political line laid down by the presidium of the New Zionist Organization. Even its militarized society, which was formed in 1935 when the Revisionists withdrew from the "labor-dominated" Haganah, retained Jabotinsky as its commander-in-chief *in absentia*.

In the meantime, a small minority of the world Revisionist Party formed an internal opposition, calling themselves "democratic Revisionists." While they continued to embrace the same totalitarian doctrines, they eschewed the separatist tendencies of the majority. At the 1933 session of the Zionist Congress the seven "democratic Revisionist" delegates bolted and formed their own Jewish State Party. Three years later the State Party was recognized as an independent world union within the Zionist Organization and established in Palestine its own labor federation. Yet the party had fewer than 1,000 members in the Yishuv in 1936 and was not represented on any of the executive organs of the quasi-government. The State Party frequently collaborated with the dissident Revisionists and constituted a self-appointed liaison between them and the Zionist Organization.[18]

CHAPTER 4

The Political Structure of the Arab Community

THE RELIGIOUS BASIS OF PALESTINE ARAB POLITICS

THE POLITICAL structure of the Arab Community differed radically from that of the Yishuv and the national home. No government statutes existed, enabling the Arabs to organize their community on a national basis. Therefore, they had no quasi-government and no elected policy-makers. The only Arab officials chosen by popular ballot were those of the municipal and village councils. The Palestine Arabs, unlike the Palestine Jews or the Arabs of the other mandated territories in the Near East, including Transjordan,[1] were receiving no experience or training in self-rule. The Arab neighbors of Palestine had adopted democratic forms, although oligarchic rule persisted. Because Britain was committed in Palestine to a policy of encouraging the establishment of the Jewish National Home, the situation in that country was unique. The eventual political structure of the local Arab Community was unpredictable. There were too many unanswered questions. How long would the British remain in effective control of the government? Would Palestine be converted into a Jewish or a binational Arab-Jewish state? Or would the Arabs succeed in establishing in all or part of Palestine an independent Arab state or one that merged with another Arab country?

If the Palestine Arab Community was not welded together as a body politic, its articulate elements were nevertheless united in national sentiment. This stemmed from the conviction that the Palestine Arabs were being made the innocent victims of external forces. The nationalist rank and file were disillusioned by the nonfulfillment of promises which they believed were given to the Arabs of Palestine as well as to the other

Arabs in the Near East during World War I. They saw no valid reason why they should suffer an alien people to take over their national patrimony. The Palestine Arabs, it was observed, were not consulted prior to the issuance of the Balfour Declaration. Subsequently, they had never given their consent to this document; or to the mandate in which it was incorporated; or to the steady stream of Jewish immigration to which both gave rise. Therefore, if the Palestine Arabs were resisting this unjust policy, it was argued, they were merely defending their national rights and possessions in the face of ultimate economic and political subjection to the Jews. These were the arguments advanced by the Arab national movement in Palestine. In the decade and a half of its existence the national movement had become the instrument by which the Arabs hoped to transform Palestine into an independent Arab state. One of the main characteristics of the movement was the fact that by 1936 it came to be dominated by a Muslim cleric. Religion was a major element at that time in the related movements of the near-by lands. But in none were clerical leaders playing the same commanding role as in Palestine.

If the Palestine Arabs had not developed a national community government which cut across religious lines, it was not due to the absence of opportunities. As early as 1923 the mandatory recommended the establishment of an Arab Agency to represent Arab national interests. But the nationalist leaders rejected the proposal, as they had turned down earlier suggestions to admit Arabs and Jews to advisory positions on the highest level of the central government. The Arab nationalists did not wish to acknowledge the legality of the mandate and the Jewish National Home, for this recognition might have undermined the claim to the entire area of Palestine and the demand for the complete stoppage of Jewish immigration. In the words of the Arab nationalist delegation to London in 1922, the Palestine Arabs could accept [2]

> no constitution which would fall short of giving the People of Palestine full control of their own affairs. . . . If [they] . . . assented . . . they would be in the position of agreeing to an instrument of Government which might, and probably would be used to smother their national life under a flood of alien immigration.

As a matter of principle, the Arab nationalists adhered with unwavering fidelity to this stand of not recognizing the validity of Jewish rights in Palestine.

That an Arab Community did not exist in a legal sense was also due to the mandatory's grant of religious autonomy. The British incorporated many features of the Turkish millet system into the religious communities organization ordinance of 1926. This ordinance stipulated that any religious community might apply to the government for the right to administer its own religious, cultural, and educational establishments as well as courts of law which would have jurisdiction over questions of personal status, such as marriage, divorce, and inheritance. By the mid-1930's there were Muslim and Druze communities and several Christian denominational communities. In the Muslim Community a highly centralized administration was created. Since Islam is a socio-political creed, this administration achieved unequalled political power. Moreover, owing to their numerical superiority, the Muslims controlled the local national movement, so that, by extension, the principal administrator of Muslim affairs was able to become the supreme political leader of the Christian as well as Muslim Arabs.

In a special regulation of December 20, 1921, the High Commissioner provided for a Supreme Muslim Council, as the most authoritative religious body in the community. The Council was empowered to administer the religious courts and the trust funds for the maintenance of mosques, shrines, and schools and to appoint or dismiss all officials. In addition to a permanent president, the Council comprised four members who were to hold office for four-year terms and were to represent various districts. The president and the members of the Council were to receive salaries from the Palestine Government as well as allowances from the religious endowments. Later enactments, it was contemplated, would define "the functions, status and precedence" of the president and would make the Council responsible to an electoral college. The electoral college was to have been entrusted with the election of the Council members, while the president was to have been chosen by a general ballot.[8] In order to set up the Council immediately, however, the Palestine Government in January 1922 allowed a general committee chosen by the surviving secondary electors of the Turkish electoral college to appoint all the initial members. Al-Hajj Muhammad Amin al-Husayni (1893–   ), recently nominated to the lifetime office of mufti of Jerusalem, was now named permanent president of the Supreme Muslim Council. An astute and ambitious politician, al-Hajj Amin took full advantage of the absence of legal restriction on his authority as the Council's president and used the unlimited rights of appointment and dismissal to build up a personal, countrywide religio-political machine.

The old Turkish secondary electors, meanwhile, were again called upon in January 1926 to select new members of the Council. Owing to irregularities, however, the High Commissioner annulled the election and himself named the new incumbents. He also appointed a Muslim committee to draw up a more precise constitution for the Council and to establish a definite procedure for future elections. The Palestine Government now endeavored to make the Council responsible to an Elected Assembly, roughly modeled after that of the Yishuv. The government also hoped to have the authority of the Council's president prescribed by an exact definition of his duties and status and to have his term of office limited to nine years. A draft ordinance incorporating these reforms was made public in June 1929. But the proposed legislation was shelved as a result of the anti-Jewish riots two months later. By 1936 the Palestine Government still had taken no further action to revise the constitution of the Muslim Community.

By that time the Jerusalem Mufti had consolidated his position as the most powerful political figure in the Palestine Arab Community. The Council's growing annual revenues were approaching $600,000 in 1936. The control of these funds furnished al-Hajj Amin with an effective lever by which to bring into line with his political policies the officials of dependent religious establishments. Through them he was able to reach the illiterate fallahin and arouse their religious fanaticism against Zionism and mandatory policy. In the multiplying schools supervised by the Council he encouraged the instruction of extreme religious conservatism, as an Islamic bulwark against Westernization. Incidentally, this established the Mufti's reputation as the protector of Islam in Palestine. Furthermore, the Husayni clan had been designated under the Turkish regime as hosts of the annual festival in honor of the birth of the Prophet Moses and as custodians of the shrine at the traditional Muslim site of Moses' tomb. Al-Hajj Amin early recognized the value of this feast as a means of exciting the fanaticism of the peasantry. His inflammatory speech to the pilgrims in 1920 was one of the chief contributory factors of the anti-Jewish outbreaks at that time. Subsequently, the festival was converted into a yearly nationalist demonstration.[4]

While religio-political authority in the Muslim Community thus tended to concentrate in a single leader, no comparable development took place in any of the Christian sectarian communities. The Greek Orthodox hierarchy consisted mostly of clerics of Greek origin. They did not enjoy the support of the rank and file, who resented the fact that the important clerical posts were filled by non-Arabs. The authority of the Latin Patriarch, a non-Arab, was also impaired, because the custodianship of the holy sites in Palestine had been retained by the Franciscan Order since the fourteenth century and because he had far fewer funds at his disposal than the European orders. The Uniate Churches—chiefly the Melkite and the Maronite—were recognized as separate communities by the Palestine Government; but they merely constituted appendages of the much larger sister-communities in the Levant States. The more important Greek Orthodox and Latin clerics, as non-Arabs, did not participate in the political life of the country. However, the local parish priests in these communities and the religious leaders on all levels of the Uniate Churches very often played active political roles.

Common opposition to Zionism provided the main basis for Christian-

Muslim collaboration in the national movement. Yet underlying differences continued to divide the two. From the start the paramount political goal of the Muslims was complete independence from foreign rule. The Christians, however, generally favored at the close of the First World War a European mandatory "which would exercise real control." The Roman Catholics desired as tutelary power a European Catholic government, preferably France. No longer able to look to Russia for aid, the Greek Orthodox Arabs endorsed Britain as their choice. These sentiments persisted under the mandate and were probably motivated by the fear that the Christians would not enjoy real freedom under a Muslim-dominated government. Christian-Muslim friction tended, at times, to take on an economic character. This was illustrated in 1932 by the campaign in the Muslim press alleging government partiality to the Christian Arabs, since they had received considerably more than their relative share of the subordinate government posts.[5]

PALESTINE ARAB NATIONALISM

The Arab national movement in Palestine formed an integral part of the general nationalist awakening in the Arab East, which traced its origin back to the cultural revival in Lebanon in the second quarter of the nineteenth century. By 1914 the movement had spread to Syria, Egypt, and Iraq. In the course of its diffusion it became increasingly political in nature. After World War I Arab nationalism acquired mass followings in Egypt and the Franco-British mandated territories of the Near East. In the postwar period there were three main currents of Arab nationalist thought, closely interwoven, yet mutually contradictory.

The first was Pan-Islamism, which advocated the religio-political unity of the Islamic countries. This drive, however, took the Muslim Arabs further afield in an effort to create a community of purpose with their non-Arab coreligionists. Less divisive was Pan-Arabism, which stressed the ethnic unity of the Arabs, whether Christian or Muslim—their common language and cultural heritage, their common history, and their common desire to liberate themselves from foreign political and economic domination. Ethnic nationalism was naturally strongest wherever there existed substantial segments of Christian Arabs, as in the Levant States, Palestine, and Egypt. Many Pan-Arabs were inspired by the ideal of uniting all Arabic-speaking peoples, or at least those in the Near East, into a single state. Others entertained less grandiose schemes, such as that of Amir 'Abdallah, who aspired to set up a Greater Syria, comprising his own Transjordan, the Levant States, and Palestine, with himself as monarch. Finally, the tempo of the nationalist awakening and the problems it faced differed from country to country. As a result, local national movements arose, whose leaders were anxious, above all, to achieve the political freedom of their separate countries and strove to preserve their hegemony. This came to be true particularly in Palestine.

On the eve of the First World War individual Palestine Arabs had participated in the general national movement, and during the war a few had even lost their lives for the cause. But within Palestine proper no organized national movement came into being until after the Armistice, when Muslim-Christian Associations were formed in the Arab towns to protest against the projected Jewish National Home. The members of these Associations were the first organized Arab nationalists in Palestine, but their movement was merely a projection of Syrian nationalism. They followed the lead of the Syrian spokesmen at Damascus in 1919–20 in their unsuccessful endeavors to create an independent, unified Syria which would embrace Lebanon, Palestine, and Transjordan.[6]

The inauguration of the British civil administration in Palestine in the early summer of 1920 marked the beginning of the transition in that country from Syrian to Palestine Arab nationalism and the transfer of headquarters from Damascus to Jerusalem. In December of that year the Muslim-Christian Associations sponsored a countrywide convention at Haifa. At this so-called third Palestine Arab Congress the local national movement was founded. For the first time the local nationalists demanded that Great Britain "embark on the establishment of a National Government in Palestine responsible to a representative Council, to be elected by the Arabic-speaking people who were living in Palestine at the outbreak of the Great War . . ."[7] The Palestine nationalists now had their own special objective. For its realization the Haifa convention set up an Arab Executive, composed of 24 Muslims and Christians, as a permanent body. The Executive continued to collaborate with the Syrian nationalists, particularly at Geneva, where until 1923 a joint Syro-Palestinian delegation lobbied against the adoption of the Syrian and Palestine mandates by the League of Nations. But the Palestine spokesmen, with few exceptions, no longer sought union with Syria or any other Arab country. Instead, they elicited the support of their Arab neighbors and even non-Arab Muslims of Iran, India, and elsewhere. Hence, for the time being at least, the ideals of Pan-Arabism and Pan-Islamism among the Palestine Arabs were largely instruments for attaining their political aspirations.

The Palestine Arab nationalist platform differed little in 1936 from what it had been at the time of the birth of the movement. The leaders still insisted upon the conversion of Palestine into a sovereign Arab state. This necessitated, in their view, the early termination of the mandate and of the Jewish National Home as well as the unqualified cessation of Jewish immigration and purchase of Arab-owned lands. They rested their case on the McMahon pledge of 1915 to the Sharif of Mecca and on

what were termed the "natural" right of "actual and long-standing possession" and the "political" right of the Wilsonian doctrine of self-
determination. What the Arabs called their natural and political rights
were sound democratic principles and constituted incontrovertible arguments.

Yet the leadership of the national movement, like that in Syria, was
limited almost exclusively to the landed gentry. This Muslim oligarchy
was anxious to preserve the old order and resisted innovation. Moreover, the lack of a statutory Arab Community deprived the Arabs of
practice in self-rule even within the limited framework of a quasi-
government. As a result, in lieu of elaborating upon plans for the kind
of government they hoped to establish, the nationalists became preoccupied with enumerating their grievances. They denied that the historical connection of the Jews with Palestine constituted a just claim to
its possession, and asserted that the Holy Land belonged to the Christian
and Moslem worlds. Syrian and Lebanese landowners, contended the
nationalists, benefited most from Jewish investments. The Palestine Arab
workers, the economic argument continued, were receiving higher wages
under the mandatory regime than under the Turkish. But these advantages were more than offset by the high taxes to maintain a bureaucratic
government, high tariffs to protect Jewish industry, and high prices for
the goods produced.

The humanitarian purpose of the national home to provide a place of
refuge for persecuted Jews was in itself laudable, conceded the Arab
nationalists. But the selection of Palestine, a country already inhabited
by a nationally conscious people, as the site of this home was worse than
misplaced philanthropy. The Palestine Arabs were not responsible for
the oppression of the European Jews and had already contributed more
than their share toward the solution of this problem. Furthermore, the
Balfour Declaration and the national home were merely screens for the
transformation of the country into a Jewish state. If this goal were attained, the Zionists would proceed to destroy "the Arabs as a national
and cultural entity." In fact, the Jews have "been allowed to occupy the
best and most productive land, from which the Arab farmers and the
Arab villages were ruthlessly swept off." [8] Palestine was unable to support further immigration, insisted the Arab nationalists, since it "can
hardly cope with the natural increase of the Arabs and Jews" already
there.[9]

These grievances were reiterated through various media. The Arab
school system was not only geared to the nationalist program but was
even more narrowly nationalistic than the Jewish. Even the government
network had become, in the view of the Royal Commission,[10]

at least as purely Arab in its character as the Jewish system is Jewish. . . .
the teaching is in Arabic only; apart from scientific subjects, the curriculum

is almost wholly devoted to the literature, history, and traditions of the Arabs; and all the schoolmasters from the humblest village teacher to the head of the Government Arab College are Arabs.

The appearance after 1929 of an Arabic daily press, which featured the nationalist demands, imparted the message to the literate public. The illiterate elements were reached through the mosques. The considerable Jewish investments in the country indirectly provided the nationalists with abundant funds for the strengthening of their movement. The unprecedented influx of Jews after 1932 added weight to the nationalist charges that the Zionists would soon dominate the Arabs. From its center at Jerusalem the national movement had fanned out by the mid-1930's to all the Arab urban areas and their rural suburbs. It had become a popular movement. It therefore represented a powerful political force in the country, one that could not be ignored.

The national movement made a promising start, and until the end of 1923 its organization remained fairly stable. The Executive sent delegations to Britain, Switzerland, Egypt, and Turkey to promote the Palestine Arab cause and won important concessions from the Colonial Office before the mandate came into formal operation. The Executive, moreover, sought popular approval by reporting on its actions to three Congresses which it convened in this period. For the most part the delegates to the Congresses were chosen by the Muslim-Christian Associations, which formed local branches of the national movement in the towns. This procedure might have evolved enduring democratic forms with an elective Executive ultimately responsible to the Arab public. But this early promise was never fulfilled, because the national movement as then constituted came to be the virtual preserve of the Husayni clan.

The Husaynis had obtained possession of large tracts of land in southern Palestine, enabling them to become one of the most powerful clans in the region during the nineteenth century. Of the thirteen Arab mayors of Jerusalem between the incorporation of the city in 1864 and the outbreak of World War I, six had been Husaynis. At the time of the British occupation of the country that post was held by Musa Kazim Pasha al-Husayni (ca. 1850–1934). After he was dismissed from office as mayor of Jerusalem in April 1920, owing to his involvement in an unauthorized nationalist demonstration, Musa Kazim Pasha devoted full time to the national movement. He presided over the Arab Executive and the several Congresses, became the acknowledged spokesman of the Muslim-Christian Associations, and headed the Arab delegations abroad. The clan's influence was further enhanced by its firm hold over the religious affairs of the Muslim Community. This it acquired through al-Hajj Amin al-Husayni and his personal followers, who were known collectively as the Councilites.[11]

Rival Muslim landowning clans resented the concentration of power in Husayni hands. As early as 1922 they began to form a nationalist Opposition, headed by Raghib Bey al-Nashashibi (1880–   ), the successor of Musa Kazim Pasha as mayor of Jerusalem. Though Raghib Bey was the first member of his clan to hold this office, the Nashashibis had amassed great wealth in the late nineteenth century and became competitors of the Husaynis even under the Turkish regime. Raghib Bey failed to obtain for his followers the posts of mufti of Jerusalem in 1921 and presidency of the Supreme Muslim Council early in the following year. He gathered about him several other Arab mayors, landed gentry, and well-to-do merchants, who founded National Muslim Societies in the Arab towns as a counterpoise to the Muslim-Christian Associations. The first opportunity to discredit the Husaynis came in the autumn of 1923, after the Council of the League of Nations had ratified the Palestine Mandate. Dependent upon the British Administration for political influence, the Nashashibi-led Opposition adopted a conciliatory attitude toward the government. They hoped thereby to undermine the Husayni position and resist Zionism more effectively within the framework of the mandate. To accomplish these purposes they established the National Party in November 1923 and even created Peasant Parties in rural areas.

The two sides now became embroiled in a bitter conflict for political leadership, and for nearly five years the national movement passed through a period of abeyance. Nationalist objectives were ignored. Even the nationalist groups vanished, leaving only al-Hajj Amin's Councilites and Raghib Bey's Opposition. The two factions organized their adherents on the basis of semifeudal principles which had been established in Palestine Arab society for centuries. They concentrated on extending throughout the community their alliances with influential landowning families, for these were the overlords of the rural clannish networks. The landed gentry themselves, in opting between the Husaynis and the Nashashibis, were prompted in part by the patronage they received and the prospects of enhancing their own prestige; and in part by clannish alignments dating back to the early period of the Islamic conquest.[12]

In this interim period the Opposition temporarily gained the upper hand, as attested by its victories in the municipal council elections of 1927–28. But the Nashashibis had previously failed to unseat the Husayni incumbents of the Supreme Muslim Council when the first quadrennial election of 1926 was declared invalid. The Husaynis' religio-political instrument was accordingly left intact. When interest was renewed in the national movement and both factions agreed to participate in the seventh Palestine Arab Congress at Jerusalem in June 1928, the Councilites were able once more to outstrip the Opposition. The Congress created an enlarged Executive, composed of 36 Muslims and 12 Christians, with Musa Kazim Pasha again as its president. The Executive opened a per-

manent office in Jerusalem and at the end of 1929 was recognized by the
Palestine Government as the official spokesman for the Arab Community.
But the Opposition was only lukewarm in its support of the new body.
As a result, the Executive was reduced for all practical purposes to a
Husayni subsidiary. No further Congresses were held. Nor were efforts
made to obtain a popular mandate or to provide for an elective leadership. Relations between the Councilites and the Opposition became increasingly strained, but the Arab Executive continued to function until
shortly after the death of Musa Kazim Pasha early in 1934. It then passed
quietly out of existence without formal dissolution.[13]

Even though the Executive had failed to unite the Palestine Arab leadership, the national movement expanded rapidly in these years. The younger,
educated generation devoted itself increasingly to the nationalist cause.
Many of these elements could not find their proper places in either of
the existing factions. Moreover, influential Muslim families which had
formerly been affiliated with the Councilites or the Opposition were now
anxious to fend for themselves. Consequently, six rival groups of leaders
including the Husaynis and the Nashashibis established separate political parties between 1932–35. With the formation of these parties the
Arab national movement in Palestine entered upon a new phase.

THE POLITICAL PARTIES

The Arab political parties in Palestine were not really political parties
in the Western sense. They were merely factions, for they could make no
constitutional appeal to the public for victory at the polls. In the neighboring Arab states where democratic forms obtained, the parties were
organized for electoral purposes. When their candidates were returned
in sufficient numbers, they were entitled to representation in the government and had a voice in the making of laws. But in Palestine the national movement had become the main field of Arab politics. It filled the
void left by the failure to develop either an Arab Community government or self-governing institutions for the country as a whole. The purpose of the Arab political parties, therefore, was to gain mastery over the
national movement, not over any government; and the national movement had no written constitution.

The Palestine Arab parties were all inflexible in their attitude toward
Zionism. Consequently, moderation could only be gauged by the degree
to which the factions cooperated with the Palestine Government and the
methods to which they resorted for realizing their ends. In this connection the factions were inclined to vary their practices in accordance with
changing conditions. Active party membership, limited to adult males, was
drawn very largely from the ranks of the influential families and the urban
intelligentsia. Individuals not uncommonly belonged to more than one

party. Differences of opinion among the factions sprang almost invariably from personal or tactical, not ideological, considerations. Party caucuses and elections did not obtain. Party conferences were irregular and were called only when the leaders desired to issue instructions. Since the factions were closely identified with powerful Muslim families, most of them were variously known by the official name of the group and by the name of the family which dominated it.[14]

Thus the Palestine Arab Party, which was founded in March 1935 by the formal reorganization of the Councilites, was also called the Husayni faction or simply the Husaynis. The faction's titular president was Jamal al-Husayni (1892–), the Mufti's cousin and most intimate aide. However, the prestige of the Palestine Arab Party, the most powerful in the community, derived mainly from its identification with al-Hajj Amin. Through him important contacts had been established in the Arab and Muslim countries, and the Supreme Muslim Council continued, as in the past, to serve for all political purposes as an adjunct of the Husayni faction. Allied with the Husaynis were a few mayors and the leaders of the Haifa and Jerusalem branches of the Palestine Arab Workers Society. As the Palestine Arab Party's vice-president, Alfred Roch (1882–1942), a wealthy citrus grower of Jaffa, attracted considerable support in the Roman Catholic community, in which he was prominent. The Husayni faction also formed in 1935 its own illegal, militarized society, which like similar groups in Syria and Iraq was called al-Futuwwah (youth or chivalry).

The Palestine Arab Party adopted as its platform the so-called National Pact. This declaration called for the repudiation of the Balfour Declaration, the end of the mandate, the full stoppage of Jewish immigration, the complete prohibition of land sales to Jews, and the immediate establishment of Palestine as an independent Arab state. The National Pact was merely a restatement of the objectives of the national movement, to which all other Arab political factions were equally dedicated. The Husaynis, however, could claim major credit for rousing popular interest in the land issue. The Mufti had taken steps as early as the 1920's to persuade the Arabs to sell their land to the Supreme Muslim Council as "a religious endowment of the Arab people in Palestine," instead of allowing these holdings to pass into Jewish hands. In 1935 and again early in the following year al-Hajj Amin, in his capacity as the Council's president, convened meetings of religious notables, who resolved to "excommunicate all Muslims selling land to Jews." The Husaynis, moreover, had been chiefly instrumental in 1931 in setting up the Arab National Fund for the purpose of pre-empting Arab realty which Jews were attempting to purchase.[15]

Second in influence to the Husayni faction was still the Opposition, which in December 1934 adopted the name of National Defense Party under the presidency of Raghib Bey al-Nashashibi. The Nashashibi faction retained most of its earlier anti-Husayni rural backing as well as the adherence of a majority of the Arab mayors. It also established close relations with Amir 'Abdallah of Transjordan. Furthermore, Ya'qub Farraj (1874–1944), the Greek Orthodox deputy-mayor of Jerusalem since 1920, was elected vice-president and carried along many coreligionists. The faction also obtained the collaboration of the leaders of the Jaffa branch of the Palestine Arab Workers Society.[16] Still, the National Defense Party was somewhat weakened by the secession of a contingent of Muslim landed gentry and their political dependents.

Raghib Bey himself had been defeated in the Jerusalem mayoralty election of 1934 by Dr. Husayn Fakhri al-Khalidi (1894–   ), an erstwhile supporter of the Opposition and a member of one of the oldest Muslim families in Jerusalem. Khalidi established his own Reform Party at Ramallah in June 1935; its following was concentrated in Jerusalem, Jaffa, Gaza, and their suburbs. Four months later 'Abd-al-Latif Salah, a Muslim lawyer of Nablus and a former member of the Supreme Muslim Council, founded the National Bloc Party. As head of a well-to-do Muslim family, possessing large estates in the vicinity of Tulkarm, he could afford to maintain his political independence and attempted to appeal to the strong parochial interest of the inhabitants of Nablus area, though the party attracted some backing in Jaffa. Meanwhile, a conference at Jaffa of young professional and business men, sponsored by the Arab Executive, elected in December 1932 a permanent steering committee called the Executive Committee of the Arab Youth Congress to encourage the active participation of the youth in the national movement. This group was converted in May 1935 at Haifa into the Arab Youth Congress Party, under the presidency of al-Hajj Muhammad Ya'qub al-Ghusayn (1899–   ), the scion of a prosperous Muslim family of Ramlah.[17]

The one Arab political group in Palestine which came close to espousing a definite political ideology was the *Istiqlal* (Independence) Party, founded in August 1932. The local faction formed part of a general Pan-Arab movement, which had been created in Damascus in February 1919, had branches in the Levant States and Iraq, and in the early 1930's looked to King Faysal I at Baghdad for leadership. Following King Faysal's death in 1933 the group in Palestine became inactive and was not revived until after the formation of the other parties in 1935. The Istiqlal President was 'Awni Bey 'Abd-al-Hadi (1889–   ), a Jerusalem lawyer and a member of a large Muslim clan whose centers of influence were Janin, Nablus, and their environs. Closely associated with him was Ahmad Hilmi Pasha 'Abd-al-Baqi (1878–   ), born in Sidon, Lebanon, allegedly of part Turkish or Albanian ancestry. Both men had been associated with Faysal in Damascus at the close of the First World War and became active in the Palestine national movement during the 1920's.

As Pan-Arabs, the members of the Istiqlal Party hoped to achieve the gradual merger of all Arab states under a single government. The individual Arab territories would first have to be liberated from foreign domination and regional federations set up. The Istiqlal spokesmen argued that Palestine belonged historically and geographically to Syria. They stated that the Zionists were merely tools of British imperialism and therefore urged that Palestine Arabs should direct their hostility primarily against the British and only secondarily against the Jews. The Istiqlal Party appealed most strongly to the young Muslim intelligentsia in the towns— lawyers, doctors, teachers, and government officials. Its main center of influence was Haifa, a city which had grown considerably under the mandate and attracted many of the progressive educated youth. Because of the party's uncompromising hostility to Britain, it also came to dominate the small number of Arab communists, affiliated with the Palestine Communist Party.[18]

The appearance of the political parties intensified for a time the interfactional quarrels. But none of the factions could claim to speak in the name of a majority of the Palestine Arabs. Consequently, even in 1935, the peak year of Jewish immigration, the Arab Community was prevented from taking united action. The Arab press therefore launched a concerted attack upon the party leaders, accusing them of placing personal interests ahead of the national welfare. In response to the resulting public pressure, the leaders of five parties formed in November 1935 a loose working agreement for representing the Arab Community in negotiations with the government. The Istiqlal spokesmen alone, insisting upon a policy of noncooperation with the mandatory, refused to join the others. Hence the national movement at the beginning of 1936, though still without an executive organ, seemed headed toward a unified leadership.

PART TWO

DEVELOPMENTS DURING THE PERIOD OF AXIS ASCENDANCY 1936-1942

CHAPTER 5

Arab Revolt and Partition Proposal

THE REVOLT: OPENING PHASE

POLITICAL tension in the Arab and Jewish communities rose sharply in the early months of 1936. One contributory factor was the mandatory's latest recommendation for a Legislative Council, which was still an unsettled matter early in April when the Colonial Office invited the Arab spokesmen to send a delegation to London for further discussions. The Italian invasion of Ethiopia in the fall of 1935 and the accompanying threat of a European war had produced a run on the Palestine banks and an economic recession. This forced a cut in the Jewish immigration schedule at a time when the Zionists were hoping to settle in the national home even more victims of Nazi oppression than in the year just ending. Moreover, the Fascist radio station at Bari had been feeding Egypt and Palestine a steady diet of anti-British propaganda. Nationalist demonstrations and strikes in Egypt and Syria procured from London and Paris by March 1936 assurances that treaties would be concluded, recognizing the independence of the two countries. In a spirited drive the Palestine Arab press was urging the local nationalists to follow their neighbors' lead. By April the Palestine Arab Community had become a virtual powder keg.[1]

On April 15 two Jews were murdered by Arabs, and in the next few days there were suspected Jewish reprisals as well as assaults on Arabs in Tel-Aviv and on Jews in Jaffa. Arab nationalists in Nablus created a national committee for that city on April 20. Before the month passed similar committees appeared in all the towns of concentrated Arab population and some of the larger villages. The Nablus Committee issued, as its first act, a plea for the enforcement of a general Arab strike until the mandatory agreed to execute the nationalist program in full. The plea was endorsed on April 21 by the spokesmen of the five political parties then in coalition. Four days later the Istiqlal leaders joined those of the other five groups to constitute a permanent ten-man executive organ, soon known as the Arab Higher Committee, under the presidency of the Jerusalem Mufti. The Husaynis were represented by two additional members, the Nashashibi and Istiqlal factions by two each, and the remaining three groups by one each.[2] The Higher Committee was the first executive body of the local national movement to function smoothly. The presence of one Roman Catholic and one Greek Orthodox notable symbolized Muslim-Christian solidarity. The local national committees furnished the leaders with an instrument for supervising the implementation of their decisions in all districts.

The Higher Committee announced soon after its formation that the purpose of the strike was to obtain the prohibition of Jewish immigration, the forbiddance of land transfers from Arabs to Jews, and the replacement of the mandate by a national government responsible to a representative council. The Arab leaders also warned that the strike would continue until the British Government indicated, by suspending Jewish immigration, that it would adjust its Palestine policy to Arab nationalist demands. From this time on the Legislative Council scheme became a dead issue. Indeed, the plan to send an Arab delegation to London, which had been accepted by the Arab spokesmen at the beginning of April, was on May 5 made contingent by the Higher Committee on the prior stoppage of Jewish immigration. The Higher Committee's stand was reaffirmed by a general conference at Jerusalem on May 8 of delegates from all the national committees, which threatened to institute a program of civil disobedience.[3]

Hence the immediate aim of the strike was to coerce the government into withholding the semiannual Jewish immigration schedule for the period of April–September 1936. The Jewish Agency had submitted on April 15 an application for 11,200 visas. The High Commissioner now advised the Agency that he would postpone his decision until the situation had crystallized. But by mid-May the Arab leaders were making the suspension of Jewish immigration their indispensable condition for ending the strike. Following notification from the Agency that it would regard the continued deferment of the schedule "a surrender to violence," the Palestine Government fixed on May 18 a labor immigrant quota of 4,500.[4] Simultaneously Colonial Secretary J. H. Thomas informed Parliament that a Royal Commission would be appointed to "investigate causes of unrest" in Palestine. However, Thomas stressed that the inquiry would be undertaken only "after order is restored"; that the proposed commission would not be empowered to bring "into question the terms of the mandate"; and that "no change of policy whatsoever could be contemplated" before the commission's report had been reviewed.[5]

The mandatory's conditions together with the continuance of Jewish immigration caused the Arab attitude to stiffen. An economic boycott of the Yishuv was instituted. By the early summer most senior and a substantial number of the junior Arab government officials formally placed themselves on record as being in full accord with the nationalists. Gradually the strike developed from sporadic acts of violence and sabotage into open rebellion. Bands of armed guerrillas were organized throughout the Arab Community, especially in the rural hill districts of southern and central Palestine. Trains were derailed, roads barricaded and mined, telephone wires cut, and the oil pipe line from Iraq pierced. The rebels sniped at interurban traffic, including that of the British soldiers and police, and assaulted outlying Jewish villages, setting fire to forests and crops. From the start the guerrillas received active popular backing from the near-by countries. "Committees for the Defense of Palestine" sprang up in most of the larger cities of the Levant States, Iraq, Egypt, and Transjordan. Syrian and Iraqi volunteers, who began to trickle into Palestine in the early weeks, arrived in sizable groups by August, among them experienced guerrilla leaders. One of these was Lebanese-born Fawzi al-Qawuqji (ca. 1890–   ), who resigned his commission in the Iraqi Army to assume supreme command of the rebel units, both native and extra-Palestine. Qawuqji styled himself generalissimo and issued communiqués and proclamations to his bands, which now even risked engagements with British troops.[6]

The High Commissioner, Sir Arthur Wauchope, enacted as early as April 19 drastic regulations, authorizing arrest and search without warrant, deportation, occupation of buildings, seizure and use of vehicles, and imposition of curfews and censorship. Less than eight weeks later additional regulations increased the penalties for firing on troops and police, bomb-throwing, and illegal possession of arms. The principle of collective punishment was introduced for imposition on villages or districts whose unidentifiable residents were responsible for such offenses. Moreover, beginning with the second week of May the local garrisons were augmented by reinforcements from Egypt and Malta, and the British section of the Palestine police was expanded. Some sixty Arab strike leaders were placed under police custody on May 23; and subsequently prominent Arabs, including the secretary of the Higher Committee, the owner of the largest Arab bank, and one of the leaders of the Palestine Arab Workers' Society, were interned. But on the whole Wauchope used his emergency powers sparingly at first in the hope that by not adding to the existing bitterness he would make the eventual restoration of peace less difficult. Troops were employed only in keeping highways open and railroads in operation and in defending key points. No offensive action against the guerrillas was taken.[7]

In response to sustained appeals from the Jewish Agency, Wauchope permitted the gradual expansion of the Yishuv's legal defense establishment. Jewish members of the regular police force—some 290 in April 1936—

were doubled in number by the summer's end. At the same time about 2,700 Jewish supernumerary police, whose maintenance costs were at first borne largely by the community, were enlisted to assist in protecting exposed villages and Jewish districts in mixed towns. The Jewish quasi-government strictly enjoined all Jews to use their arms in self-defense only. With few exceptions this policy of non-retaliation was carried out.

Moreover, the exponents of Jewish economic exclusiveness were given their first real opportunity. Because of the strike Jewish workers were able to replace Arabs on the Jewish-owned citrus plantations. Similarly many fallahin refused to sell produce on the Jewish market so that Jewish farmers were forced to increase production. Most important of all, the Agency received authority from the High Commissioner in May 1936 to unload vessels at Tel-Aviv. Jewish areas of settlement in the vicinity were therefore liberated from dependence on Jaffa, which up to that time was the only port for southern Palestine. On the other hand, the Jewish economy suffered a severe shock. The construction of new buildings slackened. The difficulties of transport had an adverse effect on commerce. Arab guerrillas destroyed 13 Jewish-owned factories and workshops, valued at more than $500,000; 38 others, located in Jaffa, were temporarily shut down and in some instances had later to be removed to other sites. The Arab boycott reduced the sale of Jewish manufactures by some 10 per cent.[8]

Meanwhile, for the first time the neighboring Arab governments officially intervened in the Palestine dispute. Amir 'Abdallah of Transjordan at his invitation met with the Higher Committee at 'Amman on June 6 and August 7 in efforts to end the strike and the uprising. But the Palestine spokesmen still insisted upon the suspension of Jewish immigration as a prerequisite. General Nuri Pasha al-Sa'id, the Iraqi Foreign Minister, arrived in Jerusalem on August 20 on a similar mediatory mission. In a private conference with Moshe Shertok, Nuri Pasha reportedly tried to persuade the Agency's political spokesman that, if the Jews voluntarily agreed to the temporary stoppage of immigration as "a spectacular gesture," they would convince "the Arabs that . . . [the Jews] were sincere in . . . [their] desire for an understanding." Shertok in reply, however, objected to the suggestion on grounds of practical politics because it would represent a concession to violence; and on grounds of principle because the Jews regarded "the right of immigration into Palestine . . . [as] an absolute Jewish right." [9] On August 30 the Higher Committee, while welcoming Iraqi mediation, warned that the Arab "Nation will continue its general strike with the same steadfastness and conviction" as theretofore.[10]

The mandatory now began to take a serious view of the crisis. The members of the projected Royal Commission had been named. But London insisted that the inquiry would not get under way until the disorders ceased. The Colonial Office therefore announced on September 7 that the mandatory would have to restore order in its own way. The Palestine Government forbade the Higher Committee ten days later to hold a conference of the local national committees. The arrival by the end of the month of more British troops raised the total in the country to about 20,000. A new defense order-in-council was issued, authorizing the High Commissioner to make any regulation considered essential for public safety, including the declaration of martial law and the denial of appeals from military to civil courts, or to delegate these powers to the commanding general. While Wauchope did not resort to these extreme steps, British troops were permitted to assume the offensive against the rebel bands.[11]

The Higher Committee was driven to the wall. Militarily the bands could not hope to withstand any determined British drive. Economically the Arab Community was suffering greater losses than the Yishuv. Even with financial assistance from their neighbors, the Palestine Arabs had to bear the major costs of the revolt. Jaffa, the most thriving Arab town, was perhaps hardest hit. It lost much of its harbor traffic and many of its Jewish commercial and industrial enterprises. But unemployment also rose sharply in all the other Arab towns because of the interruption of business, the disappearance of the tourist trade, and the stoppage of work. In the villages the fallahin had not only to give up the Jewish market but to defray expenses of billeting the guerrillas. Arab citrus growers probably contributed more than any other single group to financing the rebellion. With the approach of the citrus season in the fall, they became apprehensive over the sale of their crops and brought added pressure to bear. The hopelessness of the military and economic position was reflected in a weakening of the political unity. As early as the end of August, there were indications of differences within the Higher Committee. Khalidi and Nashashibi were reported to have concurred in the continuance of the strike only for the sake of solidarity.

The receipt on October 11 of identic notes from the rulers of Iraq, Saudi Arabia, Transjordan, and Yemen enabled the Higher Committee to make a face-saving exit from its predicament. Promising continued aid in the future, the Arab rulers urged their "sons, the Arabs of Palestine," to stop the bloodshed and to have faith in "the good intentions of our friend Great Britain, who has declared that she will do justice." On the same day the Higher Committee announced its decision, which had unanimously been endorsed by the national committees, "to respond to the appeal of Their Majesties and Highnesses, the Arab Kings and Amirs, and to call upon the noble Arab nation in Palestine to resort to quietness and to put an end to the strike and the disorders."[12] By the beginning of November British troops had surrounded the rebel bands, and most of those of foreign origin together with Qawuqji and other commanders were permitted to recross the frontiers. Desultory acts of violence still occurred, but organized Arab resistance was broken.

Now that order was restored, the Royal Commission, headed by Earl Peel, former Secretary of State for India, left for Palestine on November 5. On the same day the Colonial Office disclosed the award of 1,800 entry permits, as the Jewish labor immigration schedule for the half-year ending in March 1937. The Jewish Agency was gratified that the principle of continued immigration was upheld but dismayed that the number of visas was only 17 per cent of the amount requested. The Higher Committee on its side, apparently believing that the end of the strike would halt Jewish immigration at least for the duration of the inquiry, was outraged. The Arab Community was therefore instructed not to cooperate with the investigative body. Toward the end of the Royal Commission's hearings early in January 1937, however, the Kings of Iraq and Saudi Arabia urged the Higher Committee to appear before the Commission, stressing that the Palestine Arabs had more to gain by formally presenting their views than by leaving their case unheard. Consequently, the Palestine Arab spokesmen called off the boycott, and the Commissioners deferred their departure for England until the third week of January, so as to hear the Arab testimony.

Nearly six months elapsed before the Royal Commission's findings were published. The political uncertainty in this period kept the Arabs and Jews in a state of high tension. The persistence of Arab sniping did not warrant the presence of the military reinforcements; British garrisons were therefore reduced considerably in the winter of 1936–37. But in March 1937 the government consolidated the several ordinances dealing with emergency police and military powers, as a precaution for the future.[13] Furthermore, the economic depression in the country as a whole grew steadily worse. Nor was the strain relieved in May by the Palestine Government's award of a four-month labor immigration schedule for April–July 1937, pending the publication of the Royal Commission report. This time the disappointment of the Arabs was somewhat mitigated by the extreme irritation of the Jews. The Jewish Agency had applied for 11,250 visas but the government granted only 770. Of these a mere 120 were allocated for general distribution to the Jewish Agency, which refused on principle to accept so small a quota.[14]

THE ROYAL COMMISSION REPORT

The Royal Commission had been instructed to examine the underlying causes of the recent "disturbances" and the manner in which the mandate was being executed. The Commission was also "to ascertain whether, upon a proper construction of . . . the Mandate, either the Arabs or the Jews have any legitimate grievances" and, if satisfied that any complaints were well founded, "to make recommendations for their removal and for the prevention of their recurrence." The Commission's exhaustive report, which appeared on July 7, 1937, was based on a liberal interpretation of the instructions. It stated unequivocally that the Arab grievances about Jewish immigration, Jewish land acquisition, and the mandatory's failure to develop self-governing institutions "cannot be regarded as legitimate under the terms of the Mandate." But the mandatory obligations to the Jews under these headings, warned the Commission, could be fulfilled only by a policy of British repression against an unwilling Arab population. Such a course would run counter to the very spirit of the mandates system and accepted British principles.

The Palestine Mandate, it was observed, was originally premised on the assumption that the Arabs would acquiesce in the establishment of the Jewish National Home because of the material advantages. But no mutual understanding had been achieved. Instead "an irrepressible conflict" for the control of the government had arisen and would grow progressively more serious in the future, if the impasse were not broken. The Palestine Arabs were bound to accentuate their demands for national independence as their community prospered, their educational equipment expanded, and the Arabs of the surrounding countries realized full self-rule. The political assertiveness of the Palestine Jews was equally certain to sharpen as the national home became more firmly rooted, and the pressure of Jewish immigration to intensify as the anxieties of European Jews mounted. There was thus no hope of establishing representative government, which could operate successfully only where the population concerned was sufficiently homogeneous, so as "to enable the minority to acquiesce in the rule of the majority and to make it possible for the balance of power to readjust itself from time to time." Consequently, the Royal Commission concluded that the Palestine Mandate was unworkable.

Having arrived at this conclusion, the Commission proceeded to assess the several major proposals for a final settlement of the political impasse. The Higher Committee had urged that Palestine be established immediately as an independent Arab state. This recommendation was dismissed on grounds of injustice and violation of the mandate. The rights of the Jewish minority would not be safeguarded adequately, for the Commission recalled the Jerusalem Mufti's candid assertion that the 400,000 Jews already living in Palestine could not be assimilated into the country and that their fate would have to be left "to the future." The Revisionist proposal that Palestine and Transjordan should both be placed under a Jewish government was similarly repudiated, because it was "at plain variance with our legal and moral obligations" and its implementation would arouse the implacable resentment of the Arab and Muslim worlds. The Commission also rejected as unrealistic and impracticable the Jewish Agency's parity scheme. "If a Legislative Council were now established, and if the present Jewish minority were given an equal number of seats thereon with the present Arab majority," argued the parity proponents, "the Jews would never claim more than that equal number, whatever the future ratio between Arab and Jewish population might become." But the Commission pointed out that the Arabs would never accept an arrangement which "deprives them of a real present advantage" and "offers in return an advantage which, however sincere the Jewish undertaking may be, is only prospective and will only materialize in circumstances which . . . [the Arabs] will do their best to preclude." In any case equal representation under prevailing Arab-Zionist hostility would of necessity lead to a permanent deadlock on all vital issues.

After vetoing these schemes, the Commission recommended the only arrangement which it felt conformed to British obligations and was equitable, practicable, and best calculated to achieve a permanent settlement. Palestine was to be divided "within as short a period as may be convenient" into sovereign Arab and Jewish states and a British mandatory zone. The Jewish state would comprise the Galilee, the Jezreel Valley, and the Coastal Plain to a point midway between Gaza and Jaffa, representing about 20 per cent of the area of the country. Jaffa itself would be included in the Arab state, which would be composed of most of the rest of Palestine united with Transjordan. The zone under British mandate was to embrace permanently the Holy Places (Jerusalem, Bethlehem, a narrow corridor linking them to the Mediterranean, and possibly Nazareth as well as the Sea of Galilee) and an enclave on the northwest corner of the Gulf of 'Aqabah; and only temporarily the towns of Safad, Tiberias, Acre, and Haifa.

Arabs and Jews were to have free access to the ports of Haifa and 'Aqabah. The projected states were to conclude preferential treaties with the United Kingdom on the pattern of the Anglo-Iraqi treaty. The Arab state was to receive subventions from the Jewish state and a grant of $10,000,000 from Great Britain. Jewish land purchases and settlement in the proposed Arab area were to be prohibited during the transitional period, while Jewish immigration was to be determined by the economic absorptive capacity of the district allocated to the Jews.

In making its radical proposals for a final settlement, the Royal Commission was persuaded that the advantages to Jews and Arabs far outweighed the inevitable hardships to which partition would give rise. The Arabs would achieve their national independence. They would be able to collaborate on an equal footing with the Arabs of the near-by countries in the cause of Arab Unity. They would be liberated from the fear of Jewish domination. As for the Jews, their national home would be converted into a Jewish state. The Jews would then be able to control their own immigration. They would not be subjected to Arab rule. And they would be able to realize the primary goal of Zionism, since the Jews "will cease at last to live a 'minority life.'"[15] Although the Royal Commission discreetly omitted mention of the advantages to Britain, if partition proved successful, it may be presumed that these considerations were not ignored. The

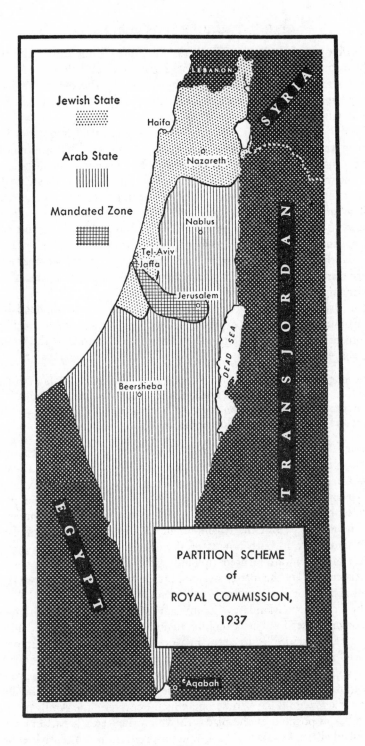

Jewish State

Arab State

Mandated Zone

LEBANON

SYRIA

Haifa

Nazareth

TRANSJORDAN

Nablus

Tel-Aviv
Jaffa

Jerusalem

DEAD SEA

Beersheba

EGYPT

PARTITION SCHEME
of
ROYAL COMMISSION,
1937

ᵉAqabah

establishment of peace would relieve the United Kingdom of the responsibility and cost of maintaining large garrisons in Palestine. Moreover, British strategic interests would be kept intact, by the recommended military alliances with the new governments and by direct control of Haifa and 'Aqabah.[16]

Recognizing that the suggested "surgical operation" might not be performed, the Commission prescribed certain "palliatives," not as a cure but as a means of reducing the inflammation. The area of close Jewish settlement, it was advised, should be restricted to the plains. The rate of Jewish influx should be fixed thereafter by "political, social and psychological as well as economic considerations" and for at least five years should be limited to the "political 'high level'" of 12,000 a year. If large-scale disorders should recur, the government was not to hesitate to enforce martial law, overhaul the police system, and introduce rigid press controls. If no effort were made to disarm both sections of the population, the system of Jewish supernumerary police should continue.[17]

The British Government, in a White Paper issued simultaneously with the Commission's report, expressed general agreement with the findings. The mandatory was "driven to the conclusion," continued the statement, that the [18]

> irreconcilable conflict between the aspirations of Arabs and Jews in Palestine . . . cannot be satisfied under the terms of the present Mandate, and that a scheme of partition on the . . . [suggested] lines . . . represents the best and most hopeful solution of the deadlock.

In an exchange of notes with London, the United States Government, in effect, announced its neutrality toward the Royal Commission's scheme, by declaring that its concern in the matter was "based exclusively on its obligation and purpose to provide for the protection of American interests in Palestine on a basis of equality with those of other Governments and their nationals." [19] But the Chamberlain Cabinet's acceptance of partition came under fire in both houses of Parliament on July 20–21, 1937. The House of Commons refused to bind itself, although it empowered the government to lay the matter before the League of Nations before framing the final plan for Parliamentary endorsement.

The Permanent Mandates Commission of the League of Nations in an extraordinary session between July 30 and August 18 was also cool to the suggested solution. Nevertheless, in a preliminary opinion the Commission declared itself favorable to the further examination of partition, subject to certain conditions. Provision would have to be made for a prolonged period of political apprenticeship for the projected states; and the ultimate arrangement would have to be one which deprived "the Arabs of as small a number as possible of the places to which they attach particular value" and enabled the Jews to embark upon a program of "intensive economic development and consequently of dense and rapid settlement." By the time the issue came before the Council of the League in mid-September, the mandatory had already decided that a technical commission would be sent to Palestine to draft the definitive blueprint. The Council approved the proposed technical investigation, but reserved final judgment. The United Kingdom was also reminded that the Palestine Mandate "remains in force until such time as it may be otherwise decided." [20]

Meanwhile, the partition proposal sharpened interparty strife among the Zionists and between the Zionist and non-Zionist adherents of the Jewish Agency. The controversy reached its climax at the twentieth Zionist Congress and the fifth session of the Jewish Agency Council in Zurich, Switzerland, in August 1937. In general the division of opinion at the Zionist Congress ran along party lines, although in complete disregard of social and economic ideologies. Those who objected to partition insisted that the Jews had an "inalienable right" to all of Palestine and that even this area was not large enough to absorb the ever-growing number of European Jews who would be compelled to migrate to the national home in the near future. These Zionists had not yet abandoned hope of eventually acquiring rights of settlement in Transjordan. Into the anti-partition ranks fell the leftist ha-Shomer ha-Za'ir, the clerical Mizrahi, the conservative wing of the General Zionists, and the rightist Jewish State Party.

Those favoring partition included primarily the moderate socialists and the progressive wing of the General Zionists, under the joint leadership of the Zionist president, Dr. Chaim Weizmann, and the chairman of the Executive, David Ben Gurion. They were prepared to exchange territorial claims and the uncertainties of continued mandatory administration for the benefits of early self-rule in an amputated Palestine. They believed that the British Government's approval of the Royal Commission's recommendations left the Zionists only these alternatives: either the "palliatives" or partition, remaining a minority in the whole of Palestine or becoming a majority in a compact Jewish state. Yet even the "pro-partitionists," as they came to be known, would not accept the particular plan advanced by the Royal Commission. But they were willing to negotiate for a larger area. Their touchstone was whether or not the contemplated Jewish state would be a viable one, adequate to reduce the Jewish refugee pool in Europe within a relatively brief period.

The Zionist Congress finally approved by a vote of 299 to 160 a course of action, which amounted to the endorsement of partition in principle without saying so directly. The Royal Commission's scheme was tagged as unacceptable. But the Zionist Executive was authorized to negotiate with the mandatory for the purpose of "ascertaining the precise [British] terms for the proposed establishment of a Jewish State." The Congress, however, bound the Executive "not to commit either itself or the Zionist Organisation, but in the event of the emergence of a definite scheme for the establishment of a Jewish State, such scheme shall be brought before a newly elected Congress for consideration and decision." [21]

The Congress also re-elected the old Executive, a majority of whose members favored partition. Immediately following the Congress' adjournment, the contest was carried to the Jewish Agency Council. Here the non-Zionists, particularly the American contingent headed by Felix Warburg (1871–1937) of New York, characterized the action taken by the Zionist Congress as contrary to the spirit and the letter of the Agency's constitution. The non-Zionists declared that they opposed partition, because as non-nationalists they had ruled out the idea of a Jewish state from the start. In the end the Council unanimously adopted a compromise formula, which substantially included the statement drawn up by the Zionist Congress, except that the Agency Executive was directed to request the mandatory to "convene a conference of the Jews and the Arabs of Palestine with a view to exploring the possibilities of making a peaceful settlement between Jews and Arabs in and for an undivided Palestine on the basis of the Balfour Declaration and the Mandate." If such a conference failed to materialize, the powers of negotiation for a settlement by partition were transferred from the Zionist to the Agency Executive, and the final authority of deciding on the acceptability of any scheme was vested in the Agency Council.[22]

Outside the Jewish Agency the dissident groups ranged themselves in unqualified opposition to any territorial reduction of Jewish claims. The militant Revisionists in mid-August 1937 called upon the Jews throughout the world to remain "faithful to [the] ideal of a Jewish State on both sides of the Jordan." [23] About the same time the Rabbinical Council of the fundamentalist Agudat Israel World Organization declared that "the frontiers of our holy land have been defined by the creator of the world. . . . It is therefore impossible for the Jewish people to renounce these frontiers." This decision was endorsed by the third World Agudat Israel Congress at Marienbad, Czechoslovakia, on August 23, 1937.[24]

As for the Palestine Arab Community, the reassertion of old quarrels had already weakened the interfactional coalition. On July 3, 1937—four days before the release of the Royal Commission report—the National Defense Party formally dissociated itself from the Higher Committee. The party accused al-Hajj Amin of arbitrary conduct and specifically charged him with responsibility for intimidating adherents of the National Defense Party and other Arabs. A further reason for the split, it was widely believed at the time, was to pave the way for the party's acceptance of partition. Both Raghib al-Nashashibi, the party's president, and Amir 'Abdallah, the ruler of Transjordan, were suspected of favoring the proposal. 'Abdallah was allegedly motivated by the desire to expand his domains, and Nashashibi by the prospects of high office.

Nevertheless, at a meeting in Jerusalem on July 11 the National Defense Party resolved that partition was incompatible with Arab nationalist aspirations and prejudicial to Arab interests. Shortly thereafter the faction addressed a memorandum to the League of Nations and the British Colonial Secretary, claiming that the Arabs could not agree to the proposed division of Palestine because the most fertile and developed part of the country was to be awarded to the Jews; a substantial proportion of Arabs was to be subjected to Jewish rule; the holy places and many Arab villages were to be placed under permanent mandate; and Jaffa would be completely isolated. The National Defense Party advocated, as an alternative, that the Palestine Mandate should be replaced by a sovereign, democratic state, in which minority rights would be "fully and constitutionally guaranteed," the existing ratio between the two sections of the population would be maintained, and Jewish land purchases would be prohibited only in those areas allocated to the Arabs under the Royal Commission plan.[25]

Much more uncompromising was the memorandum which the truncated Higher Committee addressed to the British Colonial Secretary and the Permanent Mandates Commission on July 23. The Higher Committee expressed its "repugnance to the whole of the partition scheme." In the territory of the proposed Jewish state, it was contended, the Arabs held title to four times as much land as the Jews. There were located seven-eighths of the Arab-owned citrus groves. The area left for the Arab state, stressed the Higher Committee, would never become solvent, and its dependence upon Jewish subventions would "constitute in fact Jewish control over the allegedly independent Arab State." Besides, once the Jewish state became "overfilled with Jewish immigrants," it would seek territorial expansion. The surrounding Arab countries would thus be exposed "to perpetual encroachments, political and economic." The Jews would also infiltrate into the mandatory zone, it was stated, until such time as that region became predominantly Jewish. Then it would be annexed to the Jewish state, and "the places holiest to Islamic and Christian sentiment [would be] permanently removed from the control of the Arab community." Finally, the inclusion in the mandatory enclave of the port of 'Aqabah, the airfields of Lydda and Ramlah, and the important railway junction at Lydda made it "clear that imperial and military considerations, not religious, are here at play." The Higher Committee also indicated that any attempt to carve up the country was certain to intensify Arab resistance.

The only acceptable settlement, the Higher Committee concluded, would have to be based on the following principles:

1) The recognition of the right of the Arabs to complete independence in their own land.

2) The cessation of the experiment of the Jewish National Home.

3) The cessation of the British mandate and its replacement by a treaty similar to . . . [that] existing between Britain and Iraq . . . creating in Palestine a Sovereign State.

4) The immediate cessation of all Jewish immigration and of land-sales to Jews pending the negotiation and conclusion of the Treaty.

CHAPTER 6

Retreat from Partition

THE REVOLT: SECOND PHASE

THE FOCUS of the Arab-Zionist contest shifted in the summer of 1937 from the immigration question to partition and the "palliatives." The struggle over partition was far-flung. The quarrel over the "palliatives," however, centered in Palestine itself. The Royal Commission had criticized the Palestine Government for maladministration, which was found to derive partly from difficulties inherent in the mandate and partly from the presence of unqualified personnel. The "palliatives" were intended as correctives for the duration of the mandate. The adoption of some of these recommendations was foreshadowed in the White Paper of July 1937, which warned that the most stringent military steps would be taken to suppress any serious disorders. Pending the execution of partition, it was also announced, land transactions which might prejudice the probable territorial divisions would be prohibited, and Jewish immigration of all classes—including "capitalists," whose entry was previously unrestricted—would be limited to 8,000 for the eight-month period of August 1937–March 1938.[1]

While passing over in silence the references to the preservation of public security, the Higher Committee hailed the proposed land sales and immigration restrictions as "a partial recognition of the justice of two of the principal Arab claims." [2] The Jewish Agency Council, on the other hand, condemned those "palliatives" which "involve the arbitrary curtailment of Jewish immigration, the abandonment of the principle of economic absorptive capacity as a basis for immigration policy, and severe limitations on Jewish land settlement." [3] Despite these admonitions, implied and explicit, the mandatory proceeded to put into operation some of the provisional expedients advocated by the Royal Commission. London's decision on immigration was embodied in November in a temporary amendment to the

Palestine immigration ordinance, authorizing the High Commissioner to prescribe the maximum rate of entry. The validity of the amendment was to expire on March 31, 1938, or such later date as the High Commissioner might fix with the Colonial Secretary's approval. In February 1938 the Agency urged the abrogation of this enactment. The Colonial Office agreed to take certain categories of dependents and students off the re-- stricted list and to liberalize the capitalist quota from 840 visas in the period just terminating to 2,000 in the next six months. But the life of the temporary amendment was extended until March 31, 1939, and subsequent procedure was again left open.[4]

Meanwhile, the mandatory had begun to deal firmly with the Arab Community as well. The Royal Commission had chastised the Palestine Administration for failure to discharge "the elementary duty of public security" and for having "carried the policy of conciliation [of violence and incitation to violence on the part of the Arabs] to its farthest possible limits." [5] After a nine-month comparative lull, Arab acts of terrorism were renewed with growing intensity in July 1937. The government's search of the Higher Committee's offices at Jerusalem and arrest of several members of the local national committee did not check the disorders. Not until the assassination on September 26 of L. Y. Andrews, the acting district commissioner who had served as the government liaison officer with the Royal Commission, was the administration goaded into drastic action.

Regulations were put into force on September 30, permitting the government to deport political detainees to any part of the British Empire and to dissolve any societies whose purposes might be deemed as not in accord with the administration's policy. Under these rulings the Higher Committee and the local national committees were declared unlawful, and al-Hajj Amin al-Husayni was removed from his post as president of the Supreme Muslim Council. On the following day warrants were issued for the arrest and deportation of six members of the Higher Committee, including Jamal al-Husayni, who were held "morally responsible" for the recent series of criminal acts. Jamal succeeded in escaping to Syria; the remaining five were sent to the Seychelles Islands for internment on October 2. Shortly thereafter the government formally notified Jamal and four other members of the Higher Committee then out of the country that they would be debarred from returning to Palestine until further notice. Fearing arrest, al-Hajj Amin fled secretly to Lebanon on October 15 and took up residence in the coastal village of al-Zuq, north of Bayrut. There he established contact with his exiled colleagues, and the outlawed Higher Committee was reconstituted with its seat at Damascus.[6]

In Palestine the revolt was resumed, as small rebel bands of local recruits and commanders collected in the hill districts of the northern and central parts of the country. The guerrilla tactics and objectives of 1936 remained largely unchanged, except in one fundamental respect. The Arab Community was no longer united behind the Higher Committee, and the rebels' fury was directed as much against Arab "dissidents" as against the mandatory and the Yishuv. The arrest, deportation, and banishment of most of the prominent Arab spokesmen, at a time when the Palestine problem was presumably to be settled once and for all, tended to make them nationalist martyrs. But the only leaders who were able to capitalize on the added prestige were the Husaynis. None of the smaller factions proved capable of functioning without its accredited leaders. The National Defense Party had failed to obtain government backing and for the time being also became quiescent. The reconstituted Higher Committee became for all practical purposes the creature of the Husayni party. In the absence of any effective opposition, the Mufti in exile came to exercise supreme political authority in the Arab Community, and his activities were now beyond the control of the Palestine Government.

The rebel bands thus essentially formed the Husayni military arm. Most of the locally recruited guerrillas were genuine patriots, who found their inspiration in the Mufti. But intermingled with these sincere nationalists were those who discovered in the disorders "an opportunity for paying off family vendettas and personal scores." Others were professional bandits who regarded the insurrection as "a recognized and remunerative 'racket.'" Many of the last class "were recruited, equipped and issued with instructions by rebel organisations in Beirut and Damascus" under the direction of the Higher Committee. As in 1936 the guerrillas had to depend heavily for funds on wealthy Palestine Arabs and for supplies, temporary reinforcements, and military equipment on the local fallahin. Arab notables and village headmen who did not readily comply with the rebel demands—and these by and large were Arabs who in the past had been allied with anti-Husayni groups, in a majority of cases with the Nashashibi faction—were subjected to intimidation, abduction, and murder. Under these circumstances many Arabs unsympathetic to the Husaynis found it prudent to leave the country.[7]

In the face of the challenge to its authority, the government for the first time enforced many of its emergency powers. Military courts were set up in November 1937 for trying offenses against law and order. The discharge of firearms and the carrying of bombs or unlicensed weapons were made punishable by death. All sentences were subject to confirmation by the commanding general of the British forces in Palestine; and from his decision there was no appeal. Any British commissioned officer was authorized to issue a warrant for the arrest of suspects. Before the end of 1937 the military courts tried 26 Arabs, of whom four received capital punishment. By that time, too, the number of Arabs under arrest exceeded 800. Simultaneously British troops resumed offensive action against the guerrillas. In the rural areas collective fines were imposed, and buildings housing known offenders were blown up. Steps were also taken to stamp out gun-running and the incursion of Arab volunteers from the Levant States. A road was constructed in the winter of 1937–38 along the northern frontier to enable mobile army units to patrol the area; and in the spring of 1938 a barbed wire fence, with supporting defense works, was erected along the patrol road and on stretches of the Transjordan border. Furthermore, the Mufti's continuing hold over the Supreme Muslim Council was finally broken by the mandatory's dismissal in February–March 1938 of more than a dozen of his trusted personal aides occupying key posts in that institution.[8]

In the meantime, the Jewish constabulary, composed principally of village supernumeraries, had grown from about 3,500 at the end of 1936 to somewhat less than 5,000 a year later. However, their ranks remained relatively stationary in the first six months of 1938. In this period the Jewish Agency pleaded persistently for more arms and for the training of as large a number of reservists as possible. While these pleas went unanswered, the government did permit the enlistment of about 1,000 volunteer guards in Jerusalem, and the Jewish rural police were allowed to reorganize on a regional basis. With the combined protection of the authorized constabulary and Haganah—the illegal Jewish defense establishment—the Jews did not have to abandon any villages. Indeed, from the start of the Arab revolt in 1936 new Jewish villages were established at the rate of about one a month. Many of these were located in districts where Jewish settlements previously were either few in number or wholly nonexistent. The accelerated rural settlement was motivated as much by the fear of impending restrictions on Jewish land purchases as by the desire to enlarge Jewish territorial claims under any scheme of partition and to impress upon the Arabs that the Jews would not be deterred by violence.[9]

Throughout this period of unrest and uncertainty, the countrywide economic depression deepened. At the end of 1937 the number of unemployed Arabs rose to an estimated 21,000. Nor did the plight of the Arab workers improve in the first half of 1938, as the rebellion intensified. The Yishuv's economy also continued to sag. Jewish unemployment increased from about 5,000 in December 1937 to nearly 9,000 in July 1938; of the latter some 6,400 were urban workers. For the first time in the city's history, the population of Tel-Aviv declined. The mandatory's persistent refusal to negotiate reciprocal trade agreements with European countries, moreover, placed the citrus producers at a disadvantage. In consequence, profits from citriculture withered, even though exports nearly doubled between 1935–36 and 1937–38. The disorganization of the Arab Community made it impossible to take any effective measures to check the Arab slump. In the Jewish Community, on the other hand, the severity of unemployment was mitigated somewhat by the creation of new jobs in the Haifa and Tel-Aviv ports, the constabulary, and the Jewish-owned citrus groves. Moreover, Jewish labor benefited from military contracts, while the Jewish Agency and the Histadrut jointly sponsored a semipublic works program.[10]

THE BROADENING OF THE PROBLEM

Until 1936 the parties to the Palestine dispute included only the United Kingdom as mandatory, the local Arab national movement as spokesman for the Palestine Arab Community, and the Jewish Agency—after 1929—as spokesman for the Jewish National Home. In the course of the first stage of the Arab revolt in 1936, popular and official interest in the Palestine problem was awakened in the surrounding Arab lands. This interest continued to grow in 1937 and 1938, as the Palestine Arabs sought the assistance of their neighbors to frustrate British plans to set up a Jewish state. The trend was accelerated by the international crisis in Europe. With the transparent purpose of weakening British and French prestige, Italy and Germany had begun actively to intervene in the internal affairs of the Near East, particularly in the Palestine issue.

As long as no major European powers had challenged the political arrangements in the Near East arising out of World War I and its peace settlement, the Zionist position was more powerful than that of the Arabs. The United Kingdom was committed under the mandate to the policy of facilitating the development of the Jewish National Home. Britain, moreover, had to account for its actions in Palestine to the Permanent Mandates Commission; and the Commission was also bound to uphold the mandate, as an instrument of the League of Nations. The Zionist legal position was reinforced by other factors. The Jewish Agency's permanent offices in Geneva and London defended Zionist interests formally whenever Palestine came up for consideration in these two cities and established friendly relations with members of the various delegations to the League of Nations, successive British governments, and both houses of Parliament.[11] In fact, Parliamentary sentiment, in so far as it had become articulate on Palestine, was largely sympathetic to the national home. Besides, the Zionist Organization was essentially a popular movement, and in the course of time it had developed facilities for appealing to public opinion in the many countries where Zionist branches had been formed. Consequently, the national home could boast a substantial body of sympathizers throughout the world, especially in the democratic lands.

In their quarrel with the Zionists the Palestine Arab nationalists were decidedly handicapped. They had begun only recently to pay heed to the importance of cultivating popular support in non-Arab countries. Not until 1936 was the Palestine Information Center opened in London; in the same year the Arab National League was founded in New York by Americans of Arab origin who endeavored to publicize the Palestine Arab viewpoint.[12] Although the nationalists and the governments of the surrounding Arab countries gave their blessings to the Palestine Arab cause, they were not yet organized for concerted action. Iraq was admitted to the League of Nations in 1932, and Egypt five years later. But these were the only Arab states members of the League, and neither one was represented on the Permanent Mandates Commission. Egypt, Iraq, and Saudi Arabia alone among the Arab governments maintained diplomatic missions in Britain. At that time, however, the United Kingdom did not recognize the right of the Arab states to intervene in the affairs of the Palestine Mandate. At all events, the Arabs were burdened with a legal incapacity, since, by demanding the immediate termination of the mandate and the Jewish National Home, they were striving to alter the established order.

After 1936 the circumstances for redressing the balance were auspicious. The established order in Europe and Africa was already being undermined by Italian and German territorial aggression. Both powers had withdrawn from the League of Nations and were capitalizing on the ready-made opportunities for weakening Anglo-French prestige in the Mediterranean area. The success of Arab nationalist pressures in Egypt and the Levant States in 1935–36 testified to the fact that the Western democracies, confronted with the larger European crisis, were beginning to retreat from the strongholds they had acquired in the Arab East at the close of World War I. Even after the occupation of Ethiopia Italian propaganda to the Arab countries persisted without letup, courting nationalist good will and addressing itself to existing anti-British and anti-French feeling. Regular short-wave broadcasts from Bari were supplemented by the free distribution of press releases to Arabic newspapers and the grant of scholarships to Arab students for study in Italy. The British Government viewed the results of this propaganda as sufficiently serious to merit the conclusion with Italy in April 1938 of an agreement, under which Rome promised to abandon its Arabic broadcasts. Prime Minister Chamberlain later explained to Parliament that specific oral assurances had been received from the Italian Foreign Minister that his government "would abstain from creating difficulties and embarrassment to His Majesty's Government in the administration of Palestine." [13]

Although Radio Berlin did not institute regular Arabic programs until the spring of 1939, other forms of Nazi propaganda, especially as regards Palestine, were already well developed long before that time. Indeed, the Palestine problem seemed to have been tailored by history to Hitler's specifications. Persecution in Germany and its occupied territories forced an ever-increasing number of Jews to seek visas to Palestine and added substance to the Zionist claims for greater immigration. At the same time the virulent anti-Jewish propaganda of the Nazis appeared to confirm Arab nationalist contentions. The Arab nationalists had always envied the superior organization of the Zionists, the large funds which were collected for the Jewish National Home, and the support which Zionism enjoyed in London and Geneva.[14] Consequently, Arab nationalist circles in Palestine and the near-by lands provided a receptive audience for one of the Nazi propaganda themes: that "international Jewry" controlled world politics and finance and was conspiring with Britain to wrest Palestine from the Arabs. The mandatory could not accede to Zionist pleas for large-scale immigration without pushing the Arab nationalists into the arms of the Germans and the Italians. Yet under the terms of the mandate neither could it yield to the full demands of the Arab nationalists. Hence the Nazis were able to exploit the problem to the utmost.

The German propaganda setup in Palestine integrated the activities of German shipping firms, commercial travelers, students, business men, and permanent residents with those of trained propagandists. The *Deutsches Nachrichten Büro* (official German News Agency), from its main regional office at Jerusalem, supplied the Arab press of Palestine, Transjordan, and the Levant States with news handouts; and its director, Dr. Franz Reichert, was known to have established close relations with many of the Arab political leaders, including al-Hajj Amin. Well-paid advertisements from German business agencies helped subsidize the newspapers, a common Nazi practice for influencing the "slant" of news coverage. Highly placed Nazi officials in tours of the Near East often managed to confer with Arab politicians and editors. Thus, Adolf Eichmann, one of the Nazi "experts on the Jewish question," was stated to have paid a flying visit to Palestine and the near-by countries in September 1937 and to have met at Cairo with Arab journalists, among them one of the Mufti's delegates.[15]

The most numerous carriers of the Nazi message, however, were members of the Templar movement, a German religious sect which had established seven "colonies" in Palestine in the half-century preceding World War I. Although most of the approximately 1,200 Templars were born in Palestine, they retained German citizenship and sent their youth to Germany for higher education and military service. The Templars knew Arabic well and employed large numbers of Arabs in various Templar-owned enterprises. Many Templars had become confirmed Nazis by 1936 and furnished the Third Reich with a direct line to the Arabs. Five of the seven Templar colonies lay within the area of the projected Jewish state, as recommended by the Royal Commission. These Templars reportedly feared Jewish reprisals for Nazi oppression of Jews in Germany and therefore in 1937–38 had strong personal reasons as well for aligning themselves with the Arabs against partition.[16]

The effectiveness of Nazi propaganda was reflected in the liberal use by Palestine Arab editorialists of racist clichés as early as 1936 and 1937. Typical of the period were the comments which appeared in a Palestine Arab weekly in August 1936:

. . . Hitlerism is violently but nevertheless truly symptomatic of a world which is sick to death of the pedestrian, materialistic civilisation of the industrial centuries, which gave the subversive activities of Judaism the chance to develop a strangle hold on international economics. . . . Whenever Jewry intervenes openly in politics, as to-day, it is bound to be attacked for what it is . . . a body incapable of occupying a place within another nation's democracy. As such it can contribute nothing to that nation's 'national being,' and so in these days of national renaissance it must go.

In connection with the celebration in May 1937 of the Prophet Muhammad's birthday, in which Christian Arabs as well as Muslims participated, German and Italian flags were prominently displayed, as were pictures of Hitler and Mussolini. This demonstration constituted a "significant gesture of sympathy and respect," explained an Arab editorialist.[17]

'Sympathy' because, feeling the whip of Jewish pressure and influence, the Arabs sympathize with the Nazis and Fascists in their agony and trials at the hands of Jewish intrigues and international financial pressure, and 'respect' because, knowing the strength of Jewish finance and Jewish intrigues, the Nazis and Fascists have been able to withstand the influence of the Jews.

The frequent charges that the Palestine Arab revolt was engineered and financed almost wholly by the Italians and the Germans [18] overstated the case. Nevertheless the fact that the two European powers provided the Palestine rebels with material as well as moral aid was confirmed by circumstantial evidence and by fragments of direct proof. Such secret assistance conformed to the known Italo-German propaganda objectives in Palestine in this period, to the practices of the totalitarian states in Europe, and to the later wartime collaboration between Arab leaders and the Axis. An analysis of the weapons captured from the rebels by the British security forces in Palestine between July and November 1938 revealed that a small percentage came from Germany; and in May 1939 it was reported that British frontier officials seized from Arab smugglers on the Lebanese border over 100 German rifles and thousands of rounds of ammunition.[19]

The Italo-German intrusion into the problem had a significant bearing on the extra-Palestine phase of the Arab struggle against partition. From the start, the Higher Committee elicited the enthusiastic support of those political organizations in Iraq, the Levant States, and Egypt which were not represented in their respective governments. Most of the opposition groups were affiliated with the local Committees for the Defense of Palestine. These were reactivated in the summer of 1937, and for the first time steps were taken to coordinate their activities. The Damascus committee sponsored a conference of its sister groups at Bludan, Syria, on September 8–10, 1937, attended by more than 300 delegates. Presumably to establish a basis for common action, the main speeches stressed the theme that the Zionists aspired to rule the entire Arab East. But the feelings of the delegates were expressed by the session's chairman in his opening address:

> . . . we must make Britain understand that it must choose between our friendship and the Jews. Britain must change its policy in Palestine, or we shall be at liberty to side with other European powers whose policies are adverse to Britain.

This threat was embodied in the resolutions passed by the Bludan Conference, which also rejected "the partition of Palestine and the establishment of a Jewish State therein." [20]

Parliamentary Defense Committees were formed in Egypt and Syria in the summer of 1938 and together with the opposition-led committees convened a "World Inter-Parliamentary Congress of Arab and Muslim Countries for the Defense of Palestine" at Cairo on October 7–11, 1938. Among the estimated 2,500 participants, of whom the great majority were youths, students, and Palestine emigrés, were about 60 parliamentary deputies from Egypt, Iraq, and Syria. Other delegates came from India, Yugoslavia, Yemen, Morocco, China, and the Arab communities in the Americas. But Transjordan, Saudi Arabia, and the Wafdist Party—by that time the Opposition—in Egypt boycotted the conference. The resolution adopted by the Cairo Congress reaffirmed categorically that "it refuses to recognise the partition of Palestine in any form or manner whatsoever." Britain was again threatened that, if the Arab claims were turned down, "the Arab and Muslim peoples throughout the world will be compelled to regard the attitude of the British and the Jews as inimical . . . and to adopt a similar attitude, with its natural consequences upon political, economic and social relations." [21]

One aspect of the campaign against partition involved agitation against the indigenous Jewish communities in the Arab East. The estimated quarter-million Jews in this region formed less than 1 per cent of the total population. The Yemeni Jews, it was true, had suffered persecution under the rule of an autocratic Imam even before the rise of anti-Zionism. But the position of the Jews in the remaining Arab lands improved steadily in the 1920's and early 1930's. Iraqi and Egyptian Jews had played important roles in national politics, as members of the legislatures and even as cabinet ministers. Organized anti-Jewish incitation began in mid-1936 and continued sporadically thereafter. In the spring and summer of 1938, however, the anti-Jewish drive was intensified. Inflammatory speeches were delivered in the mosques. Groups of youths carried anti-Jewish placards and shouted anti-Jewish slogans in public demonstrations. In the larger cities of Iraq, Syria, and Lebanon bombs were thrown into the Jewish quarters. Only in Egypt did Arab spokesmen openly condemn these activities. Italo-German influence was also felt in the widespread agitation. In Yemen Italian agents were implicated, while in Egypt, the Levant States, and Iraq Arabic broadsheets and pamphlets, distributed among those participating in the demonstrations, allegedly were printed in Germany.[22]

The Arab governments significantly took no action to curb the popular agitation against partition. Yet the governments themselves in general dealt with the matter gingerly. Two days after the publication of the Royal Commission report, the Higher Committee had addressed appeals to the Arab rulers, imploring them, "in the name of the sacred land . . . your Arab chivalry and your religious obligations, to work for rescuing the country from imperialism, Jewish colonisation and partition." In response to this request Syria submitted a formal protest to the French High Commissioner, and Iraq to the League of Nations. But Amir 'Abdallah of Transjordan, King ibn Sa'ud of Arabia, and the Imam Yahya of Yemen sent evasive replies; and Prime Minister Mustafa al-Nahhas Pasha of Egypt refused to make any statement whatsoever. At the Assembly of the League of Nations in September 1937 and again a year later the Egyptian and Iraqi delegates both placed themselves on record as opposed to partition. In the interim the two Arab states also approached Britain through ordinary diplomatic channels. But no attempt was made, as among the nongovernmental Arab organizations, to coordinate the efforts of all the Arab states.[23]

THE ABANDONMENT OF PARTITION

The rise of anti-British feeling in the Arab East, which was so closely associated with the prolonged impasse in Palestine, began to give the United Kingdom pause by early 1938. The clouds of war were lengthening over Europe, and threats of overtures to Britain's potential enemies, even from unofficial Arab groups, could hardly be ignored. The British Government could not afford to alienate the population of so strategic a region, which lay athwart vital imperial arteries and contained important military and naval bases and indispensable oil resources. Britain now sought Arab friendship anxiously. To counteract Italo-German propaganda, the United Kingdom inaugurated its own regular Arabic broadcasts to the Near East in January 1938. Yet it was clear that propaganda alone would not suffice, and any attempt to implement partition in the face of determined Arab opposition was bound to complicate Britain's task.

London's retreat from partition, however, was a slow process, extending over a span of more than a year. In mid-September 1937 the British Foreign Secretary, Anthony Eden, was still able to inform the Council of the League of Nations that in his government's view "partition is the only ultimate solution." By the time that the Partition Commission's terms of reference were released more than three months later, the mandatory's ardor had cooled. The Colonial Secretary, William Ormsby-Gore, announced that the British Government was "in no sense committed" to the approval of the particular partition plan advanced by the Royal Commission and that the new investigative body would enjoy "full liberty to suggest modifications of that plan." Ormsby-Gore also warned that "for some time to come, any action taken will be only of an exploratory nature." As a result of new delays, the Partition Commission did not arrive in Palestine until the end of April.[24]

Meanwhile, the Jewish Agency's proposal for an Arab-Jewish conference was transmitted to the Colonial Office. But at the end of October 1937 Ormsby-Gore dismissed this suggestion as impracticable in the prevailing circumstances. No more successful in the next few months were unofficial attempts by British and Jewish opponents of partition to bring the Agency and the Higher Committee into direct negotiations.[25] The Agency for its part possessed little political leverage. The number of Jews desirous of escaping the Nazi trap in Europe was multiplying. Since few avenues of escape existed, their eyes focused increasingly on the national home. This added moral weight to the Agency's demands. Yet the nearer war approached, the less morality counted in international relations. And in the realm of power politics, the Zionists could adduce few arguments. The anti-Jewish campaign of the Nazis, soon to be copied by the Fascists, placed almost all Jews—even those not living in democratic countries—unquestioningly on the side of Britain and the democracies. Any wooing of the mandatory's likely foes in the emerging hostilities was thus ruled out. Besides, a majority of the Zionists had been traditionally pro-British, owing to Britain's sponsorship of the national home. The one man who more than any other had shaped Zionist policy in these years—Chaim Weizmann—was himself a British citizen. In the past, under Weizmann's influence, the Zionists looked to the British press and especially to Parliament as their source of greatest support in the United Kingdom. This confidence was enhanced by the right of appeal to the League of Nations.

At all events, the Agency was sidetracked throughout this period by an internal dispute over the merits of partition. Consequently, the Zionist leaders favoring the immediate creation of a diminutive Jewish state devoted their time to winning the support, not of the League of Nations and Britain, but of the Jewish "anti-partitionists"; and the Jewish opponents of partition stepped up their own campaign even after their defeat at the sessions of the Zionist Congress and Agency Council in August 1937.[26] For these reasons the Agency Executive engaged only in defensive political action until April 1938. In the following four months the Agency spokesmen were largely preoccupied with the preparation of evidence for the Partition Commission in the hope of securing more liberal terms for the projected Jewish state than had been tentatively advanced by the Royal Commission.

As for the Arabs, the National Defense Party and Amir 'Abdallah submitted written statements to the Partition Commission, recommending solutions other than partition.[27] Otherwise the Higher Committee's boycott of the technical inquiry was strictly enforced. Indeed, during the Commission's stay in the country the terrorist operations of the Arab rebels gathered new momentum. Until the early summer of 1938 the guerrilla bands were concentrated in northern and central Palestine. But in July British troop reinforcements from Egypt drove most of the insurgents southward. Early in the following month a communiqué from the "General Command, Headquarters of the Arab Revolution in Palestine," read in the mosques, ordered all townsmen to substitute for their usual tarbush the flowing headcloth and coil of the fallahin and Beduin, so as to enable the rebels to circulate in the towns without arousing suspicion. The rebels drove British officials and police out of one Arab town and village after another. By the end of September the civil administration in the vicinity of Jerusalem and in much of the southern district —outside the Jewish areas—was almost completely disrupted. The rebels set up their own courts for "trying" Arabs charged with disloyalty to the national movement. As a rule, the suspects were abducted, forcibly brought to trial, and, if found "guilty," immediately executed.[28]

After the resumption of the Arab revolt in the fall of 1937 members of the Revisionist military arm no longer felt bound by the Jewish quasi-government's injunction of restraint. The acts of reprisal against the Arab Community were sporadic until a death sentence, imposed by a British military court on a Revisionist youth for having fired on an Arab bus, was carried out at the end of June 1938. After that date Revisionist armed units, now calling themselves the National Military Organization in Palestine (ha-Irgun ha-Zvai ha-Leumi be-Erez Israel), launched retaliatory attacks on the Arabs. The Irgun's most serious exploits occurred at Haifa in July, when on two occasions land mines were detonated in the Arab fruit market, killing 74 persons and wounding 129. Through its clandestine radio transmitter and broadsheets, the Irgun announced its responsibility for the outrages and endeavored to recruit new members.

The resort to counterviolence by the Yishuv's militant fringe drew firm rebukes from the Jewish quasi-government, whose lead the vast majority of the Palestine Jews still followed. Although negotiations over an Agency plan for the further expansion of the legal Jewish police establishment dragged on through the summer and fall without final decision, the legal constabulary as well as the illegal Haganah were given opportunities for broader experience. Jewish constables gradually came to be used for guard duty at government installations, and the British Army began the practice of calling upon the Agency to provide volunteers from the ranks of Haganah for offensive action against the guerrillas. A group of 75 volunteers formed "special night squads," under the command of Captain Orde Charles Wingate. Since these squads proved able to prevent sabotage of the Iraq Petroleum Company's pipe line, some 200 additional Haganah recruits were assigned for service with British garrisons in the Galilee District.[29]

Meanwhile, the Partition Commission completed its survey in Palestine early in August. Although the Commission's findings were not presented to Parliament until November, its recommendation that the partition scheme should be dropped was known to the British Government weeks earlier. The stage was already set for a change of policy by the appointment in February 1938 of a new High Commissioner for Palestine, Sir Harold MacMichael, and a few months later of a new Colonial Secretary, Malcolm MacDonald. At the end of September MacDonald intimated to Weizmann that a conference with Arabs and Jews would be called in London.[30]

The sponsors of the Arab revolt had thus won two major political victories by the fall of 1938. After the first phase of the uprising London admitted that the Palestine Mandate was unworkable, a claim which the Arab nationalists had advanced from the start. Now the second phase of the rebellion was followed by the scuttling of the partition scheme, even before any attempt was made to implement it. These events taught the lesson that the use of violence as a political weapon produced results which otherwise appeared unobtainable. Nor was the lesson lost upon either the outlawed Higher Committee or the militant fringe of the Yishuv. This terrorist extension of Arab-Zionist pressure politics portended future dangers, and the precedents thus established were fated to hasten the degeneration of the Palestine Mandate. The successive placating gestures in Palestine, as on the Continent, gave rise to a state of affairs which the Chamberlain Government was straining to avoid. They placed a premium on extremism, undermined the influence of the mandatory, and virtually destroyed the prospect of an agreed settlement.

CHAPTER 7

The 1939 White Paper

BEFORE THE British Government gave official notice of its intentions to hold direct parleys with Arabs and Jews, the mandatory decided to re-establish its authority in Palestine. As severe as were the mandatory's repressive measures after October 1937, the Arab insurgents retained the offensive for nearly a full year. Throughout these months the total strength of British troops stationed in the country consisted of two infantry brigades; in July 1938 two infantry battalions, two R.A.F. squadrons, and an armored-car and cavalry unit arrived from Egypt. But even these auxiliaries had to be withdrawn in September because of the Czecho-slovakian crisis. After the Chamberlain Government purchased a breathing spell with the Munich accord at the end of September, the number of British troops in Palestine rose to more than 16,000, including 18 infantry battalions and some 700 R.A.F. personnel. A virtual state of martial law was declared in mid-October. All police—Britons, Arabs, and Jews—were placed under the operational jurisdiction of the army, and civilian authority was transferred from the district commissioners to regional military commanders. Countrywide curfews were enforced, and only those possessing military identity cards and special travel permits were allowed to use the highways or trains. The reoccupation on October 19 of the Old City of Jerusalem, which had been seized by the rebels earlier in the month, marked the beginning of the British effort to stamp out Arab terrorism. Villages and towns one after another were cordonned off and searched for hidden arms and terrorist suspects. Collective penalties, including occasional large-scale demolition of houses, were inflicted where cases of communications sabotage occurred even after military warnings. By the end of the year nearly 2,500 Arabs were under arrest.[1]

German propagandists turned these operations to account, by disseminating stories of alleged British atrocities against the Palestine Arabs. The Palestine problem, moreover, threatened to spread even further afield. As soon as the Zionist leaders learned that the partition scheme was to be discarded, American Zionists sought the intervention of their government. A flood of appeals to Washington, however, elicited from Secretary of State Cordell Hull on October 18 only a cautious statement that "the American Government and people have watched with the keenest sympathy the development in Palestine of the [Jewish] National Home," but that the United States was not empowered to prevent any modification of the mandate. The Department of State would, however, "take all necessary measures for the protection of American rights and interests in Palestine." President Roosevelt confirmed this position a few days later. Nor did anything result from a pro-Zionist memorial presented to the White House by 51 Senators, 194 Representatives, and 30 state governors. While the Palestine Jews obtained scant comfort from this expression of official American disinterestedness, the Arab nationalists interpreted the American statements as evidence that the United States was pro-Zionist. Accordingly, the Defense Committees and the press in the Arab countries indulged in saber-rattling and warnings that American commerce and cultural institutions would be boycotted. Even King ibn Sa'ud sent a personal letter of protest to President Roosevelt.[2]

The Partition Commission presented its detailed negative report to Parliament on November 9. Accompanying the report was a White Paper, in which the British Government formally jettisoned partition as impracticable on account of the great "political, administrative and financial difficulties involved." The government also made public its plans for conferring in London as soon as possible with representatives of the Palestine Arabs, the near-by Arab states, and the Jewish Agency. The mandatory, however, reserved the right to disallow from participating in the talks those Palestine Arab leaders "responsible for the campaign of assassination and violence." Determined efforts would be made, it was stated, to arrive at a tripartite agreement "regarding future policy, including the question of immigration into Palestine." But the White Paper let it be known that, if no accord were achieved within a reasonable time, the mandatory would take its own decision.[3] The mandatory planned initially to hold separate discussions with the Arab and Jewish delegates, Colonial Secretary MacDonald subsequently explained to Parliament, but it was hoped that the talks would develop into a three-way conference. Egypt, Iraq, Saudi Arabia, Transjordan, and Yemen were invited, and the French Government was to be apprised of any developments which might be of interest to the Levant States. MacDonald asserted that the Mufti's "record over many years makes him wholly unacceptable" as a participant. The Colonial Secretary also declared that, while the British Government would enter the parleys bound by its international obligations to Arabs and Jews, it would not "prevent either party from presenting arguments for the modification of the Mandate." [4]

The champions of the Jewish National Home were indignant. The Agency Executive recalled that its proposal of the preceding year to convene a Jewish-Arab conference had been rebuffed by the mandatory. The Arab states, it was said, enjoyed no special status with respect to Palestine. The rights of Egypt and Iraq, as members of the League of Nations, were asserted to be no larger than those of other League members or of the United States. The mandatory was informed that the Agency could participate in the parleys only on the basis of the Balfour Declaration and the mandate. The Executive's position was upheld by the Zionist General Council and the Agency Administrative Committee.

The British Government's decision to seek a negotiated settlement before the final suppression of the Arab rebellion, following so soon the Anglo-French capitulation at Munich, did little to dispel Jewish fears; and the bitterness was heightened by the mandatory's rejection of the Yishuv's offer to adopt 10,000 German and Austrian Jewish children after the severe anti-Jewish outbursts in the Greater Reich in November 1938. Sentiment against taking part in the London discussions therefore hardened in the Palestine Jewish Community. Even the traditionally pro-British *Ha-Arez* observed that "there is no sense in our submitting politely to the role awaiting us of Czechoslovakia or of Spain, in our walking with open eyes into the pit being dug for us, and in our being respectful and cordial, moreover, to the grave-diggers." [5] Nevertheless, the Agency Executive decided to accept the mandatory's invitation, so as not to allow "the Jewish case . . . to go by default." Back in London the Agency attempted to make the Jewish conference committee as representative as possible. The delegates included non-Zionist as well as Zionist supporters of the Agency. Even the nonconformist Agudat Israel sent its spokesmen. Only the Revisionists were unrepresented in the 44-man deputation. [6]

Meanwhile, those Arab nationalists who had spearheaded the battle against partition were generally pleased with their victory and the mandatory's decision to give the Arab states a voice in determining future policy in Palestine. In terms of the ultimate nationalist objectives the victory was admittedly limited. But it seemed to vindicate the strategy of intransigence and violence. Consequently, the nationalists, in no mood for compromise, roundly condemned the announcement that certain Arab leaders would be barred from the London talks and that efforts would be made to hold trilateral discussions. At Bayrut in mid-November al-Hajj Amin issued a manifesto, enumerating the Palestine Arab nationalist demands as the only conditions under which the Arabs would agree to participate, and concluding with the blunt assertion "that there is no individual or body in Palestine, apart from the Higher Committee, which can accept the [mandatory's] invitation . . ." [7]

The Jerusalem Mufti aimed his warning at the Opposition, which was now attempting a comeback under the leadership of Fakhri Bey al-Nashashibi, Raghib Bey's cousin. Fakhri Bey and his colleagues had won the sympathy of British military commanders and district officials, who were seeking Arab cooperation in mopping up the rebels. The Arab Community itself had grown weary of the rebellion. Hundreds of Arabs had been killed or wounded by the guerrillas. Thousands of wealthy Arabs, including most of the prominent politicians not already banished by the government, fled the country to find personal safety and to avoid forced contributions to the insurgents' treasury. The disappearance of markets and the frequent closure of business necessitated by rebel-imposed strikes and army-imposed curfews produced greater unemployment in the towns than ever before. The fallahin suffered comparatively the largest losses, for the rebel operations were concentrated in the rural areas. Under these circumstances the Opposition was able to make some headway before the end of the year in reorganizing its following.

As early as November 14 Fakhri Bey opened his bid for participation in the London conferences in a memorandum addressed to the High Commissioner and the Colonial Secretary. Fakhri Bey offered the cooperation of the Opposition in the "endeavour to solve the Palestine problem in a manner which will guarantee permanent peace" and requested that the mandatory remain firm in excluding the Mufti's faction by naming as the Palestine Arab spokesmen only "those leaders who are sincere to their country." This time the Opposition was not cowed into submission by the Husaynis. The rebel court's death sentence, imposed on Fakhri Bey on November 30 for having committed "high treason" against the Arab nation, was not carried out; and the Nashashibis retaliated against Husayni attempts on the lives of dissident leaders, until by February 1939 a full-scale blood feud had developed. [8]

While the mandatory turned a deaf ear to appeals on the Mufti's behalf, the five members of the Higher Committee interned in the Seychelles were released. The Colonial Secretary declared at the beginning of December that they would be eligible for selection as delegates to London, although they would be excluded from Palestine, "where under present circumstances their admission is regarded as undesirable." [9] A month later the deportees conferred with the Mufti in Lebanon and were reinstated as members of the Higher Committee. The enlarged body released a communiqué at Bayrut on January 16, announcing the formation of a negotiating committee headed by the Mufti, which was to be represented at London by a delegation of six under the chairmanship of Jamal al-Husayni. The communiqué made it clear that the Higher Committee alone could speak for the Palestine Arabs.

The National Defense Party took up the challenge, by appointing its own negotiators and demanding the chairmanship of the Palestine Arab deputation. In contrast with the cleavage in the Palestine Arab ranks, the delegations of the Arab states, which included some of their leading statesmen, proved able to draw up a common program in preliminary discussions at Cairo. They tried also to mediate between the two rival Palestine factions, but not until after the opening of the London conferences and the Colonial Secretary's threat to consult separately with the National Defense Party were the differences composed. The Mufti finally agreed on February 9 that the Opposition might name two delegates, on condition that Fakhri Bey was not one. The National Defense Party accepted these terms, and the conferences resumed with at least an outward semblance of Palestine Arab unity.[10]

THE LONDON PARLEYS

The London conferences, which were opened at St. James' Palace with great solemnity on February 7 by Prime Minister Neville Chamberlain, Foreign Secretary Lord Halifax, and Colonial Secretary Malcolm MacDonald, could hardly have taken place under more dismal circumstances. The mandatory's relations with the Arabs of Palestine had grown steadily worse; the disaffection, abetted by Italo-German propaganda, had spread to the surrounding lands; and now the confidence of the Zionists in Britain had been severely shaken. Moreover, three years of Arab revolt had driven the two communities in Palestine further apart than ever. Thus, not only was mutual trust lacking among the three parties to the negotiations, but the Arabs refused to recognize the Jewish Agency as having any status in Palestine and declined even to enter into direct formal conversations with the Jews. Consequently, the British were forced to hold parallel talks with each side, a procedure which consumed time without encouraging mutual accommodation.

The disagreement between the Arabs and the Jews, as portrayed in the initial statements of their respective principal spokesmen, was complete. Jamal al-Husayni demanded the replacement of the mandate by an independent Arab state in accordance with McMahon's pledge to the Sharif Husayn in 1915, the immediate prohibition of Jewish immigration and land purchase, and the dissolution of the Jewish National Home. Chaim Weizmann pressed for the further development of the national home in accordance with the spirit and the letter of the mandate, Jewish immigration based on the principle of economic absorptive capacity but large enough to meet the needs of the European Jews, and effective safe-guards against minority status. Nor was any convergence of views achieved: either in more than a fortnight of separate discussions by the British Ministers with each side; or on February 23–24 in two informal trilateral meetings, in which the delegates of Egypt, Iraq, and Saudi Arabia assented to participate after they had received assurances that such meetings did not imply Arab recognition of the Jewish Agency.

The Anglo-Arab conversations had already threatened to stall because of Arab insistence upon a re-examination of British promises to the Arabs in World War I. This matter was referred on February 15 to a special Anglo-Arab committee and led to the official publication for the first time of the original text of the McMahon-Husayn letters, as corrected by new translations of certain Arabic passages, and of other British war-time statements to the Arabs. Even the committee, however, was unable to arrive at a unanimous conclusion. The Arab members contended that Palestine was actually and intentionally included in the zone in which Britain had promised to acknowledge and support Arab independence. The British members maintained the reverse position, on the ground that Palestine was not a purely Arab country; that—as the Holy Land of three religions—it contained substantial interest for non-Arabs; and that —as a country so close to the Suez Canal and Egypt—it possessed considerable practical interest for Britain. Yet the gap between the two standpoints was narrowed somewhat by the British, who conceded that [11]

> the Arab contentions . . . have greater force than has appeared hitherto.
> . . . [The British members of the committee] maintain that on a proper construction of the Correspondence Palestine was in fact excluded. But they agree that the language in which its exclusion was expressed was not so specific and unmistakable as it was thought to be at the time. . . . In the opinion of the Committee it is . . . evident . . . [in any case] that His Majesty's Government were not free to dispose of Palestine without regard for the wishes and interests of the inhabitants of Palestine.

The continuing deadlock embarrassed the Chamberlain Government. The United Kingdom was compelled by the pressure of European events to seek swift and decisive results. Even before the London conferences terminated, Germany broke its Munich pledge by proclaiming the Protectorate of Bohemia and Moravia. Britain's lease on peace was expiring. It was not renewable except on Hitler's terms. The only other choice was war. Indeed, the underlying purpose of the conferences with the Arabs and the Jews was the strengthening of imperial defenses. In the course of the negotiations it became clear that the Chamberlain Government was assessing the adjustments it sought in Palestine first with regard to their likely repercussions beyond the borders of that country and only second with regard to the deservedness of the rival claimants.[12] In the light of the Chamberlain Government's predicament early in 1939 and its record of appeasement, the bargaining power of the Arabs exceeded that of the Jews. The prolonged Palestine Arab insurgence had undermined Britain's prestige throughout a pivotal region in the Empire's defense system. Evidence had already piled up of Arab nationalist amenability to Italo-German overtures. The Zionists, on the other hand, could not possibly have been expected to court the totalitarian powers. The Chamberlain Government, it may be assumed, was not anxious to alienate the United States. But Washington had not given the Zionists any official encouragement. There remained, of course, the mandatory's obligations to the Jews and to the League of Nations, setting a limit beyond which London probably would not go. But legal terminology is flexible, and in its bid for the good will of the Arab East, the Chamberlain Government placed as narrow a construction as possible on the mandatory's pledges to the Jews and to the League.

The British unfolded their proposals in two stages. At the end of February preliminary suggestions, confined to constitutional changes, were declared wholly unacceptable by the Jewish delegation, while the conditional Arab acceptance was tantamount to rejection. A more elaborate British plan was therefore drawn up, endorsed by the Chamberlain Cabinet, and submitted to the Arab and Jewish conferees on March 15 with the warning that, if it were not accepted as a basis of agreement, the mandatory would close the conferences and would feel free to impose its own solution. The second scheme, which provided for the drastic curtailment of Jewish immigration and land purchases as well as the creation of an independent, unitary Palestine state, was turned down by the Jews without qualification, and the Jewish delegation was dissolved on March 16. The Palestine Arab delegates, with the passive compliance of their colleagues from the Arab states, again put forward conditions to which the British would not accede, so that the Anglo-Arab negotiations collapsed, and the conferences terminated on March 17.[18]

In the next two months the international situation passed from crisis to crisis. Following the German annexation of part of Czechoslovakia in mid-March, Italy invaded Albania on April 7. President Roosevelt invited Hitler and Mussolini on April 14 to settle all outstanding international disputes through peaceful negotiations. This invitation was scorned two weeks later by Hitler, who in the course of a diatribe before the Reichstag had this to say: [14]

. . . . the fact has obviously escaped Mr. Roosevelt's notice that Palestine is at present occupied not by German troops but by the English; and that the country is having its liberty restricted by the most brutal resort to force, is being robbed of its independence, and is suffering the cruellest maltreatment for the benefit of Jewish interlopers. The Arabs living in that country will therefore certainly not have complained to Mr. Roosevelt of German aggression, but they do voice a continuous appeal to the world, deploring the barbarous methods with which England is attempting to suppress a people which loves its freedom and is but defending it. . . .

The formation of the Berlin-Rome military and political Axis was announced on May 7, by which time a bill for compulsory military training in Britain had already been introduced into Parliament.

During these anxious weeks the British Government continued to exchange views with Egypt, Iraq, and Saudi Arabia on certain basic features of the projected mandatory policy. The spokesmen of the three Arab states, in a memorandum prepared at Cairo with the approval of the Higher Committee, re-submitted the Arab conditions of March.[15] While these suggestions resulted in a modification of detail, the policy statement which the mandatory finally published as a White Paper on May 17 was in most particulars virtually identical with the earlier Cabinet-endorsed British plan.[16] The 1939 White Paper comprised three sections, dealing with the constitution of the projected Palestine state, immigration, and land.

The first section announced that it was the Government's intention to develop self-governing institutions, since it was "contrary to the whole spirit of the Mandate system that the population of Palestine should remain for ever under Mandatory tutelage." The establishment of Palestine as a Jewish state was unequivocally ruled out. Simultaneously, regret was expressed over the "misunderstandings" over some of the phrases in the McMahon-Husayn correspondence. The mandatory, however, asserted that it "can only adhere . . . to the view that the whole of Palestine west of the Jordan was excluded from . . . McMahon's pledge, and . . . therefore cannot agree that the McMahon correspondence forms a just basis for the claim that Palestine should be converted into an Arab State." It was therefore contemplated to establish a Palestine state in which Arabs and Jews would jointly exercise governmental authority.

The realization of this scheme would require a decade. During that time Arabs and Jews would be given the opportunity of participating increasingly in the government, a process which would "be carried on whether or not they both availed themselves of it." The constitution would be drafted by Arab, Jewish, and British representatives five years after the restoration of peace, and would have to include safeguards concerning the Holy Places, the special position of the Jewish National Home, and British commercial and strategic interests. The grant of full independence would be conditional upon the establishment of good relations between the two peoples, which "it will be the constant endeavour of His Majesty's Government to promote." Yet the White Paper cautioned that, "if, at the end of ten years, it appears to His Majesty's Government that, contrary to their hopes, circumstances require the postponement of the establishment of an independent State, they will consult with representatives of the people of Palestine, the Council of the League of Nations, and the neighbouring Arab States before deciding on such postponement."

Regarding immigration, the White Paper observed that the principle of economic absorptive capacity had not dispelled Arab fears of eventual Jewish domination. This anxiety had often given rise to "lamentable disorders," of which "those of the last three years are only the latest and most sustained manifestation." The mandatory could, therefore, no longer overlook the harmful effect of immigration upon the political conditions in the country. The indefinite growth of the national home through immigration "against the strongly expressed will of the Arab people" would mean "rule by force," a condition contrary to the spirit of the mandate. Consequently, it was laid down that 75,000 Jews would be permitted to settle in Palestine in the five-year period beginning April 1, 1939, two-thirds to be chosen on the basis of economic absorptive capacity and the rest to constitute "a contribution towards the solution of the Jewish refugee problem." Jewish immigration after that period would depend on Arab consent. At the same time additional preventive measures to check illegal immigration would be taken, while those unauthorized immigrants who nevertheless "may succeed in coming into the country and cannot be deported will be deducted from the yearly quotas." Finally it was stipulated that the High Commissioner would be empowered generally to regulate the sale of land in certain areas and prohibit it in others with a view to avoiding the early appearance of "a considerable landless Arab population." Retroactive to the date of the White Paper, these powers would be enforced throughout the period of transition.

THE WHITE PAPER'S RECEPTION

Most Arab spokesmen acknowledged that the 1939 White Paper went a long way toward recognizing the basic claims of the Arab nationalists. Otherwise their reactions to the document varied. The Arab states did not issue any public statements. The Egyptian Prime Minister, however, informed the press that, in view of the United Kingdom's disregard of the Cairo memorandum, the Arab governments felt unable to recommend that the Palestine Arabs should collaborate with the mandatory on the basis of the new policy. Of the Arab states participating in the London conferences only Transjordan commended the White Paper. Tawfiq Pasha abu-al-Huda, the Chief Minister, stated in a press interview that, although the latest instrument of policy did not grant all of the Arab demands, it nevertheless removed fully the threats to Arab national existence in Palestine by assuring that a Jewish majority would never be established. He believed that "a new era of co-operation between the British and the Arabs in Palestine" might now be inaugurated. A similar position was taken at Jerusalem on May 29 by the National Defense Party, which endorsed the White Paper "as a good augury and a possible means for attaining . . . [in full the Arab nationalist] aspirations." The hope was expressed that, once the Arabs demonstrated through cooperation with the mandatory their readiness for complete independence, the transitional period might be shortened.[17]

The Higher Committee, on the other hand, repudiated the White Paper altogether in a statement made public at Bayrut on May 30. The very fact that the mandatory persisted in recognizing Jewish rights under the mandate prejudiced the Arab cause, it was stated, and had "made the Arabs lose hope in the new policy, as it continues to arouse their fears and fails to safeguard their rights." The promise of independence was alleged to be illusory, since the Jews by withholding their cooperation could spike all efforts to set up the Palestine government. The White Paper, it was charged, merely recommended the appointment of a few Palestine officials within the existing governmental framework, leaving in the hands of the High Commissioner and the Colonial Office all effective authority. The Higher Committee saw no justification for including British representatives in the constituent assembly. And British insistence on according the national home a special position, warned the Higher Committee, "will have no other result than the continuance of the calamities which have befallen Palestine."

The memorandum went on to declare that the continuance of Jewish immigration for five years was wholly unjustified. Besides, the Arabs had no sufficient guarantee that Jewish immigration would not be resumed in the future. At all events, the White Paper, rather than deter, would encourage unlawful entry, because those illegal immigrants "who are discovered will be deducted from the yearly quotas, while those undiscovered will be a net profit." The Arabs could consent to nothing less than "a complete and final prohibition" of Jewish immigration and land acquisition. "In deciding the fate of a living nation," the Higher Committee concluded,[18]

> the last word does not rest with White or Black Papers; it is the will of the nation itself that decides its future. The Arab people have expressed their will and said their word in a loud and decisive manner, and they are certain that with God's assistance they will reach the desired goal: Palestine shall be independent within an Arab Federation and shall remain forever Arab.

Meanwhile, in a lengthy analysis, addressed to the Permanent Mandates Commission on May 31, the Jewish Agency enumerated the legal and moral reasons for its "strongest possible protest." [19] The policy statement was denounced as a breach of the mandate and an abandonment of the national home. "The need of the Jewish people for a Home was never more acute . . . and its denial at this time is particularly harsh." Only two years earlier, it was argued, the mandatory, in urging the Jews to accept partition, had underlined the following advantages: the national home would never be subjected to Arab rule; the Jews would cease to lead a minority life; and the national home would become a Jewish state with full control over immigration. But a state in which the number of Arabs would always remain twice that of the Jews, it was contended, would in effect be an Arab state, would relegate the Palestine Jews to the position of a permanent minority, and would place the Yishuv under the domination of an Arab government. Moreover, the provisions of the White Paper on immigration and land were "based upon racial discrimination as between Jews and non-Jews, thus constituting an infringement of . . . the Mandate."

Whereas the mandate had recognized the status of Jews the world over in relation to Palestine, the Agency rebuttal continued, but had not done the same with respect to Arabs outside of Palestine, the White Paper transposed these relations. As evidence the Agency pointed to the fact that the only Jews to be consulted in determining the form of the future Palestine government were those already settled in the country, while the near-by Arab states which had participated in the London conferences were assured an active role.[20] Moreover, the Agency argued that the primary purpose of the mandate was not to develop self-governing institutions but to secure the establishment of a Jewish National Home. According to this view, Palestine still had not ripened for independence, since the growth of the national home could not securely continue without mandatory aid. In brief, the Agency accused the United Kingdom of rewarding the Arab terrorists for their campaign of violence, while punishing the Jews for their self-restraint. If Britain hoped to avoid the use of force, the statement concluded, the policy outlined in the White Paper was not designed to attain this goal, for the Jews would never acquiesce in its implementation.

The White Paper also aroused sharp hostility in Parliament, when the Chamberlain Government requested a vote of confidence from the House of Commons. A relatively few Members of Parliament welcomed the White Paper as a belated but only partial recognition of Palestine Arab rights. The numerous pro-Zionist spokesmen accused the government of again appeasing the aggressors. They voiced opinions ranging in theme from advocacy of Jewish resistance and terrorism to the warning by a Labor Party leader that the latest instrument of Palestine policy "will not be automatically binding upon . . . [the Conservative Government's] successors in office." [21] When the issue was finally put to a ballot, the Cabinet's position was upheld by a vote of 268 to 179. The Opposition included almost all of the Labor members and more than twenty Con-

servatives, among them Winston Churchill. *The Times* commented that
the majority was small "on so important a question, and the opposition
might well have been more formidable but for a general reluctance to embarrass the Government at a time of great international tension." [22]

An affirmative resolution was also passed by the House of Lords. Here
perhaps the most poignant criticism came from Viscount Samuel, who
had been the first High Commissioner for Palestine. By making Jewish
immigration after five years dependent on Arab assent and Arab sovereignty after ten years on Jewish assent, as Samuel saw it, ". . . each side
is given a veto on the aspirations of the other in order to induce both to
become friends. Both of them will, of course, exercise their veto," predicted Samuel, "and I presume His Majesty's Government proceed on
the principle that, since two negatives make a positive, that is the way to
secure a general settlement." [23]

Churchill's warning in the Commons debate that the execution of
the White Paper would alienate American sympathy for Britain did not
appear to be borne out by the immediate facts. At the end of May the
Department of State reaffirmed its evasive stand of the preceding October that Washington was powerless to prevent changes in the terms of
the Palestine Mandate. The League of Nations remained the only major
legal hurdle facing the Chamberlain Government. The mandatory presented the White Paper for review to the Permanent Mandates Commission in the second half of June. In the course of the British Colonial
Secretary's cross-examination by the Commission, MacDonald explained
that the position of the Jews in the projected Palestine state would be
safeguarded by obligatory Jewish consent to the adoption of any constitution. Also, the United Kingdom would include in its treaty with
the Palestine state a provision for protecting the rights of the national
home. At the same time, MacDonald made it clear that the land and immigration stipulations of the new policy would be enforced without
change, regardless of any opposition encountered.

The Commission members in reply observed that checks on Arab rule
to assuage Jewish fears would raise doubts among the Arabs over the
degree of independence being offered to them. Stress was also laid on the
fact that the mandate for Palestine was unique, since it contained no provision for its termination. So long as the mandate existed, the mandatory
would be required to facilitate immigration and settlement on the land.
The Commission, therefore, in reporting to the Council of the League,
unanimously concluded "that the policy set out in the White Paper was
not in accordance with the interpretation which, in agreement with the
mandatory Power and the Council, the Commission had placed upon the
Palestine mandate." Four of the seven Commission members added that
"they did not feel able to state that the policy of the White Paper was in
conformity with the mandate, any contrary conclusion appearing to them

to be ruled out by the very terms of the mandate and by the fundamental intentions of its authors." [24]

Since the Commission's opinion was merely advisory, the British Government prepared to defend its position before the next session of the League's Council, scheduled to convene early in September.[25] But the outbreak of war in Europe led to the suspension of the League's activities, so that the Council did not render a decision on the 1939 White Paper. Yet the Council's consent was required under Article 27 of the Palestine Mandate for any modification of its terms. With the support of the preliminary opinion of the Permanent Mandates Commission, the sponsors of the Jewish National Home were able to draw up a powerful legal case against the White Paper. On the other hand, the war emergency and the cessation of the League's jurisdiction over the mandates furnished the United Kingdom with powerful practical arguments for interpreting its obligations in Palestine in the manner best suited to the Allied war effort. The legality of the White Paper was destined never to be clarified. By the war's close the United Nations had come into being, and Article 79 of its Charter stipulated that the status of the existing mandates should be decided by the mandatory in conjunction with the states directly concerned.

The 1939 White Paper represented the culmination of a progressive change in the official British attitude toward the Jewish National Home, from one that was at bottom friendly to its further growth to one that was essentially the reverse. The latest instrument of policy constituted, not an agreed three-way settlement, but a unilateral compromise. Whether London could have obtained the backing of the Council of the League of Nations must remain an academic question. Without the Council's sanction, the mandatory had to assume full responsibility for its actions in Palestine.

The initial reception of the White Paper left no doubt that the Jews were implacable in their opposition and that the most powerful Palestine Arab leaders, with the tacit support of the Arab states, were holding out for even greater concessions. Hence, by the eve of World War II the Palestine Mandate had already begun to break down. Hitherto the mandatory governed the country chiefly with the cooperation of most Palestine Jews. Now the Chamberlain Government alienated the Zionists without befriending the Arabs. From then on—since the 1939 White Paper was never rescinded—the mandatory ruled in Palestine without the consent of either section of the population, and the government was gradually transformed from one that by and large was benevolent into one that was increasingly autocratic.

THE WHITE PAPER'S IMMEDIATE EFFECTS

The Arab Community at the time of the White Paper's appearance was incapable of concerted reaction. The British Army's offensive had already broken the backbone of the Arab guerrilla organization. Efforts of pro-Husayni groups in Palestine after the close of the London conferences to enforce a protest strike against the mandatory's failure to satisfy all the nationalist claims evaporated in a few days. At the end of March the rebels' titular commander-in-chief was killed in action; a fortnight later the second most powerful guerrilla leader escaped to the Levant States, where he surrendered to the French authorities. From then on the rebel-banned tarbush began to reappear as the normal headgear in the Arab urban areas. By May the large guerrilla bands either dispersed altogether or disintegrated into smaller units without coordinating command, although sporadic terrorist acts persisted until the start of World War II in September.[26]

The Jerusalem Mufti was specifically forbidden in mid-May to return to Palestine. A month later all mention of al-Hajj Amin or his movements was prohibited in the local press. Nor did the mandatory revoke the orders excluding the other members of the Higher Committee from the country. Since the exiled leaders refused to call off the rebellion or accept the White Paper, there remained no basis for organizing their followers in Palestine. Consequently, the fact that the Higher Committee still retained the allegiance of a majority of the Palestine Arabs had little political significance in the last few months of peace, except to keep alive the anti-British feeling of its adherents. Thus Radio Berlin, at the request of Jamal al-Husayni, broadcast in its regular Arabic program at the end of June the complete text of the Higher Committee's memorandum to the League of Nations, accusing the British and the Jews of torturing innocent Arabs in Palestine.

The National Defense Party spokesmen, as the only recognized Arab nationalist leaders in the country, were able to conduct their activities without local competition. Raghib Bey al-Nashashibi reappeared in Palestine in May after a prolonged period of voluntary absence. The British Army permitted the Nashashibi faction to set up its own anti-terrorist units. By mid-summer Fakhri Bey al-Nashashibi and his colleagues were trying to rouse support for the White Paper among rural notables in the country as well as Palestine emigrés in the Levant States. Yet the National Defense Party failed to replace the Higher Committee as the political directorate of the Arab Community. Eight former rebel commanders disseminated a manifesto in June, declaring that the White Paper provided "an acceptable basis for the furtherance of Arab aspirations" and charging that the Higher Committee rejected the new policy because it was serving "foreign interests in consideration of a fixed remuneration." [27] Yet in spite of their hostility to the Husaynis, these erstwhile rebels refused to join hands with the Nashashibis.

The Jewish quasi-government, on its side, did not hesitate to say that it would resist the implementation of the White Paper. A joint proclamation of the Executives of the Yishuv's National Council and the Jewish Agency, read before mass demonstrations throughout the community on May 18, declared, in part,[28]

> . . . this treacherous policy will not be tolerated. . . . No member of the Yishuv will have a hand in creating any of the administrative organs based on this policy . . . . [nor] recognize . . . any callous restriction of Jewish immigration. . . . The homeless will find their way here, and every Jew in this land will readily welcome them. . . .

The Chamberlain Government's relatively narrow margin of victory in the House of Commons encouraged the Jews in the belief that the new policy was merely a temporary expedient which would be abrogated as soon as the Chamberlain Cabinet or its successor made up its mind to prevent further Axis aggression. This belief was strengthened by the resolution of the British Labor Party's annual conference at the end of May, calling for the rescindment of the White Paper; by the warm support of Zionism on the part of Labor Members of Parliament in a second Parliamentary debate on Palestine two months later; [29] and by the reports from Geneva about the Permanent Mandates Commission's negative opinion.

Still, indignation and excitement ran at full tide in the Yishuv. Jewish notables returned British decorations. Many, particularly among the youth, were persuaded that the Agency's program of self-restraint had been discredited. Since the White Paper represented a concession to Arab terrorism, they argued, only Jewish terrorism would coerce the mandatory to abandon its new policy. The Revisionist Irgun was able to expand its ranks. In the first flush of excitement after the release of the White Paper, Jewish terrorists damaged government buildings in Jerusalem and Tel-Aviv. These crimes, the first serious outburst of violence by Jews against the mandatory, were followed by other acts of sabotage and murder, despite the fact that the Irgun's "Commander-in-Chief" in Palestine, David Raziel, was imprisoned at the end of May. The Irgun also stepped up its propaganda abroad and for the first time sent fund-raising emissaries to the United States. Although the quasi-government insisted on the continued enforcement of self-restraint, the Jewish public bodies refused to cooperate with the British security authorities in rounding up the terrorists. Moreover, the Yishuv as a whole resented the firm measures, particularly those of collective punishment, employed by the army and the police. In consequence, relations between the community and the security forces quickly became strained.[30]

While a majority of the Palestine Jews followed the quasi-government's lead in denouncing terrorism, they divided over the tactics to be pursued in combating the White Paper. The rightist and clerical parties favored an immediate program of non-cooperation with the mandatory and clamored for the resignation of the Agency Executive as well as the appointment of an emergency National Council Executive to direct the struggle. But the parties in effective power refused to take any hasty action. With a view to calming the aroused public, the Zionist leaders referred the matter of devising a program of resistance to the White Paper to a special eleven-man committee.[31] The committee never issued any public report. The Zionist strategy of resistance, however, was already beginning to take shape.

Only the immigration provisions of the new mandatory policy were put into immediate operation. The mandatory's hand was forced as early as April, when the temporary immigration enactment expired. In anticipation of the White Paper, the High Commissioner's authority to limit the total immigration into Palestine for any period or class of entrants was now made permanent. The initial schedule for the six-month period ending on September 30 was fixed in June at 10,350, of which 5,000 were allocated to regular immigrants and the remainder to refugees. To combat the restrictions, the quasi-government publicly sanctioned, and privately organized, illegal immigration. On the Continent the number of potential immigrants multiplied rapidly, as German territorial expansion uprooted thousands of Jews and menaced thousands more. Consequently illegal immigration became unusually heavy after the spring of 1939, and in July the Colonial Office announced its decision to withhold the next semiannual quota for the period ending March 31, 1940.[32]

In its official protest, the Agency contrasted the severe enforcement of the new immigration restrictions with the Palestine Government's leniency in the preceding three years toward the Arab terrorists. The Jewish people regarded the suspension of immigration, warned the Agency, "as devoid of any moral justification and based only on the use of force. . . . It is not the Jewish refugees returning to their homeland who are violating the law but those who are endeavouring to deprive them of the supreme right of every human being—the right to live." Besides furthering unauthorized immigration, the quasi-government instituted the procedure of establishing new villages without prior notice to the Palestine Government, as had been the practice since January 1938. In the last two weeks of May 1939 eight such villages were founded; two more were added by July. In this way, notice was given that any attempt to execute the proposed land restrictions would also be resisted.[33]

Meanwhile, the mandatory began to alter its attitude toward Haganah, which in the three years of the Arab revolt had come to enjoy semiofficial recognition and had almost doubled in size, for most of the Jewish constables and reservists were known to belong to the Agency's secret militia. After January 1939, when London finally approved the details of the Agency's plan for expanding the legal Jewish constabulary, the total number enrolled reached 18,600 within a few months. Lewis guns and grenade rifles were included for the first time among the arms issued to the Jews. After May 17 the mandatory promptly reversed its course. Recruitment was halted. Some of the arms were withdrawn. Captain Wingate, the pro-Zionist British leader of the special night squads, was transferred to England. It was widely suspected that Haganah would again be driven underground. The quasi-government, however, was bent on continuing to enlarge Haganah's ranks for possible emergency duties. Therefore, the National Council Executive conducted late in May a registration of all men and women between the ages of 18 and 35.[34]

At the Twenty-first Zionist Congress, which met at Geneva, Switzerland, August 16–24, the moderate delegates, who backed the Agency Executive, urged the Congress against adopting an anti-British attitude. The Zionists still had many friends in Britain, they argued, and the existing British Cabinet would not remain in office permanently. The Zionist breach with England, they contended, was not final and was confined to Palestine. The Zionist political apparatus in London should be enlarged, they advocated, a similar political office opened in the United States, and the American members of the Executive vested with adequate authority. The judgment of the Permanent Mandates Commission had proved that much could still be accomplished by argument. The parties which recommended more drastic action and a change of leadership—the Mizrahi, General Zionist B, and Jewish State parties—voiced their arguments anew.

But the moderates—the delegates of the Labor Bloc and the progressive General Zionist A—controlled 68 per cent of the votes. Consequently the resolutions passed by the Congress made no reference to a program of resistance. The Congress denied the moral and legal validity of the White Paper; asserted that the mandatory alone would be responsible for the results of its immigration policy; applauded the support Zionism had received in Parliament from "leading members of all parties"; and welcomed the negative opinion of the Permanent Mandates Commission.[35] The announcement of the Russo-German nonaggression pact of August 23 jolted the delegates into terminating the Congress. The old Executive was re-elected for a third term. The new General Council delegated its authority for the duration of the emergency to the Inner General Council, an extra-constitutional body consisting of the members or deputy-members of the General Council residing in Palestine. The fact that every party participating in the Congress was proportionately represented in the Inner General Council prevented the complete breakdown of the Zionist democratic machinery.[36]

Because of the imminence of war the regular session of the biennial Jewish Agency Council, scheduled for August 30, never took place, and the Executive automatically continued in office. The opportunity was thus lost of healing the breach between the Zionist and non-Zionist factions, which had drifted apart in the two years between the Royal Commission Report and the 1939 White Paper. The non-Zionists, although displeased over the enthusiasm with which the most influential Zionist leaders had taken up the partition scheme, were reunited with the Zionists at the London conferences in rejecting the British proposals. The non-Zionists also squarely opposed the 1939 White Paper but refused to go as far as the Zionists in criticizing the British Government or in promoting unauthorized immigration. Moreover, the non-Zionists, especially in the United States, resented the fact that their attitude was not sufficiently taken into account in the determination of Agency policy toward the mandatory and the Arabs. Added to these ideological considerations were organizational differences. In 1937 there were four non-Zionist members on the Agency Executive in Jerusalem; by 1939 the two Americans had returned to the United States in protest against their ineffectiveness, and of the two remaining in Palestine one had no portfolio.[37] The Agency now passed into the full control of the Zionists.

Nevertheless, this did not alter the attitude of the Agency toward Britain and the war. President Weizmann, in his farewell address to the Congress, made the Zionist position clear: [38]

> It is my duty at this solemn hour to tell England and through it the Western democracies: We have grievances. . . . But above our regret and bitterness are higher interests. What the democracies are fighting for is the minimum . . . necessary for Jewish life. Their anxiety is our anxiety, their war our war.

CHAPTER 8

Arab Political Stagnation

THE NATIONAL MOVEMENT IN DISREPAIR

IMMEDIATELY after the start of war, the Palestine Arabs began to reap the harvest of their insurrection. The disintegration of the national movement in the forty months since April 1936 had turned the clock back on local Arab politics. The Palestine Arabs were worse off than they had been before the rise of political parties in the early 1930's. The two main contending factions, the pro-Husayni and the pro-Nashashibi, were comparable to the old Councilites and Opposition of the 1920's, except that the Supreme Muslim Council was now closely supervised by the government and the most powerful Husayni leaders were out of the country. Caught between the strong-arm measures of the terrorists and the frequent government suspensions, many Arab political journals had passed out of existence. Only three newspapers survived,[1] and these were in serious financial straits. As the influence of the exiled leaders began to diminish, organized terrorism ceased and the rebel units were disbanded. But isolated acts of violence persisted, in part the work of those erstwhile rebels whose original occupation was brigandage, and in part the result of old blood feuds rekindled and new ones started by the revolt. While not shattered beyond repair, the political fabric of the Palestine Arab Community was rendered temporarily ineffectual.

This political breakdown was accompanied by an equally severe economic collapse. Despite substantial aid from the near-by Arab countries and from the Axis, the major costs of the rebellion were charged to the account of the Palestine Arabs themselves. From 3,000 to 5,000 Arabs were killed and at least 2,000 wounded. Many houses and other buildings were destroyed by the terrorists and even more by the British troops. The wealthy were constantly fleeced of their savings, while hundreds left the country, closing their business establishments for long periods at a time. Furthermore, the mutual Arab-Jewish boycott removed many sources of Arab income. Large numbers of other workers were often unemployed because of the recurring Arab strikes. The economic position of the fallahin, which had begun to improve in the early 1930's, reached a new low in consequence of military operations in the rural districts. Profits from citriculture shrank by more than 90 per cent in the four-year period between 1935–36 and 1938–39. Then total Arab-Jewish citrus exports—which represented about 80 per cent of the value of the country's peacetime exports—nosedived from a record of more than 15,000,000 cases in the latter season to a mere 78,000 cases in 1940–41. This drastic drop was due to the scarcity of shipping facilities and to the closing of the Mediterranean to Allied vessels after the entry of Italy into the war and the surrender of France in June 1940, when the Palestine depression reached its nadir.[2]

Amid this political and economic confusion the urban and rural masses saw in the outbreak of war only the specter of greater hardships to come. As for the politicians and their nationalist following, they were split into an anti-British majority and a pro-British opposition. The leaders of the National Defense Party were fully cognizant of the weariness of the Arab masses with the rebellion and its degeneration into fratricidal strife. Anxious to capitalize on the revolt fatigue and seeing in the 1939 White Paper the prospects of eventually realizing Arab nationalist aims, the Nashashibis redoubled their efforts to secure the government's recognition of their party as sole spokesman for the Palestine Arabs.

The Husaynis and their followers, on the other hand, were under the spell of more than three years of anti-British agitation. The stern measures taken by the British Army, especially after October 1938, to suppress the insurgence, as well as the lurid distortions of these acts emanating from Berlin and Rome, had served to aggravate the existing unrest. The Husaynis won their political victories over the mandatory in 1938 and 1939 by stirring up anti-British sentiment with the active assistance of Italy and Germany. In rejecting the latest White Paper, the Mufti and his intimates were probably prompted by a reluctance to abandon an eminently successful policy at a time when the British were bound to be more sensitive than ever to Arab flirtations with the enemy.

But for the Nashashibi as well as the Husayni groups, political frustration, issuing out of their unsuccessful twenty-year struggle for independence, narrowed their interest to the realization of their own nationalist aspirations. It blinded them to the larger political, ideological, and moral issues which were then precipitating a new world conflict. Both were motivated in their leanings toward either the democracies or the dictatorships by what each believed to be the best way of furthering the national movement and gaining unchallenged control over it.

In this climate of expediency those who counseled collaboration with Germany and Italy had the upper hand in the first three years of the war, when the threat of Axis occupation hung over the entire Near East. The myth of the invincibility of the Axis was cultivated sedulously among the Arab nationalist rank and file throughout the region. The nationalists were deeply impressed by Axis victories and were hoping to rid themselves of all vestiges of Anglo-French domination. The pro-Axis temperature, however, tended to rise and fall with the seasons, reaching its highest in the spring and summer of each year. The collapse of France and the battle of Britain in 1940, the Iraqi revolt and the joint British and Free-French occupation of the Levant States and the Anglo-Russian occupation of Iran in 1941, and the Axis break-through in the Western Desert to a point only 60 miles from Alexandria and only 400 from Jerusalem and the Nazi offensive in the Caucasus in 1942, drove the pro-Axis fever up. But with the coming of fall and winter the heat subsided again: in 1940–41 when the Nazis failed to bring Britain to its knees and the British in their seesaw battles of the Western Desert drove the Italians back from the Egyptian borders and out of Cyrenaica, and in 1941–42 when the Russians launched their first counteroffensive and the Americans entered the war on the side of the Allies.

The pro-Axis activities in Palestine were directed by the Mufti from abroad. While the Husaynis were making hay in the Axis sunshine, the national movement in Palestine remained in a state of disorganization. This resulted mainly from the fact that the British never attempted wholeheartedly either to discredit al-Hajj Amin or to back any of his local rivals. Because of the failure of the nationalists to restore the organic structure of their movement, the initiative in local Arab political affairs passed to the British. Moreover the country occupied a central position in the Near East, a region whose strategic importance was indicated by the United Kingdom's appointment, in June 1941, of an official of cabinet rank, known as the Minister of State, Resident in the Middle East, with headquarters at Cairo. Under his chairmanship a Middle Eastern War Council was set up composed of the key British military and diplomatic personnel in the area, including the High Commissioner for Palestine, for the purpose of integrating the political, economic, and propaganda activities with the military operations. Thus wartime mandatory policy in Palestine was sensitized to, and often dictated by, the over-all requirements of the region.[3]

From the government's viewpoint the line-up in Palestine in the autumn of 1939 was somewhat as follows: The Zionists from extreme left to extreme right had publicly affirmed their loyalty to Britain and the democratic cause, hoping that the execution of the 1939 White Paper would now be shelved. The National Defense Party, the only articulate Arab opposition, had expressed its satisfaction with the new statement of policy. Moreover, it was dependent on the government for retaining what political influence it had managed to muster. In any case the Opposition leaders were in the country where their actions could be closely watched. But the members of the Higher Committee were still at large in Egypt, the Levant States, and Iraq. Britain was well aware of the ever closer ties between these politicians and the Axis and was therefore anxious to have as many of them as possible return to Palestine, where their movements could be supervised.

The mandatory was thus confronted in Palestine with the delicate problem of gaining the confidence of the recalcitrant nationalist leaders, or at least rendering them and their following neutral in the European war, without entirely alienating the Arab Opposition or driving the Yishuv to revolt. Britain solved this problem—though creating in the process new ones of even greater complexity—between September 1939 and October 1942, by keeping the Arab nationalist machinery in disrepair, courting the nationalist masses with the rigid application of the White Paper's immigration and land provisions, and holding the Zionists in check at the brink of rebellion with the abandonment of the projected constitutional reform.

Whatever the motives—and the main reason appeared to have been the desire not to provide the Husaynis with additional excuses for anti-British agitation—the mandatory cold-shouldered the National Defense Party. Instead of utilizing the Nashashibi faction to round up Arab support for the war effort, the government used its own officials in the various districts to organize pro-Allied rallies. Of a series of popular demonstrations of loyalty to Britain staged in southern and central Palestine at the time of the collapse of France and Italy's entry into the war, only one was organized by the National Defense Party, when Fakhri Bey al-Nashashibi assembled some two hundred shaykhs at his home in Jerusalem early in June 1940 "to discuss measures for combating propaganda and rumours adverse to the Allied cause." Indeed, Fakhri Bey was the one leader who stubbornly persisted in trying to place his party at the helm of the national movement, despite the increasing passiveness of his colleagues in the face of the government's non-cooperation. After Fakhri Bey was murdered in Baghdad in November 1941, it was generally believed at the time by one of the Mufti's agents, the National Defense Party became entirely inactive.[4]

Meanwhile, hundreds of voluntary political emigrés began to return to Palestine in the early weeks of the war. In the Levant States the French authorities, in mid-September 1939, ordered all Palestine residents to leave before the end of the month unless they obtained special permission to remain. At the same time the British strove to persuade those politicians who had been exiled by government edict, particularly the members of the former Higher Committee, to re-establish their residence in Palestine. All charges against them were dropped, provided they promised not to participate in any political activities. Under this arrangement Ahmad Hilmi Pasha 'Abd-al-Baqi, Alfred Roch, and Fuad Saba—the first a Muslim leader of the Istiqlal Party and the last two Christian leaders of the Palestine Arab (Husayni) Party—were back by February 1940. Before the end of the year they were joined by another Istiqlal leader, Rashid al-Hajj Ibrahim; in July 1941 by 'Awni Bey 'Abd-al-Hadi (Istiqlal); in October 1941 by Ya'qub al-Ghusayn (Arab Youth Congress); and in November 1942 by Dr. Husayn Fakhri al-Khalidi (Reform).[5]

The only leaders to reassert their position in Arab public life were associated with the Istiqlal Party. Since the political avenue was officially closed, they turned off on an economic detour. Ahmad Hilmi Pasha, as chairman of the board of directors, undertook a reorganization of the Arab Agricultural Bank, changing its name in 1942 to the Arab National Bank. The new board of directors included two other Istiqlal spokesmen, 'Abd-al-Hadi and al-Hajj Ibrahim. The latter, who was manager of the bank's branch at Haifa, became chairman of the Arab Chamber of Commerce in that city in February 1941. The fact that the leaders of the Istiqlal Party had come into the Arab financial limelight was to prove useful after the government lifted the ban on Arab politics at the end of 1942.[6]

As early as November 1939 British diplomatic representatives in the Near East, assisted by the Egyptian and Iraqi prime ministers, entered into negotiations with the Mufti, then in Baghdad, with a view to securing his public endorsement of the 1939 White Paper and of the Allied cause. Yet even the strict enforcement of the White Paper provisions regarding immigration failed to win over to the British side al-Hajj Amin, who stepped up his anti-British agitation through personal agents left behind. "We have had a most stern warning from Palestine in recent weeks," declared Colonial Secretary MacDonald early in March 1940, when he defended the enactment of the Land Transfer Regulations at that time, "that . . . there was . . . a growing unrest in the Arab villages, and a growing suspicion that His Majesty's Government were not sincere in their professions that they would protect the interests of the Arab cultivators, peasants and labourers." MacDonald went on to warn that "if there was trouble in Palestine again there would be repercussions in Transjordania, Iraq, Saudi-Arabia, and Egypt and even echoes of that trouble in India." The new regulations defined more exactly and put into execution the stipulations of the White Paper, limiting the free sale of Arab-owned land to 5 per cent of the total area of the country.[7]

Members of the Higher Committee who had recently been permitted to re-enter Palestine characterized the land regulations as a "half step" which had to be supplemented by the execution of the remaining features of the White Paper. Nevertheless they were reported to have "welcomed Great Britain's action," and added that the Higher Committee had never rejected the White Paper "as a body, in spite of the personal criticism made of it by the former . . . Mufti of Jerusalem." Ahmad Hilmi Pasha endorsed Britain's move less reservedly, declaring that its effect on the Arabs would be "moral and spiritual," giving them "a new confidence in the country." But al-Hajj Amin remained unmoved, and all hope of ever obtaining the Mufti's cooperation during the war was lost in the summer of 1940, when the proposed constitutional changes were indefinitely deferred.[8]

The Mufti was officially reported to have sent envoys to Palestine in May and June 1940, at the time of the Nazi occupation of the Low Lands and the defeat of France, to explore the possibilities of inciting open rebellion. These efforts were renewed the following autumn and again in the spring of 1941, when the pro-Axis revolt took place in Iraq. After al-Hajj Amin's arrival in Europe at the end of October 1941, the Mufti's appeals on behalf of the Axis multiplied. By this time, too, the Arabs, especially the Mufti's adherents, were beginning to acquire large stocks of European arms and ammunition. "It is common knowledge," wrote the Jerusalem correspondent of the London *Times*, "that the great majority of Arabs are armed with rifles bought or stolen from allied troops (one of Gen. Dentz's last acts in Syria was to deliver French arms to the Syrian Arabs, who sold them across the border)." While organized outbreaks of violence did not occur, the Palestine Government admitted that the Mufti-inspired anti-recruitment propaganda was effective, for enlistments into separate Arab companies of an infantry regiment, known as the Palestine Buffs, were meager. Nevertheless, several of the Mufti's intimates, who had participated in the Iraqi revolt and were later seized by the British, were allowed to return to Palestine early in 1942.[9]

THE MANDATORY, THE ARABS, AND THE WAR

This handling of the Husaynis with kid gloves can only be understood within the context of Britain's new policy in the Arab East. The London conferences of 1939 and the resulting White Paper represented the turning point. Until that time Britain had followed the practice of divide and rule among the Arab successor states of the Ottoman Empire and among the diverse communities within each country. By giving the independent Arab states a voice in Palestine affairs on the eve of the war Britain had embarked on a new course, designed to promote the unity of the Arab East by fostering the interests of the Sunni Arab majority, even at the expense of the Christian, Jewish, Kurdish, and Shi'ite minorities. This program aimed at the creation of a pro-British Arab bloc to check the growing pro-Axis feeling and to marshal the greatest possible support for the war effort. Britain's espousal of the Arab Unity movement received official blessing on May 29, 1941, when Foreign Secretary Anthony Eden declared that it was "both natural and right that the cultural and economic ties between the [Arab] countries . . . . and the political ties, too, should be strengthened. His Majesty's Government for their part will give their full support to any scheme that commands general approval." Before the year was out Britain recognized the independence of Syria and Lebanon. Amir 'Abdallah of Transjordan, after his talks in the late summer of 1941 with Oliver Lyttleton, the British Minister Resident in the Middle East, announced that there was agreement of views not only on the future of his country but on that of the Arabs generally.[10]

The pro-Arab trends in Britain elicited favorable comment in the Palestine Arab press. Thus, *Filastin*, hanging its editorial on the peg of the 'Abdallah-Lyttleton meeting, went so far as to suggest in September 1941 that the realization of Arab Unity, "it is true, needs the collaboration of the British in many things," a position that most Arab nationalists would have contested. The editorial also intimated in a very guarded manner that the Palestine Arabs would have to organize, if they wished to attain their independence.[11]

> Several years ago Great Britain gave independence and self-government to the Egyptians in Egypt, the Iraqis in Iraq, and the Transjordanians in Transjordan. Now Mr. Churchill's assurance has been given to the Syrians in Syria and the Lebanese in Lebanon. The Arabs must themselves assume charge of their internal affairs. The fulfillment of the great vision of unity is an internal matter for the Arabs.

The same newspaper in the spring of 1942 took encouragement from the fact that an ardently pro-Zionist speech by Lord Wedgwood, broadcast from Britain to the United States, had given rise to considerable criticism in British Government circles. The fact that Wedgwood's remarks had "aroused a storm in London and not in Baghdad, Jerusalem, Damascus, or Amman," observed *Filastin*, "shows clearly that London is well aware of the Arab question." [12]

The degree to which pro-British comments in the Arab press at this time reflected genuine sentiments or merely official inspiration was difficult to gauge. From September 4, 1939 on, the Palestine press, Jewish as well as Arab, was at the government's mercy, with respect not only to content but, as the paper shortage became acute, to the allocation of newsprint. Strict controls were imposed on editorials, articles, and news items, especially those about Allied defeats and the peregrinations of the Mufti and his collaborators. And it was alleged that the editors of the Arab newspapers received regular monthly wages or stipends from the Public Information Office.[13]

This office was created in May 1938 to supersede the Press Bureau, which had performed merely the negative functions of punishing those journals violating government ordinances. After April 1939 increasing attention was paid to "public relations work," that is, to the utilization of newspapers as channels of government propaganda. Following the outbreak of war the Public Information Office came under the jurisdiction of the British Ministry of Information, and its propaganda services, financed largely by grants-in-aid from London, were greatly expanded. Under the sponsorship of British Institutes, which were opened in towns of concentrated Arab population, free courses in English were provided, and meetings and lectures were organized for the purpose of promoting Anglo-Arab friendship. The British established at Jaffa early in 1942 the Near East (Sharq al-Adna) Broadcasting Station, entirely devoted to Arabic programs which were beamed to the near-by countries as well as to Palestine.[14]

Evidence of the Public Information Office's hold on the Arab newspapers, even as early as June 1940, was the simultaneous appearance in *Al-Difa'* and *Filastin*—which less than a year earlier had voiced only the Mufti's views—of editorials intended to counteract the pro-Axis propaganda of the Husaynis. Italy's entrance into the war was sternly condemned, and the Arabs were urged to discredit false rumors and to remain calm. They were told that available food supplies were adequate and that the well-equipped Allied garrisons in the Near East were sufficient to make ultimate victory of the democracies certain. As the war dragged on and the Arab political machine remained stalled, the Public Information Office came to rely heavily on the newspapers for recruitment. Thus almost identically worded editorials were published in the three dailies in mid-February 1942, pleading with the Arabs to enlist in the British Army. The Arabs were reminded that their nationalist claims would carry little weight in the peace settlement unless they could point to substantial contributions to the war effort. The overtones of these editorials relating to the fact that the war was not "a struggle merely between two groups of belligerents over differences of political conceptions, but a conflict between universal social principles and the ideals of liberty and a regime of intimidation" suggested British, not Arab origin.[15]

A barometer of the prevailing Arab attitude toward the war was the number of Arab enlistees in the British armed forces. Arab recruits approximated only one-third of the 27,000 Palestinians who volunteered for British military service by December 1942. In fact, in the anxious days of the preceding July, when it seemed likely that Rommel might actually succeed in driving the British out of Egypt, although total enlistments reached an all-time monthly peak of over 2,000, Arab figures did not exceed 117, or less than 50 per cent of their monthly average for the year. The number of Arab deserters from the British armed forces was known to be considerable in the spring of 1941, and even more numerous in the summer of 1942. Indeed, Brigadier John Bagot Glubb, a tried friend of the Arabs, later claimed that "every Arab force [except the Arab Legion of Transjordan, which he commanded] previously organized by us mutinied and refused to fight for us, or faded away in desertions" at the time of the Iraqi revolt in May 1941.[16]

Arab-Jewish relations had begun to improve relatively quickly in the early weeks of the war. A meeting of Jewish and Arab citrus growers, the first since 1936, elected a joint delegation to submit to the government requests for a loan and for the abolition of the land taxes on the groves. Three months later thousands of Jews visited shrines near Bethlehem and in Hebron, a wholly Arab vicinity where such pilgrimages had been interrupted during the revolt. Jews and Arabs were appointed to serve together on the war advisory committees and boards organized by the government to elicit public cooperation in framing and enforcing emergency legislation.[17]

The unprecedented opportunity thus presented to the government for promoting Arab-Jewish harmony was not exploited, partly because the government was already overtaxed by the endless problems arising out of the war and partly because the Palestine Information Office's program was largely determined by the propaganda department of the Middle Eastern War Council at Cairo. Then, too, the War Council was concerned more with regional needs than with the peculiar wants of the individual countries. The regional emphasis of British propaganda was manifest in the establishment in May 1941 under British initiative, but with the participation of Arab journalists, of an Arab News Agency with offices in Palestine and all of the countries of the Arab East. The Arab News Agency (ANA) featured news of general Arab nationalist interest, and through British technical advisers and local managers it was able to control the news despatches and insert pro-British and pro-Allied items. In the long run the ANA was to become an invaluable agent for the promotion of Anglo-Arab amity, since it was used almost universally by the Arab newspapers. But until the end of 1942 British and Allied psychological warfare was conducted under a considerable handicap, for it had no sustained series of victories to back it up.[18]

Despite the greater cogency of Axis propaganda in this period, particularly in the summer of 1942, the Palestine Arabs did not respond to the Mufti's incessant fomentation to resume the revolt against Britain and the Jews. One reason was the disorganization of the national movement and the dispersal of its leaders. Another was the presence of thousands of British and Allied troops, for whom Palestine had become one of the Near East bases. A third important cause was economic in nature. By 1942 the country was enjoying an unparalleled prosperity which was intimately linked up with British, and later Allied, economic policy in the area.

In April 1941 the British established at Cairo the Middle East Supply Center (MESC)—which a few months later was placed under the jurisdiction of the Middle Eastern War Council—for the purpose of mobilizing agricultural and industrial production in the region so as to reduce civilian imports to a minimum and thereby relieve shipping space for the armed forces. The supply problem in the early war years was exceedingly complex because of the closing of the Mediterranean, the consequent re-routing of shipping around the Cape of Good Hope, the tremendous losses in the

U-boat campaign, and the very primitive transport facilities in the Near East. The MESC, perhaps more than any other single factor, helped keep the area in Allied hands in the critical summer of 1942. Local distresses which might have stirred up unrest were averted by carefully planned allocation of essential commodities. Although the MESC became increasingly an Anglo-American responsibility after 1942, British influence predominated. The liaison office with the MESC in Palestine was the local War Supply Board, which had been created in February 1941.[19]

While the Jewish Community was the chief beneficiary of the mobilization of local industries, the few Arab manufacturing enterprises expanded markedly. The number of workers employed more than doubled from 4,117 in 1939 to 8,804 in 1942; and Arab capital invested in industry more than trebled in the same period from $2,814,400 to $8,524,000. Military expenditures had jumped from $22,000,000 in 1940 to $104,000,000 in 1942. A substantial share was pumped into the Arab economy in the form of contracts for construction of military installations, transport, and other services. Of the 42,000 civilians employed for nonseasonal work by the armed forces alone in 1942 two-thirds were Arabs, while the total number of Arabs doing temporary and year-round work for the War Department at times soared as high as 80,000. Much of the $4,000,000 spent by troops on leave also ended up in Arab pockets. Meanwhile, the fallahin, profiting from the absence of competition and the high prices for their products, were beginning to liquidate their long-standing debts, to hoard their rapidly accumulating gains, and even to invest in additional landholdings. Perhaps the best sign of Arab prosperity was the steep rise of deposits in the two Arab banks from $982,000 in 1940 to more than $5,300,000 in 1942. Even when the widespread black market and the prevailing inflation were taken into consideration—the cost-of-living index had increased from 111 in December 1939 to 211 in December 1942—the economic gains were remarkable. With money to burn for the first time in their lives, the Arab masses lost interest in politics. Even many of the pro-Mufti politicians temporarily became more absorbed in economic gain than in political intrigue.[20]

THE ARAB LABOR MOVEMENT

Growing numbers of fallahin joined the ranks of urban labor to fill the emergency needs of the armed forces, the government and the expanding war industry. At the end of 1942 an estimated 85,000 to 100,000 Arabs were employed in manual and some 30,000 in nonmanual work, although the permanently urbanized manual workers probably did not exceed 35,000 to 37,000. Arab labor organization had been seriously disrupted by the prolonged depression of 1935–40, and interest in trade-unionism was not reasserted until the summer of 1942. Among the basic factors contributing to this revival were the mounting living costs; increasing contact with organized Jewish workers, particularly those in military and government employ; and the government's tolerant attitude toward the communists after the Soviet involvement in the war. But most important of all was the guardian role of the government itself. In line with its program for gearing the colonies to the war effort, the Colonial Office authorized in September 1940 the appointment of a labor adviser to the Palestine Government. A Labor Department was finally set up in July 1942, under the direction of the labor adviser, Richard M. Graves, a British official who had been employed by the Egyptian Government as a labor expert. The deputy-director, who served as chief inspector, the heads of the three regional offices opened in September at Jerusalem, Tel-Aviv, and Haifa, and the woman inspector, who dealt with the problems of female and child labor, were all former government factory inspectors in Britain.[21]

The Labor Department was instrumental in forming independent unions at Nablus, Nazareth, and Ramallah, of which the first was the largest, claiming over 1,000 members. Also under the department's sponsorship the first Arab women's union, consisting of some fifty Christian women employed at an army workshop in Haifa, was formed in November 1942. Thanks to government initiative, the Palestine Arab Workers Society, of which only the Haifa section had survived the lean late 1930's, reorganized its former affiliates in Jaffa and Jerusalem, and branched out into Nablus and Bethlehem. A Savings and Loan Fund was inaugurated with a capital of $12,000, and connected with the headquarters at Haifa were four producers' and two consumers' cooperatives. The total membership of the Society was officially estimated at 5,000 by the end of 1942.

Though the Palestine Arab Workers Society represented the right-wing of the labor movement, the Jaffa and Jerusalem branches were under strong and growing communist influence. The Arab communists, who, like the Jewish, had reversed their stand in June 1941 from one of opposition to "the imperialist war" to one of endorsement of "the war against Fascism," gradually came out into the open by the end of that year with the government's tacit approval. A communist group at Haifa received the department's permission in the fall of 1942 to found the Federation of Arab Trade Unions and Labor Societies. The Federation's paid-up membership was reported to have reached 1,600 at the end of 1942, although the government estimated that it probably spoke for some 3,000. The unions affiliated with the Federation were concentrated in the oil industry, naval workshops, and transport in the Haifa area and thus did not at that time come into conflict with the unions belonging to the Society, which represented chiefly the railway, tobacco, and municipality workers.[22]

Meanwhile, the Palestine Labor League, the Arab subsidiary of the Histadrut, launched its own scheme of expansion in the summer of 1942. Only the League's Haifa headquarters had weathered the Arab revolt and the five-year depression, and even its activities were drastically curtailed, as the membership shrank almost to the vanishing point. To offset Arab nationalist indoctrination against Zionism, which tended to keep the League's direct influence over Arab workers at a minimum, the Histadrut exploited every advantage. Its construction company, Solel Boneh, was the largest in the country and received many military contracts, which usually stipulated that a certain percentage of the workers employed had to be Arabs. Hence the Histadrut had jobs to offer and generally secured higher wages for its employees than were obtainable elsewhere. Moreover, the League's members were entitled to the privileges of the Histadrut medical insurance, savings, and loan plans. Associated groups were opened at Jaffa and Jerusalem early in 1943, and blueprints were drawn up for others at military installations in different parts of the country. The League claimed that it had 1,040 enrolled members, but that it represented some 2,500 to 3,000 Arab workers.[23]

Thus by the end of 1942 some 11,000 to 12,000 Arab workers, either as active members or hangers-on, belonged to unions, more than three-fourths to the government-sponsored Arab nationalist groups. With the backing of the government the labor movement had more than an even chance of striking permanent roots. As the economic and social standards of the Arab workers rose, the conversion of larger numbers of fallahin into fully urbanized workers was simplified. Moreover, Arab labor was becoming increasingly assertive, and was bound to demand a voice in local Arab politics.

CHAPTER 9

The Jewish War Effort

THE PALESTINE JEWS AND THE WAR

THE ARAB nationalists in Palestine, like those in the surrounding lands, were affected only tangentially by the Western ideological currents. Therefore the various groups could and did exercise a choice as to which of the two major sets of belligerents it would be most expedient for them to favor. That the Palestine Jews had no such option was self-evident. The Zionists could only side with Britain and the Allies, since the alternative was annihilation for themselves and the Jews of Europe. With the exception of the tiny communist splinters, whose most prominent leaders were arrested, the Palestine Jews lost no time in offering to Britain their manpower and resources in the war against the common enemy. As early as August 29, 1939, Dr. Weizmann in a letter to Prime Minister Chamberlain offered to place the Jewish Agency "in matters big and small, under the coordinating direction of His Majesty's Government." Weizmann went on to say that the Agency would like the political differences with the mandatory "to give way before the greater and more pressing necessities of the time." The Prime Minister in reply wrote, "You will not expect me to say more at this stage than that your public-spirited assurances are welcome and will be kept in mind." [1]

More outspoken than Weizmann's letter, which failed to mention the White Paper by name, was the statement addressed to the Yishuv by the Agency Executive in Jerusalem on September 3, declaring that [2]

. . . . At this fateful moment, the Jewish community has a threefold concern: the protection of the Jewish homeland, the welfare of the Jewish people, the victory of the British Empire. The White Paper of May, 1939, was a grave blow to us. . . . Our opposition to the White Paper was, however, never directed against Great Britain or the British Empire. The war

124

which has now been forced upon Great Britain by Nazi Germany is our war, and all the assistance that we shall be able and permitted to give to the British Army and to the British people we shall render wholeheartedly. . . .

Hence the Zionist leaders in Jerusalem, reflecting the dominant attitude in the Yishuv, let it be known candidly that they were offering to Great Britain the national home as a full-fledged ally in the war, but that they would under no circumstances acquiesce in the 1939 White Paper.

This declaration was accompanied by an announcement that the Agency and National Council Executives were drawing up blueprints for the total mobilization of the economy and manpower of the Yishuv. All men and women between the ages of 18 and 50 were called upon to register for national service. The volunteers would be expected to "serve the needs of the Jewish Community as regards security, economic life and other public requirements" and "to be at the disposal of the British military authorities in Palestine for such services as they may require." The number enrolled between September 10 and 21 exceeded 119,000 or 25 per cent of the entire Jewish population of the country; 71 per cent of the 86,770 men and 42 per cent of the 32,253 women who registered declared their willingness to serve in any capacity deemed necessary by the quasi-government.[3]

The Zionists doubtless hoped that they would be rewarded by Britain for their assistance by the indefinite shelving and eventual abrogation of the 1939 White Paper. They were anxious to continue the economic expansion of the national home so as to be able to rescue during and after the war an ever-larger number of the Jewish victims of Nazism. The Zionist leaders were also determined, if possible, to enlarge and legalize Haganah as a Jewish Army, trained in modern warfare. One of the basic lessons of their experience under the mandate underlined that, in the final analysis, the best defense against Arab attacks was self-defense. The reversal of mandatory policy eliminated the last remaining argument against making the fullest possible military preparations, illegally if necessary. Moreover, the Palestine Jews were resolved to make their contribution to the war effort "as a distinctive national entity, as the corporate representative of the entire Jewish People"; they hoped that the recognition of their national status in the stress of war would strengthen their case in the peace settlement.[4]

But above all they had been psychologically conditioned long before September 1939, because Nazi Germany had declared war against the Jews as early as Hitler's rise to power in 1933. "And all that has happened since 1933," noted the official Zionist monthly in September 1939, "only confirmed the view that the savage onslaught on Jews, sublimated by a false patriotism, constituted a menace to mankind."[5] Now that war was declared, the Palestine Jews were impatiently demanding immediate and full use of their military and economic potential, despite the fact that the country lay outside the theater of combat until the summer of 1940.

By contrast the tempo in Britain in the first eight months of hostilities, after the initial shock wore off, was characterized by the war's sobriquet at that time, "Sitzkrieg." British total mobilization did not get under way until the invasion of the Low Lands and France and Churchill's accession to the Premiership in May 1940. The Battle of Britain which followed kept the United Kingdom preoccupied with internal defense. Not until 1941 were real efforts initiated to organize the Near East on a total war footing. But beyond the difference in tempo lay a more important and abiding political consideration. The prevailing view in British official circles held that Zionism and the Jewish National Home were proving a liability to the United Kingdom in its efforts to wean the Arab nationalists away from the Axis. The partisans of this attitude were anxious to avoid incurring any new obligations to the Zionists.

This view, however, was not fully shared by powerful elements in Parliament and, after May 1940, in the Cabinet, including Churchill himself, who were inclined to favor military and political concessions to the Zionists. The cleavage in British official ranks was to find expression in an irresolute policy toward Zionist demands for active participation in the war effort. Every Zionist offer was minutely examined as to whether its military value exceeded its political cost. As the Near East was increasingly drawn into the operational zone in the first three years of the war, the pro-Zionist sector of the British Government was able to override by degrees the objections of the pro-Arab sector, enabling the Palestine Jews slowly to augment their recruits for the Allied armed forces.[6]

Surveying the security situation at close quarters, the Palestine Government was confronted in September 1939 with a problem in the Yishuv the exact opposite of that in the Arab Community. The loyalty of the main body of the Palestine Jews to Britain at war would remain unquestioned up to the point of extreme provocation. That point would certainly be reached by any attempted constitutional changes outlined in the latest White Paper. The one serious unknown factor was the dissident Revisionist Party. The Revisionist leaders, it was true, submitted a memorandum to the Palestine Government on September 5 expressing fidelity "to Great Britain and its Allies in the war against Hitler's tyranny." Four days later the Revisionist Irgun distributed broadsheets announcing its suspension of all terrorist activities. But the Revisionists made their truce offer contingent upon the return of mandatory policy "to the basis of the Balfour Declaration." These militant elements could not always be held in check by the quasi-government, as suggested by the Irgun's reprisals against the Arabs after the summer of 1938 and its anti-government terrorism after the issuance of the White Paper in the spring of 1939. Yet the angry Jewish demonstrations against the Land Transfer Regulations early in 1940, the government reported, "received the support of all Jewish parties except the Revisionists, who stood aside."[7] Why did the Revisionists hold back, since they were certainly no less opposed to the White Paper in March 1940 than they had been in May 1939?

Circumstantial evidence tends to bear out the allegation that the Revisionists entered into an agreement with the British security authorities. The Revisionists were reported to have assented in the first few months of hostilities to a truce for the war's duration and to supply intelligence regarding enemy agents as well as internal Zionist affairs, on condition that Irgunists arrested for political terrorism were given lenient treatment. "The Irgun went from bad to worse: it became a servile instrument in the hands of the Government and the secret police [that is, the Criminal Investigation Department]," wrote the anonymous biographer of Abraham Stern in accounting for the secession of Stern and a group of his followers from the Irgun in 1940. Those Irgunists, including Stern himself, imprisoned prior to September 1939 were actually set free in June 1940. The Irgun for its part enforced the truce in the first three years of the war. The only serious breach was a "campaign of systematic extortion from wealthy members of the Jewish community" in the summer of 1941 to replenish a depleted treasury. But the government's warning to the Executive of the Revisionist Party in August of that year brought an end to these activities at that time.[8]

MILITARY ENLISTMENTS

By the end of 1942 some 18,800 Palestine Jews—about 10 per cent women—were serving with the British armed forces, the vast majority with the army, but 1,600 with the R.A.F. and 400 with the Royal Navy. Approximately 25 per cent were combatant units. The Jewish troops had been engaged in active duty in the European, Mediterranean, and African campaigns. In Greece more than 1,000 were taken prisoner. Some special volunteers fought with the commandos in Libya and Ethiopia, while others took part in intelligence, sabotage, and scouting missions connected with the Allied occupation of the Levant States in 1941. Moreover, the number of Jewish police in Palestine, after having been scaled down in 1940, was again increased in the two following years and by August 1942 reached 24,000. About one-quarter were assigned to full-time police duties. The remainder performed "functions analogous to those of the Home Guard in . . . [Britain]." The Palestine police force already had been transferred to military command at the end of May 1942 and made subject to employment for military duties in the defense of Palestine. When a few weeks later it appeared doubtful whether British troops would be able to contain the Axis desert forces at al-'Alamayn, some 1,500 carefully selected youths, drawn from the collective villages, were secretly trained as Jewish guerrillas by the British Army with War Office approval. They were to be charged with sabotage and partisan warfare in the event of a German occupation of Palestine. The group was officially named, "the Jewish Rural Special Police." Unofficially it was soon known as *Palmah*, an abbreviation for *Plugot ha-Mahaz* or "striking units," which formed the nucleus of the later elite commando force of Haganah.[9]

Indeed, the overwhelming majority of the close to 43,000 British-trained Palestine Jews under arms at the end of 1942 had been screened by the Jewish Agency and either actually or potentially belonged to Haganah. The Zionist leaders would therefore seem to have had few grounds for complaint. These appearances, however, were misleading, for Anglo-Zionist relations in the matter of Jewish recruitment became increasingly strained. British calls for recruits in the first seven months of the war were of small proportions. Employing the political yardstick of dual obligation to the two communities, the mandatory insisted on an equal number of recruits for mixed Arab-Jewish noncombatant units, though enlistment of skilled Jews was permitted to fill a few essential vacancies in British divisions stationed in Palestine. Zionist persistence and the threat of a possible British defeat led to an agreement in July 1940 to abandon the rule of numerical equality in noncombatant enlistments and to form an equal number of Arab and Jewish companies for the newly created infantry regiment, called the Palestine Buffs.

The Zionists now redoubled their efforts for the further relaxation of what they regarded as disheartening limitations. When the British military position in the Near East became critical in the spring of 1941, the mandatory dropped the parity principle with respect to the infantry companies. "But these Jewish companies," wrote David Ben Gurion, in stating the new Zionist complaint, "contrary to all military organization in the British Army and elsewhere, were not permitted to form battalions and brigades. The Jewish companies still remain separate units, hanging, as it were, in the air." The British subsequently gave in on this point, when the Secretary for War announced in Commons, in August 1942, that the Palestine Buffs would be converted into the Palestine Regiment and existing companies would be used to form "separate Jewish and Arab infantry battalions for general service in the Middle East." The mandatory also gradually slackened its initial requirements of accepting only Palestine citizens, by admitting first those Jews who were legally residing in the country but had not yet been naturalized and then even those who had entered the country illegally.[10]

"There is, however, one supremely important aspect on which, so far, we have been refused any satisfaction," declared the Jewish Agency president in November 1941. "Like all nations, the Jews desire to serve under their own national name and flag, doing honour to their national badge, the Shield of David, which the Nazis tried to convert into a mark of shame. But the name of 'Jew' seems to be shunned as much by those who accept our services as it is flaunted by our enemies." [11] From the early months of the war Weizmann had been trying to persuade the British Government to organize a "Jewish Fighting Force" with its own flag for service with the British Army wherever required. The initial target was a Jewish Division (10,000 troops) "to be recruited in Palestine and elsewhere," under the general command of British officers but with Jewish junior officers. This plan, rejected by the Chamberlain Government, was approved in principle by the Churchill Government in October 1940, at the time of the Nazi all-out air assault on Britain.

Though a British commander had been named for the proposed Jewish Division and parleys held on the wording of the official communiqué announcing its formation, the new Colonial Secretary, Lord Moyne, finally informed Weizmann in March 1941 that "the Prime Minister has decided that owing to lack of equipment the project must . . . be put off for six months, but may be reconsidered again in four months." Lord Moyne went on to assure Weizmann that "this postponement is in no sense a reversal of the previous decision in favour of your proposal." The Jewish Agency president reopened the question at the end of August. He was now told that because of "new technical difficulties the matter . . . would have to continue in cold storage for the present," but that the question could be reconsidered in three months.[12] Weizmann, however, pressed for a final decision, declaring that "he would prefer a definite refusal to any further uncertain postponement." Six weeks later the Colonial Office let it be known that there was "no prospect of accepting the proposal under present conditions." [13]

This rebuff merely served to redirect the Agency's pressures from the closed doors of government departments to the open forum of public opinion. The Agency now undertook to organize committees for a Jewish Army in the United States, Britain, and some of the Dominions. Advertisements in the American press multiplied, as did protest meetings and mass demonstrations. By this time the objective of the appeal, which rose to its highest pitch in August 1942, had been narrowed geographically to the creation of a Palestine Jewish Fighting Force of some 20,000 combatant troops with the existing Jewish units as the core, and a Home Guard of some 40,000 to 50,000 reservists. The Agency also tried unsuccessfully to line up behind its lobbying non-Zionist groups. The Agudat Israel refused, as its world president explained, on the ground that the Zionist goal was to create "a mere political instrument for the purpose of carrying through political claims at . . . the peace-conference against Arab resistance." Representatives of the American Jewish Committee were divided over the issue, though a majority maintained that the campaign for a Jewish Army was ill-advised. "If and when Jewish Palestine becomes a commonwealth, it will have the natural right to its army," wrote the Committee's General Secretary in April 1942.

"But while it is still only in the process of development, the demand should not go beyond the idea of Jewish units as part of the British forces." While conceding that the Agency in appealing to public opinion was resorting to "a legitimate democratic process," the American non-Zionist spokesman went on to point out,[14]

> . . . I believe that pressure for its creation is proving an embarrassment to the United Nations. Obviously British policy is based on the belief that it would be dangerous to antagonize many millions of Arabs for the sake of satisfying a political design of the Zionist Organization. The British strategy may be wrong. But even if it is wrong I do not think that it is wise for the Agency to assume the grave responsibility of pressing for a measure which can in no way enhance the opportunity for service by Jews to the war effort and, being motivated purely by political considerations, is apparently, in the judgement of Britain, likely to add to the difficulties of winning the war.

Still the non-Zionist groups did not actively oppose the Agency's demands for a Jewish Military Force.

The effect of the Agency-backed appeals, however, was diluted by the emotional agitation, conducted in the United States and Britain under the auspices of the Revisionists, who had begun to set up their committees as early as 1940. Moreover, representatives in the United States of the Revisionist Irgun, who had been responsible for organizing early in 1940 the "American Friends of a Jewish Palestine"—the first of a chain of committees—instituted in December 1941 their own separate campaign for a Jewish Army, even more extreme than that of their parent body. In full-page advertisements in American newspapers the Irgun-inspired committees demanded the immediate formation of a Jewish Army, composed of Palestine Jews, the stateless Jews of Europe, and Jews from the neutral countries. "This Committee believes," ran an early advertisement,[15]

> that with America's entrance into the war against the Axis, the question of a Jewish Army, based on Palestine, has become a direct and vital concern to the United States, since this army, 200,000 strong,
> Will consolidate the Allied positions around the Suez Canal;
> Will release a considerable part of the Anzac forces from the Middle East for combat in the Pacific, and thus
> Will strengthen the defenses of this hemisphere.

A few months later the "non-partisan and non-sectarian" Committee's name was changed to the "Committee for a Jewish Army of Palestinian and Stateless Jews," a branch was formed in Britain, and their demands were repeated in Congress and Parliament by Representatives, Senators, and M.P.'s.

The attitude of the British toward the creation of a Jewish Fighting

Force resulted in arousing the general dissatisfaction of the Palestine Jews and their sympathizers abroad and in exaggerating in their minds the significance of such a Force. It also made recruiting more and more difficult, as the feeling spread in the Yishuv that Britain was not really interested in the Jewish war effort. Since the mandatory did not invoke conscription, the Jewish quasi-government employed social ostracism and other pressures against "shirkers," while more zealous and less responsible groups did not hesitate to use physical force. This, in turn, gave rise to a controversy within the community. "To my mind conscription through Government is the fair, the democratic way," declared Judah L. Magnes (1877–1948), the American-born president of the Hebrew University in June 1941, "yet as long as Government has not proclaimed the need for conscription I should like to hope that others will not attempt to make use of different forms of coercion, which are not Governmental in their character, against the Jewish youth." To this the *Palestine Post* replied that the people [16]

> must secure by their own efforts what cannot be enforced by the machinery of the law. Here if ever is a unique opportunity for a people to show its political maturity and the capacity for self-discipline which is the true hallmark of the free. And if a community possesses the means and the organization of maintaining that discipline and ensuring that response, it is not merely its right, but its duty to use them.

ECONOMIC CONTRIBUTIONS

The economic mobilization of the Jewish Community, after getting off to a belated start, proceeded smoothly. Jewish immigrants and national institutions had invested more than $500,000,000 in the national home between 1919 and 1939, and in the latter year Palestine Jews owned foreign assets (either sterling securities or bank deposits) totaling some $50,000,000. The Yishuv could also boast a large body of experienced European entrepreneurs, technicians, skilled workers, and scientists. Anxious to develop this economic potential to the full for the twin purposes of expanding the national home and advancing the common cause, the Zionist leaders created immediately after the outbreak of war a Central Economic Council, composed of financial, industrial, agricultural, and labor leaders as well as members of the Jewish quasi-government. Under the general jurisdiction of the Council were placed existing economic bodies such as the Fund for the Amelioration and Promotion of Industry and the Central Supply Commission, two bodies which had begun to place the Jewish economy on an emergency footing even before the start of the European war.

In the fall of 1939 the Agency turned to the government for assistance in providing some guarantee to the banks in granting loans to Jewish industry for building up stock piles. But this request was rejected. The Agency therefore continued the program on its own. Through the Central Economic Council it was instrumental in securing loans—amounting to more than $800,000—to Jewish manufacturing enterprises for storing up reserves. These supplies of raw materials and semi-processed goods made it possible for Jewish industry to tide over the critical period between the closing of the Mediterranean in June 1940 and the beginning of Britain's economic mobilization of the Near East early in 1941.[17]

Meanwhile, the Jewish quasi-government had to divert considerable funds to checking unemployment. The initial impact of the war on the Jewish, as on the Arab, economy was unsettling in the extreme. The recession reached its most alarming stage in July 1940, when the monthly average of Jews without work exceeded 14,000. Here the Palestine Government did eke out the appropriations for Jewish public works projects by grants-in-aid amounting to more than $186,000 or about 30 per cent of the total Jewish outlay for that purpose in 1940. In line with its policy of offering assistance only in matters affecting both sections of the population, the government also provided loans to farmers for intensifying agricultural production and to citrus growers for maintaining plantations.[18]

Despite the depression, plants producing goods formerly imported from Europe had already begun to find new markets in the near-by countries as well as in Palestine. Furthermore, the Anglo-French armies purchased about $4,000,000 worth of Jewish manufactures in 1940. To meet the growing demand some new industries were established. Meanwhile, the British attitude was becoming more cooperative. The Jewish Agency's survey of the Yishuv's industrial potential was considered at a conference which the British summoned at New Delhi early in December 1940 to consider plans for harnessing the Near and Middle East to the war effort. It was followed by the formation of the Palestine Government's War Supply Board in February 1941 and the British Middle East Supply Center two months later. Through these bodies Jewish factories were assured materials, machinery, and markets. The Agency's economic department, which gradually took over the duties of the Central Economic Council, served as liaison between the Jewish industries and the government and by means of the Amelioration Fund enabled the smaller producers to obtain low-interest loans for military production.

Allied military orders to Jewish industry jumped from approximately $14,000,000 in 1941 to some $32,400,000 in the next year, taking about 40 per cent of the total Jewish output. The military authorities employed Jewish construction companies for the erection of camps, roads, and other military installations in Palestine, the Levant States, and Bahrayn. In addition, certain specialized products—potash and other Dead Sea chemicals as well as polished diamonds—were exported to the British Empire and the United States for use in war industries. Finally, Jewish factories were able somewhat to free Allied shipping and industry for more essential military purposes by helping meet the regional civilian demands for foodstuffs, clothing, pharmaceuticals, and household appliances.[19]

An important consequence of the unheralded prosperity, exceeding in scale even the optimistic Zionist expectations, was the rapid expansion of the Histadrut's industrial holdings. By 1942 the Histadrut, while continuing with its 126,000 members to represent some three-fourths of all the workers in the Yishuv, had already become the largest industrial producer in the country, by investing its war profits in a wide variety of manufacturing enterprises. As a result political rivalry between capital and labor became further embittered. When it was announced in August 1941 that Solel Boneh, the Histadrut's building-contractor subsidiary, had acquired within a single year controlling interests in a second large factory formerly owned by private entrepreneurs unable to keep the plants in operation, resentment was voiced by private industry generally. *Ha-Arez*, which in the past had taken a sympathetic view of labor, accused the Histadrut of exploiting unfairly its dual role as a trade-union movement and an industrial employer to weaken privately owned establishments so as to be able eventually to take them over.[20] The industrialists, divided among several rival parties, could not hope to counterbalance politically the labor parties, welded into a cohesive unit by the Histadrut. The Histadrut and its affiliates in the World Zionist Organization never achieved an absolute majority. But by controlling some 35-40 per cent of the active electorate, the secular labor bloc retained its position as the most influential political force in the Yishuv.[21]

However, most significant of all, the Jewish economic expansion coupled with the relatively high rate of enlistment created a labor shortage. This, in turn, served to rivet Zionist attention to immigration. A powerful economic motive was thus added to the nationalist and humanitarian arguments against the immigration enactments under the 1939 White Paper.

CHAPTER 10

The Zionist Struggle against
the White Paper

THE LAND TRANSFER REGULATIONS

THE ONE point of agreement in September 1939 among all Palestine Jews, with the exception of the communists, was their resolve to save as many as possible of their fellow Jews in Europe. The alarming growth of anti-Semitism exceeded Herzl's pessimistic prophecy and confirmed in the minds of all Zionists the accuracy of their analysis of the Jewish problem. The champions of the Jewish National Home were stressing more and more its humanitarian function as a haven of refuge. Nor was this merely a matter of theorizing. Two out of every three Jews in Palestine had relatives in countries already, or about to be, occupied by the Nazis. The German attack on Poland was particularly foreboding. That country's 3,300,000 Jews constituted the largest Jewish community in Europe, and more than 40 per cent of the interwar Jewish immigrants into Palestine had come from there.[1] The intimate ties between the Palestine Jews and those of Europe accounted in no small measure for the almost universal support by the Yishuv of illegal immigration in defiance of the White Paper.

The White Paper policy placed a strain on Anglo-Zionist relations. The Jewish leaders, backed by a majority of the newspapers, were trying to check the growth of anti-British sentiment in the Yishuv by blaming the British Government and not the British people. "Our quarrel with Mr. Chamberlain's Government," observed the *Palestine Post* in July 1939, "is that in their latest policy for this country they have carried 'appeasement' to a point which makes it most doubtful if Palestine will continue to play its part in alleviating Jewish suffering." [2] From the Zionist viewpoint the start of the European war provided the possibility of restoring Anglo-Zionist friendship. The Palestine Jews were convinced that the White Paper would go the way of all appeasement. "There is an urgent need," declared the *Palestine Post* on September 4, 1939, "for . . . a truce, if it can be no more than that, in the war of attrition in which the British joined the Arabs when His Majesty's Government put its signature to the White Paper."

The Zionists now watched every government move closely for clues about a possible change of heart. The evidence in the first few months of war proved inconclusive. The Palestine Government formally confirmed in mid-October the Colonial Secretary's declaration of the previous July that, owing to the large volume of unauthorized immigration, no quota would be issued for the period between October 1939 and March 1940. Still, the validity of some 3,000 unused immigration visas from the preceding schedule was extended. This ordinance kindled mistrust, elicited a protest from the Jewish Agency, but did not destroy Zionist hopes. Suspicions were further stirred when 43 Haganah members were arrested while on maneuvers in October and were given long prison sentences at the end of the following month. Jewish protest demonstrations and a two-hour general strike on November 28 were orderly.[8]

But the first body blow to optimistic expectations was dealt on February 28, 1940, with the issuance of the Land Transfer Regulations, dividing Palestine into three zones. The sale of Arab-owned land to Jews was to be prohibited in the first zone (about 63.4 per cent of the land area of Palestine), comprising the hill country and parts of the Jaffa, Gaza, and Beersheba subdistricts. Land transfers were to remain uncontrolled in the second (5 per cent of the country), embracing the central portion of the Coastal Plain, the municipal areas, and the Haifa suburban industrial district. Jewish purchases were to be restricted in the rest of the country (31.6 per cent of the total), where Jews could acquire holdings freely only from owners who were not Palestine Arabs. Subsequent amendments (April 18, 1940) made it permissible for Jews to buy land in the prohibited zone from other than Palestine Arab owners.[4]

By contrast with the months of preparation for the White Paper itself, the land regulations were sprung upon the leaders and the public without warning, the Jewish Agency having been notified only a day in advance. The anti-British feeling provoked in the earlier period was now reasserted. Rigid curfews, the government's prohibition of public meetings, and the stern repressive measures by the police and troops instead of containing public excitement merely added extraneous irritants. Mass demonstrations in the first week of March in Haifa, Jerusalem, Petah Tiqvah, and Tel-Aviv often got out of hand. In the resulting brawls 74 Jews were seriously injured, two subsequently dying of their wounds,

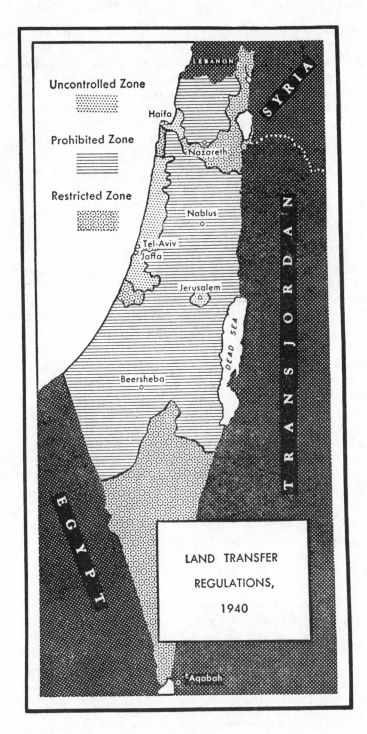

Uncontrolled Zone

Prohibited Zone

Restricted Zone

LEBANON

SYRIA

Haifa

Nazareth

Nablus

Tel-Aviv
Jaffa

Jerusalem

DEAD SEA

TRANSJORDAN

Beersheba

EGYPT

LAND TRANSFER

REGULATIONS,

1940

ʿAqabah

and 323 slightly injured; of the 25 British casualties five were seriously wounded. Press censorship forbade detailed coverage of the outbreaks, editorial comment, and even the publication of the National Council Executive's statement of protest. Consequently Haganah saw to it that deleted news and comment got to the public through its illegal broadcasting unit, called the "Voice of Israel." "The Land Transfer Regulations," read the banned National Council declaration,

> constitute a hostile attack. . . . The Jewish people are loyal to Great Britain in its war against the rule of aggression and wickedness in international relations. . . . But they will not agree . . . . to be sacrificed in their National Home for the sake of appeasing the forces of aggression and evil. . . . [The National Council] protests in the name of the Yishuv against this decree, which wantonly violates the clauses of the Mandate and nullifies the very purpose for which the Mandate was entrusted to the British Government.

Similar protests were issued by the Jerusalem and London offices of the Jewish Agency.[5]

The Palestine Jews were now involved in a two-front war. In the European hostilities they were of necessity ranged on the side of Britain. But at the same time they were forced into a second war for the preservation of their national existence. Weizmann, then in the United States, enunciated the official Zionist position before a protest rally in Boston: "Jewish loyalty to the Allies will remain steadfast, but it will not blind us to the wrong. We shall continue the struggle for our future in Palestine. The Colonial Secretary is not England. His attempts to tear the Balfour Declaration into shreds and make a mockery of the National Home will prove unavailing." [6]

The regulations were approved on March 6 by the House of Commons, which defeated the Labor Party's motion of censure by a vote of 292 to 129, although the opposition was the stoutest that the Chamberlain Government had had to face since the outbreak of war. In defense of the policy Colonial Secretary MacDonald admitted that the government would have preferred "to publish these Land Regulations in draft and hold them in suspense until the Council of the League [of Nations] had had an opportunity of pronouncing upon them," but that fear of widespread Arab unrest and its repercussions on the military position made it "expedient politically" to adopt the course that had been taken. That the mandatory's action did not receive the wholehearted blessing of the British public was reflected in *The Times'* statement that the new land policy, for "which the authors themselves are likely to feel little enthusiasm," ran counter to "fundamental principles of British political philosophy. It is against all our cherished conceptions to deny to any group of subjects in a country administered by the British Crown the full status of citizenship in that country." [7]

Nevertheless the Yishuv's indignation coupled with the calamitous military situation which soon followed caused the mandatory to stop in its tracks before endeavoring to put into effect the projected constitutional reforms of the White Paper. The immigration, and now the land, provisions were already being enforced against Jewish will. But the success of any attempted constitutional changes would depend on the co-operation of both sections of the population, particularly of the Jews because of their commanding influence over the country's economy. The risks of a likely failure were greater than any possible advantages. Moreover, with the advent in May 1940 of the Churchill Coalition Cabinet, which included many other outspoken opponents of the White Paper, the Zionists once again gained access to the top level of the government. Even under Parliamentary prompting, however, members of the War Cabinet refused to make any public statements that might be construed as departing from the basic line of policy laid down in the White Paper.[8] On the other hand, when the Zionists began to suspect in 1942 that the British might have entered into a secret agreement on Palestine with the Arabs, Viscount Cranborne, the Colonial Secretary, assured a pro-Zionist Lord that "His Majesty's Government will not enter into commitments regarding the future of that country without prior consultation with all those, including both Arabs and Jews, whom they may judge to be concerned."[9]

THE WHITE PAPER IN OPERATION

Although the constitutional features of the White Paper were allowed to languish under the Churchill Government, the land and immigration laws, contrary to Zionist hopes, were enforced with growing severity. According to the mandatory, the High Commissioner approved between February 1940 and February 1943 the transfer to Jews of about 385 acres of land in the prohibited zone and 2,660 in the restricted zone. Part of these transfers "represented exchanges of properties and so resulted in no decrease in the gross area of land in Arab hands." In the same period Jewish applications for the purchase of approximately 2,865 acres in the prohibited zone and 2,740 in the restricted zone were rejected. After the beginning of the war boom Arab owners not only became increasingly reluctant to sell their holdings but also entered the buying market, so that even in the uncontrolled zone the Jews were able to acquire only some 6,342 acres from the Arabs in the first three years. Thus the government estimate of net transfers of land from Arabs to Jews totaled some 9,387 acres.[10]

While admitting that "the interpretation of the [Land Transfer] Regulations, both by the British and the Palestine authorities, was most unfavorable to us [the Zionists]," the Jewish National Fund, the Zionist land-purchasing arm, nevertheless claimed to have acquired title to some 34,425 acres of land from September 1939 through September 1942, or roughly the same period. The National Fund obtained about 20 per cent of its new holdings from private Jewish owners. Consequently, if this appraisal is correct, then roughly 27,000 acres must have been bought from non-Jewish owners, the bulk, it must be presumed, from Arabs. This would seem to corroborate the contentions of the National Fund's director, who asserted that

> We concentrated first and foremost on the prohibited and restricted zones respectively. . . . Our major activity concerned those areas which were sparsely populated and where there still were uncultivated tracts such as in the north and south, and the central hilly region. . . . We studied the law very thoroughly with a view of discovering what possibilities, however slight, existed within the law of carrying on our work. . . .

As conflicting as these contentions may be, certain effects of the land regulations could definitely be discerned. Combined with wartime inflation, they caused the prices of salable holdings to spiral. The average price of rural land jumped from $128 per acre in the years 1933–36, to $268 in 1940 and $470 in 1942. Secondly, the process of nationalizing the land in the Yishuv was accelerated. The area in the possession of the Jewish National Fund increased from 93,000 acres or 30 per cent of the total Jewish-owned land in 1936 to 177,500 acres or 47 per cent of the total in 1944.[11]

Meanwhile, in 15 of the first 39 months of war no immigration schedules were posted. The heavy traffic in illegal immigration was the official explanation for the suspension of authorized entry between October 1939 and March 1940. Wartime travel difficulties and widespread unemployment in the Yishuv were the stated reasons for the denial of quotas for the nine-month period ending in June 1941. At the start of the war the rule was established—owing to military considerations—"not to facilitate in any way immigration of Jewish or other refugees from Germany or territory occupied by Germany." This was later modified, after ceaseless Zionist pressure in London, "to admit to Palestine Jewish holders of valid immigration certificates who had succeeded in leaving Germany and were then in Allied or neutral territory and those who arrived in such countries subsequently and were able to show that withdrawal of the certificate would involve hardship."[12]

Indicative of the government's adherence to the letter of the immigration laws was its handling of unauthorized immigration. In the first year of the war Jews arriving in Palestine without proper credentials were interned for a period of six months, pending security investigation. Despite the fact that their number was deducted from the over-all White Paper quota, they were not eligible for naturalization after release. But the tightening of this procedure because of "military risks" involved was forecast in the spring of 1940. "Nazis and Russian Communists," declared the diplomatic correspondent of *The Times*, "can easily be introduced among the shiploads of refugees from Vienna, Prague, or Poland, and once in Palestine they are not easy to detect." Moreover, the fear was expressed that the Nazis might purposely enable large numbers of Jews to escape in order to embarrass the mandatory.[13]

Deportation had been envisaged by the White Paper as one of the possible methods of combating illegal immigration. But the mandatory did not resort to this measure until the volume of unlawful traffic threatened to become substantial. In November 1940 the Palestine Government announced that the 1,771 passengers on two intercepted steamers would not be allowed to remain in the country. "His Majesty's Government are not lacking in sympathy for refugees from territories under German control," read the official statement,

> But . . . . they can only regard a revival of illegal Jewish immigration at the present juncture as likely to affect the local situation most adversely, and to prove a serious menace to British interests in the Middle East. They have accordingly decided that the passengers [of the two vessels] . . . shall be deported to a British colony . . . and shall be detained there for the duration of the war. Their ultimate disposal will be a matter for consideration at the end of the war but it is not proposed that they shall remain in the colony to which they are sent or that they shall go to Palestine. . . .

A few days later the S.S. *Patria*, to which the refugees had been transferred for deportation, was sunk at Haifa by explosives smuggled aboard, with the loss of more than 200 lives. The government permitted the survivors to remain in Palestine, "as an exceptional act of mercy," but stressed that the policy would nevertheless be applied to later arrivals. In fact, 1,584 visaless refugees were sent to the island of Mauritius on December 8. Because of the storm of protest aroused in Britain, however, no further deportations occurred during the war. But early in 1942 the Palestine Government refused to issue visas under the White Paper quota to 769 refugees on a cattle ship, the S.S. *Struma*, which had reached Istanbul in December 1941. The only concession, to award entry permits to children under 16, was made too late, for the Turkish Government had already insisted that the vessel leave its territorial waters. The S.S. *Struma* sank in the Black Sea on February 23, probably after striking a mine. Only one passenger survived.[14]

As a result of these measures, the number of Jews entering the country from April 1, 1939, the date to which the White Paper was retroactive, through December 31, 1942, amounted to 38,930, of which those who had come unlawfully accounted for 51.2 per cent. More than half of the total arrivals (53.7 per cent) in the 45-month period was recorded between April and December 1939. The monthly average of combined legal and illegal immigration declined steadily from 2,371 in the last nine months of 1939 to 311 in 1942. The White Paper, it will be recalled, explicitly established an immigration quota of 75,000 for the five-year period ending on March 31, 1944. So drastically was Jewish immigration curbed that less than 52 per cent of the total quota was filled by the end of 1942, though three-quarters of the period had already elapsed.

JEWISH IMMIGRATION (LEGAL AND ILLEGAL)

April 1, 1939–December 31, 1942 [15]

	Legal	Illegal	Total
1939 (Apr.–Dec.)	8,617	12,296	20,913
1940	4,547	3,851	8,398
1941	3,647	2,239	5,886
1942	2,194	1,539	3,733
Totals	19,005	19,925	38,930

The Jewish Agency had repeatedly solicited visas for children, community leaders, and relatives of Palestine Jews in countries about to be invaded by the Axis. Almost invariably these requests were turned down. Such an appeal was made on behalf of Balkan Jews in October 1940. High Commissioner Sir Harold MacMichael allegedly replied, "that it might be wiser . . . to save up these permits for postwar use when they might be alloted to Jews of a 'better type' than those from the Balkans." An application in April 1941, according to the Jewish Agency, "for 100 permits to be allocated to prominent members of the Jewish community in Greece, who were then in grave danger, was rejected on the ground that the saving of 100 individuals would not benefit Greek Jewry which then numbered 75,000." [16]

Zionist indignation over the government's immigration policy reached its highest pitch in this period after the sinking of the *Struma*. "Here is a tragedy which could have been prevented, even within the strait-jacket of the White Paper," declared Weizmann in London,[17]

. . . . if the slightest good will . . . would have been indicated by the Palestine Administration. . . . The arguments . . . advanced [Nazi connivance with the refugees and the infiltration of spies] in order to justify the action . . . taken . . . are merely an insult to one's intelligence. . . . The number of people who are likely to come in is not great; and . . . so far very few—if any—undesirable elements have come in. The Palestine Government, the Palestine police, are seeing to that, and we, the Jewish Agency and its organs, are only too . . . eager to help the authorities . . . weed out such elements. . . . One stands aghast at the attitude which the Palestine Government is taking up . . . systematically towards these unfortunate Jewish refugees, who flee from death . . . and try, at the risk of their lives, to find refuge in Palestine, and are, very often within sight of the shores of Palestine, cruelly, inhumanly driven back into the sea, and . . . into the jaws of death.

THE REDIRECTION OF ZIONIST PRESSURES

The attack on the Palestine Government by the Jewish Agency president demonstrated the prevailing form that anti-British sentiment had assumed among most Zionists, especially in the United Kingdom and Palestine. Relations between the Palestine Administration and the Jewish Community had soured in May 1939, but Zionist hostility was then aimed principally at the Chamberlain Government. With its downfall a year later Zionist attitudes altered overnight. The presence in the Churchill Coalition Government of a number of past friends of the national home renewed the confidence of most of its champions in the eventual resumption of a pro-Zionist policy. "In but few places outside Great Britain and France have the recent changes in the British Government been more warmly and hopefully received than in Jewish Palestine," declared one semimonthly; ". . . . the hope is revived that when the time comes for a new settlement of world affairs, the fate of the Jewish people, bound up with the National Home, will again receive fair and full consideration." [18] This faith in Churchill persisted throughout the war, as did the confidence in Parliament, where the many pro-Zionist M.P.'s often aired Zionist complaints.

But when the *Patria* incident of November 1940 made it clear that the White Paper was still being enforced, now more stringently than ever, Zionist animosity was focused on the Palestine Administration and the Colonial Office. The Churchill Government "has been placed in a predicament by an unimaginative administration in Palestine," commented the *New Judaea* in December 1940, "and its shortsighted departmental supporters in London, who are determined to pursue to the bitter end the unfortunate policy of the White Paper for which they and the former head of the Colonial Office are responsible." The officials directly charged with administering the mandate were accused of exploiting the fact that the British Government and people were distracted by the larger problems of the war. Typical of the reasoning of Zionist leadership at the end of 1941 was an analysis made by David Ben Gurion, the chairman of the Agency Executive. Why were the Jews being let down, he asked, even though they had identified themselves with the Allies in the war and many British statesmen were pro-Zionist? Ben Gurion thought he found the answer in the fact that the British colonies were not administered by the British people or Government but by a bureaucracy whose rule was absolute and "hardly under any control—unless something extraordinary happens and prominence is given to it in Parliament and the Press. And even then a reply is prepared by the very people concerned, and the Minister in charge repeats the prepared reply." [19]

The Zionists associated with the "spirit" of the White Paper the Palestine Administration's wartime censorship practices. While the customary military censorship was applied to both Arab and Jewish newspapers, government publication controls in the Yishuv otherwise differed fundamentally from those among the Arabs. The Jews were given a free hand in matters pertaining to purely internal Zionist politics. But as a rule criticism of the White Paper policy as well as coverage of and comment on incidents related to it were banned. "The purpose of the censorship as it is applied in that country is to prevent the publication of material that is likely to inflame public opinion and lead to disturbance," explained the Colonial Secretary. The Jews accepted the suppression of such information as was likely to aid the enemy. But they resented the censor's deletion of political news and comment, which they characterized as an arbitrary interference with the freedom of the press. The fact that the Palestine censors tended to interpret their instructions too broadly lent substance to Zionist grievances. One M.P. reported that "nearly three-quarters of an article by Dr. Norman MacLean in the 'Palestine Post,' written to celebrate the Jewish Feast of Lights and Christmas Day, was deleted because it was pointed out that the Jews had given the world a universal religion and contributed to the foundations of Christianity. . . ." [20]

In the face of these frustrations the Zionists were employing increasingly their traditional weapon: appeal to public opinion in friendly countries. This was revealed at a press conference in Jerusalem in November 1941 by Moshe Shertok, the head of the Agency's political department, who was asked to define the official Zionist operational objectives at that time. Shertok candidly replied that, among other things,[21]

energetic activity [must be undertaken] in Great Britain to enlighten the British Government and public opinion on the significance of the Jewish Question. . . . Similar efforts must be made in the United States of America. . . . [and] relations with the formerly great Russian Jewry must be re-established, and ways and means found to enlist the aid of the Soviet Government whose participation in the post-war settlement will be of importance.

The Zionists were best equipped in Britain for putting this scheme into effect. The Agency's London office maintained contact with pro-Zionist M.P.'s through the Parliamentary Palestine Committee, which had come into existence prior to the war. The Agency Executive was thus assured that its position would be defended in both houses. The Zionists also courted the major political parties. The most cordial relations existed with the Labor Party. At its annual conference in London in May 1942, the Labor Party passed a resolution on the international situation which included the following: [22]

> The Conference records its detestation of the sufferings inflicted upon the Jewish people. It reaffirms its determination that, in the new international order after the war, Jews shall enjoy civil, religious, and economic equality with all other citizens and that international assistance shall be given to promote by immigration and settlement the Jewish National Home in Palestine.

The information section of the Agency's London Office was expanded in December 1941. Local committees were set up in scattered cities "to undertake the work of disseminating information amongst the non-Jewish population of their districts." Pamphlets and other publications multiplied. Zionist news was regularly channeled to British papers and periodicals, press conferences held when the occasion demanded, and newspapers "scrutinised for letters on Zionist and Jewish subjects, and arrangements made for these to be answered." Provision was made for lectures and movies on the national home before non-Jewish audiences. These facilities were also used to gain a hearing among the Governments-in-Exile in London. Analogous activities on a much smaller scale were carried on in the Dominions. The Zionists were perhaps most successful in South Africa, whose Prime Minister, General (later Field Marshal) Jan Christiaan Smuts, was an outspoken advocate of the national home.[23]

The Zionist leaders attached the greatest significance to awakening public opinion in the United States, for they came to feel that Britain could not afford to disregard pressures from Washington. Weizmann, in three visits to the United States between 1940–43, conversed with President Roosevelt, Secretary Hull, and other members of the Cabinet. Since the Agency had no American office, the public relations campaign was delegated to the American Emergency Committee for Zionist Affairs (changed to American Zionist Emergency Council in 1943), which represented all of the major Zionist bodies in the country and performed functions similar to those of the Agency office in London. The Emergency Committee was instrumental in forming in April 1941 an American Palestine Committee, whose purpose was "to serve as a vehicle for the expression of the sympathy and goodwill of Christian America for the movement to reestablish the Jewish National Home in Palestine." The bipartisan Committee was composed at the time of its creation of more than 700 members, including 67 Senators, 143 Representatives, 22 governors, "distinguished jurists, educators, clergymen, publishers, editors, writers, and civic leaders." Considerable publicity was given to statements by prominent members, and the Committee itself issued a number of protests and declarations.[24]

Soon after Russia was drawn into the war in June 1941, opportunities also presented themselves for Zionist courtship of the U.S.S.R. Hard pressed by the rapid Nazi advances, the Soviet Government relaxed its traditional ban on contacts between its subjects and the outside world in order to obtain what help it could from abroad. A Jewish Anti-Fascist Committee, one of more than twenty similar committees of other religious and national groups, was organized in Moscow in August 1941. The Yishuv's response to the Committee's first appeal for aid was immediate. "They issued their call not only as citizens of the Soviet Union but as Jews," observed the *Palestine Review*. "And even as the Soviet Union is bound to take its place in the future work of reconstruction, together with the nations of the world," the journal predicted, "so will Russian Jewry again take its place in the common effort of their people to solve its tragic problem." [25] The Histadrut sponsored an "Aid-to-Russia-Week" in October, and at the start of 1942 a permanent body called the V League for Soviet Russia was created for the collection of food, clothing, medical supplies, and funds. The Agency was unable to secure permission to set up an office in the U.S.S.R., though one was opened in Tehran, Iran, in April 1942. Via that office the Agency sent Russian news bulletins and brochures about the Zionist movement to Soviet newspapers, institutions, and libraries. Moreover, Zionist leaders in London discussed their cause with the Soviet Ambassador, Ivan Maisky. But by the end of 1942 the Agency was still in the dark as to where it stood, for the Russians remained noncommittal.[26]

CHAPTER 11

Arab Collaboration Abroad

THE IRAQI INTERLUDE

WHILE THE mandatory's inflexible application of the immigration and land provisions of the 1939 White Paper had stiffened the hostility of the Yishuv, the failure to institute the proposed constitutional changes heightened the fears of the Arab Community. The suppression of Arab politics in Palestine merely served to bolster the influence of the Husaynis, for all other factions necessarily became quiescent, while al-Hajj Amin remained beyond the mandatory's reach. The Jerusalem Mufti in exile still commanded the loyalty of the majority of the Palestine Arab nationalists. In their eyes al-Hajj Amin's practice of forcibly removing his political foes was outweighed by his nationalist achievements. The Mufti, more than any other local leader, could boast of having focused nationalist attention everywhere in the Arab East on Palestine. Even though he did not go to London in 1939, his unbending attitude toward Britain and the Jewish National Home, in the last analysis, had defined the Arab position in the parleys, which were followed in May by the issuance of the pro-Arab White Paper. That instrument, the Husaynis could not help but feel, had been exacted from the mandatory as a concession to the revolt and to Arab flirtations with the Axis. Since al-Hajj Amin and his associates viewed the White Paper as inadequate, they apparently saw no reason for abandoning such productive tactics until their terms were met unconditionally.

The emergency created by the war made a renewal of the revolt in Palestine increasingly difficult. Therefore al-Hajj Amin came to place more and more emphasis on cementing relations with the Axis. At least as early as January 1941 he was already negotiating formally with Germany. By the end of 1940 the Axis had conquered Poland, occupied Denmark, Norway, and the Low Countries, and overpowered France. Although the United Kingdom managed to survive the full-scale Nazi air assault of August-October 1940, it seemed only a matter of time before the British would have to capitulate. The Mufti, following the course of the war from Baghdad where he was then residing, must have believed Britain's defeat imminent, for he could see how the distractions of the military crisis had virtually eliminated British controls over the Iraqi Government. Once convinced of an Axis victory, he must have felt the need for establishing priority with the likely victors by becoming the first Arab leader to join their camp.

The Mufti must also have had visions of getting from the Axis in World War II what the Sharif Husayn had not fully obtained from the Allies in World War I—independence everywhere in the Arab East. The victorious Axis, he could be sure, would promptly replace the pro-British Hashimi rulers of Transjordan and Iraq and would never permit the French to regain a foothold in the Levant States. The Mufti could therefore hope that, as a reward for services rendered, he might be made ruler of an Arab country stretching from the borders of Iran to the Mediterranean and from Saudi Arabia to Turkey. His dealings with the Zionists would also be abundantly simplified under the Nazis. The element of risk in collaborating with the Axis must have appeared infinitesimal. The Mufti could, it was clear, retain the allegiance of a substantial body of the nationalists in his native country. Hence, even if the unlikely should occur and Britain should win the war, he would still have to be taken into consideration in any settlement of the Palestine problem.

Years later, when the Mufti had nearly completed the circle of his ubiquitous intrigue, he described his itinerary and the motives for its selection. "When World War II broke out in 1939," declared the Mufti to the Cairo correspondent of the London *Times* in August 1946,[1]

and I felt the increased British pressure on the French authorities in the Lebanon to hand me over, I tried to take refuge in Iraq and then in Persia. The British military authorities tried to capture me there and I found myself compelled to seek refuge in Turkey; but Turkey, through diplomatic arrangement with Great Britain, refused my demand. Therefore, finding no Moslem or Arab country in which to take refuge, I had to go to Europe, which at that time was almost entirely under German domination. Since I am not a British subject and there is no treaty between us [that is, Great Britain and the Palestine Arabs] and furthermore as there existed no enmity between us [the Palestine Arabs] and Germany, I could see no reason to prevent my taking refuge there at a time when Great Britain was seeking to expel me and to suppress my nation in order to further the Zionist ambitions, which were trying to destroy utterly our national integrity.

The Mufti's explanation of motives, by referring only to British pressures, omitted the more interesting part of the narrative.

Late in September 1939 al-Hajj Amin sent letters to Gabriel Puaux, the French High Commissioner for the Levant States, and General Maxime Weygand, the Commander of the French Forces in the Near East, thanking them personally and in the name of the Higher Committee for the asylum afforded the Palestine emigrés. The Mufti assured his hosts that the Palestine Arabs, who were merely "defending their 'rights and liberties,' have no relations with any foreign powers" and would refrain from any activities detrimental to French interests. Less than a month later al-Hajj Amin arrived in Baghdad, whither his automobile and personal effects were sent by the French military and police authorities at their own expense. What were the reasons behind the Mufti's flight to Iraq and why were the French willing to defray part of the costs? Although al-Hajj Amin had been confined by the French to the vicinity of his Lebanese residence, his trusted aides could generally come and go at will. But in the last few months of peace the French Mandatory Administration began to intensify its surveillance over Husayni activities. Accordingly, as early as May 1939 al-Hajj Amin reportedly sought to transfer his base of operations from Lebanon to the Iraqi capital. The Mufti's anxiety must have deepened after the start of the European war, when he saw how the screw was suddenly being turned on all groups, including his own numerous followers, suspected of sympathizing with the enemy. In fact, the French imprisoned early in October large numbers of pro-Husayni fugitives in the Levant States who failed to return to Palestine by the end of September, as ordered.[2]

If the French no longer wished to harbor, even behind prison bars, a nationalist martyr such as the Mufti, it was understandable. They had already incurred Arab nationalist hostility by the failure to ratify the treaties of 1936, which provided for the independence of Lebanon and Syria within three years; by the cession of Alexandretta to Turkey in June 1939; and by the suspension of the Syrian and Lebanese constitutions shortly thereafter. The French could only have been reluctant to add to their difficulties by arousing Muslim fanaticism, which al-Hajj Amin's arrest would have invited. The French were alarmed by the persistent Nazi radio propaganda to the Near East, which portrayed "in lurid colours the alleged ill-treatment of the Mufti . . . in Lebanon."[3] The British for their part still appeared sanguine about being able to convince al-Hajj Amin that his real interest lay in supporting the Allies. If the one leader who enjoyed the confidence of the Arab masses in Palestine could be persuaded voluntarily to come over to the British side, the Palestine Government, with the backing of the majority of both sections of the population, would be able to devote itself to the war effort. Since pro-British General Nuri Pasha al-Sa'id was Prime Minister of Iraq at the time and could be enlisted to mediate with al-Hajj Amin, the British had no objections to his going to Baghdad. From his angle the Mufti desired to avoid imprisonment, which he had good reason to suspect would be his fate, if the fortunes of war went against the Allies while he was still in Lebanon. Moreover, he could plainly see that the arrest of his aides was crippling his political effectiveness. Since the Palestine Arab leader was obviously determined to press his advantages to the limit, he preferred to set up new headquarters in an independent Arab country such as Iraq. There he had many influential friends and could be reasonably certain that the government would not interfere with his politicizing. For these combined reasons, the Mufti was enabled in mid-October 1939 to "escape" to Baghdad, where he joined his second-in-command, Jamal al-Husayni, who had arrived a few weeks earlier.

The pro-British Iraqi Premier promptly warned al-Hajj Amin to refrain from political intrigue and propaganda and exacted from him the promise that "he would not indulge in undesirable activities." That this turned out to be an empty promise was not entirely the Mufti's fault, for the temptation of political intrigue was almost irresistible. The general mood in Iraq at that time was one of great expectancy, particularly among the anti-British chauvinists, who did not conceal their hope for a Nazi victory. Nuri Pasha's insistence on severing diplomatic relations with Germany as early as September 7, 1939, simply caused the plotters to shift their center from the German Legation to the Italian. The Fascist diplomatic pouch, thenceforth bulging with a double load, carried instructions and funds from Berlin as well as Rome to the numerous Axis agents, both native and foreign, who honeycombed the government, the army, and the country at large. Plans for eliminating the "weak-kneed, servile," pro-British leaders from office were already well advanced among pro-Axis Iraqi politicians and army officers. To the loadstone of these conspirators the Mufti was immediately drawn. But until he found his bearings, al-Hajj Amin did nothing publicly that might arouse reproach. His reputation quickly grew from that of a Palestine Arab martyr to that of a Pan-Arab hero. Even the pro-British leaders were carried along. Iraqi notables from Nuri Pasha down and the many pro-Axis societies vied with one another in tendering al-Hajj Amin elaborate receptions.[4]

In this period of the Mufti's rise to power in Baghdad, which roughly coincided with the period of "the phony war," the British made their most persistent endeavor to persuade al-Hajj Amin to accept the 1939 White Paper as a basis for settlement. But these negotiations led nowhere, for the Mufti still demanded the immediate proclamation of Palestine as an independent Arab state. A final attempt to win the Mufti over was made in July 1940 by Colonel S. F. Newcombe, a protégé of Lawrence in the First World War, who was visiting Baghdad under the auspices of the British Ministry of Information. Newcombe, together with Jamal al-Husayni and Nuri Pasha, then the Iraqi Foreign Minister, drew up a plan under which, allegedly, the Husaynis were prepared to support the British war effort and the Iraqi Government to supply two divisions for service with British forces in the Libyan campaign, provided the mandatory first complied with the Mufti's principal condition. Although Newcombe, it was reported, engaged in the talks with the knowledge of the Colonial Secretary and the British Ambassador to Iraq, he was not authorized to conclude any formal agreement. Apparently on his return to London Newcombe failed to obtain the approval of the Churchill Cabinet for the proposal. Indeed, by that time London had already shelved the constitutional provisions of the White Paper.[5]

Meanwhile, pro-Axis Rashid 'Ali al-Gaylani had replaced Nuri Pasha as Prime Minister of Iraq on March 31, 1940, a development made possible in part by the Mufti's intervention. Al-Hajj Amin now began openly to assert his influence. The new administration furnished him with an outright gift of $72,000, a monthly stipend of $4,000, and "2 per cent of the salary of each Iraqi Government official, including military and police, checked off at the source." The Axis supplemented these funds with gifts reportedly totaling $400,000. Sixty per cent was said to have come from Germany. With well-filled coffers al-Hajj Amin was now able to gather about him an estimated three hundred trusted Palestine disciples, who had previously followed him to the Levant States and, after the defeat of France, many Syrians as well. The Mufti rewarded these loyal followers by either placing them on his own payroll or obtaining employment for them in Iraqi Government departments. Before the end of 1940 al-Hajj Amin had become a towering figure in the domestic Arab politics of the Levant States and particularly Iraq, where he virtually acquired the power of appointment, promotion, and dismissal of government officials. At his request, "passports were issued . . . , refugees from Palestine were not allowed to remain in Iraq unless he agreed they were genuine 'nationalists,' [and] refugees' cars were admitted duty free and paid no taxes." The Mufti indeed was instrumental, when the Rashid 'Ali Cabinet fell in February 1941, in securing the appointment, as Prime Minister, of Taha Pasha al-Hashimi, who until 1938 had been president of the Baghdad Defense Committee for Palestine and one of al-Hajj Amin's earliest links with the Axis.[6]

When the plotting for the Iraqi revolt was already under way in January 1941, al-Hajj Amin sent an Egyptian Arab as personal agent to Berlin for "a clarification of German policy toward the Arabs." The German Foreign Office, with the knowledge and approval of the Italian Government, assured al-Hajj Amin that : [7]

Germany has never occupied any Arab countries and has no ambitions whatsoever in Arab lands. Our view is that the Arabs . . . are capable of self-government. Germany recognizes the full independence of the Arab countries, or where this has not yet been attained, their right to it.
The Germans and the Arabs have common enemies in England and the

Jews; and are united in the fight against them. Germany . . . is ready . . . to give you all possible military and financial help required by your preparations to fight against the British for the realization of your people's aspirations. In order to enable the Arabs to begin the necessary preparations for their future war against the British, Germany is prepared to deliver to you immediately military material, if the means for transporting this material can be found.

The Mufti was requested "to keep the contents of this communication secret," and was invited to send another envoy back with a view to developing further "the details of our friendly cooperation."

The Mufti and his fellow travelers now endeavored to coordinate an Arab nationalist insurrection in Iraq, the Levant States, and Palestine with the Nazi invasion of the Balkans and Crete and the Italo-German offensive in North Africa from March to May 1941. The call to arms in Palestine was made in vain. In Syria and Lebanon, however, after the French surrender, the state of public morale was ripe for disorder as a result of the political uncertainty, the spiraling inflation, and the shortage of essential commodities, which conjured up memories of the frightful starvation experienced in the First World War. The arrival of the Italian Armistice Commission in the fall of 1940 paved the way for the infiltration of many German and Italian professional agitators. These provocateurs abetted the Mufti's adherents, who played a part in most ultranationalist, anti-French factions, which blossomed anew under the Vichy Mandatory Administration and furnished an excellent medium for the dissemination of rumors that "Syria would soon come under German domination and . . . those who had not lined up with the Germans would go to a concentration camp," or "the British intended to divide Syria between a Jewish Palestine and Turkey." Also shown was the Nazi propaganda film, "Victory in the West," which made as profound an impression of Axis invincibility as it had earlier in Europe. That this incitation did not lead to more than minor riots in Aleppo, Bayrut, Damascus, and Homs late in March may be attributed to rough handling of the mobs by French troops and inadequate backing from Berlin. The Nazis at that time were probably anxious not to trample too hard on Vichy sensibilities.[8]

In Iraq a pro-Axis politico-military clique staged a *coup d'état* on April 3, while Parliament was in recess. Rashid 'Ali was again installed as Premier; Nuri Pasha, who had been retained as Foreign Minister in the two preceding cabinets, was removed from the government, as were all pro-British elements; and the pro-British Regent, Amir 'Abd-al-Ilah, was deposed. The British not only refused to recognize the regime but, invoking Article IV of the Anglo-Iraqi Treaty of 1930, landed Imperial troops at Basrah on April 18. The showdown came in less than a fortnight when the Iraqi Army invested the British Embassy in Baghdad and the British air base at al-Habbaniyyah, some 45 miles west of that city. The Mufti at that time broadcast to all Muslim countries a religious summons to a *jihad* or holy war against Britain.[9]

In Palestine, where the Imperial garrisons were alerted at once, the Husayni agitation was choked off long before it could do any serious harm. In the Levant States, where the Nazis temporarily brought pressure to bear on the Vichy High Commissioner, General Henri Dentz, al-Hajj Amin's followers were able to recruit volunteers, primarily among students, to join the Iraqi insurgents. The Mufti's personal touch was also felt in Iraq, for at the end of the revolt early in June, Arab mobs were incited to attack the Jewish quarter in Baghdad, killing and wounding men, women, and children as well as looting homes and business establishments.[10]

THE MUFTI IN AXIS EUROPE

With the crushing of the Iraqi revolt—in which, incidentally, the British-trained Arab Legion of Transjordan and a volunteer squad of the Revisionist Irgun participated—and the British assumption of sweeping powers over the Iraqi Government, the pro-Axis groups were gradually weeded out and al-Hajj Amin's adherents dispersed. The Mufti fled to Tehran and found temporary havens first in the German Legation and, following the Anglo-Russian occupation of Iran in September, in the Japanese Legation. After failing to obtain permission from Ankara to join Rashid 'Ali in Turkey, al-Hajj Amin was finally rescued by the Axis, which provided air flight via Albania to Italy, where he arrived on October 24, 1941. Thirteen of the Mufti's intimates were rounded up by the British. Seven were regarded as "unimportant people, and to that extent harmless." In February 1942 they were sent back to Palestine, where "they are under constant observation," explained Colonial Secretary Viscount Cranborne, "and they can be apprehended at any time if they misbehave themselves." Six, among them Jamal al-Husayni and Amin al-Tamimi, were classified by Viscount Cranborne as "close associates of the Mufti. They are the people who are capable of causing danger and disturbances" and consequently were sent to Southern Rhodesia for internment. Some of the less conspicuous Palestine collaborators of the Mufti remained in Iraq, a few found sanctuary in Saudi Arabia, and others fled to Turkey, where they remained throughout the war. A number first escaped to Syria, whence they soon moved on to Turkey after the British and Free French forces drove the Vichy French out in July 1941; but the Turkish Government in February 1942 expelled several who had become Axis agents and who now joined al-Hajj Amin in Europe.[11]

"Italy, which knows Husseini's feeling of friendship for the Duce and the Fascisti," read the official Italian announcement of al-Hajj Amin's arrival in Rome at the end of October 1941, "is glad to learn that he is safe and sound on her territory." [12] Radio Rome characterized the Mufti's first meeting with Mussolini and Ciano as "an important event in the future of the Arab countries." Early in November the Mufti paid his initial visit to Berlin, where a Foreign Office spokesman greeted him "as a great champion of Arab liberation and the most distinguished antagonist of England and Jewry," going on to assert that the Germans would accord "him the full honours due to his 'exalted' rank." The Axis publicity campaign, dwelling at length on the Mufti's personal history and his struggle against Britain, was most intensive in the first three months of his European sojourn. The Italian press played up the manner in which he had eluded the British and Russians in Iran, describing the event "as a British defeat." Radio Berlin referred to him as "one of the great leaders of the Arab and Moslem world who have received at the hands of Britain enough to make her the greatest enemy and hangman of Islam." [13]

The Mufti seemed determined to secure from the dictators an unequivocal statement on the position of the countries in the Arab East after the expected Axis victory. He apparently wished to establish, before the war's end, his own future status as a leader in an independent Arab world. Otherwise there was little incentive for his collaboration. But at last al-Hajj Amin had met his superiors in intrigue. Despite numerous drafts of such declarations, he was unable to obtain the signatures of either Hitler or Mussolini. Nevertheless, on November 21, 1941 the Mufti was granted a ninety-minute audience with Hitler. The Fuehrer emphasized that a public statement would have to wait until his Panzer divisions and Luftwaffe had reached the Southern Caucasus. But he gave al-Hajj Amin oral assurances, cautioning that they be kept secret for the time being, that,[14]

> Germany has no ambitions in this area [the Arab countries of the Near East] but cares only to annihilate the power which produces the Jews. . . . The hour will strike when you will be the lord of the supreme word and not only the conveyor of our declarations. You will be the man to direct the Arab force. . . .

Accompanied by Rashid 'Ali, who had fled in December 1941 from his Turkish asylum to Europe, al-Hajj Amin also managed to secure a secret, written confirmation of Italian pledges to the Arabs from Foreign Minister Count Ciano, reading in part: [15]

> The Italian Government fully appreciates the confidence placed by the Arab people in the Axis powers and in their objectives, as well as their intention of participating in the fight against the common enemy until final victory is achieved. This is in accord with the national aspirations, as conveyed by you, of the Arab countries of the Near East at present oppressed by the British. I have the honor to assure you, in full agreement with the German government, that the independence and freedom of the Arab countries, now suffering under British oppression, are also the objective of the Italian Government.

Italy is therefore ready to grant to the Arab countries in the Near East
. . . every possible aid in their fight for liberation; to recognize their sovereignty and independence; to agree to their federation if this is desired by
the interested parties; as well as to the abolition of the National Jewish
Homeland in Palestine.

Meanwhile, the Mufti was given a roving, elastic mission, amply financed
and well staffed. He and his Arab colleagues were placed at the disposal
of the Axis propaganda and foreign ministries and armed forces. The Mufti
worked closely with the Nazi specialists on the Near East, including Palestine-born Templars who had left for Germany a few days before the
outbreak of war in 1939. A special Arab Office, known in Germany as
"Das Arabische Büro" (al-Maktab al-'Arabi), was created, and al-Hajj
Amin installed as one of the directors. He styled himself "Der Grossmufti"
or Grand Mufti (al-Mufti al-Akbar), dropping altogether the territorial
qualification, "of Jerusalem," which he had used since the 1920's—further
proof that al-Hajj Amin's ambitions extended beyond Palestine's borders.
The headquarters of the Arab Office in this period were in Berlin, with
subsidiary bureaus in various cities of Germany, Italy, and the occupied
countries.[16]

The Arab Office was responsible, under the general supervision of the
Axis propaganda ministries, for the preparation and broadcast of Arabic
programs to the Near East and North Africa. On special occasions the
Mufti made personal appearances before the microphone. Copies of these
speeches and other Arabic propaganda were smuggled into Arab lands via
Turkey. There al-Hajj Amin's aides were placed on the Axis payroll and
were involved in the two-way traffic of directing the propaganda to the
Mufti's followers in the Levant States, Iraq, and Palestine and receiving
intelligence reports in return. Moreover, some of the Husayni adherents
in these Arab countries and Palestine were supplied with short-wave trans-
mitters, enabling the Axis stations to include in their Arabic news bulletins
items which were often censored from the local press by the Allies.[17]

The Mufti's propaganda was channeled to non-Arab Muslims in Axis-
occupied Europe and to those in the Japanese sphere of influence. The
Mufti took part in recruiting Muslims in Yugoslavia and Albania and Arab
prisoners of war captured in France and Greece for special Muslim and
Arab "legions," attached to the Axis armies. He also briefed Arab and
German parachutists dropped over Near East countries for purposes of
sabotage. Furthermore, he befriended Adolf Eichmann, who played a
leading role in drawing up and implementing the program for the mass
extermination of the Jews. In one of the many drafts of a declaration to
the Arabs, prepared in the Arab Office with a view to securing German
and Italian official endorsement, the following proposal appeared: [18]

Germany and Italy recognize the illegality of the "Jewish Home in Palestine." They accord to Palestine and to other Arab countries the right to

resolve the problem of the Jewish elements in Palestine and other Arab countries in accordance with the interests of the Arabs, and by the same method that the question is now being settled in the Axis countries.

Thus, al-Hajj Amin's sojourn in Axis Europe had the multiple effect of intensifying his hatred of the Jews, giving him a postgraduate course at one of the most notorious schools of international intrigue, and inflating his ambitions. By this time he no longer made any pretense of distinguishing between personal aspirations and nationalist goals. Both objectives had become fully interchangeable, and this dualism was to characterize his subsequent political strategy. Moreover, Axis support enabled the Mufti to keep his political organization in the Levant States and Iraq as well as Palestine alive even in his absence. As long as the fortunes of war favored the Axis, al-Hajj Amin enjoyed the active backing of his personal followers and the latent sympathy of a substantial number of articulate nationalists. Both groups were concerned above all with furthering their own nationalist interests. As a result, their behavior was determined ultimately more by their hope of reward for siding with the victors and fear of punishment for cooperating with the losers than by any other factor. While it was not recognized at the time, al-Hajj Amin had in fact passed the zenith of his wartime influence in the Levant States and Iraq with the crushing of the Iraqi rebellion. For after all he was a political intruder and could not have been expected to prevent native rivals from moving into his seat after it was vacated. But in Palestine, after a temporary eclipse, as will be seen later, the Mufti's sun rose again even though he was not there to bask in it.

CHAPTER 12

The Statists and Their Opponents

THE BILTMORE PROGRAM

WHILE THE Mufti and his associates were predicating their postwar plans on an Axis victory, the Zionists were also preoccupied with their own schemes for a postwar settlement under Allied sponsorship. The parties in control of the quasi-government gradually shifted from the traditional demand for the further development of the national home to the demand for the immediate establishment of a Jewish state with full control over immigration. Zionist insistence upon a Jewish state had been given up at the time of the issuance of the Balfour Declaration in 1917. It was not raised again—except by the Revisionists and their off-shoots—until twenty years later, when the Royal Commission recommended partition. Even after the White Paper's appearance in May 1939, the official Zionist demand remained that for a national home only. In fact, three months later the political resolution of the twenty-first Zionist Congress did not mention a Jewish state but merely spoke of the national home. Yet those Zionist leaders who ardently espoused the suggestion for Jewish sovereignty in a divided Palestine in 1937–38 were still hopeful that partition might be revived. This, at any rate, was what Weizmann privately told an American non-Zionist group in January 1940.[1] Not until the following year, however, did the Zionists in power begin openly to discuss the desirability of demanding the creation of a Jewish state.

The belief was spreading among Zionist leaders that an Allied victory would not automatically solve "the Jewish problem." The best preparation for the peace conference, they felt, was for the Zionists to re-define their goal unequivocally and then bring their claims to the attention of the Allies. In the summer of 1941 Berl Katznelson (1887–1944), a Mapai mentor and the editor of *Davar*, warned that it would be useless to cling to old promises [2]

> which were themselves attempts to circumscribe our work. . . . If it were possible to have a regime that assures free mass immigration and colonization in Palestine, the existence of a Jewish state as such would become of secondary importance. But our experience in recent years should have taught us that in the present period of world history there is only one type of regime that can guarantee these conditions, and that is a Jewish state. . . . If we discouraged the demands for immediate Jewish statehood in the past, it was only because we felt that our achievements to date did not yet justify it. We feared that a premature demand for statehood might cause great harm.

In an article in *Foreign Affairs* the following winter the same theme was repeated by Weizmann, who declared [3]

> it is essential to obtain such a settlement in Palestine as will help to solve the Jewish problem—one of the most disturbing problems in the world. The Arabs must, therefore, be clearly told that the Jews will be encouraged to settle in Palestine, and will control their own immigration; that here Jews who so desire will be able to achieve their freedom and self-government by establishing a state of their own, and ceasing to be a minority dependent on the will and pleasure of other nations.

Normally such fundamental changes in Zionist thinking would have led to corresponding adjustments in the official Zionist platform at the biennial Zionist Congress; and these adjustments, in turn, would have been subject to review by the Jewish Agency Council. But this was now impossible. Following the breakdown of the Agency's administrative machinery on the eve of the war, and the failure in the early war years of attempts by the Zionist leaders to bring the non-Zionists back into the fold, the Agency was converted for all practical purposes into a Zionist body. Thus, as in the case of Palestine Arab politics, wartime conditions had caused Zionist politics at the top level to revert to the situation of the mid-1920's, when the Zionists alone were responsible for the development of the national home. Non-Zionist absence from the Agency Executive made for greater administrative efficiency, but at the price of doubtful constitutionality, since the Agency could no longer rightfully claim to speak for all Jews.[4]

In contrast the emergency arrangement by which the Zionist Executive was made accountable to the Inner General Council functioned smoothly and kept alive a modified form of the democratic process. It enabled those groups not represented on the Executives to have a voice in the framing of policy. Representation on the Inner General Council was based on the composition of the 1939 Zionist Congress and hence reflected the over-all strength of the several parties throughout the world. The Inner General Council, however, consisted exclusively of Palestine Jews. Final policy-making authority was thus vested in the Yishuv. But with the Nazi destruction of the European Jewish communities, the future of the Yishuv and the national home had meanwhile become more dependent than before on the Jewish Community in the United States, the largest and wealthiest in the world. Any fundamental alteration of the official Zionist program had therefore to receive American Zionist endorsement.

The Inner General Council and the Agency Executive had been discussing this question for more than a year. A committee was actually appointed at the end of 1941 to draw up a new statement of aims for adoption by the quasi-government. It was then decided to seek American Zionist approval before submitting the platform to the Inner General Council in Jerusalem. With this end in view the American Emergency Committee for Zionist Affairs called an extraordinary political conference at the Biltmore Hotel in New York in May 1942. Among the 600 delegates were European Zionist leaders temporarily residing in the United States and three full members of the Agency Executive, including Weizmann and Ben Gurion. Accumulated grievances were aired. Assessment was made of the effects of the Nazi anti-Jewish brutalities. The consequences of openly proclaiming the demand for a Jewish state were explored. The declaration of Zionist aims, subsequently known as the Biltmore Program, adopted by the conference, disclosed that a majority of the American Zionists was in full accord with the statist leaders abroad. "The Conference declares," the statement concluded,[5]

> that the new world order that will follow victory cannot be established on foundations of peace, justice and equality, unless the problem of Jewish homelessness is finally solved. The Conference urges that the gates of Palestine be opened; that the Jewish Agency be vested with control of immigration into Palestine and with the necessary authority for upbuilding the country, including the development of its unoccupied and uncultivated lands; and that Palestine be established as a Jewish Commonwealth integrated in the structure of the new democratic world. . . .

The Biltmore Program was now referred back to the Yishuv. Here, David Ben Gurion, the Chairman of the Agency Executive, became its most ardent champion. Ben Gurion had been originally a tireless advocate of Arab-Zionist *rapprochement*. Following the appearance of the 1939 White Paper, he despaired of arriving at any political settlement with the Arabs prior to the establishment of a Jewish state. After his return from the United States in the summer of 1942, Ben Gurion barnstormed town and village and won for the proposed policy the support of the two General Zionist parties as well as Mizrahi and Mizrahi Labor. The tiny Jewish State Party, of course, required no persuasion. Nor did the Revisionists, who, as dissidents, were not represented on the Inner General Council and therefore were not entitled to any say in the adoption of a new platform.

Ben Gurion, however, encountered stiff resistance in his own party. At a Mapai conference, held at the end of October for the purpose of securing the party's endorsement of the Biltmore Program, Faction B, the intraparty leftist opposition, objected to the immediate, open espousal of statism on the ground that it could only lead to the partition of Palestine. The faction's leaders, accordingly, favored the indefinite continuation of the mandate and insisted on the right of independent action whenever it did not concur in the majority's political decisions. But the conservative Faction C, with which Ben Gurion was allied, mustered enough strength to override the anti-Biltmore group and to modify the party's constitution, making it obligatory for all members to abide by majority-approved resolutions. The Biltmore Program was finally adopted by the Inner General Council at Jerusalem on November 10, 1942 by a vote of 21 to 4. The three spokesmen of Mapai's Faction B abstained, while the delegates of ha-Shomer ha-Za'ir, the Left Zionist Workers, and the central Europeans who had just reorganized themselves into a permanent political party cast the negative ballots.[6]

THE ANTI-STATIST OPPOSITION

By the outbreak of war the Palestine Jews of central European origin numbered well over 10 per cent of the Yishuv. Most of them settled in the country after the Nazi rise to power and therefore had not taken part in the last community election of 1931. Many of the central European immigrants enrolled in existing political parties; but a greater number remained unorganized. Among the latter the feeling grew that their needs as a group could not be met so long as they were unrepresented in the quasi-government. In 1938 a number of German immigrants seceded from the General Zionist A Party to form the National Unity Party. But the new faction did not take root and passed out of existence after the 1939 Zionist Congress.

The German immigrants, now backed by Austrians, retained an active interest in local politics through their semipolitical Association of German and Austrian Immigrants. Not until November 1942, however, was the Association finally transformed into a permanent political party, called New Immigration, so as to encourage others than central Europeans to join. The party's program called for unquestioned identity with the British war effort and, therefore, postponement of the struggle against the 1939 White Paper, even though the latest mandatory policy was declared unacceptable. The New Immigration Party also rejected the Biltmore Program, since it was felt that without prior mandatory sanction the formal Zionist demand for a Jewish state was precipitate. Still, the party favored the ultimate attainment of Jewish sovereignty in Palestine and for that reason denounced binationalism.[7]

But the more vocal anti-statists were the binationalists, who argued that the Arab-Zionist deadlock in Palestine could be broken only by deliberately training the two communities for joint self-rule in a sovereign, unitary Arab-Jewish state with a governmental structure built on equal representation. In a constitutional sense, therefore, this program did not differ from the idea of parity, although its advocates commonly employed the term binationalism to describe their political objective. The leftist labor parties had incorporated binationalist principles in their party creeds, as did non-Zionist groups in their declarations on Palestine. Semipolitical societies devoted solely to the cultivation of the binationalist cause had also appeared in the community ever since the 1920's. But these groups were divided by conflicting political, economic, and religious ideologies. Nevertheless, the binationalist minority in the Yishuv were agreed on the eve of the war that the Zionist leaders in power had failed to evolve an adequate policy toward the Arabs, had neglected sufficiently to promote Arab-Jewish understanding, and to the extent of this failure and neglect bore their measure of responsibility for the Arab revolt and the anti-Zionist course of mandatory policy.

In August 1939 Hayyim M. Kalvaryski (1868–1947), one of the earliest exponents of binationalism, accused the dominant Zionist leaders of having miseducated the public "on the conception that it is not necessary to take into account the opposition of the Arabs, that in the solution of the Palestine problem England is the decisive factor." Kalvaryski, who in 1929–31 had headed an Arab Bureau operated jointly by the National Council and Agency Executives, blamed both the Agency and the Revisionists, who he said [8]

expend all their . . . energy in winning the sympathy of this or that Minister . . . and are very little concerned with winning the sympathy of the people who are as interested in this problem as we are. . . . If only we had invested one-tenth or even one-twentieth of the resources that we have sunk into securing the sympathy of remote nations and individuals . . . into winning the sympathy of the [Arab] nation . . . by creating economic, political, moral, and cultural ties . . . then our present position both in Palestine and in Europe would have been quite different. . . .

A small group of confirmed believers in Arab-Jewish amity allied themselves with Kalvaryski to found in October 1939 the League for Jewish-Arab Rapprochement and Cooperation. They aspired to organize all the binationalists in the Yishuv behind a single program, attract Arab support, and bring pressure to bear on the Agency actively to pursue Arab friendship. The League did not regard itself as a party, despite its political function and its organizational similarity to the parties, with its hierarchy of a Central Committee, a Council, and a Conference. Indeed, membership was open to existing societies, including political parties, as well as to any person above the age of 18. But the only party to affiliate with it at first was the Left Zionist Workers.[9]

Thus the League got off to a slow start. Through the Left Zionist Workers, contacts were established with Arab workers. The prevailing economic boycott of Arab products and labor were severely criticized. The League advocated combined, not separate, civil defense measures and proposed that the Agency assist Arab peasants in marketing their products. It protested against the official Zionist tendency to characterize all Arabs as Axis sympathizers, instead of trying to court the anti-Fascist elements. Early in 1940 the League in cooperation with ha-Shomer ha-Za'ir appointed a committee to draw up a blueprint of a binational solution of the Arab-Jewish problem in Palestine for consideration by the Jewish Agency. But the ruling Zionist parties greeted these proposals and protests with coolness, and sometimes with hostility.

Not until a month after the Biltmore conference did ha-Shomer ha-Za'ir formally join the ranks of the League. In a consequent revision of principles, the League acknowledged as beyond contention the right of the Jews to "return . . . to their historic homeland . . . . according to the full economic absorptive capacity of Palestine" as well as the right of the Palestine Arabs to the maintenance of ties with the Arabs in the near-by countries. The League might agree, as a temporary measure, to fixed immigration quotas. But it would "oppose any tendency to crystallize the Jewish community as a minority in Palestine." The constitutional goal would be the creation of a binational government, in which neither people would dominate the other "irrespective of the [relative] numerical strength." When this regime had once become established, the League would take a "positive attitude towards the participation of Palestine, as an autonomous binational unit, in a federation with the neighboring countries." [10]

Early in September 1942 Kalvaryski and the secretary of ha-Shomer ha-Za'ir's Arab department visited the Levant States to acquaint spokesmen in those countries with the objects of the League. On returning to Palestine they reported a "widespread distrust" in Syria and Lebanon of Zionist motives, attributable to "The lack of any declared positive program . . . [toward the Arabs], irresponsible utterances of some Jewish leaders, attacks in the Hebrew press on every effort towards Arab-Jewish understanding, the turmoil about the Jewish Army and the political tendencies which lurk behind the campaign . . ." Although Kalvaryski found no one "prepared to enter discussions on the basis of a Jewish State, there is readiness on the part of the majority of the people contacted to discuss a desirable solution of the Arab-Jewish conflict on the basis of the projected platform of the League." [11] Ha-Shomer ha-Za'ir tried to promote interest in the League among leftist Arab circles, and to rouse the Histadrut into expanding its Arab subsidiary, the Palestine Labor League. Meanwhile, relations with the dominant statist leaders had already become strained when the League's offer of cooperation was turned down by the Agency political department in June 1942. Thereupon the League decided no longer "to report to the Agency or to consult it," thus losing sight of one of its original objectives—to exert pressure on the Agency to change its Arab policy. At the same time the League came increasingly under the fire of the statist press.[12]

The statists' attacks on the League, however, were mild by comparison with those visited upon the Union (*Ihud*) Association, a new binationalist group, whose guiding light from its inception in September 1942 [13] was Judah L. Magnes. Magnes had fallen into disfavor with the irreconcilable statists as early as the mid-1920's, when he founded the first binationalist society, called the Pact of Peace (*Brit Shalom*). Following Eden's speech in May 1941 pledging British support for Arab Unity, and the promise of independence to Syria and Lebanon in June, Magnes expressed the view that, if Palestine were linked to its neighbors in a Union or Federation, the Palestine problem would be "lifted on to another plane in at least two ways: First, the Arab fear of domination by the Jewish National Home . . . [would be] mitigated by reason of the political security which the wider and more powerful background of Arab Union affords, and second, the Jewish yearning for opportunities to settle refugees from persecution could be met more generously." He appealed to "the British, the Arabs and the Jews to consider things together *now* . . . ," warning that deferment was merely courting "the pressure of propaganda and the unstable successes of diplomacy. In that event whichever side wins, Palestine loses." [14]

In the succeeding year Magnes won over to his stand a small number of community leaders, including Henrietta Szold (1860–1945), the American-born founder of Hadassah and a member of the National Council Executive since 1931, as well as the principal spokesmen of the League for Jewish-Arab Rapprochement. In September 1942 this group announced the formation of the Ihud Association. Ihud's initial public statement listed the main political aims of the Association as follows: [15]

(a) Government in Palestine based upon equal political rights for the two peoples:

(b) The agreement of a steadily growing Yishuv and of the whole Jewish people to a Federative Union of Palestine and neighbouring countries. This Federative Union is to guarantee the National rights of all peoples within it;

(c) A Covenant between this Federative Union and an Anglo-American Union which is to be a part of the future Union of the free peoples. This Union of the free peoples is to bear the ultimate responsibility for the establishment and stability of international relations in the New World after the war.

Since the new society failed to take an explicit position on immigration, rightist members of the Inner General Council demanded the expulsion of Ihud adherents from the Zionist Organization. While this action was never adopted, the Inner General Council did request from the sponsors of Ihud an elaboration of their program. The society thereupon released an amplified statement of objectives in October, declaring that it was opposed to fixing the Yishuv as a permanent minority. Rather did Ihud hope for the absorption by Palestine of the greatest possible number of Jewish immigrants in complete economic, social, cultural, and political harmony with the Arabs. Though recognizing that only the Jewish quasi-government was empowered to enter into binding negotiations with "outside factors," Ihud nevertheless claimed that every citizen and Zionist group had the right to establish contact with Jews and non-Jews for the purpose of exchanging views and formulating proposals which could then be submitted to the quasi-government.[16]

Since Ihud had no large organized popular following in the Yishuv and had not allied itself with the League for Jewish-Arab Rapprochement, an explanation of the statists' vehemence toward the new society was to be found in the repercussions of the feud in the United States. Both Dr. Magnes and Miss Szold enjoyed substantial backing in America among non-Zionists and even non-Jews. Magnes' political statements were usually featured by the New York *Times*, which also frequently printed his letters. Miss Szold in particular exerted a strong personal influence on Hadassah, the American women's Zionist organization, to whose work she had devoted a large part of her life. Her association with Ihud, it was feared in American statist circles, might lead to Hadassah's withholding approval from Biltmore, a move that would have reduced noticeably the relative strength of the statists.

The issue was by no means closed. Each participating organization of the American Emergency Committee for Zionist Affairs had still to endorse the Biltmore Program. The question had not yet come up for consideration before the Inner General Council in Jerusalem. It was therefore all the more urgent that the two largest Zionist bodies in the United States should affirm the demand for a Jewish state and dissociate themselves officially from Ihud. Accordingly, a joint meeting of Hadassah and the Zionist Organization of America in New York on October 17, 1942, passed a resolution—over the opposition of a few Hadassah leaders who staunchly supported Miss Szold—to the effect that "any program which denies these fundamental principles [proclaimed in the Biltmore Program], such as advanced by the Ichud or any other group, is unacceptable to the Zionist Organization of America and Hadassah . . ."[17]

The statists at the combined session, in discussing binationalism and the Arabs, essentially repeated the argument advanced by David Ben Gurion at the Biltmore conference the previous May. He had asserted at that time that if what the binationalists sought was equality of rights for Arabs and Jews, as national entities and individuals, "then certainly no Jew, much less a Zionist, can fail to advocate such a regime, although I am not quite convinced that the Arabs will agree to such equality, if they have the power to determine the constitution." However, if the binationalists were seeking a government based on equal representation, "not a single Arab leader has been found to agree to the principle of parity, with or without the Mandate." The Arab-Jewish problem in Palestine, Ben Gurion insisted, was,[18]

> almost exclusively, the problem of further Jewish immigration. . . . If Jewish immigration into Palestine depends on Arab consent, there will hardly be any Jewish immigration at all. It is vitally important, politically as well as morally, that our position on this crucial question should be made unequivocal. Jewish immigration to Palestine needs no consent. We are returning as of right.

The acceptance of Biltmore by a majority of the American Zionists in October and by the Inner Zionist General Council in November 1942 gave the statists as clear a mandate as they could expect in wartime. But the ideological conflict between statism and binationalism had by no means ended.

THE STERN GANG

On the extreme right, meanwhile, anti-British feeling continued to breed political terrorism. The retaliatory murder of Arabs and the attacks on government property by the Irgun Zvai Leumi in the last year of peace were intended as a warning that the Revisionists would employ the same tactics as the Arab nationalists to discourage the rebels from their assaults on Jews and to coerce the mandatory into giving up its restrictive policy. The Irgun, however, regarded itself merely as the military arm of the dissident Revisionists, and after the start of the war it suspended its terrorist activities. The new terrorist group, known to the Yishuv at large at the time as the "Stern Gang," was an outgrowth of the Revisionist Irgun, was not affiliated with any political party, and dedicated itself exclusively to political violence. Its leaders thereby hoped to drive the British "occupation" authorities out of Palestine and Transjordan, which would then be transformed into an independent Jewish state.

The Polish founder of this group, Abraham Stern (1907–1942), had settled in Palestine in 1925, studied at the Hebrew University and later at the University of Florence in Italy, earned a livelihood by teaching, and wrote Hebrew poetry in his spare time. Yair ("Illuminator"), as Stern was known among his followers, was a charter member of the Irgun and headed its "political department." He was sent to Poland in the late 1930's to assist in organizing Irgun branches in that country. Arrested by the

Palestine police at the end of August 1939, and set free in June 1940, Yair immediately let it be known to the Irgun High Command that he disapproved of its cooperation with the government at a time when "it does not depart from its White Paper policy."[19] By preventing the Jewish victims of Nazism from reaching the safety of the Land of Israel, Stern maintained, Britain "becomes an accomplice to Hitler's crimes . . . and should be fought with undiminished vigour." He urged the continuance of political terrorism even during the war as the only way to wring concessions from the British. The Irgun's refusal to end its truce induced Stern and some fifty of his intimates to leave the Revisionist military organization and to establish their own "independent, non-partisan" National Military Organization in Israel (*Irgun Zvai Leumi be-Israel*).[20]

In the furtherance of its objectives Stern's Irgun, it was reported, "sought to enlist the help of Italy after Italy had entered the war." The contention that the Sternists tried to establish contact with Italian agents in the Levant States, when the Italian Armistice Commission was there in the winter of 1940–41, had some supporting evidence in later writings of the group. But that Stern's Irgun received little, if any, tangible aid from the Italians was equally clear, for in search of funds and military equipment amid an unsympathetic Yishuv the new terrorist society resorted to theft, extortion, abduction and murder. After raiding an illegal arms cache in a Jewish village north of Tel-Aviv, the Sternists robbed in mid-September 1940 a branch of the Jewish-owned Anglo-Palestine Bank in that city of close to $20,000. This was followed by a series of similar crimes culminating in the murder in January 1942 of two Histadrut officials who resisted the seizure by Sternists of the payroll bags they were carrying. At the same time the society busied itself with enlarging its ranks from among former colleagues in the old Irgun, youthful delinquents in the Oriental Jewish slums of the larger towns, and Jewish members of the Polish troops who began to arrive in Palestine in 1941 and some of whom had belonged to the Irgun's Polish branches before the war. To propagate their aims the Sternists distributed illegal broadsheets and in the summer of 1941 began clandestine broadcasts. Their only act of political terrorism in this period was the bombing of the government immigration offices at Haifa on December 19, 1940, in protest against the deportation of illegal Jewish immigrants to Mauritius earlier that month.[21]

Stern's Irgun had not yet reached the level of political violence to which they aspired in their writings, when they were sidetracked early in 1942 to a private feud with the Palestine police. Accusing the Criminal Investigation Department (CID) of "torturing" captured Sternists for information, the terrorists "retaliated" in mid-January by killing in Tel-Aviv the Jewish deputy-superintendent of police and two detectives, one British and the other Jewish. In the next four months more than twenty members, including the most important leaders, of the group were captured. Stern and two others were shot dead early in February while resisting arrest, according to the CID communiqués. But the Sternists, insisting that their men were unarmed and offered no resistance, attempted reprisals at the end of April against the lives of the Inspector-General of the Palestine police and his assistant. By mid-May, however, with about one-quarter of its members interned and much of its equipment seized by the police, the group ceased active operations for almost two years.[22]

But this temporary throttling of Stern's Irgun could not have been accomplished without the cooperation of the Yishuv and the Jewish quasi-government. In the first half of 1942 the Palestine Jews were in no mood to abide any further political terrorism. The real threat of Axis occupation attenuated for the time being the concern of the Palestine Jews for the fate of their fellows in Axis Europe. The National Council Executive and the Jewish press urged the public to assist in eradicating "this nest of blackmailers, kidnappers, and assassins." "If terrorist activities are a scourge in normal times, they are a direct challenge to the security of the country in time of war," wrote the *Palestine Post*. "They form an essential part of the Fifth-Column activities, and their speedy suppression is as vital to the internal peace of the country as to its external defence." The mere existence of the Stern Gang provided a warning that the creed of violence arising out of political despair had already gnawed its way into the outer layer of the Community. But it was still remote from the core. Not until the later war years, when the theater of combat had receded from the frontiers of Palestine, did the sense of despair begin to take hold in the community. Only then did political terrorism begin to thrive.[23]

PART THREE

RESULTS OF THE SHARPENING EAST-WEST RIVALRY AFTER 1942

CHAPTER 13

Changing Big-Power Alignment

THE BRITISH ASPECT

THE ANGLO-AMERICAN assumption at the end of 1942 of the military offensive, which resulted in the expulsion of the Axis forces from North Africa in less than seven months, marked a political turning point in Palestine as in the rest of the Near East. With the gradual elimination of the Axis from the area, the Arab leaders lost a trump card in their power-political bargaining with Britain. Now that the Allies were on the ascendant, would new rivalries replace the old? If so, would the Arabs or the Zionists have greater advantages? If Britain neglected or proved unable either to reach an agreed settlement or to impose a solution on Arabs and Zionists, would the pressures of the two contestants draw the other Big Powers into the controversy? These questions, raised in the minds of Arabs, Zionists, and their champions, basically conditioned Arab and Zionist politics after the winter of 1942–43.

By the start of 1943 Great Britain had re-established its pre-eminence in the Near East. The British-controlled Middle East Supply Center had already placed the region's economy at the disposal of the United Kingdom and its Allies for the prosecution of the war, while political and security checks had been introduced in the individual countries. Large garrisons kept Britain's authority in mandated Palestine intact. Friendly governments were installed in Iraq and Egypt. After the Vichy regime was crushed in Syria and Lebanon, the British retained final responsibility for the security of these countries. With the wartime dwindling of pilgrimages to Mecca, Saudi Arabia leaned more heavily than ever on British (and American) subsidies. Amir 'Abdallah's hands were even more securely tied, for British grants-in-aid had from the start enabled Transjordan to balance its budget; besides, that country was still mandated and its policy was subject to veto by London. Even Yemen was entirely surrounded by territories friendly to the United Kingdom and could not reasonably have been expected to deviate from the norm. British anxiety over Axis machinations diminished steadily. Once the bubble of Axis invincibility had been pricked, the Italo-German subversive and intelligence network in the Arab East began to fall apart. Axis rumor-mongering, while it continued to focus Arab nationalist attention on Zionism, possessed nuisance value only. Its impact was cushioned by Allied propaganda agencies, whose psychological warfare became increasingly effective as it was reinforced by reports of military progress.

Now that the Axis threat to the Arab East had been contained and Britain's predominance reasserted, the United States and Russia were emerging as potential competitors. As long as Churchill remained at the helm, however, it was clear that no British interests would be liquidated willingly. The experience of the critical years of the war had demolished all doubt as to the area's importance for the security of the Empire and the survival of Britain as a Great Power. Britain's main political goal, therefore, was even more resolutely than before to encourage the Arab Unity movement. The resulting regional stability, so the theory ran, would enable Britain to reduce its political and security controls, and a grateful Arab population would assure Britain's future primacy. The Arab leaders for their part had not followed through the Foreign Office endorsement of Arab Unity in 1941. However, after the change in the war's tide the Arabs became more receptive. Nor was the significance lost upon them of Anthony Eden's reaffirmation in February 1943 of Britain's sympathy with "any movement among Arabs to promote their economic, cultural or political unity, but clearly the initiative . . . would have to come from the Arabs themselves." Prodded by one M.P. who suggested that "we send the very best men available to help in this undertaking," the Foreign Secretary in characteristic understatement replied that "we are very well represented in these countries." [1] Arab spokesmen immediately commenced a series of parleys which were to lead two years later to the creation of a League of Arab States.

Meanwhile policy makers on the Cabinet level were not unmindful of the Palestine issue. Continued support of the national home against Arab wishes might jeopardize the pro-British orientation of any emergent Arab bloc. Yet Churchill and some of his Ministers were still friendly to Zionism and, in any case, were averse to alienating the important body of American public opinion which supported the Zionist enterprise. "I have never altered my opinion," observed Churchill in August 1946, "that the White Paper constituted a negation of Zionist policy which, the House [of Commons] must remember, was an integral and indispensable condition of the Mandate." The Colonial Office, early in the period of Colonel Oliver Stanley's tenure (November 1942–July 1945), had revived partition as a possible solution. The scheme, as later outlined by Colonel Stanley, followed in essence the Royal Commission's recommendations. Palestine was to be carved into independent Arab and Jewish states in treaty relations with the United Kingdom, which would retain responsibility for administering a projected Jerusalem enclave. As in the earlier proposal of 1937–38, the Arab territory, it was contemplated, might be merged with Transjordan to "make a solid sovereign State." This plan had apparently been carefully examined, and the advantages to Arabs and Jews were thought to outweigh the technical, economic, and administrative difficulties which its execution was certain to create. "All I need say," declared Stanley in 1946, "is that during the Coalition Government, I, and some of my colleagues, worked out a plan on these lines, which I . . . and . . . many of my colleagues thought was practicable, and it was accepted as practicable by many . . . authorities on Palestine." The Colonial Office also drew up a blueprint, added Stanley, for the transformation of Palestine into a unitary, federal state with semiautonomous Arab and Jewish provinces "as an alternative, in case the final definite scheme of partition, for some reason or other, proved unacceptable." [2]

The Zionist leaders in power, it was known, would be willing to accept partition provided the Jewish area were large enough to meet immigration needs, since the principal aims of the Biltmore Program—state sovereignty and control over immigration—would thereby be attained. Presumably the Cabinet members favoring partition hoped to enlist Arab consent either prior to the crystallization of the Arab Unity movement or at the peace conference, which, it was widely believed at the time, would take place at the close of hostilities. At all events, nothing concrete was to be done until the end of the war, when the proposals were to be submitted formally to Arabs and Jews. [3] The mandatory, however, never officially released any statement about its postwar Palestine plans. Yet the realization of these plans obviously required certain modifications of the White Paper. Some changes were in fact introduced. But the official fiction was maintained that the 1939 policy was still in full operation. Only within this setting is it possible to understand the mandatory's vacillation in the later war years, the intensifying of the Zionist struggle for the formal abrogation of the White Paper, and the Arab nationalist insistence after 1943 on the government's adherence to the letter and spirit of that document.

As in the earlier period nothing was done to bring Arabs and Jews together politically. Nor were efforts made to discredit the Mufti by showing that his collaboration with the Axis was aimed, in the final analysis, against the interests of the Palestine Arabs. Instead, immediately after the inauguration of the Anglo-American campaigns in North Africa, the mandatory began progressively to restore political liberties to the Palestine Arabs. By the spring of 1944 even the Mufti's associates who had been arrested in Iran in 1941 were permitted to participate openly in politics.

At the same time press censorship regulations, which in the first three war years had stifled all but the most opaque references to Arab nationalist grievances in Palestine, were now suddenly relaxed, although direct mention of al-Hajj Amin and other Axis agents was still taboo.

On the other hand, when asked in December 1943 whether assurances could be given that Jamal al-Husayni and Amin al-Tamimi, "two of the leading assistants of the ex-Mufti of Jerusalem . . . , will not be permitted to return to Palestine from Rhodesia," Colonial Secretary Stanley replied "that there was no intention of releasing them." Pressed further as to "why no appointment has yet been made to fill the posts of Mufti of Jerusalem and President of the Moslem Supreme Council," Stanley explained that "the post of Mufti of Jerusalem is a purely religious office with no powers or administrative functions," and that "no legal machinery in fact exists for the formal deposition of the holder, nor is there any known precedent for such deposition." Though al-Hajj Amin remained the Mufti of Jerusalem, the importance of this point was academic, added Stanley, since the Government did not plan to allow that Muslim cleric, "who has openly joined the enemy, to return to Palestine in any circumstances." However, "as regards the presidency of the Supreme Moslem Council, the Government do not propose . . . to intervene in a matter which is giving rise to no trouble, and which is not impeding the adequate transaction of business in those affairs for which the Council is responsible." [4]

Meanwhile the 1939 White Paper was being whittled down. The Palestine Government, admittedly, refused to alter the Land Transfer Regulations of 1940, and the price of rural land skyrocketed from $470 an acre in 1942 to $1,050 in 1944, an increase of 820 per cent over prices prevailing in the mid-1930's. But the land laws were the one feature of the White Paper to survive the war intact. The proposed constitutional innovations had become a dead issue by 1943, even though the British did not openly admit it, the Zionists did not believe it, and the Arabs would not accept it. And the mandatory began in the later war years to retreat from the immigration provisions of the White Paper as well. The first principle to go was the time limit. "The number of Jews who entered Palestine legally or illegally up to 30th September 1943," announced the Colonial Secretary in November 1943,

against the total of 75,000 to be admitted under the existing quota system is 43,922. There are thus 31,078 who, it may be fairly assumed, would have reached it before 31st March 1944, but for the exigencies of the war. His Majesty's Government have . . . reached the conclusion that it would be inequitable to close the doors of Palestine to these persons on account of the time factor. No effort will be lacking on the part of His Majesty's Government to facilitate their arrival, subject to the criterion of economic absorptive capacity.

This move certainly could not be squared with the unconditional assurance to the Arabs that "after the period of five years [starting April 1, 1939] no further Jewish immigration will be permitted unless the Arabs of Palestine are prepared to acquiesce in it." [5]

Furthermore, as long as the mandatory remained silent on its postwar Palestine plans, the net effect of its deferment of the immigration deadline was to arouse Arab suspicions without allaying Zionist fears. It gradually became apparent that the British Government seemed determined to stretch out the residue of the White Paper's numerical quota so as to make it last until the war's end. The Colonial Office informed the Jewish Agency in July 1943 that the British passport control officer at Istanbul had been instructed "that in [the] future all Jews, whether adults or children, who may succeed in escaping to Turkey, will be eligible, after a British security screening, for onward transport to Palestine." But this step was of no immediate worth, since the Turkish Government was not advised of it until several months later. The Colonial Office then withdrew the ruling in September 1944 and notified the Agency that "for the present not more than 1,500 immigrants will be permitted to enter Palestine in any one month from 1st October." The fixed monthly rate enabled the British Government to tide over the war without having to take a final decision on immigration. But the yardstick of a "political high-level," which had been instituted on the recommendation of the Royal Commission in 1937 and had now come back to stay, did represent an improvement for the Zionists over the early war years. After declining to a monthly average of 311 in 1942, the monthly rate of Jewish immigration rose to 790 in 1943 and to 1,205 in 1944, dropping to 1,063 in 1945. [6]

Meanwhile the British Government made a significant, though tardy, concession to Zionist demands elsewhere. The Zionist campaign for a Jewish Fighting Force was resumed in the spring of 1944 when preparations for the cross-channel invasion reached their final stage. As the War Office took no action on these requests, Weizmann appealed directly to the Prime Minister in July, asking that the existing Jewish units be grouped "into a Division of their own, and that the Division . . . be permitted to carry the flag with the Star of David on the European battle-field." Churchill replied favorably a month later, and on September 19 the War Office announced that a Jewish Brigade Group—the smallest self-contained formation in the British Army—would be set up

to take part in active operations. The infantry brigade will be based on the Jewish battalions of the Palestine Regiment. . . . Supporting and ancillary units to complete the group, based on existing Palestinian units, are being prepared. . . . The details of the scheme are being discussed with the Jewish Agency, which has been invited to cooperate in its realization.

Recruitment into the Brigade was open to Palestine and British Jews as well as to the refugees who had been deported to Mauritius in December 1940. Churchill subsequently revealed that the Brigade Group would participate not only in the European "struggle but in the occupation which will follow." The creation of the Jewish Brigade Group was indicative of the sentiment among those leading members of the British Government who were no longer thinking in terms of the unitary Palestine state envisaged by the White Paper, but were reverting to the idea of establishing an independent Jewish state in a partitioned Palestine. This was probably intended as a token deposit of the postwar intentions of the Churchill Coalition Cabinet.[7]

UNITED STATES INVOLVEMENT

While Britain was trying to establish a balance between its Palestine policy and its over-all Arab policy, the United States was becoming directly involved in the Palestine issue. Both the Jewish Agency and the British Government were anxious to have the United States take an active hand in Palestine affairs. From 1943 on the Zionist propaganda campaign concentrated on winning the approval of American public opinion and Congress, and, through both, of the government, for the resettlement of European Jews in Palestine, the abrogation of the White Paper, and a pro-Zionist solution of the Palestine problem along lines of the Biltmore Program. As for the British Government, former Prime Minister Churchill declared in August 1946, "I had always intended to put it to our friends in America, from the very beginning of the postwar discussions, that . . . they should come in and help us in this Zionist problem, about which they feel so strongly, and as I think rightly, on even terms, share and share alike. . . . As I say, almost any solution in which the United States will join us could be made to work." [8]

Coordination of the Anglo-American war effort had resulted by 1943 in ever closer collaboration between the two powers on the multi-faceted Palestine issue. The point of greatest pressure was the problem of Jewish immigration. The first authentic news of the scale of Nazi atrocities against Jews reached the outside world in the autumn of 1942. This, in turn, added fresh cogency to the ceaseless Zionist appeals, backed by an expanding section of Anglo-American public opinion, to remove to Palestine as many Jews as possible from Nazi-dominated countries. But what had started out a decade earlier as essentially a Jewish refugee problem had now become a general one, affecting many millions of Europeans in all Axis-occupied countries. Except for a small percentage who continued to flow into neutral or Allied territory, they were exposed to labor conscription, deportation, and—particularly if they were Jews—probable mass slaughter. The overwhelming majority of European refugees could be and sought to be repatriated as soon as conditions permitted. However, a relatively small number, which was likely to reach several hundred thousand at the close of the war, could not, or did not wish to, return to their countries of origin. Into this class fell thousands of Jews, some of whom were managing to elude the Nazi dragnet of extermination.

The permanently displaced Jews had, in the main, become Zionists. The national home, they were persuaded, was the only place where they could find personal and group security, where there existed a community which would welcome and rehabilitate them. Some stateless Jews were able by themselves and a larger number was being assisted by the Jewish Agency's underground in Europe to slip through the Axis frontiers. But, as the Zionists and their champions pointed out, those who remained in Europe faced almost certain death. On the other hand, the question of what to do with these nonrepatriable Jews was a political as well as a humanitarian and moral question. If they were allowed to go to Palestine immediately, the White Paper's numerical quota might be exhausted before the war's end. The mandatory would then be forced to attempt a final settlement before the expected peace conference.

Accordingly, the British Government elected to view the stateless Jews as a part of the over-all refugee problem. To this view the United States adhered in principle. The two governments sponsored the Bermuda refugee conference in April 1943, which revived the Intergovernmental Committee on Refugees (ICR), and were chiefly instrumental in creating the United Nations Relief and Rehabilitation Administration (UNRRA) in November 1943. The ICR concerned itself primarily with locating new areas of settlement for the non-repatriable refugees. While the ICR was endeavoring to secure immigration visas for its charges, they were as a rule maintained by UNRRA, whose primary function, however, was the care of temporarily displaced persons. Consequently, the stateless Jews came under the jurisdiction of the ICR. But since the facilitation of Jewish immigration into Palestine was excluded from the scope of the ICR, which regarded "its activities [as] . . . purely humanitarian" and therefore avoided "being drawn into political issues or controversies," the Zionist-sponsored appeals in the United States continued unabated.[9]

In response to these pressures, President Roosevelt created in January 1944 the War Refugee Board (WRB), composed of the secretaries of State, Treasury, and War, "to take all measures . . . to rescue the victims of enemy oppression . . . in imminent danger of death, and otherwise to afford such victims all possible relief and assistance consistent with the successful prosecution of the war." The Board in February sent a representative to Turkey, where he was attached to the United States Embassy at Ankara. In conjunction with the Jewish Agency, which directed an underground railway in eastern Europe and the Balkans, the WRB was able to rescue several thousand Jewish refugees from Nazi-occupied countries and transport them safely to Palestine. But after the Colonial Office, as of October 1, 1944, revoked its order guaranteeing Palestine entry permits for all European Jews reaching Turkey, the WRB ceased its activities in that country.[10]

As in the case of Britain, the United States, in looking at the Palestine problem, had to take larger strategic and political factors, both Near Eastern and global, into consideration. A new American policy toward the Near East was in the process of evolvement, and circumstantial evidence already underlined the fact that it would break sharply with the past. In the period between the two world wars the United States protected the rights of American nationals in the region as a whole but remained steadfastly aloof from any entanglement in local internal affairs. In the area under British and French political administration, however, American private interests were consolidated. American missionary establishments studded most of the Near East. The philanthropic and individual investments of American Jews in the Zionist enterprise were greater than those of any other Jewish community in the world. In 1928 American-owned oil companies gained 23.75 per cent of the shares of the Iraq Petroleum Company, as a result of the State Department's fight against exclusive economic concessions in the mandated territories in the Near East. Their holdings expanded rapidly thereafter. American-owned corporations acquired half ownership of the Kuwayt field (1934) and exclusive concessions to the fields in Bahrayn (1929 and 1940) and Saudi Arabia (1933 and 1939).

After America's entry into World War II the United States suddenly found itself deeply enmeshed in the Near East. The American Government assumed in 1942 joint responsibility with Britain for the Middle East Supply Center. So extensive had United States economic activities become that in the following year a director of American economic operations for the area was sent to Cairo. Meanwhile, a Persian Gulf Command had been established to supervise the transport of lend-lease supplies to Russia. Although American combat troops were not stationed in the Near East, millions were sunk into American air and military repair bases, military hospitals and supply depots. The Office of War Information had in each of the countries local branches which worked with the more elaborate setup of the British Ministry of Information to counteract enemy propaganda.[11]

It was likely that the Near East would remain an American strategic outpost in the postwar period. This was accented by the Roosevelt Administration's abrupt reversal of position on American oil operations in that region. The California Arabian Standard Oil Company, later known as the Arabian American Oil Company or Aramco, proposed in 1941 that the United States Government grant the King of Saudi Arabia $30,000,000 over a period of five years. The company agreed to repay the government through the sale of oil products "virtually at cost." This offer was rejected, allegedly on the ground "that Arabia was in the British sphere of influence and that no advances could be made directly to King Ibn Saud." Yet less than three years later Secretary of Interior Ickes announced that the government's Petroleum Reserves Corporation had agreed in principle to construct a trunk pipe-line system to transport crude petroleum from the Arabian Peninsula to the Mediterranean at an estimated cost of $130,000,000 to $165,000,000. This unprecedented agreement had been authorized, declared Ickes, to help offset dwindling American oil reserves, "estimated to be adequate for this nation's needs for only a relatively few years." The oil companies were to set aside for the government a reserve of one billion barrels to help "assure an adequate supply of petroleum for the military and naval needs of the United States in view of the obligations which this country must assume for the maintenance of collective security in the postwar world." Even though the project was soon dropped, the degree of United States interest in Near East oil had been demonstrated forcefully.[12]

As long as the United States Government believed Arabian oil to be vital to the national defense, it would have to protect and assure access to American-owned concessions in Saudi Arabia. This implied that the United States would have to bear responsibility for keeping Mediterranean shipping lanes open and for maintaining the security of fields, refineries, and any pipe line that might be constructed by the companies themselves. Washington had already become concerned about the stability of the Saudi Arabian Government. Thus ibn Sa'ud received from the United States between 1943 and 1947 some $18,000,000 in direct, non-recoverable lend-lease besides a sizable share, in indirect lend-lease, of the $51,000,000 British grant to the king and "$27,000,000 in silver bullion, export-import bank loans and surplus property credits." Once entangled in Saudi Arabia and in the rivalry for control of the Near East's petroleum deposits, the United States was also directly involved in the regional as well as international politics of the Arab East. The United States, moreover, had other strategic interests besides oil in the area. Its central location astride world communications by land, sea, and especially air had made the Arab East almost as essential to America as to Britain. The United States was bound after the war to seek air and landing rights for its commercial planes, because no global, all-weather air route could omit the region. Furthermore, since the United States could no longer dodge its share of responsibility for the establishment of world peace and security, it would henceforth be in the American national interest to help maintain stability in the Arab East. This entailed taking decisions on political issues affecting not only other foreign powers but the individual countries in the area.[13]

These broader strategic, economic, and political considerations had to be taken into account in the development of any new American policy toward Palestine. In reply to a letter from King ibn Sa'ud pleading the case for an Arab Palestine, President Roosevelt assured the Arabian monarch in a confidential note that the situation in Palestine would not be modified "without full consultation with both Arabs and Jews." In response to pressures from American Zionist leaders the President permitted it to be stated in his name in March 1944 that the United States had not assented to the 1939 White Paper and that "when future decisions are reached full justice will be done to those who seek a Jewish national home." The American Consul General at Jerusalem, Lowell C. Pinkerton, was authorized by the Department of State in June 1944 to explain, in answer to a memorandum sent to President Roosevelt by the Palestine Arab (Husayni) Party, the official American attitude, as follows: [14]

> . . . Palestine is under a British Mandate and . . . the British Government is responsible for its administration. But the attitude of the United States Government is that no change should occur in the basic situation until the appropriate time (that is, until the end of the war). At that time the governments responsible for re-establishing peace and maintaining law and justice in the world will seek to reach complete agreement on all questions affecting Palestine in consultation with Arabs and Jews.

Roosevelt's confidential assurances to ibn Sa'ud of May 1943 had not yet been disclosed officially. Still, it was manifest by June 1944 that the Roosevelt Administration, while not framing a comprehensive, positive policy toward Palestine, had nevertheless accepted limited liability for finding a solution to the Arab-British-Zionist impasse. Former Secretary of State James F. Byrnes later reported that, in the stopover at Malta en route to Yalta in 1945,[15]

> The President . . . confide[d] to Churchill his plans to visit King Ibn Saud on his return trip to discuss the Palestine question. He wanted to bring about peace between the Arabs and the Jews. Churchill wished him good luck but didn't seem very hopeful that the President would meet with success. He didn't.

While the United States was dramatically entering Near East politics, France was ungracefully departing. At the time of the occupation of the Levant States in the summer of 1941, the Free French and the British promised Syria and Lebanon independence. The Free French subsequently insisted on preferential treaties, analogous to those which Britain had contracted with Iraq and Egypt. But the newly elected Arab governments refused to enter into such agreements. French efforts to achieve the preferential settlement by force in November 1943—and again in May-June 1945—brought other Big Powers around to the side of the local governments. Russia, the United States, and China recognized the unconditional independence of Syria and Lebanon in 1944, and in the following spring the two states were invited to participate in the San Francisco Conference on International Organization. In this seesaw French-Levant struggle the British alternated between supporting French demands for special treaty rights and Arab protests against French strong-arm tactics.[16]

Now that the influence of France was declining in the eastern Mediterranean, its bearing on the course of the Arab-Zionist controversy would henceforth be merely peripheral. Of potentially far greater importance was the Soviet attitude. Almost half of the Jewish survivors in Europe to the west of Russia's 1939 boundaries would be located in eastern Europe, an area that was certain to fall into the Soviet zone of influence. Many other Jews had been transferred to the Soviet hinterland after the Russian occupation of eastern Poland and the Baltic countries. Would the Soviet Union permit these Jews to emigrate to Palestine? Would the official ban on Zionism be extended to Russia's western neighbors?

From 1943 on the Soviet Union began to devote increasing attention to the Near East. The focal points of Soviet interest were Turkey and Iran, which, adjoining the southwest frontier of the U.S.S.R., formed part of the Soviet "security zone" and were of primary significance for Russian strategy and communications. The Soviet Union regarded control of the Turkish Straits as vital to prevent enemy ships from entering the Black Sea in time of war and to provide the U.S.S.R. with free access to the Mediterranean in time of peace. Russia had not been signatory to the Lausanne Convention of 1923, which gave Britain, France, and Italy responsibility for the security of the Straits. Although the Soviet Union had signed the Montreux Convention of 1936, it was nevertheless also dissatisfied with this agreement, which placed the Straits' security ultimately under Turkish jurisdiction and granted remote Japan the same rights as the U.S.S.R. As for Iran, it not only abutted on oil-rich (Russian) Azerbaijan, but itself contained extensive petroleum deposits. The British-controlled Anglo-Iranian Oil Company was exploiting a concession in the southern Persian Gulf region. The Russians, on their side, had been prospecting for oil in the Mazanderan district of north-central Iran on the eve of the war and, after the Anglo-Soviet occupation of Iran in 1941, began experimental drilling in that region. In 1943 American and British oil companies sought concessions in Iran, and toward the end of 1944 the Russians also began to press for concessions both in the Mazanderan district and in neighboring Kavir. After some hesitation the Iranian Government rejected all applications. Consequently, the Soviet policy toward the predominantly Arab zone to the south of Turkey and Iran was likely to be dictated in large measure by the extent to which the U.S.S.R. would be able to realize its unfulfilled objectives in these two Muslim, non-Arab countries, and ultimately by its postwar relations with Britain and the United States.[17]

Czarist Russia had been one of the dominant European powers in Turkey's Asiatic Arab provinces in the nineteenth century. As patron and protector of the Greek Orthodox Church after 1774, Russia won the allegiance of an important segment of the Christian Arab population. Russian religious influence in the Turkish provincial districts which later became Palestine, where a majority of the Christian Arabs were of the Greek Orthodox denomination, grew especially strong after the Crimean War (1854-56), when a permanent consulate was established at Jerusalem. The Greek Orthodox Patriarchate at Jerusalem was re-established in 1867. The Czarist Government, with the cooperation of the Russian Orthodox Society of Palestine and the Russian Ecclesiastical Mission, subsidized schools, churches, and hospices in the Holy Land. In 1900 the Imperial regime maintained, besides the Consulate General at Jerusalem, vice consulates at Jaffa and Acre and consular agencies at Nazareth and Haifa.

After the Soviet Revolution, the U.S.S.R. did not establish permanent diplomatic or consular relations with any of the new Arab governments or the Anglo-French mandated territories. All ties with the Orthodox Church outside of Russia were severed. The Russian religious properties in Palestine were taken into the mandatory's custody in 1924, and the proceeds were earmarked for the upkeep of the few hundred White Russians stranded in the country at the close of World War I. Though for a brief period in 1923-24 the Zionist Organization was permitted to communicate with Jews in the Soviet Union, Moscow's attitude toward Zionism soon chilled. Thereafter the use of Hebrew was forbidden in Russia, and Zionism outlawed as a petty bourgeois movement leading the Jews astray from their own economic interests. The only Soviet contacts with the Arab and mandated countries in these years were the small communist cells in Palestine, Syria, and Lebanon, which took their cue from the Comintern and agitated against "Anglo-French imperialism." [18]

The U.S.S.R. did not attempt to restore its bonds with the Arab East until World War II. A Soviet legation was opened in Egypt in 1943. This was followed by the establishment of diplomatic relations with the Levant States and Iraq in 1944. With the wartime softening of the official Soviet attitude toward religion, the various religious groups in Russia were permitted to resume communion with those in the Near East. Russian Orthodox clerical leaders tried to re-establish ties with the patriarchs of Constantinople, Antioch, Jerusalem, and Alexandria as early as 1942, even prior to the formal reorganization of the Russian Orthodox Church in September 1943. By February 1945 the patriarchs of Antioch and Alexandria and delegates of the patriarchs of Constantinople and Jerusalem participated in the election and investiture at the Russian capital of the Patriarch of Moscow and All Russia. Four months later the new head of the Russian Church paid a return pilgrimage to Damascus, Bayrut, Jerusalem, and Cairo. Meanwhile the Russian press and radio gave increasing publicity to the activities of the 25 million Soviet Muslims, and in November 1944 they were allowed again to make the pilgrimage to Mecca, after a twenty-year interruption.[19]

The Russian Embassy at London was reported to have approached the mandatory in 1944 regarding the return to the U.S.S.R. and the Russian Church of the extensive religious properties in Palestine. This question, however, was still unsettled at the close of the war. Soviet affairs in Palestine were transferred in 1944 from the Consulate General at Ankara, Turkey, to the recently created Legation in Egypt. Thus Russian diplomatic officials from Cairo in the spring of 1944 arrived to revise the 1939 register of some 200 Soviet subjects and invited immigrants from the Baltic countries to enter their names. While in Palestine these Soviet officials, a Muslim and a Jew, met with Arab and Zionist spokesmen. The Russian Minister to Egypt conferred with the Greek Orthodox Patriarch at Jerusalem a few weeks later. When the Russian Patriarch visited Jerusalem in June 1945 he granted audiences to religious and lay leaders of the Arab and Jewish communities.[20]

The Russians were thus promoting good will among all sections of the population in Palestine and the near-by Arab countries. But the Soviet Government until the end of the war maintained a vigilant silence on almost all political problems in the region. Moscow's only determined stand was the unconditional recognition of Syrian and Lebanese independence in July 1944. No hint was ever publicly given regarding the official Russian attitude toward the Palestine issue. The mystery of Soviet intentions, therefore, aroused both hopes and fears among the two sections of the Palestine population and contributed to the general uneasiness which underlay Arab and Zionist politics in this period.

CHAPTER 14

Arab Political Revival

IN THE EARLY months of 1943 even those Palestine Arabs who had previously advocated collaboration with the Axis gradually became convinced that the United Nations would win the war. The Arab nationalists feared Allied intentions concerning Palestine. They were pleased with Britain's espousal of the Arab Unity movement and with the Palestine Government's firm enforcement of the restrictions on Jewish immigration and land purchases. Nevertheless the local nationalists were not represented at Cairo in the preliminary Arab Unity discussions (July 1943–February 1944). They also saw that the Zionists were pressing their postwar plans in London and Washington. Consequently, the Arab nationalists suspected that under pressure from the United States, which they were convinced was pro-Zionist, and from those circles in Britain friendly to the Jewish National Home, the mandatory might revert to a pro-Jewish policy.

The 1939 White Paper, it will be recalled, had been accepted formally only by the National Defense Party, a handful of other opposition elements in Palestine, and the Prime Minister of Transjordan. Still Arab nationalists generally had come by 1943 to regard its provisions as irrevocable British pledges. Formal endorsement was unnecessary, as one Arab newspaper frankly put it, because the mandatory had undertaken to implement the policy with or without Arab and Jewish consent.[1] But as time wore on the local nationalists became increasingly suspicious over signs of a British retreat.

In order to take part in the Arab Unity talks and to fight for their political rights and aspirations, the Palestine Arab nationalists above all needed unified leadership. Now that the government restraints were being withdrawn, the struggle for the establishment of a new central body on the pattern of the old Higher Committee became their primary internal political objective in the second half of the war. The first to turn to these endeavors were the leaders of the former Istiqlal Party—Ahmad Hilmi Pasha 'Abd-al-Baqi, 'Awni Bey 'Abd-al-Hadi, and Rashid al-Hajj Ibrahim. They had been the first Arab nationalists locally to urge collaboration with Italy and Germany a decade earlier. Before the Istiqlal Party ceased functioning as a separate faction in 1936, it maintained loose ties with other Pan-Arab groups of the same name in the Levant States and Iraq. Encouraged by the mood of their erstwhile confreres abroad, who were now openly pro-British, and by the pro-Arab mandatory policy in Palestine, the local Istiqlal leaders also became staunch advocates of Arab-British amity. They tried what the National Defense (Nashashibi) Party had failed to achieve between 1938 and 1941: to unite the local national movement under their leadership with government help. They appealed to the community on the strength of their prewar reputations, without formally reconstituting the Istiqlal Party, although whenever necessary they also spoke in the name of the party.[2]

The odds in favor of the Istiqlal spokesmen in 1943 seemed considerable, for the Nashashibi faction showed no signs of reasserting itself, while the Husaynis' wartime record appeared to preclude any early overt reorganization of their party. Besides, the Arab National Bank, on whose board Ahmad Hilmi Pasha sat as chairman and 'Abd-al-Hadi and al-Hajj Ibrahim as members, acquired an interest in *Filastin*, the oldest Arabic newspaper in the country, thus providing the Istiqlal politicians with a mouthpiece. Yet they faced obstacles in the political inertia of the nationalist rank and file after three years of inactivity, the jealousies of earlier political rivals, and the absence of political groups to unite the nationalists for action. The Istiqlal spokesmen appealed to the leaders of the other defunct parties to join them in forming an executive political body which could speak for the Palestine Arabs. Al-Hajj Ibrahim, who had been interned in the Seychelles Islands in 1937–38 and was now manager of the Arab National Bank at Haifa and president of the Arab chamber of commerce in that city, convened a meeting of a group of professional and business men at the end of January 1943. They decided to organize, with government approval, a community-wide conference for the purpose of setting up the projected political directorate. Nationalist leaders in Jaffa, Jerusalem, and Nablus were invited to participate. But the spring and summer passed without visible progress.[3]

The first real opportunity came in November 1943, when the Arab chambers of commerce held their fifteenth national conference at Jerusalem. The delegates, to be sure, belonged to the commercial class. But many in the past had been affiliated with the political parties and now had substantial war profits which might be tapped for the nationalist cause.

Furthermore, the chambers enjoyed government recognition and existed in eight scattered towns of large Arab population. Among the fifty-three delegates and four observers were the three Istiqlal leaders. A resolution was adopted to call a special conference at Jerusalem the following week for organizing a general congress which, in turn, would elect an executive to represent the Palestine Arabs at the Cairo Arab Unity talks. Among those invited were the members of the national executive of the Arab chambers of commerce, those members of the former Higher Committee then in the country, the delegates to the 1939 London conferences, the Arab mayors, and the publishers of the Arabic newspapers.[4]

On the very day the chambers of commerce met in Jerusalem, the French precipitated a crisis in Lebanon by arresting the country's president and cabinet. Committees for the defense of Lebanon sprang up throughout the Palestine Arab Community. Funds were raised and protests addressed to the major Allied Powers, the neighboring Arab states, and the High Commissioner. For the first time since the early months of the revolt in 1936–37 Arab nationalist sentiment in Palestine was united. Despite this stimulus, the second conference brought the Istiqlal politicians no closer to their goal. The presidents of the former National Defense and National Bloc parties made an appearance, as did thirteen Arab mayors. But neither the heads of the quiescent Reform and Youth Congress parties, nor any of the mayors known to be Husayni supporters attended.[5] The boycott of the conference by the Husaynis served to stress their resentment of the efforts by the Istiqlal politicians to establish themselves as nonpartisan nationalist leaders.

In August 1943 Ahmad Hilmi Pasha, as presiding director, had reorganized the Arab National Fund, which before 1936 had been used by al-Hajj Amin as one of the instruments for building up the reputation of a nationalist leader who had risen above party politics. The Istiqlal spokesmen seemed determined now to use the same instrument for the same end. Conditions for the success of the enterprise were more favorable in 1943 than in the early 1930's. Nationalist concern with the literal execution of the White Paper had roused great public interest in the land issue. Even the fallahin had money to spare, so that fund-raising was no longer confined to the towns. Moreover, the Arab National Bank furnished the Istiqlal leaders with means of access to all parts of the country. Around the fourteen branches of the bank in Palestine were created the initial local chapters of the National Fund, which by the summer of 1944 had spread to all the Arab towns and larger villages. The National Fund launched a publicity drive in the Arab press. Amounts collected in the villages were listed. The practice was instituted of denouncing alleged violations of the Land Transfer Regulations in the restricted and prohibited zones. So intense had the interest in the land question become and so considerable the popularity of the National Fund that in the absence of a substitute institution no national leader dared express his opposition openly. By June 1944 even the Husaynis publicly endorsed the National Fund.[6]

The Husaynis had played a stalling game throughout 1943. They prevented the Palestine Arab politicians from closing their ranks, rather than agree to any scheme for a coalition executive which the Husaynis did not control. The Husaynis doubtless found it more and more pointless to continue the pro-Axis propaganda. Yet as long as the Mufti was still propagating the Axis gospel, his aides in Palestine could not overtly become pro-Allied, for that would have constituted a betrayal of their supreme leader. Moreover, not only al-Hajj Amin but all the other dominant leaders of the party were out of the country, either in political detention, or in exile, or in Axis Europe. The policy of negation, however, began by early 1944 to undermine Husayni prestige. As it became obvious that the Mufti had attached himself to the losing side in the war, his star was temporarily waning. To check this development and to regain their position of dominance, the Husayni politicians in Palestine decided formally to re-establish the Palestine Arab Party. At a meeting in Jerusalem on April 28, 1944, the thirty-nine delegates from the larger towns of the community set themselves up as the party's central committee and formed the nuclei of local committees. An executive of twelve, with headquarters in Jerusalem, was named under the acting-presidency of Tawfiq Salih al-Husayni, Jamal's older brother.[7]

Tawfiq Salih was not an experienced politician, and his selection was intended to symbolize the fact that the post was being held open for Jamal. The real force behind the reactivated party was its secretary, Emile al-Ghuri, a Greek Orthodox Arab who had studied journalism in the United States in the early 1930's. Ghuri was later on the staff of the pro-Husayni English weekly, *Palestine and Transjordan*, and was sent to England, the Balkans, and America in 1936–39 on propaganda and fund-raising missions for the Higher Committee. Ghuri was perhaps the only Christian Arab to join the Mufti in Iraq after the outbreak of war. Like Tawfiq Salih, he was captured by the British in Iran in September 1941 and permitted early in the following year to go back to Palestine, where he was prohibited from openly pursuing a political career until 1944.[8]

The executive committee of the Palestine Arab Party immediately addressed itself to holding frequent meetings, issuing protests and statements, feeding party propaganda to the Arabic newspapers, and organizing local branches. Permanent offices were opened at Jerusalem in July, at Haifa and Jaffa in August, and Nablus in December. The party also enlisted rural backing by sponsoring rallies of village notables. Husayni operations were allegedly subsidized by the Arab Bank, the largest in the community. Though the party had as yet no newspaper of its own, *Al-Difa'*, which was now underwritten by the Arab Bank, served as the semi-official Husayni mouthpiece.

Whereas the Istiqlal leaders demanded the execution of the White Paper, the reactivated Husayni party left no doubt that its spokesmen remained maximalists. "The Arab people who own the country and constitute a majority of its inhabitants," ran an early manifesto signed by the acting-president,[9]

> have the right to declare the basic demands of the Arab national movement in Palestine:
> 1. Independence within Arab unity.
> 2. Establishment of an Arab government to administer the affairs of the entire country.
> 3. Dissolution of the Jewish National Home.

At a meeting in Jaffa a few weeks later Ghuri assured his listeners that "the party has resumed its activities within the scope of the National Pact," which called for the immediate and absolute prohibition of Jewish immigration and land acquisition and the immediate transformation of Palestine into a sovereign Arab state. Ghuri also disclosed that the party was keeping the Arab and Muslim worlds informed of developments in Palestine and would attempt to disseminate propaganda in England and America. In fact, the Husayni leaders had already sent a cable to a New York Arabic daily in May, declaring that [10]

> The Palestine Arab Party, representing the majority of the Arabs in Palestine . . . . calls upon all Arabs in America to combat Zionism which aims at destroying all Arab nationalism in Palestine and the surrounding countries. We request from the Arabs in America immediate help and support, continued exchange of views, and aid in the national movement.

The party was able to test its strength in September 1944, when the community received an invitation to send a delegation to the Arab Unity conference at Alexandria. The community was already exercised by the personal bickerings of the politicians. The Husaynis now seized the initiative in reopening the negotiations with the leaders of the other prewar factions to form an interparty executive. Although these efforts failed, a last-minute agreement was reached in naming Musa al-'Alami the sole Palestine observer at the Arab Unity conference. Meanwhile, the search for a formula of interfactional cooperation was abandoned until after V-E Day.[11]

The Husayni defeat resulted largely from the fact that the spokesmen of the Palestine Arab Party then in the country had not yet succeeded in establishing a reputation of leadership outside of their own faction. The party strategists themselves, in fact, claimed that they were merely deputizing for the absentee leaders, al-Hajj Amin and Jamal. This claim to the stewardship of the prestige and policies of the exiled leaders had enabled the party to stage a rapid comeback, so that by September 1944 it was once again the most powerful in the community. But the leadership of the national movement was still being determined on a personal basis. As a result, the demand of the Husayni deputies for a commanding voice as an indispensable condition to their joining any interfactional coalition was calculated only to harden the hostility of the leaders of the other factions, all of whom had been in the forefront of the national movement in the prewar period and some since the 1920's.

In the last few months of the war, the Palestine Arab Party concentrated on tightening up its internal organization, sending memoranda to the High Commissioner and the British Minister Resident in the Middle East, and exploiting every opportunity to arouse popular enthusiasm. Thus, the Palestine Government allowed the Arab Community in 1944 to hold its first wartime protest meetings on November 2, the anniversary of the Balfour Declaration. Arab national groups in all of the towns staged demonstrations, but the most grandiose was that sponsored by the Palestine Arab Party at Jerusalem. The meeting-hall was unable to accommodate all the participants, and crowds gathered outside the building. Amin al-Tamimi, who had died in Southern Rhodesia less than a fortnight earlier, was martyrized. All past and present national grievances and future demands were aired. The speakers publicly demanded the return of the exiled Husayni leaders.[12]

The Palestine Arab Party was to repeat this demand with increasing frequency, particularly after V-E Day. At the same time, as it became clear that the Axis was doomed to defeat, the Mufti took steps to hasten his eventual reinstatement in Palestine. Four parachutists, two of them Palestine Templars, were dropped in October 1944 by a Nazi plane in the vicinity of Jericho. Three were captured by the military authorities. But the fourth, Hasan Salamah, was never apprehended. He had been one of the rebel commanders in the Lydda district during the revolt of 1936–39 and subsequently followed al-Hajj Amin to Iraq and Axis Europe, where he was alleged to have attained the rank of major in the German Army. Salamah, it may safely be presumed, was soon in touch with the Palestine Arab Party leaders. A second parachutist expedition, composed of four Arabs, descended late in November 1944 in the desert region west of Mosul, Iraq. An interrogation by British counterintelligence officers at Baghdad of the two Iraqi parachutists who were arrested revealed that the leader of the party, who remained at large, "enjoyed the confidence" of al-Hajj Amin. He was reported to have been fully briefed by the Mufti and to have been furnished with more than $45,000 in gold.[13]

By the war's close there were only two sets of political leaders who exercised any real influence in the Palestine Arab Community—those allied with the Palestine Arab Party and those allied with the Arab National Fund, headed by the spokesmen of the old Istiqlal Party. Neither side proved capable of imposing its will on the rest of the community. Under these circumstances each courted the backing of the other prewar political leaders and groups. These fell into two classes. 'Abd-al-Latif Salah and Ya'qub al-Ghusayn, in the Husayni manner, reconstituted their respective factions, the National Bloc Party in February 1944 and the Youth Congress Party in April 1945. But the spokesmen of the National Defense (Raghib Bey al-Nashashibi) and Reform (Dr. Husayn Fakhri al-Khalidi) parties, like the Istiqlal leaders, without reorganizing their factions, continued to issue statements and negotiate with other politicians in the name of their defunct groups. The leaders of the six parties took to meeting informally at one another's homes and offices in April 1945 at irregular intervals to discuss local political affairs. This was as close as they came in wartime to forming a new executive for the national movement.[14]

POLITICAL, ECONOMIC, AND SOCIAL CHANGES

The political practices of the old-guard leaders were beginning to be challenged in the later war years by that fragment of the new generation which had received a Western education. The young intellectuals —mostly from the upper economic stratum of Arab society—were convinced that the existing semifeudal, patriarchal parties were retarding Arab political development in Palestine. They were anxious to formulate nationalist programs with forward-looking political, economic, and social content. A few of these progressives were employed by the Arabic newspapers or the radio stations at Jerusalem and Jaffa and were afforded a limited scope for spreading their views. The majority, however, lacked leadership and, having failed to organize into separate parties, were unable to influence domestic politics.[15] The only ones to affiliate with a specific political group were those who took over the Arab communist leadership.

When the Palestine communists were accorded in 1942 a semilegal status for the first time in their history, a number of communist groups appeared in some of the larger towns, such as the Arab Anti-Fascist League at Jerusalem and the Rays of Hope Society at Haifa. Immediately following the dissolution of the Comintern in May 1943, most of the Arab communists broke away from the Arab-Jewish Palestine Communist Party. Before the year was out the Rays of Hope Society reorganized itself into a political party, called the League of National Liberation in Palestine. The League was the first communist party in the country to enjoy full government recognition. It absorbed all the Arab communist splinters and became the political arm of the Federation of Arab Trade Unions and Labor Societies at Haifa. In May 1944 this labor federation was granted government permission to publish its own weekly, *Al-Ittihad*. This first Palestine Arab trade-union journal also served as the organ of the League of National Liberation. But at first communist propaganda largely took the form of fostering friendly relations with the Soviet Union and was interspersed cautiously among articles calling for shorter working hours and minimum wage laws for Arab workers, and promoting the organization of Arab labor. The editorials also pleaded for elected municipal councils, compulsory education, and an overhauling of the Arab rural school system—since "instruction in farming techniques . . . . is more useful than studying the geography of oceans, while digging the soil is better exercise than running a one-hundred-yard dash." The weekly expressed an active interest in politics, demanding labor representation on any coalition executive which the old-guard leaders might form.[16]

The League of National Liberation established affiliates at Jaffa, Jerusalem, and Nazareth, which formed expanding cells within the local branches of the conservative Palestine Arab Workers Society. In the community at large, and especially in the national movement, the League acquired no general recognition. Still the Arab communists could probably count on the backing of some 4,000 to 5,000 workers by the beginning of 1945 and were gradually extending their power in Arab labor ranks. Indeed, the Arab trade-union movement in general expanded steadily and by V-E Day claimed to embrace approximately 20,000 workers, an increase of more than 70 per cent in less than three years. The Palestine Arab Workers Society did not have its own journal and was in consequence less articulate politically than its smaller rival. Nevertheless, the conservative labor wing also began to assert itself in nationalist politics and sent two representatives to the World Trade Union Conference at London in February 1945 to seek endorsement of the Palestine Arab cause. Despite the appreciable gains, the Arab labor movement still reached even indirectly no more than one-fifth of the total urban and semiurban labor force.[17]

Meanwhile, the Arabs, like the Jews, continued to profit from the vast British military expenditures, which averaged over $100,000,000 a year between 1943 and 1945. As a result of these unprecedented disbursements and the lack of finished goods and capital equipment, the Palestine Arabs accumulated by the close of the war more than $157,000,000 in foreign assets, almost exclusively in sterling balances. Indicative of the scale of the war-born prosperity was the phenomenal growth of deposits in the two Arab banks, from a total of $5,300,000 in December 1942 to $27,-884,000 in October 1945. Nor could this increase be attributed solely or even largely to the inflationary conditions, since the cost-of-living index rose only from 211 (prewar base = 100) in December 1942 to 259 three years later. The Arab economy remained predominantly agricultural. But Arab business men in the last year of the war became absorbed with schemes for expanding and modernizing existing firms and with the search for industrial and financial outlets for their savings. Among the new corporations registered were an airline and an insurance company, each with a capitalization of $400,000. A Palestine Arab trade delegation to Britain in April 1945 was commissioned to purchase modern machinery for a cement factory as well as a spinning and weaving establishment, the latter with a capital of $1,000,000. These economic ventures were widely applauded in the Arab press because, as *Al-Difa'* observed, "we ought to plan our future on sound and strong economic principles, for that will assist us in realizing our political aspirations." [18]

The enlarged capital reserves, if placed at the disposal of the national movement, seemed likely to make any future Palestine Arab struggle against Britain and Zionism more formidable than in the prewar years. The Arabs, moreover, who were the principal middlemen in the lucrative but illegal arms traffic, had already acquired large stores of military equipment during the war.[19] The arms were purchased on an individual basis, for there were no Arab militarized societies in Palestine at that time. But Arab military organization in the past had been largely informal and decentralized. With the prewar experience as their guide, both the British and the Zionists feared that in any emergency the Arabs might be whipped into nationalist unity.

Perhaps the most notable social achievement of the Palestine Arabs in wartime was in the realm of education. The Muslims, especially, were inclined to rely increasingly on the government school system. These schools were constructed by the municipality or village and maintained by the government. The number of government-operated schools, which in the academic year 1942–43 was 403, or only one more than existed five years earlier, jumped to 458 in 1943–44 and to 478 in 1944–45. This sudden expansion reflected primarily a new spirit in the villages. Between 1943–45 Arab peasants voluntarily contributed more than $1,500,000 for educational purposes, as compared with $187,200 for the years 1941–42. Typical was the campaign in the summer of 1944 in the village of Silwan, a Jerusalem suburb, where on the first day close to $9,000 was collected. Subsequently, the women were called upon to donate their jewelry, which netted more than $2,500. Within the space of a few weeks the village reportedly raised some $30,000 for the erection of a new school. Meanwhile, the Arab municipalities, with government encouragement, were sponsoring infant welfare projects. Moreover, in 1944 Ramallah and Jaffa drew up plans for the construction of their own hospitals; the doctors formed a Palestine Arab Medical Association; the Arab dentists held their first countrywide conference; the first Arab woman doctor in the country completed her studies in London; and at a general conference of Arab lawyers in Damascus, attended by representatives from all the neighboring countries, an Egyptian delegate reported, "When I looked around I noticed only one woman lawyer—a Palestinian." [20]

ARAB UNITY AND THE ARAB LEAGUE

The economic and social progress bolstered the confidence of the Palestine Arabs. But in the absence of any political leadership at home they tended to look to the near-by countries for guidance and support. The Arab states for their part resumed their anti-Zionist campaign in the later war years. At first the prime ministers and rulers without reference to one another issued statements to the press or sent protests through diplomatic channels to London and Washington. However, after the start of 1944 their efforts were coordinated more closely. The reassertion of Arab antipathy to Zionism was tightly interlocked with the Arab Unity movement. The prospects for forming a regional bloc in the Arab East brightened after 1943. By then an ultimate United Nations victory was no longer doubted; all Arab governments had become pro-Allied; and Foreign Secretary Eden had reaffirmed Britain's endorsement of Arab Unity. So far only Iraq, among the Arab countries, had declared war on the Axis and joined the United Nations in January 1943. But all Arab states were anxious to prepare for the peace conference so as to safeguard Arab rights more adequately than they felt had been done at Versailles. Among the problems of major importance were the attainment of complete independence for Lebanon and Syria, the elimination of British controls from Egypt and Iraq, and a settlement of the Palestine issue which would fully protect Arab interests in that country.

The concerted Arab stand at the time of the Lebanese crisis in November 1943 had contributed in part to the subsequent French retreat. Encouraged by this diplomatic victory, the Arab states again banded together in protest against the proposed passage of identical, pro-Zionist resolutions by both houses of the United States Congress in February-March 1944. The success of this démarche again underlined the feasibility of united action. The realization by the Arab governments that they could achieve through collective endeavor political ends unattainable by any one state was perhaps the most persuasive argument for reaching some sort of permanent regional agreement. Meanwhile, Mustafa al-Nahhas Pasha, who had been forcibly installed by the British as Prime Minister of Egypt in February 1942, took the lead between July 1943 and February 1944 in sounding out the views of the governments of Iraq, Transjordan, Saudi Arabia, Syria, Lebanon, and Yemen. Following these exploratory discussions, a general conference on Arab Unity, attended by delegates of the seven Arab states, met at Alexandria from September 25 to October 7, 1944.

To this conference Musa al-'Alami was sent on behalf of the Palestine Arabs as an observer, a status which did not entitle him to sit at the conference table. But at the third meeting 'Alami was admitted as a full-fledged delegate, the only one to represent a community and not a government. The conference, constituting itself a Preliminary Committee, drew up a memorandum called the "Alexandria Protocol," which announced that its signatories had agreed to form "a League . . . of the independent Arab states" in order, among other objectives, "to coordinate their political plans so as to insure their cooperation and protect their independence and sovereignty against every aggression by suitable means." Included in the Protocol was a special resolution on Palestine. "The Committee is of the opinion," ran the resolution,[21]

> that Palestine constitutes an important part of the Arab world and that the rights of the Arabs [in Palestine] cannot be touched without prejudice to peace and stability in the Arab world.
> The Committee is also of the opinion that the promises binding the British Government and providing for the stoppage of Jewish immigration, the preservation of Arab lands, and the achievement of independence for Palestine are permanent Arab rights whose prompt execution would constitute a step toward the desired goal and toward the stabilization of peace and security.
> The Committee declares its support of the cause of the Palestine Arabs and its willingness to work for the achievement of their legitimate aims and the protection of their just rights.
> The Committee also declares that it is second to none in regretting the woes which have been inflicted upon the Jews of Europe by European dictatorial states. But the question of these Jews should not be confused with Zionism, for there can be no greater injustice and aggression than solving the problem of the Jews of Europe by another injustice, that is, by inflicting injustice on the Palestine Arabs of various religions and denominations.

Part B of the resolution instructed the subcommittee on financial and economic affairs to formulate a plan for the participation of the Arab governments and peoples in the Arab National Fund to safeguard Arab-owned lands in Palestine. Moreover, the Alexandria conference, although it was not announced at the time, established a subcommittee on propaganda which was directed to draw up a scheme for information bureaus in Britain and the United States. These bureaus were to be charged with explaining the problems of the Arab states and in particular with combating Zionist propaganda. Musa al-'Alami was assigned to these two subcommittees. The hope was widespread in the Palestine Arab Community, if the local press reflected public opinion in the early months of 1945, that 'Alami would take over the leadership of the national movement. Forty-eight-year-old 'Alami belonged to one of the most respected Muslim families in the country and was related by marriage to the powerful Jabiri family in Syria and to the then Lebanese Premier, Riyad al-Sulh. 'Alami's English education and service with the government had won him many friends among the higher echelon of British officials. He was acceptable to all the party leaders, despite his past record of collaboration with the Husaynis. Ever since he was allowed to return to Palestine early in 1942 he had studiously avoided domestic partisan politics. He therefore could not be accused of trying to further the interests of any one party. 'Alami, however, resisted the pressure of public opinion and preoccupied himself with the land and propaganda plans of the projected Arab League. This proved to be a roving mission, carrying him back and forth between the capitals of the Arab states. Well acquainted with Western methods of organization, he was anxious to apply them to these schemes, so as to strengthen the Arabs in their political struggle against Zionism.[22]

Meanwhile, the Arab rulers were afforded an early opportunity of presenting their views on Palestine directly to the heads of the American and British governments. Kings Faruq of Egypt and ibn Sa'ud of Arabia met separately in mid-February 1945 with President Roosevelt and Prime Minister Churchill; President Shukri al-Quwwatli of Syria also participated in the Egyptian monarch's conversations with Churchill.[23] Of more lasting significance was the fact that between February 24 and the March 1, 1945 deadline, Egypt, Syria, Lebanon, and Saudi Arabia declared war on the Axis, raising the number of Arab states members of the United Nations to five. The Palestine Arabs were now assured of a hearing at the peace settlement. And the signing of the Pact of the League of Arab States in Cairo on March 22, 1945, guaranteed united action on Palestine not only by these five governments but by Yemen and Transjordan as well.

The Council of the Arab League, on which all of the member states were represented, was required to meet in ordinary session at least twice a year in March and October. Extraordinary sessions could be convened "upon the request of two member states . . . whenever the need arises." A permanent secretariat-general was set up with headquarters at Cairo, and an Egyptian, 'Abd-al-Rahman Bey 'Azzam, was appointed secretary-general. The Pact also contained a special annex on Palestine, which read: [24]

> Since the termination of the last great war the rule of the Ottoman Empire over the Arab countries, among them Palestine, which had become detached from that Empire, has come to an end. She has come to be independent in herself, not subordinate to any other state.
>
> The Treaty of Lausanne proclaimed that her future was to be settled by the parties concerned.
>
> However, even though she was as yet unable to control her own affairs, the Covenant of the League (of Nations) in 1919 made provision for a régime based upon recognition of her independence.

Her international existence and independence in the legal sense cannot, therefore, be questioned, any more than could the independence of the other Arab countries.

Although the outward manifestations of this independence have remained obscured for reasons beyond her control, this should not be allowed to interfere with her participation in the work of the Council of the League.

The States signatory to the Pact of the Arab League are therefore of the opinion that, considering the special circumstances of Palestine, and until that country can effectively exercise its independence, the Council of the League should take charge of the selection of an Arab representative from Palestine to take part in its work.

Hence formal provision was made for Palestine Arab participation in the Arab League Council, and Musa al-'Alami was nominated the community's representative. Owing to the continued factional deadlock, the initiative in Palestine Arab politics had thus passed in the later war years to the heads of the Arab states. Major political decisions on the organization of Arab resistance to Zionism were thereafter taken not at Jerusalem but at Cairo. The Palestine Arab cause was thereby strengthened immeasurably, for the Arab governments could bring to bear the full weight of their diplomatic machinery, their resources in manpower and wealth, and their bargaining influence with the Big Powers.

CHAPTER 15

The Biltmore Controversy

ZIONIST POLITICS in Palestine and abroad were characterized in the later war years by frustration and bitterness, stemming from the Jewish Agency's failure to persuade Britain to relax the immigration restrictions, to make any substantial headway in rescuing European Jews, and to unite the Zionists and the Jews generally behind a common program. The first reliable information on the scale of Nazi crimes against the Jews started to come out of Europe in the autumn of 1942. As recently as the previous May the Agency president told the delegates to the Biltmore Conference that perhaps as many as 25 per cent of Europe's Jews might not survive the war. Then came the stark announcement by the Big Three on December 17, 1942: [1]

> From all the occupied countries Jews are being transported, in conditions of appalling horror and brutality, to Eastern Europe. . . . None of those taken away are ever heard of again. The able-bodied are slowly worked to death in labour camps. The infirm are left to die of exposure and starvation or are deliberately massacred in mass executions. The number of victims of these bloody cruelties is reckoned in many hundreds of thousands of entirely innocent men, women and children. ⋅

The Zionists now wondered whether the number of European Jewish survivors would even reach 25 per cent at the war's close.

The sudden news plunged the Yishuv into an abiding gloom. The Big Three had warned "that those responsible for these crimes shall not escape retribution." For the Jews everywhere, however, this was but small reassurance. The Zionists in particular intensified their efforts to save as many as possible of the potential victims. Zionist pressures were chiefly instrumental in the calling of the Anglo-American refugee conference at Bermuda in April 1943 and in the creation of the American War Refugee Board in January 1944. The Agency immigration department had set up a United Rescue Committee, representing all factions in the Yishuv including the dissidents, with headquarters at Istanbul and offices at Lisbon and Geneva. This committee, with the cooperation of Jewish relief organizations abroad—notably the American Jewish Joint Distribution Committee—and of the International Red Cross, established contact with the Jewish underground in Europe. These contacts were reinforced by small missions of specially trained Haganah volunteers. They were parachuted into the Balkans in 1943–44 to collect military intelligence for the Allies, to strengthen the Jewish resistance movements, and to aid Jews and Allied prisoners of war to escape to Turkey. By these means some 10,000 Jews were rescued and resettled in Palestine.

Almost all uprooted European Jews were becoming Zionists. Zionism always exerted the strongest influence among Jews subject to persecution. During the war, Zionist propaganda constantly stressed that the Jewish position in Europe was undermined because of the absence of a sovereign Jewish state upon which Jews could call in time of distress, and where they could go to escape oppression. The Zionist spokesmen, by promising eventual settlement in the Jewish National Home, endowed the struggle for survival with a positive purpose. These arguments were employed with telling effect in the Jewish underground of eastern and central Europe, for most of its cells were built around the nuclei of the local Zionist youth training groups. The message was also carried later by relief teams from Palestine attached to UNRRA, and by Palestine Jewish military units serving in Italy and elsewhere on the Continent.[2]

But the Zionists were dejected over what they regarded as the unnecessary severity of mandatory immigration policy and the inadequate support of the United Nations. The longer the Zionists were unable to overcome these obstacles, the greater became their obsession over the fate of the European Jews, with which the political future of Zionism was indissolubly bound. This obsession became the compelling force in Zionist politics in the second half of the war. The terrorists, the statists, and the anti-statists were each persuaded that only through the adoption of their respective programs could the European Jewish remnant be resettled in Palestine.

Meanwhile, relations between the Palestine Government and the Yishuv, already impaired by nearly four years of the White Paper policy, deteriorated rapidly in 1943, now that the shooting war in the Near East was over. The government's enactment in January 1943 of a drastic regulation to curb alleged recruiting malpractices was viewed by the Agency as an effort to discourage Jewish enlistment. Ill feeling was further engendered in March, when the government announced its postwar reconstruction scheme, which appeared to the Jewish leaders as implying the retention of the White Paper. But what angered the Palestine Jews most was a succession of arms trials and searches between August and November.

That the illegal arms traffic throughout the Near East had developed into a brisk trade by 1943 was an open secret. In the early war years huge stocks of munitions, abandoned in Egypt's Western Desert by both Axis and British forces, were picked up by Beduin and Allied soldiers and sold for tremendous profits on the black market. As the frontiers of combat receded from the Near East, the black market was furnished with equipment stolen from Allied camps and dumps. Arabs, particularly the Beduins of southern Palestine and Transjordanians who were not required to obtain licenses for arms, were the primary agents. The Zionists, the highest bidders as a rule, were the chief consumers. The largest single purchaser was probably Haganah, which was preparing for a possible showdown with the Arabs and the British. But the heavy investments were also motivated by the fear that, if the matériel remained in Arab hands, it might be used ultimately against the Palestine Jews.[3]

Arabs, Jews, and Allied soldiers found in illegal possession of munitions were tried before military courts, and public announcement was customarily made of the sentences. But never was such notoriety accorded any trial as that in the late summer of 1943 of two Jews accused of purchasing arms unlawfully. During the drawn-out, public proceedings the court accused the Jewish Agency and the "Nazi-like" Histadrut of operating "a vast and dangerous" arms ring, which, by depriving Allied soldiers of weapons, menaced "the safety and defense of Palestine" and constituted an act of treason against the United Nations. While the Yishuv was still inflamed, Weizmann's former bodyguard was tried by the same court for having in his possession without authority two extra rounds of ammunition. Since one of these cartridges was the same type as those in the preceding case, the court linked the accused with the two earlier defendants and meted out a seven-year sentence. The Yishuv's Elected Assembly, in extraordinary session at Jerusalem on October 4, heard David Ben Gurion allege that the primary purpose of the wide publicity given the first trial, for the coverage of which "American correspondents were especially invited from Cairo," was to spread "slanders" against the Zionist war effort in order to justify the White Paper policy. The Assembly passed a resolution declaring that it came as a "shocking surprise" to have a British court vilify all Jews for the acts of individuals. The Palestine Government was warned that the Yishuv, "if driven to defend itself against those conspiring forcibly to block the path of its existence . . . will neither retreat nor surrender its right of self-defense."[4]

Passions were further stirred by searches conducted in two collective villages in October and November by British military and police units in conjunction with Polish troops then stationed in the country, to uncover concealed arms and Polish deserters. Small quantities of unauthorized ammunition, but no deserters, were discovered. The Yishuv, however, felt that the two outlying villages, which had suffered high casualties in the Arab revolt, required the arms for self-defense. Defying a censorship ban, ten Jewish dailies published an identical eye-witness account of the second raid, in which two villagers were wounded, one fatally. When the government suspended these newspapers at staggered intervals, the editors in united protest refused to issue their journals until the ban was rescinded eleven days later. Mass protest demonstrations were held. At Tel-Aviv government property was damaged and more than a score of persons injured, a third of them British constables.[5]

In this period the terrorist societies first took secure root. The Stern Gang, quiescent since the death of its founder and the arrest of its leaders, was revived as the Fighters for Israel's Freedom in the early summer of 1943. The Freedom Fighters busied themselves with winning converts, mostly younger than 25, among the Revisionist and Oriental youth and recently arrived illegal immigrants. Adolescents were recruited to distribute clandestine handbills and the society's Hebrew monthly, He-Hazit (The Front), which made its appearance in July 1943. The sympathy was also enlisted of a few Arabs headed by Yusuf abu-Ghosh, the twenty-three-year-old scion of a Muslim, landowning family in the village of abu-Ghosh, near Jerusalem. The Freedom Fighters, an early issue of He-Hazit disclosed, accused the Revisionists and the Jewish Agency of relying unrealistically on world democracy and Britain, and the Zionist leftists of turning with equal illusion for support to the world proletariat and Soviet Russia. Zionist politics, with its endless round of "petitions, speeches, meetings, declarations, and coalitions," had thus far not availed, because it "has been elastic in its aims and dogmatic in its means." The Freedom Fighters proposed instead the use of any means to achieve their fixed ends. They advertised themselves as the vanguard of an underground Jewish army, and "declared war" against the British "occupying" authorities for the "liberation" of Palestine and Transjordan, of which the Jews were the "sole" owners. They would seek the aid of any "power that is in conflict with our political enemy." The Freedom Fighters believed that terrorism performed "a most important function," since it served to attract world-wide attention to their cause.[6]

Freedom Fighter leadership was reinforced in the fall of 1943, when twenty members of the original gang escaped from prison. Among them was Nathan Friedman-Yellin, a thirty-year-old engineer of Polish birth, who now became commander-in-chief. The terrorist group probably numbered between 250 to 300 by the beginning of 1944. At least five times its size was the expanding Irgun Zvai Leumi. David Raziel, the

Irgun's top commander, had been killed in May 1941 in a Baghdad suburb on a special sabotage mission for the British Army. After an ensuing period of crisis the Irgun terminated its ties with the Revisionist Party in May 1943, and its ideology thereafter approximated that of the Freedom Fighters. Appeals for enlistees were made in the Irgun's secret monthly, *Herut* (Freedom), in surreptitious pamphlets and posters, and over its illegal radio transmitter. An empty treasury was refilled by systematic extortion and occasional robberies. The Irgun also received help from the Polish military units brought to Palestine in 1942–43. These troops, owing allegiance to the Government-in-Exile at London, were violently anti-Russian and were becoming increasingly anti-British. Polish commanders reportedly allowed Polish Jewish deserters to join Irgunist ranks, trained Irgunists in terrorism and sabotage, permitted the Irgun to transport munitions in Polish military vehicles, and afforded refuge in Polish army camps to Irgunists sought by the Palestine police. One of the Polish Jewish soldiers, Menahem Begin, a lawyer in his early thirties and former member of the Warsaw branch of the Irgun, was given a "leave of absence" in May 1944 to take over the Irgun supreme command, a post he retained thereafter.

The Irgun launched its "fight against the existing regime" in February 1944 by bombing the government migration offices at Jerusalem, Tel-Aviv, and Haifa. For seven months they continued to destroy government property. The assaults were carefully planned and precautions taken to avoid bloodshed. On the other hand, the terrorist campaign of the Freedom Fighters, which also started in February, was directed toward assassination. Besides renewing their old vendetta with the police, the Freedom Fighters made two unsuccessful attempts on the life of High Commissioner MacMichael. Thwarted at home, the Freedom Fighters carried their struggle beyond Palestine's borders to Cairo. There on November 6 two adherents murdered Lord Moyne, the British Minister Resident in the Middle East and a member of the War Cabinet. Following Lord Moyne's assassination no new terrorist outbreaks occurred until after V-E Day.[7]

In the meantime, emergency regulations approximating martial law, which had been invoked in the Arab revolt of 1936–39 and then rescinded by the summer of 1940, were now restored by the government. The British police, unexpectedly assisted at the end of March by an Irgunist informer, arrested some sixty central figures of the terrorist society. Large-scale screening operations, beginning early in September, increased the number of known or suspected terrorists under police arrest to 251 by mid-October. They were then transferred to military custody and deported to the former Italian colony of Eritrea, and in January 1945, by this time numbering 279, to the Sudan for detention. The mass arrests affected the Irgun more seriously than the Freedom Fighters. But few arms caches were captured, and the two commanders-in-chief were still at large. Terrorism could not be eradicated until the basic political irritants were removed. But for the government's inability even to neutralize the terrorist groups there were three main reasons: the estrangement between the government and the Yishuv, the preoccupation of Palestine Jews with local elections, and the community's lack of confidence in the police. The Jewish authorities recalled that they had assisted the police in seizing the key leaders of the Stern group in 1942, only to see most of them escape in November 1943. When a collective fine was imposed on a Jewish suburb of Jerusalem after the second attempt on MacMichael's life in August, one Hebrew newspaper stated that the failure of the government "in its war against a small band in a small country, a failure so prolonged and so conspicuous," could not be attributed to "the difficulty of the operation alone. Before the government places . . . the blame on the Jewish Community it ought first to examine very carefully the efficiency of its own institutions." [8]

Nevertheless, the Jewish quasi-government, press, and public leaders, though not cooperating actively with the mandatory, condemned terrorism as harming the Zionists themselves more than the British. "The Jewish Community . . . is not at war with His Majesty's Government, the Palestine Government, or the Palestine Police Force," noted one newspaper, which later characterized the terrorists as "misguided criminals" and "young fanatics, crazed by the sufferings of their people into believing that destruction will bring healing." The leftist press called the terrorists Jewish Fascists and warned that this domestic Fascism was far more dangerous than the foreign variety, because "in the struggle against world Fascism we have many powerful allies. But who will be concerned, if our own Fascism will completely devour us?" [9] In the past such unanimity would have exercised a powerful check on the spread of terrorism. But public opinion by itself was at best a passive influence, and this passiveness in 1944 merely played into the hands of the militant elements.

The Palestine Government and the Commander-in-Chief of the British Middle East Forces issued a joint communiqué on October 10, declaring that [10]

> Verbal condemnation . . . is not in itself enough. . . . Accordingly . . . the Jewish community in Palestine, their leaders and representative bodies [are called upon] to . . . discharge their responsibilities and not to allow the good name of the Yishuv to be prejudiced by acts which can only bring . . . dishonour on the Jewish people as a whole.

Zionist sensibilities were hurt by the communiqué's enumeration of the terrorist crimes on the debit side of the Yishuv's war ledger and the omission of any credits. Nevertheless the quasi-government now addressed itself to "cleansing" the community of terrorism. Yet as long as the White Paper remained in force, the Zionist leaders could not expect greater success than the government. Ever since the beginning of 1943 the Jewish leaders had preached that the government was hostile to Zionism and the Yishuv. They could not now suddenly urge cooperation with that government, which had made no conciliatory gestures. Some leaders were opposed to handing the terrorists over to the police, whom they did not trust. Moreover, the Irgun and the Freedom Fighters had become bolder and better organized in the year of the community's inaction. Consequently, if the measures were to be effective, use would have to be made of Haganah. But Haganah was as unconditionally outlawed by the government as were the terrorist groups; and resort to Haganah carried with it the risk of civil war in the Yishuv.

Lord Moyne's murder shocked the community into action. The hand of the quasi-government was strengthened by the arrival on November 15 on a first wartime visit of the Agency's president, Chaim Weizmann. Nor was the significance lost upon the Yishuv of the warning given in the House of Commons two days later by Prime Minister Churchill that if "this terrorism [were not brought] to a speedy end," many friends of the Jews like himself "would have to reconsider the position we have maintained so consistently . . . in the past." The quasi-government now furnished the British authorities with information about terrorist hideouts, printing presses, and arms caches, and units of Haganah kidnaped individual terrorists between December 1944 and March 1945, allegedly to extract additional information. As a result, some 200 suspects were arrested in December alone. Wealthy business men were advised to notify Haganah, if terrorists made any new efforts to fleece them. Nor was it accidental that the terrorists turned to substitute fund-raising methods, such as thefts and soliciting for bogus causes.[11]

COMMUNITY AND HISTADRUT ELECTIONS

The terrorist groups at their height in this period commanded the allegiance of less than one per cent of the Palestine Jews. The rest of the community, despite the distractions of war, was passing through a state of political turmoil. The issue on which all others converged was the controversy over the Biltmore Program. At its center stood David Ben Gurion, the chairman of the Jewish Agency Executive. Ben Gurion's engrossment with Biltmore led to his sudden resignation from his Agency post at the end of October 1943. This step seemed designed to force Weizmann to adhere to Biltmore as the irreducible minimum in his negotiations with the British Government, then taking place in London. Before Ben Gurion resumed office in March 1944, he precipitated a crisis in his own Mapai and in the Labor Federation. Mapai's left-wing Faction B refused to endorse Biltmore and threw its weight in the Histadrut behind the binationalist opposition. After three months of bitter wrangling in the councils of his party and the Labor Federation, Ben Gurion finally insisted on new Histadrut elections. He probably hoped to win a popular mandate, by directing his appeal to the 70 to 75 per cent of the Federation's members who belonged to no party. Before the electioneering got under way in earnest, Faction B formally seceded from Mapai in May to establish the Labor Unity Movement.[12]

At this stage the Biltmore controversy was drawn into the Yishuv's general election campaign which by coincidence commenced in the spring of 1944. Delegates were to be chosen to the fourth Elected Assembly, which was to be enlarged from 71 to 171 members. The life of an Assembly was constitutionally limited to four years. But because of the unsettled conditions the third Assembly had remained in office for more than thirteen years. Meanwhile the Jewish population had more than trebled from 170,000 to 550,000; and the electorate had multiplied from slightly less than 90,000 in 1931 to somewhat more than 300,000 in 1944. The National Council Executive, it was true, had been broadened in the first year of the war by co-opting members from hitherto unrepresented parties. But a majority of the eligible voters formally adhered to no party and were without voice in the community government. The electoral system, based as it was on community-wide party tickets, benefited in practice the cohesive labor parties. Other, more loosely knit factions had been recommending for years the adoption of the Anglo-American procedure of electoral districts so as to introduce "the element of local responsibility . . . [and] at least modify the slavish obedience to central party headquarters that now obtains." The semipolitical Sefardi association demanded this reform as a condition for its participation in the election. When it was turned down by the Mapai-dominated National Council Executive, the Sefardim, now joined by the rightist General Zionist B and Revisionist parties, boycotted the election. Other issues, injected into the campaign by the central Europeans' New Immigration Party, included the streamlining of the community government, the clearer division of authority between the National Council and the Jewish Agency, and the combating of wartime corruption and terrorism.[13]

The Yishuv election, originally set for May 24, was eventually deferred to August 1, only five days before the Histadrut election. Since the essence of each party's platform in the Histadrut election was its attitude toward Biltmore, Biltmore also became the central theme for each of the labor parties in the community election. Consequently, the nonlabor parties were also forced to take a stand on the statist program. Thus the community election now became concerned with basic Zionist policy, a matter normally taken up only in Zionist Congressional elections. The New Immigration Party, which remained neutral on Biltmore, incurred attack from both the statists and the binationalists. In the Yishuv election the nonpartisan voter was faced with a bewildering choice of 24 tickets, adding up to 1,694 candidates. Many tickets represented nonpolitical or semipolitical groups. Ha-Shomer ha-Za'ir and the Left Zionist Workers sponsored a joint panel under the name of the Leftist Front; the General Zionist A Party and several small centrist groups coalesced as the Democratic Center. Dissident or outlawed groups appeared under disguised names: the communists as the Popular Democratic List, one Revisionist group as the National Workers' Front, and a second as the Nation's Movement for the Jewish State.[14]

Sixty-seven per cent of the electorate—202,488 voters—appeared at the polls. Mapai retained its lead, winning 63 seats in the new Assembly. The Leftist Front ranked second with 21, the New Immigration Party third with 18, the Labor Unity Movement fifth with 16, and the Democratic Center sixth with 11. One of the unexpected results was the large gain made by the Mizrahi Labor Party, which came in fourth with 17 successful candidates, or ten more than its parent organization, the Mizrahi Party, which was seventh. The communists polled 3,948 votes, entitling them to three assemblymen. The Histadrut polling was anticlimactic. Only 72.7 per cent of the eligible voters participated, as compared with 83.4 per cent in the November 1941 elections. Mapai's percentage of the total Assembly seats declined from 43.6 to 36.8. Its relative strength in the Histadrut was even more sharply reduced, from 69.3 to 53.5 per cent. In view of the Histadrut's overwhelming power in Yishuv politics, Mapai's slim majority in the Labor Federation threatened the party's position of dominance in the community. Still Mapai outstripped its closest rival by three to one, owing largely to nonpartisan backing. After the formal separation of Faction B in the spring, Mapai's enrolled membership probably did not exceed 15,000. Yet its ticket polled 46,618 votes in the Histadrut and 73,667 in the Yishuv. But Ben Gurion had won a stronger vote of confidence for Biltmore in the community election, where the parties supporting that program obtained 66 per cent of the votes, than in the Histadrut, where the pro-Biltmore parties polled only 58 per cent of the total.[15]

Interparty squabbles over the spoils of office continued for months after the elections. No agreement was reached over the composition of the new Histadrut Executive until March 1945, when Mapai reluctantly agreed to proportional representation on the management of the Histadrut's industrial subsidiaries. On the National Council Executive, which was finally set up in December 1944, Mapai occupied five out of the eleven seats, including the presidency and chairmanship; the next six parties were awarded one seat each. But the representatives of three of these, dissatisfied with the portfolios they had received, withdrew from active membership by March 1945. Moreover, the parties boycotting the election refused to recognize the Yishuv Administration altogether.[16]

The first political debate of the new Assembly in December 1944 was devoted to a review of the Biltmore Program. But efforts to win over the Opposition were not entirely successful. Only the Labor Unity Movement agreed to vote for the political resolution, which called upon the United Nations to support the Zionist claims as formulated in the Biltmore Program, after a paragraph was added expressly rejecting partition. Of the 114 assemblymen present 82 voted for this resolution. The uncompromising Opposition, consisting of the Leftist Front, New Immigration, and the communists, abstained. The Assembly debate and resolution left the statists and their opponents as strongly confirmed in their respective beliefs as ever. But the real significance of the Assembly's decision lay in the fact that the Yishuv formally endorsed "the Jerusalem-Biltmore Program," as it had come to be known in Palestine. Hence by the war's close the Agency Executive could rely on the backing of a majority of the Palestine Jews in its demand for the creation of a Jewish state.[17]

POSTWAR PLANS

The Agency's London Office had already communicated its political claims to the British Government in October 1944 in a preliminary memorandum, which Weizmann discussed with Churchill. The Prime Minister replied that the review of the Palestine problem would have to await the end of the war with Germany.[18] The memorandum requested "a decision designating Palestine as a Jewish Commonwealth—a country where the Jewish people shall be free to work out its salvation by large-scale settlement and by the achievement of full nationhood." The area was specifically defined as "Palestine West of the Jordan," and it was hoped that the state would be "organically connected with the British Commonwealth of Nations." The Agency, it was stated, "would view with deep apprehension an attempt to revive the partition idea." In its opinion partition "is liable to be fatal to the viability of the Jewish State . . . . [and] seems bound to . . . wreck the chances of large-scale development." Yet the Agency, it appeared in this particular paragraph, had not shut the door tight against discussing partition as a possible basis for settlement. In fact, the Agency's official declaration seemed dictated largely by considerations of future diplomatic bargaining, for Churchill had informed Weizmann as early as September 1943 of the decision by the British Cabinet Committee on Palestine to grant the Jews full sovereignty in a divided Palestine. Again in November 1944 the Agency president was personally assured by the Prime Minister that he endorsed this scheme and favored the inclusion of the Negeb within the projected Jewish state.[19]

The Agency memorandum of October 1944 despaired of obtaining

Arab consent to a solution of the Palestine problem granting "justice to the Jewish people." But the Agency denied that the fulfillment of its demands would prove harmful to the Arabs, who would have "every guarantee of equality of rights, religious freedom, autonomy in cultural and municipal affairs, and a full share in the benefits of developments." The Arabs would also enjoy, it was maintained, the added security of the Arab countries surrounding Palestine. Once faced with the establishment of Palestine as a Jewish state, it was argued, the Arabs would accept "its existence . . . as an accomplished fact." Then friendly relations would follow, for "it is both the desire and the interest of the Jews to live in peace with their neighbours." The primary purpose of the projected Jewish state would be the rehabilitation of European Jews, of whom it was estimated that no more than 1,500,000 or 25 per cent of their number in 1939 would outlive the war. To offer these Jews,

> deported and broken, a return to . . . [their original status], propped up by philanthropic palliatives and paper guarantees, is morally unthinkable. For the large mass, true rehabilitation can only be achieved by a fresh start in new surroundings. . . . Apart from the survivors in Europe, the main groups of would-be immigrants are (i) refugees scattered throughout the world who have not been absorbed; (ii) Jews in those oriental countries where their safety and well-being are in permanent jeopardy; and (iii) Jews in English-speaking countries, among whom a movement to settle in Palestine is spreading.

The speedy settlement in Palestine of these prospective immigrants would lead to the creation of a Jewish majority, which in turn would "ensure the effective functioning of the Jewish State." The agency urged that it be invested with the authority to regulate this immigration.

The Agency knew that, unless its political demands could be proved economically feasible, the program would stand little chance of general acceptance. The Zionists were desirous, in the last analysis, of restoring the principle of economic absorptive capacity as the immigration yardstick. Abundant energy was therefore devoted to the reconversion of the Yishuv's economy to a peacetime basis, the creation of new jobs for war workers and expected immigrants, the cutting of production costs to meet postwar competition, and the exploitation of the country's maximum economic potentialities. A Planning Committee had been set up in 1943 by the Agency Executive to supervise the work of local economic experts. On the Planning Committee's recommendation, the Agency in conjunction with Jewish banks began to provide credit facilities in 1944 for the reconversion of war factories to civilian production and for housing. Similarly, assistance was given for the extension of rural settlement. Of the forty new villages established during the war, ten were located on desert lands of the Negeb, the most sparsely inhabited region of the country. The success of these villages might furnish a telling argument for Jewish claims to the southern third of the country.

Anglo-American Zionists financed a survey in 1944–45, undertaken by engineers formerly associated with the Tennessee Valley Authority and other power and irrigation projects in the United States, to draw up a blueprint for a Jordan Valley Authority. The scheme, as originally conceived, embraced a comprehensive system of irrigation, power, soil reclamation, reforestation, water conservation, flood control, and swamp drainage for the benefit of Palestine and Transjordan and possibly of the Levant States. The report of the investigating engineers estimated the cost of the plan at $250,000,000, which they believed could be amortized in 50 years. American and British Jews, including anti-Zionists, also provided funds for an inquiry into the prospects for the intensive economic development of Palestine so as to establish a reliable estimate of the country's absorptive capacity. The preparation of these two reports was well advanced by 1945. To the implementation of the proposals the Palestine Jews hoped to apply a quarter of a billion dollars in sterling assets accumulated during the war. Considerable economic aid could be expected from the American Jews. But these sums would have to be supplemented by an international loan; and the Agency was planning to lay claim to reparations from Germany in repayment for the Nazi expropriation of Jewish property.[20]

With these economic plans the Yishuv was in full agreement. Since the same unanimity did not exist over political objectives, Weizmann endeavored in his sixteen-week visit to the country to bring the community into line with the Agency position. The Agency president, whose personal influence had lost nothing in his five years' absence, aired his views before the Elected Assembly, in frequent public speeches on his tour of all sections of the community, at press interviews, and in private meetings with party leaders. Weizmann was anxious to dispel the prevailing illusion that a Jewish state would be set up immediately. He was desirous of bringing back into the community administration those groups which had abstained from the election, and counseled that "the Yishuv must appear united and indivisible" at this "decisive hour." Weizmann was determined to impress upon the Yishuv the imperative need for eliminating the terrorist societies. He made it clear that the Zionists had to "preserve the purity" of their enterprise, that "the end cannot, of its very nature, justify impure means." But above all he was alarmed by the state of decay in which he found Anglo-Zionist relations. He attempted to reassure the Palestine Jews that Churchill was "a man who keeps faith with us." [21]

There was indeed a noticeable improvement in Anglo-Zionist relations during the Agency chief's stay in Palestine. In no small measure this was due to the new High Commissioner, Field Marshal Viscount Gort. By the time Sir Harold MacMichael left the country at the end of August 1944 virtually no contact existed between the High Commissioner and the Jewish quasi-government. In sharp contrast Lord Gort, soon after his arrival two months later, deliberately tried to establish friendly personal relations with the local Arab and Jewish notables in town and village. The Palestine Jews were pleased by Lord Gort's decision, with Colonial Office approval, in February 1945 to allow those illegal refugees who had been deported to Mauritius in December 1940 to settle in Palestine. For the time being at least, the quasi-government was resuming a normal relationship with the Palestine Government. But Weizmann's visit was too brief to strengthen greatly the hand of the moderates or to solve any of the complex internal problems of the Yishuv. His call for unity brought no results, for the dissident parties remained outside the community government. The terrorist societies, despite the temporary stoppage of violence and the Yishuv's repressive measures, were conducting a vigorous propaganda. Most important of all, however, was the division within the Agency Executive itself.[22]

Shortly after his arrival in Palestine, Weizmann had declared that a transitional period of five to ten years would "be required before a Jewish Commonwealth emerged." In this interval, he went on, "I should like to see the beginning of considerable immigration into Palestine, something at the rate of 100,000 yearly." Before returning to England early in March 1945, Weizmann advised the Inner General Council to be neither pessimistic nor unduly optimistic. He expressed the belief, however, "that we are nearing better days, and [I] am convinced that the younger ones among you will yet be living in a Jewish state in Palestine." But Ben Gurion had talked of "a Jewish Commonwealth . . . in our time," in introducing Weizmann at a conference in Tel-Aviv at the end of December. "I wish to emphasize," declared the chairman of the Agency Executive later that day, that ". . . what is needed is not immigration on the old lines but a transfer of population; not a slow movement . . . but a quick transfer; not partial but full." Ben Gurion warned in February 1945 against "any illusions . . . about a major political decision being taken on Palestine. There might very well be no such decision, and the White Paper might remain technically in force, although the letter of it would not be adhered to." A few weeks later he urged the Jews to be prepared for every eventuality. "We should be in readiness," he stated, if the decision proved favorable, "to carry it out rapidly and to the full," and, if unfavorable, "to secure its speedy and complete frustration." Weizmann rallied to his position the moderates, the Biltmore critics, and even certain of the rightist elements. To his banner Ben Gurion gathered a majority of his own party, Mapai, and most of the anti-Weizmann factions, including some of the Revisionists.[23]

On the extremist periphery the traditional splinter factions continued to agitate for their own programs. The Revisionists were hopelessly fragmented. Before the election two small Revisionist labor groups had become affiliated with the Histadrut. Several rival leaders were contesting for control of the party machinery. As a result, the Revisionist mouthpiece, *Ha-Mashqif*, followed no consistent line, except in opposition to Weizmann, the Jewish Agency, and the labor parties. While approving the Agency's demand for a Jewish state as merely a belated recognition of "the very root of the political movement of Jabotinsky," the die-hard Revisionists did not formally endorse the Biltmore Program, for they were still laying claim to Transjordan as well as to Palestine. The religious fundamentalists of the Agudat Israel also persisted in their separatist policy, even in the face of the growing pressure from their workers' branch for closer cooperation with the Jewish Agency. The Jewish communists denounced the Biltmore Program as "based on domination despite its 'democratic' disguise" and as "a policy of conquest and jingoist isolationism." But the communists seemed to be abandoning their own isolationism. The Palestine Communist Party had participated in the Yishuv election and had begun negotiations in June 1944 for readmittance of its members into the Histadrut. A secessionist group founded in April 1945 the Communist Educational Association, which for the first time recognized the Jewish National Home and endorsed the demand for Jewish immigration into Palestine.[24]

THE BILTMORE QUARREL ABROAD

Meanwhile the Jewish Agency had stepped up its propaganda campaign in Britain and the United States. The master plan aimed at uniting all Jewish and as many non-Jewish groups as possible behind the demand for the replacement of the White Paper with the Biltmore Program. The British Zionist Federation, as a result of a membership drive, expanded its enrollment from 5,400 at the beginning of 1943 to 26,000 two years later. The Agency could also count on the backing of the Board of Deputies of British Jews, the oldest Jewish representative body in the country. The Zionists returned a majority in the triennial election of the Board in 1943. In July of that year the Board terminated its 1878 agreement with the Anglo-Jewish Association for the coordination of their activities abroad, and in November 1944 endorsed the Biltmore principles. A small core of anti-Zionist members of the Board of Deputies now formed an organization called the Jewish Fellowship, which insisted that the Jews constituted a religious, not a "politico-national," group and therefore stoutly opposed the demand for a Jewish state. The statist plank was also rejected by the more influential Anglo-Jewish Association, which after 1943 became the spokesman of the non-Zionist position. The Association in a memorandum in December 1944 called for the further "development of the Jewish National Home in an undivided Palestine" and the creation of "conditions conducive to the attainment by . . . [that country] of the status of a self-governing territory." The Board, the Fellowship, and the Association, however, were united in their objections to the White Paper and in the hope that Palestine might eventually be granted dominion status within the British Commonwealth. The ideological difference between the Zionists and the non-Zionists paralleled the statist-binationalist split in Palestine. Thus the projection of the Biltmore controversy into British Jewish life had resulted by 1945 in crystallizing the non-Zionist and anti-Zionist Opposition.[25]

The same dispute raged in American Jewish circles, producing similar results. The American Jewish Conference at its constituent session in New York in the summer of 1943 passed a resolution on Palestine embodying the essential features of the Biltmore Program. The Conference consisted of delegates from 64 nation-wide Jewish societies and 136 municipal and regional communities, and its purpose was to frame a common program of action on Palestine and on general postwar problems of the Jews throughout the world. The Conference resolution was adopted by a vote of 478 to 4 with 19 abstentions. Three of the negative ballots were cast by the American Jewish Committee spokesmen, who expressed displeasure over the incorporation of "these ultimate, divisive demands" of the Biltmore Program instead of concentrating "upon present unity of action on matters upon which there was complete agreement." The Committee therefore withdrew from the Conference and declared that it still adhered to its statement on Palestine of the preceding January. This statement advocated the conversion of the Palestine Mandate into a temporary international trusteeship responsible to the United Nations, which should expressly guarantee the future "growth and development [of the Jewish settlement] to the full extent of the economic absorptive capacity of the country." The Committee, which had consisted in the past chiefly of corporate members, was now opened to individuals agreeing with its program and purposes, by the formation of local chapters throughout the country. Although the Committee remained basically a civic protective agency, it nevertheless became, by virtue of its stand on Palestine, a nation-wide non-Zionist movement.[26]

Finally, the anti-Zionists formed their own organization, called the American Council for Judaism, which maintained that the Jews, as a religious group, were nationals of the countries in which they lived and rejected "the effort to establish a national Jewish state in Palestine or anywhere else as a philosophy of defeatism." Neither the Conference nor the Committee nor the Council favored the incorporation of Palestine into the British Commonwealth. Whereas the first two rejected the White Paper in its entirety, the Council opposed only the immigration and land clauses.[27]

At the same time the American Zionist Emergency Council shifted into high gear the machinery it had created "to educate and arouse American public opinion in behalf of the establishment of Palestine as a Jewish Commonwealth." The Emergency Council sought the cooperation of political, journalist, labor, and professional circles. Individuals were induced to join the American Palestine Committee, which by the close of the war had a membership of 6,500 public figures. Moreover, a Christian Council on Palestine was founded at the end of 1942 to enlist the aid of Christian clergy of all denominations; by V-E Day this group numbered close to 2,400 members. The American Zionist Emergency Council's public relations efforts were coordinated on a national scale by its network of 76 state and regional branches, which were further subdivided into some 380 local committees. One outcome of the campaign was the adoption of pro-Zionist planks by both major parties in the 1944 presidential election, and by the C.I.O. as well as the A.F.L. in their national conventions of that year. Another was the passage of pro-Zionist resolutions by 33 state legislatures.[28]

The confusion over Palestine in Britain and the United States was worse confounded by the activities of the Zionist dissidents, who were also seeking sympathizers. The Hebrew Committee of National Liberation was the last of the committees formed between 1940 and 1944 by a handful of Irgunists. Through demagogic, full-page advertisements in leading American newspapers it won the backing of thousands of well-intentioned non-Jews as well as Jews, unaware of the ties of the founders with the terrorist group in Palestine. The National Liberation Committee blended the doctrines of the anti-Zionists and the Revisionists, and the hybrid proved anathema to both. A distinction was drawn between "Jews" and "Hebrews"; the one was said to comprise merely the adherents of the Jewish faith who were nationals of the countries of their residence, and the other those Jews living "in the Hell of Europe" and in Palestine, whose religion was Judaism but whose nationality was Hebrew. The founders of the Committee, at its "Hebrew Embassy" in Washington, announced that they were "the sergeants and the spokesmen" of "the reborn Hebrew nation" until "our nation shall be free to elect its own . . . representatives in democratic form." The Committee claimed all of Palestine and Transjordan and demanded the status of "a co-belligerent in the United Nations' war against Axis tyranny."[29]

That these doctrines were intended solely for Anglo-American consumption was borne out by the fact that Irgun literature in Palestine made no reference whatsoever to them. Moreover, while the Irgun in Palestine was then waging "an active war against [British] slavery and oppression," the Irgunists in the United States were postponing "the settlement of the political and boundary problems of Palestine until after victory." Until the formation of the Hebrew Committee of National Liberation the Irgun delegates in the United States enjoyed Revisionist backing. Now the Revisionists disinherited their erstwhile disciples as opportunists, and concentrated on their own full-page advertisements, demanding that Britain give up the mandate and that Palestine and Transjordan be transformed into a Jewish state. The Hebrew Committee of National Liberation was denounced by the American Zionist Emergency Council as an "irresponsible" and "lunatic fringe." [30]

Despite the support taken away from the Agency by the dissidents, American Zionist ranks swelled in the later war years, from less than 250,000 in 1943 to some 400,000 two years later, and the Agency political platform was reaffirmed by the American Jewish Conference at its second session in December 1944. Although clearly not all American Jews favored a Jewish state, they appeared united in their anxiety to help those European Jewish survivors who might wish to settle in Palestine after the war. For this humanitarian objective the American Jews could count on the support of a substantial sector of American public opinion. [31]

CHAPTER 16

The Scope of the Problem
at the War's Close

As ARABS and Zionists gathered their forces in the second half of the war for the expected showdown, the last prospects of a relatively peaceful settlement were rapidly vanishing. The war, and not the White Paper, had brought into effect the Arab-Zionist truce in the fall of 1939. With the passing of the military crisis, Arabs and Zionists were turning to their pent-up grievances with a growing sense of urgency. By the war's close a vicious circle had been created. Developments in Palestine gave rise to repercussions in the near-by Arab countries, in Britain, and in the United States. These repercussions in turn affected the situation in Palestine. The 1939 White Paper had become the focus of the Arab-Zionist conflict. The Jewish Agency was demanding the unconditional annulment of this policy as a prerequisite for resettling the European Jewish survivors in an independent Jewish Palestine. The Arab countries, in the name of the Palestine Arabs, let it be known that the White Paper's terms were the absolute minimum to which they would agree, but that their goal was the conversion of Palestine into an Arab state. The Arab governments were making full use of their diplomatic machinery. The Jewish Agency's quasi-diplomatic status, however, was assured only at the League of Nations and in Britain. Yet the Permanent Mandates Commission was no longer functioning, and continuous negotiation with the mandatory had not produced the desired reversal of policy.

Consequently, the Zionists were relying increasingly on appeals to American public opinion, in the hope that the United States Government might be induced to intercede on their behalf with Britain. To check the

Zionist propaganda offensive the Arabs and their sympathizers engaged in counterpropaganda, and the Arab governments brought diplomatic influence to bear upon Washington. The Arab and Zionist pressures came at a time when Britain was seeking full-scale American cooperation in Palestine, and the United States itself was beginning to evince a growing interest in the Near East. The convergence of these four factors—Zionist pressures, Arab counterpressures, British overtures, and American self-interest—involved the United States directly in the Palestine problem. The American entanglement, at least as far as Arabs and Zionists were affected, originated with President Roosevelt's assurances to King ibn Sa'ud in May 1943 that Arabs and Jews would be given ample opportunity to express their views before any long-range decisions were taken. With this pledge the President had assumed in the name of the United States Government an obligation to participate in the final settlement of the Palestine problem. Although President Roosevelt, like his predecessors since the early 1920's, sent greetings to the annual conventions of the Zionist Organization of America, the phrasing of these messages—including the letter to the convention in September 1943—was always so careful that no formal American commitment was ever made.[1]

From the start of 1944, however, it became clear that the Arab-Zionist clash was to be reflected in the American Government. As March 31, 1944 (the original deadline for the stoppage of Jewish immigration) drew near, Zionist lobbying led to the introduction into both houses of Congress of identical resolutions urging that the United States Government "take appropriate measures" for the rescindment of the White Paper and the ultimate establishment of Palestine as a Jewish state. While the hearings were going on, the Near East Arab governments protested; and the presidents of the two chambers of the Iraqi Parliament even addressed personal remonstrations to Congressional leaders. Because of Arab opposition, Congress was persuaded in March 1944 by the War Department to shelve the resolutions temporarily on the ground that "further action on them at this time would be prejudicial to the successful prosecution of the war." The blow to the Zionists was softened by President Roosevelt's assurances that the United States had never approved the White Paper and that "when future decisions are reached full justice will be done to those who seek a Jewish national home, for which our Government and the American people have always had the deepest sympathy and today more than ever in view of the tragic plight of hundreds of thousands of homeless Jewish refugees." The President later explained that his statement did not conflict with the position taken by the War Department, since the military aspect was only temporary, whereas the views he expressed concerned "a civilian question for the future, to be worked out in connection with the peace." [2]

In the 1944 presidential election campaign both the Republican and the Democratic parties included in their platforms special planks on Palestine, calling for the removal of the barriers to Jewish immigration and land purchase. The Republicans, whose national convention took place first, merely proposed that Palestine "be constituted as a free and democratic commonwealth." Their rivals stated explicitly that this commonwealth was to be Jewish. Governor Dewey in mid-October redressed the balance by stating that his party stood for "the re-constitution of Palestine as a . . . Jewish commonwealth," and promising that, as president, he would use his best offices, in collaboration with Britain, "to achieve this great objective for a people that have suffered so much and deserve so much at the hands of mankind." President Roosevelt countered a few days later with the pledge that "efforts will be made to find appropriate ways and means of effectuating this policy [the Democratic Party's plank on Palestine] as soon as practicable . . . . and if re-elected I shall help to bring about its realization." [3]

After the election, the Arab-Zionist tug of war continued. As early as October, Secretary of War Stimson, withdrawing the objections of his department to the tabled pro-Zionist resolutions of Congress, declared that "political considerations now outweigh the military, and the issue [as to whether Congress might vote upon the resolutions] should be determined upon the political rather than the military basis." But when the resolutions were about to be reported back to both houses in December, action was again postponed, this time owing to the intervention of the Department of State, which asserted that "the passage of the resolutions at the present time would be unwise from the standpoint of the general international situation." [4]

The center of friction next shifted to the White House. President Roosevelt, describing to Congress on March 1, 1945, his talks with the Arab rulers after the Yalta conference, upset the Zionists when he said that "I learned more about . . . the Moslem problem, the Jewish problem, by talking with Ibn Saud for five minutes than I could have learned in exchange of two or three dozen letters." But a fortnight later the Zionists were again put at ease when the President reassured Dr. Stephen S. Wise, the chairman of the American Zionist Emergency Council, that he had not altered his pre-election position on Zionism and would "continue to seek to bring about its earliest realization." Shortly thereafter the President received a strongly worded letter from ibn Sa'ud, to which Roosevelt replied, a week before his death, reaffirming his assurances of May 1943. The President also reminded ibn Sa'ud of their conversation of a few weeks earlier, when Roosevelt promised that he "would take no action, in my capacity as Chief of the Executive Branch of this Government, which might prove hostile to the Arab people." These contradictory pledges, inherent in the Palestine question itself, were already implied in the American assumption of partial responsibility for resolving the deadlock to the mutual satisfaction of all concerned. [5]

In Britain, where Palestine had been an issue in domestic politics ever since 1917, the Arab-Zionist quarrel found constant echo in Parliament. And the Labor Party, which consistently supported the Jewish National Home, passed pro-Zionist resolutions at its annual conferences. In a statement of postwar international policy of April 1944, the party's national executive urged the removal of the ban on Jewish immigration and went on to recommend that

the Arabs be encouraged to move out as the Jews move in. Let them be compensated handsomely for their land and let their settlement elsewhere be carefully organized and generously financed. The Arabs have many wide territories of their own: they must not claim to exclude the Jews from this small area of Palestine. . . . Indeed, we should re-examine also the possibility of extending the present Palestinian boundaries, by agreement with Egypt, Syria, or Transjordan.

This statement was endorsed without change by the party's national conference at Blackpool in December 1944. The Liberal Party at its conference in London in February 1945 also included a pro-Zionist plank in its platform. British honor and interests, it was stated, required that the government drop the White Paper policy and "carry out faithfully its obligations under the Mandate and the Balfour Declaration." [6]

The radical views of the Labor Party drew fire even from independent British journals, one of which warned Labor to reconsider its position because any attempt to implement the Palestine proposals "would confront Great Britain with war in the Middle East." More serious, however, was the emergent Anglo-American friction over Palestine, which was only one aspect of the growing differences between the two allies in the Near East. Americans resented British efforts to retain dominance over Near East markets through stringent control of the finances of those countries in the sterling area. The British, for their part, were irked over the fact that American oil companies had developed "larger and larger . . . holdings . . . under British administration and the general safeguard of the British Navy and the British Middle Eastern Air Force." But until the start of 1944 the responsible section of the British press generally refrained from adverse comment about American statements on, or activities in, the Near East. Thereafter even those journals which had welcomed the close wartime collaboration of the United States and Britain in the area and hoped that it could develop into a permanent partnership voiced their displeasure. The British were especially annoyed by the treatment of the Palestine problem in American government and political circles. In discussing the pro-Zionist resolutions, noted the *Economist*, "Congress has afforded itself the luxury of criticizing where it has no intention of constructive action and proposing positive solutions which it has neither the power nor the intention to enforce." The adoption of pro-Zionist planks by both the Republicans and the Democrats, observed *The Times*, was "inspired no doubt by genuine sympathy with the Jews, but also by the evident necessity of carrying New York." [7]

The political statements on Palestine made in Britain and the United States had immediate repercussions among Arabs and Zionists. The postwar recommendations of the Labor Party's national executive aroused general indignation in the Palestine Arab Community. Caustic editorials in the press accused British Labor of demanding even more than the Zionists themselves. Politicians cabled protests to the rulers of the near-by Arab countries and members of the British Cabinet. While the Yishuv as a whole was pleased by Labor's stand, the quasi-government was embarrassed by the suggestion that the Arabs be encouraged to move out of the country. Ben Gurion was at pains to explain that Jewish plans did not entail the displacement of a single Arab and that, if the Arabs wished to emigrate to other lands, it was their own affair. The binationalists, going even further, declared that the Labor Party was doing a great disservice to the cause which it sought to help. Announcement of the Liberal Party's stand on Palestine caused one local Arab newspaper to place it in the same class as the Labor Party, both of which were said to have issued "a unanimous declaration of enmity" toward the Arabs. [8]

More widespread were the reactions to developments in the United States. By 1944 Arabs and Zionists were generally convinced that the United States was pro-Zionist. Yet as long as mandatory policy was not basically altered, the Arabs had not abandoned hope that the Americans might undergo a change of heart. The expectations of Arabs and Jews seesawed at the beginning and end of the year, when the Congressional resolutions were being considered. After Dewey and Roosevelt reaffirmed the Palestine planks of their respective parties in mid-October, the Arab chambers of commerce in Palestine refused to confer with an American economic mission then in the country, and the political parties and mayors addressed protests to the American Consul General at Jerusalem. The political parties in Egypt, Syria, and Iraq issued similar denunciations, and in Lebanon all parties formed a union for combating Zionism. One Egyptian daily even went so far as to decline to publish any further OWI news handouts, but was unable to persuade other Arab newspapers to do the same. Nor did anything come of threats to boycott American goods. [9]

In the Arab editorials and protests the presidential candidates were accused of hypocrisy. If Roosevelt and Dewey were so concerned about the persecuted European Jews, noted one paper, they ought to see that the refugees were admitted into the United States. The American parties were promising Jews unlimited immigration into Palestine, a provision that was not even included in the mandate, and were bartering away for votes a country which did not belong to them. Such was the reward bestowed upon the Arabs for their loyalty to the United Nations throughout the war. The American politicians, the accusation was most frequently made, were prepared in exchange for votes to violate the principles of the Atlantic Charter and the four freedoms.[10] The campaign planks on Palestine constituted an aggressive design, it was charged, since they implied forcing upon the people of one country another people.[11] This could only mean the expulsion of the Arabs from their homes, the obliteration of Arab Palestine, and the establishment of a Zionist state on its ruins. Such aggression the Arabs and Muslims of the world would resist with all the resources at their disposal.[12]

The intensity of the Arab reaction was increased because the close of the American election campaign coincided with the dual Arab efforts to set up the League of Arab States and to revive the national movement in Palestine. Interest in both causes among the masses, the politicians must have realized, could be aroused by identifying the United States with Zionism and thereby stressing the urgency of immediate action. Arab resentment and fear of American support for Zionism were becoming more articulate. Of all the Western Powers interested in the Near East, the United States alone enjoyed a record of noninterference in internal affairs. Although antagonism against the United States did not strike deep roots, except in the Palestine Arab Community, the anti-American agitation proved a handy political weapon. If the Arab politicians continued to use it after the war, American prestige in the Arab East was bound to suffer in the long run.

Representatives of American missionary and business establishments, who generally sided with the Arabs in the Palestine dispute, tried to explain away American sympathy for Zionism and pre-election pledges as "similar to promises made by candidates in Egypt and elsewhere during elections which are forgotten as soon as the elections are over." That the anti-American agitation was only spasmodic seemed to be indicated by the fact that Roosevelt's confirmation in March 1945 of his pre-election promises to the Zionists caused little stir in the Arab East. By that time the Arab states were in the midst of drawing up the Arab League pact, and the Palestine Arabs were training their sights on grievances against the Palestine Government. Roosevelt's personal assurances to ibn Sa'ud, which were apparently known to most Arab leaders, also must have had a quieting effect.[13]

The Palestine Jews, for their part, anxiously awaited concrete evidence of official American support of their cause. Experience earlier in the year, when the Congressional resolutions were tabled, had made many Zionists more cautious in their expectations from Washington. Until the American election was over the largest number of Palestine Jews followed the official line of the Jewish Agency that neither the Republicans nor the Democrats would advocate a program not shared by public opinion. While admitting that "the Jewish vote" might have influenced the adoption of the pro-Zionist planks, those adhering to the Agency position insisted that the existence of such a consideration did not diminish the value or moral importance of the promises. One paper in the Yishuv even inferred that Roosevelt would probably not have subscribed to the Democratic Party's Palestine plank "without first informing, perhaps even consulting, Britain about his intention." [14]

On the other hand, the binationalists and the Revisionists expressed a preference for fewer declarations of sympathy for the future and more action in the present. The binationalists, however, argued that Palestine would remain primarily in the British sphere of influence, and Britain's self-interest dictated its giving primary consideration to the Arab claims. To achieve the most from the American promise of aid, therefore, the statists were advised to abandon their demand for a Jewish state and to concentrate on seeking peace with the Arabs and stressing the need for mass immigration. The Revisionists, on their side, asserted that the American Zionists ought not to be satisfied with mere promises. They ought instead to insist that the United States bring pressure to bear on Britain, before the election was over, for the immediate establishment of a Jewish state. The ranks of the skeptics enlarged after the second shelving of the Congressional resolutions in December 1944 and Roosevelt's report on his talks with ibn Sa'ud in March 1945. Nor were they appreciably thinned when the President publicly informed the Zionists a few weeks later that he had not gone back on his word. [15]

ATTITUDES TOWARD EACH OTHER

The attitude of the Arab nationalists toward the Jews, as reflected in the anti-Zionist agitation of the Arab press in the last two years of the war, had not changed since 1939. The Arabs welcomed the Jews, it was stated, but could not accept political Zionism, which was merely trading on the persecution of European Jews. Once the war was over and Nazism destroyed, the refugees, and even many Palestine Jews, would be anxious to return to their countries of origin. Palestine was not big enough for Arabs and Jews. The fundamental question, therefore, was which of the two contestants "was to leave the country and which to remain there." [16] Zionism constituted a threat to the entire Arab East, for its war-expanded industry aimed at dominating all the markets in the region. The Arabs were warned to resist the efforts of Jewish industry in Palestine to transform the Arab countries into Jewish colonies. The Egyptians were urged by one Cairo daily to oppose the establishment of a Jewish state in order to prevent the transfer of the economic and financial capital of the Near East from Cairo to Tel-Aviv. The Jews living in the Arab countries, it was hinted, ought to realize that their self-interest lay in identifying themselves with the Arabs against Zionism. The American pro-Zionist statements, it was said, sprang from the immense Jewish influence in the United States, particularly over the press, the radio, and in business as well as financial circles.[17]

Many of the papers in the Yishuv, for their part, recognized that the Arab states were able to band together in opposition to Zionism. But the Hebrew press was prone, during the Arab Unity parleys in Egypt in 1943–44, to stress that the Arab countries were not yet ripe for real merger. The individual governments had not had sufficient experience in administering their own internal affairs, it was argued, while political, economic, and cultural differences between one country and another were too great and rivalries too acute to allow for abiding collaboration in the foreseeable future. At all events, the whole Arab Unity movement was alleged to have been a British creation, and "it appears that it is impossible to give . . . a group of nations a national idea emanating from outside and to convert it into a . . . practical policy when the desire to carry it out has not matured sufficiently from within." [18] One Hebrew daily, which usually analyzed Arab affairs with acumen, predicted on the eve of the Alexandria conference that decades would elapse before the Arab leaders could forge a political, economic, or even cultural unity of the Arab countries. After the conference was over and the first steps were taken to establish the Arab League, the same newspaper, voicing a more guarded opinon, warned that the Zionists had little to gain from trying to prove that Arab attempts to form closer ties had few prospects of realization. "On the contrary," continued the editorial, "we have come to realize that any emphasis placed on the failure of these efforts serves as a sort of 'injection' of new energy into the Arab politicians." [19]

The official Zionist position toward Arab unity at the war's end was outlined by Moshe Shertok, the Jewish Agency's political spokesman, before a joint session of the Zionist Inner General Council and the Elected Assembly in December 1944. The unity of the purely Arab lands was an Arab affair, declared Shertok. If the movement displayed a tendency to develop along constructive lines, the Agency was prepared to make its contribution on the basis of mutual recognition and benefit. But in view of the movement's hostility to the Jewish enterprise in Palestine, he asserted, the Zionists were compelled, for the time being at least, to entrench themselves against it. Shertok cautioned the Zionist leaders, however, to distinguish between the enmity to Zionism and the positive aspirations of the Arab countries to achieve cooperation among themselves on their internal affairs. The Jews, Shertok insisted, were solely concerned with constructive endeavor, for which there was "plenty of room for us all" in the region east of Suez, whose problem was one of a population shortage and an unexploited surplus of the means of subsistence. The charge that Jewish immigration of necessity involved the displacement of Arabs in Palestine, Shertok claimed, had no basis in fact, as attested by the country's steadily rising living standard. The contention that a Jewish state could only be established by uprooting the Arabs was equally disproved, he continued, by the position of the Arabs living in Jewish-controlled municipalities. The allegation that the Jews were hoping to infiltrate into and dominate the near-by countries was dismissed as just another "scarecrow," designed to rouse regional antipathy toward the Zionists. Shertok concluded with the assurance that "not only has the Jewish people no aspirations in respect of the countries neighbouring on Palestine, but the Zionist movement is completely opposed to the dispersal . . . of Jewish settlers in them." [20]

The Zionists viewed with dismay the admittance of four more Arab states to the United Nations as a result of their last-minute entry into the war early in 1945. They were afraid that when the Palestine problem came up for consideration the Arabs would have a distinct advantage, for five states would be defending their position whereas the Zionists could be certain of none. "We did not wait for the end of the war: we have stood up against . . . Germany ever since the Nazis came into power," asserted David Ben Gurion, voicing the opinion of all Zionists.[21]

. . . . Nevertheless, the Jews are to have no place at the first conference of the nations at San Francisco. . . . There is one reason for this: we are a people without a State, and therefore a people without credentials, without recognition, without representation, without the privileges of a nation, without the means of self-defence, and without any say in our fate.

Within Palestine itself the Arabs at first believed that the United Nations Conference at San Francisco was to be the peace conference of World War II and viewed their prospects with nervous optimism. The Arab states, observed one editorialist, would have as many votes as the British Empire, and their influence would be greater than that of any of the Big Powers, if the cooperation of such Oriental countries as Iran, Turkey and Ethiopia could be elicited. But the Palestine Arabs were afraid that the neighboring countries were not planning their offensive carefully enough. Great Britain ought to be warned, suggested one Palestine Arab paper, that friendship has its limits, that Near East stability would depend upon the establishment of Palestine as an independent Arab country, and that unless this condition were met the Arab states would not join the United Nations Organization.[22]

DISINTEGRATING DOMESTIC SITUATION

Evidence of growing Arab-Zionist tension in Palestine manifested itself by the spring of 1944, when the Arab press incriminated the entire

Jewish Community for the terrorist outrages against the government. At the end of March *Al-Difaʻ* accused the Palestine Jews of "waving a white flag with the left hand while shooting with the right" and, implying that the Jewish Agency was responsible for the terrorism, recommended its dissolution. An editorial appearing on the same day in *Filastin* contrasted this "stab in Britain's back" with the "boasts" of the Palestine Jews about their contributions to the war effort. It went on to declare that the Jews were nothing but "liars whose tongues ought to be cut off." The Jewish press in reply criticized the British censors for permitting the publication of such provocative editorials. The Arab journalists were chided for their "utterly unfounded and mischievous insinuations" and were reminded of their silence on terrorism during the Arab revolt of 1936–39. "Those . . . whose enthusiasm for law and order, the war effort and the Democratic cause is yet to be demonstrated," observed the *Palestine Post*, "should think twice before questioning the sincerity of a community which by its actions and sacrifices has given very real proof of its dedication to both Palestine security and to the war." [23]

The first serious wartime crisis between the two communities was precipitated by the death of the Jerusalem mayor in August. There had been country-wide ill feeling over that city ever since the preceding May, when the Arab mayor had offended his Jewish constituents by endorsing in the name of Jerusalem a strongly worded anti-Zionist statement. The vacancy in August was filled temporarily by the Jewish deputy mayor. The Arabs immediately began to press for the permanent appointment of a Muslim on the grounds that Jerusalem represented the entire country, a Muslim had traditionally held the office, and religious and historical associations made it imperative that a non-Arab should not be the mayor of a city holy to Islam and Christianity. The Jews argued that they formed a decisive majority of the city's inhabitants, they paid most of the municipal taxes, and the religious and historical rights of the Jews were older and no less compelling than those of the other religious communities.[24] The validity of these claims could not be recognized, replied one Arab newspaper, since the non-Arab majority had been "imposed" on the Arabs. Another inquired whether the Jews would apply the same reasoning to Palestine as a whole and permit its Arab majority to obtain all their rights. A Jewish binationalist organ pointed out that the Jews would never recognize Jerusalem as representing only Arab Palestine, and went on to deplore the fact that "short-sighted, popularity-seeking" politicians were trying to increase their influence by dividing the two peoples in a mixed town which ought to have become a training ground for bringing Arabs and Jews together in a country belonging to neither exclusively.[25]

Before any attempt was made to solve the issue, it became involved in the Arab agitation against the government. As the end of the first five years of the White Paper approached and the complete stoppage of Jewish immigration was expected, the view gained currency in the Arab Community that the second five-year period would be devoted to inaugurating self-government in Palestine. The deferment in November 1943 of the final suspension of Jewish immigration and the failure in the spring of 1944 to implement the constitutional features of the White Paper, therefore, made the Arabs uneasy. But as long as Sir Harold MacMichael remained High Commissioner, the Arabs tended to place the blame on London. After Lord Gort's arrival, however, the Palestine Government also came increasingly under Arab attack. The press continued to campaign for the execution of the White Paper in its entirety.[26] Despite "irrevocable" and "unconditional" assurances to the contrary, it was charged, the influx of Jews had persisted beyond the five-year period, so that the Jews now equaled "50 per cent" of the country's population, instead of only one-third, as laid down in the 1939 policy. The government was further accused of doing nothing to prevent evasions of the Land Transfer Regulations and at times of even colluding with the Jews in violating the enactment. So persistent had the exposés of alleged violations become in the early months of 1945, that the government agreed to appoint a commission to investigate the Arab complaints.[27]

Arab animosity toward the government, added to the existing Jewish-government and Arab-Jewish tension, had frayed the nerves of the entire country by March 1945, when Lord Gort set about solving the Jerusalem mayoralty crisis. The issue had in the interval been transformed into one of national prestige for the two communities. The High Commissioner recommended, as a provisional compromise, the rotation of the office annually between a Muslim, a Jew, and a Christian. The Jews conditionally accepted the proposal, the Arabs unconditionally rejected it, and the government soon dropped it. The possible partition of Jerusalem into separate Arab and Jewish municipal corporations was then considered for a time. But this scheme too was abandoned because of Arab objections. The management of municipal affairs was finally transferred in July 1945 —for the duration of the mandate, as it turned out—to a British commission of five, appointed by the High Commissioner.[28]

On the whole the dilemma and the deadlock in Jerusalem were characteristic of the course of Palestine events in this period. Arabs and Zionists both were victims not only of their own self-engrossed propaganda but of the hesitancy and the frequent reversal of mandatory policy. The Palestine Government itself was caught in the trap of London's indecision. The Colonial Office was thinking of partition. This implied the scrapping of the 1939 White Paper. Until such time as the Colonial Office plan might be disclosed, however, the pretense had to be made in Palestine that the principles of the White Paper remained the unswerving principles of mandatory policy. But, apart from the blind enforcement of the restrictive immigration and land laws, there was drift, not policy. The pretense had embittered the Jews and was now unnerving the Arabs. Both sides were arming to the hilt. There was no law. Therefore there could be no order.

The Jerusalem breakdown was a forewarning of what lay in store for the entire country, if no remedy were soon found. A combination of the experience of the United Kingdom and the resources of the United States might have been able to salvage the situation. The two allies enjoyed a tremendous prestige in the Near East, by reason of their victory in Europe and the presence of large garrisons throughout the region. This prestige and a coordinated, determined Anglo-American effort might have been sufficient to hammer out a compromise. Any workable solution would have had to take into consideration the equitable rights of Arabs and Jews and the realities of the two self-centered, nationalistic communities with their separate ways of life.

If a unitary, centralized regime was the least promising solution in 1937, it was even less so in 1945. To create such a governmental structure would have required undoing the achievements of an entire generation: overhauling the two educational systems, blending the two sets of political institutions, welding the two economies, and forcing bilingualism on the two sections of the population. Whether the combined resources of the two Western Powers could have forged such a regime is highly doubtful. Still, a just compromise might have assumed any one of a number of forms—partition, cantonization, or federalism—provided the essentials of early democratic self-rule and continued Jewish immigration were expressly included.

Clearly any compromise would have brought on the fury of the extremists in both the Arab and Zionist camps. But there never was a time when the Palestine problem could have been solved without the use of force. The sooner the decision was reached, the moderates given the unequivocal backing of the victorious Allies, the extremists discredited, and the necessary external force applied, the less would be the bloodshed. Delay was placing a premium on militant fanaticism. The issue was becoming firmly embedded in domestic American politics, was creating bad blood between the United States and Britain, and was stirring up unrest throughout the Arab East.

CHAPTER 17

Palestine as an Anglo-American Problem

BRITISH AND AMERICAN HESITATION

VICTORY IN Europe removed the last restraining influence from the crisis that was precipitating in and over Palestine. The issue came briefly into focus at the Conference on International Organization in San Francisco (April 25–June 26, 1945). The delegates of the Arab League states tried to have the articles on trusteeship of the projected United Nations Charter so worded as to limit Jewish rights in Palestine to the existing Jewish population in the country. This would have ended the special status accorded the Jewish Agency under the mandate. But the Charter, as finally adopted, did not in any way affect the terms of the original Palestine Mandate, and Article 77 reserved "for subsequent agreement . . . which territories . . . [including those already under mandate] will be brought under the trusteeship system and upon what terms." Aside from San Francisco, however, the Arab League was sidetracked from the Palestine question during May and June because of preoccupation with resisting French pressure on Syria and Lebanon.[1]

The Zionist cause, meanwhile, had suffered irreparable damage. The Nazi slaughter of more than 5,000,000 European Jews had largely dried up the most promising source of potential citizens of the hoped-for Jewish state. Moreover, most of the Palestine Jews had lost close relatives in Europe. The consequent personal distress endowed much of the Zionist political thinking and action with an emotional quality, which lay at the center of the steadily worsening situation in Palestine. Weizmann's moderate counsel for patience and faith in Britain could have no further meaning after V-E Day, unless Europe's Jewish survivors were soon allowed to enter Palestine freely.

The Jews "have never accepted and never can accept the moral or legal validity of the White Paper," declared the Agency president in a memorandum to Prime Minister Churchill at the end of May. In the preceding six years, the statement went on, the Jews had given paramount consideration to the war effort, even though they had "seen very large numbers of Jewish lives cruelly sacrificed, many more of which might have been saved had immigration into Palestine been regulated in accordance with the Balfour Declaration and the Mandate." But now that the war was over, the Jews "can no longer tolerate the continuance of the White Paper." After outlining the immigration needs and the Zionist political and economic plans, the memorandum requested the British Government to take "an immediate decision," specifying the establishment of Palestine as a Jewish state, and to transfer to the Agency the authority to regulate immigration and develop the country's resources. It was also recommended that the Agency be provided with "international facilities . . . for the transit of all Jews who wish to settle in Palestine" and with an international loan, supplemented by reparations in kind from Germany. As a first installment it was suggested that all German property in Palestine be given to the Jews.

Early in June, Churchill replied that the Palestine question could not be "effectively considered until the victorious Allies are definitely seated at the Peace Table." Nor was any action taken on a second Agency memorandum of mid-June, urgently pleading for 100,000 entry permits for European Jews.[2] From the British Government's viewpoint the Agency memorandum had come most inopportunely. The war in Europe was over, but the length of the war against Japan was still unpredictable. Churchill dissolved his Coalition War Cabinet late in May, and Britain was now embarked on its first general election in ten years. With the Levant crisis adding to the existing tension in the Arab East, London was not yet ready to tackle the even more complex Palestine problem. The British Government would have to revaluate its future obligations in Palestine in relation to its over-all foreign commitments. These, in turn, would depend on the postwar relations of the Big Three, particularly on the nature of Anglo-American peacetime cooperation.

Anglo-American plans for Palestine, it was true, had been coordinated in principle under Roosevelt and Churchill. Roosevelt's death in April 1945, however, ended the unprecedented, personal collaboration between the two war leaders. At the close of July, Churchill himself was swept out of office by Labor's landslide. The break in continuity was now complete. Neither Truman nor Attlee had the world-wide prestige of his predecessor. They approached the tremendous political problems arising out of the war with the irresolution and timidity of inexperienced statesmen at a time when decision and boldness were imperative. Matters were further complicated by the fact that the war-born Big Three Alliance gave evidence of breaking up. Mutual suspicions which had accumulated between Russia and the West prior to 1941, but had been submerged in the war, were now coming to the surface with added force. Moreover, the Big Three decided at Potsdam in July to entrust the drafting of peace treaties to the Big Power Council of Foreign Ministers and to submit their proposals to the United Nations for ratification. Under these circumstances, it became clear, the Palestine problem would not be taken up at a general peace conference, as envisioned by Churchill.

From Roosevelt, Truman inherited no clearly formulated Palestine policy. Congress was sensitized to American public opinion. This, in so far as it was articulate on Palestine, was markedly pro-Zionist, primarily because of the plight of the European Jews and the effective public relations program of the American Zionists. The departments of State and War were most concerned about the feelings of the Arab governments as they affected the general Near East situation and American strategic and economic interests in the region. The White House itself was exposed to all the conflicting pressures. Roosevelt and Churchill working together might have been able to reconcile Arab and Zionist claims, if certain indispensable conditions were met. Soviet acquiescence would have had to be secured in advance. London and Washington would also have had to deal with the Palestine question soon after the war's close and in conjunction with a settlement of the general Near East and certain European problems—notably the disposition of the displaced persons—which had a direct bearing on the situation in Palestine. But under Truman and Attlee none of these conditions was satisfied. Consequently the United States Government was unable to formulate a comprehensive Palestine policy which could possibly win the approval of public sentiment both in the United States and in the Near East.

President Truman, shortly after entering the White House in April, assured the Zionists that he would abide by the pre-election promises of Roosevelt and the Democratic Party. Then the President confirmed Roosevelt's pledges to the Arabs about advance consultations on Palestine. Late in June the President instructed Earl G. Harrison, the American representative on the Intergovernmental Committee on Refugees, to investigate the D.P. problem in Europe, to pay particular attention to the non-repatriable Jews, and to discover their emigration preferences. At Potsdam, Truman informed Churchill and Attlee that his government favored the admission into Palestine of as many Jews as could be settled there peacefully, but that it was opposed to the use of American troops to prevent disorder. Among the reasons for the President's unwillingness to use American troops were possible Congressional opposition, the desire to limit postwar American military commitments abroad, and the pressure of American public opinion for rapid demobilization.[3]

The British Labor Party's national executive, at the party's campaign conference in May, reaffirmed its Palestine plank of the previous year, calling for the White Paper's abrogation, unlimited Jewish immigration, the extension of Palestine territory, and Palestine Arab emigration.[4] Once in power, Labor turned in mid-August to the Palestine issue. The temporary factors—the Levant crisis, the Japanese war, and the British election—which had disquieted Churchill two months earlier were no longer operative. Labor's overwhelming victory indicated on the surface that the new government would have public support for whatever Palestine policy it might choose. Still the Labor Government hesitated.

The war had left the British economy in a state of near-prostration. The United Kingdom, therefore, could not undertake costly ventures in the Arab East, as vital as the area was. Besides, the war had changed the United Kingdom's relationship to Egypt, Palestine, and Iraq from a creditor to a debtor nation, thereby further diluting British authority. Fear of Soviet intentions regarding the Near East had suddenly become very acute, because of Russian pressures on Turkey and Iran and Moscow's demand for a trusteeship over one of the Italian colonies. Britain alone could not check the Soviet Union, if it should seek to expand into the Near East. Yet the United States, whose peacetime collaboration in the region the Labor Government would have welcomed, seemed determined to quit that area after V-J Day as rapidly as it had entered three years earlier. This undue haste derived from the Truman Administration's tendency not to resist the will of American public opinion to return from a war to a peace footing and from the American failure to frame an integrated policy for the Near East. Finally, when Arab representation in the United Nations was augmented from one to five states early in 1945, London was deprived of maneuverability in its diplomatic negotiations with the Arab countries. Admittance to the United Nations could no longer be used as a reward for Arab cooperation. In fact, the Labor Government soon came to feel that all of its Near East decisions would have to be based on winning Arab friendship.[5]

Labor's victory in Britain momentarily checked the anxiety of the Zionists, who hoped that pre-election pledges would soon be honored, at least in part. A world Zionist conference, attended by more than 100 delegates and observers from 17 countries, including five formerly occupied by the Nazis, met in London early in August. In the six years since the Twenty-first Zionist Congress of August 1939 the Zionist movement had undergone basic structural changes. Interest in Zionism on the Continent had become more intense among the Jewish survivors, but the branches of the movement had either been destroyed or driven underground. The principal Zionist centers were now Palestine and the United States. The conference accordingly made some adjustment of the leadership by enlarging the Zionist, and therefore the Jewish Agency, Executive from twelve to eighteen members. The delegates were split into the followers of Weizmann, who still accented gradualism, and those of Ben Gurion, who emphasized immediate action, if the White Paper were not soon rescinded. But British Labor's consistent sympathy with Zionism gave the moderates a temporary edge over the activists. Nevertheless even their tone was desperate. "The remnants of European Jewry cannot and will not continue their existence among the graveyards of the millions of their slaughtered brethren," warned the political resolutions adopted by the conference.

> Their only salvation lies in their speediest settlement in Palestine. . . . The vast majority of the Jewish people throughout the world feel that they have no chance of "freedom from fear" unless the status of the Jews, as individuals and as a nation, has been made equal to that of all normal peoples, and the Jewish State in Palestine has been established.

The Agency's demands of May, consideration of which had been postponed by Churchill, were renewed, and an appeal for amity was addressed to the Arabs and "other peoples" in the Near East.[6]

Also in the summer and fall of 1945 the Arab League states, principally Iraq, had launched their comprehensive propaganda scheme under the general supervision of Musa al-'Alami, and allocated to it a first year's budget of about $2,000,000. The project was designed to inform and influence official and public opinion in the United States and the United Kingdom on all aspects of Arab life. Offices were opened in Washington, London, and Cairo, with headquarters in Jerusalem. The constitution specifically counseled the staff not to confine themselves to Palestine propaganda but to "try to show events in Palestine as particular examples of general tendencies in the Arab World." Despite this admonition the Arab offices, as the Arab struggle against Zionism intensified, tended to concentrate on counteracting Zionist propaganda. On this subject the constitution instructed the Arab offices to avoid "anti-British elements" in the United States and anti-Jewish propaganda. They were directed to base their work upon "a thorough analysis" of the

> main Zionist arguments . . . particularly (i) the strategic arguments that it is in Great Britain's and America's interest to have a Jewish State in Palestine; (ii) the social and economic arguments; (iii) the religious and ethical arguments; (iv) the question: What have the Arabs done during the war?

This publicity was to be addressed mainly to "influencing . . . M.P.'s, higher civil servants, journalists, business men and finance, the [armed] Services, the universities, the churches, labour, [and] non-Zionist Jews."

The London office was to be both political and propagandist, and the constitution recommended the appointment as its director of "a responsible statesman able to work on the highest level and ensure that the Arabs are not forgotten when great decisions are taken." The Washington office, however, was visualized as almost solely one of public relations, so that there was "not so much need for a statesman at its head." In the United States, moreover, the Arab League's publicity efforts were eked out in New York by the Institute of Arab American Affairs, which had been founded in the spring of 1945 by Americans of Arab descent.[7]

The Arab bureau in London advised the Labor Government a few days after it assumed office that the Arab world would never accept a Jewish homeland in Palestine, even if it secured the blessings of the Big Three. Any reversal of the White Paper, continued the Arab statement, "would be viewed as another breach of faith by England and would cause the utmost prejudice to Anglo-Arab relations." Then in mid-August at a press conference in Alexandria 'Abd-al-Rahman Bey 'Azzam, the Secretary-General of the Arab League, turned his guns on President Truman, who had just announced at Potsdam his support of Zionist claims for immigration into Palestine. The encouragement of Zionist aspirations, warned 'Azzam Bey, might touch off a new crusaders' war between Christianity and Islam. The Arabs had placed their confidence throughout the war in the United States and built on its sense of justice their dreams of a new world. But "we are in duty bound to remind" President Truman of "the last promise made to the Arabs by the great and lamented President Roosevelt a few weeks before his death. Placing his hand in that of King 'Abd-al-'Aziz ibn al-Sa'ud, he pledged his word that he would not support the Zionist cause against the Arabs in Palestine." [8]

The Labor Government now took its first move to deal with the Palestine problem. Over the opposition of the Labor Party's national executive and several Ministers favoring a pro-Zionist policy, the Attlee Cabinet adopted the recommendations of a special subcommittee on Palestine, headed by Foreign Secretary Ernest Bevin. After analyzing the estimates by British Near East experts, the subcommittee concluded that the United Kingdom alone could not carry out a pro-Zionist program. Bevin therefore proposed that, as an interim measure, Jewish immigration should continue at the rate of 1,500 a month even after the expiry of the White Paper quota. The Colonial Office communicated the Cabinet decision to Weizmann on August 25, but the Agency president rejected the offer as entirely inadequate.[9]

At about this time President Truman received a preliminary report from Earl G. Harrison, describing the deplorable conditions of the D.P.'s in Europe. Many were still kept behind barbed wire in unsanitary, crowded camps, where the death rate remained high, the morale low, and where they lived "in complete idleness. . . . Beyond knowing that they are no longer in danger of the gas chambers, torture and other forms of violent death, they see—and there is—little change." The estimated 100,-000 stateless European Jews outside the Russian zone, declared Harrison, required special treatment. "While admittedly it is not normally desirable to set aside particular racial or religious groups from their nationality categories," he explained,[10]

> the plain truth is that this was done for so long by the Nazis that a group has been created which has special needs. Jews as Jews (not as members of their nationality groups) have been more severely victimized than the non-Jewish members of the same or other nationalities.

The vast majority of the displaced Jews were anxious to leave Germany and Austria. "With respect to possible places of resettlement," the report continued,

> . . . Palestine is definitely and pre-eminently the first choice. Many now have relatives there, while others, having experienced intolerance and persecution in their homelands [for] years, feel that only in Palestine will they be welcomed and . . . given an opportunity to live and work.

Others chose Palestine, it was asserted, because they were devoted Zionists or because they realized that the possibility of settling in the United States or the Western Hemisphere was slight.

President Truman immediately forwarded the Harrison report to Prime Minister Attlee, recommending that "as many as possible of the non-repatriable Jews, who wish it," be evacuated to Palestine. The British Government reportedly agreed to let these refugees enter Palestine on condition that the United States assume joint responsibility, including the use of troops, if necessary. But the President again vetoed American military intervention, and there the matter stalemated for several weeks. Reflecting official as well as public displeasure, the British press commented on the generosity of American advice and the parsimony of American helpfulness. Even a pro-Zionist publication declared that Truman's action was motivated by his awareness "of the 5,000,000 Jews who form so influential a body of voters in the United States"; another pointed out that "America's request would be more impressive had she herself opened her doors wider to Hitler's victims." [11]

For a brief while the Labor Government toyed with the idea of referring the Palestine issue to the United Nations. But this was quickly dropped, as a result of dissension with the Soviet Union at the first session of the Council of Foreign Ministers in London, which concluded in an impasse on October 2, and the consequent sharpening of British fears of Russian motives in the eastern Mediterranean and Iran. Finally the Attlee Cabinet suggested to President Truman, as a compromise between the British and American positions, that the two governments undertake a joint investigation of the Palestine and related problems. This proposal was accepted by the United States at the end of October, but its details were not released by London and Washington for more than a fortnight.[12]

The vacillation of the Labor Cabinet kept Arab nationalists and Zionists on tenterhooks. The longer the decision was delayed the more both protagonists were emboldened to try to influence that decision. The suspense was all the greater because they both feared that any settlement imposed so soon after the war was likely to be permanent. The Arab League's Secretary-General proceeded to London at the end of September to confer with Bevin and declared publicly that the League would demand the immediate independence of Palestine, if Britain attempted to convert the mandate into a trusteeship. "The essence of the Palestine problem," stated 'Azzam Bey, "is the clash between the rights and interests of . . . [the] indigenous [Arab] population, on the one hand, and the challenge to it of a mixed and alien population on the other." The Arabs harbored no hostility toward the Jews, he continued, but they recognized that "the driving power behind this immigration is a political and racial will to domination . . . . backed by European imperialism." In Washington the legations of Iraq, the Levant States, and Egypt presented to Secretary of State Byrnes on October 12 a joint memorandum, warning that "there obviously can be no peace in . . . [the Arab world] by sacrificing Arab interests for the sake of the Jews. A Zionist political state can be created in Palestine, but only with the help of external force." [13]

In the Arab countries incitation against Zionism, Britain, and the United States became increasingly serious after the beginning of October. Threats were voiced about suspending concessions to American-owned oil companies and applying economic sanctions against the United States. The Levant States and Iraq began to follow the practice, instituted by Egypt in May, of neither honoring nor granting transit visas for Palestine-bound Jews. Iraq reportedly refused to allow its Jewish subjects to visit Palestine even on business unless they first deposited a bond of $20,000. The climax was reached on November 2, the anniversary of the Balfour Declaration, when anti-Zionist demonstrations took place in Egypt, Syria, Lebanon, and Iraq. Spurred on by agitators, crowds in Cairo, Alexandria, and other Egyptian towns attacked Jews and other minorities, foreigners, and even Muslims, burning synagogues, stoning churches, and looting stores. Before peace was restored at the end of three days, the unrest spread to the former Italian colony of Tripolitania, where the recently organized, secret National Party provoked Arab mobs from November 4 to 7 to massacre over 100 native Jews and wound 50 others.[14]

For their part the Jewish Agency and its affiliated bodies in Britain and the United States brought to bear after the end of September the full weight of the support they had amassed during the war. In Britain, Agency leaders at extraordinary meetings of the Zionist Federation and the Board of Jewish Deputies served notice that the Jews would resist efforts to retain the White Paper and that its further execution would necessitate the use of force. The same theme was developed by Weizmann before the pro-Zionist Parliamentary Committee on October 9, the day that the British legislature reconvened. More outspoken were the statements of American Zionist leaders. The Palestine Jews "will not sit calmly by," declared the co-chairman of the American Zionist Emergency Council, who had been elevated a few weeks earlier to membership on the Agency Executive, "and watch the final destruction, after 'liberation,' of the surviving remnants of their brothers and sisters in Europe." An estimated 150,000 participants in a mass Zionist demonstration in New York heard the president of the Zionist Organization of America declare,

> We refuse to recognize as "illegal" any Jewish immigrant who enters Palestine without a certificate. . . . Illegal is the hand and the Government that attempts to bar the Jew from the Jewish national home.

The American Christian Palestine Committee held a conference in New York in October and another, attended by foreign delegates, in Washington in November. Pro-Zionist congressmen participated in these meetings and on the floor of the House endorsed President Truman's appeal for the transfer of the 100,000 displaced Jews to Palestine.[15]

In this twilight period the tension in the Yishuv became noticeably worse. The short-lived optimism over the Labor Party's victory gradually gave way to a deeper anxiety than before, as disturbing reports flowed in from London. An emergency session of Jewish leaders at Jerusalem on September 27 issued a proclamation, declaring that the immigration ban after the war's close was [16]

> tantamount to a death sentence upon . . . those liberated Jews . . . still languishing in the internment camps of Germany. . . . Jewish immigrants will stream to Palestine by all means. . . . The Hebrew Book of Books will, by its eternal strength, destroy the White Paper. . . . The Jewish State will be established.

That the quasi-government was planning to carry out its threats of organized mass illegal immigration was borne out by incidents in the early fall. A Jewish village on the Lebanese border resisted attempts by the frontier police to search for Jews who had entered the country without proper credentials. Some 200 illegal European immigrants, held in a detention camp near Haifa, were set free by Haganah units after rumors that they were going to be deported. Two villages, suspected of complicity in this action, refused to pay collective fines. Two coastal patrol launches were damaged and a third sunk. Early in October, Haganah began daily broadcasts over its mobile, unlawful "Voice of Israel" station, unused since June 1940. One of the first broadcasts advised the British not to "delude themselves that there will be peace here if Jewish immigration is restricted." [17]

From these developments it was clear that the activists were now gaining the upper hand for the first time. When on the night of October 31 the Palestine railway system was blown up in 153 places, paralyzing the service for 24 hours, the action was defended by most of the press. "There was a time when the overwhelming majority of the Yishuv was vigorously opposed to acts of violence," wrote *Ha-Arez.*

> In the depth of our hearts we still feel that this path is fraught with danger. But it is not up to us alone to prevent grave dangers. If the British Government has arrived at a decision that can open a gate of hope to the Jewish people—let us hear it.

In the sabotage of the railways Haganah collaborated with the Irgun. Indeed, Haganah commanders were reportedly seeking a permanent working agreement with the terrorist groups, despite strong opposition from the Agency Executive and the leftist labor parties. As for the Irgun and the Freedom Fighters, they had recommenced their terrorist activities in May by bombing police installations, blowing up telegraph poles, and piercing the Iraq Petroleum Company pipe line. After a brief "truce," during August and the first half of September when the new Labor Government was placed "on trial," the violence was resumed.[18]

Relations also remained strained between the Palestine Arabs and the government, and on the surface the sentiment in the Arab Community toward the Zionists as well as the government was united. But in reality the acute rivalries among the politicians precluded organized action like that of the Yishuv. This contrasted starkly with the Arab states' unity on Palestine. Even when the League offered direct material assistance to the national movement in Palestine, its efforts often became hopelessly enmeshed in the personal squabbles of the local politicians.

An example was Musa al-'Alami's Constructive Scheme. The project, as originally conceived, was to be dedicated to the dual objective of saving Arab land from passing to Jewish ownership and of helping the peasants to modernize their farming techniques and equipment. 'Alami's proposal was adopted by the Arab Unity conference at Alexandria in October 1944, and the Arab states agreed to contribute to it $4,000,000 a year over a period of five years. But in Palestine the Istiqlal spokesmen sought to have 'Alami's plan incorporated into the Arab National Fund, which was under their control. The Palestine Arab (Husayni) Party, on the other hand, saw in the Constructive Scheme the possibility of undermining their rivals' influence. The Husaynis therefore sided with 'Alami, who insisted that the new project remain completely independent. Finally in June 1945 the Palestine Arab Party leaders resigned from the board of directors of the National Fund. Thereupon the Istiqlal politicians withdrew their support from 'Alami as the Palestine delegate to the Arab League. Under these circumstances the Constructive Scheme was temporarily dropped from the Arab League's agenda.[19]

Amir 'Abdallah's endeavor to mediate between the Palestine Arab politicians early in August with a view to setting up a Higher Committee also foundered on the rock of factional jealousies, for the Husaynis refused to appear with the other politicians. Even the established newspapers, which were identified with the parties, censured the politicians for their chronic disagreement, which was stated to be a "blot on our name and an obstacle to Arab League efforts." And a new independent weekly lashed at the politicians as "charlatans" and "professional nationalists" and exclaimed that, if they had any self-respect, the Palestine Arab politicians would have "folded their tongues within their mouths and removed their dirty linen from the lines, where it is exposed to full public view." But despite the censure of the press Palestine Arab politics continued as usual. The party leaders themselves had ceased their periodic informal meetings in June, as the split in the national movement widened. The young intellectuals who were anxious to reform the movement and regarded themselves as nonpartisan were forced under the circumstances to side with the Istiqlal or the Husayni bloc. Even the labor ranks were thus divided. In August 1945 the left-wing Federation of Arab Trade Unions merged with the communist-dominated branches of the Palestine Arab Workers Society to form the Arab Workers Congress. The Arab Workers Congress, which was already tied to the communist League of National Liberation, followed the Istiqlal lead. The truncated, right-wing Palestine Arab Workers Society cooperated on the political level with the Husaynis.[20]

Of the two rival blocs, that dominated by the Husaynis was the more aggressive. The Palestine Arab Party held frequent meetings, the most spectacular of which, a tenth-anniversary celebration at Jerusalem on June 1, 1945, was attended by an estimated 5,000 persons. Resolutions passed by these meetings called for the repatriation of al-Hajj Amin, his cousin Jamal, and the other exiled or interned leaders. These demands were embodied in party appeals to members of the British Government, Parliament, the Archbishop of Canterbury, and the Arab kings and heads of government. Although Jamal was still detained by the British in Southern Rhodesia in November 1945, the Mufti had managed on the eve of the Nazi surrender to reach France. There he was placed under house arrest and "treated with every consideration due an outstanding personality of the Islamic world." In July the Yugoslav Government entered al-Hajj Amin's name on the list of war criminals "for inciting brutalities and for pro-German activities among the Bosnian Moslems." But Belgrade later withdrew its charges at the request of the Arab League.[21]

Because of their political disunity the Palestine Arabs were not yet ready for a show of force. Consequently the only serious threat to peace came from the Yishuv. That the mandatory was determined to deal firmly with the Jews was indicated in the steps taken after the end of September. The Palestine Government's sweeping police and military powers were consolidated in a fifty-page enactment. Military reinforcements included a division of airborne troops, veterans of the Normandy invasion. By early November there were four destroyers and two cruisers in Palestine waters; coastal and frontier patrols were strengthened by additional aircraft. Security measures on highways and at government buildings were noticeably tightened. When Lord Gort unexpectedly resigned as High Commissioner early in November for reasons of health, he was succeeded by another professional soldier, Lieutenant-General Sir Alan Gordon Cunningham. But a full-scale British-Zionist conflict was postponed by the announcement on November 13 of the proposed Anglo-American inquiry.[22]

CHAPTER 18

The Anglo-American Committee
of Inquiry

THE ANGLO-AMERICAN Committee of Inquiry was instructed to examine the status of the Jews in former Axis-occupied countries and to determine how many could be reintegrated into their lands of origin or present residence, and how many sought or were "impelled by their conditions to migrate to Palestine or other countries outside Europe." An estimate was to be made, in consultation with "representative Arabs and Jews," of the prospects of Jewish immigration into Palestine under the prevailing "political, economic and social conditions." The committee was directed to recommend provisional and permanent solutions for all these questions. The Inquiry Committee, under alternating British and American chairmanship, consisted of six Americans and six Britons, whose names were not disclosed until December 10.[1]

In elaborating upon the announcement of the proposed inquiry, Foreign Secretary Bevin declared that mandatory policy would be developed in three stages. The Arabs were being consulted—and "he felt confident that they would agree"—about the continuation of Jewish immigration at the monthly rate of 1,500, once the 2,000 visas remaining under the White Paper were consumed. The British Government, after considering the Inquiry Committee's interim proposals, would "explore, with the parties concerned, the possibility of devising other temporary arrangements for dealing with the Palestine problem until a permanent solution of it can be reached." The mandatory would then propose a final settlement, "if possible an agreed one," for submission to the United Nations. Palestine was to become a temporary trusteeship, and in time an independent, "Palestinian, not Jewish, state." Until the trusteeship agreement came into being the United States' role would be purely advisory.

The British Government, the Foreign Secretary declared, had tried vainly for a quarter of a century to find common ground between Arabs and Zionists. But this had proved impossible, owing chiefly to the absence of a clear definition of mandatory obligations to both sides. The Zionists, he went on, had won great humanitarian sympathy in Anglo-American countries and elsewhere as a result of the persecution of European Jews, while the Palestine Arabs had rallied to their side the entire Arab world and the 90,000,000 Muslims of India. The Inquiry Committee would, therefore, have to find a balance between equity, humanitarianism, and world peace. But the British Government, Bevin asserted, could not "accept the view that the Jews should be driven out of Europe," nor that Palestine alone could solve the problem of rehabilitating European Jews. Bevin expressed his gratitude to the Arabs for their cooperation and his resentment over the Jewish Agency's obstructive tactics. "If the Jews, with all their sufferings, want to get too much at the head of the queue," said Bevin, "you have the danger of another anti-Semitic reaction through it all." He appealed to the Jews of the world, "apart from the Zionist organization," to assist in finding a solution of the Palestine issue. He warned that the problem could only be settled by discussion and conciliation, and that any resort to force would be handled resolutely.[2]

The Arabs deplored and the Zionists welcomed American participation. Nevertheless, both regarded a new investigation as superfluous. Despite minority pressures to the contrary, the Arab League Council and the Jewish Agency Executive agreed to testify. But the League warned that presentation of testimony "does not imply recognition on our part of the right of the Anglo-American Committee . . . to decide the Palestine issue, nor . . . the right of Great Britain and the United States . . . to handle this problem exclusively." The Agency also said that it would not be bound by the committee's findings and accused the British Foreign Secretary of prejudging the committee's proposals. As regards the interim mandatory policy, the Palestine Jews denounced it "as maintaining the spirit and the letter of the White Paper"; the Palestine Arabs as repudiating the explicit promises of the White Paper.[3]

Bevin's distinction between Zionism and the problem of the European Jews, his assertion that Palestine could not absorb all the European refugees and that in any case they should not be transferred forcibly to Palestine pleased the Arabs and outraged the Zionists. "The age-old Jewish question is torn out of its historic context," declared the Jewish Agency, "and reduced, in time, to the period of the Nazi persecution; in space, to liberated Europe; and, in substance, to the relief of displaced Jewish individuals in that continent—this at a time when, as demonstrated by recent outbreaks in Tripoli and elsewhere, the position of Jews in many lands is more precarious than it has ever been." Even the moderate Weizmann asked, "Is it 'getting too much at the head of the queue' if, after the slaughter of six million Jews, the remnant . . . implore the shelter of the Jewish homeland?" The Agency president was disturbed by the charge that Zionism aimed to drive the Jews out of Europe. "We take it for granted that every Jew is morally entitled to remain in his land of birth or choice," asserted Weizmann. "But no Jews should be forced to return to countries where they saw their wives mutilated and burned, their sons and daughters buried alive, their parents turned into white ash." [4]

Arab and Zionist anxiety gave rise to a new round of pressures and counterpressures. The Arab League announced early in December that its member states would impose a boycott, effective January 1, 1946, of goods produced by the "war-enriched" Zionist industry. Jewish-owned factories in Palestine, the League explained, were being used to establish a Jewish state, a goal which constituted a serious threat to the entire Arab world. The Jewish Agency protested against this action to the United Nations General Assembly. Meanwhile, the Zionists were belatedly satisfied in mid-December 1945 when both houses of Congress finally passed pro-Zionist resolutions, overriding the objections of President Truman and Secretary Byrnes, who had urged that no such step be taken until the inquiry committee had reported its findings. The spirit of the Palestine Arabs was in turn uplifted by the joint communiqué which kings Faruq and ibn Sa'ud issued a month later during the Arabian monarch's unprecedented visit to Egypt, reaffirming the Arab rulers' "belief . . . that Palestine is . . . and . . . should remain an Arab country." [5]

In the Yishuv the Bevin statement of interim policy confirmed the feeling of betrayal that had been welling up since September, and his unflattering references to Zionism intensified the anger. The binationalists as well as the statists were now certain that the Labor Government had decided upon a course of cynical expediency, for the Foreign Secretary had decreed that, if Jewish immigration were to continue, it would do so only on a very small scale and on Arab sufferance. "Bevin has offered us a cup of poison with a frigid diplomatic hand," observed the binationalist *Mishmar*. "Does he think we shall accept it?" The Palestine Jews were "interested in an alliance with democratic England, which has vital interests here," declared Ben Gurion at an extraordinary session of the Elected Assembly on November 28,

> but [we] reject any policy designed to liquidate our existence as a nation. . . . We do not want to die, we believe we have the right to live as individuals and as a nation like you English and others, but there are some things dearer than life. We are prepared to be killed for the right to come here and build, for the right of independence in our own country.

The decision to sponsor large-scale illegal immigration was now formally endorsed by the Elected Assembly, the Zionist Inner General Council, and the Jewish Agency Executive. Even Dr. Judah L. Magnes, who remained an advocate of passive resistance, publicly declared early in December that he was not "against that immigration called illegal." [6]

Against the possibility of an attempt by Britain to halt Jewish immigration altogether and end its support of the national home, an eventuality which the Palestine Jews hoped might be averted, they had been steeling themselves for more than five and a half years. Haganah had been forged during the war into a well-organized illegal army of an estimated 60,000 troops, with a striking force, a static defense force, and reservists. To these units belonged most of the enlistees in the Jewish Brigade and various branches of the British armed forces, now being demobilized gradually. Moreover the equivalent of one year's compulsory military training for high-school seniors was inaugurated in November 1945. The considerable military supplies acquired in the war years had been distributed throughout the community. Wartime contacts with the Jewish underground in Europe had netted volunteers for Haganah on the Continent. This well-disciplined organization was now alerted to direct the traffic of unauthorized immigration from the D.P. camps in Europe to Palestine. With the overland routes virtually sealed up owing to the measures taken by the Arab countries, Haganah was forced to transport the refugees by ship. This necessitated running the British blockade, maintained by reconnaissance planes as well as warships.

Also in mid-November the Arab League Council, then in session at Cairo, sent its president, Jamil Bey Mardam of Syria, as head of a delegation to Jerusalem. Now that the mandatory appeared to be seeking a final solution of the Palestine problem, the need for unified leadership in the local Arab Community was imperative. Mardam was able in a week of mediation to impose on the Palestine politicians what they themselves had been unable to achieve in nearly three years of negotiation. A new Higher Committee was established, with five of the twelve seats allocated to the Palestine Arab Party, one each to the heads of the remaining five prewar parties, and the last two to Musa al-'Alami and Ahmad Hilmi Pasha 'Abd-al-Baqi. The presidency was left open for the exiled Mufti, and the acting presidency was to be rotated among the various party chiefs. To placate the Istiqlal spokesmen, who still refused to surrender control over the National Fund, it was decided that the Higher Committee, and not 'Alami alone, would supervise the Arab League's publicity and projected land schemes. [7]

Criticism immediately came from the left wing of the labor movement, which decried the "undemocratic" character of the Higher Committee, since it did not include any of "the new elements." The Higher

Committee, it soon became apparent, was nothing more than a coalition of the Husayni and Istiqlal leaders. Neither the heads of the other parties nor 'Alami participated in its meetings. 'Alami continued to perform his Arab League duties without reference to the political leaders in Palestine. Moreover, the greatest influence in the Higher Committee was in the hands of the Palestine Arab Party. The importance of this fact was further enhanced at the end of December by the arrival in the Near East of Jamal al-Husayni, after his release from detention in Southern Rhodesia. Although Jamal was still not permitted to enter Palestine, the way was thus being cleared for the return to unchallenged supremacy of the exiled Husayni leaders. Still, the Higher Committee provided the Arab Community with an official spokesman and was recognized as such by the Arab League at once and by the Palestine Government early in January 1946.[8]

THE ACTIVISTS IN CONTROL

A month after the formation of the Higher Committee the White Paper's immigration quota was finally exhausted. The conflicting attitudes of the mandatory and the two sections of the local population now came into sharp focus. The Palestine Jews maintained that the express intent of the mandate was to facilitate Jewish immigration, and that its restriction under the 1939 White Paper, which had never been approved by the Council of the League of Nations, violated the mandate. Consequently, the Zionists argued that their encouragement of Jewish entry into Palestine, even without government authority, was not illegal. The Arabs, on the other hand, claimed that the mandate itself was illegal, since it had been imposed on them, as the original inhabitants of the land, against their will, and that all Jews who had come into Palestine under the British regime, whether or not with government authorization, were unlawful residents. The British Government for its part contended that as long as the mandate remained in existence, the mandatory would have to insure at least a token flow of Jewish immigration, and, since the League of Nations was no longer supervising the mandate, the mandatory, as the governing authority, not only had the right to lay down immigration limits but was obligated to resist any efforts to exceed these quotas.

The British Government early in January 1946 requested the Higher Committee and the Arab states to approve the Foreign Office proposal that Jewish immigration continue at the monthly rate of 1,500, pending the completion of the Anglo-American inquiry. The Higher Committee, however, rejected the Bevin formula on January 19, declaring that "the Arab people in Palestine . . . holds fast to its national and acquired right in regard to the final stoppage of Jewish immigration." Continued Jewish immigration, the Higher Committee announced, would be regarded as "a concession to the aggressive demand of the Jews. . . . This will not conduce to . . . the desired atmosphere of peace and tranquility, but will encourage the Jews to intensify their terrorist activities in order to secure further concessions." The Palestine Arab position was endorsed a week later by each of the Arab League's member states.[9]

The mandatory's hand was forced at this time when British naval units intercepted a vessel with over 900 unauthorized Jewish immigrants. The likely repercussions had been foreshadowed by a test case two months earlier. At that time British coastal patrols had succeeded in capturing only 21 of a shipload of 200 visaless refugees. Not only did Haganah units blow up two coast-guard stations in reprisal, but British military searches of Jewish villages met with stiff passive resistance, resulting in death to nine Jews and injury to over ninety, including twelve members of the British security forces. When the Palestine Government denied that it was hunting out the illegal immigrants, as the Agency charged, the Arabs accused the British of appeasing the Yishuv by allowing it to smuggle Jews into the country without hindrance and by releasing those originally arrested. In January 1946 there was no quota from which to deduct. If the 900 were deported, the Yishuv was likely to rebel. Indeed, Haganah had already retaliated by destroying another coast-guard station and by trying to damage R.A.F. radar installations in Haifa. If the 900 were permitted to remain, British efforts to promote Arab good will would be seriously weakened. The Labor Government tried to extricate itself by declaring on January 30 that "His Majesty's Government could not divest themselves of their . . . responsibilities under the Mandate while the Mandate continued." Since consultations with the Arabs had reached "no conclusive result," the British communiqué stated, "His Majesty's Government have now decided for cogent reasons that they must allow immigration to continue provisionally at the proposed rate of 1,500 a month." Simultaneously the Palestine Government announced that the exclusion order against Jamal al-Husayni had been rescinded.[10]

The compromise satisfied neither community. The Jewish Agency characterized the monthly quota as an "outrage on the feelings of martyred Jewry and a cruel prolongation of the agony of the survivors." The British Government was accused of trying to "crystallize the Jewish population of Palestine at its present relative strength" and was warned that the Jews would "redouble their efforts to secure . . . the restoration of their fundamental rights." The Higher Committee denounced the immigration decision as an act of aggression which had shaken the Arabs' confidence in British intentions, since the decision was made "under pressure of Jewish propaganda and armed terrorism." Protest strikes staged on separate days enabled Arabs and Jews to let off steam. But in the Arab Community the persistence of old rivalries within the Higher Committee ruled out united counteraction.[11]

For this reason great significance attached to Jamal al-Husayni's return to Palestine in the first week of February. Jamal's prestige exceeded that of any other Arab political leader in the country at that time. His reinstatement was regarded by the Arabs as a British vindication of his wartime activities. He had not been involved in the intense political and personal dissensions of the preceding three years. The hope was therefore raised that he might be strong enough to weld the Higher Committee into an effective political directorate of the community. Once back in the country, Jamal attempted to gain the cooperation of the nonconformist members of the Higher Committee. When no agreement was attained by the end of March, Jamal finally reorganized the body with himself as acting-president, still leaving the presidency vacant for al-Hajj Amin. The Committee was to consist of twenty-eight members. Besides the twelve selected in November, the Palestine Arab Party was to nominate two others and the remaining prewar parties one each. The rest of the seats were to be filled by delegates from various groups in the community, including one from the conservative branch of the labor movement. The Istiqlal and nonconformist leaders, however, challenged Jamal's authority to take such a step without their concurrence and refused to associate with the reorganized body. Hence what had been a Husayni-Istiqlal coalition was reduced in four months' time to an adjunct of the Palestine Arab Party, and the local leadership was now as deeply rent as it had been before.[12]

In the Jewish Community the activists seemed temporarily to draw closer to the terrorists. At the end of February Palmah (Haganah's striking force), the Irgun, and the Freedom Fighters by common plan carried out a series of assaults on installations used to curb illegal immigration. Palmah blew up a radar post at Haifa and attacked three mobile police stations; and the terrorist groups raided three military airfields, destroying or damaging fifteen planes. The degree of popular approval was illustrated by the participation of some 50,000 persons, including the chairman of the National Council Executive, in the funeral procession at Tel-Aviv of four Palmah men killed in action. Anti-British feeling in the Yishuv was doubtless heightened at the time by the British Army's decision to bring into Palestine hundreds of German prisoners to construct military installations in the Gaza district. But the countenance of political violence by the activists was denounced by the moderates, whose influence declined steadily as the community lost faith in the Labor Government. In fact, the one remaining non-Zionist member of the Jewish Agency Executive, David Werner Senator, had resigned from that body in December over this very issue. By such acts the Jews were courting disaster, warned the moderate press, since they could not possibly withstand full-scale military suppression by Britain. Armed opposition, these papers added, should be confined to self-defense and to resistance against government efforts to curb immigration and the establishment of new settlements.[13]

The activists and the terrorists were still far from united. Haganah was accountable to the Jewish quasi-government; the commanders of the Irgun and the Freedom Fighters were accountable only to themselves. When Haganah attacked government installations, in the words of its own spokesmen, "we take strict precautions not to injure those manning them, even if by so doing we endanger the success of the undertaking and the safety of our own men." The Freedom Fighters never had any regard for human life, while the Irgun had long since abandoned efforts to prevent bloodshed. During the first four months of 1946 the two terrorist groups accelerated their campaigns of robbery and murder, aimed principally at replenishing military supplies and monetary reserves. That the community as a whole still distinguished between the terrorists and the activists was manifest in the public behavior when the security authorities undertook mopping-up operations following each outbreak of violence. If the Irgun or the Freedom Fighters were responsible, the Yishuv passively submitted. But if Haganah was involved, the community resisted military and police searches.[14]

Only the moderates inveighed against the political criminals, until the Irgun, in an arms theft in Tel-Aviv in April, killed seven British soldiers. This prompted the activist press to state that the Yishuv was not at war with His Majesty's forces or civilian personnel but with the mandatory's anti-Zionist policy. British-Zionist relations, however, had become so hostile, that the Jewish quasi-government would no longer cooperate in apprehending the terrorists. Until now the British troops had shown considerable restraint in the face of terrorist provocation. But a group of soldiers, in retaliation for the murder of their comrades, went berserk in Natanyah and the village of Beer Tuviyyah, smashing windows, destroying furniture in houses, and mauling innocent people. The Hebrew press connected these events with an army communiqué invoking the principle of collective responsibility for the terrorist crimes. Such a communiqué, the newspapers asserted, constituted an invitation to the soldiers to take reprisals against innocent citizens. "The residents of Beer Tuviyyah and Natanyah are no more responsible for the acts committed in . . . Tel-Aviv," observed one daily, "than the airborne troops are responsible for British policy in Palestine." If the Yishuv ought to curb its riotous elements, the editorial went on, the mandatory ought also to discipline its troops.[15]

The fine distinctions between Haganah and the terrorists were not made by the Arabs, who placed the blame for all terrorist acts on the entire Jewish Community and its leaders.[16] The Arabs more persistently than ever urged that the Yishuv be treated with severity equal to that meted out to the Arab Community before the war. In the Arab revolt of 1936–39, Jamal al-Husayni pointed out a few days before his return to Palestine, many Arabs were sentenced to death, Arab houses blown up, large collective fines imposed on poverty-stricken Arab villages, and the prisons filled with Arabs. But no similar measures had yet been taken against the Jews. The Arab press demanded that the government dissolve the Jewish Agency as it had the first Arab Higher Committee, stop illegal immigration at its source and deport all Jews caught entering the country unlawfully, and disband the Jewish "armies" as it had disbanded the Arab scout movement before the war. The mandatory, it was suggested, was either conspiring with the Jews, or was fearful of Jewish propaganda from abroad, or like the United States was subservient to world Jewish influence. As for the United States, all Americans were declared to be Zionists and "for the sake of the dollar the American would sell Christ, the land of Christ, and, if need be, the religion of Christ." The same newspaper revived the suggestion that the Arab governments apply economic sanctions against the United States.[17]

THE COMMITTEE'S REPORT

Thus when the Anglo-American Committee of Inquiry reached Jerusalem on March 6 it found both Arabs and Jews under activist domination. Full committee hearings had been conducted in Washington and London during January. Throughout February subcommittees had studied the question of the displaced Jews in various parts of Europe west of the Soviet Union and the Balkan countries. On February 28 the full Committee had listened to the testimony of the Arab League in Cairo. The Jerusalem hearings were interrupted to allow subcommittees to tour the two communities and to meet with Arab spokesmen in Damascus, Bayrut, Baghdad, Riyad, and 'Amman. Among those who appeared before the Committee in its three months of hearings were Zionist, non-Zionist, and anti-Zionist Jews, Christian and Muslim Arabs, and their respective non-Jewish and non-Arab champions as well as Palestine Government and British Near East officials, past and present. The only political groups which refused to submit testimony in Palestine were the Arab parties unaffiliated with the Higher Committee, and the Revisionist Zionists. The mass of repetitious and conflicting evidence, oral and written, was then taken at the end of March to Lausanne, Switzerland. There in three weeks' time it was boiled down to a unanimous report of less than one hundred pages.[18]

The report substantiated the Harrison findings that the overwhelming majority of the displaced Jews wished to settle in Palestine. The number of persons in the Jewish assembly centers was growing steadily, as refugees streamed in from the Soviet-controlled area to the American and British zones. There was "no hope of substantial assistance" in settling these Jews outside of Palestine, although that country alone, it was said, could not meet fully the pressing needs. The United States and Britain were accordingly urged, in concert with other governments, to make special provision for the absorption of all D.P.'s, non-Jews as well as Jews. At the same time the Committee recommended that visas be issued, "as far as possible in 1946," for the entry into Palestine of 100,000 Jewish victims of Nazi and Fascist persecution and "that actual immigration be pushed forward as rapidly as conditions will permit."

The Committee established as axiomatic that as a country holy to Christianity, Islam, and Judaism, Palestine

> is not, and can never become, a land which any race or religion can justly claim as its very own. . . . The Jews have a historic connection with the country. The Jewish National Home, though embodying a minority of the population, is today a reality established under international guarantee. It has a right to continued existence, protection and development. Yet Palestine . . . . lies at the crossroads of the Arab world. Its Arab population, descended from long-time inhabitants of the area, rightly look upon Palestine as their homeland.

In consequence the Committee emphatically endorsed the binationalist position, which envisaged setting up an independent, democratic government based on equal rather than proportional representation. By this means it was hoped to put an end to the bedeviling struggle between Arabs and Jews for a numerical majority. But since the determination of Arabs and Jews "to achieve domination, if necessary by violence," precluded the possibility of establishing independence "now or for some time to come," it was recommended that the mandate be converted into a United Nations trusteeship.

The primary duty of the Trustee was to prepare the two communities for binationalism. This would require raising Arab economic standards to the Jewish level, developing a sense of democratic political responsibility in the Arab Community, and weeding out the aggressively nationalist aspects of the Arab and Jewish educational systems. The existing immigration restrictions were pronounced discriminatory. After the admission of the 100,000 a compromise would have to be found between the demands of Arabs and Jews. Moreover, it was declared that "any immigrant Jew who enters Palestine contrary to its laws is an illegal immigrant." The Land Transfer Regulations of 1940 were stated to be both discriminatory and segregative and would have to go, as would the practice by the Jewish National Fund of employing only Jews on land to which it had acquired title. The Jewish Agency and the National Council would have to resume their cooperation with the Palestine Government in the suppression of terrorism and illegal immigration. Finally, the Committee recommended that "it should be made clear beyond all doubt to both the Jews and Arabs that any attempt from either side, by threats of violence, by terrorism, or by the organization or use of illegal armies to prevent . . . [the] execution [of its report, if adopted] will be resolutely suppressed." [19]

The Committee had made a conscientious attempt to appraise fairly the Arab and Zionist cases, but in making recommendations its hands had been tied from the start by the conditions imposed by Bevin, that Palestine be converted into a trusteeship, and by Truman, that 100,000 Jews be admitted to Palestine immediately. In trying to meet these conditions the Committee had proposed a solution which under the best of circumstances was the least practicable. But the positions taken by Bevin and Truman and the interim mandatory policy had brought into power the uncompromising elements in the Yishuv and the Arab Community, so that any serious attempt to put binationalism into operation in 1946 was foredoomed to failure. The inquiry report also did not consider forthrightly the larger strategic and political issues with which the Palestine question had become interlocked. That the Labor Government was giving the highest priority to these issues was demonstrated by the fact that the Foreign Secretary had assumed responsibility for appointing the British members of the Inquiry Committee and for settling the Palestine problem, even though the administration of the mandate was still directed by the Colonial Office. The only possibility of enforcing a solution of the Palestine problem lay in Big Three agreement. But the Soviet Union was not a party to the investigation and its relations with the Western Powers, particularly Britain, had gone from bad to worse in the early months of 1946.

The U.S.S.R. had given evidence even prior to the completion of the Anglo-American inquiry that it was going to play a mischievous role in the Near East. The Soviet-precipitated crisis in Iran coupled with the Kremlin's war of nerves against Turkey and its persistent demands for a trusteeship over one of the former Italian colonies aroused deep apprehension in London. To deflect attention from itself, Moscow accused Britain and the United States of imperialist designs throughout the Near East, particularly in the Arab core. Articles on these countries suddenly appeared with regularity in the *New Times,* then a semimonthly dealing with international problems and published in several languages primarily for foreign consumption. Digests were broadcast by Radio Moscow in Arabic to the Near East and in English to the West. Britain was charged with deliberately fomenting unrest in all the Arab states, with resisting efforts on the part of Iraq and Egypt to revise their treaties which deprived these Arab lands of full sovereignty, and with having no intention of withdrawing its troops from Syria, Lebanon, and Egypt. The United States was declared to be seeking economic penetration into Saudi Arabia, the Levant States, and Yemen.

As regards the Anglo-American Inquiry Committee, Soviet propagandists challenged the authority of London and Washington to by-pass the United Nations and the Arab states, which were directly concerned in the Palestine problem. By denying that the creation of "a Zionist-Jewish state in Palestine" could solve the problem of the European Jewish refugees, Moscow seemed to be currying Arab nationalist favor. But subsequent propaganda left no doubt that Soviet support might be expected only if the "progressive" leaders took over the direction of Arab League affairs from the "reactionary" elements. Such progressive leadership, it was implied, would indicate its "genuine defense of Arab national interests" by having the Arab League abandon its subservience to Britain, cease its function as a British-controlled anti-Soviet bloc, and cooperate "with Jewish democratic organizations to carry on the joint struggle for Palestine independence" and for the evacuation of British troops from the country.[20]

American interests in the Near East, meanwhile, were growing apace and the United States appeared anxious to demonstrate its friendliness to the Arab East. Aramco received in January 1946 a concession from the Palestine Government for the construction of a pipe line from its fields in Arabia to the Mediterranean and was seeking a similar concession from Transjordan. The United States Army was finishing the construction of an airfield in Saudi Arabia, begun immediately after V-J Day. This airfield was to be capable of handling the largest craft and, by agreement with ibn Sa'ud, it was to remain in American military hands for three years. The Department of State was negotiating with Cairo for the transfer to Egypt at nominal cost of a large United States Army airport near Cairo, constructed during the war, and with that country and its neighbors for bilateral air transport agreements, the first of which was concluded with Lebanon in April. In the same month an American mission arrived in Yemen to establish diplomatic and commercial relations. But the Truman Administration still did little to develop a comprehensive policy toward the Near East, despite the President's realization that the region "might become an arena of intense rivalry between outside powers, and . . . such rivalry might suddenly erupt into conflict." [21]

The Soviet and American attitudes were basic considerations of the Labor Government in formulating its Near East policy. By the spring of 1946 there were indications that the Attlee Cabinet was as determined as its predecessor to preserve British predominance in the Near East, but in a guise that would be appropriate for a Labor Government, and in a manner that would not entail huge operating costs to a nation heavily in debt. The paramount objective was to dispel mistrust of Britain. Once the Anglo-American Middle East Supply Center was disbanded, Bevin announced in November 1945 that the Foreign Office had decided to continue on its own the advisory functions of that agency through a Middle East Office at Cairo. Sir Kinahan Cornwallis, one of the Arab specialists of the Conservative and Coalition eras, was appointed head of the Middle East Secretariat at the Foreign Office. As for political questions, Bevin stated that the Labor Government wished to "maintain our relations with the countries of the Middle East on the basis of free and equal partnership.

. . . We have no intention to interfere in the local politics of the different countries." [22]

In May 1946 Prime Minister Attlee informed Parliament that the British Government had agreed to withdraw all naval, military, and air forces from Egypt in gradual stages. But this withdrawal would be contingent upon Egyptian consent to negotiate a new treaty of alliance which would make Britain jointly responsible in time of war or emergency for the defense of Egypt and the Suez Canal and would guarantee to His Majesty's Government "the facilities that will enable it to do so." Under pressure from the Conservative Opposition, which expressed the fear that the Labor Government was not making adequate provision to safeguard imperial communications, Attlee admitted that, if the talks broke down, "there is still, of course, the 1936 Treaty," which was not due to expire until 1956.[23] In brief, what the Labor Government was seeking in Egypt was a preferential status in time of crisis without the burdens of local nationalist displeasure and high costs in time of peace. If the parleys with Egypt proved successful, it could reasonably be expected that the agreement would provide the pattern for a later settlement with Iraq.

Meanwhile, in January 1946 Bevin notified the United Nations General Assembly that the United Kingdom would "take steps in the near future for establishing . . . [Transjordan] as a sovereign, independent state." Two months later a preferential treaty modeled after those with Iraq and Egypt was concluded, enabling Britain to retain the same military rights in Transjordan that it had exercised under the mandate. But the military privileges in Transjordan could not offset the inevitable retreat from Egypt and Iraq, a development which enhanced the strategic importance of Palestine. Here the United Kingdom could substitute the naval base at Haifa for that at Alexandria, while control of the Negeb would keep Britain on the northern flank of the Suez Canal. That the British had no intentions of leaving Palestine at that time was indicated by the erection of large, permanent military camps in the Gaza district and the decision to construct a new pipe line, 60 per cent larger than the existing one, from the Iraqi oil fields to Haifa.[24]

CHAPTER 19

Provincial Autonomy

THE ANGLO-AMERICAN Committee's report was released simultaneously in Washington and London on May 1, 1946. On the same day, President Truman approved the recommendation that the 1939 White Paper's immigration and land laws be rescinded and expressed pleasure over the fact that the Inquiry Committee had unanimously endorsed his original request for the immediate admission of 100,000 Jews into Palestine. The President, however, reserved judgment on the long-range political questions. Prime Minister Attlee for his part, in explaining the Labor Government's position to the House of Commons, stated that the report would have to be considered "as a whole in all its implications." His Majesty's Government would not desire to undertake such heavy commitments alone, continued Attlee, and would therefore seek "to ascertain to what extent . . . the United States would be prepared to share the . . . additional military and financial responsibilities." At all events, the 100,000 immigrants could not be admitted "unless and until" the illegal armies had been disbanded, their arms surrendered, and the Jewish Agency's cooperation in the suppression of terrorism resumed.[1] Thus, the joint inquiry, it was manifest, far from bringing Anglo-American policy on Palestine into accord, had left the two governments roughly where they were in September 1945.

The President's statement encouraged the Zionists and angered the Arabs, while the Prime Minister's remarks had the reverse effect. Just as Truman and Attlee had singled out certain sections of the report for approbation, so the Jewish Agency initially welcomed the immigration and land proposals. But since "the central problem of the homeless and stateless Jewish people has been left untouched," the Agency voiced the "firm conviction . . . that the National Home cannot be really secured save

249

within the framework of a Jewish State." The Arabs rejected the Inquiry Committee's proposals in their entirety. In an *aide-memoire* to the Secretary of State, the Arab diplomatic representatives in Washington warned on May 10 that their governments would consider American support of these proposals as hostile to the Arab people and that "the adoption of such a policy would result in a state of . . . conflict in Palestine and in the Near and Middle East." [2]

Three weeks elapsed before Washington and London invited the formal reactions to the Anglo-American report of the governments and organizations which had taken part in the hearings. The Committee's proposals were merely advisory and therefore not binding, declared the Department of State, trying to steer a middle course, but the United States was giving the report careful consideration because it had been unanimously approved by the Committee's members. After another three weeks it was announced that President Truman had set up a special committee, comprising the secretaries of State, War and the Treasury, to assist him in formulating and executing "such policy with regard to Palestine and related problems as may be adopted by this government." The work of the Cabinet Committee was delegated to a board of alternates, appointed by the three secretaries, with Henry F. Grady, the recent head of the American section of the Allied mission to observe the elections in Greece, as chairman. The Cabinet Committee was empowered to negotiate with a similar British group in order to define a joint Anglo-American program and allocate the economic, military, and technical responsibilities between the two governments. The United States had already offered to transport the 100,000 Jews to Palestine and to help defray the costs of their resettlement. The Department of State, therefore, sent an advance mission to London to iron out the details of the American offer. But the Cabinet Committee itself did not reach the British capital until mid-July.[3]

Anglo-American indecision raised Arab hopes, exacerbated Zionist feelings, and did nothing to discourage the efforts of both parties to influence the final decision. General strikes were held in the Palestine Arab Community, the Levant States, Iraq, and Egypt. Individuals suggested that the Arabs might impose economic sanctions against American and British business men. Palestine Arab politicians, particularly the Husaynis, threatened to seek Soviet aid. The Cairo meeting at the end of May of the rulers of five of the Arab League states and the sons of Imam Yahya and King ibn Sa'ud demonstrated Arab solidarity against the Anglo-American report.[4] But concrete countermeasures were not considered until the special five-day session of the Arab League Council at Bludan, Syria, early in June.

The League Council sent vehement memoranda to Washington and London containing its views on the Inquiry Committee's report. In its note to the Department of State the legal right of the United States to intervene in Palestine was challenged. The League charged that "a clamorous and noisy band of Jews" were trying to direct American public opinion toward a goal which was calculated to undermine United States interests in the Arab world. The Arabs "would not stand by with their arms folded," if the Zionists continued to accumulate military equipment. Furthermore, the Arab League did not consider its latest exchange of memoranda with Washington as the consultation promised by President Roosevelt to ibn Saʻud. The note to Britain declared that approval of the Inquiry Committee's recommendations would constitute "an unfriendly action" and that the two Western Powers would bear responsibility for the "disturbances that will occur in Palestine and the whole Arab East." The request was made to stop Jewish immigration into Palestine and to deport all unauthorized entrants. Each League state, in a second memorandum to London, proposed that the United Kingdom enter into direct negotiations as soon as possible, so as to reach a final Anglo-Arab agreement on Palestine before the next session of the United Nations General Assembly. Until that time Britain was urged not to deviate from the White Paper's immigration and land clauses.[5]

The Bludan session also formed a Palestine Committee to direct the struggle against Zionism. The Arab states were called upon to increase their monetary contributions and to tighten the economic boycott of the Palestine Jews. The League Council approved a number of secret resolutions to become operative if any international action were taken that might "affect [adversely] the right of Palestine to be an independent Arab state." These decisions provided for material, military, and moral aid to the Palestine Arabs and for political and economic sanctions against Britain and the United States.[6]

In the wake of the strong reaction against the Anglo-American report, meanwhile, the Palestine Arab leaders had made fresh efforts in May to unite in a single Higher Committee. But the negotiations broke down when Jamal al-Husayni refused to admit two Opposition nominees to membership, because they were not personally acceptable to him. Consequently, the Istiqlal-led Opposition parties early in June formed their own Arab Higher Front.[7] The rival claims of the Husaynis and the Opposition to Arab political leadership in Palestine were placed on the agenda of the League Council at Bludan. The resolution of the dispute was greatly simplified by the dramatic appearance in Egypt at the end of May of al-Hajj Amin al-Husayni.

Ever since the Mufti had been seized by the French at the war's end the British Government had been under pressure to have him tried as a war criminal. But the Labor Government refused to prefer charges against him. Moreover, despite steady Parliamentary pressure, the Foreign Office made no formal demand for al-Hajj Amin's extradition, and in May 1946 even the half-hearted attempts to have him transferred to British custody were given up. The Mufti, placed under "discreet surveillance" by the French

Government in a Paris suburb, was permitted freedom of movement, after "he had given his word not to change his residence without informing the French authorities." After a year al-Hajj Amin, allegedly disguised and carrying a Syrian passport, escaped from France on an American plane. Arriving in Cairo on May 29, he went into hiding until late in June.[8] Word of his escape, however, was publicized when the French police discovered his absence at the time of the Bludan session, although his presence in Egypt was already known to the Arab League spokesman.

The Palestine Arabs were psychologically prepared for al-Hajj Amin's resumption of leadership, thanks to his disciples' untiring devotion and to the government's failure to bring him into disgrace. In the eyes of his followers the Jerusalem cleric was dedicating his life to the cause of national independence, and his wartime performance was now rationalized as part of this struggle. "The Grand Mufti," it was stated, was the Palestine Arabs' "first leader . . . for whom they can accept no substitute." The British had been persecuting him, it was charged, ever since he left Palestine in 1937. By the time al-Hajj Amin reached Iran at the end of the second year of the war, he feared for his life and, therefore, took sanctuary in the only country open to him, with Germany, the mortal enemy of Britain. Yet the Mufti did not really collaborate with the Nazis, it was stressed. "He was only seeking to get something out of them in case they were victorious." His sole concern was "for the interests of his people who had no direct interest, at least, in the controversy [World War II]." Although the Palestine Arabs had been neutral as between the two major sets of belligerents in the late war, they were nevertheless aiding the Allied cause, for "our people here stopped our war with the British when the British were in difficulty." And since the Mufti "in his heart . . . was with his people who were then helping you," he too was on the side of the democracies.[9]

If the mandatory did not elect to mete out punishment to the Mufti, his followers could hardly have been expected to do less than demand his recall. The Palestine Arab Party, and through it the Arab governments and the League, had been pressing for his readmission into Palestine. The Mufti's reputation among the Palestine Arabs was now greater than at any time since his presidency of the first Higher Committee in 1936–37. He once again became the symbol of the Palestine Arab struggle against Zionism, imperialism, and the West. His influence derived not only from the Palestine Arab Party but from the hope that he could end the chronic political stalemate.

Consequently, in arranging a settlement of the Palestine Arab impasse, the League Council ordered the dissolution of both the Higher Committee and the Higher Front, and created in their stead an Arab Higher Executive, with the Mufti as chairman. Jamal al-Husayni was nominated vice-chairman, Dr. Husayn Fakhri al-Khalidi, the head of the defunct Reform

Party, secretary, and Emile al-Ghuri, the secretary of the Palestine Arab Party, and Ahmad Hilmi Pasha 'Abd-al-Baqi, an Istiqlal leader, members. So far as the mandatory was concerned, however, the chairmanship of the Higher Executive was vacant, since al-Hajj Amin was not allowed to re-enter Palestine. Jamal was accordingly recognized as the acting-chairman in formal dealings with the government. But the Higher Executive was managed by the Mufti from Egypt. There he was granted asylum as a political refugee, and after a few weeks the political restraints imposed on him by the Egyptian Government were removed.[10]

REPRESSION OF THE JEWISH AGENCY

While the Mufti was being restored under Arab League auspices, the Zionists were disturbed by "the stalling tactics" of the British Government. Pro-Zionist Senators charged in Congress that the Office of Near Eastern and African Affairs of the Department of State was also "promoting delay." In its official reactions to the Anglo-American report the Agency expressed grave concern over "the hesitation . . . in implementing the positive recommendations" of the Inquiry Committee. "The fact that Jews are still confined to displaced persons' camps a year after the defeat of Germany and the continuing deterioration in the position of the Jews in Europe make such procrastination indefensible." The Agency offered to discuss the problems arising out of the Anglo-American Committee's report, once it was convinced that the proposal for the settlement of the 100,000 refugees in Palestine was being executed "in good faith." [11]

Zionist chagrin was intensified by the British Foreign Secretary's defense of his Palestine policy before the Labor Party conference at Bournemouth in mid-June. The agitation in the United States, especially in New York, for the admission of 100,000 Jews into Palestine, exclaimed Bevin, arose from the fact that Americans "did not want too many of them in New York." He was not prepared to send to Palestine the additional division of troops which the settlement there of so many Jews would require. Moreover, the costs of implementing the Anglo-American proposals were so great that His Majesty's Government could not shoulder them alone. Bevin was definitely opposed to a Jewish state, because he did "not believe in the absolutely exclusively racial states." These remarks offended liberal and pro-Zionist public opinion in the United States and drained further the influence of the moderate Zionist leaders who hoped that Anglo-American negotiations might yet lead to tangible results. The two Senators from New York protested direct to the British Foreign Secretary, designating his reference to their state a "false and anti-Semitic utterance," and accused him of repudiating the Inquiry Committee's unanimous recommendations. To soften the impact of Bevin's speech the Foreign Office explained that Britain had not rejected the Anglo-American Committee's proposals and was most anxious to expedite the endeavors to find a solution of the Palestine problem.[12]

Except for a passing reference to Egypt, Bevin had made no mention of the strategic and regional motives for the Labor Government's attitude. But it was precisely these omissions which appeared ominous to the activists in the Yishuv. They saw that Britain's opening talks with Egypt for treaty revision had broken down, that the flood of anti-British agitation in that country was still rising, and that the evacuation of British garrisons from Syria had already been completed and the British troop withdrawal from Lebanon was well under way. When the activists coupled these developments with the heavy troop concentration and the erection of large, permanent military camps in Palestine, they concluded that Britain was planning to regroup its Near East bases around that country. Britain "is therefore concerned to strengthen her hold over the mandate, and is using her responsibility to the Jewish people merely as a means to that end," announced Haganah over its transmitter as early as mid-May. "But this double game will not work," the warning was sounded. "Britain . . . cannot exploit the tragic Jewish question for her own benefit as mandatory power, while attempting to wriggle out of the various responsibilities which that mandate confers." Bevin's speech helped to provoke Haganah's third act of political violence in less than eight months. On June 16 Palmah destroyed or damaged four rail and four road bridges on Palestine frontiers, disrupting traffic with the neighboring states. Haganah explained that its action was intended to show that the Yishuv was capable of thwarting the plans of the British and the Arabs of the near-by countries "who talked so much about coming to fight the Jews." [13]

Indeed, Anglo-Zionist relations had deteriorated to such a degree that the Cabinet finally authorized the Palestine Government to crack down on the Jewish Agency. The Yishuv was placed under virtual military siege on June 29. For almost a fortnight British soldiers and police conducted intensive searches in Tel-Aviv, the Jewish sections of Jerusalem and Haifa, and twenty-seven collective villages. The army occupied the Agency headquarters in Jerusalem and its offices in Tel-Aviv and removed their files. Other public buildings were also seized. Rigid censorship was imposed. Communications with the outside world were severed. Some 2,700 persons, almost wholly from the ranks of Agency supporters, were arrested, among them four members of the Agency Executive and the chairman of the National Council Executive. Other members of the Agency Executive, including David Ben Gurion, then out of the country, were subject to arrest.[14]

These drastic measures were "not directed against the Jewish community as a whole," declared High Commissioner Cunningham at the start of the operations, "but solely . . . . to root out terrorism and violence" and "to restore those conditions of order without which no progress can be made toward the solution of the problem of Palestine." But after the operations had commenced, official quarters in Palestine stated that they were primarily striving "to demobilize the Jewish standing army," that is, Haganah's striking force, Palmah. Only one large Haganah armory, however, was discovered in a collective south of Haifa. Furthermore, about 600 detainees were released before the military operations ceased, and a majority of the remainder shortly thereafter, although three members of the Agency Executive, the chairman of the National Council Executive, and approximately 700 others were incarcerated in detention camps.[15]

The mandatory's sudden change of heart was motivated largely by the repercussions in the United States. In an audience with American Zionist leaders President Truman revealed that the British military operation had been undertaken without his prior knowledge and expressed the hope that the members of the Agency Executive would soon be released. Moreover, the proposed American loan to Britain, which had been passed by the Senate in May, was coming up for debate in the House. At the time of the Bevin speech in mid-June, Dr. Abba Hillel Silver, the chairman of the American Zionist Emergency Council and the leader of the activist Zionist wing in the United States, declared that "American citizens have the right to turn to their representatives in . . . Congress . . . and inquire whether . . . the United States can afford to make a loan to a government whose pledged word seems to be worthless." Now the American Zionists were further offended by the refusal of the mandatory to grant Palestine visas to two moderate American members of the Agency Executive, Rabbi Stephen S. Wise and Louis Lipsky, who had decided to proceed to Jerusalem immediately in view of the crisis. If many of the pro-Zionist Representatives joined the isolationists, it was feared in London that the loan might be voted down. Declaring that "the British Government has made it very difficult for me, as an American Jew and Zionist, to continue in support of the loan," Rabbi Wise nevertheless urged the House during the debate on the measure (July 8–13) to approve it as an imperative necessity.[16]

By then, however, the Palestine Government had already decided to suspend its disciplinary steps, although it had neither disarmed nor impaired Haganah's striking force. If the government's objective was to secure the cooperation of the Agency and the Yishuv, its action produced the opposite results. The military drive may have discouraged those activist leaders who had sponsored acts of violence as a protest against mandatory policy. But, of far greater importance, the government had seriously undermined the authority of the Jewish quasi-government, which alone could have held the terrorists in check, and practically destroyed the influence of the moderate leaders. The Palestine Jews were persuaded that the British Government had accepted only the negative, but none of the positive, recommendations of the Anglo-American Committee. Even the pro-British Weizmann commented that "the Mufti of Jerusalem, 'a war criminal and sworn enemy of Britain,' sat in a palace at Cairo, while Moshe Shertok, who raised an army of 25,000 Jewish Palestinians to fight shoulder to shoulder with Britain in World War II, was imprisoned in Latrun detention camp." [17]

The Labor Government's handling of Zionism was playing directly into the hands of the terrorists, against whom no similar action was taken at this time. In fact, two incidents illustrated the further weakening of the mandatory's grip over the country's security and the increasing boldness of the terrorists. The Irgun had held three British officers as hostages since mid-June, warning that they would be killed unless the death sentences of two Irgunists were rescinded. Despite the intervention of the quasi-government and Haganah, the Irgun refused to free the officers until after the High Commissioner had commuted the sentences to life imprisonment early in July. This incident was followed at the end of that month by the Irgun's blasting of the government offices in the King David Hotel at Jerusalem, killing about eighty British, Arab and Jewish civil servants and wounding some seventy others. The quasi-government called upon the Palestine Jews "to rise up against these abominable outrages." But before any practical measures were taken, the British Government issued a formal statement on acts of violence in Palestine, explaining its earlier repression of the Agency. Coming as it did immediately after the King David bombing, the statement implied that the Agency was responsible for the terrorism.[18]

The security authorities with the backing of the Cabinet and public opinion in Britain, now took severe punitive measures against the entire Jewish Community in an endeavor to apprehend the terrorists. Tel-Aviv was placed under a twenty-two-hour curfew for four days and isolated from the rest of the country. Some 20,000 troops, aided by 600 police, with orders to shoot to kill all curfew-breakers, conducted a house-to-house search and screened more than half the city's population. To this the residents of the all-Jewish city submitted passively, as had the Jewish residents of Jerusalem in similar searches a few days earlier. But the Yishuv as a whole took umbrage at the wording of a non-fraternization order issued three days after the King David blast by Lieutenant-General Sir Evelyn Barker, the British commander in Palestine. Barker accused all Palestine Jews of complicity in the terrorist crimes and the Jewish leaders of "hypocritical sympathy." All Jewish establishments and homes were placed out of bounds, and no British soldier was "to have any social intercourse with any Jew" in order to punish "the Jews in a way the race dislikes as much as any, by striking at their pockets and showing our contempt for them." Although Barker was rebuked by Prime Minister Attlee for "the terms in which the letter was couched," the fact that the general was not transferred from Palestine until February 1947 did nothing to improve relations between the armed forces and the community.[19]

Hence British makeshift in Palestine was in effect consolidating the position of the militant elements in the two communities and rapidly dissipating what little remained of the government's authority. Besides, in the three months since the appearance of the Anglo-American Inquiry Committee's report, the attitudes of London and Washington toward Palestine showed few signs of converging. London's deference to the Arab viewpoint on Palestine was assured by the breakdown of Anglo-Egyptian treaty talks in May, and by the persistent Soviet propaganda attacks on the British search for military bases in the Near East and suggestions that the Palestine problem be submitted to the United Nations. The biennial elections in the United States, on the other hand, made the President more amenable to the Zionist lobby. But the departments of State, War, and Navy, having in mind the strategic importance of Near East oil, the projected trans-Arabian pipe line, the conclusion of bilateral air agreements with the Arab countries, and allegedly military and naval concessions in the Arab East, were receptive to the oil and air lobbies and for that reason anxious not to offend Arab nationalist sensitivities. Moreover, although Congressmen generally voiced support of Zionism and the demand for large-scale Jewish immigration into Palestine, sentiment in Congress strongly opposed the relaxation of American immigration laws, which might have relieved the pressure on Palestine, and objected to the use of American troops in that country.[20]

Yet while the American Cabinet Committee was preparing itself for the July negotiations in London, the Foreign Office let it be known that Britain was bent on securing military as well as financial assistance from the United States. The White House with equal persistence did not budge from its demand for the entry of 100,000 Jews into Palestine, skirted the issue of American military intervention, but expressed a willingness to assume financial obligations.[21] Under the circumstances, the prospects of the negotiations between the Anglo-American experts, as the Cabinet Committee and its British counterpart were then known, were hardly encouraging.

The results of the talks were formally outlined to Parliament on July 31 by the Lord President of the Council, Herbert Morrison. The scheme, henceforth called the Morrison-Grady plan, envisaged converting the mandate into a trusteeship and dividing the country into a Jewish province, an Arab province, and the districts of Jerusalem and Negeb. The execution of the plan might lead ultimately either to a unitary, binational

state or to partition. The central government under a British High Commissioner would rule directly the Jerusalem enclave and the Negeb (the
southern third of the country) and would have exclusive authority over
defense, foreign relations, customs and excise and "initially" over police,
prisons, courts, railways, Haifa harbor, communications, civil aviation,
broadcasting, and antiquities as well. In purely intra-community matters
the two provinces would be given autonomy. Each province would elect
a legislative chamber. But for five years the presidents of the chambers
would be appointed by the High Commissioner, whose approval would be
required before any legislation passed by the two bodies became law. The
Negeb would remain under direct British administration "pending a survey of its development possibilities."

As regards immigration, the 100,000 Jews would be admitted in the first
year after "it is decided to put into effect the scheme as a whole"; and the
United States would be asked "to undertake sole responsibility for the
sea transportation" of the refugees to Palestine. Thereafter, the British
would retain final control over immigration. Each province, however,
would be empowered to make recommendations to the central government, which would then base its decisions on "the economic absorptive
capacity" of that province. The full implementation of the plan would
depend upon United States cooperation and its acceptance by Arabs and
Jews. President Truman would be asked to "recommend legislation granting 50 million dollars to the Government of Palestine for the purpose of
financing development schemes" and, "in the event that adequate finance
from other sources such as the International Bank is not available, to recommend . . . legislation authorizing . . . loans through an appropriate
agency for the development of the Middle East region, including Palestine,
up to 250 million dollars." [22]

The conference of Anglo-American experts, it was clear, had not resolved the basic differences between the Attlee Government and the
White House. Since the British request for American military intervention had obviously been rejected, the Cabinet Committee must have had
little bargaining leverage. For that reason the Morrison-Grady plan was
fundamentally not an Anglo-American, but a British, plan. This exposed
the Labor Government to the criticism of the Opposition in the United
Kingdom as well as anti-British and isolationist circles in the United States.
"His Majesty's Government by their precipitate abandonment of their
treaty rights in Egypt, and, in particular, the Suez Canal zone, are now
forced to look for . . . a jumping-off ground in Palestine in order to protect the Canal from outside Egypt," declared former Prime Minister
Churchill. "By this unwisdom . . . we can now be accused of having a
national strategic motive for retaining our hold on Palestine." [23]

In the United States one isolationist newspaper observed that, "if England wants to buy the Arabs off, let her use her own dough." President

Truman recalled to Washington the American members of the Anglo-American Inquiry Committee, who pointed out that the Morrison-Grady plan was "virtually identical" with one that had been submitted to the Inquiry Committee and rejected in its entirety, and that it represented "a repudiation" of the original Anglo-American report. In consequence, Truman did not endorse the Morrison-Grady scheme, and by mid-August temporarily withdrew from efforts to find a solution for the Palestine impasse.[24]

Britain had already gone ahead on its own to consider the provincial autonomy plan with Arabs and Jews in London. On July 23 Egypt and Iraq had filed with the United Nations Secretariat copies of memoranda they had sent to London the preceding month, requesting bilateral negotiations on Palestine before the next session of the General Assembly at the end of September. Though this was not a formal demand to place the question on the Assembly's agenda, the British Foreign Office must have expected that such a move might be taken. Accordingly, the British Government informed the Arab states on July 25 that it accepted their proposals for Palestine parleys. The Foreign Ministers of the seven Arab League states, after meeting at Alexandria on August 12–13, agreed to attend the conference provided that the Arabs were free to discuss their own plan, the independence of Palestine as an Arab state, and that the Zionists and the Americans were excluded from the talks. Spokesmen of the Arab Higher Executive, endorsing these conditions, added one of their own, that the Mufti be permitted to participate.[25]

The Labor Government originally hoped that the conference would be co-sponsored by the United States and that it would begin by mid-August with Jewish as well as Arab delegates present. However, the plans were upset by the United States disavowal of the Morrison-Grady scheme and by a new Anglo-Zionist crisis over the issue of illegal immigration. Until June unauthorized immigrants fell within the monthly quota of 1,500, and after a few weeks' detention they were generally released. But in July three ships, bearing more than 4,000 would-be immigrants, were intercepted by the British Navy. Since the movement of even larger numbers in the future was indicated, the Attlee Cabinet decided early in August to tighten the blockade of Palestine. Naval and air patrols were augmented. European governments were requested to check the transit of Jews without proper credentials. Favorable response was received from Italy and France, but not from Russia and the countries of eastern Europe. The military commander of the British zone in Germany closed the frontiers to infiltrees, and General McNarney, the commander of the American zone, followed suit.[26]

Finally, on August 12, a day on which two ships carrying a total of 1,300 refugees arrived in Palestine waters, the British Government announced that thereafter all illegal immigrants, including those of the preceding month, would be deported to the near-by island of Cyprus "or elsewhere," where they would be "housed in camps . . . until a decision can be taken as to their future." The British statement declared that the mandatory "cannot tolerate this attempt by a minority of Zionist extremists to exploit the sufferings of unfortunate people in order to create a situation prejudicial to a just settlement [of the Palestine problem]." Announcement of the deportation scheme coincided with the meeting of the Arab Foreign Ministers in Alexandria and prompted 'Azzam Pasha to observe that this was merely a "step on the right road." But the Palestine Jews and the Zionists everywhere were inflamed. On the day of the first deportation a demonstration of 1,000 unarmed Jewish curfew-breakers trying to make their way to the port area in Haifa ended in a struggle with soldiers and resulted in the death of three Jews and the hospitalization of seven others. The following week the two ships used to ferry refugees to Cyprus were damaged by bombs.[27]

The Jewish Agency Executive, then meeting in Paris because its chairman was on the Palestine Government's proscribed list, had already spurned the Morrison-Grady plan as unacceptable, since it provided no genuine independence for either Arabs or Jews. The Jews, continued the Agency, would not control immigration in their diminutive province, an area even smaller than that of the Jewish state recommended by the Royal Commission nine years earlier. "There is nothing of finality in the proposed plan except that it denies Jewish rights in 85 percent of the country," observed the Agency. Still, the Agency Executive, abandoning its previous demand for the whole of Palestine, adopted a secret resolution in favor of the establishment of an independent Jewish state in a partitioned Palestine, and communicated its details to the American and British governments in August.[28] The Agency was prepared to forego some of its territorial claims in return for "a viable Jewish State in an adequate area of Palestine," and proposed that the area allotted to the Jews should include the Galilee and the Coastal Plain—as recommended by the Royal Commission in 1937—plus the Negeb. The rest of the country, comprising the hill districts of east-central Palestine, Jaffa, and a corridor connecting the two, would go to the Arabs. The proposed Jewish state would exercise full autonomy with control over immigration and economic policy. Britain would be assured preferential rights, similar to those of the Anglo-Transjordan treaty, including naval and military bases. The reasons adduced in favor of partition, when it was first put forward by the Royal Commission and approved in principle by the British Government of that day, it was argued, were no less compelling now. "Beyond this scheme," wrote Weizmann, ". . . no Jewish representative could go without being repudiated by the Jewish people." [29]

When Colonial Secretary George Hall finally extended an invitation to the Agency Executive on August 15 to join in the London parleys, the

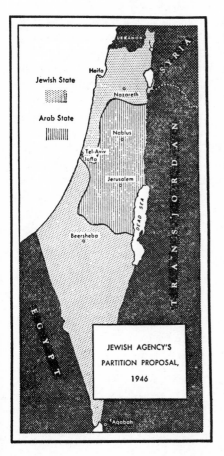

Jewish State

Arab State

Haifa
Nazareth
Nablus
Tel-Aviv
Jaffa
Jerusalem
Beersheba

LEBANON

SYRIA

TRANS-JORDAN

DEAD SEA

EGYPT

'Aqabah

JEWISH AGENCY'S
PARTITION PROPOSAL,
1946

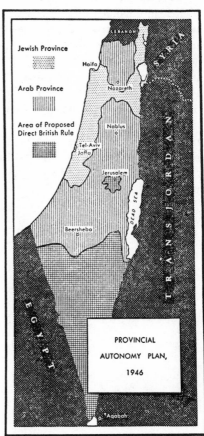

Jewish Province

Haifa
Nazareth

Arab Province

Area of Proposed
Direct British Rule

Nablus
Tel-Aviv
Jaffa
Jerusalem
Beersheba

LEBANON

SYRIA

TRANS-JORDAN

DEAD SEA

EGYPT

'Aqabah

PROVINCIAL
AUTONOMY PLAN,
1946

Zionist body insisted that it would take part in the discussions only on the basis of its partition scheme. The Agency demanded freedom to name its own representatives, including "any who are detained or are subject to detention," and the right to invite, in consultation with the British Government, all the members of the Jewish delegation, on the understanding that others than Zionists would also be designated. The Attlee Cabinet accepted none of these conditions. The Morrison-Grady plan, Hall informed Weizmann, would be the first subject on the agenda, but every delegation would be permitted to advance counterproposals. The Labor Government, moreover, reserved the right to determine the final composition of the Jewish delegation.[30] The British later announced that the Mufti would be ineligible as a conferee and that the High Commissioner would nominate Palestine Arab delegates from outside the ranks of the Higher Executive. This move failed to induce the Agency to attend and led to the boycott of the conference by the Arab Higher Executive, which stated that it could not proceed to London "except on the principles and conditions [it had already] laid down." Nor did the British effort to by-pass the Agency by inviting spokesmen of Jewish organizations in the United Kingdom and the Yishuv bear any fruit.[31]

CHAPTER 20

The London Conference

DEADLOCK

THE LONDON Conference on Palestine opened on September 10, 1946, with only the Arab states and the British Government participating. In the absence of the Zionists and the Palestine Arabs, the two parties most intimately concerned, and the United States, whose cooperation was indispensable, the parleys had no chance of success. The Arab states' delegates refused to meet the British half-way and insisted that they would not confer with the Zionists, even if the latter were present. Nor were they any more willing than the Zionists to accept the Morrison-Grady plan as the basis for negotiation, asserting that trusteeship was unnecessary and that provincial autonomy would pave "the way towards the establishment of a Jewish State." The Arabs would be prepared to recognize the Palestine Jews as a religious community only. Therefore Jewish immigration would have to stop, since it was "the effective weapon of Zionism in the building of a Jewish State" and was inconsistent with the 1939 White Paper. After three weeks the Arabs made their own counterproposals, calling for the transformation of the Palestine Mandate into an independent Arab state "not later than 31st December, 1948." [1]

Under this scheme the High Commissioner would, "notwithstanding the non-cooperation of any section of the Palestine citizenry," nominate a provisional government composed of seven Arab and three Jewish ministers, of "Palestine nationality." The provisional government, in turn, would conduct elections, based on adult male suffrage, for a constituent assembly of sixty members. The Arabs did not define the kind of constitution visualized, other than stating that the government would be "democratic" and its legislature "elected." Jewish immigration was to be entirely prohibited and the existing land laws were to remain unaltered. The immigration and land laws could be modified only with "the consent of . . . a majority of the Arab members of the legislative assembly." Jewish representation in the assembly would be constitutionally limited to a maximum of one-third. Citizenship would be open only to persons legally residing in Palestine "for a continuous period of ten years." The government would control all schools, Jewish and Arab, with a view to "preventing subversive teaching," and Arabic, the official language of the country, would be compulsory. The Jews would be permitted to use Hebrew "as a second official language in districts where they form an absolute majority."

Two days after the Arab scheme was placed on the agenda, the British suddenly suspended the conference, stating that time was needed to study the proposals. Two tactical advantages, it was unofficially observed, also influenced the Labor Government. By the time the conference reconvened, the United Nations General Assembly would have ended its session without the Arabs having raised the Palestine issue. Besides, the American biennial election would be over, so that the United States might more readily resume an active interest in the negotiations. By then, too, it was hoped that an agreement might be reached with the Agency regarding its entry into the parleys. But informal talks between members of the Agency Executive in London and the Foreign and Colonial secretaries in the latter half of September had struck a snag over the question of the detained and proscribed Agency leaders. The British refused to yield on this point. Though certain members of the Agency Executive were prepared to give in, they were voted down by the Zionist Inner General Council. Informal British conversations with the Agency spokesmen, however, now reinforced by a fresh contingent from Jerusalem, continued even after the suspension of the London Conference. Foreign Secretary Bevin believed he had advanced to a more hopeful stage with the Zionist leaders, when he suggested that the British might be willing to consider "the idea of an interim arrangement, leading ultimately to self-government." [2]

At this point the bargaining position of the Zionists was unexpectedly strengthened by the American election. Criticism of the Administration's inaction on Palestine and the D.P.'s was sufficiently strong to weaken Democratic chances in the state of New York. In order to bolster his party's position in that key state and anticipate Governor Dewey, a candidate for re-election, President Truman in a public statement on October 4 reviewed his Administration's efforts to persuade Britain to admit the 100,000 into Palestine and said that he was prepared to recommend to Congress the liberalization of American immigration laws. The President also expressed the belief that a solution of the Palestine problem along the lines of the Agency's partition plan "would command the support of public opinion in the United States." But he urged that "substantial" immigration into Palestine, which "cannot wait a solution to the . . . problem," should commence immediately.[3]

Since it did not make available all the facts in the case and omitted altogether the Arab side, the President's endorsement of the Zionist program was more of a political than a policy statement and allegedly was made against the counsel of his foreign affairs advisers.[4] But the Department of State had never developed an integrated American policy toward the Near East, into which Zionism, not in its most extreme form to be sure, could fit. Since Zionism was as much a European, and now, in part because of the Department's default, an American as well as a Near East problem, the matter of adjustment was never simple. But accommodation was all the more difficult because of the Department's failure to win the confidence of American Zionists and their supporters. The Near East division of the American Foreign Service was too preoccupied with anxiety over the impact of American pro-Zionist statements on American prestige in the Arab East to look beneath the surface of pro-Zionist agitation in the United States. American Foreign Service personnel in the Arab East, whose duties almost exclusively concerned the promotion of American economic and philanthropic interests, came to view Zionism as merely an intrusive force in the region. But the more the Department of State ignored the cause of the Jewish National Home, the less it shielded the White House from the pro-Zionist lobbies and the Arab counterpressures.

The Truman statement provoked immediate response among the Arabs, despite the advice of some Arab spokesmen "to wait until after the [American] election . . . before tackling Washington." Syria and Iraq were already declining to discuss air agreements with the Department of State, and Syria refused to grant transit rights to Aramco, whose projected pipe line was now to terminate in Lebanon and by-pass Palestine altogether. But the two Arab states later changed their minds, when Pan American Airways announced that it would overfly Syria and Iraq and the Trans-Arabian Pipeline Company (Tapline) warned that the terminus would be shifted back to Palestine. King ibn Sa'ud in a letter to President Truman implied that the President had broken earlier American promises to the Arabs, because of his support of the Zionists whose "ambitions . . . have now been extended beyond the Palestine boundaries, even to . . . the confines of our Holy Lands." President Truman, in a cordial but firm reply, expressed the conviction that "the responsible Jewish leaders do not contemplate a policy of aggression against the Arab countries adjacent to Palestine," and went on to deny that his pleas for large-scale immigration and his backing of the Agency's partition plan "in any sense represent an action hostile to the Arab people."[5]

In making his Palestine pronouncement Truman had also flouted the appeals of the British Government, which had been notified in advance. The chagrined Foreign Office labelled the President's action "most unfortunate" and asserted that it "may very well jeopardize a settlement of this difficult problem." Nor was the Labor Government's task eased by the fact that the Opposition in Britain, largely for domestic political reasons, was also capitalizing on the Palestine impasse. Churchill, addressing the Conservative Party's annual conference at Blackpool on the day after the Truman statement, noted that the "lavish" pre-election promises to the Zionists by the Labor Party and its victory at the polls had "excited passionate expectation throughout the Jewish world. These promises were no sooner made than they were discarded, and now all through this year the Government stand vacillating without any plan or policy, holding on to the Mandate in which they have no vital interest, gaining the distrust and hostility both of the Arab and the Jew and exposing us to worldwide reprobation for their manifest incapacity." [6]

The claim of the Foreign Office that it was on the verge of a truce with the Zionists at the time of the Truman bombshell had little foundation. The American Jews were entitled to a voice in the policy of the Agency, which under the mandate was the spokesman for the Jewish National Home. The fact that the British Government, by Bevin's own later admission, had tried to exclude American Jews from the London Conference was calculated only to intensify their pressures on the United States Government. The British Foreign Secretary had also seriously misjudged another basic aspect of the problem. According to his view "the Jewish Agency . . . [was] very largely dominated by New York . . . and it was with gentlemen from there that I had to deal so much." [7] Though a majority of the American Zionists had endorsed the statist program, the leadership of the Agency was firmly in the grip of the activists in Jerusalem. These activists controlled the Zionist Inner General Council, a purely Palestine body, which had to pass on all Agency decisions.

And the members of the Inner General Council, reflecting the prevailing opinion in the Yishuv, were not prepared to make concessions unless there was an immediate enlargement of the monthly immigration quota, as a down payment of Britain's good intentions. But the Foreign Office had already given the delegates of the Arab states a tacit undertaking that Jewish immigration "would not be increased before the [London] conference reconvenes." Moreover, the decision to deport illegal immigrants to Cyprus rankled anew in the Jewish Community each time a captured ship was escorted into Haifa harbor by British naval vessels. On September 9 the National Council Executive in cooperation with the municipal and rural councils had voted to allocate at once $400,000 for illegal immigration." [8]

Despite the setback the British felt they had suffered from the Truman statement, the new Colonial Secretary, Arthur Creech-Jones, a past friend of Zionism, now aimed at reaching an agreement to reduce the tension in the Yishuv, as a preliminary measure to Zionist participation in the second stage of the London Conference. The mandatory ruled out any increase of the immigration quota, even though the Agency spokesmen insisted that this was one of the root causes of the Yishuv's disaffection. The British Government explained that it was primarily seeking the cooperation of the Agency in curbing the terrorists. The Zionist leaders on their side aired the Yishuv's grievances: the continued detention without formal charge or trial of the three members of the Agency Executive and a large number of non-terrorist Jews, the severe repressive methods of the security authorities, and the search for arms in outlying rural areas where no terrorism existed. Neither the British nor the Zionists achieved their wishes in full. The Inner General Council passed a resolution on October 29 calling upon the Yishuv to outlaw the terrorist groups and "to deny them all encouragement, support and assistance." At the same time Britain was accused of disregarding its mandatory obligations and was warned that "no power on earth can prevent the homeless Jews of the Diaspora from reaching the shores of their homeland." The mandatory accepted this resolution "as an earnest of the intention of the Jewish Agency and of representative Jewish institutions in Palestine to dissociate themselves entirely from the campaign of violence." A week later the Palestine Government released from internment the three Agency leaders and more than one hundred others who had been arrested four months earlier.[9]

FAILURE

The second stage of the London Conference was again put off until early in 1947 to enable the Agency to refer the question of its attendance to the Twenty-second Zionist Congress, scheduled to sit in Basel, Switzerland, in December. Since the eve of the war the world Jewish population had been reduced by more than one-third, from close to 17,000,000 to an estimated 11,000,000. But because of the Nazi anti-Jewish policy and the United Nations failure to take adequate action for the rehabilitation of the European Jewish survivors, world Zionist enrollment had more than doubled from one million in 1939 to well over two million in 1946. The relative number of Jews who had become members of the Zionist Organization more than trebled in the same period from 6.2 per cent to 19.6 per cent. The number of countries with Zionist branches rose from fifty-one to sixty-three, and the United States now replaced Poland as the chief Zionist center, with almost half the world membership.

The political complexion of the world Zionist movement had also altered. In Palestine these developments had been foreshadowed during the war and had partly crystallized in the 1944 Yishuv election. In the year and a half since V-E Day, political disillusionment and uncertainty as well as mandatory repression had further hardened Zionist thinking. The wartime spread of statism and the activists' postwar rise to power were largely responsible for bringing the Revisionists in the spring of 1946 back into the World Zionist Organization, from which they had seceded eleven years earlier. The prolonged Palestine crisis, moreover, resulted in that year in the merger of many splinter factions. On the right, the United Zionists-Revisionists had been formed by the union of the Revisionist and the Jewish State parties; in the center the A and B groups formed a single General Zionist Party; and on the left, ha-Shomer ha-Za'ir absorbed its urban affiliate, the Socialist League, while the Labor Unity Party fused with the Left Zionist Workers, retaining the name of the first.

These changes were reflected in the Yishuv in the returns of the election of delegates to the Zionist Congress in October 1946. The three labor parties together had polled more than 60 per cent of the votes, as compared with 65 per cent in 1939. But the ideological differences between Mapai and the two enlarged leftist parties were too ingrained to be resolved; and even ha-Shomer ha-Za'ir and Labor Unity, whose social, economic, and political thinking were akin, found it impossible to close ranks. Consequently, though Mapai was still by far the strongest single party, it returned only twenty-eight of the seventy-nine delegates from the Yishuv, far short of a majority. Under these circumstances, the Revisionists with eleven successful candidates came in second, and the two leftist labor parties tied for third with ten each. Though the General Zionist Party, including its labor affiliate, won only four delegates in Palestine, the overwhelming strength of that party in the United States gave it first place at the Congress, with 123 of the 385 delegates. The world Union of Zionist Labor—Mapai in Palestine—with only 101 delegates had to relinquish the position of pre-eminence it had held for more than thirteen years. Third place was occupied by Mizrahi and its labor branch with fifty-eight delegates, fourth by the Revisionists with forty-one, and fifth by the two leftist parties with twenty-six each.[10]

In the political debate, which occupied most of the sixteen-day session of the Congress (December 9–24), Weizmann denounced the terrorists and warned that the growth of this "cancer in the body politic of Palestinian Jewry" must be checked, "for, if not, it will devour the Movement and the Yishuv and will destroy all that we have built up." The question of partition divided most of the parties. Even the religious Mizrahi Party, with its theory of the divinity of the Jewish right to Palestine in its Biblical boundaries, found its labor subsidiary in the pro-partition camp. Only ha-Shomer ha-Za'ir, which clung to its plank for converting Palestine into a binationalist state, and, on the other extreme, the Revisionists, who did not budge from their claim to Transjordan as well as Palestine as the area of an exclusively Jewish state, remained undivided. As the vote on partition went, so went the vote on the London Conference. The moderates, following the lead of Weizmann, Shertok, and Stephen Wise, favored participation in the London parleys and endorsed the partition formula advanced by the Agency Executive the preceding August. But the activists, whose chief exponents were Ben Gurion and Abba Hillel Silver, argued that for tactical reasons the partition proposal ought to come from the British.

That the activists had won the day was evident when the Congress resolved "that in the existing circumstances the Zionist movement cannot participate in the London Conference," but empowered the General Council to reconsider, "if a change should take place in the situation." The delegates reaffirmed the three demands of the Biltmore Program. Another resolution repudiated the terrorists, but did not refer to the Irgun and the Freedom Fighters by name, euphemizing them instead as "dissident groups." The close vote on the political resolutions, 171 to 154, indicated that, if the mandatory gave any encouragement to the moderates, their counsel might again prevail. Weizmann was not re-elected president because he exemplified cooperation with Britain, but out of deference to his prestige and past service, the post was left vacant. The new coalition Executive comprised 19 members, apportioned relatively among the three strongest parties at the Congress. Ben Gurion retained the chairmanship and Silver headed the American section, consisting of six members, including Shertok, who was made roving coordinator of Zionist political activities with his seat in Washington.[11]

While the Agency's participation in the second phase of the London Conference appeared doubtful, the Arab League spokesmen seemed pleased with the results of the September talks and 'Azzam Pasha declared on their behalf that they felt "much nearer agreement [with the British] than we ever thought we would be." The Morrison-Grady plan, though not discarded, was not being implemented. The Arabs had been able to present their own counterproposals. Assurances that no change would occur in the interim immigration policy in Palestine before the parleys were resumed were being kept, despite pressure from President Truman. In September the Arab states' representatives had requested an amnesty for five Palestine Arabs who had been associated with the Mufti in Axis Europe and had been interned in the Seychelles Islands in February 1946 by the British. The Colonial Office fulfilled this demand early in November, when the Jewish Agency leaders were set free. At the same time the Palestine Government granted a general amnesty to a dozen other followers of the Mufti who had been excluded from Palestine ever since the revolt and some of whom had records of collaboration with the Axis.[12]

Three of these exiles and two other Husayni followers, one of whom was still excluded from Palestine, were nominated members of the Arab Higher Executive in January 1947. With eight of the ten-man Executive belonging to the Palestine Arab Party, the Husaynis once again had gained supreme control over the local national movement. The Mufti continued to direct Palestine Arab political affairs from Egypt, where many meetings of the Executive were held. Furthermore, the Arab League Council in December 1946 decided to transfer to the Higher Executive all funds earmarked for Palestine. And the Executive itself, for purposes of greater efficiency, set up a treasury and special departments. The department of national economy was concerned chiefly with supervising the boycott of Jewish manufactures; the department of lands with preventing the sale of Arab-owned realty to Jews; the department of national aid with dispensing relief to dependents of Arabs killed or imprisoned in the revolt; and the department of national reconstruction with directing the Arab paramilitary organizations.[13]

The illegal militarized societies, alternately known as youth or scout movements to avoid official proscription, were the outgrowth of the political uncertainty, the postwar spread of Jewish terrorism, the rising militancy of the Husayni leadership, and the government's failure to disband Haganah or suppress the Irgun and the Freedom Fighters. The first Arab group, al-Najjadah (Helpers), was formed at Jaffa in October 1945 by a Muslim lawyer, Muhammad Nimr al-Hawari, who aspired to make his group the Arab counterpart of Haganah. Hawari successfully resisted attempts by Jamal al-Husayni, shortly after the latter's return to Palestine, to convert the Najjadah into the military arm of the Palestine Arab Party. As a result, the Husaynis reorganized their own body, al-Futuwwah, which they had first created in 1935 but which went out of existence during the Arab revolt. Both the Najjadah and the Futuwwah expanded steadily in the summer of 1946, as the situation in Palestine became more critical. Surplus American army uniforms were purchased at Cairo. A growing stream of military equipment, mostly small arms, came out of hiding, was smuggled across the frontiers from near-by Arab countries, or was purchased from British soldiers. Training was entrusted to experienced soldiers; public parades and drill in uniform with rifles and side arms frequently took place, at times under the very nose of government officials. After prolonged negotiations between Hawari and the Mufti in Cairo, Najjadah and Futuwwah, whose combined membership was variously estimated from less than 10,000 to about 30,000, reached a short-lived agreement whereby both were placed under a joint command and became the Higher Executive's "army." [14]

Despite the bolstering from within and without the Executive had not silenced the Opposition, which kept insisting on popular elections. The Husayni reply was a promise, made at the time of the creation of the Executive's treasury, to hold elections in the near future and to declare eligible for voting all who paid "taxes." A further indication of the persistence of the Opposition was the Executive's intimidation of Arab shopkeepers selling Jewish-made wares in defiance of the boycott and Arab middlemen involved in Jewish land purchases. In fact, Jamal al-Husayni declared that these were the two main immediate functions of the Arab militarized groups. But he went on to elucidate that the Palestine Arabs were in reality organizing themselves for war against a Jewish state, if it should be established, and that they would employ the same guerrilla tactics used in the earlier revolt. Time was the Arabs' ally, explained the Mufti's deputy, because the British-Zionist struggle and the internal Zionist dissension were sapping the Yishuv's strength. Jamal stressed that the Arabs "would accept help from any power, including the Soviet Union, willing to back the Arabs against partition" and that all the Arab states would come to their aid.[15]

Indeed, the Arab League Council had already rejected partition outright and announced that it would continue to oppose "any drastic change in . . . [the] Arab status" of Palestine. Though the Arab delegates to the United Nations had not directly raised the Palestine issue, evidence was not wanting that the problem was on their minds. In the deliberations on the constitution of the proposed International Refugee Organization, the Arab delegates tried unsuccessfully to have inserted the principle that the question of the European Jewish refugees should be divorced from that of Palestine. Horse-trading between the Latin-American and Arab blocs resulted in the election of Syria to the Security Council and Iraq to the Trusteeship Council. When the ballot was taken on New York as the United Nations permanent site, the Arab delegates refused to go along with the overwhelming majority, despite the pleas of the chairman of the Headquarters Committee that they "forget their prejudices." [16]

Thus, in the four-month interval between the first and second installments of the London Conference the views of the Zionists and the Arabs had stiffened. With the activists in power the Agency spokesmen were even more uncompromising than they had been in September. They would accept nothing less than a Jewish state. They were prepared to consider partition, but the proposal would have to come from the British. With the Husaynis in the saddle, the Higher Executive was equally unbending and served notice that it even regarded the Arab states' constitutional scheme of September as too generous. The Higher Executive, it was announced, would urge in particular that the proportion of Jews in the proposed Arab government be based on the Palestine population figures of 1919. But, above all, the Executive declared that it would under no circumstances consider partition. As for the United States, Secretary of State Byrnes had agreed at the beginning of December to send an American observer to London, if the Jews as well as the Arabs attended.[17]

The second and final phase of the London Conference opened on January 27, 1947, under circumstances even more dismal than those of the preceding September. The Palestine Arab Higher Executive, it was true, was now formally represented. But the Agency Executive, though eight of its nineteen members were in London, continued to boycott the conference; and for that reason the United States did not appoint an observer. Jamal al-Husayni repeated the historical, legal, and constitutional arguments of the Palestine Arabs and warned that they would fight partition "with all the means at their disposal." The Arab states' delegates refused to deviate from their position of four months earlier. Nor did Bevin and Creech-Jones, in informal conversations, find the Agency spokesmen in a pliant mood.[18]

Foreign Secretary Bevin then submitted to the Arabs and Jews a modified version of the Morrison-Grady plan as the final British proposal. The new scheme differed from the old in several major respects. A definite time limit of five years was suggested for the trusteeship term. During this transition the country would be progressively prepared for independence in a unitary, Arab-Jewish state. The possibility of partition was entirely removed. The High Commissioner would exercise supreme legislative and executive authority. But the Palestine population would be accorded cantonal self-government instead of provincial autonomy. The cantons, whose areas would be defined according to whether Arabs or Jews constituted a majority in the locality, would not necessarily be contiguous and would enjoy "wide" legislative, administrative, and financial powers, "including some share in responsibility for the police." The Jewish Agency would be dissolved immediately after the trusteeship agreement was concluded, and the Jews, like the Arabs, would be represented by delegates on an advisory council. The 100,000 Jewish immigrants would be admitted over a period of two years, instead of one. In the last three years of trusteeship the Arabs would be assured a voice in determining immigration policy, though the ultimate decision would rest with the United Nations Trusteeship Council. The constituent assembly of the projected unitary state would be elected at the end of four years, and, in the event of a disagreement over the constitution, the dispute would be referred to the Trusteeship Council.[19]

The latest Bevin proposal was rejected unconditionally by Arabs and Jews. The conference with the Arabs and the informal talks with the Zionists came to an abrupt end with the announcement on February 14 that "His Majesty's Government had decided to refer the whole problem to the United Nations." [20]

CHAPTER 21

Britain's Legacy to the United Nations

LABOR'S RECORD IN PALESTINE

DISTRACTED by the greater urgency of other international issues, the British Labor Government from the very start had merely gone through the formal motions of tackling the Palestine problem. The question, consequently, became increasingly critical and its repercussions more widespread. The mandatory's plight was not eased by the Attlee Cabinet's division of responsibility for Palestine. The Colonial Office, as heretofore, administered the mandate. But the Foreign Office was charged with resolving the impasse. After the collapse of the London Conference, the Labor Government had to account to Parliament for its dilatory treatment of the Palestine problem and its inability after a year and a half in office to devise a policy.

Foreign Secretary Bevin started out by explaining his desire to remove existent ambiguities about the 1939 White Paper. Until that statement of policy, which had been approved by Parliament, was replaced by another, His Majesty's Government was bound by its terms, he pointed out, for the sake of continuity and of keeping a solemn pledge. Still at the very outset the Labor Cabinet had notified the Arabs that a substitute policy would have to be negotiated. Meanwhile, when the White Paper's immigration quota had been exhausted in December 1945, "we agreed that it should continue at 1,500 a month. I will not say, and it would be wrong of me to say, that there was an agreement by the Arabs to do that, but there was at least acquiescence . . ." Since that time immigration had been proceeding at the rate of 18,000 a year, a rate exceeded only "five times in the whole history of the Mandate."

Bevin observed that he and his colleagues, despite warnings from every quarter that any final solution would have to be enforced, felt obliged first to exhaust all efforts to reach a negotiated settlement. His Majesty's Government could not be blamed, he insisted, for the failure to achieve an agreement. In retracing the negotiations with Americans, Arabs, and Jews, the Foreign Secretary charged that the Americans invariably intervened for the admission to Palestine of the 100,000 just when he was at the point of obtaining concessions from either Arabs or Jews. Of the two, however, he felt that the Arabs were more reasonable because, though they had never acknowledged the validity of the Balfour Declaration and the mandate, they were nevertheless "willing to recognize the results of this policy so far as the present residents in Palestine were concerned." Bevin believed that, "if it were only a question of relieving Europe of 100,000 Jews," the Arabs might still be persuaded. But "from the Zionist point of view the 100,000 is only a beginning, and the Jewish Agency talk in terms of millions."

Bevin found the Arab claim difficult to answer. The Arabs saw no justifiable reason why "an external agency, largely financed from America, [should] determine how many people should come into Palestine and interfere with the economy of the Arabs, who had been there for 2,000 years." But the Agency would consider nothing less than a Jewish state. In opposing a unitary, Arab-Jewish state, the Agency spokesmen had argued that "the Jews, as Jews, will not be in the United Nations." Bevin thought that this was "raising a very big question. Are we in the United Nations as a religion [or] . . . as a people geographically situated, or how are we in it?" The Zionist claim to statehood might be satisfied through partition, it was advanced. But Palestine could never be so divided as to create two viable states; the Arabs would never agree to it; such a solution would "set going a conflict which will be worse than the conflict we have tried to settle"; and, in any case, the mandatory had no authority to take a decision on partition, for its position in the United Nations would be indefensible.

"If I could get back to the contribution on purely humanitarian grounds of 100,000 . . . into Palestine, and if this political fight for a Jewish State could be put on one side, and we could develop self-government by the people resident in Palestine, without any other political issue," concluded Bevin, "I would be willing to try again." [1] The Foreign Secretary's public indulgence in wishful thinking underlined the bankruptcy of the Labor Government's Palestine policy and its failure adequately to assess the scope of the problem. At the time of the dissolution of the League of Nations in April 1946 the United Kingdom gave assurances that, until "fresh arrangements" had been concluded, Palestine would be governed in conformity with "the general principles" of the existing mandate.[2] Therefore, until the mandate was terminated, the Agency was the recognized spokesman of the Jewish National Home. By its constitution the Agency was an international body, deriving its support and authority from Jews the world over. Clearly the Agency could never be expected willingly to surrender its rights under the mandate, unless convinced that the status of the national home was secured. Strong public interest in Palestine, predominantly pro-Zionist, accounted in part for United States involvement. But the American Government was also drawn into the question originally by its approval, in its capacity as one of the Principal Allied Powers at the close of World War I, of assigning the mandate to Britain and most recently by British invitation. Washington, however, had not yet evinced any real appreciation of its obligations in helping to maintain peace in the Near East. The Arab states were first accorded a voice in Palestine by the mandatory in 1938 and were subsequently re-assured by both Britain and the United States that they would be consulted before any basic decision was taken. Holding the views that the mandate was invalid, Palestine was an Arab country, and its Arab population was entitled to rule that country, the Arab states would never voluntarily yield on any one of these points.

To reach a negotiated settlement, the Labor Government would have had to find a balance among these divergent interests. But one of Britain's most urgent concerns in its Near East strategic planning in 1946 was the fear of Soviet expansion toward the Mediterranean Sea and the Indian Ocean. This fear was reinforced by captured German Foreign Office archives, which showed that the Kremlin's aspirations in this region had been articulated as early as 1940. Yet the United Kingdom could no longer sustain the costs of large military establishments in the area and was in an awkward relationship with Egypt and Iraq by reason of its war-accumulated debts to the two countries, approximating two billion dollars. Nevertheless London viewed the Near East as vital to imperial strategy and communications, the major source of petroleum for British domestic consumption, a means of securing dollar credits by the sale of crude oil to American companies, and an important market for British manufactures. The Labor Government's avowed objectives were to give the Arab countries full independence, treat them as equals, remove the irritants which were keeping alive anti-British feeling, establish an identity of interest between the Arab East and the United Kingdom, and conclude new treaties which would provide for permanent joint defense boards and military bases in time of emergency. Egypt was the first Arab country with which the Attlee Cabinet endeavored to negotiate such an agreement, beginning in the spring of 1946.[a]

To avoid additional unrest and unpopularity in the Arab East and, if possible, to obtain Arab cooperation on other regional issues, the Labor Government was apparently prepared to make the maximum possible concessions to the Arabs in Palestine within the framework of the mandate. The Arabs, however, refused anything less than the complete fulfillment of their basic demands. Indeed, the demand for setting Palestine up as an independent Arab state was but one aspect of the Arab struggle for unconditional release from Western domination. Moreover, the Arabs were made even more truculent by the knowledge of Britain's weakness and Soviet overtures. Consequently, the Labor Government, which could not bring itself to capitulate, was unable to obtain Arab consent even to the generous conditions of the latest Bevin plan for an independent, unitary Palestine state at the end of five years. The final breakdown of the London Conference on Palestine and the standstill in Egyptian talks after eleven months were adding to the general restiveness in the Arab countries.

The Labor Government, in the meantime, hoped to bolster the Near East defenses against potential Soviet aggression by prevailing upon Washington to share postwar responsibilities for the region's security. The question was complicated by the fact that the American Government had no preferential treaties or mandates in the area and, therefore, no permanent military bases. If Britain had been able to persuade the United States, either at the time of the Inquiry Committee or the subsequent Anglo-American parleys in London, to partake of the military burdens in Palestine, the Americans would have been placed squarely in the center of the Near East. But this the Labor Government had proved incapable of doing. As a result, Anglo-American relations over Palestine grew steadily cooler. Bevin's critical remarks in his apologia about President Truman, American Jews, and Americans generally, reflected widespread British annoyance with what was regarded as irresponsible American intervention. His assertions were warmly endorsed by most British newspapers. But they were greeted by the White House as "most unfortunate and misleading" and by pro-Zionist Congressmen in less restrained language, while leading American newspapers expressed resentment over Bevin's "tactlessness" and "foolish performance." [4]

The Labor Government's inflexible disregard for the Zionist position coupled with Bevin's blunt statements had contributed substantially to the emergence of the very situation which the Foreign Secretary now deplored. The United States was the last remaining trump in the Zionist hand, so far as Big-Power support was concerned. Consequently, the more the British tried to coerce the Zionists into submission, the greater became the Zionist pressures on American public opinion and on the American Government. By this time the United States had developed into a veritable depository of Zionist groups. Besides the Agency, the Histadrut, and the several Zionist parties, each of which had an American affiliate, the Irgun and the Freedom Fighters were also represented, the first by the Hebrew Committee of National Liberation and its multifarious off-shoots and the second by the so-called Political Action Committee for Palestine.[5]

The American Government for its part was not making matters easier. The Army-Navy petroleum board and the Department of State's petroleum division, it was true, continued to regard Near East oil as of "extreme importance," in view of the dwindling resources at home. A $10,000,000 loan was granted in August 1946 to Saudi Arabia, where the largest American concessions were located, and in January-February 1947 the Arabian Crown Prince, Amir Sa'ud, visited the United States as the government's guest to gather information about modernizing his father's realm. But the Department of State had not yet defined, or at least not publicized, except in the vaguest terms, the principles of United States over-all policy toward the Near East.[6] Moreover, President Truman's repeated requests for the admission of 100,000 Jewish D.P.'s into Palestine and his approval of the Jewish Agency's partition plan had little immediate practical value. Congressmen, many of whom also readily endorsed the Zionist platform, were generally reluctant to send American troops to Palestine. Nor had Congress taken any steps whatsoever to admit D.P.'s into the United States. This weakened the moral influence of American demands for resettling Jewish refugees in Palestine and did nothing to alleviate the pressure of emigration to the British-held mandate.

While preoccupied with these unsuccessful attempts to gain Arab good will and to enlist American cooperation, the Labor Government had failed to come to grips with essentials. The espousal of the Morrison-Grady and Bevin schemes, it must be assumed, indicated that the Labor Government believed provincial autonomy an equitable compromise that would offer some prospects of realization. But the political realities in Palestine did not bear out this belief. The Yishuv was already a democratically organized, self-governing community. Its leaders enjoyed more authority with the Jewish population than did the officials of the Palestine Government. The Arab Community was not similarly constituted and, in fact, had no machinery for self-government on a national (Muslim-Christian) basis. Even the largest of its autonomous religious institutions, the Supreme Muslim Council, was still controlled by the government.[7] The political spokesmen, appointed by the Arab League and later by the Mufti himself, exercised their authority largely through the national movement and, though their prestige was considerable, they were not elected leaders. The Morrison-Grady and the Bevin schemes, therefore, offered the Arabs much more than they already enjoyed and the Jews much less.

As long as the mandate remained in force, the Jews demanded that its provisions for the facilitation of Jewish immigration and close settlement on the land be honored. The Arabs, on the other hand, were relying on the pledges of the 1939 White Paper. Since the provincial and cantonal autonomy schemes provided for the entry of 100,000 Jews into Palestine and were not explicit about eventual prohibition of Jewish immigration, even the Bevin plan, which offered the Arabs basically what they wanted at the end of five years, proved unacceptable. The Palestine Arabs had had their fill of unkept British promises. By the same token, no Zionist from moderate to terrorist would ever agree to the eventual cessation of immigration, even if in the interval all European Jewish D.P.'s, now numbering over 200,000, were to be resettled in Palestine. That would have amounted to forsaking the supreme aspiration of Zionism: the creation of a national home, where Jews would be masters of their own political destiny and where all Jews who desired or were forced by circumstances could settle.[8]

RESULTS OF LABOR'S POLICY

While London thus seemed to be faltering toward a binationalist solution, the Attlee Cabinet's resolute execution of an irresolute interim policy produced results precisely the reverse of those sought. Aside from the insuperabilities of undoing the developments of a generation, the chances of putting binationalism into successful operation depended ultimately on both Arab and Jewish consent. In the Arab Community the handful of binationalists consisted largely of the ineffectual communists. The likelihood of inducing the anti-Husayni politicians to share the government with the Jews was very small; the possibility of securing Husayni cooperation entirely nonexistent. Yet under the Labor regime most of the exiled Husaynis and their fellow travelers received unconditional amnesties. This action was not calculated to enhance British prestige either in Palestine or the near-by Arab countries, since it seemed to vindicate the anti-British agitation of those politicians who had collaborated with the Axis. Nor could the Arab nationalists understand why the mandatory, in granting amnesties, should have stopped short of the Mufti, particularly since no formal charges had been preferred against him.[9] In the Yishuv there was a substantial binationalist minority, which the moderate statists of the Weizmann stripe might possibly have been persuaded under certain conditions to join in trying out binationalism. But London's procrastination, Bevin's impatient utterances, and the Labor Government's imperviousness to the Zionist viewpoint brought the activists to power; and the arrest of members of the quasi-government, the occupation of the Agency and Histadrut offices, and the attempts to disarm Palmah alienated binationalists and moderate statists as well. With the activist Zionists and the militant Husaynis at the helm, binationalism did not have the slightest chance.

Similarly Labor's provisional immigration policy infuriated Arabs and Zionists alike. The Palestine Arab leaders regarded as a breach of faith the continuance of Jewish immigration, even at the rate of 1,500 a month, after the exhaustion of the White Paper quota. The Jews believed that this rate was paltry, especially in relation to the pressing needs of rehabilitating the European D.P.'s, and in contravention of the mandate. The Royal Navy and Air Force were able effectively to blockade the Palestine seacoast against unlawful entrants. Despite diplomatic intervention with the European governments, however, the British proved singularly unsuccessful in checking the traffic at the source. Thus, of the 18,000 Jewish immigrants in 1946, more than half were unauthorized. In the first seven and one-half months of that year some 8,900 illegals and eight vessels were apprehended, while in the next six months, after the system had been instituted of deporting such Jews to Cyprus, some 12,500 refugees and twelve vessels had been seized. By April 1, 1947, there were 11,900 Jews in Cyprus detention camps. When the Colonial Secretary announced in December 1946 that maintenance costs of the camps would be met by the Palestine Government, the secretary of the Higher Executive threatened that Arabs would refuse to pay taxes, "if it meant underwriting Jewish immigration." Palestine Arab spokesmen generally felt that Britain could do more than it was doing to dry up the flow of illegal immigration. They argued that "if Britain allows a great number of immigrants to arrive in Palestine waters in defiance of established quotas, it is Britain's financial concern." [10]

The most portentous development in the eighteen months of Labor's administration of the mandate, however, was the deterioration of security. In addition to units of the Transjordan Arab Legion and some 16,000 British and local police, the mandatory had stationed in tiny Palestine at the end of 1946 more than 80,000 British troops—including the equivalent of two and one-half combat divisions—or nearly one-tenth the total manpower strength of the British Army at that time. There was one soldier or constable for every eighteen persons in the country. The combined military-police establishment was over four times as large as it had been eight years earlier, at the height of the Arab revolt. For the upkeep of the forces, British taxpayers spent an estimated $200,000,000 during Labor's year and one-half in office and the Palestine Government at least another $20,000,000. Besides extensive army camps, some sixty police structures—a few as large as a city block—were erected between 1940–44 throughout the country at a cost to the Palestine citizens of $6,000,000. Designed to billet the police, their families, and essential government offices, they were equipped with the most modern police and semimilitary facilities and "were capable of being defended as forts in an emergency." [11]

By the war's end the Palestine Government, under the emergency regulations, exercised rigid press censorship and authorized troops and police to arrest or search without warrant and to impose collective fines and forfeiture of property. The jurisdiction vested in the High Commissioner under the Attlee Cabinet was extended until it reached a climax in January 1947, when Cunningham was empowered, at his own discretion, to enforce statutory martial law in any area of the country. In the first week of February the families of British civilian personnel and "nonessential" officials, some 2,000 persons altogether, were evacuated from the country. All remaining nonmilitary Britons were placed behind heavily guarded, wire-enclosed security zones in former residential areas of the larger towns, where hundreds of Jewish inhabitants were evicted on 48-hour notice.[12] Yet with this elaborate arrangement and the broadest police powers Britain was unable to re-establish the Palestine Government's authority.

Except for brief lulls during August 1946 and part of December, the Irgun and the Freedom Fighters had stepped up their political terrorism after the King David disaster. The Irgun added to its list of "tactical victories" against the mandatory at the end of December by flogging a British officer and three sergeants in reprisal for the caning of a young Irgunist. A month later two British civilians were kidnapped and not released until Cunningham had granted a reprieve to an Irgunist under death sentence. Haganah's only act of violence after August was an attack at Haifa in February 1947 on two Government launches used in transferring illegal immigrants from their "floating slums" to deportation ships. Meanwhile, the scale of Jewish violence had largely obscured the fact that two unlawful Arab militarized societies, both of which had come into existence during the period of the Attlee Government, were terrorizing their own community. Most of the victims were violators of the economic and land-sale boycott against the Yishuv. But between November 1946 and February 1947 six alleged political opponents of the Husaynis were murdered.[13]

The Palestine Government tended to overlook Arab terrorism for the time being, since that of the Jews was a more serious and immediate danger and was directed in the main against the British. Thus, for example, Fawzi al-Qawuqji, who after his leadership of the Palestine Arab rebels in 1936 had worked closely with the Mufti in Iraq and in Axis Europe, managed at the end of February 1947 to "escape the vigilance" of the British frontier control at the Lydda airport in Palestine, despite the $8,000 reward for his capture. As for Jewish terrorism, punitive action had failed, because, though the Labor Government had succeeded in transforming the mandate into a police state, it was a police state with a conscience. As the High Commissioner was later to observe, the terrorist activities could have been "brought to an end in a matter of hours," if the armed forces had been allowed to employ "the full power of their weapons against the whole Jewish community." But Cunningham stressed that "such measures have never been contemplated by His Majesty's Government, nor have they ever been recommended, nor desired by the Army." He went on to commend the behavior of the British soldiers, declaring that "no other troops in the world would have exercised such restraint and tolerance in the face of such continued provocation." [14] Since the British were not prepared to be absolutely ruthless, the only chance of rounding up the terrorists lay in obtaining the active assistance of the Yishuv.

The Agency and National Council Executives were eager to rid the community of the multiplying terrorists, who did not acknowledge the quasi-government's authority and were endangering Zionist prospects. But the Jewish authorities from the time of Bevin's first public statement on Palestine had refused to cooperate with the Labor Government, which gave them no basis for believing that they would receive an equitable hearing. The Yishuv cannot "be called upon to place itself at the disposal of the Government," insisted the Jewish Agency, "for fighting the evil consequences of a policy which is of that Government's own making and which the Yishuv regards as a menace to its own existence." Moreover, the mere existence in Palestine of a police government and the presence of thousands of troops, interfering as they must with normal pursuits, served as provocation to the Yishuv. No matter how exemplary the conduct of most British soldiers, there were those who handled the civilian population roughly, destroyed property wantonly, and engaged in their own campaign of counterviolence against innocent Jews. The Yishuv remembered, not the restraint of the many, but the excesses of the few.[15]

Hence, the Attlee Cabinet in the short period of a year and a half had arrived at an intolerable position in Palestine. The British Government was seeking economy; its security costs in Palestine had risen far beyond the means of the British taxpayer. As a result of the intensifying terrorism, public pressure in the United Kingdom increased to "bring the boys home." London was striving for a negotiated settlement; expediency had ensconced militant elements in power in the Arab and Jewish communities and rendered peaceful negotiation impossible. Britain's need for military bases in Palestine appeared to be growing; muddling had made the possibility of their retention infinitely more precarious. The machinery for a police state had been set up, but since this was alien to democratic tradition in Britain and came to be embarrassing because the Zionists were able to bring the situation to the attention of the Western world, the entire governmental structure in Palestine lay condemned. Law could no longer be enforced. Instead, the British officials themselves had become captives. At the end of February 1947 only eleven British civilians resided outside the security zones. Those inside lived for all practical purposes under a dusk-to-dawn curfew and ventured forth only under armed escort.[16]

The wartime Anglo-American harmony over Palestine had been dissipated. This was as much Washington's fault as it was London's. Besides, the two Western Powers were losing the initiative. In its persistent, but as yet unrewarding, efforts to win Arab friendship, Britain seemed prone to follow the lead of the Arab League. Owing to the lack of an integrated, well-defined Near East policy, the Truman Administration's position on Palestine had become more ambiguous than ever, precluding any effective decision one way or another. As the war receded, Anglo-American prestige declined and with it the moral authority of the two Western Powers. The rift between the Soviet Union and the West was widening steadily. Consequently, Russia's interest in the problem would probably be motivated by the desire to ease the British out of Palestine and prevent the Americans from coming in. This was the problem and these were the conditions which the Mandatory Power was now bequeathing to the United Nations.[17]

CHAPTER 22

United Nations Inquiry

REFERENCE OF the Palestine problem to the United Nations did not alter the prerequisites for a final settlement. Without provision for military enforcement, United Nations decisions were no more binding than the Big Powers were prepared to make them. Unless London, Washington, and Moscow saw eye-to-eye on any proposed solution, their differences were certain further to promote Arab-Zionist strife. But the prospects in the spring of 1947 of Big-Three agreement on Palestine, as on any other issue of immediate or potential strategic importance, were more remote than at any time since 1945. The appointment in January of General George C. Marshall as Secretary of State marked the inception of a stiffening in the Truman Administration's attitude toward unilateral Soviet action in international affairs. With the enunciation of the Truman Doctrine two months later Washington replaced London as the center of Western resistance to Moscow. In assuming British military and financial commitments in Greece and Turkey, the United States dedicated itself to hardening the northern crust of the Near East against Soviet infiltration and could thus be expected to resist possible efforts by Moscow to gain an entering wedge in Palestine. Hence Britain, the United States, and the U.S.S.R. were bound to view the Palestine issue, as heretofore, in the light of their respective national interests.

The Labor Government, it was clear, did not intend to relinquish control over Palestine. "We are not going to the United Nations to surrender the Mandate," declared Colonial Secretary Creech-Jones. "We are . . . setting out the problem and asking for their advice as to how the Mandate can be administered. If the Mandate cannot be administered in its present form we are asking how it can be amended." Had Bevin obtained Arab and Jewish approval for a trusteeship along the lines of provincial or cantonal autonomy, the question would have been placed on the Trusteeship Council agenda. There now remained the alternatives of submitting the problem to either the Security Council or the General Assembly. The Security Council possessed the theoretical advantages of speed and limited power of enforcement, since that organ functioned continuously and could order the application of sanctions and other punitive measures against non-cooperative states. The Attlee Cabinet, however, ruled the Security Council out as "an imperfect instrument." This left the General Assembly as the last choice, and the Labor Government was at first inclined to wait until that body reconvened in the fall. But under pressure from the Conservative Opposition and the worsening crisis in Palestine the British Government finally requested the United Nations Secretary-General on April 2 "to summon, as soon as possible, a special session of the General Assembly for the purpose of constituting and instructing a special committee to prepare for the consideration" of the problem of Palestine and its future government at the next regular session.[1]

The five Arab states members of the United Nations gave advance notice of their desire to include on the agenda a supplementary item concerning "the termination of the mandate over Palestine and the declaration of its independence." [2] Had this proposal been adopted, the British objective of setting up an investigative body would certainly have been delayed and might have been defeated, and at the very least all aspects of the Palestine question would have been thrown open to debate. But the Arab request was voted down, and, despite frequent Arab excursions into political discussion, the Assembly debate was confined essentially to the composition of the proposed inquiry committee and its terms of reference. The Soviet delegate agreed to a fresh inquiry, but urged that the five permanent members of the Security Council should assume, "together with the United Nations as a whole, the responsibility not only for final decisions . . . taken by our Organization . . . but also for the preparation of these decisions." He therefore proposed Big-Five membership on the projected committee and saw "no grounds for objecting to the inclusion . . . of one of the Arab States." The United States delegate, however, favored the creation of a "neutral" body from which the Big Five would be explicitly debarred because of their "special interests." This position was endorsed by the United Kingdom, whose spokesman also recommended that the Arab states be excluded, owing to their direct interest in the problem. The Anglo-American view was upheld in the end. The eleven-nation investigative board, known as the United Nations Special Committee on Palestine or UNSCOP, was composed of Australia, Canada, Czechoslovakia, Guatemala, India, Iran, Netherlands, Peru, Sweden, Uruguay, and Yugoslavia.[3]

As for the terms of reference, the Arab delegates insisted that the problem of the displaced European Jews be divorced from that of Palestine and that the committee concern itself solely with the situation in Palestine and the grant of independence to its population under a unitary government. The United States delegation, however, objected to the Arab demands as prejudging the inquiry and recommended that the instructions be as broad as possible. This view was shared by the British delegation. The terms of reference, as finally approved, invested UNSCOP with "the widest powers to ascertain and record facts, and to investigate all questions and issues relevant to the problem of Palestine." The committee was to "conduct investigations in Palestine and wherever it may deem useful" and to "give most careful consideration to the religious interests . . . of Islam, Judaism and Christianity." Its report, which was to include "proposals . . . for the solution of the problem of Palestine," was to be completed no later than September 1, 1947. When the final ballot on the terms of reference was taken, only the five Arab states, Afghanistan, and Turkey cast negative votes.[4]

Throughout the special session (April 28–May 15) the Arab spokesmen stressed again and again that the only just solution was the Arab solution. They repeatedly warned that any other proposal would have to be enforced against the will of the Palestine Arabs and all the Arab states. Most Arab delegates spoke of the consequent threat to the peace in the Near East, while the Iraqi delegate, Fadhil al-Jamali, declared "that supporting the national aspirations of the Jews means very clearly a declaration of war, and nothing less." After the adoption of UNSCOP's terms of reference, each Arab delegate expressly "reserved the right of . . . [his] Government as to its future attitude. . . ."[5] The Arab states had thereby, in effect, given advance notice that they would not necessarily be bound by the ultimate recommendations.

Representatives of the Arab Higher Committee—as the Higher Executive now began to call itself—and the Jewish Agency, the only nongovernmental organizations accorded the privilege, were allowed to present testimony before the First (Political and Security) Committee, and to express their opinions on the directives to the inquiry committee. The conflicting claims were thus brought into sharp focus. "The establishment [in Palestine] of the Jewish national home is a process," declared Moshe Shertok on behalf of the Agency. "The setting up of a Jewish state is its consummation." Emile al-Ghuri, the secretary of the Higher Committee delegation, answered that "it is . . . the determined and unequivocal will of the Arabs to refuse to consider any solution which . . . even implies the loss of their sovereignty over . . . any part of their country, or the diminution of such sovereignty in any form whatever."[6]

By the time the first special session adjourned, it was clear that the United Kingdom and the United States were on the defensive. The two

Western Powers were already inescapably entangled in the ever-widening meshes of the Palestine problem. As a result, the British and the American representatives studiously avoided discussing substantive aspects of the Palestine question and refrained from expressing any preference regarding possible solutions. The British delegate, Sir Alexander Cadogan, even under the most persistent prodding as to whether his government would accept the United Nations recommendations, refused to elaborate upon two conditions which he stated would guide London in taking its final decision. "If the United Nations can find a just solution which will be accepted" by both Arabs and Jews, declared Sir Alexander, "it could hardly be expected that we should not welcome such a solution." But, he went on, "we should not have the sole responsibility for enforcing a solution which is not accepted by both parties and which we cannot reconcile with our conscience." [7]

Similarly the American spokesmen made no mention of previous American statements on Palestine or pledges to Arabs and Zionists, but strove instead to establish the "neutrality" of the projected inquiry committee and its terms of reference. Thus, while they resisted Arab efforts to bias the instructions, they did not urge the adoption of any terms which would prejudice the committee's findings in Zionist favor. Indeed, Secretary Marshall, in answer to a petition from twenty-nine pro-Zionist Congressmen for a statement of American policy toward Palestine, asserted early in May that the United States Government considered it "premature . . . to develop its policy with regard to the substance of this question in such a way as to limit the full utilization of . . . [the United Nations inquiry] committee's recommendations and its report." [8]

The Soviet delegate, on the other hand, could afford to be entirely unrepressed. The U.S.S.R. was not burdened by commitments to Arabs or Zionists, and its only past interest had been negative, dictated chiefly by the propaganda value of the Palestine controversy as a small but useful element in Moscow's war of nerves against the West. The Kremlin, to be sure, had been consistently anti-Zionist. But this antagonism was largely a projection of Soviet propaganda against "capitalist colonialism," for in Russian eyes Zionism was merely a tool of British imperialism. Now that the Anglo-Zionist partnership had dissolved, however, the Soviet attitude toward the national home did not have to remain hostile. Hence in theory the Soviet delegate, Andrei A. Gromyko, could elect to be cooperative or obstructive or both; to support the Arabs or the Zionists or both; to flail the British or the Americans or both. In practice, Gromyko's strategy aimed at securing the mandate's early windup and thwarting possible British or American efforts to preserve the tutelary status of Palestine. He therefore followed an independent course, which encouraged Arabs and Zionists and, at times, brought him into conflict with the British and American position. Thus aside from the clash over UNSCOP's composition, the Big Powers collided over nongovernmental participation in the Assembly's meetings. The representatives of Poland and Czechoslovakia, with Soviet backing, had urged that the Jewish Agency be authorized to appear before the plenary Assembly; but the delegate of the United States, supported by the United Kingdom, believed that "the plenary meeting should be reserved for the views only of the Member States" and that "the First Committee would afford the proper forum for . . . the Jewish Agency." Gromyko supported Arab appeals for a full-dress debate and for directing UNSCOP to recommend early independence for Palestine. Yet he also backed the Zionist contention that the Jewish D.P. question was closely "linked with the problem of Palestine and its future administration." [9]

Toward the close of the special session Gromyko for the first time disclosed the Soviet substantive position, assailing "the bankruptcy of the mandatory system of administration of Palestine" and endorsing "the aspirations of the Jews to establish their own State." He implied that the primary responsibility for the pressure of European Jewish emigration to Palestine arose from "the fact that no western European State has been able to ensure the defense of the elementary rights of the Jewish people." He declared that the Soviet delegation's first choice of a solution would be "the establishment of an independent dual, democratic, homogeneous Arab-Jewish State." Gromyko did not elaborate upon this proposal, which in execution could have assumed any form from the Jewish binationalist scheme of equal representation to the Arab scheme of proportional representation. But he went on to explain that if it "proved impossible to implement [the plan for a unitary state], in view of the deterioration in the relations between the Jews and the Arabs . . . then it would be necessary to consider the second plan which . . . provides for the partition of Palestine into two independent autonomous States, one Jewish and one Arab." [10] While thus fairly consistently opposed throughout the special session to the details of the Anglo-American stand, the U.S.S.R. nevertheless favored the creation of an inquiry committee and in the end voted for setting up the neutral, small-power committee and giving it broad directives, even though both were in the main American in origin.

APPROACHING ERUPTION IN PALESTINE

The maneuvers of the Big Powers in the General Assembly's first special session had been carefully scrutinized by the population of Palestine. There the Arabs and Jews suspected an Anglo-American conspiracy. Both believed that Britain had no intention of leaving the country. The Arabs, convinced that the United States was irrevocably pro-Zionist, interpreted the American emphasis on the neutrality of the proposed investigation as a subtle design to assure findings favorable to the Zionists. The

Jews, on the other hand, thought that American neutrality merely served as a cover for Washington's recoil from previous pro-Zionist declarations. Up to the time of Gromyko's speech the feeling prevailed in Palestine that Moscow would not abandon its traditionally anti-Zionist outlook and would in the end rally to the Arab side. The Zionists were, therefore, elated by the final Soviet statement. With the backing of the U.S.S.R. and of American public opinion the Zionists now felt that their claims would not pass unnoticed. The Arabs, however, were stunned by what they regarded as a sudden about-face. Only a week before Gromyko's address, Jamal al-Husayni had told foreign correspondents in Jerusalem that the Higher Committee was establishing contact with the Soviet Union to send an Arab delegation to Moscow; and only a day before the Russian statement, the director of the Arab Office in Palestine asserted that "the Arabs 'in despair' might accept aid from Russia." [11]

Persuaded that the Big Powers were exploiting the United Nations for their own private purposes and that the inquiry's outcome would be detrimental to the cause of an independent Arab Palestine, the Higher Committee elected to boycott UNSCOP. It adhered to this position even after the Political Committee of the Arab League, meeting in Cairo on June 7, had agreed to keep an open mind on whether or not to cooperate, a move presumably designed to pressure UNSCOP into omitting from its itinerary the Jewish D.P. camps in Europe. But UNSCOP allayed Arab fears by announcing that no decision on its consideration of the refugee question would be taken until after the committee's arrival in Palestine. The proposal to conduct hearings in the United States was turned down. The Higher Committee, the Agency, and the Palestine Government were invited early in June to appoint liaison officers, who would be authorized "at the discretion of the committee to present such information as they might think advisable." This invitation the Higher Committee rejected. The Palestine Government, apparently nettled by having been placed in the same class as the nongovernmental bodies, also declined at first to designate "a liaison officer in the sense of the rule of procedure" adopted by UNSCOP. Still, "a representative of the Palestine Government" was named to furnish information which the committee might require while in Palestine. Not until mid-July did the Palestine Government officially declare this representative to be its liaison spokesman with UNSCOP. [12]

Jamal al-Husayni notified the United Nations Secretary-General on June 13 that the Palestine Arabs would "abstain from collaboration [with] and desist from appearing before" UNSCOP. When the committee held its first hearings in Jerusalem three days later, the Higher Committee staged a general protest strike in the Arab Community. UNSCOP's chairman, Emil Sandstroem of Sweden, in a radio appeal on June 16, emphasized that he and his colleagues had "come to Palestine with a completely open mind," that they represented "eleven different countries . . . no one of which has any direct concern with the Palestine question," and that they intended "to make an impartial report to the United Nations." This and subsequent overtures to the Higher Committee, however, were of no avail. Consequently, only the Palestine Government, the Anglican Bishop of Jerusalem and other British religious spokesmen, as well as various Jewish organizations formally testified, generally doing little more than bringing up to date evidence prepared early in 1946 for the Anglo-American Inquiry Committee. Chairman Sandstroem also conferred privately with the Irgun high command, as did on a separate occasion the representatives of Guatemala and Uruguay. Moreover, UNSCOP devoted about half of its five weeks in Palestine to a tour of all sections of the country, Arab as well as Jewish, and gathered Arab political views unofficially.[13]

In the six-month period before the completion of UNSCOP's inquiry at the end of August the mounting tension between Arabs and Jews and between both and the government had reached a postwar peak. The mandatory altered neither its "interim" immigration policy of January 1946 nor its rule by repression. Nor was the growth of militancy among the two sections of the Palestine population and their respective champions abroad checked by the General Assembly's adoption of a resolution calling upon "all Governments and peoples, and particularly upon the inhabitants of Palestine, to refrain . . . [pending action on UNSCOP's report] from the threat or use of force or any other action which might create an atmosphere prejudicial to an early settlement. . . ."[14] Instead, the very creation of UNSCOP, which carried with it the promise of a final decision, introduced a new element into the passions controlling the political life of Palestine.

Jewish terrorism thrived as never before, despite the statutory martial law and the execution of condemned terrorists. Four Irgunists were hanged at Acre prison on April 16. Less than three weeks later the Irgun blasted open the walls of that prison, setting free 251 inmates. Of five accomplices captured by the British, three received a death sentence from the military court on June 16, the day on which UNSCOP launched its Palestine hearings. Acting on a clemency appeal from the families of the condemned, UNSCOP intervened to prevent "possible unfavorable repercussions." But the committee was rebuffed by the Palestine and British governments. The Irgun abducted two British sergeants on July 12 and warned that, if the sentence against the Irgunists were carried out, the British hostages would suffer a like fate. On two occasions in the preceding year the Palestine Government had yielded to such tactics. But in the face of the latest threats the government remained resolute. The three Irgunists were executed at the end of July 1947, and the bodies of the British sergeants were found two days later. These were the gravest of an uninterrupted series of crimes committed by the Freedom Fighters as well as the Irgun.[15]

Ever since the beginning of 1947 the Jewish quasi-government had been employing Haganah, even without mandatory countenance, to protect the Yishuv against terrorist blackmail and propaganda. Now during UNSCOP's stay in the country Haganah's anti-terrorist vigil was intensified, at times with specific British sanction. But what little restraining influence Haganah might have exerted was squandered after mid-July by the affair of the *Exodus 1947*. Between February 28 and May 31, 1947, some 11,000 unauthorized immigrants had reached Palestine, despite London's renewal of diplomatic pressures on European governments to prevent the departure of illegal-immigrant vessels. Following the General Assembly's truce resolution, therefore, the British delegation to the United Nations urged Secretary-General Trygve Lie to request that member nations do "all in their power to discourage illegal immigration" while the Palestine question was under consideration. Lie acted upon this request early in June. But the Jewish Agency protested against the action as not falling within the scope of the General Assembly's resolution, since the British delegation at the special session had not sought to include any clause dealing with illegal immigration. "Had the British Government sought to do so," the Agency protest continued, "its action would undoubtedly have been challenged on the ground that it was bringing into issue the very matter for which the special committee on Palestine was being appointed." [16]

For whatever reason, the illicit traffic came to a full stop in June. But on July 18 the *Exodus 1947*, bearing some 4,550 refugees, the largest number up to that time ever carried on a single voyage, was escorted into Haifa harbor. British sailors met with stiff resistance in the boarding operation, which resulted in the death of three Jews, including an American member of the crew, and injury to over one hundred. Instead of interning the would-be immigrants in Cyprus, Foreign Secretary Bevin chose "to make an example of this ship" by returning the refugees to the port of origin in southern France. The French Government offered to accept the D.P.'s only if they went ashore voluntarily. At the end of three weeks, when only 130 Jews had disembarked, the British Cabinet decided to take the remainder to D.P. camps in the British zone of Germany.[17]

The fact that the incident was spread over a period of nearly two months kept anti-British agitation seething in the Yishuv and throughout the Zionist world. Nor were the contradictory statements by the Foreign Office calculated to enhance Britain's moral position. One official spokesman at first explained that the refugees had to be sent elsewhere because "Cyprus was overcrowded." But it had been reported in the spring that the refugee camps on that island were being enlarged in anticipation of a sharp rise in illegal immigration. Indeed, the Foreign Office later admitted that the

Cyprus accommodations were sufficient. But the "only" other territory under British rule, it was claimed, "where such a large number of people can be adequately housed and fed at short notice" was the British zone of Germany. The choice of Germany was interpreted by Zionists as personal "vindictiveness" on the part of Bevin and "the height of wickedness" on the part of the government. London's action was avowedly motivated by the twin objectives of disciplining the Zionists and placating the Arabs. But these purposes were negated by the transfer of some 1,100 would-be unauthorized immigrants to Cyprus less than a fortnight after the seizure of the *Exodus 1947*.[18]

The last traces of the mandatory's thesis that its role was that of disinterested mediator between two conflicting communities were rapidly disappearing. Having lost all control over the situation and most of its governmental authority, Britain became as subjectively involved in the dispute as either Arabs or Zionists. This was illustrated by the Foreign Office's propaganda techniques with respect to illegal immigration. Such charges as the recruitment of mercenaries among non-Jewish European D.P.'s to swell the terrorist ranks in Palestine and the operation by ha-Shomer ha-Za'ir of a "strikingly inhuman kidnapping ring" in Hungary for the purpose of taking children to Palestine against their parents' wishes were made, never substantiated, but never withdrawn. Nor was detached self-assurance indicated when the Palestine Government saw fit, after the Jewish Agency had submitted its testimony to UNSCOP, "to correct some of the mis-statements made to the Committee" by Zionist spokesmen; "comment on the calumnies which some of this evidence contains" was omitted, explained the government, and no attempt was being made "to cover all the inaccuracies," since that "would require a document of greater length than the circumstances justify." [19]

Perhaps the most serious aspect of the mandatory's subjectivity was the Palestine Government's growing insensitiveness to attacks on the lives and property of innocent Jews by members of the British security forces, particularly after the Irgun's hanging of the two British sergeants. A flagrant abuse of British legal traditions was the case of Major Roy Alexander Farran, a British war hero assigned by the army to a special anti-terrorist police unit. A sixteen-year-old Jew mounting Freedom-Fighter posters on Jerusalem walls was forcibly arrested by Farran's unit early in May, was reportedly tortured to death, and his body never recovered. Farran at first fled to Syria, was brought back to Palestine, escaped from military detention, later surrendered, and was finally tried by a military tribunal. But Farran was acquitted because the court permitted his superior to decline to testify "on the ground that he might incriminate himself" and ruled inadmissible as evidence Farran's own written notes.[20]

During this time, the Higher Committee continued to tighten its grip over the Arab Community. The Higher Committee's authority sprang for the most part from external sources. Its leadership over the Palestine Arabs was acknowledged in the first instance by the Arab League, which had created the organ and still held most of its purse strings. The Palestine Government did not extend full recognition to the body as the legitimate voice of Arab Palestine until January 1947, when it was allowed to nominate the community's delegates to the London conference. Finally in May the Higher Committee was recognized as the sole political spokesman for the community by the United Nations General Assembly, after Sir Alexander Cadogan agreed "unhesitatingly" that the body was "representative of the views of the Arab population of Palestine." [21] Though external recognition reinforced the prestige of the Higher Committee within the Palestine Arab Community, its real influence internally derived from its identification with the Palestine Arab (Husayni) Party. This party had restored its prewar political machine in town and village at a time when the other prewar factions, which had been reorganized in 1944–45, once again became quiescent and their leaders were for all practical purposes removed from the political scene. Furthermore, Musa al-'Alami fell into Husayni disfavor because he insisted on keeping the Arab League's propaganda offices out of Palestine Arab politics. 'Alami rallied to his side most of the anti-Husayni Opposition. But absorption with the Arab offices required his absence from the country for prolonged periods, and his refusal to enter the political arena left a substantial body of the intelligentsia unorganized.

The organized opposition was thus reduced to the communist wing of the Arab labor movement—the Arab Workers Congress and its affiliated League of National Liberation—and the Najjadah. But the communists, never very powerful, were further weakened after the General Assembly's special session, owing to Soviet support of Zionism. The first attempted merger between the Najjadah and the Husayni-controlled Futuwwah had collapsed in February. The Najjadah, admittedly, was not a political party. The mere existence of an independent militarized society, however, diluted the Higher Committee's authority and reduced its military potential. Moreover, as long as the Najjadah, which retained its numerical lead over the Futuwwah, remained free of the Higher Committee's supervision, the possibility of its alliance with the disaffected politicians could not be overlooked. Indeed the danger of a general political vendetta threatened to engulf the Arab Community in the spring of 1947, because the Husayni's intimidation of their rivals was giving rise to retaliation.[22]

The Opposition press criticized the Higher Committee's handling of the Palestine Arab case at the United Nations and reacted unfavorably at first to the proposed boycott of UNSCOP. Yet when the Higher Committee decided on a policy of non-cooperation, even the communists, who had planned to present testimony, obeyed the injunction. The boycott's effectiveness could be attributed in part at least to the Mufti's success in again uniting the Najjadah and the Futuwwah, this time under the supreme command of Mahmud Labib. A former Egyptian army officer, Labib had organized the military branch of the Muslim Brethren, a fanatical religio-political society, with headquarters and the bulk of its adherents in Egypt and small branches in Palestine and the near-by countries. The negotiations for fusing the two Palestine societies into a single "Youth Organization," owing allegiance to the Higher Committee, were completed a few days before UNSCOP began its hearings in Jerusalem.[23]

The resurgence of the Husaynis meant that the Arab Community was dominated by their political thinking, which came through the war remarkably unaffected by the changed conditions. Their platform still called for complete ostracism of the Jews, and their campaign was simplified by the Labor Government's indecision and the rise to power in the Yishuv of the statists who themselves espoused the tenets of exclusive nationalism. Within a year the Husaynis had snuffed out most of the surviving sparks of Arab-Jewish harmony. Where persuasion did not work, coercion was applied. Hence an Arab who had delivered an address of welcome at the founding ceremony of a new Jewish village was subsequently murdered. Arabs were enjoined to resign from the few societies with mixed national enrollment. They were "permitted" to remain on essential joint committees, such as the Citrus Board, but when its members went to London, the Arabs "were obliged to travel separately, live separately, and refrain from social relations with the Jewish members." [24]

From mid-June on the Husaynis, with one eye on UNSCOP, became increasingly belligerent. Jewish liaison officers and journalists accompanying UNSCOP were not allowed to visit certain Arab establishments or municipalities. The Husaynis staged mass demonstrations in Haifa, Jaffa, and Jerusalem and roused their followers not only against the Zionists, the British, and the Americans, but against the Arab "traitors" who continued to violate the land and economic boycotts. "Zionists must not have an inch of this country," declared a message from the Mufti. "It is your duty to gain back every inch of your land." Jamal warned that "revolt . . . . is inevitable unless the Arab struggle succeeds and the United Nations gives us justice." In a speech before an estimated 5,000 members of the Youth Organization, Labib stated that "We are talking no longer. Let others do the talking." So persistent was the agitation that a week-long series of clashes occurred on the Jaffa-Tel-Aviv border in mid-August. The disorders were quelled by the prompt action of the British security forces and the municipal leaders in the two towns. While the National Council issued to the Yishuv an appeal for restraint, significantly the Higher Committee remained silent. The government suspended *al-Difa'* for publishing an inflammatory article by Labib only a few days before the border incidents, and deported the Higher Committee's military commander. The Youth Organization once more split into its components, for the Najjadah chief refused to accept supreme command without assurances of complete freedom from Higher Committee directives. Moreover, the conservative Palestine Arab Workers Society at its annual conference at Haifa joined the ranks of the Opposition, by endorsing 'Alami instead of the Higher Committee.[25]

UNSCOP left Palestine on July 20 for Bayrut, Lebanon, where all the Arab League states except Transjordan testified. On behalf of the six governments, Hamid Bey Franjiyyah, the Lebanese Foreign Minister, warned that "the partition of Palestine and the creation of a Jewish State would result only in bloodshed and unrest throughout the entire Middle East." The spokesmen of each government, explained Franjiyyah, felt that "the safety of their own country is at stake and this gives them the right to oppose Zionism by every means at their disposal and even makes it their duty to do so." [26] On July 27 UNSCOP arrived in Geneva, Switzerland, where it was decided, by a vote of 6 to 4, to have a subcommittee investigate the Jewish D.P. camps in Germany and Austria. The committee's report and proposals were finished on August 31.

After analyzing the problem and summarizing the main solutions previously advanced, UNSCOP unanimously endorsed eleven guiding principles, among which the following were the most significant. The mandate should be terminated and independence granted at the earliest practicable date. The political structure of the new state or states should be "basically democratic, i.e., representative, in character" and should provide constitutional guarantees, accepting "the obligation to refrain in . . . international relations from the threat or use of force against the territorial integrity or political independence of any State, or in any manner inconsistent with the purposes of the United Nations." The economic unity of Palestine, which the committee regarded as "indispensable to the life and development of the country and its people," should be maintained. The sacred character of the holy places should be preserved and access to them assured according to existing rights. The General Assembly should initiate and execute immediately an international arrangement for solving the urgent problem of the 250,000 displaced Jews in Europe. A twelfth principle, adopted with two dissenting votes, stated that "it be accepted as incontrovertible that any solution for Palestine cannot be considered as a solution of the Jewish problem in general." Applying these principles, UNSCOP divided into a majority (the delegates of Canada, Czechoslovakia, Guatemala, Netherlands, Peru, Sweden and Uruguay) recommending partition and a minority (the delegates of India, Iran, and Yugoslavia) recommending federalism, with the delegate of Australia abstaining.

The majority scheme—political partition with economic union—called for carving Palestine into independent Arab and Jewish states and an internationalized zone of Jerusalem. The Arab area was to comprise western Galilee, the hill country of central Palestine with the exception of the Jerusalem enclave, and the Coastal Plain from Isdud to the Egyptian border. The Jewish territory was to consist of eastern Galilee, the Coastal Plain from a point south of Acre to one north of Isdud (including the predominantly Arab town of Jaffa), and the Negeb, which was defined as embracing the whole of the Beersheba subdistrict and part of the Gaza subdistrict. Jerusalem, Bethlehem, and their rural suburbs were to form the city of Jerusalem, which the United Nations was to administer under a permanent trusteeship agreement. In the two-year probationary period starting September 1, 1947, the United Kingdom, either alone or jointly with one or more members of the United Nations, was to administer Palestine under United Nations auspices.

Arabs and Jews in Jerusalem who so designated would be entitled to vote in the Arab and Jewish states. The constitutions of the two states would have to provide for universal suffrage for persons above the age of twenty. The 1939 White Paper's provisions on land purchases in the area of the proposed Jewish state were to be abrogated. Jewish immigration, to be organized by the Jewish Agency, was to continue at the monthly rate of 6,250 in the first two years and 5,000 thereafter, if the transitional period had to be extended. The economic unity of the country was to be preserved by a ten-year treaty between the Arab and Jewish states, providing for common customs, currency, and communications and the promotion of "joint economic development, especially in respect of irrigation, land reclamation and soil conservation." An economic board, composed of three Arabs, three Jews, and three members appointed by the United Nations Economic and Social Council, was to be responsible for organizing and administering the economic union. In justifying its support of partition, the majority argued that it provided the only prospect of an equitable and workable solution and contained the hope of finality, which would end the persistent pressures of the interested parties and would allay Arab fears of further Jewish expansion.

But the minority considered partition impracticable, unworkable, and anti-Arab, and argued that "the well-being of the country and its peoples as a whole" outweighed "the aspirations of the Jews [for a separate and sovereign state]." The minority therefore proposed the development of the mandate, after a three-year transitional United Nations administration, into an independent federal government, comprising Arab and Jewish states with Jerusalem as capital. The transitional regime was

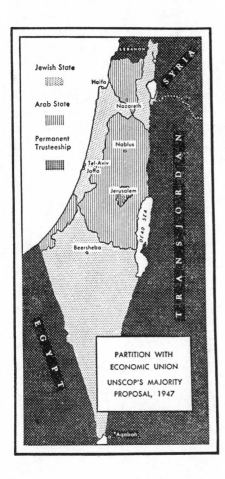

Jewish State

Arab State

Permanent
Trusteeship

Haifa
Nazareth
Nablus
Tel-Aviv
Jaffa
Jerusalem
Beersheba

LEBANON

SYRIA

TRANSJORDAN

DEAD SEA

EGYPT

ʿAqabah

PARTITION WITH
ECONOMIC UNION

UNSCOP'S MAJORITY
PROPOSAL, 1947

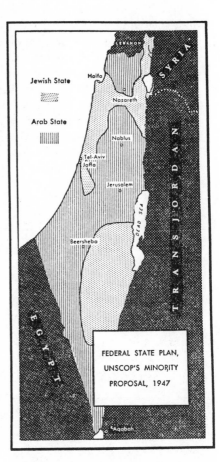

Jewish State

Arab State

Haifa
Nazareth
Nablus
Tel-Aviv
Jaffa
Jerusalem
Beersheba

LEBANON

SYRIA

TRANSJORDAN

DEAD SEA

EGYPT

ʿAqabah

FEDERAL STATE PLAN,
UNSCOP'S MINORITY
PROPOSAL, 1947

to be "entrusted to an authority to be decided by the General Assembly." The area of the projected Arab state was more generous than in the majority plan. The jurisdiction of the state governments was to cover "education, taxation for local purposes, the right of residence, commercial licenses, grazing rights, interstate migration, settlement, punishment of crime, social institutions and services, public housing, public health, local roads, agriculture, and local industries." Immigration, foreign relations, and national defense were to be directed by the central government, whose legislature was to be bicameral, with equal representation in one house and proportional representation in the other. A majority of both houses would be required for the enactment of all laws. In case of deadlock "the issue shall be submitted to an arbitral body" of five, including not less than two Arabs and two Jews. Jewish immigration into the Jewish state was to be allowed for three years "in such numbers as not to exceed . . . [its] absorptive capacity . . . having due regard for the rights of the population then present within that state and for their anticipated natural rate of increase." [27]

CHAPTER 23

Partition

ARAB AND Zionist reactions to UNSCOP's recommendations crystallized in the fortnight between the completion of the committee's report and the opening of the second regular session of the General Assembly on September 16. The Arab League's publicity office in New York charged UNSCOP with an advance pro-Zionist bias and served notice that the General Assembly's approval of either the majority or the minority scheme would precipitate a war in the Near East, which would probably develop into a world conflict. The Higher Committee labeled the two plans "absurd, impracticable and unjust." The United Nations was warned that "not a single Jew will be allowed to migrate to Palestine. . . . The Arabs will fight to the last man to defend their country, to defend its integrity and to preserve it as an Arab country." While dismissing federalism as "wholly unacceptable," the Zionist General Council, then meeting in Zurich, Switzerland, expressed satisfaction with the partition proposal. But final judgment was reserved until "after the General Assembly has taken a decision." [1] The Arabs had gained voting strength between May and September, by the admission to membership in the United Nations of Yemen, a sixth Arab League state, and Pakistan, a fourth non-Arab Muslim state. The Zionists, on the other hand, could now rely on the moral influence of the recommendations made by UNSCOP's majority.

The international situation had deteriorated, following Russia's rejection of the Marshall European aid program in July and the creation of the Cominform in September. That the East-West rift would have repercussions in the United Nations was indicated in the opening meetings of the General Assembly. Secretary Marshall enumerated charges of Soviet obstructionism; Deputy Foreign Minister Andrei Y. Vyshinsky countered with a blast against American "warmongers" whom he accused of trying to wreck the United Nations.[2] Like other issues the Palestine problem was bound to become involved in the larger quarrel. But the West was not united on Palestine, for Anglo-American differences had not been eradicated. True, both Western Powers were anxious to protect their common or complementary oil investments in the Near East, to prevent Soviet infiltration, and to promote Arab friendship. These were powerful inducements for harmonizing Anglo-American policy on Palestine, and, indeed, American diplomatic and military circles were inclined to follow the Labor Government's lead in the matter. But while the Foreign and Colonial offices had come to enjoy broad backing in Britain by the summer of 1947, the departments of State and Defense were confronted on the subject of Palestine with a generally hostile public opinion. This led to extreme caution and frequent reversals in Washington.

The British press, M.P.'s, and Government were prone to lump together the Agency-promoted illegal immigration and the acts of the terrorist groups. They had become irritated over the fact that most of the funds for both were provided by Americans. Official representations were made to Washington as to why American citizens were allowed to finance a "war" against citizens of a friendly nation and why the fund-raising organizations were tax exempt. Government circles in Washington, however, made a distinction between American support for the official Zionist program, including illegal immigration, and support for the terrorists. Therefore, President Truman's response was merely to urge "every citizen and resident of the United States . . . to refrain, while the United Nations is considering the problem . . . from engaging . . . in any activities which tend further to inflame the passions of the inhabitants of Palestine." But no action was taken against American organizations financing illegal immigration, because of the American public's strong pro-Zionist sympathy, which incidents such as the *Exodus 1947* tended to keep alive. By exploiting this sympathy and the attached immunity, American backers of the Irgun and the Freedom Fighters had themselves acquired influential adherents.[3]

The pro-terrorist advertisements in the American press provoked bitter reaction in Britain. There the declining pro-Zionist feeling had sunk to a new low after the affair of the two British sergeants. This coupled with efforts by the Freedom Fighters to blast the Colonial Office, to murder prominent British statesmen with letter bombs, and to carry out an "air raid" over London, gave every advantage to the British Fascists, who were already trading on the serious economic crisis in Britain. Anti-Jewish incitation and destruction of synagogues and other Jewish property reached serious proportions in many of the larger British cities in August and

September. Meanwhile the British attitude toward the Arabs remained unchanged, although the Government's policy had as yet shown no promise of practicability. No real progress had been made toward the grand plan of "disinterested" sponsorship by Britain through its Middle East Office in Cairo of the economic and social development of the Arab countries. The execution of such a scheme required surplus funds and the confidence of the Arabs. Britain could claim neither. The key to the British political and strategic position in the Arab East was Egypt. Here although British troops had been evacuated from Alexandria and Cairo by the end of March 1947, treaty negotiations had broken down two months earlier. In August Egypt carried its complaints to the Security Council. When the case was suspended on September 10, Egyptian nerves remained frayed. Nevertheless the Attlee Cabinet clung tenaciously to its Arab program, and in the long run its policy toward Palestine was certain to be governed by the more inclusive imperial and regional considerations.[4]

Hence the Palestine issue in the fall of 1947 was an Arab-Zionist contest within an Anglo-American controversy about to be drawn into the Soviet-American "cold war." In view of the crowded agenda and the anticipation of a stormy debate, the General Assembly, upon the suggestion of the United Nations Secretariat, referred the item on September 23 to a special committee on the Palestine question, consisting of all the member nations.[5] The Palestine Committee consumed fourteen meetings and twenty-four days in open discussion in which the Arab Higher Committee and the Jewish Agency were invited to participate. The Arab states formally joined the Higher Committee in rejecting without qualification both partition and federalism, and revived their pleas for a unitary, Arab Palestine. The Jewish Agency formally accepted UNSCOP's partition plan as "the indispensable minimum."

On October 21 the Palestine Committee assigned the task of modifying UNSCOP's majority proposal in the light of objections raised in the debate to a subcommittee of nine supporters of partition, including the United States and the Soviet Union. To a second subcommittee, comprising the six Arab states, the two Muslim states of Afghanistan and Pakistan, and Colombia, was referred the formulation of a plan for a unitary Palestine state, in accordance with proposals submitted by Saudi Arabia, Iraq, and Syria. A third subcommittee on conciliation failed to reduce the area of disagreement. The proposal of the subcommittee on a unitary state was defeated by the Palestine Committee on November 24 by a vote of 29 to 12. On the following day the Palestine Committee introduced further changes in the partition subcommittee's scheme and then approved the amended plan by a vote of 25 to 13. Four days later the plenary General Assembly endorsed the Palestine Committee's partition proposal by a vote of 33 to 13, thus giving it the necessary two-thirds majority.[6]

The refinements of the revised partition scheme chiefly concerned questions of boundaries, the transition period, and implementation. The proposed Jewish state was to be reduced in size from 6,000 to 5,500 square miles and was to include roughly 55 per cent of the total land area of Palestine. The most significant territorial changes were the transfer to the projected Arab state of the city of Jaffa and of some 500,000 acres in the Negeb, in the vicinity of the town of Beersheba as well as along the Mediterranean Sea and the Egyptian frontier. The mandate was to terminate at the earliest possible date but no later than August 1, 1948, by which time Britain was to withdraw all its armed forces. The independent Arab and Jewish states and the special regime for the City of Jerusalem were to come into existence two months after the British military evacuation but not later than October 1, 1948. A Commission composed of the representatives of Bolivia, Czechoslovakia, Denmark, Panama, and the Philippines was to supervise the implementation of partition. The mandatory was instructed to dovetail its plans for retirement with those of the Commission for assuming administrative responsibility. Britain was also enjoined "not to take any action to prevent, obstruct or delay the implementation by the Commission of the measures recommended by the General Assembly."

The Palestine Commission was charged with establishing in each of the proposed states a provisional council of government which would receive progressive administrative authority in the transitional period. Each council was also to be empowered to recruit "within the shortest time possible" an armed militia among the residents of its state, "sufficient in number to maintain internal order and to prevent frontier clashes." Finally, the Security Council was requested to "determine as a threat to the peace . . . any attempt to alter by force the settlement envisaged" by the partition resolution; and if it were decided that such a threat existed, the Security Council was to "supplement the authorization of the General Assembly by taking measures, under Articles 39 and 41 of the Charter, to empower the United Nations Commission . . . to exercise in Palestine the functions . . . assigned to it by this resolution." [7]

MANEUVERS BEHIND THE ADOPTION OF PARTITION

The steps leading up to the General Assembly's partition resolution and the changes in the plan itself reflected the clashing purposes of the Big Three. As the mandatory, the United Kingdom held most of the controls and, as the Big Power with the largest stakes in the Near East, felt constrained to exercise the utmost caution. The Labor Government's policy of winning Arab friendship remained the fundamental determinant of Britain's position toward United Nations decisions on Palestine. Creech-Jones informed the General Assembly's Palestine Committee at the outset of its deliberations that the United Kingdom accepted UNSCOP's unanimous recommendations to end the mandate and grant

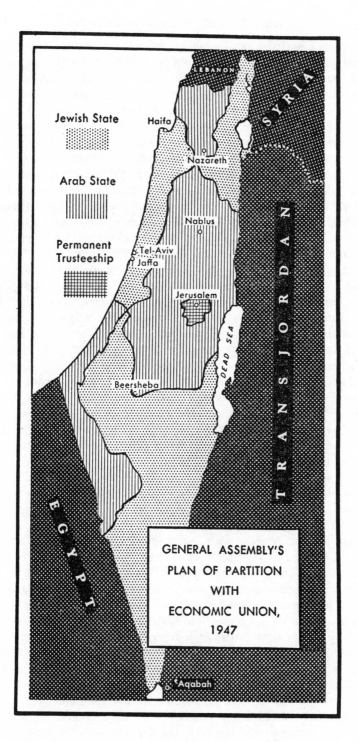

Jewish State

Arab State

Permanent
Trusteeship

LEBANON

SYRIA

Haifa

Nazareth

Nablus

Tel-Aviv
Jaffa

Jerusalem

TRANSJORDAN

DEAD SEA

Beersheba

EGYPT

GENERAL ASSEMBLY'S
PLAN OF PARTITION
WITH
ECONOMIC UNION,
1947

ʿAqabah

independence to Palestine. In taking this decision, which represented a reversal of the Colonial Secretary's assurances to Parliament only six months earlier, the Labor Government had the overwhelming support of British public opinion. The cost in manpower, resources, and prestige far outweighed the strategic, political, and economic value of retaining its rule over the country against the wishes of Arabs and Jews. Once it had resolved to give up the mandate, London's overriding consideration was to salvage as much good will as possible in the Arab East. The Labor Government's strategy at the General Assembly, therefore, was to resist to the fullest extent UNSCOP's majority scheme. Its tactics primarily consisted in establishing the legal fiction of neutrality, as if Britain had never held the mandate and had no vital interests in the Near East.

Creech-Jones, Cadogan, and the British adviser to the partition subcommittee served notice time and again that the United Kingdom would play neither a lone nor a leading role in implementing partition on the ground that the scheme was not accepted by both Arabs and Jews. In the end Britain declined to play any role whatsoever. The United Kingdom refused to fix a date for the evacuation of its troops until the partition subcommittee's work was nearly completed. The equally important date of the termination of the mandate was withheld altogether until after the General Assembly had approved the partition resolution. The British balked at the suggested gradual transfer of authority to the proposed United Nations Commission, allegedly because such a procedure would create confusion and disorder. Nor would they concur in any arrangement transferring authority direct to the projected Arab and Jewish councils of government, since, it was argued, this would amount in practice to the implementation of the partition scheme.[8]

For almost a month and a half after the release of UNSCOP's report, the only United States pronouncement was a vague remark by Secretary Marshall in the General Assembly on September 17 that Washington gave "great weight" to the majority proposals. Then on October 11 Herschel V. Johnson, the American representative on the Palestine Committee, endorsed "the basic principles" of partition, subject to "certain amendments and modifications," and proposed that the United Nations might recruit a volunteer constabulary to keep the peace during the transition. Twenty more days elapsed before the United States delegation clarified its position. The United States now advocated eliminating the transitional period by advancing the date of independence from September 1, 1949, to about July 1, 1948. The coordinating and directing agency would be a small United Nations commission, responsible to the General Assembly, though questions affecting peace and security would be referred to the Security Council. This procedure, argued Johnson, would obviate the need for either a brief trusteeship or a special United Nations armed force. But not until the last week of the General Assembly's session, after the blueprint for implementation had been drawn up, did Johnson bring the full influence of his country to bear in favor of partition. In an impassioned plea before the final vote was taken by the Palestine Committee, he declared that "the governments who believe in partition think that it is not perfect, but that it is humanly just and workable and if adopted will make a genuine and notable contribution to the solution of one of the most thorny political problems in the world today." [9]

The hesitant unfolding of United States support of partition suggested that Washington was experiencing difficulty in reconciling the traditional pressures. The Joint Chiefs of Staff and the Near East experts in the Department of State reportedly advised against backing partition for fear it would alienate the Arabs, endanger American strategic interests in the region, and threaten the invaluable American oil investments. On the other hand, public opinion favored Zionism more than ever, now that a neutral United Nations inquiry seemed to have substantiated many of the Zionist claims. Although the White House appeared to be following public opinion on the Palestine issue, the Truman Administration was still opposed to committing American troops and, in this respect, was apparently taking the counsel of not only its military but its Congressional advisers. [10] The American proposals, finally, indicated that the United States was trying to devise some means of overcoming British obstructionism while avoiding the possibility of direct Soviet entanglement.

Unlike the United States, the Soviet Union was under no pressure and could afford to wait until after the United States had announced in the Palestine Committee its conditional acceptance of the majority scheme. On October 13 the Soviet spokesman, Semyon K. Tsarapkin, endorsed partition as the plan which "under the present circumstances . . . could be better put into practice" than the minority scheme. In the partition subcommittee the Soviet spokesman aimed at assuring Moscow a voice in the execution of partition, if Washington and London were to be involved. The Soviet delegation at first insisted that the Security Council should be responsible for administering Palestine in the transitional period and that the United Nations supervisory commission should consist of representatives of those states belonging to the Security Council. The Russians were also determined to have the British cleared out of Palestine. Even after the United Kingdom had reaffirmed its resolve to wind up its tutelary regime at an early date, the Soviet delegation still proposed that the mandate be terminated on January 1, 1948, and that British troops be withdrawn not more than four months later. British failure in Palestine, declared Tsarapkin, automatically disqualified the mandatory, "even if Great Britain should offer her services," from any part in the United Nations creation of independent Arab and Jewish states. The divergent Soviet and United States recommendations produced a deadlock which was finally broken by a compromise arrangement under which the transitional period was considerably reduced and a small commission was to be selected by the General Assembly but was to be guided by the Security Council.[11]

Again, as at the first special session, the interests of the Big Three collided, but this time the two Western Powers were ranged against each other. Creech-Jones spoke acridly of "the connivance of some governments" in furnishing arms, ships, and money for illegal immigration and of "the freedom enjoyed by the nationals of other states to employ every means to defeat . . . [Britain's] efforts" in Palestine. Toward the end of the session Johnson countered that Britain was laying down its mandate in a unilateral manner and was setting as a price for cooperation in any United Nations settlement a "condition [Arab-Jewish accord] . . . impossible to fulfill." The United States and Britain, it may be fairly assumed, were equally anxious to prevent the Soviet Union from becoming too deeply involved in Palestine. Nevertheless the two Western Powers were unable to arrive at a common program because the United Kingdom would not soften its opposition to partition, while the United States was becoming increasingly committed to that solution. Hence when Washington notified London in advance of its plan to eliminate the transitional period so as to skirt the issue of Big-Power enforcement, Britain did not accede to the American request to hand over governmental authority direct to the nascent Arab and Jewish states. Moreover, despite the Soviet-American agreement, unprecedented in the prevailing cold war, in accepting the compromise plan, Washington and Moscow were prompted by contradictory motives. From Johnson's statements it was patent that the United States delegation hoped for observance of the United Nations Charter by all member states.[12] It therefore took the calculated risk that the execution of partition would proceed peacefully without need for Security Council intercession. By the same token the Soviet delegation must have reasoned that sooner or later the issue would probably come before the Security Council, where the U.S.S.R. could veto any action in which it did not concur.

The Soviet endorsement of a Jewish state was not motivated by any change of heart about Zionism, still outlawed in the U.S.S.R., although no anti-Zionist statements had appeared in the Russian press since May 1947. The Russians could argue that partition harmonized with their fundamental practice of advocating the principle of self-determination in the U.S.S.R. and in all colonial or dependent areas; and with basic Marxist propaganda which inveighed against imperialism and favored independence for all subjected peoples. But more practical considerations were also present. The Kremlin must have believed that the creation of a Jewish state with its vigorous nationalism would lead more certainly to the elimination of the British than would a unitary Arab state. This thought, combined with the realities of the almost complete separation between the Arab and Jewish communities in Palestine, probably contributed to Moscow's abandonment of its earlier preference for a binational state. Moreover, the Soviet policy-makers possibly hoped that the emergence of a new sovereign state would intensify the ferment of nationalism and the anti-British agitation throughout the Arab East. Nor could Moscow have been unmindful that any British withdrawal, without a corresponding increase of American influence, would result of necessity in a relative improvement of the Soviet strategic and political position in the entire Near East. At all events, Anglo-American friction over Palestine which was likely to persist, if partition were implemented, would serve Soviet purposes in the cold war.

On the other hand, Gromyko reminded the Arab delegates that his government's backing of partition was "not directed against the Arabs." The Soviet Government and people, he stated,

> still entertain a feeling of sympathy for the national aspirations of the nations of the Arab East. . . . The USSR delegation is convinced that . . . . the Arab States will still, on more than one occasion, be looking towards Moscow and expecting the USSR to help them in the struggle for their lawful interests, in their efforts to cast off the last vestiges of foreign dependence.

Indeed, at the start of the General Assembly's second session in September, the Arab delegates had not despaired of acquiring Soviet backing. They must have been encouraged in the belief that Washington and Moscow would never take the same side. This was attested in the opening days of the session by the unconcealed pleasure of the Arab delegates over Vyshinsky's tirade against American warmongering, coming as it did on the day following Marshall's oblique and incidental approval of UNSCOP's findings. Furthermore, the delegation of Syria included its Minister to the Kremlin and one of his predecessors. And up to the very day that the Russian stand on partition was disclosed, the Arab delegates abstained from voting against any Soviet resolution.[13] This formed part of the larger Arab campaign to forestall the General Assembly's adoption of partition.

Since the ten Arab and Muslim votes were insufficient, the Arab delegates concentrated on persuading the members of the Latin-American bloc, with which close working relations had already been established at the United Nations, and other small powers either to oppose partition or to abstain from voting. The Arab delegates also met with Marshall and members of the American delegation, who were reportedly notified that American economic interests, including the oil concessions, would suffer irreparable harm, if Washington sanctioned the founding of a Jewish state. The Arabs challenged the General Assembly's competence to adopt partition, arguing that the United Nations "cannot be treated as the successor of the League of Nations insofar as the administration of mandates is concerned . . . . unless . . . the Mandatory . . . negotiates a Trustee-ship Agreement in accordance with Article 79 and presents it to the General Assembly . . . for approval." The Arabs therefore moved that the question be referred to the International Court for an advisory opinion. After the partition plan had finally reached the plenary Assembly, the Arabs pressed for a vote when it seemed likely that the required two-thirds majority could not be mustered and urged delay when it was feared that the scheme might be accepted.[14]

In pleading their cause the Arabs adduced all the arguments that had already become familiar to the General Assembly at its special session and had been summarized by UNSCOP. Jamal al-Husayni told the Pales-tine committee that, if the Arab demands were not fulfilled, the Palestine Arabs would drench "the soil of our beloved country with the last drop of our blood in the lawful defense of all and every inch of it." The spokesmen of the Arab states followed with warnings of war through-out the Near and Middle East. Arab propaganda in the General Assem-bly was at times characterized by the racist clichés which had pervaded Arab nationalist thinking since the late 1930's. Faris Bey al-Khuri of Syria, dean of the Arab delegates, declared that, though the Jews formed only one-thirtieth of the United States population, "they have extended their influence into all circles" and the Americans ought, therefore, to "be careful for the future which awaits them." [15]

In countering these statements, the Zionist and pro-Zionist spokesmen were inclined to play up Arab wartime associations with the Axis. Moshe Shertok said that the Arabs had contributed "nothing" to the victory in World War II, "in which they had finally joined at the last moment . . . to qualify for membership of the United Nations," and that the only Near East community which had actively assisted the Allies was the Yishuv. Dismissing as libelous charges by the Iraqi and Syrian dele-gates that Zionism was a form of Nazism, Weizmann questioned their qualification to pass judgment on Zionism, though he did "not dispute the right of those two gentlemen to speak with . . . intimacy on the nature of Nazism." Abba Hillel Silver, head of the American section of the Agency Executive, declared that the Jews were neither intimidated nor impressed by the Arabs' "idle threats" of war and that, while not seeking an open clash, "the Jewish people in Palestine is prepared to defend itself." [16] The Zionists, like the Arabs, repeated their historical, legal, political, and economic contentions.

Since the Agency did not belong to the United Nations, it was unable to engage in logrolling. But the Zionists had accepted UNSCOP's major-ity recommendations. They accordingly benefited from the advantage of the findings of a neutral committee, which gained many adherents, in-cluding certain members of UNSCOP's majority, themselves delegates to the United Nations. These pro-partition delegates, with United States and Soviet assistance, marshaled enough votes to pass the scheme in the Palestine Committee, where only a simple majority was needed. Yet the partition backers were still one short of the necessary two-thirds for the final vote in the plenary Assembly. At this stage, the lobbying and publicity facilities which the Zionists had built up over the years came to their good stead. The Zionists were able to bring their case to the White House and to win the help of "friendly, unofficial Americans," who approached the heads of certain governments which the Arab and Muslim delegates thought they had already lined up against partition. In the end, the Zionist maneuvers proved more successful than the Arab.[17]

END OF MANDATE AND START OF WAR

Once again the Arabs and Zionists had been sucked into the vortex of Big-Power rivalries, which served to obscure the merits of the Palestine problem and to vitiate the findings of an impartial investigation. The Big-Three clash of interest and the absence in the partition resolution of enforcement provisions furnished the Arabs with loopholes through which to evade the General Assembly's recommendations. Immediately after the Assembly adjourned the Arab delegates jointly condemned the resolution as "doubly invalid," alleging that the United Nations had exceeded its authority under the Charter and that the vote on partition had been taken "under great pressure and duress." The initial outburst of violence in the Arab East lasted until mid-December. The local Jewish communities perhaps suffered most seriously. In the next six months the Arab League progressively put into effect its program, developed over the preceding year and a half, of supplying men, munitions, and money to the Palestine Arabs until the British civil administration terminated. If no prior political settlement were reached, the program called for the occupation of Palestine by the armies of the League's member states and the forcible prevention of the establishment of a Jewish state.[18]

With these plans the Higher Committee had articulated its own at 'Alayh, Lebanon, where the Arab League Council convened in special session in the second week of October. At that time the Mufti moved his headquarters from Egypt to Lebanon, whence the Higher Committee was now directed. Internal strife in the Palestine Arab Community had abated after mid-September under the impact of the UNSCOP report and the United Nations developments. To close the ranks it was decided to set up local national committees, responsible to the Higher Committee and comparable to those formed on the eve of the Palestine Arab revolt in 1936, but on a more comprehensive scale, embracing all the Arab towns and some 275 villages. These committees were to direct local fundraising and recruitment. The first was created at Jaffa in November. Once the partition decision was taken, the Higher Committee immediately condemned it as "null and void" and announced that it would not co-operate in its implementation but would request "the British Government to hand over Palestine forthwith to its Arab people." [19]

Sporadic attacks against the Jews began on November 30 and gradually expanded into organized countrywide warfare. The immediate objectives, like those of a decade earlier, appeared to be the severance of communication lines, the isolation of outlying villages, and the disruption of urban life. But the goal was to compel the Zionists by force of arms to accept a final political settlement on Arab terms. The Palestine Arab guerrilla forces were apparently built around the Futuwwah and the Najjadah, which were augmented by part-time recruits. In the second half of January 1948 some 2,000 volunteers crossed the borders from Syria under the sponsorship of the Arab League. The two principal military commanders of this "Arab Liberation Army" were 'Abd-al-Qadir al-Husayni and Fawzi al-Qawuqji, both of whom had participated in the earlier revolt. Husayni owed allegiance to his cousin, the Jerusalem Mufti. Qawuqji, who maintained headquarters at Damascus until early in March, took orders from the Arab League.[20]

Hence, for the Arabs the struggle for political independence had now been reduced essentially to a military undertaking. As for the Zionists, the military phase of their struggle was but one element in the process of transforming the quasi-government of the Yishuv and the national home into the government of the coming Jewish state. While the General Assembly was still discussing the Palestine problem, the Agency and National Council Executives were making arrangements for the maintenance of government services, in the event of a British departure, and for the preservation of security, in the event of Arab resistance. The political plans included everything from the drafting of a constitution and a legal code to the establishment of a school for diplomatic and administrative personnel and the canvassing of Arab, British, and Jewish civil servants as to their willingness to serve the future Jewish government. At the same time Jewish veterans of Allied armies were sought abroad to strengthen the high command and specialized branches of Haganah; local recruitment was stepped up; refresher training was given to reservists; a civic guard was formed in the towns; and rural fortifications and communications were kept in repair.[21]

"Our right to independence . . . , now . . . confirmed in principle, must be translated into fact," declared a National Council manifesto after the Assembly's partition vote, "by the building of a progressive state whose high standard of democracy and culture will compensate for the smallness of its size and for the complicating conditions besetting its inception." While not resisting partition, the terrorists, whose anti-British exploits had become less sustained since September, nevertheless refused to accept as final anything less than a Jewish state over Palestine and Transjordan. The same tack was taken by the Revisionists. At the other extreme the Ihud continued its opposition to the political division of Palestine on the ground that it could never lead to peace with the Arabs. On the other hand, binationalist ha-Shomer ha-Za'ir merged in January 1948 with the Labor Unity Party to form the United Labor Party or Mapam, whose founding platform declared that the party "has determined to support the establishment of a Jewish State and its defence under present conditions despite its rejection, in principle, of the Partition solution." [22]

Moreover, developments at the United Nations had contributed to uniting behind partition the Jews abroad, particularly those in the United States. The non-Zionist American Jewish Committee believed that the General Assembly's resolution "decreed that partition was a measure that made for the peace of the world. The world must support that decree." Such prominent American Jews as Bernard Baruch, who in the past had taken no interest in the national home, by the autumn of 1947 actively supported the UNSCOP majority plan. Even the anti-Zionist American Council for Judaism, though it had lobbied against partition at Lake Success and remained "unalterably opposed to the Zionist political program," declared that it "accepted" the General Assembly's resolution. But the Council continued to warn American Jews against dual loyalties. [23]

The partition recommendations were thus rendering academic the debate between the statists and the binationalists, the activists and the gradualists, and the pro- and anti-partitionists. This along with the threat posed by the Arab guerrilla war tended in the Yishuv to draw together all shades of conviction, from the communists to the Agudat Israel. After a few days of non-retaliation, the community found itself in a civil war with the Arabs. The strategy of the Jews, as revealed in the first two or three months of strife, was to gain control over the territory allotted to them by the United Nations, to preserve intact areas of Jewish settlement in the proposed non-Jewish zones, and to keep open the lines of communication, particularly with the city of Jerusalem, where more than 100,000 or some 16 per cent of the total Palestine Jewish population lived.

At the United Nations a month had passed before the five members of the Palestine Commission were named by their respective governments, and the Commission did not buckle down to its assignment until January 9, 1948. Meanwhile the Colonial Secretary had informed Parliament in mid-December that the Palestine Mandate would be terminated on May 15, 1948. But the mandatory held firm in its refusal to transfer any authority to the United Nations Commission prior to that date; or to allow the members of the Commission to go to Palestine before May 1; or to accede to any of the fundamental requests advanced by the Commission in accordance with the General Assembly's resolution, such as those regarding the delimitation of the frontiers, the creation of armed militias, and immigration. The mandatory admitted that hundreds of armed Arabs were entering Palestine from the neighboring states, but contended that "the nature of the border country makes it extremely difficult to secure the entire frontier against illegal entry, especially at night." The mandatory, it was true, established Arab and Jewish constabularies in some of the towns and larger villages, but the Commission reported that only the Arabs "were being armed in part with arms of the Palestine Government." [24]

The United States was equally uncooperative. No sooner was the partition resolution passed, in no inconsiderable measure owing to the strong American stand in the last week of the Assembly session, than Washington began to recoil from its pro-Zionist position. In the first week of December 1947, the Department of State announced its discontinuance "for the present" of licensing of arms shipments to the Near East. Since the Arab states were procuring weapons from Britain, the American arms embargo worked to the detriment of the Yishuv. This led to efforts by Palestine Jews to secure military supplies illegally in the United States. Meanwhile, anti-American agitation in the Arab East, which had become menacing during the Assembly session, reached new heights after November. The violence was accompanied by pressures both on Washington and on private American interests, particularly the oil companies. This lent weight to the arguments of those officials in the departments of State and Defense who insisted that the United States espousal of partition would cause irreparable harm to vital national interests.[25] As a result, the United States became evasive at a time when the United Nations Palestine Commission was in dire need of Big-Power endorsement.

On February 16, 1948, the Commission reported to the Security Council that it would be unable to discharge its responsibilities at the close of the mandate without armed assistance. The first public hint at the United Nations of the United States retraction came in the opening Security Council debate on Palestine on February 24, when Warren Austin declared that his government was prepared to consider the use of armed force to restore peace but not to enforce partition. Austin then recommended on March 19 that action on partition be suspended and that the General Assembly be convened in special session to consider the establishment of a temporary trusteeship over Palestine "without prejudice . . . to the character of the eventual political settlement." This about-face vitiated American prestige among the smaller powers, whose cooperation was necessary to assure acceptance of such a proposal. Furthermore, the United States and the United Kingdom were still at odds, as manifested by British balking at American suggestions of even a brief extension of the mandate. The Soviet delegation for its part insisted on the retention of the original partition resolution and was therefore in a position to criticize the Western Powers for undermining the United Nations authority. When it seemed that the United States trusteeship plan had even a remote chance of acceptance, the Russian boycott of the Trusteeship Council was lifted, presumably to assure Moscow a voice in such a settlement.[26] The result of the Big-Three division and Arab as well as Jewish opposition to the trusteeship proposal was that the British mandate came to an end before the Assembly could agree on any course of action.

The Palestine Commission, which continued to function until May 17, failed to elicit the cooperation not only of the mandatory, but of the Higher Committee, which did not even provide consultants. However, until April 19, when it suspended these efforts, the Commission was able, in close cooperation with the Jewish Agency, to make considerable progress in planning a Jewish provisional council of government.[27] The dissolution of the British civil administration in Palestine proceeded rapidly after February, as did the military evacuation. But since the British did not hand over to any other authority the responsibilities they were relinquishing and the United Nations did not provide armed forces or even moral backing, the Commission was unable to prevent the situation in Palestine from developing on its own.

Until the end of March the Arabs, with the aid of an estimated 6,000 to 7,000 volunteers from the near-by countries under the command of Qawuqji, appeared to be achieving their military objectives. They succeeded in blocking the Tel-Aviv–Jerusalem highway against all Jewish traffic. They strengthened Arab military morale by such exploits as the bombing of the Jewish Agency headquarters in Jerusalem on March 11 and ambush near Bethlehem two weeks later of a Haganah party which surrendered its arms and armored vehicles. But early in April Haganah dealt the Arab forces telling blows by reopening the Jerusalem highway, killing 'Abd-al-Qadir al-Husayni, and routing Fawzi al-Qawuqji's troops who had attempted to capture a key Jewish village south of Haifa. This was soon followed by a rapid chain of victories which placed in Jewish possession most of the important towns, including Tiberias, Haifa, Safad, Jaffa, Acre, and the bulk of the new city of Jerusalem.[28]

The Higher Committee had made primarily military plans. These had so far miscarried. So did a last-minute attempt to take over central governmental authority from the departing British. The Higher Committee in the last weeks of the mandate requested all Arab civil servants of the Palestine Government to carry on their respective duties and named the senior official of each department as its provisional director. Supervisory jurisdiction over the civil servants in each district was to have been exercised by the local national committee. But as early as February 4, 1948, the High Commissioner had reported that "panic continues to increase . . . throughout the Arab middle classes, and there is a steady exodus of those who can afford to leave the country." When the massacre on April 9 by Irgunists and Freedom Fighters of a hundred women and children in the Jerusalem Arab suburb of Dayr Yasin was added to the military defeats and the lack of political leadership, there were causes enough for general Arab demoralization. By mid-May panic overcame all classes, and an estimated 200,000 Arabs had already fled their homes, many seeking sanctuary in neighboring countries. When the mandatory finally laid down its governmental authority, there were no Arab political institutions to fill the void.[29]

The Jews for their part had begun to establish their authority over zones assigned to them by the General Assembly's resolution. They consolidated their hold over the Coastal Plain and eastern Galilee, but their ability to retain the Negeb was still in doubt. Within the territory under its control the Jewish provisional council of government took over the operation of all government services. A Provisional National Council of thirty-eight members, based on the estimated relative strength of the several political parties and including delegates from all groups except the terrorist, elected a Provisional Cabinet of thirteen, with David Ben Gurion as Premier and Minister of Defense. On May 14 the Provisional Government issued its declaration of independence and announced the creation in the partitioned area of Palestine of the state of Israel.[30]

Epilogue

THE PALESTINE WAR

IN THE SPRING of 1948 three principal organs of the United Nations were, in the parlance of Lake Success, "seized of" the Palestine problem. Faced with a civil war in Palestine and threats by the Arab states to employ their full military might to subdue the Zionists, once the British had abandoned their authority, the Security Council on April 17 called on Arabs and Jews in Palestine and on the governments of the near-by states to "cease all activities of a military or para-military nature." The Security Council on April 23 entrusted the negotiation of the cease-fire to a Truce Commission, comprising the American, Belgian, and French consuls in Jerusalem. The General Assembly, convoked in special session at the Security Council's request, in turn asked the Trusteeship Council on April 26 "to study . . . suitable measures for the protection of the city [of Jerusalem] and its inhabitants." The Trusteeship Council's proposals led to the General Assembly's recommendation on May 6 that the United Kingdom appoint before the mandate's end "a neutral acceptable to both Arabs and Jews, as Special Municipal Commissioner" to administer the affairs of Jerusalem. As for the over-all Palestine problem, however, the General Assembly impotently watched its deliberations being outrun by events. Not until a few hours after the state of Israel had come into existence and the mandatory administration formally expired, did the Assembly, without withdrawing its earlier partition resolution, finally dissolve the Palestine Commission and recommend the appointment by the Big Five of a Mediator to "promote a peaceful adjustment of the future situation in Palestine." [1]

On May 15 units of the regular armed forces of Transjordan, Syria, Lebanon, Iraq and Egypt, together with token troops from Saudi Arabia, were sent to Palestine for combat against Israel. Harold Evans, a Quaker attorney of Philadelphia, had already been named Special Municipal Commissioner for Jerusalem on May 13, but resigned his post less than five weeks later without setting foot on Palestine soil. Nor was the

Security Council's Truce Commission any more successful in effectuating a cease-fire. Meanwhile, on May 20 Count Folke Bernadotte, president of the Swedish Red Cross who had served as intermediary between Nazi Germany and the Allied Powers in the closing days of World War II in Europe, was selected as United Nations Mediator. Backed by a Security Council resolution of May 29 threatening sanctions for non-compliance, Count Bernadotte was able to negotiate a four-week truce, beginning June 11. But when the Arab states had turned down the Mediator's appeals for its prolongation, the Security Council, after six days of renewed fighting, decided on July 15 that "the situation in Palestine constitutes a threat to the peace" and ordered the parties to conclude an indefinite truce. The second truce went into effect in Jerusalem on July 16 and in the rest of the fighting area two days later.[2]

Nevertheless, breaches of the truce by both parties, largely the work of irregulars, continued. By mid-August the Mediator reported that "not only has firing practically never ceased in Jerusalem but [the] situation is gradually getting out of hand" and expressed the fear that the truce as a whole might be endangered. Nor was the tension lessened after the Security Council on August 19 directed the attention of each party to its responsibilities for preventing further truce violations by regular and irregular forces under its authority or in territory under its control. Toward the end of June both the Irgun and the Freedom Fighters had disbanded their underground movements in Israel proper but transferred their activities to Jerusalem, which they proposed to annex to Israel. Count Bernadotte was assassinated in that city on September 17, presumably by the Freedom Fighters. Dr. Ralph J. Bunche, Secretary-General Lie's personal representative on Count Bernadotte's staff, was immediately named Acting Mediator. Before the month's end the two terrorist groups accepted an ultimatum from the Provisional Government of Israel to dissolve in its occupied territory as well.[3]

At the time of the Arab states' invasion of Palestine in mid-May, the Arab League's secretary-general, 'Abd-al-Rahman Pasha 'Azzam, had explained that this action was unavoidable, because the end of the mandate left "no legally constituted authority behind to administer law and order in the country and afford the necessary and adequate protection of life and property." The war had been started by "Jewish aggression" and Zionist "imperialistic intentions." The Arab states proposed to restore peace, establish law and order, and then hand over the government to the Palestine Arabs. Egypt, Transjordan, and Iraq, under their treaties with the United Kingdom, had been acquiring arms from Britain and therefore had an initial advantage over Israel, especially in tanks, planes, and heavy guns. To defeat the Israelis in the field, however, the Arab armies had to act swiftly and decisively, for the Tel-Aviv Government began to receive in the second half of May its heavy military equipment from Europe and elsewhere. But the League states failed to achieve their objective before the first United Nations truce. Thereafter time favored the new state, as demonstrated by its victories between the two truces, when Israel re-established and widened the corridor to Jewish Jerusalem.[4]

Immigration into the new state, which in the first nine months exceeded the number of Jews who had settled in Palestine in the last nine years of British rule, augmented Israel's manpower resources. Haganah, now transformed into the Defense Army of Israel, was strengthened by recruitment of combat pilots and other veterans of Allied armies and more especially by the training which a substantial number of its soldiers had received in the British armed forces in World War II. The Jewish economy had been securely established in the mandatory period, particularly after 1939, and the trained economists of the quasi-governmental era were now formulating the economic policies of Israel. The Jewish Agency, which continued to be underwritten by American Jews, was converted in September 1948 into an international body for financing immigration and settlement in Israel and promoting good will for the new state. To make it clear that the Tel-Aviv Government was not directing the Zionist movement, the members of the Provisional Israeli Cabinet resigned their seats on the Zionist and Agency Executives. The election of the first permanent government took place in January 1949. The Provisional Cabinet, in which all the political parties were represented, gave way in March 1949 to a small coalition Cabinet, still dominated by Mapai and resembling in composition the old quasi-government. Although consideration of the draft constitution was indefinitely shelved, the unicameral constituent *Kneset* (Assembly)—comprising 120 deputies, of whom three were Arabs—buckled down to the job of legislating and keeping close check on the Administration. By the spring of 1949, moreover, Israel was recognized by more than forty governments, including the Big Five.[5]

Meanwhile in the place of Palestine Arab governmental authority, there was either military administration by the armed forces of the Arab League states or administrative chaos. The Palestine Arabs had turned a deaf ear in the early 1920's to British proposals for self-government. At that time the opposition to the mandate and the Jewish National Home stimulated the growth of the local Arab national movement. But it never developed into a stable community government, and the rivalries of the leaders drained most of its political influence. The defeat of the Legislative Council scheme in 1936, the Husayni rejection of the 1939 White Paper, and al-Hajj Amin's alliance with the Axis were further reasons for the postwar failure. The reinstatement of the Jerusalem Mufti in particular meant adherence to the original nationalist dogma of the exclusive Arab rights to Palestine and its government, and the preservation in power of the semifeudal, conservative elements. Instead of facing up to the changed conditions of 1947–48, the Palestine Arabs under al-Hajj Amin's guidance prepared for the last war against partition, and, in the end, squandered most of their economic and social gains of the mandatory period.[6]

At the close of September 1948 the Higher Committee tried to form an Arab "Government of All-Palestine," with a temporary capital at Gaza. This move precipitated a crisis in the Arab League. The Mediator in mid-September had already suggested the merger of Arab Palestine with Transjordan, a proposal which promised to upset the existing balance of power in the Arab East and was accordingly resisted by most Arab states, which now backed the Gaza regime. King 'Abdallah, however, refused to recognize the All-Palestine Government, using as a pretext the fact that al-Hajj Amin had been elected president of its Assembly. In December 'Abdallah was acclaimed King of a united Palestine and Transjordan by anti-Husayni Palestine Arabs, a measure approved by the Transjordan Parliament. This was followed by 'Abdallah's appointment of al-Shaykh Husam-al-Din Jarallah (1884–   ), the former Chief Justice of the Muslim religious courts in Palestine, as Mufti of Jerusalem and Raghib Bey al-Nashashibi as military governor of those portions of Arab Palestine occupied by Transjordan forces. Since the two appointees were traditional foes of al-Hajj Amin, 'Abdallah thereby let it be known that he, and not the Husaynis, would be directing the future political affairs of Arab Palestine.

There was brief talk about expelling Transjordan from the Arab League, but long after it had subsided the crisis in the Arab bloc persisted. Even in the opening weeks of the war the Arab states had not placed their armies under a united command. Each participating army was assigned a particular sector, so that any resulting mutual assistance was purely fortuitous. Now even the nominal military solidarity disappeared. When sporadic fighting broke out again in the last quarter of 1948, the Israelis cleared the Egyptians out of the western Negeb and occupied western Galilee as well as the southeastern corner of Lebanon. By March 1949 the token Transjordan forces were compelled to retire from the eastern Negeb. Tel-Aviv thus established its control not only over the areas originally allocated to the Jews by the General Assembly but over certain Arab zones as well.[7]

The Arab defeats made further fighting useless by the beginning of 1949. Besides, the Arab governments were encountering growing discontent at home. Added to the military fiasco were the economic dislocations caused by the huge costs of the war and—in Syria, Lebanon, and the Egyptian-occupied Gaza strip—of helping to maintain thousands of Arab D.P.'s. The Syrian Cabinet, reshuffled in August 1948, was replaced with difficulty in December, only to be arrested at the end of March 1949, when the army staged a *coup d'état*. In Iraq a new Cabinet came to power in January, and only the exceptional ability of the new Premier,

General Nuri Pasha al-Sa'id, staved off serious trouble. In Egypt the government was forced in December 1948 to outlaw the ultranationalist Muslim Brethren, who maintained close relations with al-Hajj Amin; a few weeks later the Brethren retaliated by assassinating the Prime Minister, Mahmud Fahmi Pasha al-Nuqrashi. In Lebanon the crisis was delayed until the summer of 1949, when the government had to resort to mass arrests of the quasi-Fascist Syrian National Party members and the execution of its leader to avert open rebellion. Transjordan alone escaped internal crisis, for its Legion was the only Arab army with a creditable record in the field and its treasury was buttressed by British grants-in-aid, including a special subsidy for the care of the Palestine refugees.[8]

Under these circumstances, Acting Mediator Bunche was able to help bring the Palestine war to a formal close. On November 16, 1948 the Security Council had called upon the parties to seek an immediate general armistice "by negotiations conducted either directly or through the Acting Mediator on Palestine." By January 1949 Bunche had opened negotiations between Israel and Egypt at his headquarters on the island of Rhodes. The two countries concluded on February 24 a permanent armistice agreement, demarcating lines between the Israeli and Egyptian forces and providing for the reduction of garrisons and the demilitarization of certain areas. The execution of the armistice was entrusted to a mixed commission, consisting of three Israelis, three Egyptians, and a senior United Nations official as chairman. By July 20 Israel entered into similar bilateral agreements with Lebanon, Transjordan, and Syria. Iraq had already agreed to honor the armistice terms accepted by Palestine's Arab neighbors and Saudi Arabia to abide by the decision of the Arab League.

The armistice lines left in Israel's *de facto* possession almost all the territory occupied by its troops within the boundaries of the former Palestine Mandate: the entire Galilee, the Negeb (including Beersheba but excluding al-'Awja and the Gaza strip), the Coastal Plain, and a sizable corridor to Jewish Jerusalem. Now that Egyptian and Iraqi troops had been withdrawn from the interior of central Palestine, the military administration of that district—extending from north of Janin to south of Hebron and including the Old City of Jerusalem—was taken over wholly by 'Abdallah, who soon requested that his realm henceforth be called "the Hashimite Kingdom of Jordan." On August 11 the Security Council took formal cognizance of the end of the war in Palestine by terminating the office of Acting Mediator.[9]

The armistice agreements gave provisional assurance of stabilizing the existing boundaries and administrative arrangements. This made it possible to restore many normal routines, even though the final peace settlement should prove long in coming. But the question of the Arab refugees was becoming increasingly urgent and complicated. By the summer of 1949 there remained in Israeli-held territory 133,000 Arabs out of an original

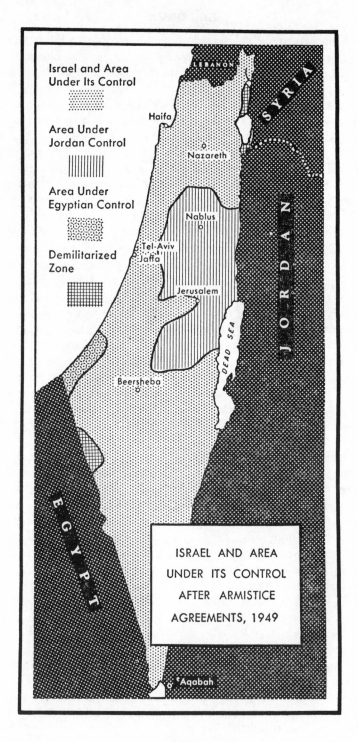

Israel and Area
Under Its Control

Area Under
Jordan Control

Area Under
Egyptian Control

Demilitarized
Zone

LEBANON

SYRIA

Haifa

Nazareth

JORDAN

Nablus

Tel-Aviv
Jaffa

Jerusalem

DEAD SEA

Beersheba

EGYPT

ISRAEL AND AREA
UNDER ITS CONTROL
AFTER ARMISTICE
AGREEMENTS, 1949

ʿAqabah

estimated Arab population of 859,000. Of those who had abandoned their original homes, 470,000 found temporary refuge in Arab Palestine, 40 per cent crowding into the Gaza strip. Another estimated 256,000 had fled to the near-by Arab countries, Lebanon receiving about 100,000, Jordan 75,000, Syria 70,000, Egypt 7,000 and Iraq 4,000.[10]

The Israeli Government disclaimed any responsibility for the mass exodus, which, it contended, stemmed directly from the war forced on the new state by the Arab governments. Therefore the problem, in Israel's view, could only be solved as an integral part of the general and final peace settlement, for the rehabilitation of the displaced Arabs "could not take place . . . while considerations of military security were still paramount . . . and while the [requisite] economic and social effort . . . was paralysed by mobilisation. . . ." Israel also let it be known that it would be willing to repatriate only a limited number of carefully-screened refugees; that it reserved the right to resettle them in places where the new state's economy and security dictated; and that, in its belief, the best solution for the peace of the Near East would be to resettle the majority in near-by Arab lands which are "akin to them in spirit and tradition and in which their smooth integration would be immediately possible." Meanwhile, starting early in the war, the Tel-Aviv Government settled Jewish immigrants in all areas vacated by Arabs and deemed militarily strategic for the new country's defenses, particularly in the Jerusalem corridor and the Galilee. But as the wave of immigration reached tidal proportions, far outstripping the state's ability to provide housing, the government placed the immigrants in all unoccupied Arab dwellings. Spokesmen of the Arab states, for their part, charged that Israel alone was responsible for "driving three-quarters of the lawful population of Palestine from their homes." They insisted "for humanitarian and political reasons" that the refugee problem would have to receive absolute priority over all other questions and that Israel would have to accept in advance the principle of repatriating all those displaced Arabs willing to return to their homes.[11]

As early as July 1948 the Arab League, whose member states had already found the refugee-relief burden too great to shoulder by themselves, appealed for United Nations assistance. Accordingly, in August Count Bernadotte enlisted the cooperation of the United Nations specialized agencies as well as voluntary welfare and religious societies and sought governmental contributions to carry out a provisional relief program. On the basis of Bernadotte's posthumous proposals and further reports by Bunche, the General Assembly in mid-November recommended the allocation of $32,000,000 for emergency aid to the displaced Arabs and the appointment of a Director of United Nations Relief for Palestine Refugees. Named to this post a fortnight later, Stanton Griffis, the American Ambassador to Egypt, coordinated the activities of the private and international agencies already in the field. The contribution of the United States, which agreed to underwrite half the required outlay, was authorized by Congress in March 1949.[12]

While Bernadotte and Bunche were struggling to bring the Palestine war to a halt, the Big Powers continued jockeying for position. For almost a year after the mandate's end, the British Labor Government's policy toward Israel and the Arab East did not change in any major respect. At the United Nations, Great Britain had opposed sanctions against the Arab states when they were on the offensive early in the war. Later it advocated sanctions against Tel-Aviv, when the Israelis refused to give up advanced positions in the Negeb wrested from the Egyptians. Great Britain was the first non-Arab country to offer aid to the Arab refugees. But the Labor Government would not release some 11,000 Jewish detainees on Cyprus until the move was dictated in January 1949 by the rising British criticism over its Israel policy. Moreover, the British representative in the International Refugee Organization was chiefly responsible for its withholding of funds from Jewish relief agencies engaged in transporting D.P.'s from Europe to Israel, until he was finally overruled early in 1949.

The Foreign Office had apparently not lost hope of regaining control over strategic points in Palestine. Thus, Bevin informed the General Assembly in September 1948 that "the United Kingdom . . . had decided to support Count Bernadotte's plan in its entirety. . . ." This plan recommended that the Negeb and the interior of central Palestine be merged with Transjordan and that "the port of Haifa, including the oil refineries and terminals" and "the airport of Lydda . . . be declared . . . free" so as to assure the "interested Arab countries" access to both. The execution of these proposals would have afforded Britain, under its treaty with Transjordan, the possibility of re-establishing bases and protecting directly its oil interests and air rights in Palestine. Therefore the British delegation strove at the General Assembly in November to salvage as many of the Bernadotte recommendations as possible.[13]

The United States for its part continued to gyrate in its course. President Truman granted Israel *de facto* recognition a few minutes after the announcement of the formation of the Provisional Government. Under American influence, the British agreed early in June to stop shipping arms to the Arab states. Washington then aligned itself with London in September, when Secretary Marshall strongly urged at the General Assembly the acceptance of the Bernadotte conclusions "in their entirety as the best possible basis for bringing peace to a distracted land." A month later, in the heat of the presidential election campaign, President Truman reaffirmed the Democratic Party's promise not to approve any changes in the boundaries of the General Assembly's partition resolution not "fully acceptable" to Israel. Less than a week later the American representative on the Security Council was prepared to back an Anglo-Chinese resolution calling for sanctions against Israel, only to reverse himself the next day on instructions from the White House; this performance was repeated immediately after the election. Toward the end of November, the American delegation again encouraged British designs on the Negeb, when Dr. Philip C. Jessup declared in the General Assembly that any reduction in the territory originally given the Jews by the partition resolution "should be agreed upon by Israel and if Israel desired additions, it would have to offer an appropriate exchange through negotiations." Early in 1949 Washington once more swung over to the Israeli side, granting Tel-Aviv a $100,000,000 loan on the eve of the new state's first general election and *de jure* recognition immediately thereafter.[14]

Behind the frequent American shifts lay Washington's mistrust of Soviet motives and its determination to exclude Moscow from any direct role in settling the Palestine dispute. Hence in April 1948, when the Security Council adopted the United States proposal to set up a Truce Commission composed of "representatives of those members of the Security Council which have career consular officers in Jerusalem," the Soviet Union was automatically disqualified. But the U.S.S.R. was equally determined to participate in any United Nations measures on Palestine to which the United States was a party. In June, therefore, when Count Bernadotte requested that the member nations of the Truce Commission—Belgium, France, and the United States—and his native Sweden furnish military personnel to supervise the first truce, Gromyko notified the Security Council that "the Soviet Union has grounds which are certainly no less cogent than those of the United States for including a small group of military observers." However, a Soviet proposal, which would have allowed all member states of the Security Council so desiring, except Syria, to appoint observers, was rejected, as were later Russian moves in the General Assembly as well as the Security Council to have all military observers recalled.[15]

The United States' rivalry with the Soviet Union sometimes went to absurd lengths. *De facto* recognition of Israel by the White House was given even before the American delegation to the United Nations was apprised of the step. Three days later the Kremlin accorded *de jure* recognition, and the Soviet Minister, as the ranking diplomat, became the dean of the Tel-Aviv diplomatic corps. Shortly after the United States recognized Israel *de jure* at the end of January 1949, Washington decided to raise its mission to an embassy, so that the American Ambassador replaced the Soviet Minister as ranking diplomat.[16]

Moscow's unwavering support of the original partition resolution aimed at preventing Britain from regaining and the United States from obtaining any strategic foothold in Palestine. Thus in November 1948 the Soviet spokesman charged that the Bernadotte plan "had been prepared in the British Foreign Office" and was "clearly contrary to the Assembly's decision" of November 29, 1947. He therefore accused Britain and the United States of trying "to strengthen their influence in the Middle East . . . . in the interests of the American and British General Staffs and oil monopolies." Although the U.S.S.R. and the eastern European states generally supported Israel at the United Nations, and sizable amounts of Israeli arms came from Czechoslovakia, there was evidence of reasserting hostility to Zionism by the end of 1948. In part this animosity derived from Jewish communists who did not wish to be identified with the Zionist "mystics" and "homeless cosmopolitans" or the "bourgeois" Israeli regime, presumably because they feared that their loyalty to the party might be questioned. But the general curbs on Jewish emigration from eastern Europe to Israel after the winter of 1948–49 indicated that the mistrust was shared by non-Jewish communists.[17]

As late as the end of November 1948, meanwhile, Acting Mediator Bunche had warned that "there was no guarantee that it would be possible to bring about an armistice" and "expressed his full support for the establishment of a conciliation commission," to replace the Mediator's office. Accordingly, on December 11, 1948 the General Assembly created the United Nations Conciliation Commission for Palestine, consisting of France, Turkey, and the United States and transferred to it all the functions which the Assembly had given the Mediator. The Assembly also recommended that the Security Council might hand over to the Commission the duties "now assigned to the . . . Mediator . . . or the . . . Truce Commission by resolutions of the Security Council" and that when this had been done, the Mediator's office would be terminated. The Conciliation Commission, moreover, was instructed to present to the next Assembly session "detailed proposals for a permanent international regime for the Jerusalem area . . . [providing] maximum local autonomy for distinctive groups consistent with the special international status of Jerusalem"; "to seek arrangements . . . which will facilitate . . . economic development . . ."; and "to facilitate the repatriation, resettlement and . . . rehabilitation of the refugees and the payment of compensation, and to maintain close relations with the Director of the United Nations Relief for Palestine Refugees."

By the time the Conciliation Commission began its work in Jerusalem at the end of January 1949, the situation in Palestine appeared ripe for an armistice. Indeed, to this end Bunche was already negotiating on Rhodes with Israelis and Egyptians. So that the armistice talks might not be jeopardized, Bunche was permitted to conclude the agreements between Israel and its four Arab neighbors. Nevertheless, the Conciliation Commission immediately embarked on exploratory talks with the parties and by the end of April invited Israel, Egypt, Jordan, Lebanon, and Syria to

Lausanne, in the hope of negotiating a formal peace settlement. In Switzerland, however, there was no meeting of minds, and the Conciliation Commission recessed the discussions in the first half of July.[18]

Israel's initial application for admission to the United Nations was turned down in December 1948 by the Security Council, which, however, reversed itself less than three months later, and early in May the General Assembly admitted the new state as the fifty-ninth member. Thereafter, relations between Israel and Britain grew less tense. By the end of May the two countries signed a financial and trade accord, whereby London released $28,000,000 or about a quarter of Israel's estimated sterling balances, which had been blocked ever since February 1948, when Palestine had been dropped from the sterling area. Talks were resumed in Tel-Aviv in July 1949 to settle financial claims and counterclaims arising out of the British departure. By October London permitted Israel to process for domestic consumption Venezuelan crude oil in the Haifa refineries, which had been closed since the spring of 1948. On the other hand, Britain had no intention of alienating the Arab countries. Immediately after the Security Council lifted its arms embargo on countries involved in the Palestine war, Britain resumed sales of military matériel to the Arabs. Egypt was reported in November to have placed orders in the United Kingdom for equipping "a full armored division" and "five squadrons" of jet-propelled planes. Moreover, the British Government jointly with the Iraq Petroleum Company granted the depleted Baghdad treasury a $42,000,000 loan for railway development and public works.

The United Kingdom's acceptance of Israel as a permanent feature on the Near East map required a reassessment of British regional policy. Late in July the heads of the British diplomatic missions in the area assembled in London for the first time in four years to review developments with key officials in the Foreign Office, Treasury, and Ministry of Defense, including the Chiefs of Staff. The security problems created by the rise of Israel, the exposure of the military weakness of the Arab East, and the loss of Palestine as a British base doubtless received the highest priority. But the government communiqué announced that special attention had been given to the relief and resettlement of the Arab refugees as part of a plan for promoting the over-all economic and social welfare of the Arab countries.[19]

Now a new opportunity presented itself for Anglo-American cooperation on constructive action in the Near East. Indeed, as early as June it had been reported that the new Assistant Secretary of State for Near Eastern and African Affairs, George C. McGhee, favored a plan much like the one recommended by the British diplomatic conference in July. The agency for blending the American and British schemes was provided by the Conciliation Commission, which on August 23 established an

Economic Survey Mission. The Mission was to investigate the economic situation in the countries affected by the Palestine war and to recommend an integrated program enabling the governments concerned "to overcome economic dislocation created by the hostilities; . . . to reintegrate the refugees into the economic life of the area on a self-sustaining basis within a minimum period of time; and . . . to promote economic conditions conducive to the maintenance of peace and stability. . . ." Gordon R. Clapp, chairman of the board of directors of the TVA, was appointed head of the Mission; assisting him were not only representatives named by the two other member states of the Conciliation Commission but also one by the United Kingdom.[20]

On the basic issues under negotiation the Conciliation Commission made little headway in talks with the parties between July 18 and September 12. By the time it reconvened in New York five weeks later, its deliberations were overshadowed by developments at the General Assembly. The Economic Survey Mission, whose interim report reached the Assembly in mid-November, found that "tens of thousands [of Arab refugees] are in temporary camps; some are in caves; the majority have found shelter in Arab towns and villages, in mosques, churches, monasteries, schools and abandoned buildings." The Mission proposed that "a programme of useful public works [be established] for the employment of able-bodied refugees as a first measure towards their rehabilitation; and that . . . relief, restricted to those in need, be continued throughout the coming year." Since rations were being issued, under United Nations auspices, to 1,019,000 recipients, and since only some 652,000, including 25,000 borderline cases, represented needy refugees from Israeli-held territory, the Mission recommended that rations be reduced to the lower figure by the end of 1949.

The General Assembly created on December 8 a United Nations Relief and Works Agency for Palestine Refugees in the Near East to implement the Mission's proposals in collaboration with the local governments at a cost of $54,900,000 over a period of a year and a half. The Relief and Works Agency was instructed to terminate direct doles not later than the end of 1950 and to consult with the Near East governments concerned on "measures to be taken by them preparatory to the time when international assistance . . . is no longer available." The Agency was also to absorb by April 1, 1950, the responsibilities of the existing United Nations refugee relief body and to consult with the Conciliation Commission, particularly on the question of those refugees wishing to return to their former homes.[21]

The adoption of this rehabilitation scheme encountered no opposition. The question of Jerusalem, however, gave rise to bitter controversy. King 'Abdallah let it be known that he had no intention of surrendering Arab Jerusalem, while to Jewish Jerusalem Israel began progressively to transfer its government departments. Nor had the Conciliation Commission been able to arrest this process. Nevertheless, in response to the General Assembly's instructions of December 1948 the Commission drafted a proposal calling for a permanent United Nations regime over a demilitarized Jerusalem area with limited municipal autonomy for the Arab and Jewish zones.[22]

The Israeli Foreign Minister, Moshe Sharett [Shertok], in explaining his government's objections, pointed to the centrality of Jerusalem in Jewish history, the Jewish religion, and the Zionist movement. But of more immediate concern, he went on, was the experience of the Jerusalem Jews, who in the early weeks of the Palestine war faced possible starvation and capitulation. In rescuing them, the Israeli Army was required to forge a land bridge and construct a water pipe line at a cost of many lives. The Israeli Army continued its responsibility for the defense of the city "even after the mortal peril had been averted," and subsequently the city had been incorporated into the state of Israel in every administrative respect, "since it would have been ludicrous to attempt to set up a separate legislative system for Jerusalem." Sharett, moreover, declared that, since Jewish Jerusalem was surrounded on three sides by Arab territory, "a complete bilateral disarmament [of the Jerusalem district] . . . would leave the Jewish area . . . extremely vulnerable to sudden attack." Sharett expressed greater confidence in the Israeli-Jordan armistice agreement, under which a partial reduction of garrisons had already been effected, and once formal peace was attained, "a further reduction would undoubtedly take place." He reiterated Israel's proposals on the eve of its admission to the United Nations in May 1949: either a limited internationalized area, encompassing only that part of the city "which contained the largest number of religious and historic shrines," or "an international regime applying to the whole city . . . but restricted functionally, so that it would be concerned only with the protection of the Holy Places. . . ."

The spokesman for Jordan, Fawzi Pasha al-Mulqi, observed that Jerusalem had been "in Arab hands since time immemorial" and that its sacred sites had been provided "with the best guardianship the world has ever witnessed." Mulqi gave assurances that "the Holy Places in the Holy City and its environs under the control of my Government are safe and secure. . . ." He, too, pointed to the lesson of the Palestine war, stating that "were it not for . . . [the] genuine effort on the part of the Jordan Kingdom, Jerusalem, like the rest of Arab Palestine, now under Jewish control, would have been overrun . . . and . . . we would not be discussing the future of the Holy City . . ." The Jordanian also referred to the armistice lines, which, he contended, were drawn with Jerusalem in mind. The demilitarization of the city would weaken the defenses of the kingdom and expose it to the "imminent dangers of Jewish territorial expansionist motives, to say nothing of the domination of the entire Holy City by the Jews . . ." [23]

In the end a resolution far more drastic than that suggested by the Conciliation Commission was adopted. The General Assembly requested the Trusteeship Council to complete its original statute for Jerusalem, drafted in connection with the 1947 partition resolution and proposing to place the Jerusalem area under a special international regime administered by the Trusteeship Council. The Council was directed to "proceed immediately" with the execution of this plan and not to "allow any actions taken by any interested Government or Governments to divert it." This resolution was passed by the substantial margin of 38 to 14, despite the warnings from Israel that "such a plan would replace the order and freedom reigning in Jerusalem by anarchy and discontent, endangering both the secular and religious peace" of Jerusalem and from Jordan that "such measures . . . are harmful to its vital interests and to [the] security of its territory . . . . and that it will oppose the execution of whatever is decided contrary to its rightful wishes." The United States and Britain also disapproved of the resolution, but the fact that they supported the Conciliation Commission's proposal, which was also objectionable to Israel and Jordan, did not give the Western Powers any constructive alternative around which to rally the opposition. [24]

The vote, which was even more decisive than that on the partition resolution, was secured by an alliance of the Arab states, the Catholic countries (particularly those of Latin America), and the Soviet bloc. The six Arab states members of the United Nations were probably motivated by the wish to prevent Israel from retaining possession of New Jerusalem, so as to strengthen Arab claims for the return of the Israeli corridor to Jerusalem. Besides, the defeat of Israel on this important issue would, in the words of Charles Malik, the Lebanese delegate, provide "a moral bolstering of the Arab world in its present anxieties." Another consideration of the anti-Hashimite Arab states might have been to loosen Jordan's hold over Old Jerusalem, thereby depriving 'Abdallah of the third most sacred city in Islam and possibly paving the way for his government's eventual displacement from all of Arab Palestine. The Arab-Latin combine had been a feature of the United Nations politics from the beginning, most recently in the action on the former Italian colonies. More important in influencing the Latin American states, however, and such countries as France—which took the unorthodox step of abandoning the Conciliation Commission's scheme in whose framing it had participated—were the appeals from the Vatican to the Catholic episcopacy throughout the world. This unusual alliance was led by the delegation of Australia, which had consistently favored the internationalization of Jerusalem. [25]

Obviously nettled because the Soviet Union had been excluded from the Palestine truce supervision and from representation on the Conciliation Commission, the Kremlin now aired its cumulative grievances. The Soviet representative, Semyon Tsarapkin, stressed the consistent record of his government in upholding the letter of the original partition resolution. The Jewish state had already come into being, he observed, and all that remained was the creation of the Arab state and the international regime for Jerusalem. Tsarapkin accused the United States and Britain, "bound by common imperialist considerations," of having delayed "the implementation of General Assembly decisions by means of intrigue, threats and military, political and economic pressure." The United Kingdom, it was charged, "had never left Palestine; they had merely replaced their own troops by troops from 'Transjordan'," which, "as everyone knew, was a British puppet." The Conciliation Commission had been created by Anglo-American "manoeuvres" for the purpose of enabling "the United Kingdom . . . [to] gain control of a large part of Palestine and the United States . . . [to] obtain a solid foothold in that country." The U.S.S.R. delegation therefore proposed that the Conciliation Commission be dissolved. While this proposal was defeated, Soviet backing helped assure the Jerusalem resolution more than a comfortable lead.[26]

CONCLUSION

On the road to partition, Palestine was inflated to a global problem of prime importance, involving the prestige and authority of the United Nations. The assessment of its record in handling the dispute would have to await the final settlement. Yet it was already clear that, though the United Nations proved incapable of preventing the outbreak of war, it nevertheless did stop the fighting and help the belligerents to arrive at a formal armistice. The United Nations also enabled the British to get out of an impossible situation and provided the Palestine Jews with an opportunity for setting up their state. This entailed the creation of a serious refugee problem. But the United Nations did assume responsibility for the hapless victims of the war and tried to put into operation a constructive program for rehabilitating not only the uprooted Arabs but the Arab states as well. The United Nations seemed to have taken on an assignment in Jerusalem that was calculated to bring embarrassment to itself and to retard the final peace. But the fact remained that the United Nations was providing the machinery for the peace settlement.

Between the armistice and the peace there lay the Palestine problem in a new guise. The old issues of immigration, land sales, and statehood had been solved with the attainment of sovereignty by the Palestine Jews and with their military victory. These issues were now replaced by others:

the legal delimitation of Israel's frontiers, the legal disposition of the Arab remnants of Palestine, the future status of Jerusalem, and the rehabilitation of the refugees.

Mutual distrust between Israel and the Arab states appeared to persist in as virulent a form as ever. The Israelis were convinced that they had survived because of their own efforts, without the help of the international community at the most critical juncture. Besides, they had won the war and saw no reason why they should have to lose the peace. The Arab spokesmen were persuaded that the United States and Great Britain through the United Nations had enabled the Zionists to triumph. The Arabs therefore refused to accept the defeat as final and did not regard themselves as vanquished. So they, too, were in no mood to concede. Nor had the Big-Power rivalry died down. The United States seemed to be succeeding in its efforts to keep the Russians out of any direct role in settling the Palestine problem, for neither the U.S.S.R. nor any eastern European state took part in the truce supervision, the armistice negotiations, the conciliation talks, and the refugee and economic rehabilitation programs. Yet as long as general peace was not established, it would be impossible to foresee precisely the final consequences of either the Arab-Israel or the Big-Power competition. The familiar pressures and counterpressures were still capable of producing capricious results, as the United Nations decision on Jerusalem demonstrated.

Nevertheless, it was instructive that, once the mandate expired, the local Arab national movement which had never developed a stable community government dissipated itself in complete chaos. On the other hand, the two corporate entities—the Jewish National Home and 'Abdallah's original Amirate—which had received experience in self-rule not only outlived the mandate but in the first flush of the post-mandate excitement divided the spoils of the Palestine Arab Community between them. Whether the territorial forms as molded by the armistice agreements would harden into permanence or not depended ultimately on the extent to which the conflicting forces at play neutralized one another.

Israel's viability had been tested and proved in the crucible of war. But once the floodgates of Jewish immigration, damned up for so long, were opened, the new state's economy was nearly overwhelmed. In less than twenty months Israel's Jewish population expanded from 650,000 to about 1,000,000, an increase of over 50 per cent. The economic crisis was, of course, far from solved, but the initial shock appeared to have been absorbed, a further demonstration of Israel's staying powers. As Near East countries go, Israel seemed destined not to be the smallest, for if immigration continued even at half the post-mandate pace for a few years longer and the armistice boundaries were not radically changed, the new land would be larger in area than Lebanon, and in population than Lebanon or Jordan. Yet in the long run size alone was unimportant. For better or for worse, Israel was in the midst of the Arab East. Israel's survival and the region's stability would be determined as much by the outcome of the East-West cold war as by the ability of Israel and the Arab states to establish relations of mutual friendship and cooperation.

Notes

ABBREVIATIONS

AACI—Anglo-American Committee of Inquiry

AE—Jewish Agency Executive

AH—*Ad Hoc* Political Committee of the United Nations General
Assembly

AHC—Arab Higher Committee

AL—Arab League

Cmd.—Command Paper

C.O.—Colonial Office

FC—First (Political and Security) Committee of the United Nations
General Assembly

F.O.—Foreign Office

G.A.—General Assembly

G.B.—Great Britain

JA—Jewish Agency for Palestine

Jer—Jerusalem

Lon—London

ManGuard—The Manchester Guardian

MEJ—The Middle East Journal

*MPMC—The Establishment in Palestine of the Jewish National Home:
Memorandum on the Development of the Jewish National Home,
[Year], Submitted by the Jewish Agency for Palestine to the Secretary-
General of the League of Nations for the Information of the Permanent
Mandates Commission, June [Year]*

NJ—The New Judaea

NY—New York

OR—Official Records of the United Nations General Assembly and
Security Council

PalGaz—The Palestine Gazette

PalPost—The Palestine Post

PalRev—Palestine Review
PalTrans—Palestine and Transjordan
PalYear—The Palestine Year Book
PD—Parliamentary Debates
P.G.—Palestine Government
PM—Plenary Meeting of the United Nations General Assembly
PP—Parliamentary Papers
RPA—Report by His Majesty's Government in the United Kingdom of Great Britain and Northern Ireland to the Council of the League of Nations on the Administration of Palestine and Trans-Jordan for the Year. . . .
S.C.—United Nations Security Council
S.D.—United States Department of State
SIA—Survey of International Affairs
Supp. Mem.—Supplementary Memorandum by the Government of Palestine, including Notes on Evidence given to the United Nations' Special Committee on Palestine up to the 12th July, 1947
Survey—A Survey of Palestine Prepared in December 1945 and January 1946 for the Information of the Anglo-American Committee of Inquiry
Survey Supp.—Supplement to Survey of Palestine, Notes Compiled for the Information of the United Nations Special Committee on Palestine
U.K.—The United Kingdom
U.N.—The United Nations
UNPAC—United Nations Palestine Commission
UNSCOP—United Nations Special Committee on Palestine
U.S.—The United States
WashPost—The Washington Post
ZE—Zionist Executive

(page 17)

CHAPTER 1

[1] The literature on the early history of the Palestine Mandate is vast. The Palestine Royal Commission Report (G.B., *PP, 1936–37,* Cmd. 5479) remains the classic British treatment. A briefer, less reliable statement is Royal Institute of International Affairs, *Great Britain and Palestine, 1915–1936.* The Arab viewpoint is presented not only by Tawfiq Canaan, *Conflict in the Land of Peace* and George Antonius, *The Arab Awakening,* but by J. M. N. Jeffries, *Palestine: the Reality* and Nevill Barbour, *Nisi Dominus,* which appeared in the U.S. as *Palestine: Star or Crescent?* Esco Foundation, *Palestine: a Study of Jewish, Arab, and British Policies,* 2 vols., develops the Jewish position

(pages 17–21)

in greatest detail. A dispassionate analysis is that by Paul L. Hanna, *British Policy in Palestine,* though it focuses on the U.K. more than on Palestine. British wartime promises to Arabs and Jews have been subjected to conflicting interpretation. The McMahon-Husayn correspondence appeared officially for the first time in G.B., *PP, 1938–39,* Cmd. 5957, while the divergent British and Arab attitudes toward this correspondence may be found in Cmd. 5974. The most exhaustive Jewish study of the Balfour Declaration is N. M. Gelber, *Hazharat Balfur we-Toldoteha;* the Arab viewpoint is explained in W. F. Boustany, *The Palestine Mandate: Invalid and Impracticable.*

[2] Article 25 of the final draft.

[3] U.S., 67th Cong., 2nd Sess., House

Committee on Foreign Affairs, *Report No. 1038, Accompanying H.J. Res. 322,* p. 1.

4 G.B., *PP, 1922,* Cmd. 1700, pp. 17–21.
5 Cmd. 5479, p. 33.
6 G.B., *PP, 1930–31,* Cmd. 3692.
7 Text in G.B., *PD, Commons,* vol. 248, cols. 751–57.
8 The number of districts was increased to six in 1939.

CHAPTER 2

1 The statistical data in this section is derived primarily from the following: *Survey,* I, chap. 6; P.G., Office of the Census, *Census of Palestine, 1931,* by E. Mills, 2 vols.; P.G., Dept. of Statistics, *Statistical Abstract of Palestine, 1942;* D. Gurevich, A. Gertz, and R. Bachi, *The Jewish Population of Palestine* (Heb. text with Eng. summary); A. Boehm and A. Pollak, *The Jewish National Fund;* ZE and AE, *Reports, 1937* and F. W. Notestein and E. Jurkat, "Population Problems of Palestine," *The Milbank Memorial Fund Quarterly,* 23 (Oct.), 307–52. No precise Beduin statistics are available; after 1931 the Palestine Government automatically assumed that they numbered 66,553. This estimate is somewhat lower than that in Ya'aqov Shim'oni, *'Arvei Erez Israel,* which is the best comprehensive analysis of the Palestine Arab Community. For general reference on the Druzes, see P. K. Hitti, *The Origins of the Druze Religion,* while reliable information on the Christian Arabs may be found in C. T. Bridgeman, *Religious Communities in the Christian East.*

2 Most of the illustrative material in this section has come from: R. R. Nathan, O. Gass, and D. Creamer, *Palestine: Problem and Promise;* S. B. Himadeh, ed., *Economic Organization of Palestine;* David Horowitz, *Ha-Kalkalah ha-Arzisraelit be-Hitpathutah; Survey,* I and II, chaps. 9, 13, 14, and 16; and *MPMC, 1936.* For detailed descriptions of the Histadrut, see G. Muenzner, *Jewish Labour Economy in Palestine* and Histadrut, *Memorandum to AACI.* Arab Office, Jer, *Evidence to AACI* (stenciled), items C.46–54 and Khalil Totah, *Arab Progress in Palestine* are accounts of Arab economic development, as seen by Arabs. Zionist efforts to organize Arab labor are traced by Abba Khoushi in *The Palestine*

Labour League; and an Arab description of Arab labor unions may be found in J. Asfour, "Arab Labour in Palestine," *Royal Central Asian Society Journal,* 32 (May 1945), 201–05. In converting prewar Palestine currency into the American equivalent, the value of the Palestine pound is assumed to equal five dollars.

8 For further reference on topics covered in this section see: Cmd. 5479; *Survey,* II, chap. 16; *RPA* for 1925, 1929, and 1937; N. Nardi, *Zionism and Education in Palestine;* G.B., C.O., No. 201, *The System of Education of the Jewish Community in Palestine;* H. F. Infield, *Cooperative Living in Palestine;* E. Samuel, *Handbook of the Communal Villages in Palestine* (2nd Eng. ed.); JA, Economic Research Institute, *Housing in Jewish Palestine,* pp. 4–68; Shim'oni, *op. cit.,* chaps. 11 and 16; P.G., Dept. of Statistics, *General Monthly Bulletin of Current Statistics,* vols. 10 and 11, which contain the results of an intensive survey of the social and economic conditions in five typical, medium-sized Arab villages; and Omar el-Baghuthi, "Judicial Courts among the Bedouin of Palestine," reprinted from the *Journal of the Palestine Oriental Society,* 2 (Jer, 1922), 34–65, which deals with the legal customs of the Beduin and fallahin of southern Palestine.

CHAPTER 3

1 From address of Zionist President Chaim Weizmann at 1931 Zionist Congress, *NJ,* July–Aug. 1931, p. 214; also JA, *Memorandum to Royal Commission,* chap. 7.
2 ZE, *Reports, 1935,* p. 12.
3 Text of government regulations, enacted on Dec. 30, 1927, in *RPA, 1927,* pp. 81–93; the mandatory did not recognize the National Council Executive until 1934, *PalGaz,* No. 427, Mar. 15, 1934, Supp. No. 2, p. 219. Histories of the community government are M. Burstein, *Jewish Self-Government in Palestine* and M. Attias, *Kneset Israel be-Erez Israel.*
4 A readable history of Zionism is I. Cohen, *The Zionist Movement.*
5 Non-Partisan Conference to Consider Palestinian Problems, *Verbatim Report,* p. 9.
6 Text of Agency constitution in *MPMC, 1929,* app. II, pp. 36–49.
7 Cmd. 5479, pp. 118 and 335–36.

[8] Text of electoral regulation in *Official Gazette of the Government of Palestine*, No. 254, March 1, 1930.

[9] For European origins of the labor parties, see A. G. Duker's introd. to Ber Borochov, *Nationalism and the Class Struggle*, pp. 17-55.

[10] Mapai, *Ketavim we-Te'udot*, p. 187. This volume is a source book of Mapai's ideology in the early 1930's; also B. Katznelson, *Revolutionary Constructivism*.

[11] Hashomer Hatzair, *Pioneer Saga*, p. 17. Indispensable for an understanding of the party's program in its formative years is *Sefer ha-Shomrim*, ed. by J. Guthelf and A. Cohen.

[12] Left Zionist Workers, Tenth World Conference, *Report* (Yiddish), pp. 23, 26-27; for further reference on party's platform see Left Zionist Workers, *Zionist Labor in the Present Period* (Yiddish) and *Red Book* (Yiddish).

[13] B. Sherman, *The Communists in Palestine*, p. 5; on enrollment cf. Burstein, *op. cit.*, pp. 111 and 120.

[14] ZE, *Reports, 1933*, p. 15; a brief account of the schism appears in *Reports, 1935*, pp. 29-33, 212-13.

[15] S. Rosenblatt, *The Mizrachi Movement*, p. 8; on history and ideology of Mizrahi and its labor offshoot, see A. L. Gellman and P. Hurgin, eds., *Mizrahi Jubilee Miscellany*; and Ha-Po'el ha-Mizrahi, *Memorandum to AACl*.

[16] Agudas Israel World Organization, Lon Executive, *Agudist Essays* and *Memorandum to AACl*; J. Rosenheim, *Agudist World-Problems*; and Wa'ad Leumi, "Histadrut Poalei Agudat Israel in Palestine" (typescript).

[17] V. Jabotinsky, *An Answer to Ernest Bevin*, pp. 6, 19, 29; this pamphlet is a reprint of a hearing before the Palestine Royal Commission on Feb. 11, 1937; details of the Revisionist program may be found in J. Schechtmann, *Die staatszionistische Bewegung* (stenciled).

[18] ZE and AE, *Reports, 1937*, pp. 156-59, 411.

CHAPTER 4

[1] While remaining part of the Palestine Mandate and under the British High Commissioner's jurisdiction, Transjordan was granted limited self-government under Amir 'Abdallah.

[2] Cmd. 1700, p. 2.

[3] Text of regulation establishing Council in *Official Gazette of the Government of Palestine*, Jan. 1, 1922.

[4] On al-Hajj Amin's rise to power, see Cmd. 5479, pp. 174-81; G.B., *PP, 1929-30*, Cmd. 3530, pp. 31-32, 73, 172-73; *Survey*, II, 900-03; *SIA, 1925*, I, 364-65; *1930*, p. 275; and *1936*, p. 727; Shim'oni, *op. cit.*, pp. 68-70; Hanna, *op. cit.*, pp. 69-72; Esco, *op. cit.*, I, 260-62; and R. F. Woodsmall, *Moslem Women Enter a New World*, pp. 196-97, 381-85, 404-05.

[5] "King-Crane Report," *Editor and Publisher*, Dec. 2, 1922, Section Two, p. vi; see also W. F. Albright's analysis in Esco, *op. cit.*, I, 533-53; and *RPA, 1932*, p. 13.

[6] On history of Arab nationalism, cf. Antonius, *Arab Awakening*; E. A. Speiser, *The United States and the Near East*, pp. 41-91; Shim'oni, *op. cit.*, pp. 240-78; Hanna, *op. cit.*, pp. 39-68; Esco, *op. cit.*, I, 120-64; for Greater Syria scheme, see Transjordan Government, *Al-Kitab al-Urdunni al-Abyad—Suriyya al-Kubra*.

[7] M. E. T. Mogannam, *The Arab Woman and the Palestine Problem*, p. 126. This was the first such conference in Palestine; the earlier sessions, attended by Palestine Arabs, were the General Syrian Congresses of June-July 1919 and Feb.-March 1920 at Damascus.

[8] AHC, *Memorandum to Royal Commission*, pp. 10, 12; other arguments from AHC, *Memorandum to Permanent Mandates Commission* (1937); Antonius, *op. cit.*, pp. 407-09; Mogannam, *op. cit.*, pp. 125-27; and *RPA, 1935*, p. 15.

[9] Canaan, *op. cit.*, p. 32.

[10] Cmd. 5479, p. 133.

[11] After the Supreme Muslim Council; for brief sketches of the more important Muslim clans in Palestine, see Shim'oni, *op. cit.*, chap. 10; also Thabit al-Khalidi, "Arab Clan Rivalry in Palestine" (typescript). A convenient list of Arab mayors of Jerusalem may be found in *Al-Difa'*, Aug. 31, 1944.

[12] Friction between those who traced their origin back to the North Arabian (*Qaysi*) and to the South Arabian (*Yamani*) tribes still divided many influential Muslim clans in Palestine. Since the Husaynis, as Yamanis, attracted clans of this class, many Qaysis joined the Nashashibi ranks, even though Raghib Bey was neither a Qaysi nor a Yamani. P. K. Hitti, *History of the Arabs* (1940), pp. 280-81; and al-Khalidi, *op. cit.*

13 *Survey*, II, 946–47.

14 *Ibid.*, p. 945; *SIA*, *1936*, pp. 720–21; and Shim'oni, *op. cit.*, pp. 335–37.

15 *Ibid.*, pp. 293, 352; see also pp. 376–78; *Oriente Moderno*, 15 (Apr. 1935), 160; *Survey*, II, 947–48; *Survey Supp.*, p. 142; Mogannam, *op. cit.*, pp. 241–42; *RPA*, *1935*, p. 17; and P.G., "The Sanduq al-Ummah: a Statement Prepared for the AACI" (typescript).

16 *Oriente Moderno*, 15 (Jan. 1935), 15–17; Mogannam, *op. cit.*, pp. 237–39; and Shim'oni, *op. cit.*, p. 365.

17 *Oriente Moderno*, 15 (Aug. 1935), 392 and 19 (Feb. 1939), 81; Mogannam, *op. cit.*, pp. 242–44; *Survey*, II, 947–50; Shim'oni, *op. cit.*, pp. 293–94.

18 *Oriente Moderno*, 12 (Sept. 1932), 437–38; *RPA*, *1935*, p. 15; Antonius, *op. cit.*, pp. 111, 292; Shim'oni, *op. cit.*, pp. 229–30; and J. Waschitz, *Ha-'Arvim be-Erez Israel*, pp. 308–09.

CHAPTER 5

1 Cmd. 5479, pp. 90–95; Hanna, *op. cit.*, pp. 117–21; Esco, *op. cit.*, II, 782–89; AE, *Political Report*, *1937*, pp. 5–10; text of Legislative Council scheme in G.B., *PP*, *1935–36*, Cmd. 5119.

2 Original composition of Higher Committee in Cmd. 5479, p. 96.

3 *Ibid.*, p. 97; Mogannam, *op. cit.*, pp. 296–301; and *RPA*, *1936*, p. 24.

4 AE, *Political Report*, *1937*, pp. 26–27.

5 G.B., *PD*, *Commons*, vol. 312, cols. 837–38.

6 Cmd. 5479, pp. 98–101, 401–03; *SIA*, *1936*, pp. 719–48; and Shim'oni, *op. cit.*, pp. 296–314.

7 Text of emergency regulations in *PalGaz*, Extraordinary, No. 584, Apr. 19, 1936, Supp. No. 2, pp. 259–68 and Extraordinary, No. 603, June 12, 1936, Supp. No. 2, pp. 609–13; for other details, see Cmd. 5479, p. 98; *Survey*, II, 584–85; *SIA*, *1936*, pp. 732–34; Hanna, *op. cit.*, pp. 122–24; and *PalTrans*, Aug. 22, 1936.

8 AE, *Political Report*, *1937*, pp. 32–48; *MPMC*, *1936*, pp. 23, 30, 36; *SIA*, *1936*, p. 730; and Cmd. 5479, p. 106.

9 JA, Political Dept., "Minute of a Conversation with H.E., the High Commissioner, on Monday, August 24th, 1936" (stenciled).

10 Text in *RPA*, *1936*, p. 30.

11 G.B., *PD*, *Commons*, vol. 315, cols. 1509–15; *The Times* (Lon), Sept. 8, 1936;

SIA, *1936*, p. 739; text of Martial Law Order in Council, 1936, in *PalGaz*, Extraordinary, No. 634, Sept. 30, 1936, pp. 1070–72.

12 Cmd. 5479, pp. 101–02.

13 Hanna, *op. cit.*, p. 135; text of consolidated ordinances in *PalGaz*, Extraordinary, No. 675, Mar. 24, 1937, Supp. No. 2, pp. 267–73.

14 *MPMC*, *1937*, p. 5 and par. 6 of the covering letter.

15 Cmd. 5479, pp. ix, 141–43, 360, 361, 365, 370, 373, 380–95.

16 *Cf.*, for example, G.B., *PD*, *Lords*, vol. 106, col. 815; and *SIA*, *1937*, I, 556.

17 Cmd. 5479, pp. 363–68.

18 G.B., *PP*, *1936–37*, Cmd. 5513.

19 *Ibid.*, Cmd. 5544.

20 G.B., *PP*, *1937–38*, Cmd. 5634, pp. 5, 7–8, 11; see also Hanna, *op. cit.*, pp. 132–33.

21 Text in *NJ*, Aug.–Sept. 1937, p. 227; verbatim records of the political debate in Twentieth Zionist Congress and Fifth Session of Jewish Agency Council, *Stenographic Report* (Hebrew); see also C. Weizmann, *Trial and Error*, pp. 385–87.

22 Text in *NJ*, Aug.–Sept. 1937, pp. 235–36; verbatim records in *Stenographic Report*; also M. J. Karpf, "Partition of Palestine and its Consequences," *Jewish Social Service Quarterly*, 14 (Mar. 1938), reprint.

23 *ManGuard*, Aug. 19, 1937.

24 Agudas Israel World Organization, Lon Executive, *Memorandum to AACI*, p. 9; see also *PalPost*, Aug. 24, 1937.

25 *The Times* (Lon), July 6, 7, 12, 14, 1937; *PalPost*, July 4, 12, 22, 1937; and *SIA*, *1937*, I, 550.

CHAPTER 6

1 Cmd. 5513; immigrants possessing $5,000 or more were classified as "capitalists." For criticism of Palestine Government, see Cmd. 5479, pp. 163–64 and 365.

2 AHC, *Memorandum to Permanent Mandates Commission* (1937).

3 Text in AE, *Political Report*, *1939*, app. I, p. 3.

4 Immigration amendment ordinances in *PalGaz*, No. 736, Nov. 11, 1937, Supp. No. 1, pp. 285–88; *ibid.*, Extraordinary, No. 767, Mar. 15, 1938, pp. 256–58 and No. 779, May 5, 1938, Supp. No. 2, pp. 519–20; Agency protest in AE, *Political Report*, *1939*, pp. 50–51 and apps. V and VI.

[5] Cmd. 5479, pp. 140 and 201.
[6] Defense regulations in *PalGaz*, Extraordinary, No. 723, Sept. 30, 1937, Supp. No. 2, 911–13; text of government communiqué in *RPA, 1937*, pp. 20–21; for daily catalogue of incidents of terrorism, see *PalPost*, July–Sept. 1937; list of deported and exiled Higher Committee members, *ibid.*, Oct. 3, 15, 1937; on Mufti's activities, see *SIA, 1937*, I, 570–71; *NYTimes*, Oct. 17, 1937; and *PalPost*, Nov. 16, 1937.
[7] *The Times* (Lon), Nov. 28, 1938; text of British War Office statement in *Man-Guard*, Jan. 10, 1939; and *Survey*, I, 44–45. For details of rebel organization and exploits and general Arab exodus in this period, see *SIA, 1937*, I, 567–70; *1938*, I, 414–18, 443–44; *RPA, 1937*, pp. 8–18; *RPA, 1938*, pp. 11–17; and AE, *Political Report, 1939*, pp. 65–66.
[8] *Cf.* official communiqué in *RPA, 1937*, p. 23; *The Times* (Lon), Dec. 31, 1937; *Survey*, I, 43 and II, 585; *SIA, 1937*, I, 573; list of government dismissals of Council employees may be found in *PalPost*, Feb. 23, Mar. 22, 23, 25, 1938.
[9] AE, *Political Report, 1937*, pp. 37–41; *Political Report, 1939*, pp. 59–63, 67–69; A. Bein, *Ha-Hityashvut ha-Haqlait shel ha-Yehudim be-Erez Israel*, p. 41; and *Survey*, II, 600. Most of the Jewish police, especially the supernumeraries, belonged to Haganah; but Haganah members as such were not authorized to bear arms and, when seized by the British security forces, were given prison terms; *ibid.*, I, 45.
[10] *SIA, 1937*, I, 567; *Survey*, II, 734; Nathan, *op. cit.*, pp. 210–11; P.G., Dept. of Statistics, *Statistical Abstract of Palestine, 1944–45*, p. 72; *MPMC, 1937*, pp. 12–18; *MPMC, 1938*, pp. 29–31; AE, *Political Report, 1939*, pp. 74–75.
[11] *Cf.* Weizmann, *Trial and Error*, pp. 375–78.
[12] *PalTrans*, Aug. 22, 1936.
[13] G.B., *PD, Commons*, vol. 335, col. 538; for Italian activities see *NYTimes*, June 8, 1937 and *The Times* (Lon), Dec. 22, 1937.
[14] *Cf.*, for example, Antonius, *op. cit.*, pp. 387–89.
[15] Sworn testimony of Dieter Wisliceny, an East Prussian who worked with Reichert in Germany in World War II; affidavit signed on Dec. 2, 1946, before the National Tribunal of Bratislava; see also

The Times (Lon), Nov. 28, 1938 and June 29, 1939; *NYTimes*, June 28, 1939; and *PalPost*, Dec. 3, 7, 1937 and June 21, 1939.
[16] On history of Templar colonies, see H. Seibt, *Moderne Kolonisation in Palästina*, 2 vols.; and The Temple Society, *The Temple Society in Palestine*. For details of Templar activities in this period, *cf. The Times* (Lon), July 12, 28, 1937 and Mar. 14, 1939; *NYTimes*, July 17, 1937; and *PalPost*, Dec. 9, 1938.
[17] *PalTrans*, Aug. 15, 1936 and May 29, 1937; see also *NYTimes*, May 23, 1937.
[18] *Cf.*, for example, Nation Associates, *The Palestine Problem and Proposals for Its Solution* (Apr. 1947), p. 43.
[19] *The Times* (Lon), Nov. 28, 1938, Feb. 23, 1939; *NYTimes*, Sept. 15, 1938; and *PalPost*, May 29, 1939.
[20] *NYTimes*, Sept. 10, 1937 and *PalTrans*, Sept. 18, 1937; for a contemporary analysis of the Bludan conference, see R. G. Woolbert, "Pan-Arabism and the Palestine Problem," *Foreign Affairs*, 16 (Jan. 1938), 309–22; *cf.* also message to the conference from the Jerusalem Mufti, in his capacity as president of the Higher Committee, portraying Zionism as a modern crusade against Islam; text in *Filastin*, Sept. 10, 1937.
[21] From text of resolution distributed by Arab Center in London; brief accounts of the Inter-Parliamentary Congress may be found in *The Times* (Lon), Oct. 8, 1938; and Shim'oni, *op. cit.*, p. 308.
[22] Cmd. 5479, pp. 123–24; *PalTrans*, Aug. 22, Oct. 17, Nov. 14, 1937, July 9, 1938; *PalPost*, May 2, Aug. 7, 8, 14, Oct. 27, 1938; editorial in *Al-Misri* [Cairo], Nov. 5, 1938; *NYTimes*, July 18, 1937, May 2, 16, 1938; *The Times* (Lon), Nov. 28, 1938; and H. Scott, *In the High Yemen*, pp. 89 and 121. Regarding Jewish communities in Arab East *cf.* I. Yesha'yahu and S. Greidi, *Mi-Teiman le-Ziyyon* (Yemen); A. J. Brauer, *Avaq Derakhim* (Iraq, Syria, Lebanon); and M. Fargeon, *Les Juifs en Égypte*.
[23] *PalTrans*, July 17, 1937; for other details, see *SIA, 1937*, I, 551–54, 567; text of Iraqi protest in *League of Nations Official Journal*, 18 (Aug.–Sept. 1937), 660–61; *PalPost*, Jan. 20 and June 2, 1938; and *The Times* (Lon), Oct. 6, 1938.
[24] Cmd. 5634, pp. 1–3 and 10.
[25] AE, *Political Report, 1939*, p. 6; and Esco, *op. cit.*, II, 881–85.

26 See, for instance, ZE and AE, *Reports, 1939*, pp. 33, 116–17.

27 Text of National Defense Party statement in *PalTrans*, May 14, 1938; extracts from 'Abdallah's memorandum *ibid.*, June 4, 1938.

28 *SIA, 1938*, I, 418–19; *PalPost*, Aug. 31–Sept. 2, 1938.

29 *Survey*, I, 45 and II, 601; AE, *Political Report, 1939*, pp. 72–76; also *NYTimes*, Apr. 1, 2, 1944.

30 AE, *Political Report, 1939*, p. 10.

CHAPTER 7

1 G.B., *PD, Commons*, vol. 341, cols. 40 and 861; *SIA, 1938*, I, 419–22; Defense (Military Commanders) Regulations in *PalGaz*, Extraordinary, No. 827, Oct. 18, 1938, Supp. No. 2, p. 1361; and *Survey*, I, 46.

2 Text in *NYTimes*, Oct. 15, 1938; see also *ibid.*, Oct. 19, 22, 29, Nov. 3, 6, 1938; *The Times* (Lon), Nov. 2, 1938, Jan. 10, 1939; for editorial reaction in Yishuv *cf.* *Ha-Arez*, Oct. 20 and Dec. 30, 1938; and *Ha-Boqer*, Jan. 9, 1939.

3 G.B., *PP, 1938–39*, Cmd. 5893 (White Paper); Partition Commission's report appeared as Cmd. 5854.

4 G.B., *PD, Commons*, vol. 341, cols. 302–05.

5 *Ha-Arez*, Jan. 30, 1939; text of Agency statement in AE, *Political Report, 1939*, app. viii, pp. 88–89; resolutions of General Council and Administrative Committee in ZE and AE, *Reports, 1939*, pp. 20–21, 273–74.

6 AE, *Political Report, 1939*, p. 10; list of delegates in app. xiv, pp. 115–16.

7 *PalPost*, Nov. 18, 1938; *cf.* also editorial in *Al-Lahab*, Nov. 10, 1938; and statements by Palestine Information Center in London and Cairo Inter-Parliamentary Congress delegation to Britain in *PalPost*, Nov. 10–11, 1938.

8 Text (extracted and abbreviated), *ibid.*, Nov. 16, 1938; see also extracts from Fakhri Bey's pamphlet in issue of Jan. 6, 1938; *cf.* *The Times* (Lon), Dec. 1, 29, 1938, Jan. 7, 9, 10, Feb. 7, 23, Mar. 6, 1939; and *SIA, 1938*, I, 422, 433–44.

9 *The Times* (Lon), Dec. 8, 1938.

10 List of delegations of Arab states and Higher Committee, *ibid.*, Jan. 30, 1939; text of Colonial Secretary's statement, *ibid.*, Feb. 8, 1939; see also issues of Feb. 2–4, 6–10 for other details.

11 From Anglo-Arab committee's report in G.B., *PP, 1938–39*, Cmd. 5974, pp. 10–11; McMahon-Husayn correspondence appears in Cmd. 5957; other British wartime statements in Cmd. 5964; for other details of the conference, see *The Times* (Lon), Feb. 11, 14, 23, 25, 1939; and AE, *Political Report, 1939*, pp. 12–15.

12 In talks with the Jews the British constantly stressed the "administrative necessity" of ensuring the support of the Arab countries in the event of war; *ibid.*, p. 15 and Weizmann, *Trial and Error*, pp. 401–12.

13 Text of first British proposals in *NYTimes*, Feb. 27, 1939 and AE, *Political Report, 1939*, pp. 15–17; text of second British plan, *ibid.*, pp. 21–24; for official Jewish and Arab reactions to each, see *ibid.*, pp. 18–21, 24; and *The Times* (Lon), Mar. 4, 7, 9, 14, and 18, 1939.

14 From text, *ibid.*, Apr. 29, 1939 (Reuters' translation); text of Roosevelt's letter in R. J. Bartlett, comp., *The Record of American Diplomacy*, pp. 596–98.

15 *SIA, 1938*, I, pp. 458–59; *Survey*, I, 51; for more details, see *The Times* (Lon), Apr. 12, 13, 24, May 1, 2, 1939; and *NYTimes*, Apr. 27, 29, May 1, 2, 15, 1939.

16 G.B., *PP, 1938–39*, Cmd. 6019.

17 *The Times* (Lon), May 22 and 30, 1939; see also *ibid.*, May 19, 1939; and *NYTimes*, May 30, 1939.

18 AHC, *Reply to the White Paper*; also summary in *NYTimes*, June 1, 1939.

19 Text of Weizmann's letter to Permanent Mandates Commission in JA, *The Jewish Case against the Palestine White Paper*, pp. 5–14.

20 The Colonial Secretary later explained to the Permanent Mandates Commission that "there was no suggestion of getting away from consultation with the Jewish Agency"; League of Nations, Permanent Mandates Commission, *Minutes of the Thirty-sixth Session*, p. 179. This explanation did not diminish the Agency's hostility to the consultative rights which Britain granted to the Arab countries, which, it was contended, "have under the terms of the Mandate [for Palestine] no *locus standi* whatsoever in relation to that country"; JA, *Jewish Case against the Palestine White Paper*, p. 6.

21 G.B., *PD, Commons*, vol. 347, col. 2154, from the speech of Herbert Mor-

rison; the records of the debate, *ibid.*, cols. 1947–2207.

[22] *The Times* (Lon), May 24, 1939.

[23] G.B., *PD, Lords,* vol. 113, col. 104.

[24] Permanent Mandates Commission, *Minutes of Thirty-sixth Session,* p. 275; the White Paper was reviewed at meetings held between June 15 and 29, 1939, *ibid.,* pp. 95–275. Churchill's warning in G.B., *PD, Commons,* vol. 347, col. 2186; statement by Department of State in *NYTimes,* May 30, 1939.

[25] *Cf.* Colonial Secretary's statement in G.B., *PD, Commons,* vol. 350, cols. 806–07.

[26] *The Times* (Lon), Mar. 28, Apr. 14, May 4, 1939; *PalPost,* Mar. 21, 22, Apr. 20, 28, May 4, 1939; and *Survey,* I, 48.

[27] *PalPost,* June 30, 1939; for other details, *cf.* G.B., *PD, Commons,* vol. 347, cols. 1442–43; *NYTimes,* June 18, 1939; *PalPost,* May 20, June 22, 1939; and *The Times* (Lon), July 12, 25, Aug. 15, 22, 1939.

[28] Text in *PalPost,* May 19, 1939.

[29] G.B., *PD, Commons,* vol. 350, cols. 761–884; text of Labor Party's resolution, *ibid.,* col. 762.

[30] *PalPost,* May–Aug. 1939; *Survey,* I, 54; AE, *Political Report, 1939,* pp. 75–76; *PalRev,* May 26, 1939, p. 94 and June 9, 1939, pp. 115–16; on Irgun's emissaries to the U.S., see *NYHerald-Tribune,* July 11, 1939; *NYWorld-Telegram,* July 13, 1939; and *New Republic,* Aug. 9, 1939.

[31] *PalRev,* June 30, 1939, p. 163; for rightist and clerical opinion, see editorials *ibid.,* June 23, 1939; *Ha-Boqer,* June 20, 1939; *Bustnai,* June 22, 1939; and *Ha-Zofeh,* July 11, 1939.

[32] Immigration ordinance in *PalGaz,* No. 877, Apr. 6, 1939, Supp. No. 1, p. 26; Colonial Secretary's statement in G.B., *PD, Commons,* vol. 350, cols. 811–12; details of first semi-annual immigration schedule in *NYTimes,* June 15, 1939.

[33] Text of Agency protest in AE, *Political Report, 1939,* app. xiii, p. 114; on Agency's land policy, see p. 65.

[34] See Shertok's figures in Twenty-first Zionist Congress, *Stenographic Report* (Heb.), p. 168; AE, *Political Report, 1939,* p. 70; *Survey,* II, 590–91; also *PalPost,* May 26, 1939 and *Ha-Arez,* June 19, 1939

[35] Text of resolutions in Twenty-first Zionist Congress, *Stenographic Report,* pp. 249–51; for views of moderates, see speeches of Weizmann, Ben Gurion, Gruenbaum, Brodetsky, Silver, Berl Katznelson, and Shertok, *ibid.,* pp. 1–8, 33–47, 80–87, 104–08, 127–32, 134–36, 142–46, and 165–76; for opposing views, *cf.* speeches of Suprassky, Bernstein, Berlin, Shagrai, and Grossman, pp. 53–62, 65–71, 99–103, and 116–18.

[36] ZE and AE, *Reports, 1946,* pp. 11–13; on origins of this *ad interim* body, see ZE and AE, *Reports, 1937,* pp. 49–50, 56 and *Reports, 1939,* pp. 16–17, 27.

[37] See, for example, M. Madzini, "The Question of the Non-Zionists," *Ha-Arez,* Aug. 18, 1939.

[38] Twenty-first Zionist Congress, *Stenographic Report,* pp. 222–23.

CHAPTER 8

[1] *Filastin, Al-Difaʻ,* and *Al-Sirat al-Mustaqim,* all published at Jaffa.

[2] On Arab losses, see *Survey,* I, 38, 43, 46, 49; economic data from *ibid.,* p. 474 and Nathan, *op. cit.,* pp. 155, 207–12, 427–43.

[3] A description of the War Council's scope of activities appears in G.B., *PD, Commons,* vol. 374, cols. 727–28; a compact analysis of Arab nationalist sentiment in the early war years and Britain's wartime strategic interest in the Near East may be found in Speiser, *op. cit.,* pp. 92–116.

[4] *PalPost,* June 7, 1940; for other details, see issues of Sept. 17, Oct. 2, 1939, June 26, July 4, 15, 16, 18, Aug. 7, 1940, and Nov. 11, 1941.

[5] *Ibid.,* Sept. 17, 1939, Feb. 3, 1940, Apr. 17, July 17, 1941, Apr. 23, Nov. 13, 1942; and *The Times* (Lon), June 13, 1940.

[6] Arab Office, Jer, *Evidence to AACI,* C.50, "Banks and Investment Companies"; and *PalPost,* Feb. 24, 1941.

[7] G.B., *PD, Commons,* vol. 358, cols. 444–45; the Land Transfer Regulations were published as G.B., *PP, 1939–40,* Cmd. 6180; on negotiations with Mufti in early weeks of war, see *The Times* (Lon), Nov. 2, 1939; *NYTimes,* Nov. 18, 1939; and *PalPost,* Nov. 23, 1939.

[8] Hilmi Pasha's statement from *NYTimes,* March 6, 1940; *The Times* (Lon), March 1, 1940; on indefinite deferment of constitutional changes *cf. Survey,* I, 53.

[9] *The Times* (Lon), Dec. 4, 1943; Gen. Henri Dentz was the Vichy High Commissioner for the Levant States from Jan.

1941 until the British and Free French forces occupied these mandated territories in July of that year. Other data from *Survey*, I, 58–60; G.B., *PD, Commons*, vol. 378, cols. 178, 660; and *PD, Lords*, vol. 122, col. 216.

[10] Text of Eden's Mansion House speech in *The Times* (Lon), May 30, 1941; *cf.* Speiser, *op. cit.*, pp. 108–09 and 173–78, for an analysis of British policy in the Arab East; other data from Hourani, *Syria and Lebanon*, pp. 233–52; and *PalPost*, Sept. 26, 1941.

[11] As translated *idem*.

[12] As quoted and summarized *ibid.*, June 15, 1942.

[13] Shim'oni, *op. cit.*, p. 406, note 48.

[14] *Survey*, II, 877; other details on pp. 873–78; *PalPost*, Sept. 24, Dec. 9, 1940, Nov. 6, 1941, Mar. 4, 9, Apr. 24, 1942; the general manager of the Near East Broadcasting Station until the summer of 1944 was Shams-al-Din Marsak, a British major who professed to have become a Muslim; *Al-Difa'*, Aug. 30, 1944.

[15] Summary in *PalPost*, Feb. 18, 1942 of editorials appearing on preceding day in *Al-Difa'*, *Filastin*, and *Al-Sirat al-Mustaqim;* see also *PalPost*, June 14, 1940.

[16] App. to S. de Chair, *The Golden Carpet*, p. 244; *cf.* also J. B. Glubb, *The Story of the Arab Legion*, pp. 251–94; statistics from *The Times* (Lon), Aug. 6, Dec. 9, 1942; and *PalPost*, July 8, Aug. 4, 1942.

[17] *Survey*, II, 1047–70, contains a list of these committees and boards and their composition; other information from *PalPost*, Sept. 11, 1940; and *NYTimes*, Jan. 18, Apr. 9, 1940.

[18] G. B., *PD, Commons*, vol. 374, col. 728; and Shim'oni, *op. cit.*, p. 408.

[19] A brief history of the MESC was issued by G.B., Ministry of Information, Cairo, *The Work of the Middle East Supply Centre* (July 1945); on Palestine War Supply Board, see *Survey*, II, 985.

[20] In converting the Palestine pound into American dollars for the period after 1939, it is assumed that each pound is worth four dollars. The statistical and other data are based on *Survey*, II, 559, 562, 728, 733, 835, III, 1298–1301; P.G., Dept. of Statistics, *Statistical Abstract of Palestine, 1944–45*, p. 51; Nathan, *op. cit.*, pp. 162, 303, 329; Shim'oni, *op. cit.*, p. 365; and *PalPost*, July 9, 1942.

[21] P.G., Dept. of Labour, *Annual Report for 1942* (abr. ed.), pp. 3–6; Shim'oni, *op. cit.*, pp. 189–90, 359; *The Times* (Lon), Nov. 2, 1940; and *PalPost*, Oct. 18, 1940, July 21, Sept. 16, 1942.

[22] P.G., Dept. of Labour, *Annual Report for 1942*, pp. 3, 15; *Survey*, II, 764; a penetrating analysis of the Arab trade-union movement may be found in Shim'oni, *op. cit.*, pp. 359–71; see also *PalPost*, Oct. 6, 13, Nov. 10, 1942.

[23] A. Khoushi, *Palestine Labour League*, pp. 4–5; the Palestine Government's Labor Dept., on the other hand, declared that the League had an enrollment of only 500, but could speak for some 1,200 Arab workers; *Annual Report for 1942*, p. 16.

CHAPTER 9

[1] Text in *NJ*, Sept. 1939, p. 318; as for the communists in Palestine, they were still being placed under police custody as late as Sept. 1941; *PalPost*, Sept. 9, 1941.

[2] Text, *ibid.*, Sept. 4, 1939.

[3] *Idem; cf.* also issue of Sept. 7, 1939; statistics from ZE and AE, *Reports, 1946*, p. 95; these figures were lower than those appearing in *PalPost*, Oct. 3, 1939 and AE, *Political Report, 1946*, p. 32, which declared that 136,043 had registered.

[4] ZE and AE, *Reports, 1946*, p. 94; also *cf.* D. Ben Gurion, "Jewish Army," *Jewish Frontier*, Feb. 1942, pp. 4–7.

[5] *NJ*, Sept. 1939, p. 317.

[6] See, for example, text of memorandum by Prime Minister Churchill to Colonial Secretary Lord Lloyd, June 28, 1940, in Winston Churchill, *Their Finest Hour*, pp. 173–74.

[7] Revisionist quot. from *PalPost*, Sept. 6, 1939; govt. statement from *Survey*, I, 59; reference to Irgun statement in *PalPost*, Sept. 11, 1939.

[8] Lohamei Herut Israel, *Yair* (stenciled), p. 30 and *Survey*, II, 602; other data from *Eshnav*, No. 103, Oct. 5, 1945, pp. 2–3; J. Z. Lurie, "The Inside Story," *The New Palestine*, Feb. 21, 1947, p. 80; G.B., *PD, Commons*, vol. 362, col. 428; and *PalRev*, Aug. 15, 1941, p. 59.

[9] Sir James Grigg, Secretary of State for War, in G.B., *PD, Commons*, vol. 382, cols. 1271, 1273; enlistment figures from same source and *Survey*, III, 1316–17; other data from *The Times* (Lon), June 6, Dec. 9, 1942, and Mar. 4, 1943; G.B., *PD, Commons*, vol. 374, col. 2019; ZE and

AE, *Reports, 1946*, pp. 94–103; I. Cohen, *Britain's Nameless Ally* (1942); and M. P. Waters, *Haganah: Jewish Self-Defence in Palestine*, pp. 30–42.

[10] D. Ben Gurion, "Jewish Army," *Jewish Frontier*, Feb. 1942, p. 7 and Sir James Grigg in G.B., *PD, Commons*, vol. 382, col. 1272; other information from AE, *Political Report, 1946*, pp. 32–37; and ZE and AE, *Reports, 1946*, p. 95.

[11] Text in *NJ*, Nov.–Dec. 1941, p. 23.

[12] AE, *Political Report, 1946*, pp. 34–36.

[13] From Lord Moyne's account in G.B., *PD, Lords*, vol. 121, cols. 102–04.

[14] Agudas Israel World Organization, NY Branch, *Second Confidential Report, Jan. 1–June 30, 1942* (stenciled), p. 13; American Jewish Committee, unpublished correspondence, M. D. Waldman to Dr. A. D. Margolin, Apr. 3, 1942. For outline of Agency plan, see speech of Col. V. A. Cazalet in G.B., *PD, Commons*, vol. 382, cols. 1242–48.

[15] *NYTimes*, Jan. 5, 1942; on earlier activities of Irgun spokesmen in U.S., see *American Jewish Chronicle*, Feb. 15, 1940, pp. 2, 10–11; Marie Syrkin, "Revisionists at Work," *Jewish Frontier*, Mar. 1940, pp. 15–18.

[16] Magnes statement in *PalPost*, June 29, 1941; editorial *ibid.*, July 1, 1941; regarding pressures against shirkers, see *ibid.*, July 22, 1942 and Feb. 28, 1943.

[17] Nathan, *op. cit.*, pp. 326–27; JA, *Report, 1940 with Addenda for 1941*, pp. 9–10; ZE and AE, *Reports, 1946*, pp. 407, 415–16; *NJ*, Oct. 1939, p. 4; and *PalPost*, Sept. 4, 1939.

[18] *Survey*, II, 734; JA, *Report, 1940*, p. 12; *NJ*, Jan. 1940, pp. 42–44; Nathan, *op. cit.*, p. 212.

[19] *Ibid.*, pp. 231–37, 253–55, 333–37, 495–98, 510–14; JA, *Report, 1940*, pp. 8–9; ZE and AE, *Reports, 1946*, pp. 407–17; *Survey*, I, 526, 528–29; Histadrut, *Memorandum to AACI*, 144–51; *NYTimes*, Dec. 8, 1940; and *NJ*, Sept. 1941, p. 185.

[20] From translation of editorial in *PalRev*, Sept. 1, 1941, p. 69–70; see also editorials in *Davar*, Sept. 8, 1941 and *HaArez*, Sept. 10, 1941; Histadrut statistics from Muenzner, *Jewish Labour Economy in Palestine*, pp. 11–15, 87–113.

[21] At the Zionist Congress in 1939 Mapai, ha-Shomer ha-Za'ir, and their world-wide counterparts were represented by 216 or 41 per cent of the 527 delegates; Twenty-first Zionist Congress,

Stenographic Report, p. xxvi. The members of the Histadrut and their families numbered about one-third of the entire Palestine Jewish population; Muenzner, *op. cit.*, p. 11.

CHAPTER 10

[1] The precise figure was 43.5 per cent for the years 1919–42; Gurevich, *Jewish Population of Palestine*, p. 8.

[2] *PalPost*, July 17, 1939.

[3] Text of Agency protest in *NJ*, Nov.–Dec. 1939, pp. 21–22; for other details, *cf.* *PalPost*, Oct. 31, Nov. 28, 29, Dec. 24, 1939, Jan. 11, 1940; and *Survey*, I, 58.

[4] The Land Transfer Regulations in Cmd. 6180; amendments in Nathan, *op. cit.*, p. 187.

[5] Text of censored statement in *NJ*, Mar.–Apr. 1940, p. 77; other data in G.B., *PD, Commons*, vol. 358, cols. 1194–95; "Uncensored," *Jewish Frontier*, May 1940, pp. 10–12; *PalPost*, Feb. 29, Mar. 1, 3–8, 1940; *NJ*, Feb. 1940, p. 53 (statement by Agency's Lon Office), 54–55 (Jer Office), and Mar.–Apr. 1940, p. 77.

[6] *PalPost*, March 6, 1940.

[7] Colonial Secretary's statement in G.B., *PD, Commons*, vol. 358, col. 448 [the full debate, cols. 411–530] and *The Times* (Lon), Feb. 29, 1940.

[8] Thus, for instance, Churchill, asked whether the British Government "still adheres to the policy of the Balfour Declaration," replied that "there has been no change in the policy . . . with respect to Palestine." The identical answer was repeated a moment later in reply to the question as to whether "the Government stand by the principle laid down in the White Paper"; G.B., *PD, Commons*, vol. 373, col. 1396. On Zionist entrée to the War Cabinet, *cf.* Weizmann, *Trial and Error*, pp. 424–37.

[9] G.B., *PD, Lords*, vol. 122, cols. 943–44; see also Weizmann in *Jewish Frontier*, June 1942, p. 9.

[10] *Survey*, I, 263–71.

[11] A. Granovsky, "The Struggle for Land," *PalYear*, 2 (1945–46), pp. 424–25, 428; other data not only from this article but from Jewish National Fund, *Pe'ulot* (1945), and Nathan, *op. cit.*, p. 188.

[12] *Survey*, I, 177–78; other details from G.B., *PD, Commons*, vol. 350, cols. 807, 811–12; *NJ*, Nov.–Dec. 1939, p. 21, Jan. 1941, pp. 41–42, May 1941, p. 124; *NY-*

Times, Dec. 28, 1940; and *PalPost*, Dec. 29, 1940.

[13] *The Times* (Lon), Mar. 28, 1940; see also Colonial Secretary's references to same subject in G.B., *PD, Commons*, vol. 358, cols. 1961–62 and vol. 359, cols. 147–48; and *NJ*, Mar. 1942, p. 76.

[14] Official communiqués in *PalPost*, Nov. 21, 25, 1940; other information, including report of the government's investigative commission, in issues of Dec. 19, 1940, Mar. 18, 1941, Feb. 27, 1942; ZE and AE, *Reports, 1946*, p. 80; *NJ*, Mar. 1942, p. 74, Apr. 1942, p. 93.

[15] Based on ZE and AE, *Reports, 1946*, p. 154; *Survey*, I, 185; and official figures in *PalPost*, Apr. 18, 1943.

[16] ZE and AE, *Reports, 1946*, pp. 78–79.

[17] *NJ*, Mar. 1942, p. 76.

[18] *PalRev*, May 24, 1940, p. 26; similar editorials in *Ha-Arez* and *Ha-Zofeh*, May 12, 1940; and *NJ*, May 1940, p. 121.

[19] Editorial, *ibid.*, Dec. 1940, p. 25 and D. Ben Gurion, "The Palestine Administration and the Jews," *ibid.*, Nov.–Dec. 1941, pp. 19–20; *cf.* also Jan. 1941, p. 42.

[20] G.B., *PD, Lords*, vol. 122, col. 218 and *Commons*, vol. 377, col. 371; other examples, *ibid.*, vol. 358, cols. 1195–96; vol. 359, cols. 547–48; vol. 374, cols. 1765–66; vol. 378, cols. 640–41.

[21] *PalRev*, Dec. 1, 1941, p. 122; *cf.* also *NJ*, Nov.–Dec. 1941, p. 27.

[22] S. Levenberg, *The Jews and Palestine*, pp. 240–41.

[23] AE, *Political Report, 1946*, p. 8; Smuts' statements in *NJ*, May 1941, pp. 140–41 and Nov.–Dec. 1941, p. 29.

[24] American Palestine Committee, *Proceedings of Second Annual Dinner* (1942); see also AE, *Political Report, 1946*, p. 8.

[25] *PalRev*, Sept. 1, 1941, p. 67.

[26] ZE and AE, *Reports, 1946*, pp. 172, 199; AE, *Political Report, 1946*, p. 8; *Pal-Post*, Oct. 22, 1941, Mar. 9, 1942.

CHAPTER 11

[1] *Middle East Opinion* [Cairo], Aug. 26, 1946; *cf.* the Mufti's later statement to H. J. J. Sargint, foreign correspondent of the North American Newspaper Alliance, *ibid.*, Oct. 28, 1946 and *NYTimes*, Oct. 6, 1946.

[2] *Ibid.*, Sept. 27, 1939; photostat of voucher prepared in the office of the French Inspector General of Police in the Levant States in Nation Associates, *The Arab Higher Committee* (1947), unpaginated; other information from *The Times* (Lon), May 12 and 13, 1939; *Pal-Post*, Sept. 17, 1939; and *NYTimes*, Oct. 19, 1939.

[3] *The Times* (Lon), Oct. 18, 1939; see also Speiser, *op. cit.*, pp. 86–87; and Hourani, *op. cit.*, pp. 210–30.

[4] Information derived mainly from two British intelligence reports from Baghdad, entitled "A Short History of Enemy Subversive Activity in 'Iraq 1935–1941" (April 1945) and "The Ex-Mufti's Role in the 'Iraqi Revolt" (Dec. 1941); selected passages of the first report and a verbatim reproduction of the second appeared in American Christian Palestine Committee, *The Arab War Effort*, pp. 30–40; quot. in text from p. 33. The second report formed the basis of despatches sent from the Near East by C. L. Sulzberger in *NYTimes*, Feb. 2, 3, 1942 and of his article on "German Preparations in the Middle East," section II, *Foreign Affairs*, 20 (July 1942), pp. 666–71. For other contemporary accounts of pro-Axis activity in the Arab East, see *NYTimes*, May 11, 16, 18, June 1, 1941, Feb. 1, 1942. An article sympathetic to the Mufti is that by V. Sheean, "Personal Opinion: the Mufti of Jerusalem," *Asia and the Americas*, 46 (Aug. 1946), pp. 373–74; reprinted in *Middle East Opinion*, Feb. 10, 1947.

[5] Newcombe's version of the negotiations in R. Maugham, *Approach to Palestine*; Arab versions in M. F. Abcarius, *Palestine through the Fog of Propaganda*, p. 212 and *Middle East Opinion*, Nov. 11, 1946, which translated from the Arabic an interview granted to another Cairo weekly, *Al-Usbu'*, by Dr. Ahmad Bey al-Qadri, director-general of the Syrian Public Health Dept., who claimed to have taken part in the talks.

[6] American Christian Palestine Committee, *The Arab War Effort*, pp. 35–36; other data not only from this intelligence report but from Sulzberger in *NYTimes*, Mar. 12, 1942; for detailed lists of Palestine Arabs who joined the Mufti in Baghdad, see *Arab War Effort*, pp. 35–40 and Shim'oni, *op. cit.*, p. 315, note 1.

[7] Text in Nation Associates, *Arab Higher Committee*.

[8] *NYTimes*, Apr. 7, 1941; *cf.* also issues of Jan. 12, Mar. 6, 7, 20, 24, 27, 29, Apr. 5, May 26, 1941.

9 Text of the *fatwa* in *Oriente Mo-derno*, 21 (1941), pp. 552–53; see also *NYTimes*, Apr. 20, May 14, 18, 1941.

10 On Levant recruits, cf. *ibid.*, May 26, 1941; for details of attack on Jewish quarter in Baghdad, see Nation Associates, *Arab Higher Committee*, p. 5 of introd. and E. A. Mowrer in *NYPost*, June 4, 1946; both quote from the report of an official Iraqi investigative commission.

11 G.B., *PD, Lords*, vol. 122, col. 216; other information from Glubb, *Story of Arab Legion*, pp. 261–94; P. van Paassen, *That Day Alone*, pp. 326–34; *The Times* (Lon), Sept. 15, 22, 1941; and *NYTimes*, Oct. 28, 1941. For dispersal of Mufti's Palestine followers, see Shim'oni, *op. cit.*, pp. 315–16 and *The Times* (Lon), Feb. 16, 1942.

12 *NYTimes*, Oct. 28, 1941. The following account of the Mufti in Axis Europe roughly covers the period between Oct. 1941 and Dec. 1942 and is not intended to be exhaustive, but merely accents those factors bearing on internal Palestine Arab politics. It is based on contemporary sources as well as documents seized by the Allies after V-E Day. Photostats of many of these documents appeared in Nation Associates, *Arab Higher Committee;* extensive quots. from the same and other documents were reproduced by Nation Associates, *The Palestine Problem and Proposals for its Solution* and by E. A. Mowrer in his series on the Mufti in *NYPost* and *The Philadelphia Record*, June 3–7, 10–13, 15, 1946.

13 Quots. on Italian and German broadcasts from Mowrer, *NYPost*, June 5, 1946; statement by Wilhelmstrasse spokesman in *The Times* (Lon), Nov. 8, 1941.

14 From the English translation of the Mufti's diary of this conversation in Nation Associates, *Arab Higher Committee*, which also contains a photostat of the original Arabic.

15 From English translation, *ibid.*, where a photostat of the original Italian also appears.

16 Photostat of Mufti's Arab Office stationery in American Christian Palestine Committee, *Arab War Effort*, p. 23; on Templars, see *PalRev*, Sept. 8–15, 1939, p. 324 and *PalPost*, July 6, 1944.

17 Shim'oni, *op. cit.*, p. 317; and *The Times* (Lon), March 20, 1942.

18 From translation in Nation Associates, *Arab Higher Committee*. When

Eichmann was Gauleiter of Vienna in 1938, an unsigned article in *Ha-Arez*, Nov. 27, 1938, declared that he was a German Templar, born in Sarona, Palestine. This theory was widely believed in the Yishuv thereafter; see, for example, editorial in *PalPost*, as late as June 20, 1945. On the other hand, Wisliceny, a war criminal who had worked with Eichmann, stated in his sworn affadavit of Dec. 2, 1946, that Eichmann was born in Germany and had visited Palestine only once in Sept. 1937.

CHAPTER 12

1 Weizmann speech to Executive Committee of American Jewish Committee, Jan. 20, 1940 (unpub.); quot. from *NJ*, Sept. 1939, p. 347.

2 *Jewish Frontier*, Sept. 1941, p. 23; the article, entitled "The Zionist Situation Today," on pp. 22–24.

3 From "Palestine's Role in the Solution of the Jewish Problem," *Foreign Affairs*, 20 (Jan. 1942), p. 337; see also *NJ*, Sept. 1941, p. 195.

4 Nominally, the non-Zionist members of the Agency Executive elected in 1937 —D. W. Senator, A. Ruppin, Mrs. R. Jacobs, M. B. Hexter, and M. J. Karpf [the last three Americans]—retained their posts; ZE and AE, *Reports, 1946*, p. 71. But the three Americans ceased active duty; Ruppin died in Jan. 1943; and Senator had no portfolio. For non-Zionist position, see M. J. Karpf, "Zionist and Non-Zionist Relationships in the Enlarged Jewish Agency," *Universal Jewish Encyclopedia*, 6, pp. 92–93; L. N. Shub, "The Jewish Agency and the Non-Zionists," prepared for Foreign Affairs Dept., American Jewish Committee (unpub.). On Agency negotiations with American non-Zionists in this period, cf. *NJ*, Aug. 1941, p. 174, Sept. 1941, p. 195 [for Zionist viewpoint]; American Jewish Committee, *Thirty-fifth Annual Report*, pp. 46–47, *Thirty-sixth Annual Report*, pp. 26, 39–41, 43–50.

5 *Jewish Frontier*, May 1942, pp. 3–4; *PalPost*, May 27, 1942.

6 *Ibid.*, Nov. 12, 1942, for results of vote; on internal Mapai split cf. *Ha-Po'el ha-Za'ir*, Nov. 9, 1942, pp. 2, 5–14; *Pal-Post*, Oct. 28, Nov. 1, 1942; *Ha-Arez*, Nov. 1, 1942; *PalRev*, Dec. 1, 1942, p. 123;

Furrows, Apr. 1944, pp. 17–21, July 1944, pp. 8–12.

[7] Based on report in *Ha-Arez*, Nov. 2, 1942 and editorial in issue of the following day; on prewar antecedents, see *Pal-Rev*, Sept. 9, 1938, p. 325.

[8] From an article entitled "Our Path after the White Paper," *Darkenu* (Heb. brochure), pp. 6–10.

[9] *PalPost*, Oct. 9, 12, 1939; the League's draft constitution may be found in *Darkenu*, pp. 49–50.

[10] From the English translation in Esco, *op. cit.*, II, 1162–63; other details on pp. 1161–62 and *PalRev*, Aug. 30, 1940, p. 82.

[11] From internal circular of League, dated Oct. 1942.

[12] From internal circular of League, dated Dec. 20, 1942; other data from ha-Shomer ha-Za'ir Arab Dept., Bulletin No. 8, Nov. 20, 1942, translated into Eng. by Hadassah, Committee for the Study of Arab-Jewish Relations, *Bulletin* [stenciled], May 1943, pp. 10–11; and A. Cohen, "Inactivity—How Long, an Open Letter to the Histadrut Executive," *Ha-Shomer ha-Za'ir* [Heb.], Jan. 13, 1943, p. 4.

[13] *Cf.* editorials in *Ha-Boqer*, *Ha-Mashqif*, and *Ha-Zofeh*, Sept. 2, 1942; *PalRev*, Sept. 1–16, 1942, pp. 76–77; and *Ha-Arez*, Sept. 14, 1942.

[14] J. L. Magnes, "Palestine and Arab Union" (June 22, 1941) and "Palestine and Arab Union: Two Initial Steps" (July 28, 1941); reprints.

[15] Text in M. Buber, J. L. Magnes, and M. Smilansky, *Palestine, a Bi-National State*, p. 29.

[16] *PalRev*, Sept. 1–16, 1942, p. 76; *Ha-Zofeh*, Sept. 2, 1942; *PalPost*, Sept. 25, Oct. 7, 1942.

[17] *The New Palestine*, Nov. 6, 1942, p. 2; Hadassah with its close to 90,000 members was the second largest Zionist body in the U.S. The American affiliates of Mizrahi and Mapai approved Biltmore at a later date; Esco, *op. cit.*, II, 1087. Meanwhile, the American branches of ha-Shomer ha-Za'ir and the Left Zionist Workers withdrew from the American Emergency Committee for Zionist Affairs, following its espousal of statism.

[18] *Jewish Frontier*, June 1942, p. 14; full text pp. 11–18.

[19] Lohamei Herut Israel, *Yair*, p. 30; other biographical data pp. 6–8, 25–31; see also *PalPost*, Feb. 13, 1942.

[20] Lohamey Heruth Israel, *For Justice, Freedom and Peace*, p. 23; the founders of the new terrorist society selected this name to distinguish it from the Revisionist group, which, in full, was called the National Military Organization in Palestine (*Irgun Zvai Leumi be-Erez Israel*); *Survey*, II, 604.

[21] G.B., *PD, Lords*, vol. 123, col. 69; also *Eshnav*, No. 103, Oct. 5, 1945. For supporting evidence of these charges, *cf.* *He-Hazit* [illegal Heb. organ of the Freedom Fighters, as the Stern Gang called itself after 1943], No. 2, Aug. 1943, in which it was argued that, since Fascist Italy had remained "neutral" on the Palestine problem, there was no reason why its assistance should not be courted. Other data from *Survey*, II, 604; *PalPost*, Sept. 17, Oct. 8, 1940, Dec. 4, 1941, Jan. 11, 13, 1942; *The Times* (Lon), Sept. 23, 1940, Feb. 10, 1942; G. Frank, "The Truth about the Terrorists," *The Nation*, 159 (Dec. 2, 1944), pp. 685–86; interviews with leaders of the terrorist group by H. Bigart in *NYHerald-Tribune*, May 1, 1947 and C. Daniel, *NYTimes*, Aug. 25, 1947; and Lohamey Heruth Israel, *For Justice, Freedom and Peace*, p. 24.

[22] *PalPost*, Jan. 21, 22, 27, 28, Feb. 1, 3, 5, 9, 13, Mar. 5, 23, Apr. 23, 24, May 5, 6, 10, 1942; *Survey*, II, 604–05; G.B., *PD, Lords*, vol. 123, col. 69; and Lohamey Heruth Israel, *For Justice, Freedom and Peace*, pp. 24–25.

[23] *PalPost*, Jan. 25, Apr. 24, 1942; *cf.* editorials in issue of Jan. 27, 1942 and in *PalRev*, Feb. 1, 1942, p. 157.

CHAPTER 13

[1] G.B., *PD, Commons*, vol. 387, col. 139; *cf.* also Eden's remarks in vol. 445, Dec. 12, 1947, col. 1394. For other data, see Speiser, *op. cit.*, pp. 96–99, 116, 175—81; *Survey*, II, 877, III, 1347; and Sulzberger in *NYTimes*, May 6, 9, 1943.

[2] G.B., *PD, Commons*, vol. 426, cols. 986–89, 1254.

[3] *Ibid.*, col. 989 and Churchill's report on the Yalta conference in *NYTimes*, Feb. 28, 1945.

[4] G. B., *PD, Commons*, vol. 395, cols. 346–48; although the Palestine Government issued no formal statements at the time, it was manifest—by the gradual resumption of activities on the part of the Arab politicians and the sudden airing of

nationalist grievances in the Arab press after the beginning of November 1942—that the prohibiting orders had been allowed to lapse.

[5] Text of Colonial Secretary's statement in G.B., *PD, Commons*, vol. 393, col. 1152; quot. from White Paper in Cmd. 6019, p. 11; for other data, see *Survey*, I, 263–71 and Nathan, *op. cit.*, p. 188.

[6] *Survey*, I, 182; other information from ZE and AE, *Reports, 1946*, pp. 157–58; AE, *Political Report, 1946*, p. 47; *Statistical Abstract of Palestine, 1944–45*, p. 36.

[7] Weizmann quot. in AE, *Political Report, 1946*, p. 38; War Office statement in *The Times* (Lon), Sept. 20, 1944; and Churchill quot. from text in *NYTimes*, Sept. 29, 1944.

[8] G.B., *PD, Commons*, vol. 426, cols. 1259, 1261.

[9] Intergovernmental Committee on Refugees, *Report of the Fourth Plenary Session*, p. 22; this report includes a brief history of the ICR through the summer of 1944; for the official British report of the Bermuda conference, see G.B., *PD, Commons*, vol. 389, cols. 1117–1203.

[10] *The Christian Science Monitor*, Jan. 24, 1944; see also personal accounts of WRB representative in Turkey, I. A. Hirschmann: "Palestine—as a Refuge from Fascism," *Survey Graphic*, May 1945, pp. 195–97, 265–69; and *Life Line to a Promised Land*.

[11] On background of American part-ownership of the Iraq Petroleum Company, see U.S., S.D., *Mandate for Palestine*, p. 25 ff.; American oil investments in the Arabian Peninsula are treated by Speiser, *op. cit.*, pp. 125–33; R. F. Mikesell and H. B. Chenery, *Arabian Oil*, pp. 44–70; and K. S. Twitchell, *Saudi Arabia*, pp. 122–23, 148–56. For lack of American official interest in the Near East as late as 1941, cf. R. E. Sherwood, *Roosevelt and Hopkins*, pp. 315–16. Regarding U.S. involvement in the Middle East after 1942, see G. S. McClellan, "Palestine and America's Role in the Middle East," *Foreign Policy Reports*, 21 (July 1, 1945), pp. 100, 104–05; J. M. Landis, "Middle East Challenge," *Fortune*, Sept. 1945 (repr.); and Sulzberger in *NYTimes*, May 5, 6, 8, Aug. 16, 1943.

[12] First quot. from statement by J. A. Moffett, the oil company's representative in the negotiations, *ibid.*, March 24, 1944, March 29, 1947; text of Ickes state-

ment, *ibid.*, Feb. 6, 1944. *Cf.* also H. Feis, *Seen from E.A.*, pp. 93–190.

[13] From statement by Senator Owen Brewster and based on Dept. of State report on the subject, *NYTimes* and *NYHerald-Tribune*, Oct. 30, 1947; on other data, cf. Landis, "Middle East Challenge," *Fortune*, Sept. 1945 (repr.) and G. A. Brownell, "American Aviation in the Middle East," *MEJ*, 1 (Oct. 1947), pp. 401–16.

[14] Letter to ibn Sa'ud, dated May 26, 1943, as cited by B. Crum, *Behind the Silken Curtain*, p. 39; statement to American Zionist leaders in *NYTimes*, March 10, 1944; Pinkerton letter, as reported in *Al-Difa'*, June 21, 1944.

[15] J. F. Byrnes, *Speaking Frankly*, p. 22.

[16] Speiser, *op. cit.*, pp. 100–06; for more extended treatment, see Hourani, *Syria*, pp. 146–57, 163–230, 279–307.

[17] For a Russian view of the Straits question, see G. Meiksins, "Russia, Britain and the Straits," *The American Review on the Soviet Union*, 7 (May 1946), pp. 3–15; Byrnes, *Speaking Frankly*, p. 77 reveals the position of Stalin and Molotov at Potsdam in 1945; on Russian interest in Iranian oil, *cf.* W. S. Haas, *Iran*, pp. 238–39 and G. Lenczowski, *Russia and the West in Iran, 1918–1948*, pp. 216–34.

[18] For a catalogue of Czarist Russia's interests, *cf.* N. Verney and G. Dambmann, *Les puissances étrangères dans le Levant*, pp. 127–34; for other data, see F. H. Kisch, *Palestine Diary*, pp. 66, 90, 127, 134, 142; and definition of "Sionizm" in *Brief Soviet Encyclopedia* (Rus., 1943).

[19] Speiser, *op. cit.*, p. 185; J. S. Curtiss, "The Russian Orthodox Church during World War II," *The American Review on the Soviet Union*, 7 (Aug. 1946), pp. 32–44; "The Non-Orthodox Religions in the U.S.S.R. during and after World War II," *ibid.*, 8 (Nov. 1946), pp. 3–14; K. Bayastan, "Moslems in the USSR," Soviet Embassy, Washington, *Information Bulletin*, Aug. 14, 1946. For examples of local press coverage of Patriarch Alexei's visit to the Near East in May–June 1945, see *Filastin*, May 31, June 1–3, 5–7, 1945; *Al-Difa'*, May 31, June 1, 3–7, 1945; *La Bourse Égyptienne* and *Le Journal d'Égypte*, June 6–8, 1945.

[20] *PalPost*, May 2, 7, June 4, 11, Aug. 17, 1944; *Davar*, May 22, 1944; *Ha-Arez*, June 11, 1944; *Al-Difa'*, May 3, June 1, 4, 1944; and *NYTimes*, June 1, 1944.

CHAPTER 14

[1] *Al-Sirat al-Mustaqim*, March 29, 1943; see also *Al-Difa'*, Sept. 9, 1943 and *Filastin*, June 23, 1944.

[2] Among the leaders of the extra-Palestine branches of the Istiqlal movement were the then premiers of Iraq and Lebanon, Nuri Pasha al-Sa'id and Riyad al-Sulh, as well as the then President of Syria, Shukri al-Quwwatli. 'Awni 'Abd-al-Hadi issued political statements as "the chief of the Istiqlal Party" (*'Amid Hizb al-Istiqlal*) and was thus regarded by the other Arab politicians; *cf. ibid.*, Sept. 26, 1944.

[3] Shim'oni, *op. cit.*, pp. 406–07; *Filastin*, Jan. 26, 1943; and *PalPost*, Feb. 16, 1943.

[4] A detailed account of the conference, including a complete list of the delegates, appeared in *Filastin*, Nov. 12, 1943. There were branches of the chamber of commerce in Jerusalem, Jaffa, Nablus, Haifa, Gaza, Nazareth, Acre, and Tulkarm.

[5] For details of the second conference, see *Al-Difa'*, Nov. 19, 1943; on repercussions of the Lebanese crisis, *cf. ibid.*, Nov. 14–18, 1943 and *Filastin*, Nov. 14, 16–18, 1943.

[6] Although the Fund remained inactive between 1936–41, a new board of directors, headed by Ahmad Hilmi Pasha with al-Hajj Ibrahim as one of the members, had taken over the administration in 1941. When the board was enlarged in Feb. 1944, 'Abd-al-Hadi was added; P.G., "The Sanduq al-Ummah" (typescript); see also Shim'oni, *op. cit.*, pp. 352–53. At the end of 1943 the Arab National Bank had branches in Jerusalem, Hebron, Haifa, Jaffa, Nablus, Gaza, Tulkarm, Acre, Ramlah, Tiberias, Baysan, Lydda, Safad, and Nazareth; Arab National Bank, *Tenth Annual Report* (Arabic, 1944). Other data from *Al-Difa'*, June 23, July 19, Oct. 12, 13, 29, Nov. 15, 1944; and *Filastin*, June 30, Aug. 21, 1944, Jan. 15, 1945.

[7] *Survey*, I, 66; Shim'oni, *op. cit.*, p. 319; and *Al-Difa'*, May 1, 2, 4, 1944.

[8] Tawfiq Salih was pensioned on the eve of the war from the government Dept. of Migration, where he had risen to the rank of chief clerk; Shim'oni, *op. cit.*, p. 218. For biographical details of Ghuri, see *Oriente Moderno*, 16 (1936), pp. 401, 462; *PalPost*, Oct. 12, 1937, June 12, 1939.

[9] *Al-Difa'*, July 16, 1944; other details, *ibid.*, May 2, 4, July 5, 11, Aug. 13, Oct. 18, 29, Dec. 28, 1944; *Filastin*, May 31, Aug. 10, 1944; and Shim'oni, *op. cit.*, pp. 406–07, 410.

[10] *Al-Difa'*, Aug. 13, 1944 and *Al-Hoda* (NY), May 27, 1944.

[11] *Filastin*, Aug. 4, Sept. 5, 26, 1944; *Al-Difa'*, Sept. 4, 6, 10, 13, 17, 18, 22, 1944.

[12] *Ibid.*, Oct. 23, Nov. 3, Dec. 1, 1944, Jan. 11, Feb. 28, 1945; *Filastin*, Nov. 3, 10, 1944.

[13] Extracts of the British counterintelligence reports on the Iraqi expedition in American Christian Palestine Committee, *Arab War Effort*, pp. 43–47; other details from *PalPost*, Oct. 11, 17, 1944; Shim'oni, *op. cit.*, p. 317; S. P. Brewer in *NYTimes*, Jan. 24, 1948.

[14] One or more of the leaders absented themselves from most of these meetings; *cf. Filastin*, Apr. 7, 14, 21, 1945; for other details, see *ibid.*, Sept. 26, 1944, Jan. 14, Apr. 15, 1945; *Al-Difa'*, May 2, 3, 5, 7, 1944; *PalPost*, Feb. 28, Apr. 2, 1944.

[15] Shim'oni, *op. cit.*, pp. 340–42.

[16] *Al-Ittihad*, June 25, 1944; other data from issues of June 18, July 9, Aug. 6, 13, Sept. 10, 1944; *Survey Supp.*, p. 138.

[17] *Survey*, II, 763–66; *Filastin*, Feb. 9, 1945.

[18] *Al-Difa'*, Aug. 22, 1944; other data from issues of Sept. 5, 29, 1944, Apr. 26, 1945; *Filastin*, July 5, Aug. 15, Sept. 1, 24, 1944; *Survey*, II, 562, 565–66, 569, III, 1300–01; *Survey Supp.*, p. 65; Nathan, *op. cit.*, pp. 336–37.

[19] *Cf.* arms seizures from Arabs in *Survey*, II, 592–94.

[20] *Akhir Sa'ah* (Cairo), Sept. 10, 1944, p. 13; other information from *Statistical Abstract of Palestine, 1944–45*, pp. 185–86, 197; *Survey*, II, 729; *Al-Difa'*, July 12, Aug. 2, 27, Sept. 17, Dec. 24, 1944; *Filastin*, July 25, Aug. 21, Sept. 24, 1944; and *PalPost*, March 31, Apr. 10, May 15, 19, 1944.

[21] From the Arabic text which appeared in *Al-Ahram* (Cairo), Oct. 8, 1944 and in *Al-Difa'*, Oct. 9, 1944; since 'Alami did not represent a government, he did not sign the Protocol. For analyses of the background of the conference, see Speiser, *op. cit.*, pp. 107–10; and C. A. Hourani, "The Arab League in Perspective," *MEJ*, 1 (Apr. 1947), pp. 128–30.

[22] For a brief biographical sketch of 'Alami, see Shim'oni, *op. cit.*, pp. 219–20; on local opinion, *cf.* editorials in *Filastin*,

Feb. 11, Mar. 29, Apr. 3, 4, 1945; *Al-Difaʿ*, Apr. 2, 1945.

23 The precise nature of these talks has not yet been disclosed, though President Roosevelt revealed that he had discussed Palestine with ibn Saʿud; *NYTimes*, March 2, 1945; and in a letter, published after the President's death, Roosevelt alluded to his conversations on Palestine with the Arabian King; *ibid.*, Oct. 19, 1945; finally, 'Azzam Bey related his account of the meeting; *ibid.*, Aug. 25, 1945.

24 The Arabic text appeared in *Al-Ahram*, March 23, 1945; a French translation in *Le Progrès Égyptien*, same date; an English text, from which these quots. have been taken, was printed by the Arab Office, Washington, entitled "Pact of the Arab League" (1946). Analyses of the pact may be found in Speiser, *op. cit.*, pp. 111–13 and Hourani, *MEJ*, 1 (Apr. 1947), pp. 132–33.

CHAPTER 15

1 Text in *NJ*, Dec. 1942, pp. 39–40; Weizmann estimate in *Jewish Frontier*, June 1942, pp. 7, 10.

2 ZE and AE, *Reports, 1946*, pp. 85, 152–90; Waters, *Haganah*, pp. 38–42; Hirschmann in *Survey Graphic*, May 1945, pp. 195–97, 265–69; statistics based on *Survey*, I, 200, 202.

3 Regulation on recruitment in *PalGaz*, Extraordinary, No. 1264, Jan. 23, 1943; see also correspondence between Agency and government in *PalPost*, Feb. 28, 1943; text of official Jewish rejection of government's reconstruction scheme in Attias, *op. cit.*, pp. 225–27; for other details, see *Survey*, II, 592–95 and Sulzberger in *NYTimes*, Aug. 1–3, 1943.

4 Trial quots. from A. C. Sedgwick, *ibid.*, Aug. 13, 15, 18, 1943; Ben Gurion quot. *ibid.*, Oct. 7, 1943; text of Assembly resolution in Attias, *op. cit.*, p. 229.

5 *PalPost*, Nov. 19, 21–26, 28–29, 1943; J. Lurie, "Guns in Palestine," *The Nation*, 158 (Jan. 22, 1944), pp. 92–94.

6 *He-Hazit*, No. 2, Aug. 1943; on Arab members, *cf.* J. L. Meltzer, *NYTimes*, Aug. 16, 1948.

7 *Survey*, II, 602–03, 605; Lohamey Heruth Israel, *For Justice, Freedom and Peace*, p. 25; *Eshnav*, No. 103, Oct. 5, 1945, p. 3; A. Altman press interview, *Ha-Mashqif*, Oct. 30, 1944; *The Answer*, June 1946, p. 9; K. Bilby's interview of Begin,

NYHerald-Tribune, Aug. 8, 1948; G. Frank, "The Truth about the Terrorists," *The Nation*, 159 (Dec. 2, 1944), pp. 685–86; F. Gervasi, "Terror in Palestine," *Collier's*, Aug. 11, 1945 [Gervasi and Frank accounts based on Haganah intelligence]; *The Times* (Lon), Feb. 9, 15, 1944; *NYTimes*, Feb. 26, 28, Mar. 26, Apr. 11, Nov. 7, 1944; *PalPost*, Feb. 16, May 19, July 16, Aug. 9, 23, 24, Oct. 1, 1944.

8 *Davar*, Aug. 24, 1944; *'Uvdot we-Sikkumim* [illegal Haganah broadsheet], Apr. 1945, relates story of Irgun informer; other details from *NYTimes*, Mar. 26, 1944; *PalGaz*, Mar. 30, 1944; *PalPost*, Mar. 30, Apr. 9, Oct. 20, Nov. 24, 1944, Jan. 30, 1945.

9 *PalPost*, Mar. 26, July 18, 1944 and *Mishmar*, Aug. 24, 1944; editorials rebuking the terrorists appeared in the Jewish newspapers after each act of violence, and by the summer of 1944 even the Revisionist *Ha-Mashqif* joined the rest of the press; *cf.* editorials on July 16, Aug. 9, 1944.

10 Text in *The Times* (Lon), Oct. 12, 1944; for typical reaction in Yishuv see editorials in *PalPost* and *Ha-Boqer*, Oct. 12, 1944; *Davar* and *Ha-Zofeh*, Oct. 15, 1944.

11 Churchill quot. in *NYTimes*, Nov. 18, 1944; for other details, see Hebrew press—editorials and news items—from mid-Nov. 1944 to mid-Feb. 1945.

12 Ben Gurion's letter of resignation in *Palcor Bulletin*, Nov. 11, 1943; on resolution of crisis see *PalRev*, Jan. 1944, p. 115 and *Ha-Arez*, March 3, 1944. For split in Mapai and its repercussions see *Davar* and *Mishmar*, Jan. 11, Feb. 27, Mar. 6–8, Apr. 7, 1944; on formation of Labor Unity Party, *cf. ibid.* and *Davar*, May 21, June 1, 1944.

13 *PalRev*, Dec. 6, 1940, pp. 141–42; see also Nov. 8, 1940, p. 125, Mar. 5, 1942, pp. 177–78. An emergency National Council Executive, under the presidency of Pinhas Rutenberg (1879–1942), had been created in Oct. 1939, when the body was enlarged from 6 to 18 members. Rutenberg resigned in Aug. 1940 and the Executive was reduced to 11 members; *PalPost*, Oct. 13, 18, 1949; *Ha-Arez*, Aug. 23, 1940. For attitude of three boycotting factions see editorials and statements in *Hed ha-Mizrah*, July 16, 1944; *Ha-Boqer*, July 6, 16, 23, 1944; and *Ha-Mashqif*, July 23, 1944. New Immigration views in *Mitteilungs-*

blatt, June 23, 30, July 7, 14, 21, 28, 1944.

14 For attacks on New Immigration Party see *Davar*, July 5, 1944; *Ha-Zofeh*, July 9, 1944; and *Mishmar*, Aug. 3, 1944. A list of the tickets including the number of candidates on each and the names of the leading candidates in *Davar*, July 25, 1944.

15 Results of Assembly election in *Ha-Arez* and *PalPost*, Aug. 15, 1944, *Mitteilungsblatt*, Aug. 18, 1944; names of new Assemblymen in *Davar*, Aug. 21, 1944; results of Histadrut election *ibid.*, Sept. 17, 1944.

16 The Histadrut Executive, which had been expanded from 6 to 20 members, was now further enlarged to 33; a committee was set up to nominate the candidates for managerial posts; *ibid.*, *Mishmar*, and *PalPost*, Mar. 11, 19, 1945. The representatives of the Leftist Front, Mizrahi Labor, and New Immigration ceased active participation in the National Council Executive; see G. Swett, "Within the Portals of the National Council," *Ha-Arez*, Mar. 11, 1944. For views of boycotting groups see editorials in *Ha-Boqer*, Sept. 12, Oct. 5, 1944; *Ha-Mashqif*, Sept. 12, 1944; *Hed ha-Mizrah*, Oct. 1, 1944.

17 Detailed report on political debate in Assembly, including text of resolution and ballot thereon, in JA, *Digest of Press and Events*, No. 47, Supp. No. 1, Dec. 13, 1944; for continuing dispute over Biltmore see, *e.g.*, editorials in *Mishmar*, Dec. 10, 1944 and *Ha-Zofeh*, Dec. 11, 19, 1944.

18 Text of memorandum and reference to Churchill-Weizmann talks in AE, *Political Report, 1946*, pp. 14–17.

19 *NJ*, Dec. 1946–Jan. 1947, pp. 65–66; Weizmann, *Trial and Error*, pp. 436–37.

20 E. Kaplan, "Our Preparations for the Transition Period," *PalYear*, 1 (1944–45), pp. 45–59; S. Schwartz, "Blueprint and Vision: the Jordan Valley Authority," *ibid.*, 2 (1945–46), pp. 83–100; the projected JVA was first given wide publicity by W. C. Lowdermilk in *Palestine, Land of Promise* (1944); for a tentative statement of the Palestine Government on this scheme cf. *Survey*, I, 412–14 and II, 565–66 for Jewish sterling assets in London; the economic inquiry was directed by R. R. Nathan, former chairman of the central planning division of the U.S. War Production Board, and its report—R. R. Nathan, O. Gass, and D.

Creamer, *Palestine: Problem and Promise* —appeared in 1946.

21 JA, *Digest of Press and Events*, No. 47, Supp. No. 1, Dec. 13, 1944, pp. 3–4.

22 On Lord Gort's influence see daily accounts in Hebrew press during Nov. 1944–Mar. 1945; a typical summary is that in JA, *Digest of Press and Events*, Dec. 13, 1944, pp. 1–3.

23 Weizmann quots. from *NYTimes*, Nov. 27, 1944 and JA, *Digest of Press and Events*, No. 60, Mar. 14, 1945, p. 5; Ben Gurion quots.: *ibid.*, No. 50, Supp., Jan. 4, 1945, pp. 2, 42; *ibid.*, No. 55, Feb. 6, 1945, p. 2; and *ibid.*, No. 61, Mar. 21, 1945, p. 4. On support for Weizmann cf. editorials in *Ha-Boqer*, Nov. 30, 1944, Mar. 8, 1945; *Mishmar*, Dec. 5, 1944, Mar. 8, 1945; *Ha-Arez*, Mar. 7, 1945; and *'Amudim*, Mar. 9, 1945; on support of Ben Gurion see JA, *Digest of Press and Events*, No. 54, Jan. 31, 1945, p. 11, *PalRev*, Jan. 1945, pp. 149–50 and Mar. 1945, p. 185.

24 From editorial in *Ha-Mashqif*, Dec. 11, 1944 and article by H. Ben Israel in *Qol-ha-'Am*, Feb. 21, 1945; other details from JA, *Digest of Press and Events*, No. 39, Supp. No. 15, Sept. 20, 1944; article entitled "Degeneration and Decline in the Revisionist Camp," *Davar*, Aug. 25, 1944; and news items in *Mishmar* and *Ha-Arez*, Apr. 8, 1945.

25 Anglo-Jewish Association, *Memorandum on Palestine* (1944), p. 7; other information from Board of Deputies of British Jews, *Statements on Post-War Policy and Policy on Palestine* (1944); AACI, London, *Hearings* (stenographic report), Jan. 30, 1946, morning session, pp. 38–63; S. Rowson, "Review of the Year 5704—Great Britain," *American Jewish Yearbook*, 46 (1944–45), pp. 187–95; and *NJ*, Jan. 1945, p. 47.

26 Statement on Palestine in American Jewish Committee, *Thirty-sixth Annual Report*, pp. 13–15 and statement of withdrawal in *Thirty-seventh Annual Report*, pp. 104–11. For details of Committee's reorganization cf. *ibid.*, pp. 39–42; see also American Jewish Conference, *The Jewish People in the Post-War World* (1945), p. 5 and *Statement to AACI* (1946), p. 6; text of Conference resolution in *NYTimes*, Sept. 2, 1943.

27 Text of Council's declaration of principles in *ibid.*, Aug. 31, 1943; cf. also American Council for Judaism, *Palestine, Haven of Refuge or Power Politics*

(1944), p. 5; AACI, Washington, *Hearings*, Jan. 10, 1946, p. 63.
[28] A. Lourie, "The American Zionist Emergency Council," *PalYear*, 1 (1944–45), pp. 368–73.
[29] Hebrew Committee of National Liberation, "A Call by the Hebrew Nation" (Wash; May 18, 1944), repr. in circular soliciting monetary contributions; *cf.* series of articles by G. Lubar and E. F. van der Veen in *WashPost*, Oct. 3–6, 8, 1944.
[30] Irgun Zvai Leumi, *Ziyyon Lohemet* [illegal Heb. brochure; somewhere in Palestine, Oct. 1944], p. 8; HCNL, "A Call by the Hebrew Nation" and *NYHerald-Tribune*, May 19, 1944; and *NYTimes*, May 19, 1944. Other information from B. Netanyahu, "The Fiasco of the Hebrew Committee," *Zionews*, July 1944, pp. 12–16; editorial in *Ha-Mashqif*, May 24, 1944; and New Zionist Organization of America, *Ten Political Statements* (1945) and *Fighting for a Jewish Homeland* (1946).
[31] Statistics from Lourie, "American Zionist Emergency Council," *PalYear*, 1 (1944–45), p. 368; and reindorsement of Biltmore from American Jewish Conference, *Statement to AACI*, pp. 18–19.

CHAPTER 16

[1] See, for instance, *The New Palestine*, Sept. 10, 1941, p. 1, Nov. 6, 1942, p. 31; *NYTimes*, Sept. 12, 1943.
[2] War Dept. quot., *ibid.*, Mar. 18, 1944; Roosevelt quots., *ibid.*, Mar. 10, 31, 1944. While the immigration deadline had already been deferred in Nov. 1943, the end of the White Paper's first five-year period still exercised a strong psychological influence on the Zionists. The resolutions in Congress had bipartisan sponsorship; for details see *ibid.*, Jan. 28, Feb. 2, 29, Mar. 1, 2, 5, 6, 1944.
[3] Text of party platforms, *ibid.*, June 28, July 21, 1944; Dewey and Roosevelt statements in issues of Oct. 13, 16, 1944.
[4] Statements by Stimson and Dept. of State in *NYHerald-Tribune*, Oct. 14, 1944 and *NYTimes*, Dec. 12, 1944.
[5] *Ibid.*, March 2, 17, Oct. 19, 1945.
[6] Text of Labor Party statement in *ManGuard*, Apr. 24, 1944; see also Dec. 14, 1944; on Liberal Party *cf. PalPost* and *NYHerald-Tribune*, Feb. 4, 1945.
[7] *The Economist*, Apr. 29, 1944, p. 569,

Mar. 11, 1944, pp. 328, 329; and *The Times* (Lon), July 24, 1944. On the American side *cf.* J. M. Landis, "Middle East Challenge," *Fortune*, Sept. 1945 (repr.); R. J. Barr, "Postwar Trade Prospects in Egypt, Iraq, Palestine," *Foreign Commerce Weekly*, June 30, 1945; and the financial page of *NYTimes*, Jan. 24, Mar. 21, 23, Apr. 14, 1944.
[8] Editorial in *Filastin*, Feb. 7, 1945; see also editorials, *ibid.* and *Al-Difa'*, Apr. 25, June 20, 1944; for Arab protests *cf.* issues of both papers of Apr. 30, May 1–4, 1944. On reactions in Yishuv, see editorials in *Ha-Arez*, *Davar*, and *Ha-Zofeh*, Dec. 15, 1944 for favorable comments, and in binationalist *Mishmar*, May 3, Dec. 18, 1944 for unfavorable; Ben Gurion statement in *PalPost*, May 11, 1944.
[9] *Al-Difa'*, Oct. 15–20, 22–27, 1944; *Filastin*, Oct. 14–15, 17–22, 24–29, 1944; *Al-Wafd al-Misri* on Oct. 23, 1944 announced its decision to boycott the OWI; see also editorials in issues of Oct. 24, 27, 1944; for threats against purchase of American products, see *Al-Difa'*, Oct. 23, 25, 1944.
[10] First three arguments in *Filastin*, Oct. 14, 1944; *Al-Muqattam* (Cairo), July 10, 1944; and *Al-Balagh* (Cairo), July 10, 1944; fourth in *Filastin*, July 25, Oct. 14, 1944; *Al-Difa'*, Aug. 2, Oct. 23, 1944; *Al-Balagh*, and *al-Muqattam*, July 10, 1944; *Al-Ahram* (Cairo), July 27, 1944; and *Al-Wafd al-Misri*, Oct. 18, 1944.
[11] *Cf.* statement by secretary-general of the Arab Unity Society of Egypt, As'ad Daghir, in *Al-Ahram*, July 27, 1944; the protest of the National Bloc Party in Palestine in *Filastin*, Oct. 21, 1944; and editorial in *Al-Difa'*, Oct. 22, 1944.
[12] Arguments in *Al-Balagh*, July 10 and Oct. 16, 1944, *Al-Musawwar* (Cairo), July 28, 1944, and *Al-Difa'*, Oct. 22, 1944.
[13] Editorial in *Al-Ahram*, July 27, 1944; see also *Al-Misri*, Oct. 19, 1944, which cited similar statements made by staff members of the American University at Cairo. In March 1945 anti-American demonstrations were reported only in Damascus; *Al-Difa'* and *PalPost*, March 21, 1945.
[14] *PalPost*, Oct. 17, 1944; see also Shertok's speech in December in JA, *Digest of Press and Events*, No. 47, Supp. No. 1, Dec. 13, 1944, p. 6; and editorials in *Ha-Arez*, June 30, July 24, Oct. 18, 24, 1944; *Ha-Zofeh*, June 29, July 24, Oct. 18, 1944;

Ha-Boqer, June 29, Oct. 18, 1944; *Mittei-lungsblatt,* Oct. 20, 1944.

[15] *Mishmar,* July 3, 26, Oct. 17, Dec. 17, 1944; *Ha-Mashqif,* July 4, Oct. 15, 17, 1944, Mar. 11, 1945; *Ha-Boqer,* Mar. 5, 1945; *Ha-Zofeh,* Mar. 6, 19, 1945.

[16] *Filastin,* June 3, 1944; first contention from *NYTimes,* Mar. 18, 1945, citing 'Azzam Bey, who was to be the first secretary-general of the Arab League; second contention in *Al-Muqattam,* July 10, 1944, *Filastin,* Aug. 18, 1944, *Al-Balagh,* Oct. 16, 1944, and *Al-Difa',* Dec. 4, 1944.

[17] Arguments from *Al-Difa',* Oct. 18, 1944 (also 'Azzam Bey's statement in *Le Progrès Égyptien,* Apr. 14, 1944 and letter in *Filastin,* Apr. 18, 1945, from its publisher to 'Azzam Bey); *Al-Balagh,* Oct. 16, 1944; *Al-Ahram,* July 27, 1944; and *Al-Balagh,* July 10, Oct. 16, 1944.

[18] *Davar,* Sept. 6, 1944; *Ha-Arez,* July 8, 1943, July 16, Sept. 20, 1944; *Ha-Boqer,* July 5, Sept. 26, 1944; *Ha-Zofeh,* Sept. 7, 1944; *Ha-Mashqif,* Aug. 18, Sept. 6, 1943, July 6, 10, 1944.

[19] *Ha-Arez,* Jan. 10, 1945; *cf.* with issue of Sept. 20, 1944.

[20] JA, *Digest of Press and Events,* No. 47, Supp. No. 1, Dec. 13, 1944, pp. 8–9.

[21] *Ibid.,* No. 59, Mar. 7, 1945, pp. 1–3.

[22] *Filastin,* Mar. 6, Apr. 24, 1945; *Al-Difa',* Apr. 3, 25, 26, 1945.

[23] *Ibid., Filastin,* Mar. 26, 1944, and *PalPost,* Mar. 30, 1944; see also *Ha-Arez, Davar, Ha-Zofeh, Mishmar, Ha-Boqer,* and *Ha-Zman,* Mar. 28, 1944.

[24] Arab arguments from *Al-Difa',* Aug. 30, Sept. 1, 4, 1944; *Filastin,* Aug. 30, Sept. 1, 1944; *Al-Ittihad,* Sept. 10, 1944; Jewish arguments from *Yediot Aharonot,* Aug. 30, 31, 1944; *Ha-Arez,* Aug. 31, 1944; *Ha-Mashqif,* Sept. 1, 6, 1944; *Davar,* Sept. 4, 1944; *Mishmar,* Sept. 5, 1944.

[25] *Filastin,* Sept. 1, 1944; *Al-Difa',* Sept. 4, 1944; and *Mishmar,* Sept. 5, 1944.

[26] On Arab attitude toward Mac-Michael, *cf.* editorials in *Filastin,* July 21, Aug. 10, 31, 1944; *Al-Difa',* Aug. 2, 10, 31, 1944. In welcoming Lord Gort, *Al-Difa',* Oct. 31, 1944 expressed the hope that the "last phase" of the White Paper, "which was to have commenced on March 31, 1944, but was delayed for unknown reasons," would now get under way; see also unsigned article on same subject, *ibid.,* as early as Sept. 9, 1943. On press campaign for execution of White Paper, *cf.* edi-

torials in *Filastin,* Nov. 17, 21, 24, Dec. 28, 1944, Jan. 5, Feb. 21, Mar. 15, 21, 1945; *Al-Difa',* Dec. 29, 1944, Jan. 5, Mar. 15, Apr. 4, 17, 19, 1945.

[27] See, for instance, *Filastin,* Mar. 10, 13, 15, 18, Apr. 18, 1945; *Al-Difa',* Oct. 29, Nov. 5, 1944, Feb. 6, Mar. 11, 13, 15, 20, Apr. 4, 9, 10, 15, 18, 1945; and *Al-Sirat al-Mustaqim,* Jan. 15, Mar. 19, 1945; *cf.* also *Survey,* I, 270–71.

[28] Rotation plan in *PalPost,* Mar. 22, 1945; for examples of its cool reception in Yishuv, see *ibid., Ha-Arez, Ha-Boqer,* Mar. 22, 1945; *Davar, Ha-Mashqif,* and *Ha-Zofeh,* Mar. 23, 1945; for Arab response, see *Filastin,* Mar. 22–25, 1945; *Al-Difa',* Mar. 22, 23, 25, 1945. Partition plan in *NYTimes,* Apr. 21, 1945; *PalPost,* Apr. 23, 1945. For government summary, see *Survey,* II, 936–38; at the time that the British municipal commission was set up by the Chief Justice, Sir William Fitzgerald, was instructed to investigate the problem afresh. But Fitzgerald's proposal to place the Old City with its historic shrines sacred to Christianity, Islam, and Judaism under a British administrative council, and to divide the rest of Jerusalem into two independent boroughs, one Arab and one Jewish, was shelved. Fitzgerald's analysis was completed on Aug. 30, 1945, but was not made public until Dec. 18, 1946; *PalPost,* Dec. 19, 1946.

CHAPTER 17

[1] J. Robinson, *Palestine and the United Nations,* pp. 3–6; Speiser, *op. cit.,* pp. 102–04; *NYTimes,* May 27, 30, 31, June 2, 3, 6, 24, 1945.

[2] Text of Agency memorandum and citation from Churchill's reply in AE, *Political Report, 1946,* pp. 17–21; reference to second memorandum regarding immigration on p. 23; the text of a third memorandum dealing specifically with the Templar and other German property in Palestine may be found in JA, *The Jewish Case before the AACI,* pp. 326–30; see also "German Property in Palestine and Jewish War Claims," in *The Palestine Tribune,* May 10, 1945.

[3] President Truman's assurances to Dr. S. S. Wise, the chairman of the American Zionist Emergency Council, in *NYTimes,* Apr. 21, 1945; the President's assurances to Arabs, as subsequently reported by 'Azzam Bey in *Al-Ahram,* Aug. 20, 1945

and in an *aide-memoire* by the Arab ministers in Washington to the Secretary of State in *NYTimes*, May 17, 1946; for other details, see *WashPost* and *NYTimes*, Aug. 17, 1946 and text of Harrison report, *ibid.*, Sept. 30, 1946.

[4] *PalPost*, May 23, 25, 1945.

[5] Byrnes, *Speaking Frankly*, pp. 74–75; Speiser, *op. cit.*, pp. 187–89, 225–31; R. J. Barr, "Postwar Trade Prospects," *Foreign Commerce Weekly*, June 30, 1945; U.S. Dept. of Commerce, Bureau of For. and Dom. Commerce, *International Reference Service*, 2 (Nov. 1945), pp. 12–13; E. Monroe, "British Interests in the Middle East," *MEJ*, 2 (Apr. 1948), pp. 129–46. *NYTimes*, Sept. 2, 12–14, 19, 1945; *ManGuard*, Sept. 19, 27, 1945.

[6] Text of resolutions in AE, *Political Report, 1946*, pp. 73–80; summary records of conference in *NJ*, Aug.–Sept. 1945, pp. 169–88; for Zionist attitude toward Labor victory see *ManGuard*, July 28, 1945; *NYTimes*, July 29, 1945; and editorials in *Ha-Mashqif*, July 29, 1945; *Mishmar* and *Ha-Boqer*, July 31, 1945; *Davar*, Aug. 3, 1945. List of new members of Agency Executive in ZE and AE, *Reports, 1946*, pp. 6–7.

[7] Text of Arab Office constitution in *ManGuard*, Aug. 4, 1945; five Palestine Arabs were appointed to the London office and four to the Washington office; *Al-Difa'*, Apr. 14, May 11, 1945; on American Institute, see *Al-Misri*, Mar. 31, 1941.

[8] Arab Office quot. from *NYTimes*, July 31, 1945 (see *Al-Misri*, same date, for greater detail); 'Azzam quot. from *Al-Ahram*, Aug. 20, 1945.

[9] *NYTimes*, Sept. 23, 25, Oct. 2, 7, 21, 1945; *ManGuard*, Sept. 25, 1945.

[10] From text in *NYTimes*, Sept. 30, 1945.

[11] *The Department of State Bulletin*, 13 (Nov. 18, 1945), p. 795, editorial in *ManGuard*, Sept. 24, 1945, and in *The New Statesman and Nation*, Sept. 29, 1945, p. 208; for other details, see *NYTimes*, Sept. 24, Oct. 2, 1945; *ManGuard*, Sept. 25, 1945.

[12] *NYTimes*, Sept. 24, Oct. 7, 26, Nov. 11, 1945; *ManGuard*, Sept. 25, 1945.

[13] 'Azzam citations *ibid.*, Oct. 4, 1945 and *NYTimes*, Oct. 5, 1945; text of Arab Washington memorandum, *ibid.*, Oct. 21, 1945.

[14] For typical anti-American incitation, see editorials in *Al-Balagh* and *Al-Muqat-*

tam, Oct. 22, 1945; Iraq had denied passage to orphaned Polish Jewish children en route to Palestine from the U.S.S.R. at the end of 1942, *NJ*, Dec. 1942, p. 34, but the issue was not raised again until 1945. On other details, see *Mishmar*, May 20, 1945; *PalPost*, May 22, Oct. 7, 12, 25, 1945; *Ha-Arez*, Nov. 2, 1945; *NYTimes*, Oct. 15, 24, 25, Nov. 3–5, 8–9, 1945.

[15] *Ibid.*, Sept. 24, Oct. 25, 1945; other data from *ManGuard*, Sept. 25, Oct. 8, 1945; *JTA Bulletin*, Oct. 10, 1945; *NYTimes*, Oct. 16, 17, Nov. 3, 1945; Sen. Bailey (D., N.C.) warned the Secretary of State that he would carry an opposition fight to the floor of the Senate, if the Administration attempted to take a hand in setting up a Jewish state in Palestine; text, *ibid.*, Oct. 29, 1945.

[16] Text in *PalPost*, Sept. 28, 1945.

[17] As cited in *PM*, Oct. 11, 1945; other details from *PalPost*, Oct. 7, 11, Nov. 2, 1945; *NYTimes*, Oct. 9, 11, 13, Nov. 2, 3, 1945.

[18] *Ha-Arez*, Nov. 2, 1945; see also editorials in *PalPost*, Nov. 2, 1945; *Ha-Boqer* and *Ha-Mashqif*, Nov. 5, 1945; *Yediot Aharonot*, Nov. 6, 1945; for binationalist position, *cf. Mishmar*, Nov. 6, 1945. On relations between Haganah and the terrorist groups, *cf.* G.B., *PP, 1946*, Cmd. 6873, pp. 3–5. "Truce" declaration of Irgun in *Fighting Judea* [illegal monthly], Sept. 1945; that of Freedom Fighters in a broadsheet, dated Aug. 1945. For a detailed list of terrorist activities after V-E Day, see AACI, *Report* [Washington edit.], pp. 84–85.

[19] For details of 'Alami's scheme, see his statement in *Al-Difa'* and *Filastin*, June 19, 1945; text of Husayni resignations from Fund in both papers on June 8, 1945; 'Abd-al-Hadi and Khalidi (the latter then allied with the Istiqlal leaders) did not sign the telegram to the League endorsing 'Alami's candidacy, *Filastin*, June 7, 12, 1945 and Arab News Agency despatch in *Al-Difa'*, June 8, 1945; *cf.* also Shim'oni, *op. cit.*, pp. 357–59.

[20] *Al-Difa'*, June 21, 1945 and *Al-Wahdah*, June 16, 1945; for other editorials on same subject, see *ibid.*, June 23, 30, 1945; *Al-Difa'*, June 18, 22, July 3, Aug. 3, 1945; *Filastin*, July 6, 17, 1945; *cf.* also articles by the publisher of *Filastin* in issues of Aug. 3, 8, 1945. The Istiqlal bloc at this time included, besides Khalidi (of the defunct Reform Party), some

politicians who formerly supported the now quiescent National Defense Party, and the Arab communists. The Husayni bloc consisted of the leaders of the remaining prewar factions, the young intelligentsia grouped around 'Alami, and the right-wing of the Arab labor movement. On split in Arab labor, see *Survey*, II, 763–66 and Shim'oni, *op. cit.*, pp. 368–69.

[21] *JTA Bulletin*, June 1, 1945 and Sulzberger from Paris in *NYTimes*, Aug. 29, 1945; other data from *Filastin*, June 2, Aug. 3, Nov. 1, 1945; *Al-Difa'*, June 3, 30, Sept. 14, 26, 1945; *NYTimes*, Aug. 25, 1945; *Le Progrès Égyptien*, Sept. 7, 1945.

[22] Summary of regulations in *PalPost*, Sept. 27, 1945; other data in issues of Sept. 28, Oct. 3, 7, 11, 12, Nov. 4, 11, 1945; *NYTimes*, Oct. 9, 23, Nov. 3, 9, 1945; *WashPost*, Oct. 4, 1945.

CHAPTER 18

[1] Texts of Truman and Bevin statements in *NYTimes*, Nov. 14, 1945; see also *ibid.*, Dec. 11, 1945.

[2] H. L. Matthews from London, *ibid.*, Nov. 14, 1945; the dipl. corr., *ManGuard*, same date; and citations from text of American Zionist Emergency Council statement in *NYTimes*, Nov. 15, 1945.

[3] AL, Secretariat-General, *Memorandum to AACI* (stenciled; March 6, 1946), p. 9; and resolution of the Yishuv's Elected Assembly, text in *PalPost*, Nov. 29, 1945. Agency's statements, *ibid.*, Dec. 14, 1945, Feb. 14, 1946; Arab Higher Committee's statements in *Filastin*, Feb. 2, 14, 1946.

[4] Agency statement in *PalPost*, Dec. 14, 1945 and Weizmann address delivered to ZOA convention in Atlantic City, Nov. 19, 1945 (verbatim rec.); for Arab reactions, *cf. Filastin*, Nov. 16, 1945; and statement of Arab League Council, *Al-Ahram*, Dec. 7, 1945.

[5] *NYTimes*, Jan. 17, 1946; Fr. text of League's economic boycott in *Le Journal d'Égypte*, Dec. 4, 1945; see also AACI, London, *Hearings*, Feb. 1, 1946, morning session, pp. 16–17; for Agency protest, see M. Shertok to Chairman, General Assembly, United Nations Organization, JA, Pol/1/46, Jan. 4, 1946; on Congressional resolutions, *NYTimes*, Nov. 30, Dec. 13, 18, 20, 1945.

[6] *Mishmar*, Nov. 14, 1945; *PalPost*, Nov. 29, 1945; and J. L. Magnes, *Rebel-*lion (Dec. 6, 1945), pres. address on diploma day at Heb. Univ.; other data from *PalPost*, Nov. 29, Dec. 12, 1945.

[7] *Filastin*, Nov. 16–18, 20–24, 1945; *Al-Difa'*, Nov. 16, 18–23, 1945; and *NYTimes*, Nov. 20, 1945. On continuing discord among Arab politicians, see *PalPost*, Nov. 18–21, 23, 1945; *Al-Difa'*, Feb. 20, 1946; and article in *Al-Hurriyyah*, Feb. 19, 1946.

[8] *Al-Ittihad*, Nov. 24, 1945; other data from *Survey*, I, 84; *PalPost*, Jan. 4, Feb. 20, 1946; *Filastin*, Jan. 4, 1946; *Al-Difa'*, Feb. 20, 1946.

[9] Text in Abcarius, *op. cit.*, pp. 238–40; other data from *Supp. Mem.*, p. 5; *NYTimes*, Jan. 26, 1946.

[10] *Ibid.* and *PalPost*, Jan. 31, 1946; other data from *NYTimes*, Nov. 26–28, 1945, Jan. 19, 22, 1946; *PalPost*, Nov. 27, 1945; editorials in *Filastin* and *Al-Difa'*, Nov. 27–28, 1945.

[11] *NYTimes*, Jan. 31, 1946 and *Filastin*, Feb. 2, 1946; see also *NYTimes*, Feb. 1, 3, 1946.

[12] G. Currivan from Jerusalem, *ibid.*, Feb. 1, 2, 8, 1946; Arab News Agency from Bayrut, *Al-Difa'*, Feb. 4, 1946 and editorial, Feb. 20, 1946; *PalPost*, Mar. 26, 1946; editorial and statements in *Filastin*, Mar. 30, 1946; *Survey Supp.*, p. 139.

[13] *NYTimes*, Feb. 21, 22, 25, 26, 1946; on German prisoners, see government press officer's statement in *PalPost*, Feb. 21, 1946 and editorials in Hebrew press, Feb. 21–Mar. 5, 1946. Senator's letter of resignation appears in *Commentary*, 2 (Oct. 1946), pp. 384–86. For moderate viewpoints in Yishuv, *cf.* editorials in *Mishmar*, Feb. 25, 1946 and *Ha-Arez*, Feb. 27, 1946.

[14] Haganah evidence to AACI, repr. in *Palestine Affairs*, July 1946, p. 3; for difference in public reactions to terrorist and Haganah exploits, *cf.* descriptions by disinterested American observers in despatches from Jerusalem in *NYTimes*, from Nov. 26, 1945 to Apr. 27, 1946.

[15] *Davar*, Apr. 29, 1946; on views of activist press, see editorials *ibid.*, *Ha-Boqer* and *Ha-Zofeh*, Apr. 28, 1946; the only earlier serious incident involving Br. troops occurred in Feb. when some E. African native troops, after the murder of one of their number, ran amuck in a Jewish village, killing one person and wounding many others; *NYTimes*, Feb. 7, 1946; details of later incident, *ibid.*, Apr. 29,

1946; text of army communiqué in *Pal-Post*, Apr. 28, 1946.

[16] See editorials in *Al-Difa'*, Dec. 30, 1945, Jan. 1, Mar. 6, 19, Apr. 1, 4, 29, 1946; *Filastin*, Dec. 31, 1945, Apr. 2, 9, 1946.

[17] *Filastin*, Dec. 23, 1945; other data from Jamal al-Husayni's statement in Arab News Agency despatch, Bayrut, *Al-Difa'*, Feb. 4, 1946; and editorials, *ibid.*, Nov. 27, Dec. 30, 1945, Jan. 1, 23, 24, 31, Apr. 29, 1945; *Filastin*, Nov. 27, 30, Dec. 23, 30, 31, 1945, Jan. 22, Feb. 28, Mar. 1, Apr. 2, 1946; and *Al-Wahdah*, Nov. 17, 1945.

[18] Only the public hearings in Jerusalem were published for UNSCOP's benefit; the Washington hearings were dittoed and the London hearings stenciled. Two members of the committee subsequently published personal accounts of the inquiry board's activities: R. Crossman, *Palestine Mission*, and B. C. Crum, *Behind the Silken Curtain*. The report was published separately by the American and British Governments: U.S., S.D., AACI, S.D. Publication No. 2536 [hereafter referred to as AACI, *Report*] and G.B., *PP, 1946*, Cmd. 6808.

[19] AACI, *Report*, pp. 1–2, 4, 5, 8, 12.

[20] *New Times*, Feb. 1, 1946, pp. 15–16 and article by Victor Lutsky in *Trud* [the trade-union newspaper which published *New Times*], as summarized and cited by Reuters from Moscow, *PalPost*, Mar. 20, 1946. See also articles in *New Times* between Jan. and Aug. 1946; C. Daniel from Cairo, *NYTimes*, Feb. 5, 1946; and A.P. despatch from Cairo, *WashPost*, Feb. 7, 1946.

[21] Pres. Truman's Army Day speech on Apr. 6, 1946 in *NYTimes*, Apr. 7, 1946. Aramco agreements noted in *PalPost*, Jan. 24, Aug. 11, 1946 [plans to terminate pipe line in Palestine were later abandoned]; on American airport in Saudi Arabia, see U.S., Senate, 80th Congress, 2nd Session, Special Committee Investigating the National Defense Program, Rep. No. 440, Part 5, *Navy Purchases of Middle East Oil*, pp. 17–18; Brownell, "American Aviation in the Middle East," *MEJ*, 1 (Oct. 1947), pp. 401–16; text of U.S. agreement with Yemen, *ibid.*, 1 (Jan. 1947), pp. 86–88; an evaluation of American policy toward the Arab East in Speiser, *op. cit.*, pp. 225–31.

[22] G.B., *PD, Commons*, vol. 416, cols.

774–75; see also vol. 460, Jan. 26, 1949, cols. 928–29.

[23] *Ibid.*, vol. 422, cols. 856–60.

[24] *NYTimes*, Jan. 18, 1946; U.K. treaty with Transjordan appeared as G.B., *PP, 1946*, Cmd. 6799 [replaced in 1948, Cmd. 7368]; other data from Monroe, "British Interests in Middle East," *MEJ*, 2 (Apr. 1948), p. 130; *NYTimes*, Dec. 22, 1945, Apr. 22, May 8, 1946; *PalPost*, Jan. 30, Feb. 4, 1946.

CHAPTER 19

[1] G.B., *PD, Commons*, vol. 422, cols. 195–97; text of Truman statement in *NYTimes*, May 1, 1946.

[2] Text of Agency statement in *PalPost*, May 2, 1946 and text of *aide-memoire* in *NYTimes*, May 17, 1946. For non-Zionist position, see American Jewish Committee, *Fortieth Annual Report*, p. 74; American anti-Zionist attitude in *NYTimes*, May 2, June 3, 1946.

[3] Text of Dept. of State note, *ibid.*, May 22, 1946; Executive Order creating Cabinet Committee in *The Department of State Bulletin*, 14 (June 23, 1946), p. 1089; see also Truman statement in *NYTimes*, June 7, 1946; other data, *ibid.*, June 13, 14, 1946.

[4] *Ibid.*, May 4, 5, 7, 9, 11, 13, 1946; *NYHerald-Tribune*, June 9, 1946; editorial in *Filastin*, May 2, 1946; and news despatches *ibid.*, May 28–31, 1946.

[5] Texts of Egyptian and Iraqi second memoranda to the U.K. in *NYTimes*, July 24, 1946; extracts from the first memorandum to the U.K. and the note to the U.S. appeared, *ibid.*, July 9, 1946 and *Middle East Opinion*, July 15, 1946, pp. 13–14.

[6] *NYTimes*, June 14, Aug. 13, 1946, Oct. 10, 1947; *Middle East Opinion*, July 15, 1946, p. 14.

[7] *Survey Supp.*, p. 139; *PalPost*, May 30, 1946; *NYTimes*, May 30, June 13, 1946.

[8] H. Callender from Paris, *ibid.*, June 13, 1946; also issues of May 9, June 9–12, 21, 1946; and G.B., *PD, Commons*, vol. 417, col. 383; vol. 421, cols. 2346–47.

[9] From testimony of Jamal al-Husayni in AACI, Jerusalem, *Hearings*, Mar. 12, 1946, pp. 20–27.

[10] See *ibid.*, p. 20 for reference to Arab pressures for Mufti's return; also *Filastin*, Jan. 4, Feb. 14, Mar. 10, Apr. 10, 1946; other data from *Survey Supp.*, pp. 139–40;

NYTimes, June 10, 20, 21, 26, July 21, Aug. 5, 16, 1946.

[11] Text of Agency statement in ZE and AE, *Reports, 1946*, p. 124; other data from *NYTimes*, June 7, 13, 1946.

[12] *Ibid.*, June 13, 16, 1946; other data from issues of June 15, 26, 1946.

[13] Cmd. 6873, pp. 8, 9.

[14] *NYTimes*, June 30, July 1–4, 6, 7, 10, 11, 1946; ZE and AE, *Reports, 1946*, pp. 129–34; *Supp. Mem.*, p. 13.

[15] Text of Cunningham statement in *NYTimes*, June 30, 1946; other quot. as cited by C. Daniel from Jerusalem, *ibid.*, July 3, 1946 and later confirmed by U.K. memorandum to UNSCOP, *The Political History of Palestine under British Administration*, para. 119, which read in part, "Orders were then given to undertake operations against the Palmach." In later editions of the memorandum this sentence was changed to read, "Orders were then given to implement the plan directed against the whole network of armed organizations"; *cf.* corrigendum inserted in copies distributed at second regular session of the U.N. General Assembly, A/AC.14/8, Oct. 2, 1947. See also Sir Alan Cunningham, "Palestine—the Last Days of the Mandate," *International Affairs*, 24 (Oct. 1948), p. 485. Other data from *Survey Supp.*, p. 83 and *NYTimes*, July 12, 13, 1946.

[16] *Ibid.*, June 13, July 10, 1946; other data from issues of July 1, 3, 4, 9, 1946.

[17] *Ibid.*, July 10, 1946; see also Cunningham in *International Affairs*, 24 (Oct. 1948), p. 485; and Agency statement of July 9, 1946 in ZE and AE, *Reports, 1946*, pp. 130–31.

[18] *NYTimes*, July 23, 1946; other details from *ibid.*, June 19, 20, 22, 25–27, July 1, 4, 5, 1946; ZE and AE, *Reports, 1946*, p. 125; the U.K. statement on violence (Cmd. 6873) appeared in *NYTimes*, July 25, 1946; Agency spokesmen denied the authenticity of the telegrams cited in this statement; *ibid.*, July 26, 1946.

[19] Text of non-fraternization order in ZE and AE, *Reports, 1946*, pp. 134–35; Attlee statement in G.B., *PD, Commons*, vol. 426, col. 963. Other data from *NYTimes*, July 24, 27, 31, Aug. 1–3, 1946; *PalPost*, Feb. 14, 1947.

[20] On Soviet propaganda, *cf. Daily Worker* (NY), May 24, June 1, 1946; K. Serezhin, "A Seat of Unrest in the Middle East," *New Times*, June 1, 1946, pp. 14–17; Reuters' summary in *PalPost*, May 31, 1946 of *Isvestia* article; despatches from Moscow in *NYTimes*, May 31, June 1, July 5, 1946; J. Reston's summary, *ibid.*, July 24, 1946 of V. D. Lutsky's speech in Moscow on July 17 and official reports thereof in *Pravda*. Other data from Reston, *NYTimes*, May 1–2, 1946; W. H. Stringer, *The Christian Science Monitor*, May 2, 1946; and Brownell, "American Aviation," *MEJ*, 1 (Oct. 1947), pp. 404–10.

[21] *NYTimes*, June 12, July 3, 6, 13, 1946.

[22] Based on Morrison's statement in G.B., *PD, Commons*, vol. 426, cols. 967–75; advance report in *NYTimes*, July 26, 1946; and extracts from original plan in Drew Pearson's column, *WashPost*, Aug. 17, 1946.

[23] G.B., *PD, Commons*, vol. 426, col. 1262; on British origins of plan, see Secretary Byrnes' comment, *NYTimes*, July 27, 1946.

[24] *NYDaily News*, July 31, 1946; other data from *NYTimes*, Aug. 6, 8, 9, 14–17; see also statements by two British members of the inquiry committee, Crossman and Manningham-Buller, in G.B., *PD, Commons*, vol. 426, col. 1029.

[25] Texts of Egyptian and Iraqi memoranda in *NYTimes*, July 24, 1946; other data from issues of July 26, Aug. 13–16, 19, 22, 1946; and *Survey Supp.*, p. 14.

[26] *Ibid.*, pp. 11–13, 15; *NYTimes*, July 26, Aug. 8–13, 1946.

[27] Text of British communiqué *ibid.*, Aug. 13, 1946; 'Azzam cited *ibid.*, Aug. 14, 1946; for other data *cf. ibid.*, Aug. 15 [statement by American Zionist Emergency Council], 19, 23, 1946.

[28] *Ibid.*, Aug. 6, 1946; reference to secret resolution and more thorough Agency critique of Morrison-Grady plan in JA, *Political Survey, 1946–47*, pp. 12–18, 28–29.

[29] Weizmann's letter of Sept. 4, 1946 to Colonial Secretary Hall in AE, *Political Report, 1946*, pp. 82–84; other details from *Palestine Affairs*, Sept. 1946, pp. 4–6; F. Belair, Jr., from Washington in *NYTimes*, Aug. 14, 1946; and statements by Nahum Goldman, a member of the Agency Executive, *ibid.* and *NYHerald-Tribune*, Oct. 24, 1946.

[30] Text of Weizmann's letter and Hall's

reply in AE, *Political Report, 1946*, pp. 81–82.

[31] *NYTimes*, Sept. 1, 1946; see also issues of Aug. 30, Sept. 17; *NYHerald-Tribune*, Sept. 5, 1946. For Arab editorial reaction in Palestine, see *Al-Wahdah*, Sept. 2, 3, 5, 6, 1946; *Filastin*, Sept. 3, 1946. Only the non-Zionist Anglo-Jewish Association appointed delegates but observed that this was merely an "empty gesture," since the Agency, the "responsible and recognized voice of the Jews in Palestinian affairs," was not participating; *NYTimes*, Sept. 13, 1946.

CHAPTER 20

[1] Text of Arab comments on Morrison-Grady plan, presented by Arab delegates on Sept. 16, in *Middle East Opinion*, Nov. 25, 1946, pp. 9–10; text of Arab counterproposals in G.B., *PP, 1946–47*, Cmd. 7044, pp. 9–11; or in Arab Office, Washington, *Palestine, the Solution*, pp. 16–19; or in Arab Office, London, *The Future of Palestine*, app. A, pp. 91–95. See also Bevin's report to Parliament in G.B., *PD, Commons*, vol. 433, col. 1913, for Arab delegates' attitudes.

[2] *Ibid.*, cols. 1913–14; also *NYHerald-Tribune*, Oct. 3, 1946; *NYTimes*, Sept. 17, Oct. 3, 1946; *PalPost* and *Ha-Arez*, Sept. 20, 22–25, 29–30, Oct. 1–4, 1946.

[3] Text in *NYTimes*, Oct. 5, 1946; Dewey statement, *ibid.*, Oct. 7, 1946.

[4] Cf. James Reston, *idem*.

[5] *NYHerald-Tribune*, Oct. 6 [Arab spokesmen], Oct. 18 [ibn Sa'ud], and Oct. 29, 1946 [Truman]. Cf. also *Middle East Opinion*, Oct. 7, 1946, p. 12, and Oct. 14, 1946, pp. 10–12; *NYTimes*, Sept. 2, 4, Oct. 5, 1946; *MEJ*, 1 (Oct. 1947), pp. 407–08.

[6] *NYTimes*, Oct. 6, 1946 [F.O.]; and Reuters despatch in *PalPost*, same date [Churchill].

[7] G.B., *PD, Commons*, vol. 433, cols. 1913–14; on Foreign Office claim, see Reston in *NYTimes*, Oct. 7, 1946.

[8] C. Daniel, citing Arab delegates, *ibid.*, Oct. 5, 1946; confirmed by Foreign Office spokesman, *PalPost*, Oct. 9, 1946; other data from ZE and AE, *Reports, 1946*, p. 136.

[9] Text of Inner General Council resolution in *PalPost*, Oct. 30, 1946; Colonial Secretary's statement, issued as Palestine Government communiqué 98, *ibid.*, Nov.

6, 1946. Details of British-Zionist talks (Oct. 8–18), *ibid.*, Oct. 11, 13–15, 18, 27, 1946; *NYTimes*, Oct. 8, 9, 11, 14–15, 19, 1946.

[10] Statistical and other factual data from *Survey*, II, 907; *Survey Supp.*, pp. 129–35, 145, 147, 149; ZE and AE, *Reports, 1946*, chart opp. p. 1 and pp. 17–18; ZE, *Stenographic Report of Twenty-first Zionist Congress* (Heb.), p. xxvi. The Revisionists did not formally dissolve their New Zionist Organization until April 1947; *PalPost*, May 19, 1947.

[11] Summary records of the Congress, with verbatim records of Weizmann's speeches, in *NJ*, Dec. 1946–Jan. 1947, pp. 34–79; Weizmann quot. from p. 66; text of political resolutions, pp. 79–81; results of vote thereon, p. 78; on election of new Executive and its composition see *PalPost* and *Ha-Arez*, Dec. 26–27, 29–31, 1946.

[12] *NYTimes*, Oct. 4, 1946; other data from Palestine Government communiqués 98 and 99, *PalPost*, Nov. 6, 1946; the Husaynis, however, were displeased with the release of the Zionist leaders, which they ascribed to British partiality to Zionism and to Jewish "influence"; cf. editorials in *Al-Difa'*, Nov. 8, 1946; *Al-Wahdah*, Nov. 10, 1946.

[13] *Survey Supp.*, pp. 140–42; Arab Office, Washington, *Arab News Bulletin*, Feb. 1, 1947; *NYTimes*, Dec. 13, 1946; *PalPost*, Jan. 2, 1947.

[14] *NYTimes*, July 19, Sept. 1, 4, 14, Nov. 1, 2, 26, Dec. 28, 1946; H. Bigart in *NYHerald-Tribune*, Jan. 9, 1947.

[15] As cited by Bigart, who interviewed Jamal, *idem;* see also Jamal's statement to correspondents of *Middle East Opinion*, Oct. 28, 1946, p. 11 and Feb. 17, 1947, p. 12. On continuance of Opposition, cf. editorials in *Al-Ittihad*, Oct. 21, 1946, *Al-Sha'b*, Nov. 28, 1946, and article by Musa Nasir in *Filastin*, Nov. 1, 1946. Other data from Ghuri's statement in *Al-Wahdah*, Dec. 15, 1946; *NYTimes*, Oct. 22, Dec. 19, 26, 1946; and *PalPost*, Oct. 22, 1946.

[16] Arab Office, Washington, *Arab News Bulletin*, Feb. 1, 1947 and G. Barrett, *NYTimes*, Dec. 15, 1946; other information from Reston, *ibid.*, Nov. 20, 1946; F. S. Adams, *ibid.*, Dec. 15, 1946; Robinson, *Palestine and the United Nations*, pp. 15–25.

[17] See statements by Jamal al-Husayni, *Al-Difa'*, Dec. 15, 1946, *Al-Wahdah*, Dec. 15, 23, 1946; text of Higher Executive's

statement, *ibid.* and *Al-Difa'*, Jan. 10, 1947; text of Bevin-Byrnes letters of Dec. 2, 1946, in *NYTimes*, Dec. 7, 1946.
18 *Ibid.* and *NYHerald-Tribune*, Jan. 28, 1947; other data from both papers, Jan. 11, 29–31, Feb. 1–8, 1947; *Survey Supp.*, p. 141 [composition of Palestine Arab delegation]; *PalPost*, Jan. 12, 1947; *Filastin* and *Al-Difa'*, Jan. 23, 1947.
19 Text in Cmd. 7044, pp. 11–14; *NYTimes*, Feb. 11, 1947.
20 *Ibid.*, Feb. 15, 1947; other data, *ibid.* and *NYHerald-Tribune*, Feb. 11–14, 1947.

CHAPTER 21

1 G.B., *PD, Commons*, vol. 433, cols. 1907–26; also *ibid.*, cols. 989–98.
2 *League of Nations Official Journal*, Spec. Supp. 194, p. 28.
3 Byrnes, *Speaking Frankly*, p. 290; U.S., S.D., Publication 2023, *Nazi-Soviet Relations 1939–41*, pp. 258–59 [pertinent captured documents]; Monroe, "British Interests in Middle East," *MEJ*, 2 (Apr. 1948), p. 134; J. A. Loftus, "Middle East Oil: the Pattern of Control," *ibid.*, (Jan. 1948), p. 30; *NYTimes*, Dec. 27, 1946.
4 *Ibid.* and *NYHerald-Tribune*, Feb. 26–27, 1947; editorials in these two papers as well as *WashPost*, Feb. 27, 1947.
5 On Political Action Committee, see *NYPost*, July 9, 1946; *NYTimes*, July 14, 1947; *NYHerald-Tribune*, Sept. 7, 1947.
6 *Ibid.* and *NYTimes*, Aug. 18, 1946; other details from Mikesell, *Arabian Oil*, pp. 58–70; R. H. Sanger, "Ibn Saud's Program for Arabia," *MEJ*, 1 (Apr. 1947), pp. 180–90; statement by L. W. Henderson, director of Office of Near Eastern and African Affairs in the Dept. of State, *ibid.*, pp. 85–86; *NYHerald-Tribune*, Aug. 10, 1946, Jan. 19, Mar. 13, 1947; *NYTimes*, Jan. 28, Feb. 17, 19, 1947.
7 *Survey Supp.*, pp. 130–31.
8 On number of Jewish D.P.'s, *cf.*, U.N., G.A., UNSCOP, *Report to the General Assembly*, I, 44.
9 On Arab binationalists, see *ibid.*, III, 198–203; for the Arab League's intervention on the Mufti's behalf, *cf.* Arab Office, Washington, *Arab News Bulletin*, Feb. 1, 1947.
10 *NYTimes*, Dec. 22, 1946; other data from AACI, *Report*, pp. 6–8; *Survey Supp.*, pp. 17, 22; *Supp. Mem.*, pp. 6–27.
11 AACI, *Report*, p. 76; *Survey*, II, 538; article by Jerusalem corr., "Palestine

Police Force," *The Times* (Lon), Feb. 21, 1944. Statistics based on *NYHerald-Tribune*, March 4, 1947 [citing War Office figures for Dec. 31, 1946]; C.O. and F.O., *Palestine: Termination of the Mandate*, p. 10; *Survey Supp.*, pp. 72–73.
12 AACI, *Report*, pp. 76–77; *NYTimes* and *NYHerald-Tribune*, Feb. 1–7, 15, 1947.
13 UNSCOP, *Report*, III, 201–02; *NYTimes*, Jan. 27–30, Feb. 15–16, Apr. 16, 1947; *NYHerald-Tribune*, Jan. 27–30, 1947; *PalPost*, Nov. 25, Dec. 30, 1946, Feb. 16, 1947.
14 From extracts of High Commissioner's report in *Supp. Mem.*, p. 57; on Qawuqji, see *NYTimes* and *NYHerald-Tribune*, Feb. 24–25, 1947.
15 Text of Agency's reply to government's "ultimatum" for Jewish cooperation in Feb. 1947 from *PalPost*, Feb. 11, 1947. Other details from ZE and AE, *Reports, 1946*, pp. 134–35, 139–41; *NYTimes*, Sept. 2, Nov. 19, 24, Dec. 27, 1946; and *NYHerald-Tribune*, Jan. 8, 1947.
16 *Cf.* C. Daniel from Jerusalem, *NYTimes*, Mar. 1, 1947.
17 For a penetrating British appraisal of the Labor Govt.'s Palestine policy and the causes of Anglo-American divergency, see G. L. Arnold, "Lessons of Palestine," *The Nineteenth Century and After*, 144 (Oct. 1948), pp. 192–201.

CHAPTER 22

1 G.B., *PD, Commons*, vol. 433, cols. 2013, 2014; and U.N., G.A., *OR, 1st Spec. Session*, I, 183; see also Bevin's statements in G.B., *PD, Commons*, vol. 433, cols. 993–94, 997, 1926.
2 U.N., G.A., *OR, 1st Spec. Session*, I, 184–86.
3 *Ibid.*, III, 149–50 [Soviet statement]; 80–81, 132 [U.S. statement]; 86, 131 [U.K. statement]; I, 174–75 [UNSCOP's composition]; II, 81 and I, 59–60 [votes on Arab agenda proposal in committee and in plenary meeting].
4 *Ibid.*, III, 184–85, 188, 218–21, 240, 262, 284–90, 294–95; I, 125–26, 142, 145, 155–56 [Arab statements]; III, 201–03, 296; I, 152; II, 48–49 [U.S. and U.K. statements]; I, 176–77 [vote on terms of reference]; terms of reference in U.N., G.A., resolution 106 (S-1).
5 U.N., G.A., *OR, 1st Spec. Session*, III, 260 [Jamali; for similar statements by

other Arab spokesmen, see pp. 188, 241, 261–63, 290, 295; I, 143] and I, 127, 135, 145, 157, 158 [Arab reservations].

⁶ *Ibid.*, III, 256 [Shertok], 269 [Ghuri]; in its dealings with the United Nations, the Palestine Arab political directorate reverted to the old name of "Higher Committee," although in the Palestine press it continued for some time thereafter to be designated "the Higher Executive." For further details concerning the appearance of the Higher Committee before the First Committee, see *NYTimes* and *NYHerald-Tribune*, May 7–8, 1947.

⁷ U.N., G.A., *OR, 1st Spec. Session*, III, 183–84; see also II, 4, 6, 11.

⁸ *Ibid.*, II, 81–83, 296 [W. R. Austin], 201–03 [H. V. Johnson]; Marshall's statement as cited in *NYHerald-Tribune*, May 7, 1947.

⁹ U.N., G.A., *OR, 1st Spec. Session*, II, 103 [Austin] and I, 131 [Gromyko]; see also I, 131–32, II, 108–11, III, 203–04, 294 [Gromyko]; II, 88–93 [Poland], 99 [Czechoslovakia], 112–13 [U.K.].

¹⁰ *Ibid.*, I, 127–35.

¹¹ Bigart from Jerusalem in *NYHerald-Tribune*, May 14, 1947; on Jamal's statement, see Daniel from Jerusalem in *NYTimes*, May 8, 1947; for local Arab and Jewish reactions in Palestine to developments at U.N., cf. editorials in *Al-Sha'b* and *Filastin*, May 14, 1947; *Al-Difa'*, May 16, 1947; *Ha-Boqer*, May 6, 9, 1947; *Ha-Arez*, May 9, 15, 1947; *PalPost*, May 16, 1947; also summary of Ben Gurion's speech before Elected Assembly, *ibid.*, May 23, 1947.

¹² UNSCOP, *Report*, I, 3–4 and A/AC.13/NC/12, June 16, 1947 [see also A/AC.13/SR.37 for Palestine Govt.'s formal appointment of liaison officer]; *NYTimes*, May 16, 18, 25, June 8, 11, 14, 1947; *NYHerald-Tribune*, May 16, 18, 25–26, June 3, 1947. Note the warning [as cited *ibid.*, May 25, 1947] by Faris Bey al-Khuri, the head of the Syrian delegation, that inclusion of the D.P. camps in the investigation "would be a cause of cutting off relations with the committee."

¹³ UNSCOP, *Report*, II, 5–6; verbatim records of the public hearings may be found in *ibid.*, III; verbatim records of the government's evidence in private hearings, *ibid.*, IV, 1–13, 19–32. Other data from *NYTimes*, June 17, July 1, 9, 11, 17, 27, 1947; *NYHerald-Tribune*, June 17, July 1, 9, 11, 13, 1947.

¹⁴ U.N., G.A., resolution 107 (S-1).

¹⁵ Text in UNSCOP, *Report*, II, 13; details from *NYTimes* and *NYHerald-Tribune*, April 17, May 5, Aug. 1, 1947.

¹⁶ Text in UNSCOP, *Report*, II, 12–13 [British] and *NYHerald-Tribune*, June 10, 1947; data from *ibid.*, Feb. 20, Apr. 11, June 7, July 14, 1947; *PalPost*, Jan. 21, June 10, 11, 1947; *NYTimes*, Mar. 1, 9, 13, 15, 31, Apr. 11, 16, 23, May 18, 24, June 1, 7, 1947; JA, *Political Survey, 1946–47*, pp. 41–42.

¹⁷ "The Exodus 1947: the British Case," by Thomas Cadett, a BBC corr., in *NYHerald-Tribune*, Sept. 17, 1947; *ibid.*, July 19–21, 31, Aug. 22, 1947; *NYTimes*, July 10, 19–21, Aug. 22, 1947.

¹⁸ J. Tait from London, *NYHerald-Tribune*, July 22, 1947; Foreign Office statement, issued as Palestine Government communiqué 127, *PalPost*, Aug. 22, 1947 [see also editorials in Hebrew press on that day]. The Arab press and the Higher Committee had been urging all along that the government return illegal immigrants to the countries of embarkation; cf. editorials in *Al-Difa'*, Nov. 18, 27, Dec. 2, 5, 8, 16, 18, 1946; *Al-Wahdah*, Nov. 20, 29, 1946; *Filastin*, Dec. 1, 22, 1946; *Al-Sha'b*, Dec. 1, 8, 1946. The Higher Committee addressed its latest demand on this subject to the High Commissioner immediately after the interception of the *Exodus 1947; NYTimes*, July 22, 1947. For other data, see *ibid.*, Mar. 20, July 24–25, Aug. 23, 26, Sept. 10, 11, 1947; *PalPost*, July 29–30, 1947.

¹⁹ *Supp. Mem.*, p. 3; F.O. propaganda on illegal immigration from *NYTimes* and *NYHerald-Tribune*, May 28, Sept. 6, 1947.

²⁰ *Ibid.*, June 13, 14, 24–25, July 18, Aug. 1–5, 22–23, 30, Sept. 4, 25, Oct. 1–3, 1947; *NYTimes*, June 14, 16, 20, 22, July 2, Aug. 1–5, 22–23, Sept. 4, 25, Oct. 2–3, 1947; Farran's version may be found in Roy Farran, *Winged Dagger*, pp. 348–84.

²¹ U.N., G.A., *OR, 1st Spec. Session*, III, 32.

²² *NYHerald-Tribune*, Feb. 22, Apr. 14, 1947; *NYTimes*, Mar. 21, Apr. 14, 1947; *PalPost*, Apr. 16, 17, 20, 22 [statement by Arab Workers Congress], 23, 1947 [statement by Ghuri]; *Filastin*, Apr. 17, 1947 [statement by Ahmad Hilmi Pasha].

²³ For criticism by Arab Opposition of the Committee's action at U.N., see editorials in *Al-Ittihad*, May 18, June 1, 8,

1947; *Filastin*, May 26, 29, June 1, 10, 1947; and *Al-Sha'b*, June 1, 1947; other data from *PalPost*, May 22, 28, June 13, 15, 1947; *NYHerald-Tribune*, May 14, 1947; *NYTimes*, June 2, 1947.

²⁴ Clifton Daniel from Jerusalem, *ibid.*, Mar. 23, 1947; on difficulties encountered by Jewish binationalists, see UNSCOP, *Report*, III, 198–203.

²⁵ *NYHerald-Tribune*, July 7, 1947 [Mufti]; *NYTimes*, July 7 [Jamal], Aug. 9, 1947 [Labib]. Other data, *ibid.*, July 14, Aug. 11–16, 22, 1947; *NYHerald-Tribune*, June 20, 25, 29, July 14, Aug. 11–16, 22, 1947; *PalPost*, Aug. 15, 20, 27, 31, 1947.

²⁶ UNSCOP, *Report*, III, 244; Chairman Sandstroem and seven members of the committee, in their private capacities, visited the Transjordan capital, but the statement by Samir Pasha al-Rifa'i, the Premier and Foreign Minister, was not included in the published hearings; *ibid.*, I, 7; for extracts from Transjordan statement, see *NYTimes*, July 25, 1947.

²⁷ UNSCOP, *Report*, I, 42–46 [the twelve principles], 47–58 [majority scheme], 59–64 [minority scheme].

CHAPTER 23

¹ *NYHerald-Tribune* and *NYTimes*, Sept. 9, 1947 [Arab Higher Committee]; *ibid.*, Sept. 4, 1947 [Zionist General Council]. Arab League's statement in New York, *NYHerald-Tribune*, Sept. 16, 1947. The Palestine Arab press joined the chorus of rejection: see editorials in *Filastin*, Sept. 2, 1947; *Al-Sha'b*, Sept. 5, 1947; *Al-Ittihad*, Sept. 7, 1947. For reactions in Yishuv: editorials in the statist *Ha-Boqer*, *Ha-Zofeh*, and *Ha-Arez*, Sept. 2, 1947, expressed restrained pleasure; the Revisionist *Ha-Mashqif*, Sept. 2, 1947, rejected the idea of "false independence in a toy state"; and the binationalist *Mishmar*, same date, objected to both the majority and minority proposals.

² Texts of speeches in U.N., G.A., *OR, 2nd Session, PM*, I, 19–27 [Marshall], 81–106 [Vyshinsky].

³ Text of Truman statement in *NYTimes*, June 6, 1947. On British irritation with fund-raising in the U.S. for illegal immigration and terrorism in Palestine, cf. *ibid.*, Aug. 14, Oct. 31, Nov. 16, 1946, Jan. 7, May 20, 1947; *NYHerald-Tribune*, Oct. 26, Nov. 16, 1946, Jan. 8, Mar. 21, Apr. 24, May 20, 31, 1947. For effect of *Exodus 1947* affair on American public opinion, see editorials *ibid.*, Aug. 21, 1947 and *NYTimes*, Sept. 11, 1947. Bartley C. Crum, who had been a member of the AACI, became chairman of the national council of a group called "Americans for Haganah," whose avowed object was to promote illegal immigration; *ibid.*, July 3, 1947 and *NYHerald-Tribune*, Oct. 17, 1947.

⁴ The most inflammatory advertisement, written by Ben Hecht, appeared *ibid.*, May 13, 1947; for a summary of American and British response, see *Time* (Mag.), June 16, 1947, pp. 31–32. For other data connected with the terrorists and their American sympathizers, see *NYHerald-Tribune*, Apr. 17, June 6–7, Aug. 2–7, 9, 11, Sept. 7–10, 19, 21–22, 29, 1947. On Labor Government's policy, cf. Bevin's speech before the annual Labor Party conference on May 29, 1947: *ibid.* and *NYTimes*, May 30, 1947, and Robinson, *Palestine and the United Nations*, pp. 60–61. Regarding the Egyptian question before the Security Council, see *NYTimes*, Jan. 27, 28, Mar. 30, 31, 1947; and U.N., S.C., *OR, 2nd Year*, Nos. 70, 73, 75, 80, 82, 84, 86, 87, 88.

⁵ As of the time of writing, the records of the *Ad Hoc* Committee on the Palestinian Question have not yet been published; the U.N. documentation symbol for this committee is A/AC.14/.

⁶ Results of the final vote on the partition resolution in U.N., G.A., *OR, 2nd Session, PM*, II, 1424–25; for details of the *Ad Hoc* Committee's work, see document A/516, *ibid.*, annex 33, pp. 1628–37; cf. also reports of partition subcommittee, A/AC.14/34, and of subcommittee on a unitary state, A/AC.14/32.

⁷ U.N., G.A., resolution 181 (II).

⁸ A/AC.14/SR.2 [Creech-Jones]; A/AC.14/SR.15 [Creech-Jones]; A/AC.14/SR.25 [Cadogan]; U.N., G.A., *OR, 2nd Session, PM*, II, 1323–24 [Cadogan]; see also verbatim text of Cadogan's statement to partition subcommittee, *NYTimes*, Nov. 14, 1947. Not until Dec. 11, 1947 did the Colonial Secretary disclose the date on which Britain had decided to end the mandate; G.B., *PD, Commons*, vol. 445, col. 1219.

⁹ Text in *NYTimes*, Nov. 23, 1947 [off. documentation is only a summary record, A/AC.14/SR.28]; see also U.N., G.A., *OR, 2nd Session, PM*, I, 21 [Marshall];

A/AC.14/SR.11 [Johnson]; and text of Johnson statement before partition subcommittee in *NYTimes*, Nov. 1, 1947.

[10] A. Krock, *ibid.*, Sept. 3, 1947; T. J. Hamilton, *ibid.*, Sept. 25, Oct. 13, 1947; Reston, *ibid.*, Oct. 13, 1947; editorials, *ibid.*, Oct. 12, 15, 1947 and in *NYHerald-Tribune*, Sept. 27, Oct. 1, 11, 12, 14, Nov. 2, 12, 15, 23, 28, 1947; for political pressures on White House, see *NYTimes*, Sept. 12, 15, 22, Oct. 7, 1947.

[11] Texts *ibid.*, Oct. 14, Nov. 4, 1947; also *ibid.* and *NYHerald-Tribune*, Nov. 5–11, 1947.

[12] *NYTimes*, Oct. 17, Nov. 23, 1947; other data, *ibid.*, Nov. 1, 2, 14, 1947.

[13] Gromyko quot. from U.N., G.A., *OR, 2nd Session, PM*, II, 1360; on Arab delegates attitude toward the U.S.S.R. in the early part of the session, see *NYTimes*, Sept. 19, Oct. 14, 1947; Farid Zayn-al-Din, Minister to Moscow, and Faiz al-Khuri, his predecessor, were members of the Syrian delegation; U.N., G.A., *OR, 2nd Session, PM*, II, p. xxxviii.

[14] Report of subcommittee on a unitary state, A/AC.14/32, p. 13; see also draft resolution 1, pp. 57–58, regarding International Court proposal. On Arab lobbying, *cf.* Sir M. Zafrulla Khan, *Palestine in the U.N.O.*, pp. 16–23; J. García-Granados, *The Birth of Israel*, pp. 263–65; in the final vote six Latin American countries abstained and one voted against partition; U.N., G.A., *OR, 2nd Session, PM*, II, 1424–25. For Arab meetings with Marshall and other members of the American delegation, see *NYTimes*, Sept. 24, Oct. 10, 1947; other data, *ibid.*, Nov. 27, 29–30, 1947.

[15] *Ibid.*, Sept. 30, 1947; and U.N., G.A., *OR, 2nd Session, PM*, II, 1421; on threats of war by Arab delegations, see *ibid.*, pp. 1317, 1338, 1340, 1345, 1391–95, 1418; also A/AC.14/SR.11–13, 15, 28–30.

[16] A/AC.14/SR.17 [Shertok]; texts in *NYTimes*, Oct. 3 [Silver], 19, 1947 [Weizmann].

[17] UNSCOP members who championed partition were García-Granados [Guatemala], Fabregat [Uruguay], Lisicky [Czechoslovakia]; see A/AC.14/SR.4–6, 15. On Zionist maneuvers, *cf.* L. Shultz, "The Palestine Fight—an Inside Story," *The Nation*, 165 (Dec. 20, 1947), pp. 675–78; Weizmann, *Trial and Error*, 456–59; J. Rogers in *NYHerald-Tribune*, Nov. 30, 1947; T. J. Hamilton, "Partition

of Palestine," *Foreign Policy Reports*, 23 (Feb. 15, 1948), pp. 290–91; and political advertisement by the late Rep. Sol Bloom (D., N.Y.) in *NYTimes*, Oct. 19, 1948. On condemnation of Zionist pressure politics by Arabs and their sympathizers, see memorandum to UNPAC from 'Isa Nakhlah, the New York representative of the Arab Higher Committee, in A/AC.21/10; Zafrulla Khan, *op. cit.*, pp. 16–23; K. Roosevelt, "The Partition of Palestine," *MEJ*, 2 (Jan. 1948), pp. 14–16.

[18] Text in *NYTimes*, Nov. 30, 1947; see also U.N., G.A., *OR, 2nd Session, PM*, II, 1425–27. On violence in Arab East in first half of December, *cf.* *NYTimes* and *NYHerald-Tribune*, Dec. 1–15, 1947; official account of anti-Jewish disorders in Aden Colony in G.B., *PD, Commons*, vol. 445, col. 1013. For development of Arab League plans, see *NYTimes*, Sept. 23, Oct. 9–12, 1947; *NYHerald-Tribune*, Oct. 9–12, 1947; also statement by Ahmad Sharabati, the Syrian Defense Minister, *ibid.*, Nov. 5, 1947.

[19] *NYTimes*, Dec. 1, 1947. The last serious Arab political murder was that of Sami Taha, the secretary of the Palestine Arab Workers Society, at Haifa on Sept. 12, 1947, although coercive incidents against Arab shopkeepers suspected of trading with Jews occurred even as late as the end of Oct.; *ibid.*, Sept. 13–14, Oct. 23, 1947. The national committee at Jerusalem was not formed until late in Jan. 1948; *NYHerald-Tribune*, Nov. 26, 1947; *NYTimes*, Jan. 28, 1948.

[20] UNPAC, "First Special Report to the Security Council," A/AC.21/9, citing reports from High Commissioner Cunningham; F. Turner from Jerusalem, *NYHerald-Tribune*, Feb. 2, 1948; D. A. Schmidt from Jerusalem, *NYTimes*, Mar. 7, 1948. By decision of the Arab League Council at its session of Dec. 8–16, 1947, recruitment took place chiefly in the Levant States, Iraq, and Egypt; all volunteers were reportedly sent to assembly centers in Syria for training and equipment; *ibid.*, Dec. 17, 1947, Feb. 23, 1948.

[21] *Cf.* Ben Gurion's statement in *PalPost*, Oct. 16, 1947; *NYTimes*, Sept. 21, 24, Oct. 14–15, 17, 19, 20, 23, Nov. 9, 12, 30, 1947; *NYHerald-Tribune*, Oct. 15, 23, 1947.

[22] *NYTimes*, Nov. 30, 1947 [National Council] and *PalPost*, Jan. 26, 1948 [Ma-

pam]; *cf.* also: T. F. Reynolds from Jerusalem, *PM*, Nov. 10–11, 1947; *NYTimes*, Nov. 5, 1947, Feb. 3, Mar. 9, 12, 1948; *NYHerald-Tribune*, Mar. 9, 1948 [terrorists]; *NYTimes*, Sept. 12, 1947 [American Revisionist advertisement]; *ibid.*, Sept. 28, 1947, Feb. 6, 1948 [Magnes' letters to editor] and despatches from Jerusalem, *ibid.*, Jan. 30, Mar. 5, 11–12, 1948 [Ihud].

23 Letters to editor by presidents of Committee and Council respectively, *NYHerald-Tribune*, Jan. 21, Feb. 15, 1948; other data from Weizmann, *Trial and Error*, pp. 437–56.

24 UNPAC, "First Special Report to the Security Council," U.N., S.C., S/676 [A/AC.21/9], p. 7 and UNPAC, "Report to the General Assembly," *OR, 2nd Spec. Session*, Supp. No. 1, p. 17; other data from *ibid.*, pp. 35–36 and G.B., *PD, Commons*, vol. 445, col. 1219.

25 *NYTimes*, Sept. 2, Oct. 14, 25, Dec. 2–6, 19, 1947, Jan. 4, Feb. 1, 1948; *NYHerald-Tribune*, Feb. 13, 1948; see also statements by Secretary of Defense Forrestal, *NYTimes*, Jan. 20, 30, 1948; articles by Reston, *ibid.*, Jan. 27, Feb. 15, 18, 20, 1948. The view of officials that Arabian oil was strategically indispensable to the U.S. was challenged by some authorities; *cf.* B. Brodie, "American Security and Foreign Oil," *Foreign Policy Reports*, 23 (March 1, 1948), pp. 298–311.

26 U.N., S.C., S/PV.271; other details from S/PV.253 [Austin, Creech-Jones]; S/PV.260, 275 [Gromyko]; *OR, 3rd Year*, No. 52, pp. 26–27 [Cadogan]; UNPAC, "First Special Report to the Security Council," A/AC.21/9; Reston's despatch from Lake Success, *NYTimes*, Feb. 26, 1948; V. Clemmer, *NYHerald-Tribune*, Mar. 22, 1948; on the Soviet entry into the Trusteeship Council, *NYTimes*, Apr. 26, 1948.

27 U.N., G.A., *OR, 2nd Spec. Session*, Supp. No. 1, p. 6; *NYTimes*, Apr. 20, 1948.

28 *Ibid.*, Mar. 12, 21, 29, Apr. 3, 6, 9, 17–18, 20, 23, 25, May 11, 14–15, 1948.

29 Extracts of High Commissioner's report in A/AC.21/9, p. 7; Higher Committee's scheme in Jamal al-Husayni's telegram of May 24, 1948 to U.N. Secretary-General, S/775; other data from *NYHerald-Tribune*, Apr. 10, May 3, 12, 1948.

30 *Ha-Arez*, May 16, 1948.

EPILOGUE

1 Security Council resolutions S/723 and S/727; General Assembly resolutions 185–87 (S-2).

2 Security Council resolutions S/801, S/902; *NYTimes*, May 14, 21, June 22, 1948.

3 U.N., S.C., S/977, S/983, S/1002, and *OR, 3rd Year*, No. 110, p. 2; *NYTimes*, Sept. 18, 1948.

4 Cable from Secretary-General of Arab League to U.N. Secretary-General, May 15, 1948 in U.N., S.C., *OR, 3rd Year*, Supp. for July 1948, pp. 83–88 [S/745]; *NYTimes*, Jan. 14, May 19, 21–28, July 10–19, 1948.

5 Only Eliezer Kaplan, the Finance Minister, now remained on the Agency Executive in an advisory capacity; *PalPost*, Sept. 3–5, 1948; other data in *Davar*, Mar. 8, 1949.

6 On Arab failure to make adequate preparations, *cf.* Musa al-'Alami, *'Ibrat Filastin*, pp. 9–21; a translation of this brochure, partly condensed, appears in *MEJ*, 3 (Oct. 1949), pp. 373–405.

7 U.N., G.A., *OR, 3rd Session*, Supp. No. 11, p. 18 [Mediator's proposal]; other data from *The Times* (Lon), Oct. 13, Dec. 15–16, 1948; *NYTimes*, Oct. 6, Dec. 2, 4, 11–16, 1948.

8 *Ibid.*, Dec. 2, 9, 17, 29, 1948, Jan. 7, Mar. 31, June 12, July 5, 7–9, 1949; U.N., G.A., A/1106, p. 17.

9 U.N., S.C., S/1080 [resolution]; S/1357 [Acting Mediator's final report] contains a summary of the armistice negotiations; S/1376 [resolution terminating Acting Mediator's office].

10 Statistics from U.N. Economic Survey Mission for the Middle East, Interim Report, A/1106, App. B & C, pp. 22–25.

11 U.N., G.A., *OR, 3rd Session, Part II, AH*, pp. 237–41 [Israel], pp. 198, 220, 267, 269, 290 [Arab states]; A/927 and A/992 [Conciliation Commission, 3rd & 4th Progress Reports]; Bilby, *NYHerald-Tribune*, Nov. 7, 1948; A. O. McCormick, *NYTimes*, Jan. 17–18, 1949.

12 U.N., G.A., resolution 212 (III); *OR, 3rd Session*, Supp. Nos. 11 & 11A; Report of Secretary-General, "Assistance to Palestine Refugees," A/1060; *NYTimes*, Dec. 5, 8, 1948, Jan. 5, 22, Feb. 22, Mar. 17, 1949.

13 *Cf.* U.N., S.C., *OR, 3rd Year*, No. 69, pp. 2–6 and U.K. draft resolution S/755,

p. 6; No. 100, pp. 4–7; No. 122, pp. 9–13 and U.K.–Chinese draft resolution S/1059, pp. 12–13; U.N., G.A., *OR, 3rd Session, Part I, PM*, p. 144 and Annexes, pp. 524–35, especially U.K. draft resolutions A/C.1/394, Revs. 1 & 2; *OR, 3rd Session*, Supp. No. 11, p. 18 [Mediator's proposals]; *NYTimes*, Jan. 19, 27, 29, 1949.

14 *Ibid.*, Sept. 22, 1948 [text of Marshall statement]; U.N., G.A., *OR, 3rd Session, Part I, FC*, p. 682 [Jessup]; other data, *NYTimes*, May 21–June 4, Oct. 25, 29–31, Nov. 5, 9, 1948, Jan. 20, Feb. 1, 1949; *NYHerald-Tribune*, Oct. 29–31, Nov. 5, 9, 1948.

15 U.N., S.C., *OR, 3rd Year*, No. 62, pp. 32–33 [U.S. proposal, as amended S/727]; No. 80, p. 3, No. 82, p. 44, No. 84, pp. 6–8, 11–13 [Gromyko]; S/1368 and U.N., G.A., *OR, 3rd Session, Part I, FC*, Annexes, p. 75 [Soviet draft resolutions].

16 U.N., G.A., *OR, 2nd Spec. Session, PM*, pp. 36–37; *NYTimes*, Mar. 29, 1949.

17 U.N., G.A., *OR, 3rd Session, Part I, FC*, pp. 694–95 [Soviet statement]; *NYTimes*, Sept. 22, Oct. 22, Dec. 4, 5, 13, 1948, Jan. 10, 19, 23, Feb. 11, Mar. 5, 1949; Lt.-Gen. W. B. Smith, *My Three Years in Moscow*, pp. 273–76; J. Newman, "Moscow Uncensored," *NYHerald-Tribune*, Nov. 8, 1949.

18 U.N., G.A., *OR, 3rd Session, Part I, FC*, pp. 770–71 [Bunche]; resolution 194 (III); A/819, A/838, & A/927 [Conciliation Commission, 1st–3rd Progress Reports].

19 U.N., G.A. resolution 273 (III);

NYTimes, May 31, July 1, Aug. 13, 29, Oct. 16, Nov. 15, 1949; on Middle East diplomatic conference, *ibid.*, July 12, 22, 29, 1949.

20 U.N., G.A., A/992 [Conciliation Commission, 4th Progress Report], Annex I, pp. 13–14 for Mission's terms of reference; *NYTimes*, June 12, Aug. 27, 1949; *The Times* (Lon), Sept. 3, 1949.

21 U.N., Conciliation Commission for Palestine, *Final Report of the United Nations Economic Survey Mission for the Middle East*, I, 14–30 [the Mission's interim report]; resolution 302 (IV).

22 *NYTimes*, Apr. 8, Oct. 9, 1949 ['Abdallah on Jerusalem]; Currivan, *ibid.*, Feb. 2, 18, Mar. 28, 1949 [Israel on Jerusalem]; U.N., G.A., A/973 [Conciliation Commission, Draft Instrument for Jerusalem].

23 U.N., G.A., *OR, 3rd Session, Part II, AH*, pp. 231–37; *OR, 4th Session, AH*, pp. 262–64, 352–55 [Israeli statements]; *ibid.*, pp. 276–77; A/1231; *NYTimes*, Nov. 27, 1949 [Jordan statements].

24 U.N., G.A., resolution 303 (IV); *OR, 4th Session, AH*, p. 353 [Israel]; and A/1231 [Jordan].

25 Reston, *NYTimes*, Nov. 23, 1949 [Italian Colonies]; *ibid.*, Dec. 10, 1949 [Malik]; *ibid.*, Oct. 24, 1948, Apr. 16, 1949 [Papal Encyclicals], Nov. 19, 1949 [statement by Catholic hierarchy in U.S.]; Rogers, *NYHerald-Tribune*, Dec. 10, 1949; see also Australian draft resolution of Nov. 23, 1948, A/C.1/396, para. 4.

26 U.N., G.A., *OR, 4th Session, PM*, pp. 589–92; see also *OR, 4th Session, AH*, pp. 302–05 [statements by Tsarapkin]; A/1238/Rev.1 [Soviet draft resolution].

Bibliography

No ATTEMPT has been made to draw up an exhaustive list of titles. Only those titles which have had a direct bearing on the preparation of the text have been included. Readers seeking to inquire further into any of the many facets of the Palestine problem will find the general bibliographical references at the end helpful. The titles marked with an asterisk (*) were illegal at the time of their appearance. The entries under Palestine newspapers and periodicals date back to the period prior to May 15, 1948, and their circulation figures are those of the Palestine Government.

DOCUMENTS, UNPUBLISHED MATERIALS, AND OFFICIAL PUBLICATIONS

AGUDAS ISRAEL WORLD ORGANIZATION:
New York Office. Confidential Report for the Chawerim Nichbodim of the Agudas Israel World Organization. Issued semiannually between July 1941 and June 1944; annually thereafter. Reports 1–8, July 1941–September 1946. Stenciled. New York, 1942–1947.

AMERICAN JEWISH COMMITTEE:
Stenographic transcript of remarks by Dr. Chaim Weizmann at Executive Committee Meeting, January 20, 1940.
Unpublished correspondence. Letter from Morris D. Waldman to Dr. Arnold D. Margolin, April 3, 1942.
Foreign Affairs Department. The Jewish Agency and the Non-Zionists, a confidential report prepared by Louis N. Shub. New York, June 14, 1944.

ANGLO-AMERICAN COMMITTEE OF INQUIRY:
Hearings at London. Stenciled. 6 vols., dated January 25, 28–31, and February 1, 1946. London, 1946.
Hearings at Washington. Dittoed. 7 vols., dated January 7–12 and 14, 1946. Washington, 1946.
Public Hearings at Jerusalem. 10 vols., dated March 8, 11–15, 21, 23, 25, and 26, 1946. Jerusalem, 1947.
Report to the United States Government and His Majesty's Government in

the United Kingdom, Lausanne, Switzerland, April 20, 1946 [American edition]. Department of State Publication, No. 2536, Near Eastern Series No. 2. Washington, 1946.

Report of the Anglo-American Committee of Enquiry regarding the Problems of European Jewry and Palestine, Lausanne, 20th April, 1946 [British edition]. Cmd. 6808. London, 1946.

ARAB HIGHER COMMITTEE:
A Memorandum Submitted to the Royal Commission on January 11, 1937. Jerusalem, 1937.

Memorandum to the Permanent Mandates Commission and the Secretary of State for the Colonies. Jerusalem, July 23, 1937.

Reply of the Arab Higher Committee for Palestine to the White Paper issued by the British Government on May 17, 1939. London, 1939.

ARAB LEAGUE:
Arab Office, Cairo. Draft Constitution of the Arab Publicity Bureaus. Text in *The Manchester Guardian*, August 4, 1945.

———, Jerusalem. Evidence to the Anglo-American Committee of Inquiry. Stenciled. Jerusalem, 1946.

———, London. The Future of Palestine. London, August 1947.

———, Washington. *Arab News Bulletin*, 1946–48. This semimonthly ceased publication in May 1948.

———. Iraq's Point of View on the Palestine Question: Statement Submitted by M. Fadhel Jamali, Minister of Foreign Affairs of the Iraq Government, to the United Nations Special Committee on Palestine. Washington, 1947.

———. Pact of the Arab League. Washington, 1946.

———. Palestine: the Solution; the Arab Proposals and the Case on which they Rest. Washington, April 1947.

———. The Problem of Palestine: Evidence Submitted by the Arab Office, Jerusalem, to the Anglo-American Committee of Inquiry, March 1946. Washington, 1946.

Secretariat-General. Memorandum to the Anglo-American Committee of Enquiry. Stenciled. Cairo, March 2, 1946.

ARAB NATIONAL FUND:
Qarar Majlis Idarat Sanduq al-Ummah al-'Arabi (Resolution of the Board of Directors of the Arab National Fund). Jerusalem, 1945.

COMMITTEE ON CONSTITUTIONAL DEVELOPMENT IN PALESTINE:
Report. Volume I. Stenciled. Jerusalem, June 1941.

GENERAL FEDERATION OF JEWISH LABOUR IN PALESTINE:
A Survey of Arab Labour Organisation in Palestine: a Memorandum addressed to the World Trade Union Conference in London in February 1945. Stenciled. Tel-Aviv, January 1945.

GREAT BRITAIN:
The Political History of Palestine under British Mandate; Memorandum by His Britannic Majesty's Government presented in 1947 to the United Nations Special Committee on Palestine. Jerusalem, 1947.

Colonial Office. Colonial No. 20. Report by His Britannic Majesty's Government to the Council of the League of Nations on the Administration of Palestine and Trans-Jordan for the Year 1925. London, 1926.

――――. Colonial No. 26. Report by His Britannic Majesty's Government to the Council of the League of Nations on the Administration of Palestine and Trans-Jordan for the Year 1927. London, 1928.

――――. Colonial Nos. 40, 47, 59, 75, 82, 94, 104, 112, 129, 146, 166. Report by His Majesty's Government in the United Kingdom of Great Britain and Northern Ireland to the Council of the League of Nations on the Administration of Palestine and Trans-Jordan for the Year 1928 [–1938]. 11 vols. London, 1929–1939.

――――, Commission of Enquiry. Colonial No. 201. The System of Education of the Jewish Community in Palestine. London, 1946.

Colonial and Foreign Offices. Palestine: Termination of the Mandate 15th May, 1948; Statement prepared for Public Information. London, May 1948.

Foreign Office. Communique on Palestine with Reference to the Deportation of the Illegal Immigrants on the Exodus 1947 to the British Zone in Germany (British Information Services, New York, No. ID 752). New York, August 21, 1947.

Ministry of Information, Cairo. The Work of the Middle East Supply Centre. Cairo, July 1945.

Parliament. The Parliamentary Debates. House of Commons, Fifth Series, vols. 317–449. London, 1936–1949.

――――. The Parliamentary Debates. House of Lords, Fifth Series, vols. 103–158. London, 1936–1948.

Parliamentary Papers. Command Paper [Cmd.] 1540. Palestine: Disturbances in May, 1921. Reports of the Commission of Inquiry with Correspondence Relating Thereto. London, October 1921.

――――. Cmd. 1700. Correspondence with the Palestine Arab Delegation and the Zionist Organisation (The Churchill Memorandum). London, June 1922.

――――. Cmd. 3530. Report of the Commission on the Palestine Disturbances of August, 1929 (The Shaw Report). London, 1930.

――――. Cmd. 3692. Palestine: Statement of Policy by His Majesty's Government in the United Kingdom (The Passfield White Paper). London, October 1930.

――――. Cmd. 5479. Palestine: Royal Commission Report. London, 1937.

――――. Cmd. 5513. Palestine Statement of Policy by His Majesty's Government in the United Kingdom. London, July 7, 1937.

――――. Cmd. 5634. Policy in Palestine: Despatch dated 23rd December, 1937, from the Secretary of State for the Colonies to the High Commissioner for Palestine. London, January 1938.

――――. Cmd. 5854. Palestine Partition Commission Report. London, 1938.

――――. Cmd. 5893. Palestine Statement by His Majesty's Government in the United Kingdom. London, November 1938.

――――. Cmd. 5957. Correspondence between Sir Henry McMahon, His Majesty's High Commissioner at Cairo, and the Sherif Hussein of Mecca, July 1915–March 1916. London, March 1939.

――――. Cmd. 5964. Statements made on behalf of His Majesty's Government during the year 1918 in regard to the Future Status of Certain Parts of the Ottoman Empire. London, March 1939.

————. Cmd. 5974. Report of a Committee Set Up to Consider Certain Correspondence between Sir Henry McMahon [His Majesty's High Commissioner in Egypt] and the Sharif of Mecca in 1915 and 1916. London, March 16, 1939.

————. Cmd. 6019. Palestine Statement of Policy (The White Paper of May 1939). London, May 17, 1939.

————. Cmd. 6180. Palestine Land Transfer Regulations. London, February 28, 1940.

————. Cmd. 6799. Treaty of Alliance between His Majesty in Respect of the United Kingdom and His Highness the Amir of Trans-Jordan. London, March 22, 1946.

————. Cmd. 6873. Palestine Statement of Information Relating to Acts of Violence. London, July 1946.

————. Cmd. 7044. Proposals for the Future of Palestine July, 1946–February, 1947. London, February 1947.

Privy Council. Statutory Rules and Orders, No. 1282 of 1922, the Palestine Order in Council. London, August 10, 1922.

*HAGANAH:
[Ha-Magen ha-'Ivri]. Haverim Msaprim, I: Bimei Meura'ot (Comrades Relate, I: In the Days of the Disturbances [of 1936–39]). Anti-terrorist pamphlet, explaining the difference between defense and terrorism. Palestine, April 1945.

————. Yeriyot ba-Afelah (Shots in the Dark). Anti-terrorist pamphlet, underlining the differences between the Agency's struggle against the 1939 White Paper and terrorism. Palestine, 1944 or 1945.

[Mishmar ha-Ummah]. Mi-Lehi el Dehi (From Fighters for Israel's Freedom to Defeat). Anti-terrorist pamphlet, published in reply to a Freedom Fighters' brochure. Palestine, 1944.

[Mizrahi branch]. Milhemet Ya'aqov: Davar la-No'ar ha-Dati (Jacob's Struggle: a Word to the Religious Youth). Anti-terrorist pamphlet, stressing that terrorism is contrary to Jewish religious teachings. Palestine, 1944 or 1945.

[Neemanei Tel-Hai]. Zehu ha-Revizionizm (This is Revisionism). Anti-terrorist pamphlet, endeavoring to prove that the Revisionists support the terrorists. Palestine, 1945.

HAPOEL HAMIZRAHI:
Memorandum to the Anglo-American Committee of Inquiry. Stenciled. Jerusalem, March 1946.

HEBREW COMMITTEE OF NATIONAL LIBERATION:
Memorandum to the Anglo-American Committee of Inquiry. Typewritten. Washington, January 3, 1946.

INTERGOVERNMENTAL COMMITTEE ON REFUGEES:
Report of the Fourth Plenary Session, August 15–17, 1944, London. Washington, n.d.

IRAQ:
Iraq's Point of View on the Question of Palestine: Memorandum submitted

to the Anglo-American Committee of Inquiry by Mohammed Fadhel Jamali, Director-General of the Foreign Office. Stenciled. Cairo, March 1946.

*Irgun Zvai Leumi:

Anu Maaminim (We Believe). Palestine, 1944.

Anu Mered Niqra (We Shall Rebel). Palestine, 1944.

The Hebrew Struggle for National Liberation: a Selection of Documents on Its Background and History. Submitted to UNSCOP. Stenciled. Palestine, July 1947.

Memorandum to the United Nations Special Committee on Palestine. Stenciled. Palestine, June 1947.

Mishpat ha-'Esrim (The Sentence of the Twenty). Pamphlet warning of retaliation against the Palestine Government's imprisonment of twenty Irgunists. Palestine, October 1945.

Yehudah ha-Lohemet (Fighting Judaea). Statement of objectives and declaration of "truce" until the new Labor Government in Britain announced its policy on Palestine. Palestine, September 1945.

Ziyyon ha-Lohemet (Fighting Zion). Recruitment pamphlet. Palestine, 1944.

The Jewish Agency for Palestine:

Constituent Meeting of the Council held at Zurich, August 11th–14th, 1929. London, 1930.

The Establishment in Palestine of the Jewish National Home: Memorandum on the Development of the Jewish National Home, 1929 [–1938], submitted to the Secretary-General of the League of Nations for the Information of the Permanent Mandates Commission. 10 vols. London, 1930 [–1939].

Memorandum submitted to the Palestine Royal Commission. London, November 1936.

The Jewish Case against the Palestine White Paper: Documents submitted to the Permanent Mandates Commission. London, June 1939.

Memorandum submitted to the United Nations Conference on International Organization, San Francisco, California, by the Jewish Agency for Palestine, n.p., April 1945.

The Jewish Case before the Anglo-American Committee of Inquiry on Palestine as presented by the Jewish Agency for Palestine: Statements and Memoranda. Jerusalem, 1947.

The Palestine Issue: Preliminary Memorandum submitted to the Special Committee of the United Nations. Jerusalem, 1947.

Some Legal Aspects of the Jewish Case: Memorandum submitted to the United Nations Special Committee on Palestine. Jerusalem, July 1947.

Political Survey 1946–1947: Memorandum submitted to the United Nations Special Committee on Palestine. Jerusalem, July 1947.

Observations on the Supplementary Memorandum by the Government of Palestine including Notes on Evidence given to the United Nations Special Committee on Palestine up to the 12th July, 1947: submitted to the United Nations Special Committee on Palestine. Jerusalem, August 1947.

Reply to the Government of Palestine's Memorandum on the Administration of Palestine under the Mandate: submitted to the United Nations Special Committee on Palestine. Jerusalem, August 1947.

Economic Research Institute. Housing in Jewish Palestine. Jerusalem, 1938.

Executive. Report to the Second Meeting of the Council. London, 1931.

———. Report to the Third Meeting of the Council. London, 1933.

———. Report to the Fourth Meeting of the Council at Lucerne, September 4th-5th, 1935. London, 1935.

———. Political Report submitted to the XXth Zionist Congress and the Vth Session of the Council of the Jewish Agency. Jerusalem, 1937.

———. Political Report submitted to the Twenty-first Zionist Congress and the Sixth Session of the Council of the Jewish Agency. Jerusalem, 1939.

———, London Office. Political Report submitted to the Twenty-second Zionist Congress at Basle, December, 1946. London, 1946.

Information Section. Digest of Press and Events, 1943–   . Weekly summary of editorial opinion in Palestine, chiefly culled from the Hebrew press but containing briefer extracts from the Arabic press of Palestine and the near-by countries.

London Office. Report of the Jewish Agency for Palestine for the Year 1940 with Addenda for 1941. London, 1942.

New York Office. Book of Documents submitted to the General Assembly of the United Nations relating to the Establishment of the National Home for the Jewish People. New York, May 1947.

Political Department. Memorandum addressed to the High Commissioner, requesting 100,000 immigration certificates, June 18, 1945, POL/67/45.

———. Minute of . . . [Moshe Shertok's] Conversation with H.E., the High Commissioner, on Monday, August 24th, 1936, in the morning at Government Offices. Stenciled.

———. Protest against Arab boycott of Zionist goods. Moshe Shertok to the Chairman of the General Assembly, United Nations Organization, January 4, 1946, POL/1/46.

———. Yalqut ha-Mizrah ha-Tikhon, 1935–   . Hebrew monthly on Near East Affairs.

JEWISH NATIONAL FUND, Jerusalem:

Pe'ulot ha-Qeren ha-Qayemet le-Israel, 1945 (Activities of the Jewish National Fund in 1945). Jerusalem, 1945.

EL-KHALIDI, HUSSEIN F.:

The Arab Case: a Reply to Dr. Walter C. Lowdermilk's Jordan Valley Scheme. Stenciled. Jerusalem, 1945.

AL-KHALIDI, THABIT:

Arab Clan Rivalry in Palestine. Manuscript. Jerusalem, August 5, 1945.

LEAGUE OF NATIONS:

Assembly. Records of the Twentieth (conclusion) and the Twenty-first Ordinary Sessions. Texts of the Debates at the Plenary Meetings and Minutes of the First and Second Committees. League of Nations Official Journal, Special Supplement No. 194 (April 1946).

Permanent Mandates Commission. Thirty-second Session (extraordinary); Minutes, 30 July–18 August 1937. Geneva, 1937.

————. Thirty-fourth Session; Minutes, 8–23 June 1938. Geneva, 1938.
————. Thirty-sixth Session; Minutes, 9–29 June 1939. Geneva, 1939.

LEBANON:
Memorandum on the Palestine Problem [to the Anglo-American Committee of Inquiry]. Stenciled. Cairo, March 1946.

*LOHAMEI HERUT ISRAEL [Fighters for Israel's Freedom]:
Avnei Yesod le-Torat ha-Herut ha-'Ivrit (Fundamental Doctrines of Hebrew Freedom). A statement of objectives and principles. Stenciled. Palestine, December 1943.
Ha-Derekh le-Herut: 'Aliyah we-Hityashvut, Mediniyut 'Ivrit, Milhamah be-Shilton ha-Zar (The Road to Freedom: Immigration and Settlement, Jewish Diplomacy, War against the Foreign Regime). Stenciled. Palestine, 1944.
Eikh Naflu Lohamei Herut (How Freedom Fighters Fell). Brochure giving the Freedom Fighters' version of how Abraham Stern, the founder of the terrorist group, was killed by the British police in February 1942. Stenciled. Palestine, 1943.
For Justice, Freedom and Peace: Memorandum submitted to the United Nations Special Committee on Palestine. Stenciled. Palestine, June 1947.
Gilui Da'at, Av 1945 (Declaration, August 1945). Broadsheet announcing "truce" until Labor Government announces its Palestine policy. Stenciled. Palestine, August 1945.
Ha-Mahteret ha-'Ivrit (The Hebrew Underground). Palestine, 1943.
Min ha-Mishpat 'ad ha-Teliyah (From the Sentence to the Hanging). Broadsheet issued after the execution in Egypt of the two Freedom Fighters who had assassinated Lord Moyne. Stenciled. Palestine, April 1945.
Ha-Neeshamim Maashimim: Lohamei Herut bifnei Bet-ha-din ha-Zvai ha-Briti bi-Yrushalayim (The Accused Accuse: Freedom Fighters before the British Military Court in Jerusalem). Stenciled. Palestine, November 1944.
Le-Or ha-Gardom (In the Light of the Gallows). Broadsheet, issued after the execution in Egypt of the two Freedom Fighters who had assassinated Lord Moyne. Stenciled. Palestine, April 1945.
Yair (Illuminator, name by which Stern was known to his followers). Brochure in commemoration of the second anniversary of Stern's death. Stenciled. Palestine, February, 1944.

MAGNES, J. L.:
Correspondence relating to negotiations with Jewish Agency and Arab Higher Committee in the winter of 1937–38 for a political settlement in Palestine on the basis of the Hyamson-Newcombe proposals. Cover letter, dated February 21, 1938. Stenciled.

PALESTINE ARAB PARTY:
Qanun al-Hizb al-'Arabi al-Filastini (Constitution of the Palestine Arab Party). Jerusalem, n.d. (probably 1935).

PALESTINE COMMUNIST PARTY:
Central Committee. Memorandum to the Anglo-American Inquiry Commis-

sion on Palestine including supplementary statement on the Question of European Jewry and Palestine. Stenciled. Tel-Aviv, March 1946.

———. Memorandum to the United Nations Special Committee on Palestine. Stenciled. Tel-Aviv, July 1947.

PALESTINE COMMUNIST UNION:
Central Committee. Memorandum on the problem of Palestine to the United Nations Special Committee on Palestine. Stenciled. Tel-Aviv, June 1947.

PALESTINE GOVERNMENT:
Official Gazette of the Government of Palestine, 1920–32.

The Palestine Gazette, 1932–48.

Report by Sir William Fitzgerald on the Local Administration of Jerusalem, 28th August, 1945. Jerusalem, 1946. (Also issued by United Nations, Trusteeship Council, Second Session, Working Committee on Palestine. T/AC.7/1, December 3, 1947.)

The Sanduq al-Ummah, a statement prepared for the Anglo-American Committee of Inquiry. Typewritten. Jerusalem, March 1946.

Staff List of the Government of Palestine as on the 1st October, 1943. Jerusalem, 1943.

Supplementary Memorandum by the Government of Palestine, including Notes on Evidence given to the United Nations' Special Committee on Palestine up to the 12th July, 1947. Jerusalem, July 17, 1947.

Supplement to the Survey of Palestine, Notes Compiled for the Information of the United Nations Special Committee on Palestine. Jerusalem, June 1947.

A Survey of Palestine: Prepared in December 1945 and January 1946 for the Information of the Anglo-American Committee of Inquiry. 3 vols. Jerusalem, 1946.

Department of Education. Annual Report for the School Year 1937–1938. Jerusalem, 1939.

———. Annual Report for the School Year 1938–1939. Jerusalem, 1940.

Department of Labour. Annual Report for 1942. Abridged edition. Jerusalem, 1943.

———. *Department of Labour Bulletin,* issued at irregular intervals between 1943–48.

Department of Statistics. *General Monthly Bulletin of Current Statistics,* 1936–48.

———. Statistical Abstract of Palestine, 1942. Jerusalem, 1943.

———. Statistical Abstract of Palestine, 1944–45. Eighth edition. No. 15 of 1946. Jerusalem, 1946.

Office of the Census. Census of Palestine, 1931. By Eric Mills. 2 vols. Alexandria (Egypt), 1933.

PARIS PEACE CONFERENCE:
Inter-Allied Commission on Mandates in Turkey. "Report of American Section of Inter-Allied Commission on Mandates in Turkey," *Editor and Publisher,* 55 (December 2, 1922), section two, pp. iv–xxvi.

SCHECHTMANN, J.:
Die staatszionistische Bewegung: Programm, Entwicklung, Struktur. Stenciled. London, March 1939.

SEPHARDIC COMMUNITIES IN PALESTINE:
Memorandum presented to the Anglo-American Committee of Inquiry on Palestine. Stenciled. Jerusalem, February 1946.

STATUTORY JEWISH COMMUNITY IN PALESTINE:
National Council [Wa'ad Leumi]. Histadrut Po'alei Agudat Israel in Palestine. Typewritten. Jerusalem, December 1939.

SYRIA:
Supplementary Memorandum to the Anglo-American Committee on Palestine, signed by Faris al-Khoury. Typewritten. London, February 1, 1946.

TRANSJORDAN:
Al-Kitab al-Urdunni al-Abyad: Suriyya al-Kubra (The Transjordan White Paper: Greater Syria). 'Amman, 1947.

UNITED NATIONS:
General Assembly, Official Records. First Special Session.
———. Second Session, including Supplement No. 11, Report of United Nations Special Committee on Palestine to the General Assembly (5 vols.). The records of the *Ad Hoc* Committee on the Palestinian Question (A/AC.14/SR.1–34 and A/AC.14/1–46) were still not published as of the beginning of 1950.
———. Second Special Session, including Supplement No. 1, Report of United Nations Palestine Commission to the General Assembly.
———. Third Session, Parts I and II, including Supplement Nos. 11 and 11A, Progress Reports of the United Nations Mediator and Acting Mediator on Palestine.
———. Fourth Session, including reports of Secretary-General, "Assistance to Palestine Refugees," A/1060 and Add.1, and A/C.5/366.
———. Palestine Commission, Reports, A/AC.21/7, 9, 14 and S/720.
———. Conciliation Commission for Palestine: Progress Reports, A/819, 838, 927, 992; Proposals for a Permanent International Regime for the Jerusalem Area, A/973 and Add.1; Final Report of the United Nations Economic Survey Mission for the Middle East (2 vols., Interim Report in vol. I, 14–30); and Protection of the Holy Places, A/1113.
Security Council, Official Records. Second Year, No. 106.
———. Third Year, S/PV.243, 253–55, 258, 260, 262–63, 267, 270–71, 274–75 [unpublished as of beginning of 1950] and Nos. 52, 57–58, 62, 64–80, 82, 84, 92–98, 100, 103, 106–08, 110, 112, 116, 118, 121–26, 128–30, 136–37. Supplements for April–December 1948 include the more important documents.
———. Fourth Year, Nos. 16–17, 36–38, 49. Supplements for March and August 1949 include the more important documents. Special Supplements Nos. 1–4 contain the armistice agreements; the first two include maps.
———. Documents (cablegrams, draft resolutions, resolutions, letters, protests, and reports): S/663–1459 (*passim*).

Trusteeship Council, Official Records. Second Session. As of the start of 1950 only the records of the 36th through the 46th meetings were published.

————. Third Session, pp. 2–12 and 468–75.

UNITED STATES:
78th Congress, House, Committee on Foreign Affairs. Hearings on H.Res. 418 and H.Res. 419; Resolutions relative to the Jewish National Home in Palestine, February 8, 9, 15, and 16, 1944; with Appendix of Documents relating to the Jewish National Home in Palestine. Washington, 1944.

————. The Jewish National Home in Palestine; H.Res. 418 and H.Res. 419. Washington, 1944.

80th Congress, 2nd Sess., Senate, Subcommittee No. 5: National and International Movements. Report [on] the Strategy and Tactics of World Communism: Supplement III, Country Studies, B, Communism in the Near East. Washington, 1948.

————, Special Committee Investigating the National Defense Program. Navy Purchases of Middle East Oil. Report No. 440, Part 5. Washington, 1948.

Department of Agriculture. *Foreign Agriculture.*

Department of Commerce. *Foreign Commerce Weekly.*

Department of State. *The Department of State Bulletin,* 1939–

————. Nazi-Soviet Relations 1939–1941: Documents from the Archives of the German Foreign Office. Publication No. 2023. Washington, 1948.

————, Division of Near Eastern Affairs. Mandate for Palestine. Near Eastern Series No. 1. Washington, 1931.

Library of Congress, Legislative Reference Service, General Research Section. Public Affairs Bulletin No. 50. The Palestine Problem: an Analysis Historical and Contemporary, by Charles R. Gellner. Washington, March 1, 1947.

WORLD INTER-PARLIAMENTARY CONGRESS OF ARAB AND MUSLIM COUNTRIES FOR THE DEFENCE OF PALESTINE:
Resolution of the Congress, Cairo, 7th–11th October, 1938. London, 1938.

ZIONIST ORGANIZATION:
The New Judaea, 1924– . Official monthly, published at London.
Ha-'Olam, 1906– . Official Hebrew weekly, published at Jerusalem.
Executive. Constitution of the Zionist Organisation. Jerusalem, 1938.

————. Report to the XVIIth Zionist Congress. London, 1931.

————. Report to the XVIIIth Zionist Congress. London, 1933.

————. Report to the XIXth Zionist Congress. London, 1935.

————. Ha-Qongres ha-Ziyyoni ha-Khaf-alif, Geneva, 16–25 August 1939, Din-we-Heshbon Stinografi (The Twenty-first Zionist Congress, Geneva, 16–25 August 1939; Stenographic Report). Jerusalem, 1939.

————. The World Zionist Organisation during the War. Stenciled. Jerusalem, August 1943.

ZIONIST ORGANIZATION AND JEWISH AGENCY:
Executives. Report to the XXth Zionist Congress and the Vth Session of the Council of the Jewish Agency. Jerusalem, 1937.

————. Report to the XXIst Zionist Congress and the VIth Session of the Council of the Jewish Agency. Jerusalem, 1939.

————. Reports to the Twenty-second Zionist Congress at Basle December 1946. Jerusalem, 1946.

————. Ha-Qongres ha-Ziyyoni ha-'Esrim weha-Moshav ha-Hamishi shel Mo'ezet ha-Sokhnut ha-Yehudit, Zurich, 3–21 August 1937, Din-we-heshbon Stinografi (The Twentieth Zionist Congress and the Fifth Session of the Jewish Agency Council, Zurich, 3–21 August 1937: Stenographic Report). Jerusalem, 1937.

BOOKS AND BROCHURES

ABCARIUS, M. F. Palestine Through the Fog of Propaganda. London, 1946.

ABRAMOVITZ, Z. AND GUELFAT, I. Ha-Mesheq ha-'Arvi (The Arab Economy). Tel-Aviv, 1944.

AGUDAS ISRAEL ORGANISATION OF GREAT BRITAIN. Agudist Essays. London, 1944.

AGUDAS ISRAEL WORLD ORGANISATION, LONDON EXECUTIVE. Memorandum to the Anglo-American Committee of Enquiry into the Jewish Problem in Europe and the Future of Palestine. London, January 1946.

AL-'ALAMI, MUSA. 'Ibrat Filastin (The Lesson of Palestine). Bayrut, 1949.

THE AMERICAN CHRISTIAN PALESTINE COMMITTEE. The Arab War Effort: a Documented Account. New York, 1947.

AMERICAN COMMITTEE FOR ANTIFA. Program and Aims of Antifa. New York, 1936.

AMERICAN COUNCIL FOR JUDAISM. Let us Reason Together: Reflections on the Palestine Question, by Lessing J. Rosenwald. Interpretive Pamphlet No. 3. Philadelphia, 1944.

————. Palestine, Haven of Refuge or Power Politics, Statements presented . . . before the Committee on Foreign Affairs of the House of Representatives, February 8–16, 1944. Philadelphia, 1944.

AMERICAN JEWISH COMMITTEE. Thirty-fifth Annual Report. New York, 1942.

————. Thirty-sixth Annual Report. New York, 1943.

————. Thirty-seventh Annual Report. New York, 1944.

————. Ways to Human Freedom: being the 40th Annual Report. New York, 1947.

————. To the Counsellors of Peace: Recommendations of the American Jewish Committee. New York, 1945.

————. The London Conference of Jewish Organizations, February 23–March 2, 1946. New York, 1946.

————. Our Duty as Americans—Our Responsibility as Jews: the Presidential Address of the Hon. Joseph M. Proskauer at the 41st Annual Meeting of the American Jewish Committee, New York, January 18, 1948. New York, 1948.

AMERICAN JEWISH CONFERENCE. The Jewish People in the Post-War World, a Memorandum submitted to Secretary of State Stettinius on the eve of the United Nations Conference at San Francisco. New York, 1945.

————. Statement to the Anglo-American Committee of Inquiry. New York, 1946.

AMERICAN JEWISH JOINT DISTRIBUTION COMMITTEE. The Rescue of Stricken Jews in a World at War: a Report of the Work and Plans of the American Jewish Joint Distribution Committee, as contained in Addresses delivered at its

Twenty-ninth Annual Meeting, December 4th and 5th, 1943. New York, 1944.

——. Preliminary Memorandum on the Condition of Jews Overseas submitted to the Anglo-American Committee of Inquiry. New York, January 1946.

AMERICAN JEWISH TRADE UNION COMMITTEE FOR PALESTINE. British Labor and Zionism. New York, 1946.

AMERICAN PALESTINE COMMITTEE. Proceedings of the Second Annual Dinner. New York, 1942.

——. The Voice of Christian America: Proceedings of the National Conference on Palestine, March 9, 1944. New York, 1944.

ANGLO-JEWISH ASSOCIATION. Memorandum on Palestine. London, 1944.

ANKORION, A. The Government of Palestine. Jerusalem, 1945.

ANTONIUS, GEORGE. The Arab Awakening: the Story of the Arab National Movement. London, 1938.

ASSAF, MICHAEL. The Arab Movement in Palestine. New York, 1937.

ARAB NATIONAL BANK. Tenth Annual Report of the Board of Directors, 1943. Arabic. Jerusalem, 1944.

ATTIAS, MOSHE. Kneset Israel be-Erez Israel: Yesudah we-Irgunah (The Community of Israel in Palestine: Its Foundation and Its Organization). Jerusalem, 1944.

BARBOUR, NEVILL. Palestine: Star or Crescent? New York, 1947. [Appeared in Britain as Nisi Dominus. London, 1946.]

BARON, SALO W. Social and Religious History of the Jews. 3 vols. New York, 1937.

BARTLETT, RUHL J., ed. The Record of American Diplomacy: Documents and Readings in the History of American Foreign Relations. New York, 1947.

BEIN, ALEXANDER. Ha-Hityashvut ha-Haqlait shel ha-Yehudim be-Erez Israel (Agricultural Colonization of the Jews in Palestine). Jerusalem, 1944.

BEN GURION, DAVID. Anahnu u-Shkhenenu (We and Our Neighbors). Tel-Aviv, 1931.

BENTWICH, NORMAN. The Mandates System. London, 1930.

BERGER, ELMER. The Jewish Dilemma. New York, 1945.

BERTRAM, SIR ANTON AND LUKE, HARRY CHARLES. Report on the Orthodox Patriarchate of Jerusalem. London, 1921.

BIN-NUN, AARON, ed. Jew and Arab on the Border: a Story of Religious Pioneering. New York, 1940.

BLISS, FREDERICK JONES. The Religions of Modern Syria and Palestine. New York, 1912.

BOARD OF DEPUTIES OF BRITISH JEWS. Statements on Post-War Policy and Policy on Palestine. London, 1944.

——. Memorandum submitted to the Anglo-American Committee of Inquiry into the Jewish Problem in Europe and the future of Palestine. London, January 23, 1946.

BOEHM, ADOLF AND POLLAK, ADOLF. The Jewish National Fund: Its History, Function and Activity. Jerusalem, 1939.

BOROCHOV, BER. Nationalism and the Class Struggle: a Marxian Approach to the Jewish Problem. Selected Writings of Ber Borochov. Introduction by Abraham G. Duker. New York, 1937.

Palestine Royal Commission, House of Lords, London, February 11, 1937. Reprinted under the auspices of the Jabotinsky Foundation. New York, 1946.

JEFFRIES, J. M. N. Palestine: the Reality. London, 1939.

JEWISH SOCIALIST LABOUR PARTY IN GREAT BRITAIN. British Labour Policy on Palestine: a Collection of Documents, Speeches, and Articles, 1917–1938. London, 1938.

JEWISH SOCIALIST LABOUR PARTY (Poale Zion). World Labour and the Jewish People: the Jewish Case before the World Trade Union Conference, London, February 6th to 17th, 1945. Submitted to the Delegates of the 44th Annual Conference of the Labour Party. London, May 1945.

KALVARYSKI, HAYYIM M., ed. ʿAl Parashat Derakhenu (At Our Crossroads). Jerusalem, 1939.

KATZNELSON, BERL. Revolutionary Constructivism: Essays on the Jewish Labor Movement in Palestine. New York, 1937.

KHOUSHI, ABBA. The Palestine Labour League. Tel-Aviv, 1943.

KISCH, FREDERICK H. Palestine Diary. London, 1938.

KURLAND, SAMUEL. Cooperative Palestine: the Story of Histadrut. New York, 1947.

LEFT POʿALEI ZIYYON. Poʿalei Ziyyon in der Iztiqer Tequfeh (Poʿalei Ziyyon in the Present Period). Yiddish. Tel-Aviv, 1934.

———. Royt Buch: vegen die Blutiqe Gesheenishen in Palestine in Yor 1936 (Red Book: concerning the Bloody Events in Palestine in the Year 1936. Yiddish. Lodz (Poland), 1936.

———. Zente Velt-Qonferenz fun Farband Linqe Poʿalei-Ziyyon, December 1937 (Tenth World Conference of the Left Zionist Workers, December 1937). Yiddish. Tel-Aviv, 1938.

LENCZOWSKI, GEORGE. Russia and the West in Iran, 1918–1948. Ithaca, 1949.

LEVENBERG, S. The Jews and Palestine: a Study in Labour Zionism. Preface by J. S. Middleton, former secretary of the British Labour Party. London, 1945.

LOCKER, BERL. What is Poale Zionism? Palestine Labour Studies No. 6. London, 1938.

———. Palestine and the Jewish Future. London, June 1942.

LOWDERMILK, WALTER CLAY. Palestine, Land of Promise. New York and London, 1944.

LUKE, HENRY CHARLES AND KEITH-ROACH, EDWARD. The Handbook of Palestine and Trans-Jordan. 2nd ed. London, 1930.

MACIVER, R. M. The Web of Government. New York, 1947.

MAGNES, J. L. Rebellion, Presidential Address on Diploma Day at the Hebrew University. Jerusalem, December 6, 1945.

MARLOW, JOHN. Rebellion in Palestine. London, 1946.

MARRIOTT, J. A. R. The Eastern Question: a Study in European Diplomacy. Oxford, 1915.

MASSE, HARRY. Islam. Translated from the French by Halide Edib. New York, 1938.

MAUGHAM, ROBIN. Approach to Palestine. London, 1947.

MIFLEGET POʿALEI EREZ ISRAEL [Mapai]. Ketavim we-Teʿudot, 1929–1933 (Sources and Documents, 1929–1933). Tel-Aviv, 1935.

MIKESELL, RAYMOND F. AND CHENERY, HOLLIS B. Arabian Oil: America's Stake in the Middle East. Chapel Hill, 1949.

MILLER, WILLIAM. The Ottoman Empire and Its Successors, 1801–1927. 3rd ed. Cambridge, 1927.

MIZRACHI FEDERATION OF GREAT BRITAIN AND IRELAND. Memorandum to the Anglo-American Committee of Enquiry. London, January 1946.

MOGANNAM, MRS. MATIEL E. T. The Arab Woman and the Palestine Problem. London, 1937.

MUENZNER, G. Jewish Labour Economy in Palestine. London, 1945.

NAMIER, L. B., LOCKER, BERL, BEN GURION, DAVD, AND FREEMAN, D. Palestine and Jewish Freedom: a Symposium. Introduction by Shlomo Grodzensky. New York, 1942.

NARDI, NOACH. Zionism and Education in Palestine. New York, 1934.

NATHAN, ROBERT R., GASS, OSCAR, AND CREAMER, DANIEL. Palestine: Problem and Promise. Washington, 1946.

NATION ASSOCIATES. The Arab Higher Committee, Its Origins, Personnel and Purposes: the Documentary Record submitted to the United Nations. New York, 1947.

——. Could the Arabs Stage an Armed Revolt against the United Nations? Memorandum submitted to the General Assembly of the United Nations. New York, October 1947.

——. The Palestine Problem and Proposals for Its Solution: Memorandum submitted to the General Assembly of the United Nations. New York, April 1947.

——. Police State: Nazi Model; Palestine under British Rule; a Study of the Police State created by the Mandatory Power; Memorandum to General Assembly of the United Nations. New York, September 1947.

NEW ZIONIST ORGANIZATION OF AMERICA. Fighting for a Jewish Homeland. New York, 1946.

——. The New Zionist [Revisionist] Organization of America: Its Aims, Principles, and Policies. New York, 1944.

——. Ten Political Statements. New York, January 1945.

NON-PARTISAN CONFERENCE TO CONSIDER PALESTINIAN PROBLEMS. Verbatim Report of the Proceedings, February 17, 1924. New York, 1924.

NON-ZIONIST CONFERENCE CONCERNING PALESTINE. Verbatim Report of the Proceedings, October 20–21, 1928. New York, 1928.

ORENSTEIN, MORDEKHAY. Palestine: Plea for Jewish-Arab Unity. London, 1939.

PEARLMAN, MAURICE. Mufti of Jerusalem: the Story of Haj Amin el-Husseini. London, 1947.

POALE ZION ZEIRE ZION OF AMERICA. Labor Zionist Handbook: The Aims, Activities, and History of the Labor Zionist Movement in America. New York, 1939.

ROBINSON, EDWARD AND SMITH, ELI. Biblical Researches in Palestine, Mount Sinai, and Arabia Petrea: a Journal of Travels in the Year 1838. 3 vols. London, 1841.

ROBINSON, JACOB. Palestine and the United Nations: Prelude to Solution. Washington, 1947.

ROSENBLATT, SAMUEL. The Mizrachi Movement: Its Philosophy, Achievements, and Prospects. New York, 1944.

ROSENHEIM, JACOB. Agudist World-Problems. New York, 1941.

ROYAL INSTITUTE OF INTERNATIONAL AFFAIRS. British Security: a Report by a Chatham House Study Group. London and New York, 1946.

———. Documents on International Affairs, 1928 [-1938]. London, 1929 [-1943].

———. Great Britain and Palestine, 1915–1945. 3rd ed. London, 1946.

———. Survey of International Affairs, 1920–1923 [-1938]. Edited by Arnold J. Toynbee. London, 1925–1941.

SAMUEL, EDWIN. Handbook of the Communal Villages in Palestine. 2nd Eng. ed. Jerusalem, 1945.

SCOTT, HUGH. In the High Yemen. London, 1942.

SEFER HA-ISHIM [Palestine Jewish Who's Who]. Tel-Aviv, 1937.

SEIBT, HANS. Moderne Kolonisation in Palästina: I. Teil, Die Kolonisation der deutschen "Templer." Jerusalem, 1933.

SHERMAN, BEZALEL. The Communists in Palestine. New York, 1939.

SHERWOOD, ROBERT E. Roosevelt and Hopkins: An Intimate History. New York, 1948.

SHIM'ONI, YA'AQOV. 'Arvei Erez Israel (The Arabs of Palestine). Tel-Aviv, 1947.

SMITH, GEORGE ADAM AND BARTHOLOMEW, J. G. Atlas of the Historical Geography of the Holy Land. London, 1915.

SMITH, WALTER BEDELL. My Three Years in Moscow. Philadelphia & New York, 1950.

SPEISER, E. A. The United States and the Near East. Cambridge (Mass.), 1947.

STAVSKI, MOSHE. Ha-Kfar ha-'Aravi (The Arab Village). Tel-Aviv, 1946.

SOKOLOW, NAHUM. History of Zionism. 2 vols. London, 1919.

SYRKIN, DR. NAHMAN. Essays on Socialist Zionism. New York, 1935.

THE TEMPLE SOCIETY. The Temple Society in Palestine. London, n.d.

THOMSON, WILLIAM H. The Land and the Book. 3 vols. New York, 1886.

TWITCHELL, K. S. Saudi Arabia, with an Account of the Development of Its Natural Resources. Princeton, 1947.

ULITZUR, A. Two Decades of Keren Hayesod: a Survey in Facts and Figures, 1921–1940. Jerusalem, 1940.

VAN PAASSEN, PIERRE. That Day Alone. New York, 1941.

VERNEY, NÖEL AND DAMBMANN, GEORGE. Les puissances étrangères dans le Levant en Syrie et en Palestine. Paris, 1900.

VON GRUNEBAUM, GUSTAVE E. Medieval Islam: a Study in Cultural Orientation. Chicago, 1946.

WASCHITZ, J. Ha-'Aravim be-Erez Israel (The Arabs in Palestine). Tel-Aviv, 1947.

WATERS, M. P. Haganah: Jewish Self-Defence in Palestine. London, 1946.

WEIZMANN, CHAIM. Trial and Error, the Autobiography of Chaim Weizmann. New York, 1949.

WOODSMALL, RUTH FRANCES. Moslem Women Enter a New World. New York, 1936.

WRIGHT, QUINCY. Mandates under the League of Nations. Chicago, 1930.

Ya'ari, Meir. 'Im Haqamat Mifleget Po'alim ha-Shomer ha-Za'ir (With the Establishment of the Young Watchman Labor Party). Tel-Aviv, 1946.

Yesha'yahu, Israel and Greidi, Shim'on. Mi-Teiman le-Ziyyon (From Yemen to Zion). Tel-Aviv, 1938.

Zurayq, Qostantin. Ma'na al-Nakbah (The Meaning of the Disaster). Bayrut, 1948.

Zafrulla Khan, Sir Muhammad. Palestine in the U.N.O. Karachi, 1948.

ARTICLES

Alami, Musa. "The Lesson of Palestine," The Middle East Journal, 3 (October 1949), pp. 373–405.

Arnold, G. L. "Lessons of Palestine," The Nineteenth Century and After, 144 (October 1948), pp. 192–201.

Arsenian, Seth. "Wartime Propaganda in the Middle East," The Middle East Journal, 2 (October 1948), pp. 417–29.

Asfour, John. "Arab Labour in Palestine," Journal of the Royal Central Asian Society, 32 (May 1945), pp. 201–05.

Babcock, F. Lawrence. "The Explosive Middle East," Fortune, October 1944, pp. 113–16 and 263–69.

el-Barghuthi, Omar. "Judicial Courts among the Bedouin of Palestine," Journal of the Palestine Oriental Society, 2 (1922). Reprint.

Barr, Robert J. "Postwar Trade Prospects in Egypt, Iraq, Palestine," Foreign Commerce Weekly, June 30, 1945. Reprint.

Bayastan, Kamil. "Moslems in the USSR," Information Bulletin (of the Embassy of the Union of Soviet Socialist Republics in the U.S.A.), August 14, 1946, pp. 19–20.

Ben Gurion, David. "The Palestine Administration and the Jews," The New Judaea, 18 (November 1941), pp. 19–20.

Bentwich, Norman. "Impressions of American Jewry," The New Judaea, 17 (August 1941), pp. 173–74.

Berlin, Meir. "The Mizrahi Programme," Palestine Review, 2 (July 30, 1937), pp. 270–71.

Brodie, Bernard. "American Security and Foreign Oil," Foreign Policy Reports, 23 (March 1, 1948), pp. 298–311.

Brownell, George A. "American Aviation in the Middle East," The Middle East Journal, 1 (October 1947), pp. 401–16.

Cadett, Thomas. "The Exodus 1947: the British Case," The New York Herald-Tribune, September 17, 1947.

Cohen, Aaron. "Inactivity—How Long? An Open Letter to the Histadrut Executive," Ha-Shomer ha-Za'ir [Hebrew], January 13, 1943.

Cunningham, Sir Alan. "Palestine—the Last Days of the Mandate," International Affairs, 24 (October 1948), pp. 481–90.

Curtiss, John S. "The Non-Orthodox Religions in the U.S.S.R. during and after World War II," The American Review on the Soviet Union, 8 (November 1946), pp. 3–14.

———. "The Russian Orthodox Church during World War II," The American Review on the Soviet Union, 7 (August 1946), pp. 32–44.

FARRELL, MAURICE L. "Eastern Oil Empire," *Wall Street Journal*, July 25, 1946.

FEDERAL COUNCIL OF THE CHURCHES OF CHRIST IN AMERICA, Department of Research and Education. "Conflict over Palestine," *Information Service*, October 7, 1944.

FRANK, GEROLD. "The Truth about the Terrorists," *The Nation*, 159 (December 2, 1944), pp. 685–86.

"German Property in Palestine and Jewish War Claims," *The Palestine Tribune*, May 10, 1945.

GERVASI, FRANK. "Terror in Palestine," *Collier's*, August 11, 1945.

GIBB, H. A. R. "The Islamic Congress at Jerusalem in December 1931," *Survey of International Affairs, 1934*, pp. 99–109.

———. "Toward Arab Unity," *Foreign Affairs*, 24 (October 1945), pp. 119–29.

GRANOVSKY, ABRAHAM. "The Struggle for Land," *The Palestine Yearbook*, 2 (1945–46), pp. 423–35.

"The Great Oil Deals," *Fortune*, May 1947, pp. 138–43 and 175–82.

HAMILTON, THOMAS J. "Partition of Palestine," *Foreign Policy Reports*, 23 (February 15, 1948), pp. 286–95.

HIRSCHMANN, IRA A. "Palestine—as a Refuge from Fascism," *Survey Graphic*, 34 (May 1945), pp. 195–97 and 265–69.

HOURANI, CECIL A. "The Arab League in Perspective," *The Middle East Journal*, 1 (April 1947), pp. 125–36.

HOWARD, HARRY N. "An American Experiment in Peace-Making: the King-Crane Commission," *The Moslem World*, 32 (April 1942), pp. 122–46.

"Interchange of Correspondence between the Histadrut and the Palestine Communist Party," *Digest of Press and Events*, No. 39, Supplement No. 15, September 20, 1944.

JABOTINSKY, VLADIMIR. "Evacuation." A speech delivered in 1937 and reprinted in *Zionews*, 4 (September 1, 1942), pp. 30–31.

JEFFERY, ARTHUR. "The Political Importance of Islam," *Journal of Near Eastern Studies*, 1 (October 1942), pp. 383–95.

JEWISH RESISTANCE MOVEMENT, Head of Command. "The Jewish Resistance Movement in Palestine, evidence submitted to the Anglo-American Committee of Inquiry, March 25, 1946," *Palestine Affairs*, 1 (July 1946), pp. 1–6.

KAHN, A. E. "Palestine: a Problem in Economic Evaluation," *American Economic Review*, 34 (September 1944), pp. 538–60.

KALVARYSKI, HAYYIM M. "Our Path after the White Paper," *Darkenu* [a brochure containing articles on the subject of Arab-Jewish cooperation]. Hebrew. Jerusalem, August 1939.

KAPLAN, ELIEZER. "Our Preparations for the Transition Period," *The Palestine Yearbook*, 1 (1944–45), pp. 45–59.

KARPF, MAURICE J. "Partition of Palestine and Its Consequences," *Jewish Social Service Quarterly* [New York], 14 (March 1938). Reprint.

———. "Zionist and Non-Zionist Relationships in the Enlarged Jewish Agency," *Universal Jewish Encyclopedia*, vol. 6, pp. 92–93.

KHUSHI, ABBA. "The Palestine Labor League: the Record of a Fight for Arab-Jewish Labor Cooperation," *Jewish Frontier*, March 1944.

KRAEMER, ERICH. "The Revival of the Centre," *Palestine Review*, 3 (March 10, 1939), p. 749.

LANDIS, JAMES M. "Middle East Challenge," *Fortune*, September 1945. Reprint.

LIEBESNY, HERBERT J. "International Relations of Arabia: the Dependent Areas," *The Middle East Journal*, 1 (April 1947), pp. 148–68.

LOFTUS, JOHN A. "Middle East Oil: the Pattern of Control," *The Middle East Journal*, 2 (January 1948), pp. 17–32.

LOURIE, ARTHUR. "The American Zionist Emergency Council," *The Palestine Yearbook*, 1 (1944–45), pp. 368–73.

LURIE, JESSE. "Guns in Palestine," *The Nation*, 158 (January 22, 1944), pp. 92–94.

MAGNES, J. L. "Palestine and Arab Union." Jerusalem, June 22, 1941. Reprint.

———. "Palestine and Arab Union: Two Initial Steps." Jerusalem, July 28, 1941. Reprint.

MATTHEWS, CHARLES D. "Palestine—Mohammedan Holy Land," *The Moslem World*, 33 (October 1943), pp. 239–53.

McCLELLAN, GRANT S. "Palestine and America's Role in the Middle East," *Foreign Policy Reports*, 21 (July 1, 1945), pp. 98–107.

McKAY, VERNON. "The Arab League in World Politics," *Foreign Policy Reports*, 22 (November 15, 1946), pp. 206–15.

MEIKSINS, GREGORY. "Russia, Britain and the Straits," *The American Review on the Soviet Union*, 7 (May 1946), pp. 3–15.

MONROE, ELIZABETH. "British Interests in the Middle East," *The Middle East Journal*, 2 (April 1948), pp. 129–46.

NETANYAHU, B. "The Fiasco of the Hebrew Committee," *Zionews*, 6 (July 1944), pp. 12–16.

NOTESTEIN, FRANK W. AND JURKAT, ERNEST. "Population Problems of Palestine," *The Milbank Memorial Fund Quarterly*, 23 (October 1945), pp. 307–52.

PEREJDA, ANDREW D. "The Position of Russia in the Oil Age," *The American Review on the Soviet Union*, 7 (August 1946), pp. 3–19.

PERLMANN, M. "Chapters of Arab-Jewish Diplomacy, 1918–22," *Jewish Social Studies*, 6 (April 1944), pp. 123–54.

ROOSEVELT, KERMIT. "The Partition of Palestine: a Lesson in Pressure Politics," *The Middle East Journal*, 2 (January 1948), pp. 1–16.

ROWSON, SHABTAI. "Review of the Year 5704—Great Britain," *American Jewish Yearbook*, 46 (1944–45), pp. 187–95.

SANGER, RICHARD H. "Ibn Saud's Program for Arabia," *The Middle East Journal*, 1 (April 1947), pp. 180–90.

SCHWARTZ, SULAMITH. "Blueprint and Vision: the Jordan Valley Authority," *The Palestine Yearbook*, 2 (1945–46), pp. 83–100.

SENATOR, DAVID WERNER. Letter of resignation from the Jewish Agency Executive, *Commentary*, 2 (October 1946), pp. 384–86.

SEREZHIN, K. "The Anglo-Transjordan Treaty," *New Times*, April 15, 1946, pp. 11–14.

———. "Contemporary Palestine (Geographical Sketch)," *New Times*, August 1, 1946, pp. 18–22.

———. "The Events in Egypt," *New Times*, March 1, 1946, pp. 7–10.

———. "Iraq Today (Geographical Sketch)," *New Times*, March 15, 1946, pp. 21–26.

———. "The Problems of the Arab East," *New Times*, February 1, 1946, pp. 12–16.

——. "A Seat of Unrest in the Middle East," *New Times*, June 1, 1946, pp. 14–17.

SHEEAN, VINCENT. "Personal Opinion: the Mufti of Jerusalem," *Asia and the Americas*, 46 (August 1946), pp. 373–74; reprinted in *Middle East Opinion*, February 10, 1947.

SHULTZ, LILLIE. "The Palestine Fight—an Inside Story," *The Nation*, 165 (December 20, 1947), pp. 675–78.

SHWADRAN, BENJAMIN. "Palestine in Anglo-American Relations," *Palestine Affairs*, 1 (September 1946), pp. 1–7.

SULZBERGER, CYRUS L. "German Preparations in the Middle East," *Foreign Affairs*, 20 (July 1942), pp. 663–78.

SYRKIN, MARIE. "Revisionists at Work," *Jewish Frontier*, March 1940.

TANNOUS, AFIF I. "Land Tenure in the Middle East," *Foreign Agriculture* (United States Department of Agriculture monthly bulletin), August 1943. Reprint.

VAN PAASSEN, PIERRE. "An Open Letter," *The Protestant* and *Jewish Frontier*, April 1944.

VOLINSKY, L. "The Situation in Syria and Lebanon," *New Times*, January 15, 1946, pp. 14–16.

WEIZMANN, CHAIM. "Palestine's Role in the Solution of the Jewish Problem," *Foreign Affairs*, 20 (January 1942), pp. 324–38.

WELTSCH, ROBERT. "Jewish Political Parties in Palestine," *Contemporary Jewish Record*, 7 (October 1944), pp. 487–96.

WOOLBERT, ROBERT GALE. "Pan-Arabism and the Palestine Problem," *Foreign Affairs*, 16 (January 1938), pp. 309–22.

WYSNER, GLORIA M. "Dilemma in Palestine," *Foreign Missions Conference Bulletin* (New York), No. 6, November 1944.

NEWSPAPERS AND PERIODICALS

ARAB STATES

Al-Ahali, Baghdad, 1932– . In early years of Iraqi independence it was organ of a populist movement.

Al-Ahram, Cairo, 1875– . Oldest Arabic newspaper in Egypt and largest in the Near East.

Al-Akhbar, Baghdad, 1932 (?)– . Pro-Hashimi (court) and pro-British.

Akhir Sa'ah, Cairo. Independent Arabic weekly.

Al-Balagh, Cairo, 1924– . Pro-Wafdist during World War II; an afternoon daily.

Bayrut, Bayrut, 1931– . Muslim Arabic daily, favoring Arab Unity movement.

La Bourse Égyptienne, Cairo, 1899– . Conservative pro-French and pro-British French-language daily.

The Egyptian Gazette, Cairo, 1879– . Conservative pro-British, English-language daily.

Le Journal d'Égypte, Cairo. Conservative, usually pro-Palace, French-language daily.

Middle East Opinion, Cairo, 1946–47. English-language weekly.

Al-Misri, Cairo, 1937– . Largest Wafdist daily.

Al-Muqattam, Cairo, 1888– . Christian-owned, afternoon daily; pro-British until 1924, thereafter nationalist.

Al-Musawwar, Cairo. Arabic weekly, usually pro-Government.

L'Orient, Bayrut, 1924– . Christian-owned, French-language daily; favors independent Lebanon and Christian ascendancy.

Le Progrès Égyptien, Cairo, 1893– . Conservative, pro-British and pro-French French-language daily.

Al-Wafd al-Misri, Cairo. Afternoon Arabic daily; ceased publication shortly after the dissolution of the Nahhas (Wafdist) Government in October 1944.

GREAT BRITAIN

The Economist, London. Weekly.

International Affairs, London, 1922– . Quarterly published by the Royal Institute of International Affairs.

Journal of the Royal Central Asian Society, London, 1914– . Quarterly.

The Manchester Guardian, Manchester.

The New Statesman and Nation, London. Weekly.

The Spectator, London. Weekly.

The Times, London.

ITALY

Oriente Moderno, Rome, 1921– . Monthly.

PALESTINE

*A-B. See *Eshnav.*

*Af 'Al Pi. Monthly bulletin, first issued by the Irgun toward the end of the war.

Al-Akhbar, Jaffa, 1936–39 (irregular appearance). Published whenever *Filastin* suspended by Palestine Government in Arab Revolt of 1936–39.

'Al ha-Mishmar, Tel-Aviv, 1948– . Organ of the United Labor Party or Mapam, formed by the merger of ha-Shomer ha-Za'ir and Labor Unity parties in January 1948.

'Amudim, Tel-Aviv, 1944– . Hebrew-language weekly of the New Immigration Party.

Ha-Arez, Tel-Aviv, 1918– . Independent, centrist; oldest Hebrew daily with second largest circulation—about 14,000 in 1946.

He-'Atid, Tel-Aviv. Hebrew weekly of Agudat Israel Labor; ceased publication in 1940.

Ha-Boqer, Tel-Aviv, 1936– . General Zionist B Party's daily organ; circulation in 1946 estimated at 9,000.

Davar, Tel-Aviv, 1925– . Although technically the daily of the Histadrut, it has been for all practical purposes the mouthpiece of Mapai. It boasted the largest circulation of all the Hebrew newspapers in the country—19,000 in 1946. See also *Hegeh.*

Ha-Derekh, Tel-Aviv, 1941–44. Hebrew weekly of Agudat Israel Labor.

Al-Difa', Jaffa, 1934–48; Old City of Jerusalem, 1949– . Muslim-owned; had the largest circulation of all Arabic newspapers in Palestine—about 13,000 in 1946. From 1934–39 it was the Istiqlal mouthpiece; from 1939–43 it was independent; and from 1944–48 it voiced the opinions of the Palestine Arab (Husayni) Party and the Arab Higher Committee. Publication interrupted from fall of Jaffa until early in 1949. See also *Al-Fajir*, *Al-Hayah*, and *Al-Jihad*.

Eshnav, ca. 1941– . Hebrew fortnightly of Haganah, at times issued under alternative title, *A-B*.

Al-Fajir, Jaffa, 1936–39 (irregular appearance). Substituted for *Al-Difaʻ*, whenever latter suspended by Palestine Government.

Fighting Judea, 1946–48. Irgun English monthly, stenciled and distributed to foreign correspondents in Palestine and mailed clandestinely to institutions and individuals abroad.

Filastin, Jaffa, 1911–48; ʻAmman, 1949– . Oldest Arabic newspaper in Palestine; publication interrupted between 1914 and 1921. Christian-owned, it had the second-largest circulation in the Arab Community, about 9,000 in 1946. During the 1930's it supported the National Defense (Nashashibi) Party; 1940–43 it was independent; 1943–46 it supported the Istiqlal spokesmen; in 1947 it was anti-Husayni. Publication interrupted from fall of Jaffa until early in 1949. See also *Al-Akhbar*.

Front de Combat Hébreu, 1944–45. Freedom Fighters' bi-monthly, stenciled and distributed to Free French in the Levant States.

Hadashot ha-Yom, Jerusalem, November 1943. Hebrew daily news bulletin, issued by the Palestine Government when the Hebrew press struck in protest against the staggered suspension of several Hebrew dailies.

Al-Hayah, Jaffa, 1937–39 (irregular appearance). Substituted for *Al Difaʻ* whenever latter suspended by Palestine Government.

He-Hazit, July 1943– . Stenciled Hebrew monthly of the Freedom Fighters.

Hed ha-Mizrah, Jerusalem, 1942– . Hebrew weekly of the Sefardim.

Hedim, Merhavyah. Hebrew monthly of ha-Shomer ha-Zaʻir world movement.

Hegeh, Tel-Aviv. In the late 1930's substituted for *Davar*, whenever latter suspended by the Palestine Government; from 1940 on published regularly in basic Hebrew for benefit of new immigrants; its circulation was estimated at 3,500 in 1946.

Herut, 1941–48. Irgun's Hebrew monthly.

Herut, Tel-Aviv, 1948– . Daily newspaper of Irgun's legal successor, the Freedom Movement.

Ha-Homah. Hebrew monthly of Haganah's labor branch. Published during World War II.

Al-Hurriyyah, Jaffa, 1945– . Arabic weekly which supported the Istiqlal spokesmen and the Arab National Fund; converted for a brief period in the summer of 1946 into an afternoon daily.

Al-Ittihad, Jaffa, 1944– . Arabic weekly of the pro-communist wing of the Palestine Arab labor movement; until April 1945 published at Haifa. Publication interrupted after mandate's end until early in 1949.

Al-Jamiʻah al-ʻArabiyyah, Jerusalem, 1927–35. Earliest Arabic organ of the Husayni faction; started out as a weekly, then became a semiweekly.

Al-Jamiʻah al-Islamiyyah, Jaffa, 1932–39. This Muslim-owned Arabic daily supported the National Defense (Nashashibi) Party in the mid-1930's; appeared only irregularly after 1937.

Al-Jihad, Jaffa, February–May 1939 (irregular appearance). Substituted for *Al-Difaʻ* and its allied publications whenever they were suspended by the Palestine Government.

Al-Lahab, Jerusalem, February 1938–April 1939 (irregular appearance). Intended to replace *Al-Liwa*, as the Husayni daily newspaper.

Al-Liwa, Jerusalem, 1933–38. Arabic daily newspaper of the Palestine Arab (Husayni) Party; after its suspension by the Palestine Government in October 1937, it appeared for only a few days at a time every three months until October 1938, when it ceased publication altogether.

Ha-Mashqif, Tel-Aviv, 1938– . Revisionist Hebrew daily with a circulation of about 4,000 in 1946.

Mishmar, Tel-Aviv, 1943–48. Ha-Shomer ha-Za'ir Hebrew daily with a circulation of about 7,000 in 1946.

Mitteilungsblatt, Tel-Aviv, 1937– . German-language weekly of the New Immigration Party.

Neie Velt, Tel-Aviv. Yiddish-language weekly of the Left Zionist Workers Party.

*Nidal al-Sha'b, 1940–42. Arabic monthly of the Palestine Communist Party.

*'Oz, 1946– . Palmah fortnightly.

Palestine and Transjordan, Jerusalem, 1936–38. Arab-owned, English-language weekly, which supported the Husaynis and the first Higher Committee.

The Palestine Post, Jerusalem, 1932–50. Independent, pro-Mapai English-language daily with the largest circulation in the country—about 20,000 in 1946.

Palestine Review, Jerusalem, 1936– . English-language weekly until 1940, semi-monthly until the end of 1941, and monthly thereafter. Independent but often voiced the opinions of the General Zionist B Party.

The Palestine Tribune, Tel-Aviv, 1945– . General Zionist B Party's English-language weekly.

Ha-Po'el ha-Za'ir, Tel-Aviv, 1906– . Hebrew weekly of Mapai.

*Qol ha-'Am, Tel-Aviv, 1937– . Hebrew organ of the Palestine Communist Party. Illegal until December 1944, when it converted into a weekly; became a daily early in 1947.

Qol Israel, Jerusalem. Hebrew weekly of Agudat Israel.

*Raq Kakh. Issued irregularly by the Irgun from 1943 on either as a broadsheet or a pamphlet, chiefly for purposes of recruitment or announcing responsibility for terrorist exploits.

Sha'arim, Tel-Aviv, 1944– . Hebrew weekly organ of Agudat Israel Labor.

Al-Sha'b, Jaffa, 1946–48. Arabic daily.

Ha-Shomer ha-Za'ir, Merhavyah. Hebrew organ of ha-Shomer ha-Za'ir. Fortnightly until 1939; weekly until 1943, when it was replaced by *Mishmar*.

Al-Sirat al-Mustaqim, Jaffa, 1925–48. Muslim-owned Arabic weekly until 1929; afternoon daily thereafter. Wartime circulation about 1,300.

*'Uvdot we-Sikkumim, December 1944–April 1945. Haganah weekly broadsheet for the purpose of counteracting the terrorists.

*Volksstimme, Tel-Aviv. German-language fortnightly of the Palestine Communist Party, which usually carried articles translated from *Qol ha-'Am*.

Al-Wahdah, Jerusalem, 1945–48. Commenced publication in June 1945 as an independent Arabic weekly; transformed into a daily in July 1946, when it became the mouthpiece of the Palestine Arab (Husayni) Party.

Ha-Yarden, Tel-Aviv, 1932–38. Revisionist Hebrew weekly.

Yedi'ot Aharonot, Tel-Aviv, 1939–. Independent Hebrew afternoon daily; often voiced Revisionist sentiment. Its circulation in 1946 was estimated at 10,000.

Ha-Zman, Tel-Aviv, 1943–44. Daily of the General Zionist A Party.

Ha-Zofeh, Tel-Aviv, 1937– . Mizrahi Hebrew daily, circulation about 3,500 in 1946.

SOVIET UNION

New Times, Moscow. Periodical devoted to international affairs and published by the trade-union newspaper *Trud*. Semimonthly through 1946; weekly thereafter.

UNITED STATES

American Jewish Chronicle, New York, 1939–40. Revisionist monthly.

American Jewish Yearbook, Philadelphia, 1899– .

The American Review on the Soviet Union, New York. Quarterly of the American Russian Institute.

The Answer, New York, 1942–48. Published by American friends of the Irgun; monthly until 1947; weekly thereafter.

Bulletin of the Institute of Arab American Affairs, New York, 1945– Monthly.

The Christian Science Monitor, Boston.

Collier's.

Commentary, New York, 1945– . Monthly published by the American Jewish Committee.

The Daily Worker, New York.

Foreign Affairs, New York. Quarterly.

Foreign Policy Reports, New York. Semimonthly.

Fortune, New York. Monthly.

Furrows, New York, 1943– . Monthly of Habonim, Zionist labor youth group, affiliated with Mapai in Palestine.

Hashomer Hatzair, New York, 1931– . English-language monthly of the American branch of ha-Shomer ha-Za'ir.

Information Service, New York. Published weekly, except during July and August, by the Federal Council of the Churches of Christ in America.

Jewish Frontier, New York, 1934– . Monthly, published by American labor Zionists affiliated with Mapai in Palestine.

Jewish Social Studies, New York, 1939– . Quarterly devoted to contemporary and historical aspects of Jewish life.

JTA Bulletin, New York. Daily, published by the Jewish Telegraphic Agency.

Journal of Near Eastern Studies, Chicago, 1942– . Quarterly, published by the Department of Oriental Languages and Literatures at the University of Chicago.

The Middle East Journal, Washington, 1947– . Quarterly of the Middle East Institute.

The Moslem World, Hartford, 1911– . Quarterly review of history, culture, religions, and the Christian mission in Islamdom, published by the Hartford Seminary Foundation. Appeared as *The Muslim World* from 1948 on.

The Nation, New York.

The New Palestine, New York, 1921– . Semimonthly of the Zionist Organization of America.

New Republic, New York.

New York Daily News.

New York Post.

New York Herald-Tribune.

The New York Times.

Palestine Affairs, New York, 1946–49. Monthly information bulletin of the American Zionist Emergency Council.

The Palestine Year Book, New York, 1945– . Published by the Zionist Organization of America; the first volume appeared in Washington.

The Philadelphia Record.

PM, New York.

Time (Magazine), New York.

Wall Street Journal, New York.

The Washington Post.

The Washington Star.

Zionews, New York, 1938– . Monthly of the New Zionist (Revisionist) Organization of America.

BIBLIOGRAPHICAL REFERENCES

"Bibliography of Periodical Literature on the Near and Middle East," *The Middle East Journal*, 1947– . Prepared by the Near East Section of the Library of Congress.

Esco Foundation, *Palestine: a Study of Jewish, Arab, and British Policies*, vol. II, pp. 1238–80.

Johnsen, Julia E., comp. *Palestine: Jewish Homeland?* [*The Reference Shelf*, vol. 18, No. 6]. New York, 1946. Pp. 312–41.

Zionist Archives and Library, New York. *Palestine and Zionism: a Bimonthly Bibliography of Books, Pamphlets and Periodicals*, 1945– . The years 1946–48 have appeared in book form: *Palestine and Zionism, a Three Year Cumulation, January 1946–December 1948*. New York, 1949.

INDEX

'Abd-al-Baqi, Ahmad Hilmi Pasha, 62, 115, 116, 183, 184, 239, 253; quoted, 117

'Abd-al-Hadi, 'Awni Bey, 62, 116, 183

'Abd-al-Ilah, Amir, 151

'Abdallah, Amir, 20, 55, 62, 70, 78, 90, 92, 118, 169, 234; King, 318, 319, 326, 328, 330

Abu-al-Huda, Tawfiq Pasha, 102

Abu-Ghosh, Yusuf, 198

Acre, 74, 180, 290, 296, 313

Aden Settlement, 17

Afghanistan, 286, 301

A.F.L., pro-Zionist plank of (1944), 210

Africa, 86

Agudat Israel Labor Federation, 48

Agudat Israel World Organization, 48, 129, 208, 311; Rabbinical Council of, quoted, 78

Ahmad Hilmi Pasha, 62, 115, 116, 117, 183, 184, 239, 253

Al-. Names containing this Arabic article appear alphabetically, according to the first letter following the article

al-'Alamayn, 127

al-'Alami, Musa, 186, 191 ff., 228, 234, 239, 240, 293, 295; Constructive Scheme of, 233

'Alayah, 309

Albania, 100, 152, 154

Aleppo, 19, 151

Alexandretta, 148

Alexandria, 26, 114, 180, 219, 229, 231, 233, 248, 259, 260, 301; Arab Unity conference at, 186, 191

Alexandria Protocol, quoted, 192

Allied Powers (the), 19

Allies (the), 124

America, 36, 163, 174, 177, 185, 186, 275. *See also* United States

American Christian Palestine Committee, 232

American Council for Judaism, 209, 311

American Emergency Committee for Zionist Affairs, 144, 158, 163

"American Friends of Jewish Palestine," 130

American Jewish Committee, 129, 209, 311

American Jewish Conference, 209, 211

American Jewish Joint Distribution Committee, 196

American Palestine Committee, 210; membership of, 144

American Zionist Emergency Council, 144, 209 ff., 214, 232, 255

Americas, the, 89

'Amman, 20, 70, 118, 244

Andrews, L. Y., 82

Anglo-American Committee of Inquiry, 259, 290; report of, 253, 255, 257, 259

Anglo-American Zionists, 47

Anglo-Arab negotiations, 100

Anglo-Iranian Oil Company, 25, 179

Anglo-Iraqi treaty (1930), 74, 80, 151

Anglo-Jewish Association, 208

Anglo-Palestine Bank, 30, 165

Anglo-Transjordan treaty (1946), 260

Ankara, 152, 175, 181

Antioch, 180

Anti-Zionists (Jewish), 209, 210, 244, 311

Anzacs, 130

'Aqabah, 76, 79; Gulf of, 74

Arab Agency, recommended, 52

Arab Agricultural Bank, 116

Arab Anti-Fascist League (communist), 188

Arab College (of Palestine Government), 58

Arab Community (Palestine), 25, 29 ff., 35 ff., 58, 72, 78, 82, 83, 115, 146, 187, 189-90, 217, 220, 221, 239, 240, 246, 250, 271, 278, 279; and Britain, 82, 98, 113, 118, 119, 216, 222, 233, 240, 271-72, 278-79, 280, 290; clans in, 35; communism in, 63, 188-89, 234, 279, 293; economy of, 31-32, 71, 84, 112-13, 121, 189-90; labor